MARVEL MASTERWORKS
PRESENTS

VOLUME 3

COLLECTING

CAPTAIN AMERICA NOS. 101-113

STAN LEE • JACK KIRBY • JIM STERANKO

Collection Editor
Cory Sedlmeier

Book Design
Nickel Digital

Senior Editor, Special Projects
Jeff Youngquist

Editor in Chief
Joe Quesada

Publisher
Dan Buckley

MARVEL MASTERWORKS: CAPTAIN AMERICA VOL. 3. Contains material originally published in magazine form as CAPTAIN AMERICA #101-113. First printing 2006. ISBN# 0-7851-2063-7. Published by MARVEL PUBLISHING, INC., a subsidiary of MARVEL ENTERTAINMENT, INC. OFFICE OF PUBLICATION: 417 5th Avenue, New York, NY 10016. Copyright © 1968, 1969 and 2006 Marvel Characters, Inc. All rights reserved. $49.99 per copy in the U.S. and $80.00 in Canada (GST #R127032852); Canadian Agreement #40668537. All characters featured in this issue and the distinctive names and likenesses thereof, and all related indicia are trademarks of Marvel Characters, Inc. No similarity between any of the names, characters, persons, and/or institutions in this magazine with those of any living or dead person or institution is intended, and any such similarity which may exist is purely coincidental. **Printed in the U.S.A.** ALAN FINE, President & CEO Of Marvel Toys and Marvel Publishing, Inc.; DAVID BOGART, VP Of Publishing Operations; DAN CARR, Executive Director of Publishing Technology; JUSTIN F. GABRIE, Managing Editor; STAN LEE, Chairman Emeritus. For information regarding advertising in Marvel Comics or on Marvel.com, please contact Joe Maimone, Advertising Director, at jmaimone@marvel.com or 212-576-8534.

10 9 8 7 6 5 4 3 2 1

MARVEL MASTERWORKS
CREDITS

CAPTAIN AMERICA
Nos. 101-113

Writer: **Stan Lee**

Pencilers: **Jack Kirby** (Nos. 101-109, 112)
Jim Steranko (Nos. 110, 111, 113)

Inkers: Syd Shores (Nos. 101-103, 107-109)
Dan Adkins (Nos. 104, 105)
Frank Giacoia (No. 106)
Joe Sinnott (Nos. 110, 111)
George Tuska (No. 112)
Tom Palmer (No. 113)

Letterers: Art Simek (Nos. 101-104, 107-109, 112, 113)
Sam Rosen (Nos. 105, 106, 110, 111)

Color Reconstruction: Wesley Wong (Nos. 101-104)
Tom Mullin (Nos. 105-108)
Wil Glass & All Thumbs Creative (Nos. 109-113; Covers)

Art Reconstruction: Wesley Wong (Nos. 101-104)
Tom Mullin (Nos. 105-108)
Wil Glass & All Thumbs Creative (Nos. 109-113; Covers)

Special Thanks: Tom Brevoort, Ralph Macchio, Harry Mendryk & the Richard Howell/Carol Kalish Collection

Captain America created by Joe Simon & Jack Kirby

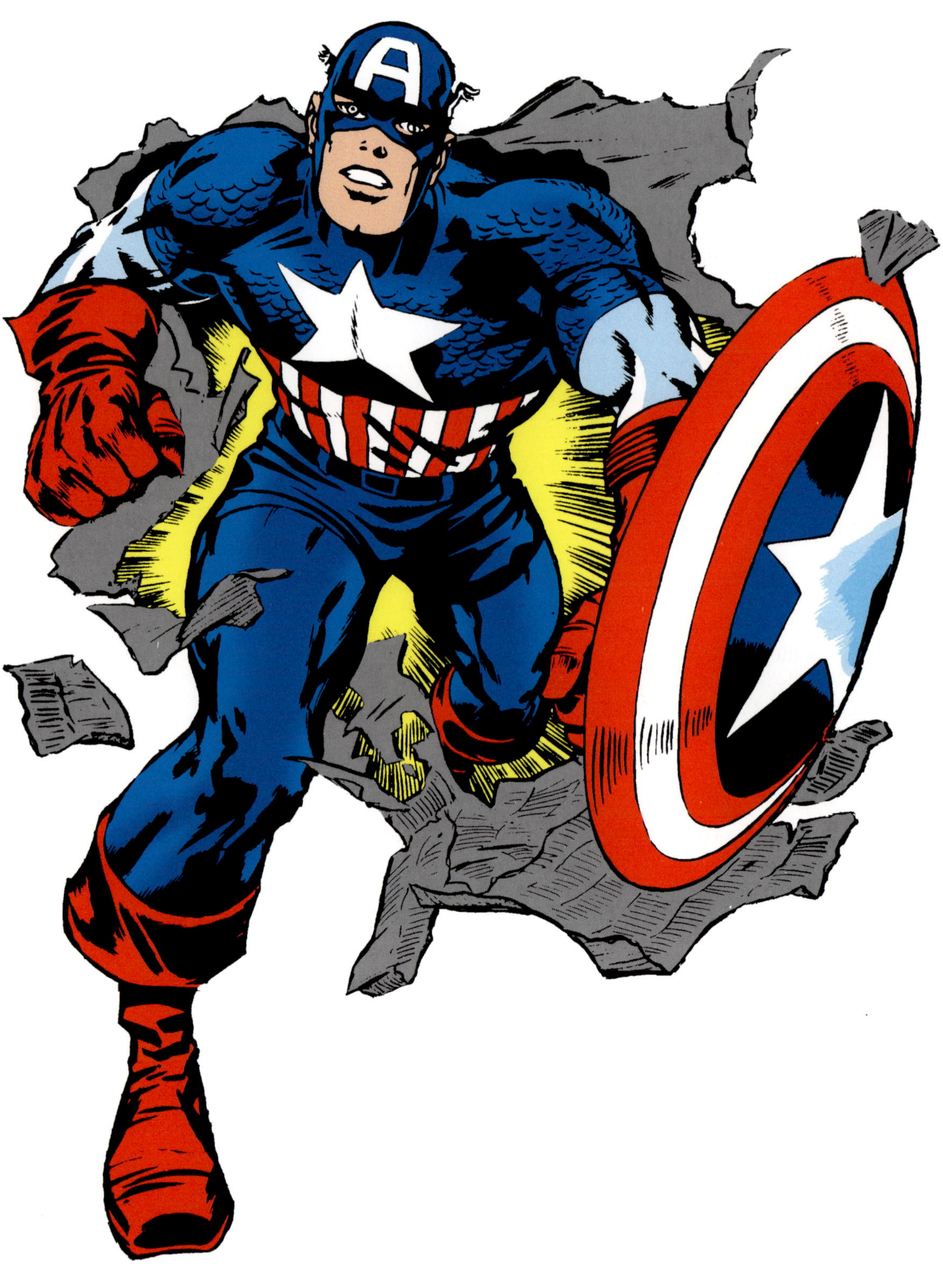

MARVEL MASTERWORKS
Contents

Introduction by John Morrow......vi

Captain America #101, May 1968
   "When Wakes the Sleeper!"......1

Captain America #102, June 1968
   "The Sleeper Strikes!"......21

Captain America #103, July 1968
   "The Weakest Link!"......42

Captain America #104, August 1968
   "Slave of the Skull!"......63

Captain America #105, September 1968
   "In the Name of Batroc!"......84

Captain America #106, October 1968
   "Cap Goes Wild!"......105

Captain America #107, November 1968
   "If the Past Be Not Dead--"......126

Captain America #108, December 1968
   "The Snares of the Trapster!"......147

Captain America #109, January 1969
   "The Hero That Was!"......168

Captain America #110, February 1969
   "No Longer Alone!"......190

Captain America #111, March 1969
   "Tomorrow You Live, Tonight I Die!"......212

Captain America #112, April 1969
   "Lest We Forget!"......233

Captain America #113, May 1969
   "The Strange Death of Captain America"......254

LEAVE 'EM WANTING MORE
BY JOHN MORROW

The volume you hold in your hands presents stellar work by two of my favorite artists of all time. Just the same, it's a bittersweet experience to pen the introduction to this book, because I had to go back and re-read the stories—and they always leave me wanting more.

The first artist represented is Jack Kirby, who, together with Stan Lee, ushered in the Marvel Age back with *Fantastic Four* #1 in 1961. But Kirby's career had flourished long before that, and his first big hit was in co-creating (with partner Joe Simon) Captain America in 1941. Prior to his 1960s run, Kirby had only drawn the first dozen of the Star-Spangled Avenger's appearances in the 1940s, but the course was set. Kirby came back to the character two decades later without missing a beat, taking a hero who could've easily been seen as passé in those socially-relevant 1960s, and injecting a new sense of vitality to him. But not long after penciling the stories in this collection, Kirby left Marvel, and left me, and countless other readers, wishing for just one more 1960s Kirby *Cap* story.

The other artist here is Jim Steranko; musician, magician, designer, publisher, escape artist, and not least of all, comic book artist. While the actual number of comics stories he's drawn is few compared to a prodigious creator like Kirby, his innovations in the field are many, and several are on display here. One thing that's always stuck in my mind is the way Steranko portrayed the Hulk in issue #110. The character's essentially there just as a vehicle to get Rick Jones into the storyline, but in only 20 panels, Jim manages to convey the wild, rampaging nature of ol' Greenskin better than any other artist to this day, including Kirby. (Note his use of rear views, severe angles, and cropping on the Hulk to keep the reader off-balance as the city gets destroyed; it's really disconcerting that we never get a good straight-on shot of the character until he finally departs. Steranko kept us wanting to see more the whole time.)

On the surface, these two comic book legends would seem to be polar opposites of one another—Kirby's all about power, Steranko's all about atmosphere. But upon closer inspection, it's clear these two gents actually work well together in this collection, even if they're not in the same issues. (Although sharp-eyed readers will spot some Steranko faces on the Nick Fury figures in the Kirby stories—probably done to carry through the look that Steranko had established in his popular S.H.I.E.L.D. series running around the same time.)

Here are two men, separated by decades in age, but both with similar storytelling sensibilities, if not similar styles. Both men really know how to tell a story well. They don't do it the same way; with Kirby, it's effortless and transparent. You get the sense that it just flows out of him, like water from a faucet. With Steranko, it's much more labored, more intentional, but equally as potent. Sit and read any issue in this volume, and see if you aren't totally absorbed in the story by the last page. And see if reading one story doesn't (you guessed it) leave you wanting more.

There is an unintentional pairing of the two presented here. Sandwiched in between Steranko's second and third story is a Kirby fill-in (issue #112). Legend has it that Jim was running late with the final installment of the tale, and as insurance against missing the deadline, Stan Lee called up Kirby and asked him to pencil an issue that'd fill 20 pages, without actually advancing the plot. Steranko swears he got his pages in by deadline, but I guess Marvel didn't want to waste a Kirby story they'd already paid for. So, the Kirby story ran in #112, complete with some admirable last-minute inks by George Tuska, and Steranko left the strip after the following issue, never to return. Once again, we got just a taste—this time, of Steranko on Cap—and were left wanting more, more, more.

Of course, we shouldn't overlook the contributions of the inkers on the stories presented here—and what a mixed bag Marvel used! Golden Age great Syd Shores, who worked on the original 1940s incarnation of Cap, continued his inking run from the previous two issues. His fussy, heavily rendered inks seem to be in direct opposition to Kirby's bold, powerful, in-your-face penciling, but after removing him from the book for a few issues, Stan Lee reassigned him, no doubt due to fan response. In between Shores' stints was Dan Adkins, who turned in inks very faithful to Kirby's pencils of the period. Then, in #106, we're treated to the lush work of Frank Giacoia, with (in my opinion) just the right balance of spotting blacks and slick brushwork. But it's only for one issue; once again, I wanted (and didn't get) more Giacoia, who, to my mind, supplied the finest inking Kirby gets in this volume.

It's not, however, the finest inking in this book; that honor has to go to Joe Sinnott. It's here, inking Steranko's first two Cap tales, that you get, for my money, one of the best pairings of penciler and inker in comics history, ever. While Tom Palmer did a fine job on the final Steranko story, Sinnott's inks add an extra degree of polish to Jim's inventive layouts. After seeing Joe ink the first two installments of Steranko's story arc, I couldn't wait to see him ink the final one. True to form for this collection, it didn't happen.

Add Stan Lee's quick, snappy patter to all this visual wonderment, and you've got one heck of a collection of stories. Sure, there's a few plot holes big enough to drive a Hydra vehicle through, but this is arguably the best run the good Captain ever had in his 65 years of existence—and unfortunately, the end of the line for both Kirby and Steranko on the strip.

Don't get me wrong; I'm thankful for the fabulous stories I *did* get to read here. But if you're like me, once you've finished this book, you'll still want more.

Kirby's no longer with us; if someone could just convince Steranko to do one last *Cap* story...

2006

John Morrow founded TwoMorrows Publishing in 1994 with the release of the first issue of The Jack Kirby Collector, *his magazine celebrating the life and career of the prodigious comics creator. Still going strong after 45 issues and five softcover collections, the Kirby Collector is the flagship of the TwoMorrows magazine line, which includes* Alter Ego, Draw!, Write Now, *and* Back Issue, *all dedicated to bringing new life to comics fandom.*

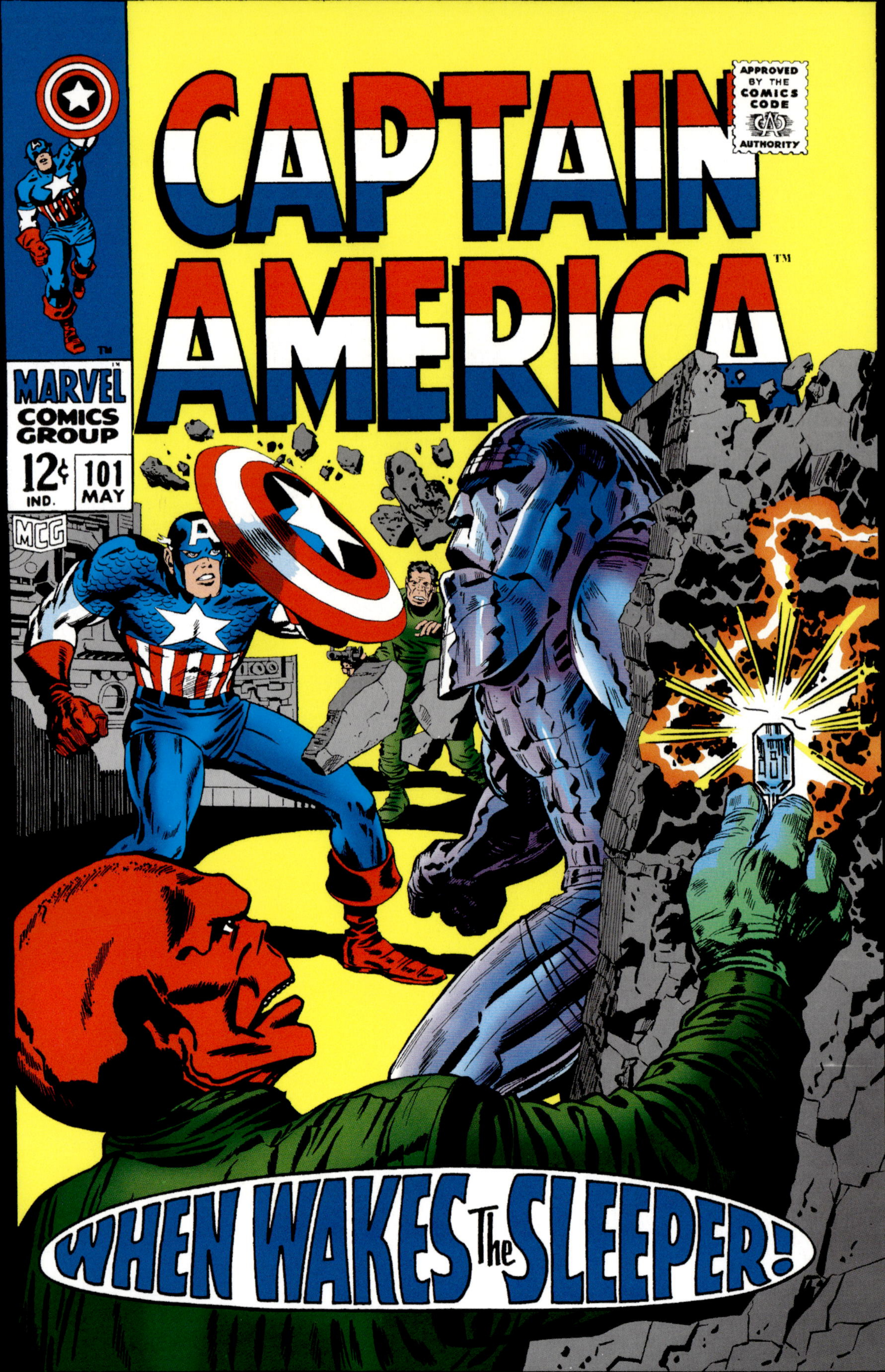
CAPTAIN AMERICA™
MARVEL COMICS GROUP
12¢ IND.
101 MAY
MCG
APPROVED BY THE COMICS CODE AUTHORITY
WHEN WAKES The SLEEPER!

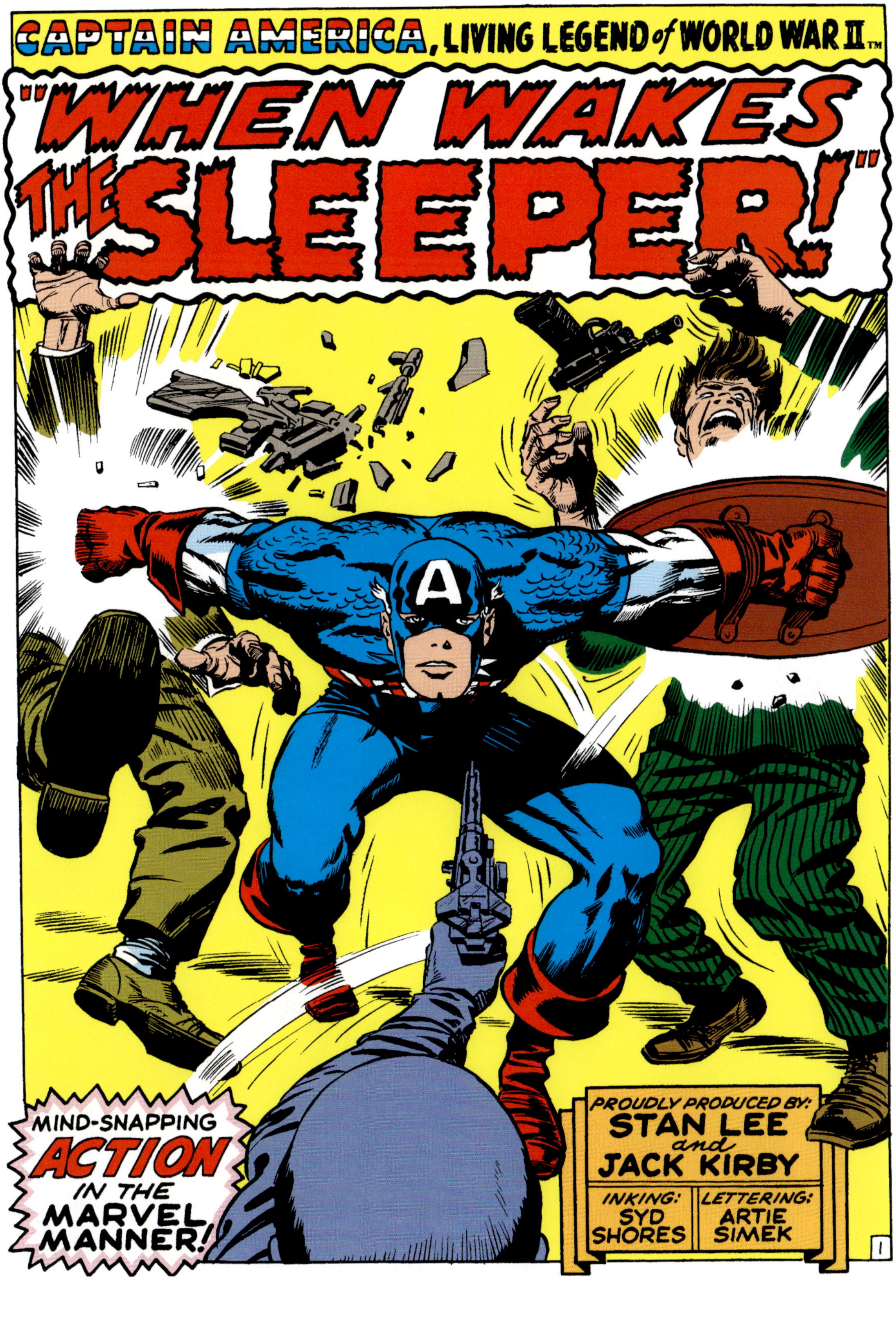
CAPTAIN AMERICA, LIVING LEGEND of WORLD WAR II™
"WHEN WAKES THE SLEEPER!"
MIND-SNAPPING ACTION IN THE MARVEL MANNER!
PROUDLY PRODUCED BY: STAN LEE and JACK KIRBY
INKING: SYD SHORES
LETTERING: ARTIE SIMEK
1

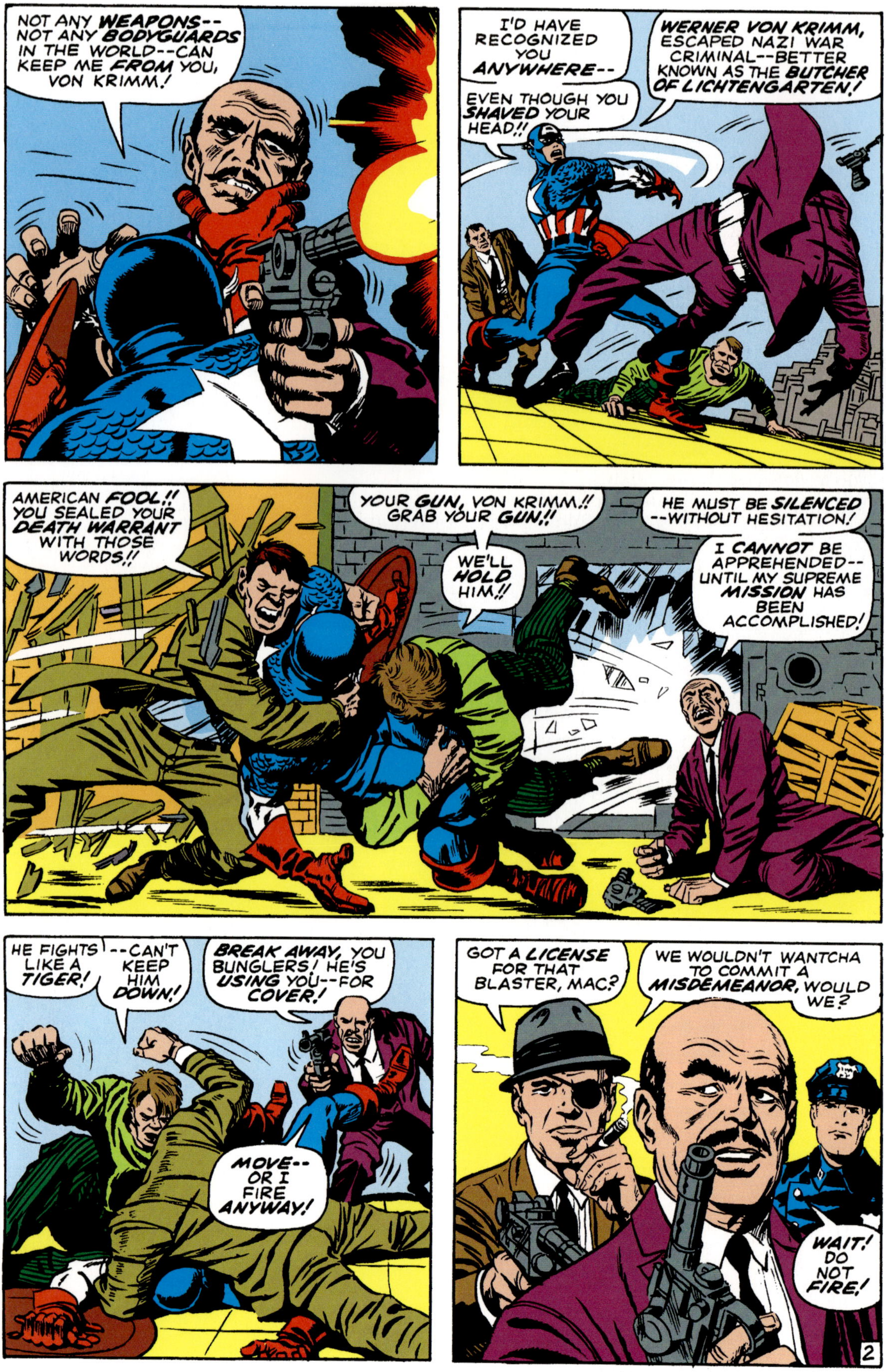
NOT ANY WEAPONS--
NOT ANY BODYGUARDS IN THE WORLD--CAN KEEP ME FROM YOU, VON KRIMM!
I'D HAVE RECOGNIZED YOU ANYWHERE--
EVEN THOUGH YOU SHAVED YOUR HEAD!!
WERNER VON KRIMM, ESCAPED NAZI WAR CRIMINAL--BETTER KNOWN AS THE BUTCHER OF LICHTENGARTEN!
AMERICAN FOOL!! YOU SEALED YOUR DEATH WARRANT WITH THOSE WORDS!!
YOUR GUN, VON KRIMM!! GRAB YOUR GUN!!
WE'LL HOLD HIM!!
HE MUST BE SILENCED --WITHOUT HESITATION!
I CANNOT BE APPREHENDED-- UNTIL MY SUPREME MISSION HAS BEEN ACCOMPLISHED!
HE FIGHTS LIKE A TIGER!
--CAN'T KEEP HIM DOWN!
BREAK AWAY, YOU BUNGLERS! HE'S USING YOU--FOR COVER!
MOVE-- OR I FIRE ANYWAY!
GOT A LICENSE FOR THAT BLASTER, MAC?
WE WOULDN'T WANTCHA TO COMMIT A MISDEMEANOR, WOULD WE?
WAIT! DO NOT FIRE!
2

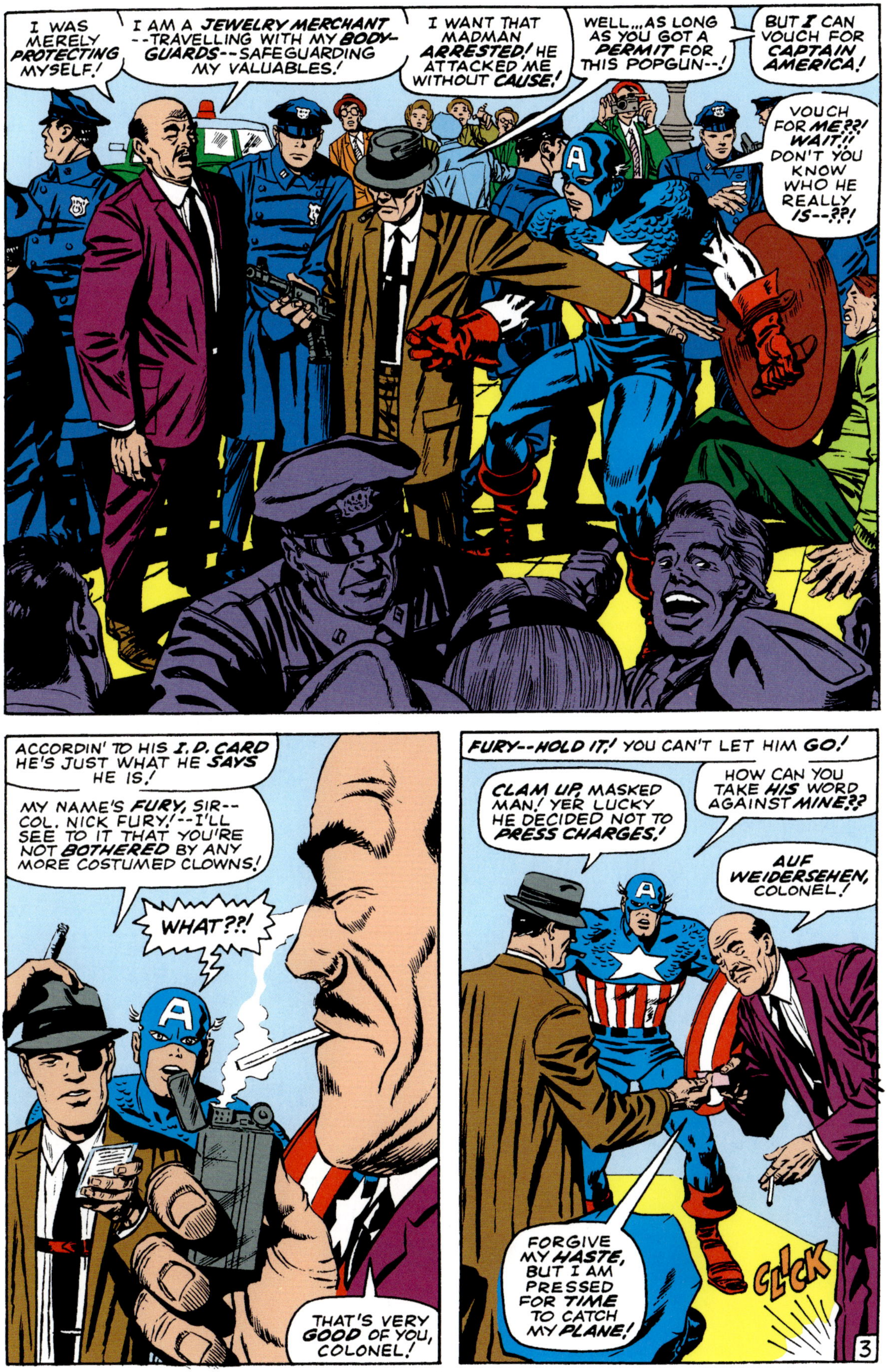
I WAS MERELY PROTECTING MYSELF.!
I AM A JEWELRY MERCHANT --TRAVELLING WITH MY BODY-GUARDS--SAFEGUARDING MY VALUABLES.!
I WANT THAT MADMAN ARRESTED! HE ATTACKED ME WITHOUT CAUSE!
WELL...AS LONG AS YOU GOT A PERMIT FOR THIS POPGUN--!
BUT I CAN VOUCH FOR CAPTAIN AMERICA!
VOUCH FOR ME??! WAIT!! DON'T YOU KNOW WHO HE REALLY IS--??!
ACCORDIN' TO HIS I.D. CARD HE'S JUST WHAT HE SAYS HE IS.!
MY NAME'S FURY, SIR--COL. NICK FURY!--I'LL SEE TO IT THAT YOU'RE NOT BOTHERED BY ANY MORE COSTUMED CLOWNS!
WHAT??!
THAT'S VERY GOOD OF YOU, COLONEL!
FURY--HOLD IT! YOU CAN'T LET HIM GO!
CLAM UP, MASKED MAN! YER LUCKY HE DECIDED NOT TO PRESS CHARGES!
HOW CAN YOU TAKE HIS WORD AGAINST MINE??
AUF WEIDERSEHEN, COLONEL!
FORGIVE MY HASTE, BUT I AM PRESSED FOR TIME TO CATCH MY PLANE!
CLICK
3

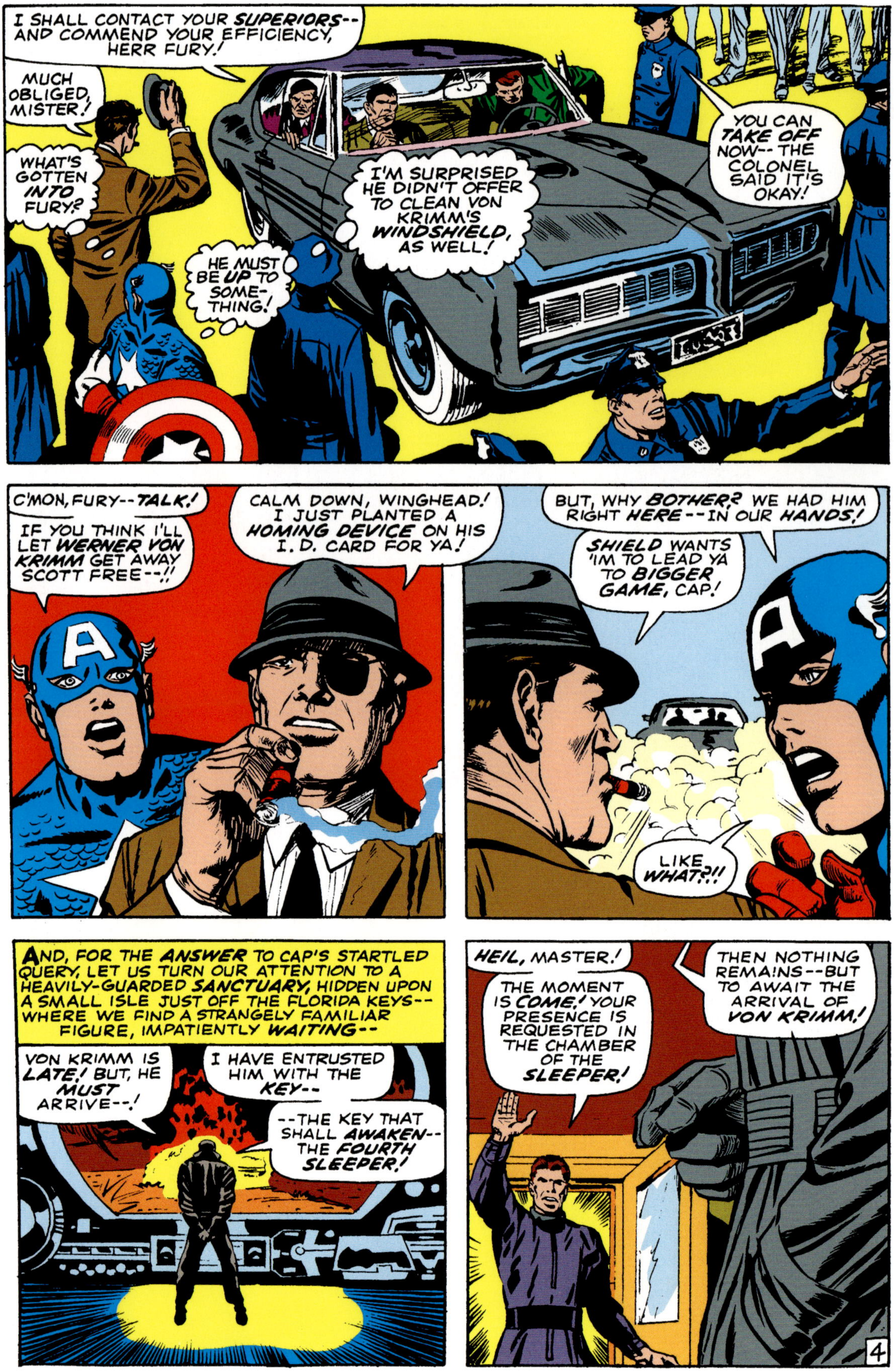

I SHALL CONTACT YOUR SUPERIORS-- AND COMMEND YOUR EFFICIENCY, HERR FURY!
MUCH OBLIGED, MISTER!
WHAT'S GOTTEN INTO FURY?
HE MUST BE UP TO SOME-THING!
I'M SURPRISED HE DIDN'T OFFER TO CLEAN VON KRIMM'S WINDSHIELD, AS WELL!
YOU CAN TAKE OFF NOW-- THE COLONEL SAID IT'S OKAY!
C'MON, FURY-- TALK!
IF YOU THINK I'LL LET WERNER VON KRIMM GET AWAY SCOTT FREE--!!
CALM DOWN, WINGHEAD! I JUST PLANTED A HOMING DEVICE ON HIS I. D. CARD FOR YA!
BUT, WHY BOTHER? WE HAD HIM RIGHT HERE--IN OUR HANDS!
SHIELD WANTS 'IM TO LEAD YA TO BIGGER GAME, CAP!
LIKE WHAT?!!
AND, FOR THE ANSWER TO CAP'S STARTLED QUERY, LET US TURN OUR ATTENTION TO A HEAVILY-GUARDED SANCTUARY, HIDDEN UPON A SMALL ISLE JUST OFF THE FLORIDA KEYS-- WHERE WE FIND A STRANGELY FAMILIAR FIGURE, IMPATIENTLY WAITING--
VON KRIMM IS LATE! BUT, HE MUST ARRIVE--!
I HAVE ENTRUSTED HIM WITH THE KEY--
--THE KEY THAT SHALL AWAKEN-- THE FOURTH SLEEPER!
HEIL, MASTER!
THE MOMENT IS COME! YOUR PRESENCE IS REQUESTED IN THE CHAMBER OF THE SLEEPER!
THEN NOTHING REMAINS--BUT TO AWAIT THE ARRIVAL OF VON KRIMM!
4

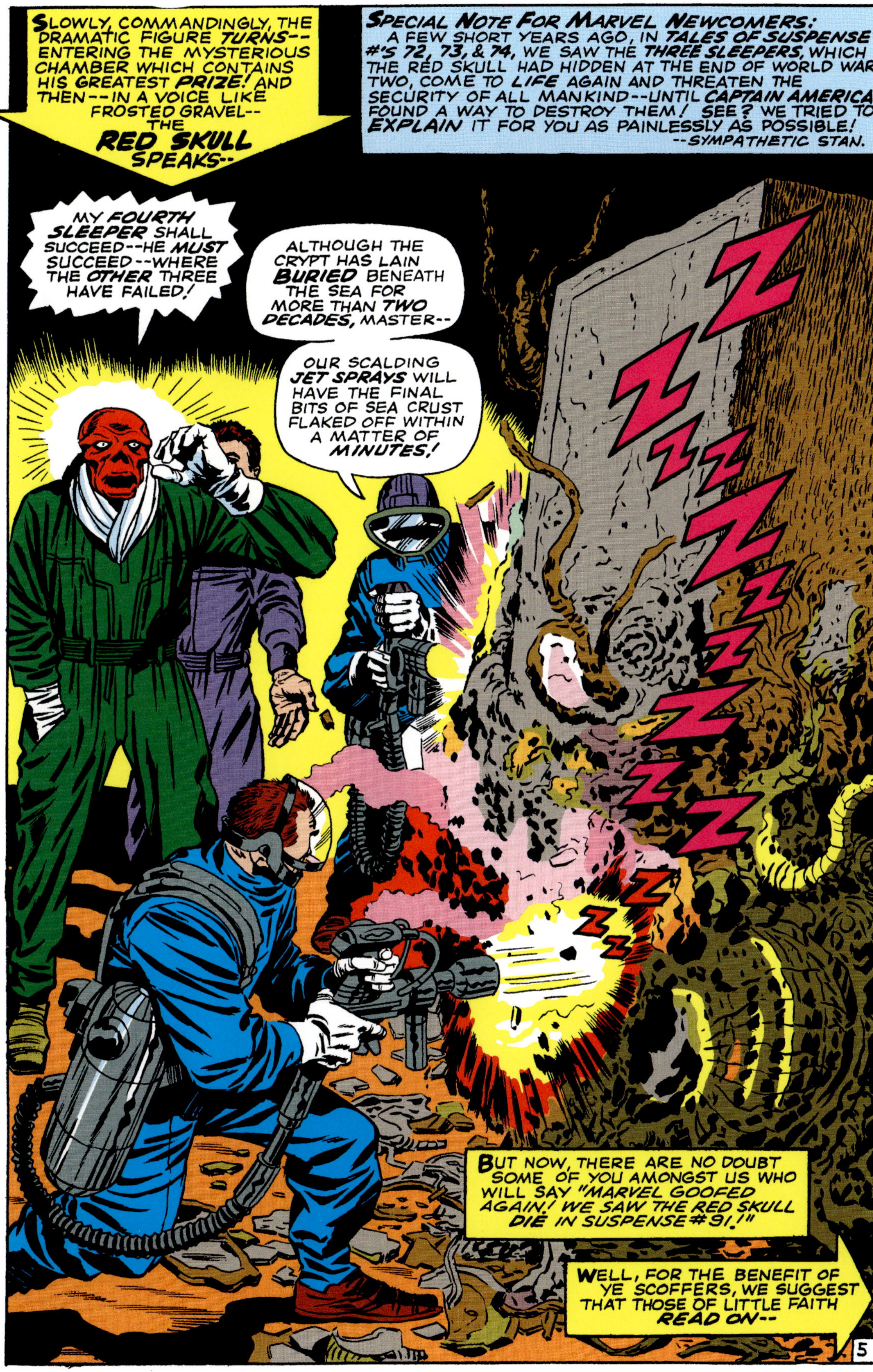
SLOWLY, COMMANDINGLY, THE DRAMATIC FIGURE TURNS-- ENTERING THE MYSTERIOUS CHAMBER WHICH CONTAINS HIS GREATEST PRIZE! AND THEN--IN A VOICE LIKE FROSTED GRAVEL-- THE RED SKULL SPEAKS--
SPECIAL NOTE FOR MARVEL NEWCOMERS: A FEW SHORT YEARS AGO, IN TALES OF SUSPENSE #'S 72, 73, & 74, WE SAW THE THREE SLEEPERS, WHICH THE RED SKULL HAD HIDDEN AT THE END OF WORLD WAR TWO, COME TO LIFE AGAIN AND THREATEN THE SECURITY OF ALL MANKIND--UNTIL CAPTAIN AMERICA FOUND A WAY TO DESTROY THEM! SEE? WE TRIED TO EXPLAIN IT FOR YOU AS PAINLESSLY AS POSSIBLE! --SYMPATHETIC STAN.
MY FOURTH SLEEPER SHALL SUCCEED--HE MUST SUCCEED--WHERE THE OTHER THREE HAVE FAILED!
ALTHOUGH THE CRYPT HAS LAIN BURIED BENEATH THE SEA FOR MORE THAN TWO DECADES, MASTER--
OUR SCALDING JET SPRAYS WILL HAVE THE FINAL BITS OF SEA CRUST FLAKED OFF WITHIN A MATTER OF MINUTES!
ZZZZZZZZZZ
ZZZ
BUT NOW, THERE ARE NO DOUBT SOME OF YOU AMONGST US WHO WILL SAY "MARVEL GOOFED AGAIN! WE SAW THE RED SKULL DIE IN SUSPENSE #91!"
WELL, FOR THE BENEFIT OF YE SCOFFERS, WE SUGGEST THAT THOSE OF LITTLE FAITH READ ON--
5

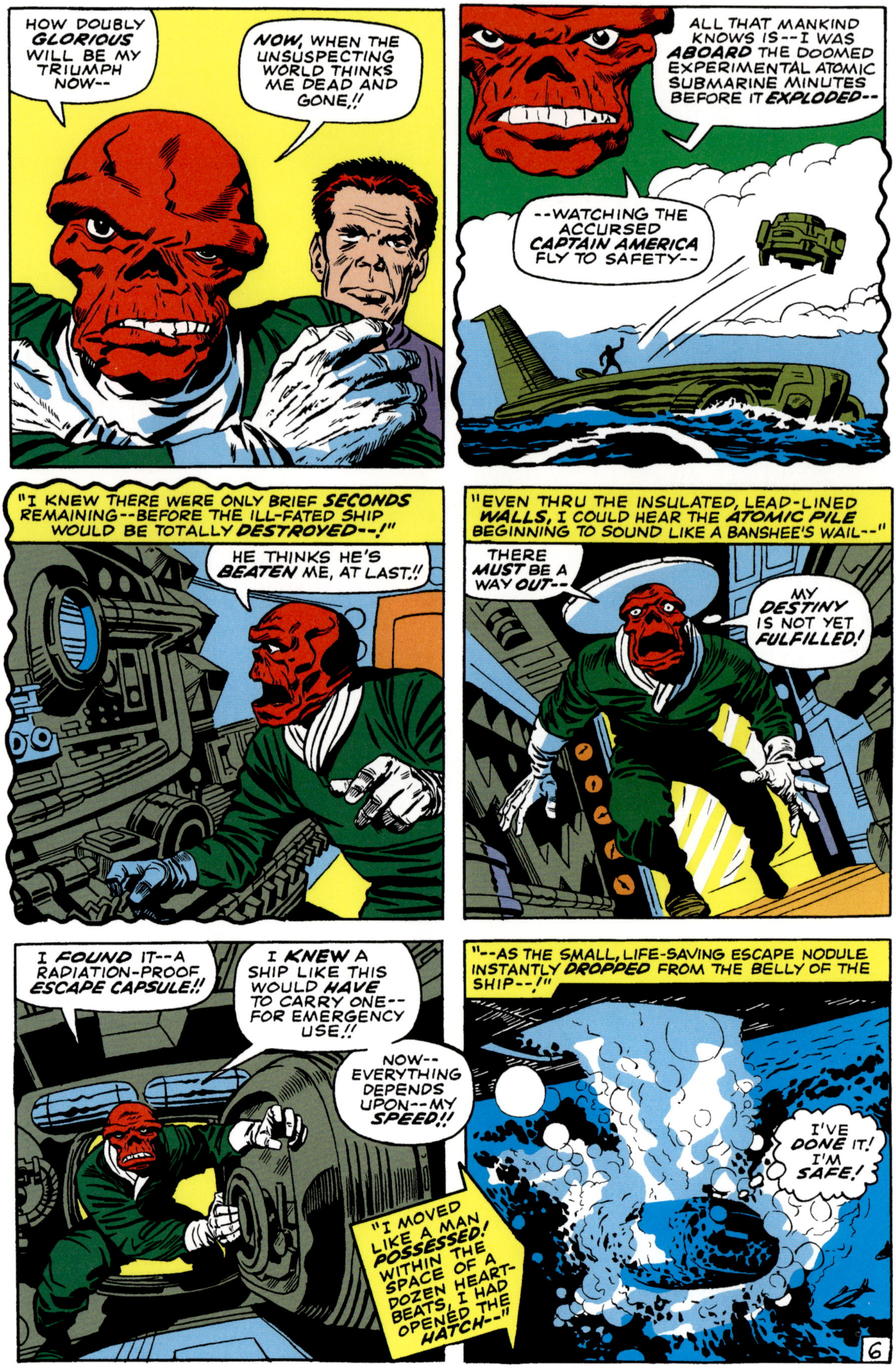
HOW DOUBLY GLORIOUS WILL BE MY TRIUMPH NOW--
NOW, WHEN THE UNSUSPECTING WORLD THINKS ME DEAD AND GONE!!
ALL THAT MANKIND KNOWS IS--I WAS ABOARD THE DOOMED EXPERIMENTAL ATOMIC SUBMARINE MINUTES BEFORE IT EXPLODED--
--WATCHING THE ACCURSED CAPTAIN AMERICA FLY TO SAFETY--
"I KNEW THERE WERE ONLY BRIEF SECONDS REMAINING--BEFORE THE ILL-FATED SHIP WOULD BE TOTALLY DESTROYED--!"
HE THINKS HE'S BEATEN ME, AT LAST!!
"EVEN THRU THE INSULATED, LEAD-LINED WALLS, I COULD HEAR THE ATOMIC PILE BEGINNING TO SOUND LIKE A BANSHEE'S WAIL--"
THERE MUST BE A WAY OUT--
MY DESTINY IS NOT YET FULFILLED!
I FOUND IT--A RADIATION-PROOF ESCAPE CAPSULE!!
I KNEW A SHIP LIKE THIS WOULD HAVE TO CARRY ONE--FOR EMERGENCY USE!!
NOW--EVERYTHING DEPENDS UPON--MY SPEED!!
"I MOVED LIKE A MAN POSSESSED! WITHIN THE SPACE OF A DOZEN HEART-BEATS, I HAD OPENED THE HATCH--"
"--AS THE SMALL, LIFE-SAVING ESCAPE NODULE INSTANTLY DROPPED FROM THE BELLY OF THE SHIP--!"
I'VE DONE IT! I'M SAFE!
6

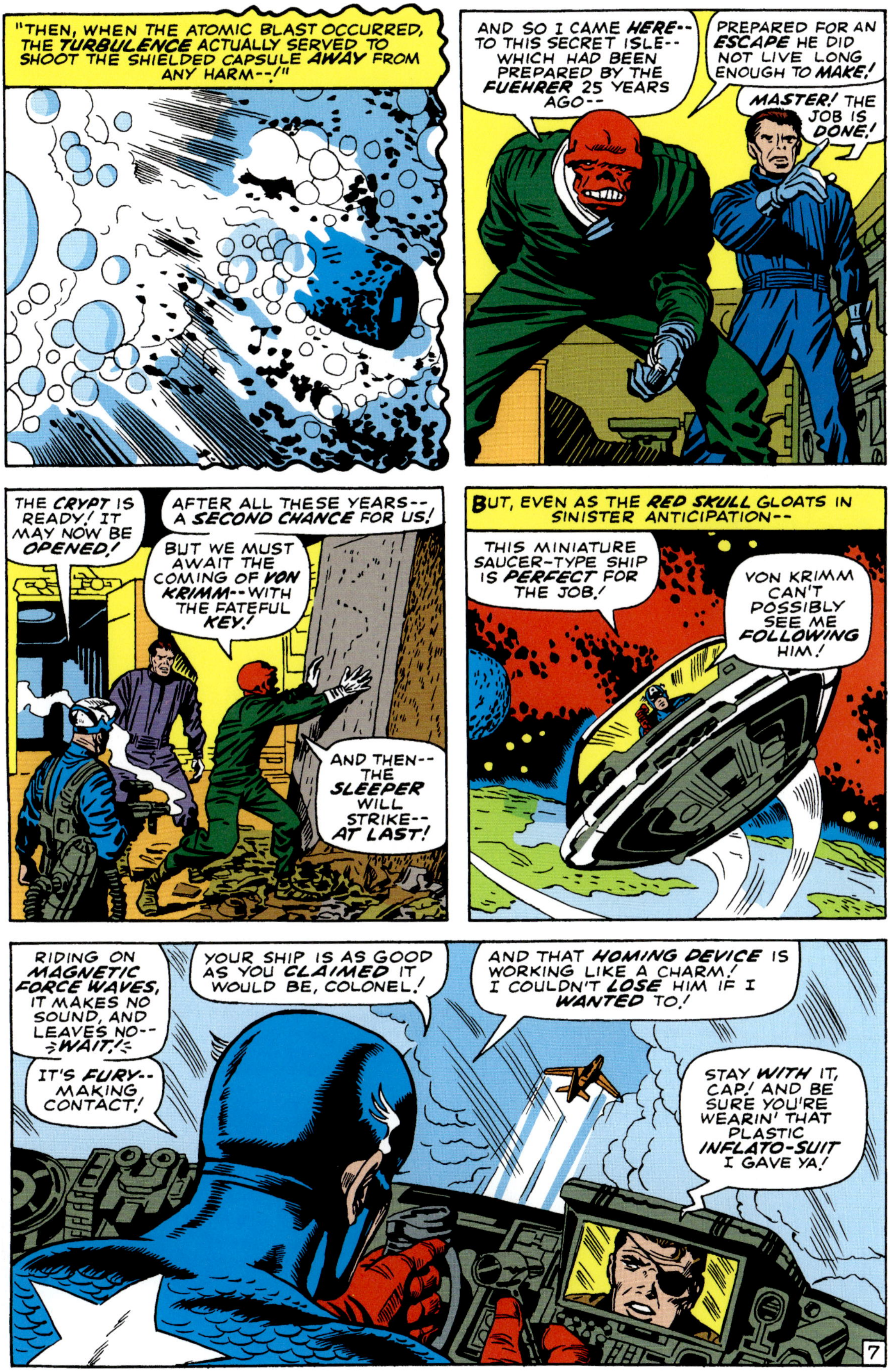
"THEN, WHEN THE ATOMIC BLAST OCCURRED, THE TURBULENCE ACTUALLY SERVED TO SHOOT THE SHIELDED CAPSULE AWAY FROM ANY HARM--!"
AND SO I CAME HERE-- TO THIS SECRET ISLE-- WHICH HAD BEEN PREPARED BY THE FUEHRER 25 YEARS AGO--
PREPARED FOR AN ESCAPE HE DID NOT LIVE LONG ENOUGH TO MAKE!
MASTER! THE JOB IS DONE!
THE CRYPT IS READY! IT MAY NOW BE OPENED!
AFTER ALL THESE YEARS-- A SECOND CHANCE FOR US!
BUT WE MUST AWAIT THE COMING OF VON KRIMM--WITH THE FATEFUL KEY!
AND THEN-- THE SLEEPER WILL STRIKE-- AT LAST!
BUT, EVEN AS THE RED SKULL GLOATS IN SINISTER ANTICIPATION--
THIS MINIATURE SAUCER-TYPE SHIP IS PERFECT FOR THE JOB!
VON KRIMM CAN'T POSSIBLY SEE ME FOLLOWING HIM!
RIDING ON MAGNETIC FORCE WAVES, IT MAKES NO SOUND, AND LEAVES NO-- WAIT!
IT'S FURY-- MAKING CONTACT!
YOUR SHIP IS AS GOOD AS YOU CLAIMED IT WOULD BE, COLONEL!
AND THAT HOMING DEVICE IS WORKING LIKE A CHARM! I COULDN'T LOSE HIM IF I WANTED TO!
STAY WITH IT, CAP! AND BE SURE YOU'RE WEARIN' THAT PLASTIC INFLATO-SUIT I GAVE YA!
7

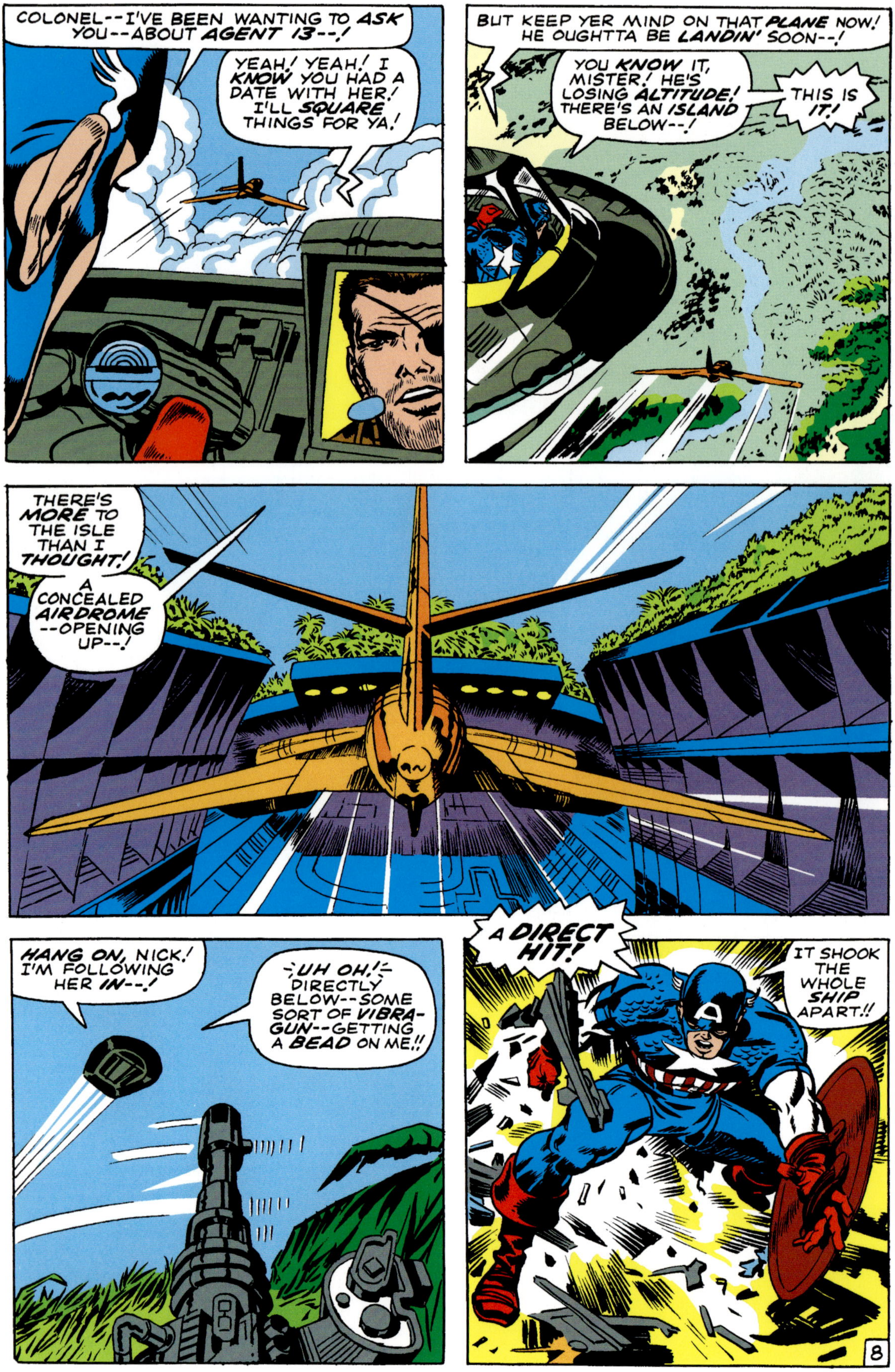
COLONEL--I'VE BEEN WANTING TO ASK YOU--ABOUT AGENT 13--!
YEAH! YEAH! I KNOW YOU HAD A DATE WITH HER! I'LL SQUARE THINGS FOR YA!
BUT KEEP YER MIND ON THAT PLANE NOW! HE OUGHTTA BE LANDIN' SOON--!
YOU KNOW IT, MISTER! HE'S LOSING ALTITUDE! THERE'S AN ISLAND BELOW--!
THIS IS IT!
THERE'S MORE TO THE ISLE THAN I THOUGHT!
A CONCEALED AIRDROME --OPENING UP--!
HANG ON, NICK! I'M FOLLOWING HER IN--!
UH OH! DIRECTLY BELOW--SOME SORT OF VIBRA-GUN--GETTING A BEAD ON ME!!
A DIRECT HIT!
IT SHOOK THE WHOLE SHIP APART!!
8

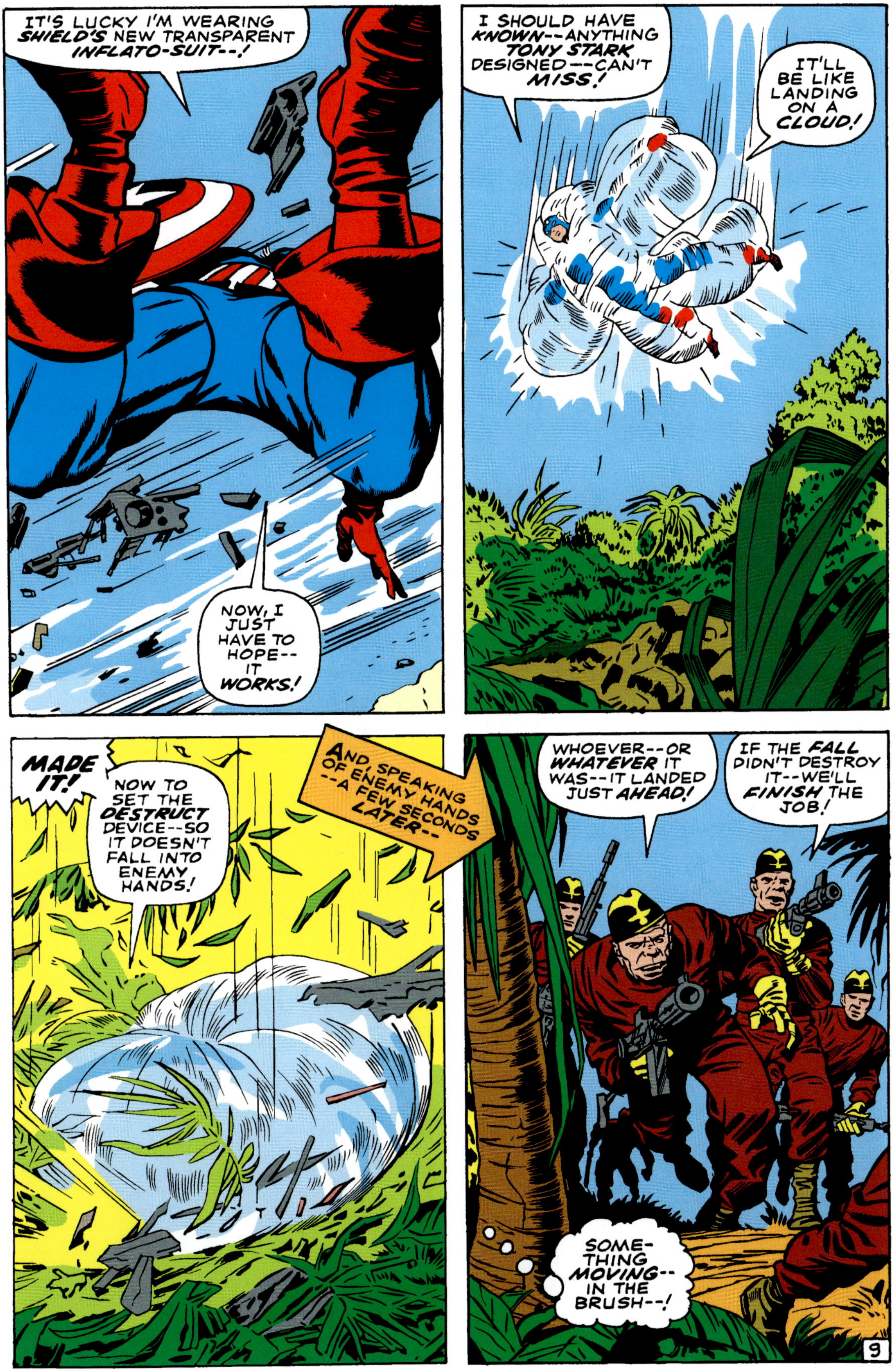
IT'S LUCKY I'M WEARING SHIELD'S NEW TRANSPARENT INFLATO-SUIT--!
NOW, I JUST HAVE TO HOPE-- IT WORKS!
I SHOULD HAVE KNOWN--ANYTHING TONY STARK DESIGNED--CAN'T MISS!
IT'LL BE LIKE LANDING ON A CLOUD!
MADE IT!
NOW TO SET THE DESTRUCT DEVICE--SO IT DOESN'T FALL INTO ENEMY HANDS!
AND, SPEAKING OF ENEMY HANDS --A FEW SECONDS LATER--
WHOEVER--OR WHATEVER IT WAS--IT LANDED JUST AHEAD!
IF THE FALL DIDN'T DESTROY IT--WE'LL FINISH THE JOB!
SOME-THING MOVING-- IN THE BRUSH--!
9

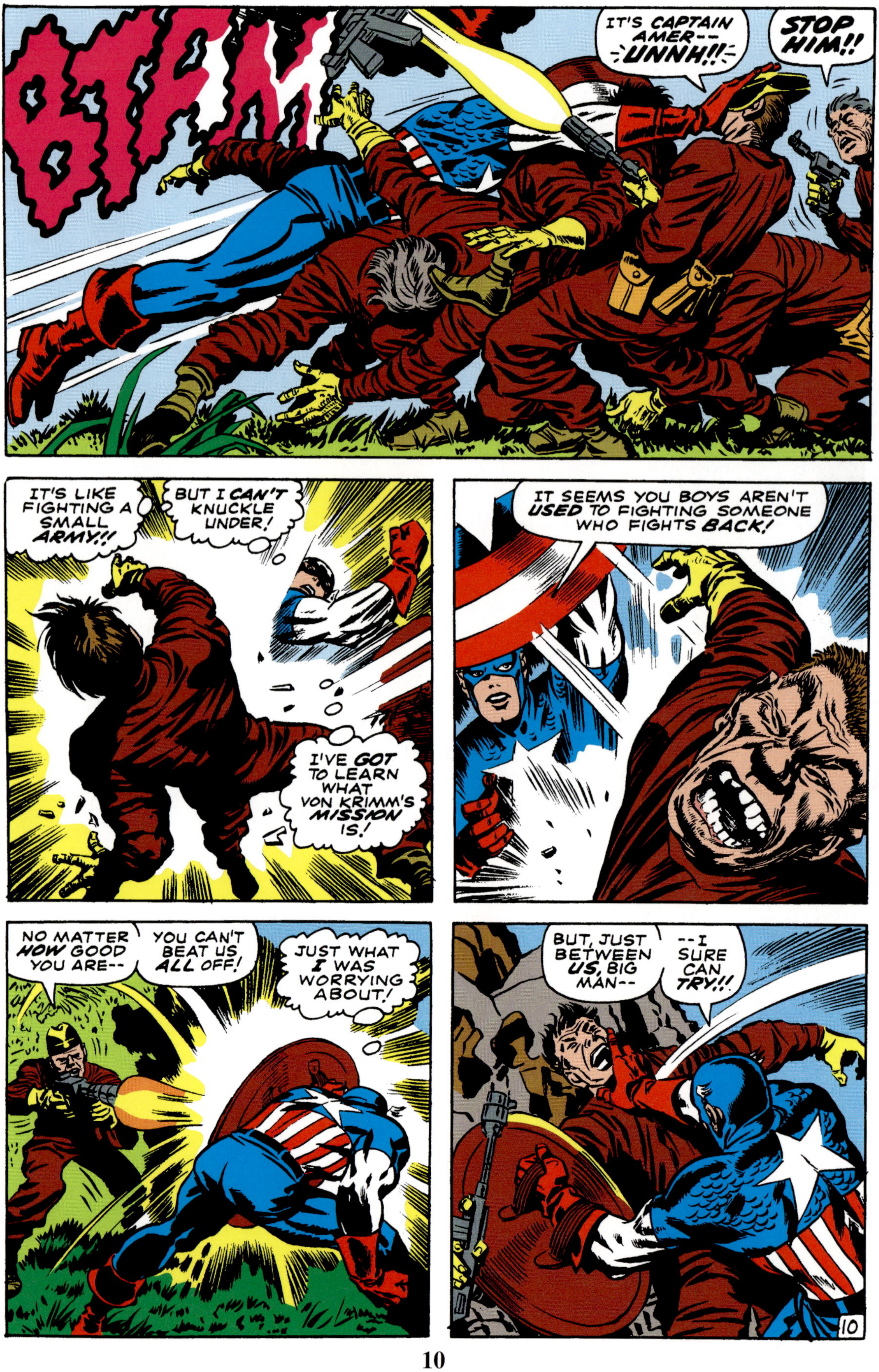
BTAM
IT'S CAPTAIN AMER-- -UNNH!!-
STOP HIM!!
IT'S LIKE FIGHTING A SMALL ARMY!!
BUT I CAN'T KNUCKLE UNDER!
I'VE GOT TO LEARN WHAT VON KRIMM'S MISSION IS!
IT SEEMS YOU BOYS AREN'T USED TO FIGHTING SOMEONE WHO FIGHTS BACK!
NO MATTER HOW GOOD YOU ARE--
YOU CAN'T BEAT US ALL OFF!
JUST WHAT I WAS WORRYING ABOUT!
BUT, JUST BETWEEN US, BIG MAN--
--I SURE CAN TRY!!
10

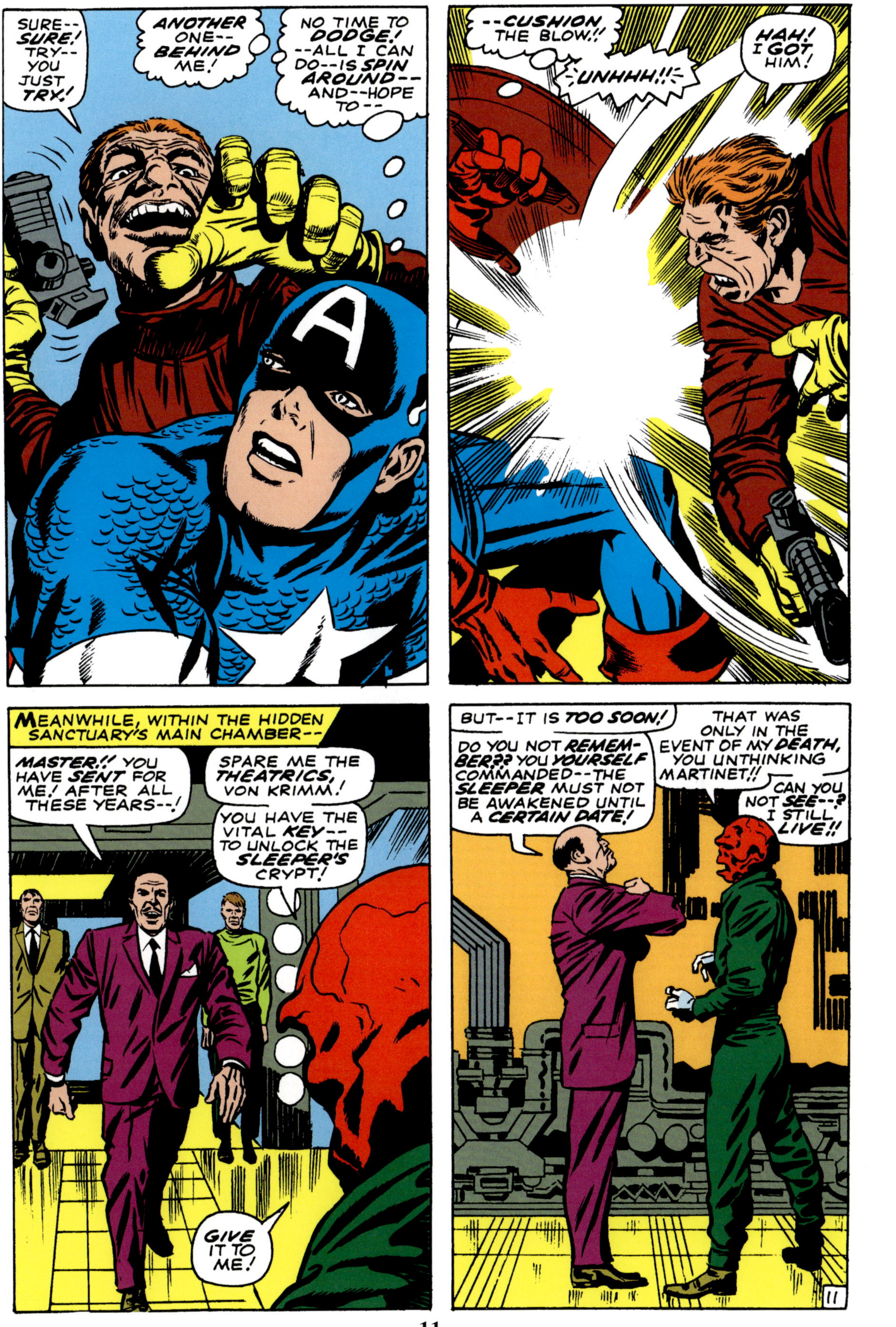
SURE--SURE! TRY--YOU JUST TRY!
ANOTHER ONE--BEHIND ME!
NO TIME TO DODGE! --ALL I CAN DO--IS SPIN AROUND--AND--HOPE TO--
--CUSHION THE BLOW!!
UNHHH!!
HAH! I GOT HIM!
MEANWHILE, WITHIN THE HIDDEN SANCTUARY'S MAIN CHAMBER--
MASTER!! YOU HAVE SENT FOR ME! AFTER ALL THESE YEARS--!
SPARE ME THE THEATRICS, VON KRIMM!
YOU HAVE THE VITAL KEY--TO UNLOCK THE SLEEPER'S CRYPT!
GIVE IT TO ME!
BUT--IT IS TOO SOON!
DO YOU NOT REMEMBER?? YOU YOURSELF COMMANDED--THE SLEEPER MUST NOT BE AWAKENED UNTIL A CERTAIN DATE!
THAT WAS ONLY IN THE EVENT OF MY DEATH, YOU UNTHINKING MARTINET!!
CAN YOU NOT SEE--? I STILL LIVE!!
11

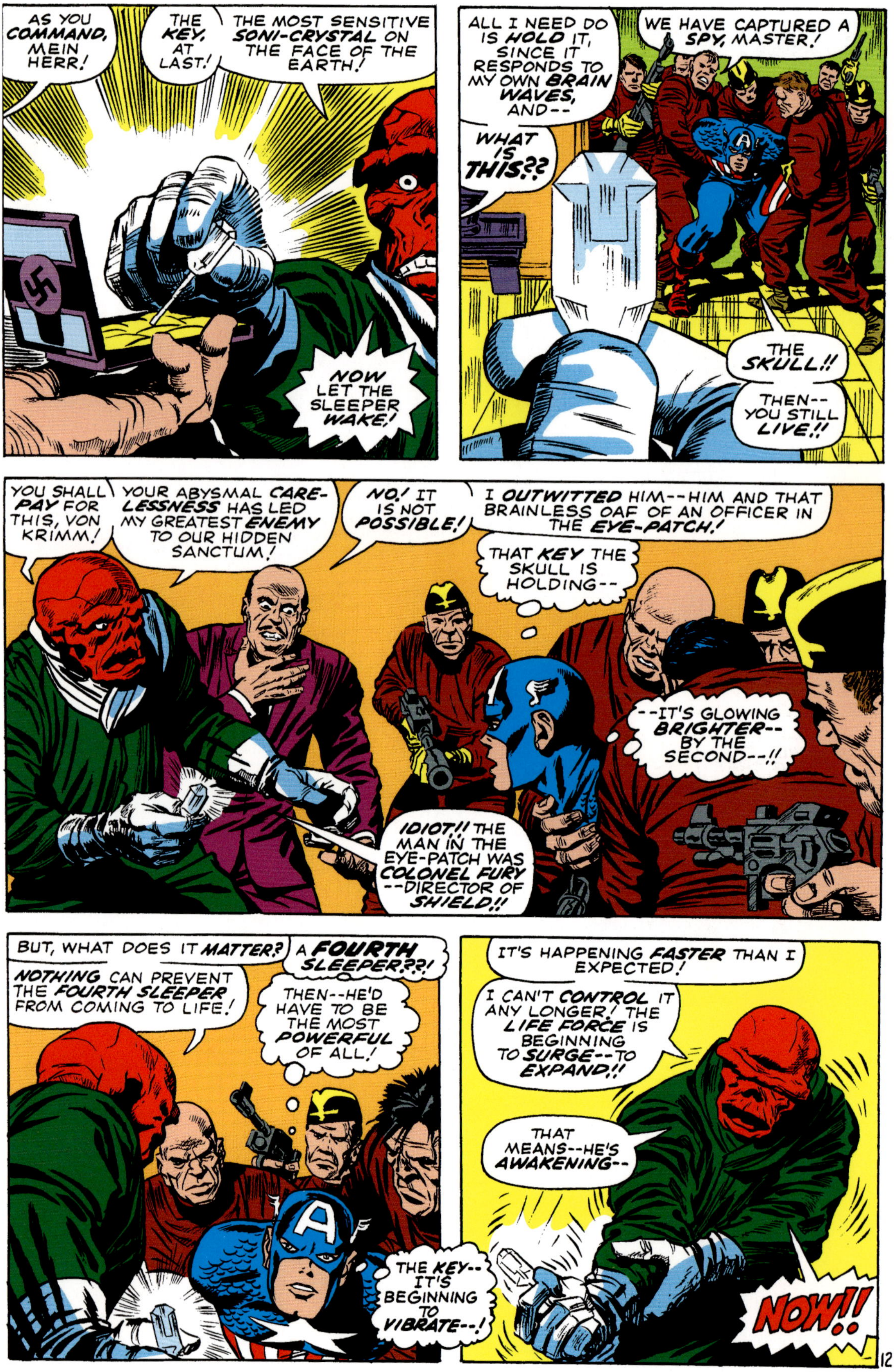
AS YOU COMMAND, MEIN HERR!
THE KEY, AT LAST!
THE MOST SENSITIVE SONI-CRYSTAL ON THE FACE OF THE EARTH!
NOW LET THE SLEEPER WAKE!
ALL I NEED DO IS HOLD IT, SINCE IT RESPONDS TO MY OWN BRAIN WAVES, AND--
WHAT IS THIS??
WE HAVE CAPTURED A SPY, MASTER!
THE SKULL!!
THEN--YOU STILL LIVE!!
YOU SHALL PAY FOR THIS, VON KRIMM!
YOUR ABYSMAL CARELESSNESS HAS LED MY GREATEST ENEMY TO OUR HIDDEN SANCTUM!
NO! IT IS NOT POSSIBLE!
I OUTWITTED HIM--HIM AND THAT BRAINLESS OAF OF AN OFFICER IN THE EYE-PATCH!
THAT KEY THE SKULL IS HOLDING--
--IT'S GLOWING BRIGHTER--BY THE SECOND--!!
IDIOT!! THE MAN IN THE EYE-PATCH WAS COLONEL FURY--DIRECTOR OF SHIELD!!
BUT, WHAT DOES IT MATTER?
NOTHING CAN PREVENT THE FOURTH SLEEPER FROM COMING TO LIFE!
A FOURTH SLEEPER??!
THEN--HE'D HAVE TO BE THE MOST POWERFUL OF ALL!
THE KEY--IT'S BEGINNING TO VIBRATE--!
IT'S HAPPENING FASTER THAN I EXPECTED!
I CAN'T CONTROL IT ANY LONGER! THE LIFE FORCE IS BEGINNING TO SURGE--TO EXPAND!!
THAT MEANS--HE'S AWAKENING--
NOW!!
12

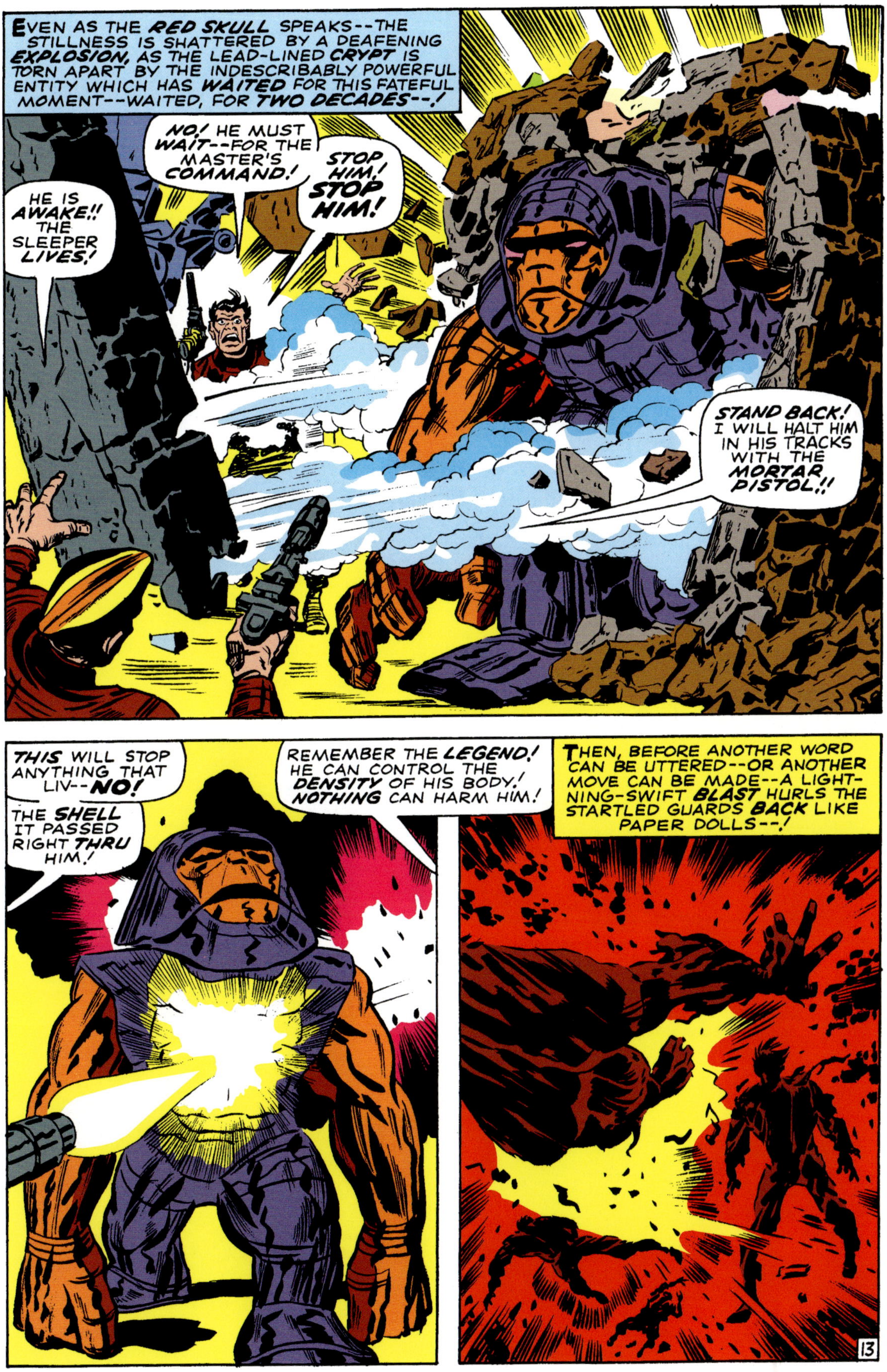
EVEN AS THE RED SKULL SPEAKS--THE STILLNESS IS SHATTERED BY A DEAFENING EXPLOSION, AS THE LEAD-LINED CRYPT IS TORN APART BY THE INDESCRIBABLY POWERFUL ENTITY WHICH HAS WAITED FOR THIS FATEFUL MOMENT--WAITED, FOR TWO DECADES--!
HE IS AWAKE!! THE SLEEPER LIVES!
NO! HE MUST WAIT--FOR THE MASTER'S COMMAND!
STOP HIM! STOP HIM!
STAND BACK! I WILL HALT HIM IN HIS TRACKS WITH THE MORTAR PISTOL!!
THIS WILL STOP ANYTHING THAT LIV--NO!
THE SHELL IT PASSED RIGHT THRU HIM!
REMEMBER THE LEGEND! HE CAN CONTROL THE DENSITY OF HIS BODY! NOTHING CAN HARM HIM!
THEN, BEFORE ANOTHER WORD CAN BE UTTERED--OR ANOTHER MOVE CAN BE MADE--A LIGHTNING-SWIFT BLAST HURLS THE STARTLED GUARDS BACK LIKE PAPER DOLLS--!
13

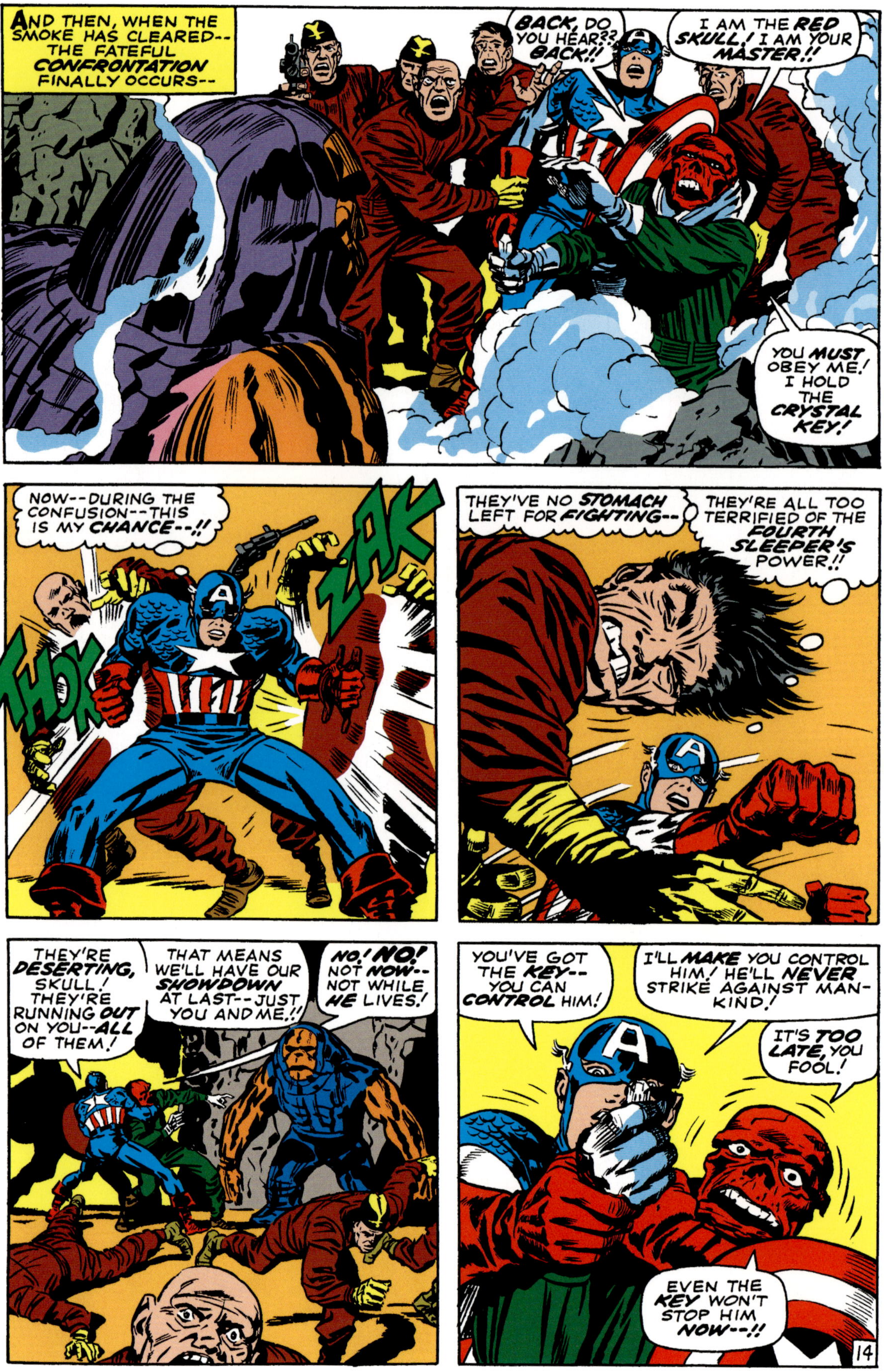
AND THEN, WHEN THE SMOKE HAS CLEARED-- THE FATEFUL CONFRONTATION FINALLY OCCURS--
BACK, DO YOU HEAR?? BACK!!
I AM THE RED SKULL! I AM YOUR MASTER!!
YOU MUST OBEY ME! I HOLD THE CRYSTAL KEY!
NOW--DURING THE CONFUSION--THIS IS MY CHANCE--!!
ZAK
THOK
THEY'VE NO STOMACH LEFT FOR FIGHTING--
THEY'RE ALL TOO TERRIFIED OF THE FOURTH SLEEPER'S POWER!!
THEY'RE DESERTING, SKULL! THEY'RE RUNNING OUT ON YOU--ALL OF THEM!
THAT MEANS WE'LL HAVE OUR SHOWDOWN AT LAST--JUST YOU AND ME!!
NO! NO! NOT NOW--NOT WHILE HE LIVES!
YOU'VE GOT THE KEY--YOU CAN CONTROL HIM!
I'LL MAKE YOU CONTROL HIM! HE'LL NEVER STRIKE AGAINST MAN-KIND!
IT'S TOO LATE, YOU FOOL!
EVEN THE KEY WON'T STOP HIM NOW--!!
14

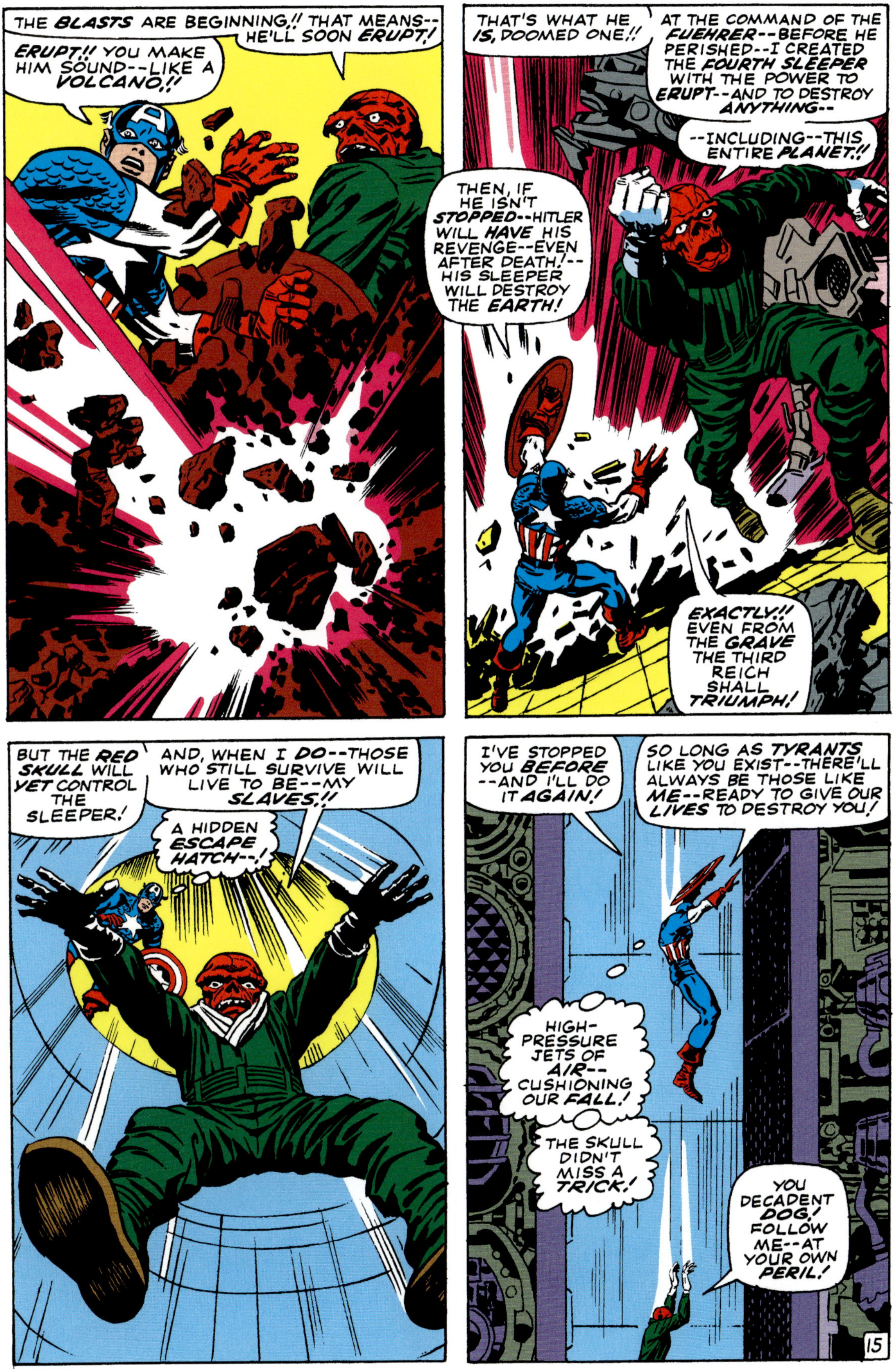
THE BLASTS ARE BEGINNING!! THAT MEANS-- HE'LL SOON ERUPT!
ERUPT!! YOU MAKE HIM SOUND--LIKE A VOLCANO!!
THAT'S WHAT HE IS, DOOMED ONE!!
AT THE COMMAND OF THE FUEHRER--BEFORE HE PERISHED--I CREATED THE FOURTH SLEEPER WITH THE POWER TO ERUPT--AND TO DESTROY ANYTHING--
--INCLUDING--THIS ENTIRE PLANET!!
THEN, IF HE ISN'T STOPPED--HITLER WILL HAVE HIS REVENGE--EVEN AFTER DEATH!--HIS SLEEPER WILL DESTROY THE EARTH!
EXACTLY!! EVEN FROM THE GRAVE THE THIRD REICH SHALL TRIUMPH!
BUT THE RED SKULL WILL YET CONTROL THE SLEEPER!
AND, WHEN I DO--THOSE WHO STILL SURVIVE WILL LIVE TO BE--MY SLAVES!!
A HIDDEN ESCAPE HATCH--!
I'VE STOPPED YOU BEFORE --AND I'LL DO IT AGAIN!
SO LONG AS TYRANTS LIKE YOU EXIST--THERE'LL ALWAYS BE THOSE LIKE ME--READY TO GIVE OUR LIVES TO DESTROY YOU!
HIGH-PRESSURE JETS OF AIR--CUSHIONING OUR FALL!
THE SKULL DIDN'T MISS A TRICK!
YOU DECADENT DOG! FOLLOW ME--AT YOUR OWN PERIL!
15

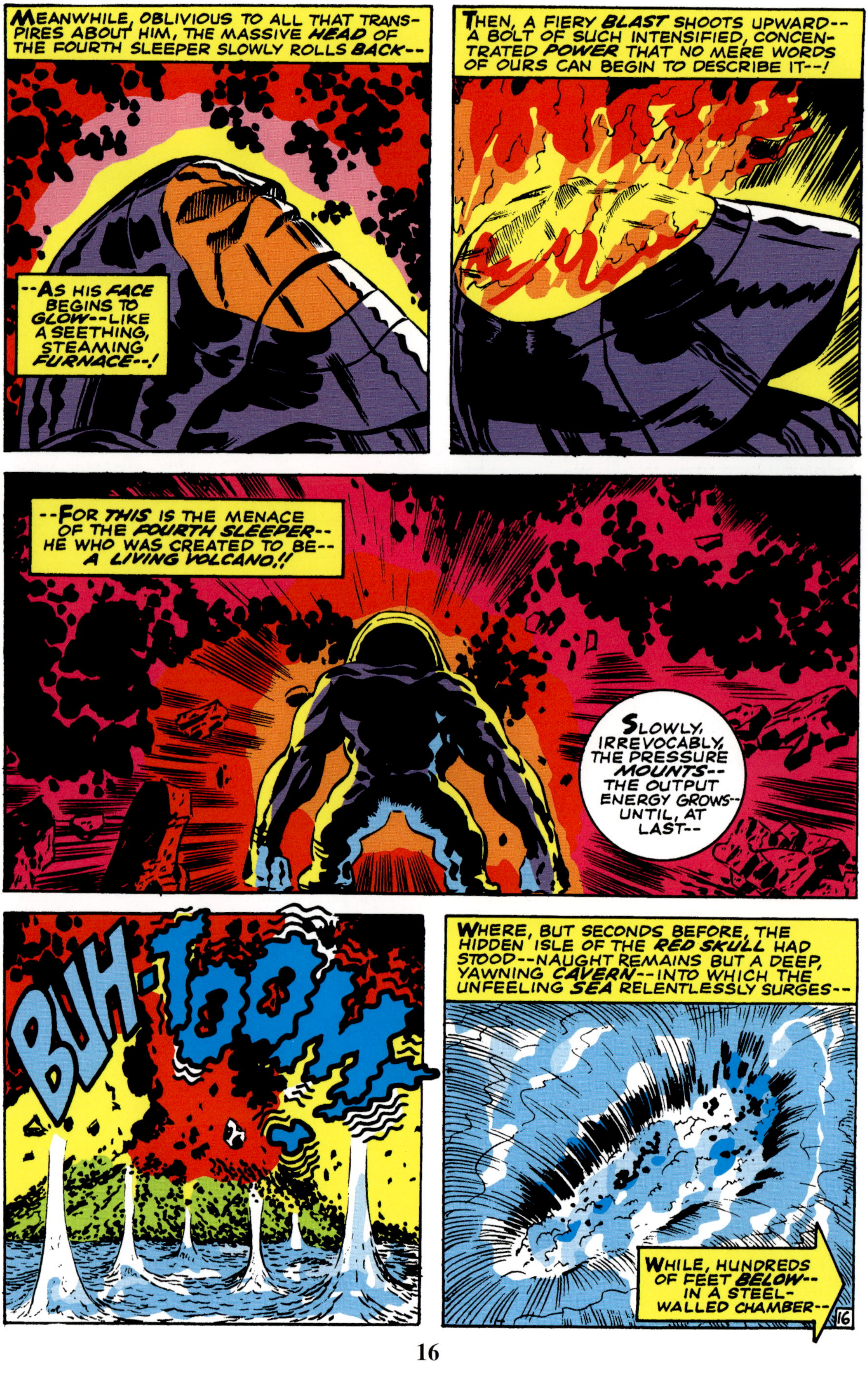
MEANWHILE, OBLIVIOUS TO ALL THAT TRANSPIRES ABOUT HIM, THE MASSIVE HEAD OF THE FOURTH SLEEPER SLOWLY ROLLS BACK--
--AS HIS FACE BEGINS TO GLOW--LIKE A SEETHING, STEAMING FURNACE--!
THEN, A FIERY BLAST SHOOTS UPWARD--A BOLT OF SUCH INTENSIFIED, CONCENTRATED POWER THAT NO MERE WORDS OF OURS CAN BEGIN TO DESCRIBE IT--!
--FOR THIS IS THE MENACE OF THE FOURTH SLEEPER--HE WHO WAS CREATED TO BE--A LIVING VOLCANO!!
SLOWLY, IRREVOCABLY, THE PRESSURE MOUNTS--THE OUTPUT ENERGY GROWS--UNTIL, AT LAST--
BUH-TOOM
WHERE, BUT SECONDS BEFORE, THE HIDDEN ISLE OF THE RED SKULL HAD STOOD--NAUGHT REMAINS BUT A DEEP, YAWNING CAVERN--INTO WHICH THE UNFEELING SEA RELENTLESSLY SURGES--
WHILE, HUNDREDS OF FEET BELOW--IN A STEEL-WALLED CHAMBER--
16

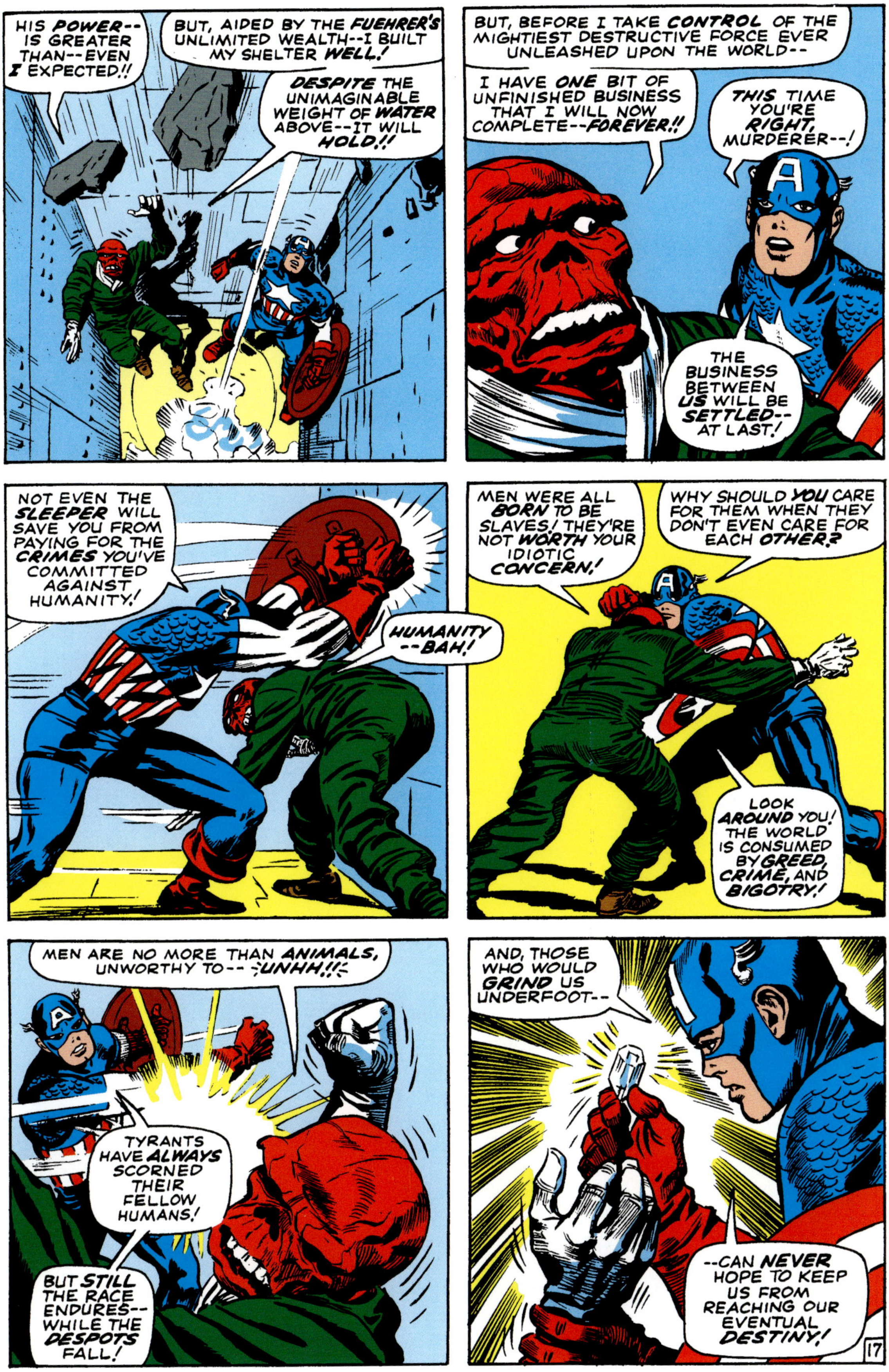
HIS POWER-- IS GREATER THAN--EVEN I EXPECTED!!
BUT, AIDED BY THE FUEHRER'S UNLIMITED WEALTH--I BUILT MY SHELTER WELL!
DESPITE THE UNIMAGINABLE WEIGHT OF WATER ABOVE--IT WILL HOLD!!
BUT, BEFORE I TAKE CONTROL OF THE MIGHTIEST DESTRUCTIVE FORCE EVER UNLEASHED UPON THE WORLD--
I HAVE ONE BIT OF UNFINISHED BUSINESS THAT I WILL NOW COMPLETE--FOREVER!!
THIS TIME YOU'RE RIGHT, MURDERER--!
THE BUSINESS BETWEEN US WILL BE SETTLED-- AT LAST!
NOT EVEN THE SLEEPER WILL SAVE YOU FROM PAYING FOR THE CRIMES YOU'VE COMMITTED AGAINST HUMANITY!
HUMANITY --BAH!
MEN WERE ALL BORN TO BE SLAVES! THEY'RE NOT WORTH YOUR IDIOTIC CONCERN!
WHY SHOULD YOU CARE FOR THEM WHEN THEY DON'T EVEN CARE FOR EACH OTHER?
LOOK AROUND YOU! THE WORLD IS CONSUMED BY GREED, CRIME, AND BIGOTRY!
MEN ARE NO MORE THAN ANIMALS, UNWORTHY TO-- UNHH!!
TYRANTS HAVE ALWAYS SCORNED THEIR FELLOW HUMANS!
BUT STILL THE RACE ENDURES-- WHILE THE DESPOTS FALL!
AND, THOSE WHO WOULD GRIND US UNDERFOOT--
--CAN NEVER HOPE TO KEEP US FROM REACHING OUR EVENTUAL DESTINY!
17

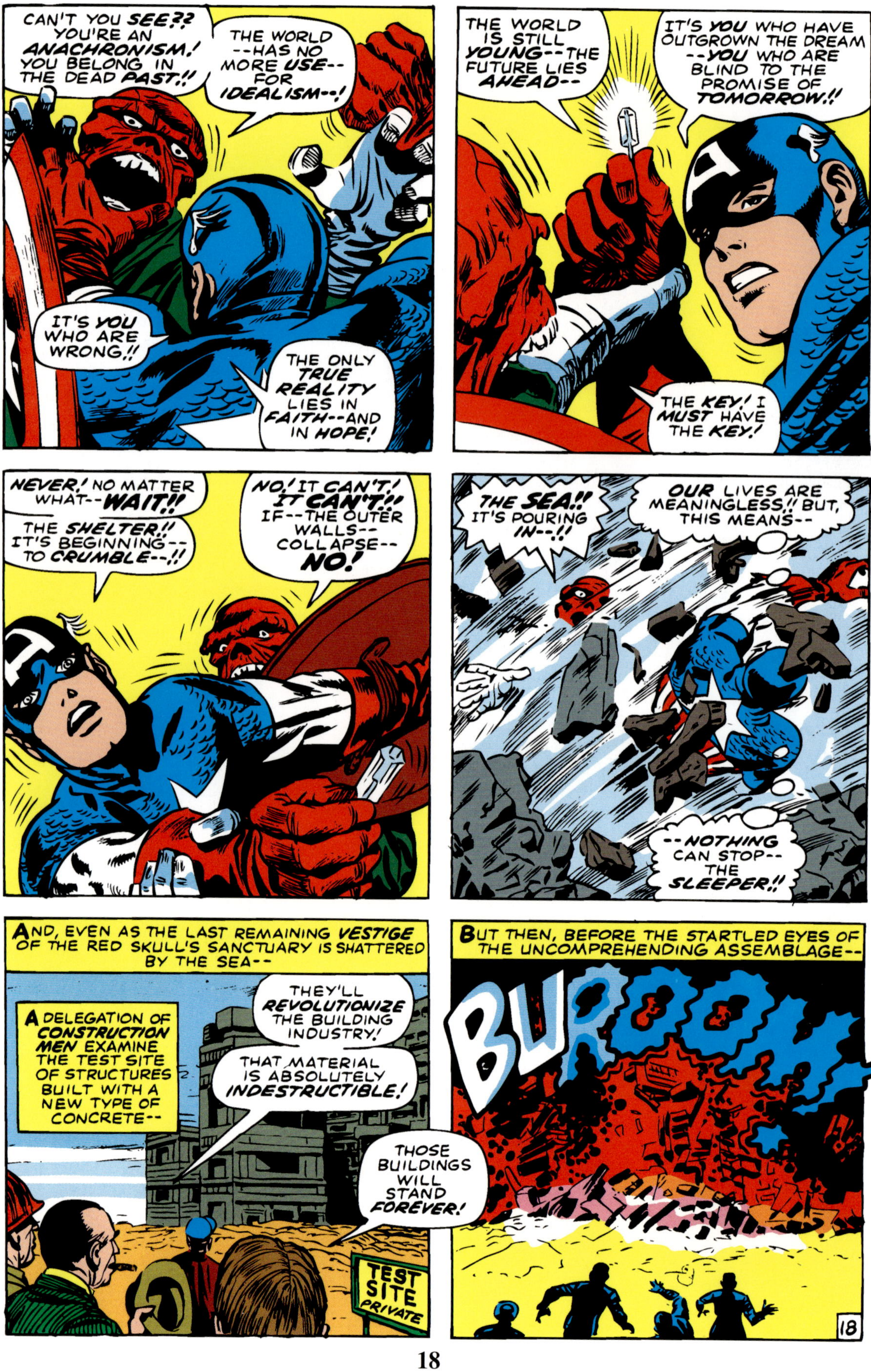
CAN'T YOU SEE?? YOU'RE AN ANACHRONISM! YOU BELONG IN THE DEAD PAST!!
THE WORLD --HAS NO MORE USE-- FOR IDEALISM--!
IT'S YOU WHO ARE WRONG!!
THE ONLY TRUE REALITY LIES IN FAITH--AND IN HOPE!
THE WORLD IS STILL YOUNG--THE FUTURE LIES AHEAD--
IT'S YOU WHO HAVE OUTGROWN THE DREAM --YOU WHO ARE BLIND TO THE PROMISE OF TOMORROW!!
THE KEY! I MUST HAVE THE KEY!
NEVER! NO MATTER WHAT--WAIT!!
THE SHELTER!! IT'S BEGINNING-- TO CRUMBLE--!!
NO! IT CAN'T! IT CAN'T!! IF--THE OUTER WALLS--COLLAPSE-- NO!
THE SEA!! IT'S POURING IN--!!
OUR LIVES ARE MEANINGLESS!! BUT, THIS MEANS--
--NOTHING CAN STOP-- THE SLEEPER!!
AND, EVEN AS THE LAST REMAINING VESTIGE OF THE RED SKULL'S SANCTUARY IS SHATTERED BY THE SEA--
A DELEGATION OF CONSTRUCTION MEN EXAMINE THE TEST SITE OF STRUCTURES BUILT WITH A NEW TYPE OF CONCRETE--
THEY'LL REVOLUTIONIZE THE BUILDING INDUSTRY!
THAT MATERIAL IS ABSOLUTELY INDESTRUCTIBLE!
THOSE BUILDINGS WILL STAND FOREVER!
TEST SITE PRIVATE
BUT THEN, BEFORE THE STARTLED EYES OF THE UNCOMPREHENDING ASSEMBLAGE--
BUROOOM
18

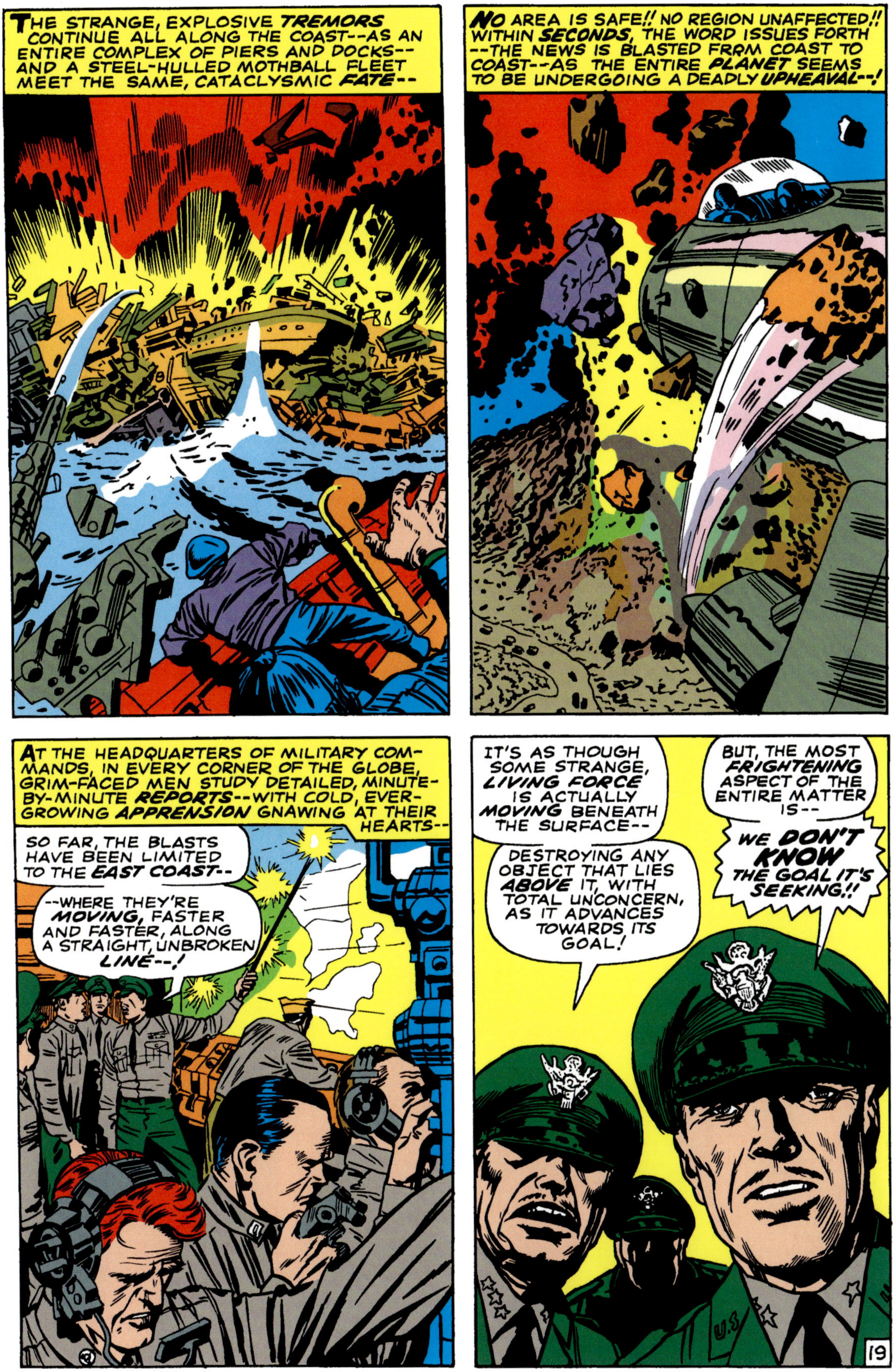
THE STRANGE, EXPLOSIVE TREMORS CONTINUE ALL ALONG THE COAST--AS AN ENTIRE COMPLEX OF PIERS AND DOCKS--AND A STEEL-HULLED MOTHBALL FLEET MEET THE SAME, CATACLYSMIC FATE--
NO AREA IS SAFE!! NO REGION UNAFFECTED!! WITHIN SECONDS, THE WORD ISSUES FORTH --THE NEWS IS BLASTED FROM COAST TO COAST--AS THE ENTIRE PLANET SEEMS TO BE UNDERGOING A DEADLY UPHEAVAL--!
AT THE HEADQUARTERS OF MILITARY COMMANDS, IN EVERY CORNER OF THE GLOBE, GRIM-FACED MEN STUDY DETAILED, MINUTE-BY-MINUTE REPORTS--WITH COLD, EVER-GROWING APPRENSION GNAWING AT THEIR HEARTS--
SO FAR, THE BLASTS HAVE BEEN LIMITED TO THE EAST COAST--
--WHERE THEY'RE MOVING, FASTER AND FASTER, ALONG A STRAIGHT, UNBROKEN LINE--!
IT'S AS THOUGH SOME STRANGE, LIVING FORCE IS ACTUALLY MOVING BENEATH THE SURFACE--
DESTROYING ANY OBJECT THAT LIES ABOVE IT, WITH TOTAL UNCONCERN, AS IT ADVANCES TOWARDS ITS GOAL!
BUT, THE MOST FRIGHTENING ASPECT OF THE ENTIRE MATTER IS--
WE DON'T KNOW THE GOAL IT'S SEEKING!!
19

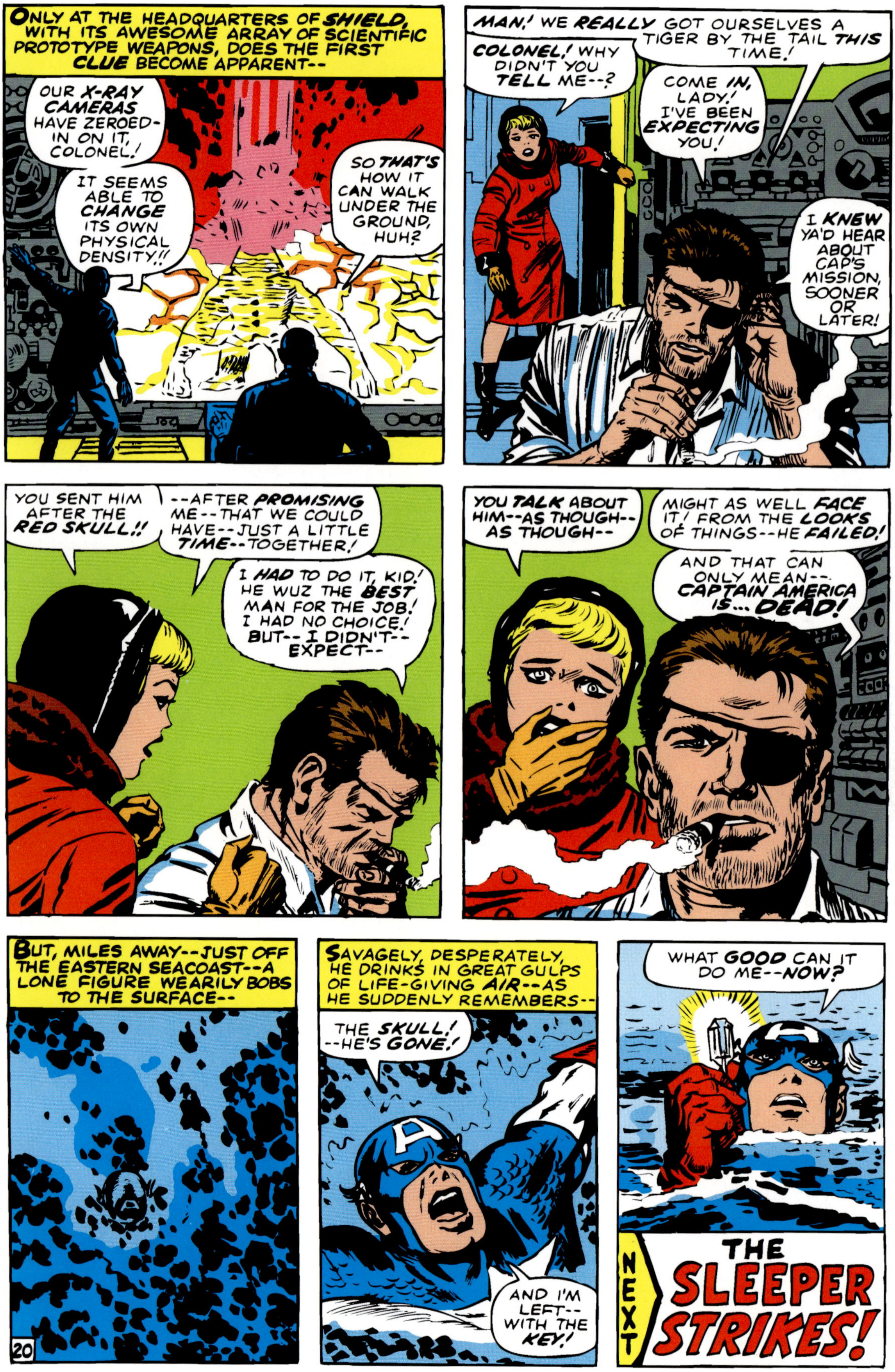

ONLY AT THE HEADQUARTERS OF SHIELD, WITH ITS AWESOME ARRAY OF SCIENTIFIC PROTOTYPE WEAPONS, DOES THE FIRST CLUE BECOME APPARENT--
OUR X-RAY CAMERAS HAVE ZEROED-IN ON IT, COLONEL!
IT SEEMS ABLE TO CHANGE ITS OWN PHYSICAL DENSITY!!
SO THAT'S HOW IT CAN WALK UNDER THE GROUND, HUH?
MAN! WE REALLY GOT OURSELVES A TIGER BY THE TAIL THIS TIME!
COLONEL! WHY DIDN'T YOU TELL ME--?
COME IN, LADY! I'VE BEEN EXPECTING YOU!
I KNEW YA'D HEAR ABOUT CAP'S MISSION, SOONER OR LATER!
YOU SENT HIM AFTER THE RED SKULL!!
--AFTER PROMISING ME--THAT WE COULD HAVE--JUST A LITTLE TIME--TOGETHER!
I HAD TO DO IT, KID! HE WUZ THE BEST MAN FOR THE JOB! I HAD NO CHOICE! BUT--I DIDN'T--EXPECT--
YOU TALK ABOUT HIM--AS THOUGH--AS THOUGH--
MIGHT AS WELL FACE IT! FROM THE LOOKS OF THINGS--HE FAILED!
AND THAT CAN ONLY MEAN--CAPTAIN AMERICA IS... DEAD!
BUT, MILES AWAY--JUST OFF THE EASTERN SEACOAST--A LONE FIGURE WEARILY BOBS TO THE SURFACE--
20
SAVAGELY, DESPERATELY, HE DRINKS IN GREAT GULPS OF LIFE-GIVING AIR--AS HE SUDDENLY REMEMBERS--
THE SKULL! --HE'S GONE!
AND I'M LEFT--WITH THE KEY!
WHAT GOOD CAN IT DO ME--NOW?
NEXT
THE SLEEPER STRIKES!

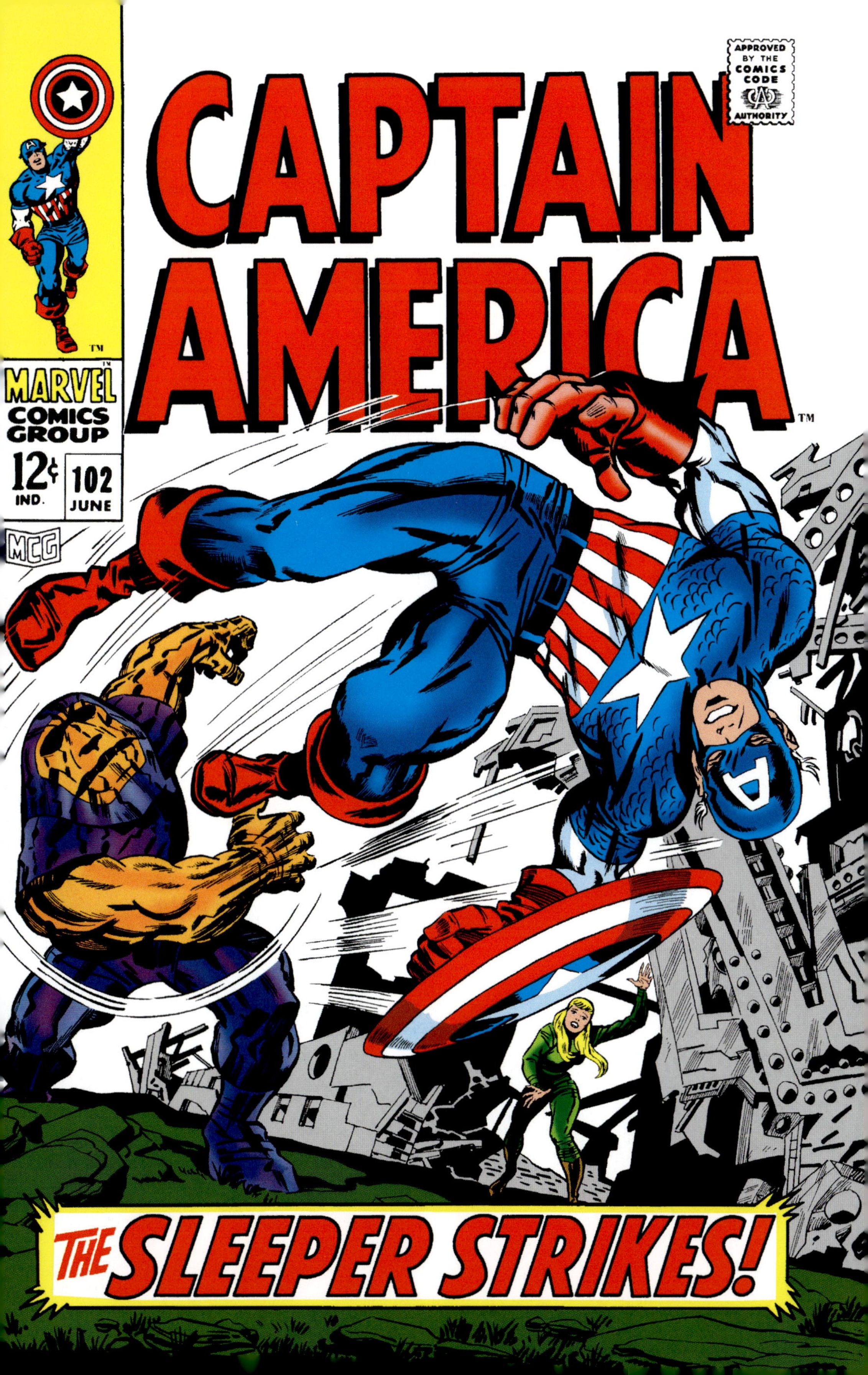

APPROVED BY THE COMICS CODE AUTHORITY
CAPTAIN AMERICA
MARVEL COMICS GROUP
12¢ IND.
102 JUNE
MCG
THE SLEEPER STRIKES!

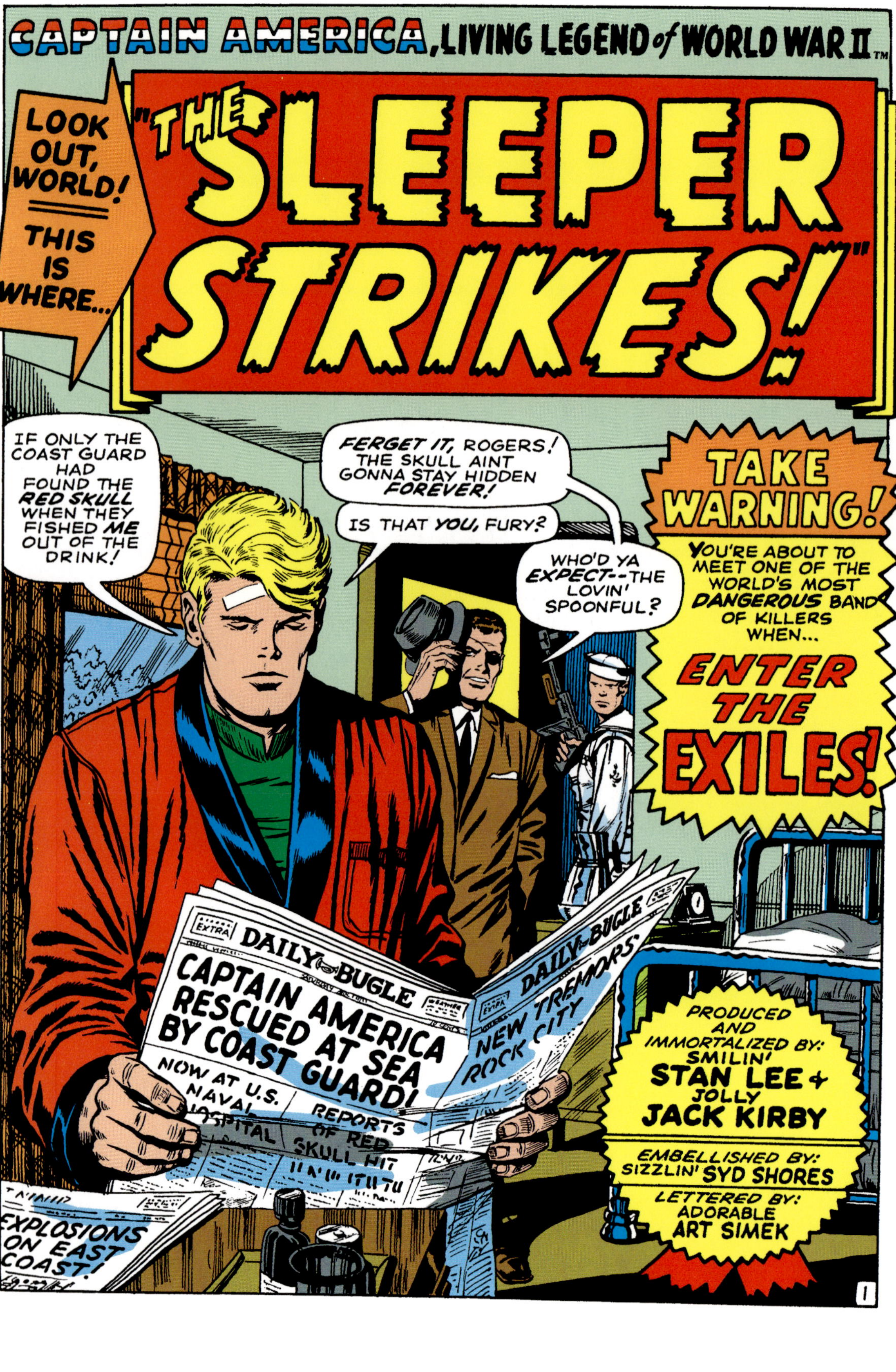
CAPTAIN AMERICA, LIVING LEGEND of WORLD WAR II
LOOK OUT, WORLD! THIS IS WHERE...
"THE SLEEPER STRIKES!"
IF ONLY THE COAST GUARD HAD FOUND THE RED SKULL WHEN THEY FISHED ME OUT OF THE DRINK!
FERGET IT, ROGERS! THE SKULL AINT GONNA STAY HIDDEN FOREVER!
IS THAT YOU, FURY?
WHO'D YA EXPECT--THE LOVIN' SPOONFUL?
TAKE WARNING!
YOU'RE ABOUT TO MEET ONE OF THE WORLD'S MOST DANGEROUS BAND OF KILLERS WHEN...
ENTER THE EXILES!
DAILY BUGLE
CAPTAIN AMERICA RESCUED AT SEA BY COAST GUARD!
NOW AT U.S. NAVAL HOSPITAL
REPORTS OF RED SKULL HIT
DAILY BUGLE
NEW TREMORS ROCK CITY
EXPLOSIONS ON EAST COAST!
PRODUCED AND IMMORTALIZED BY: SMILIN' STAN LEE & JOLLY JACK KIRBY
EMBELLISHED BY: SIZZLIN' SYD SHORES
LETTERED BY: ADORABLE ART SIMEK
1

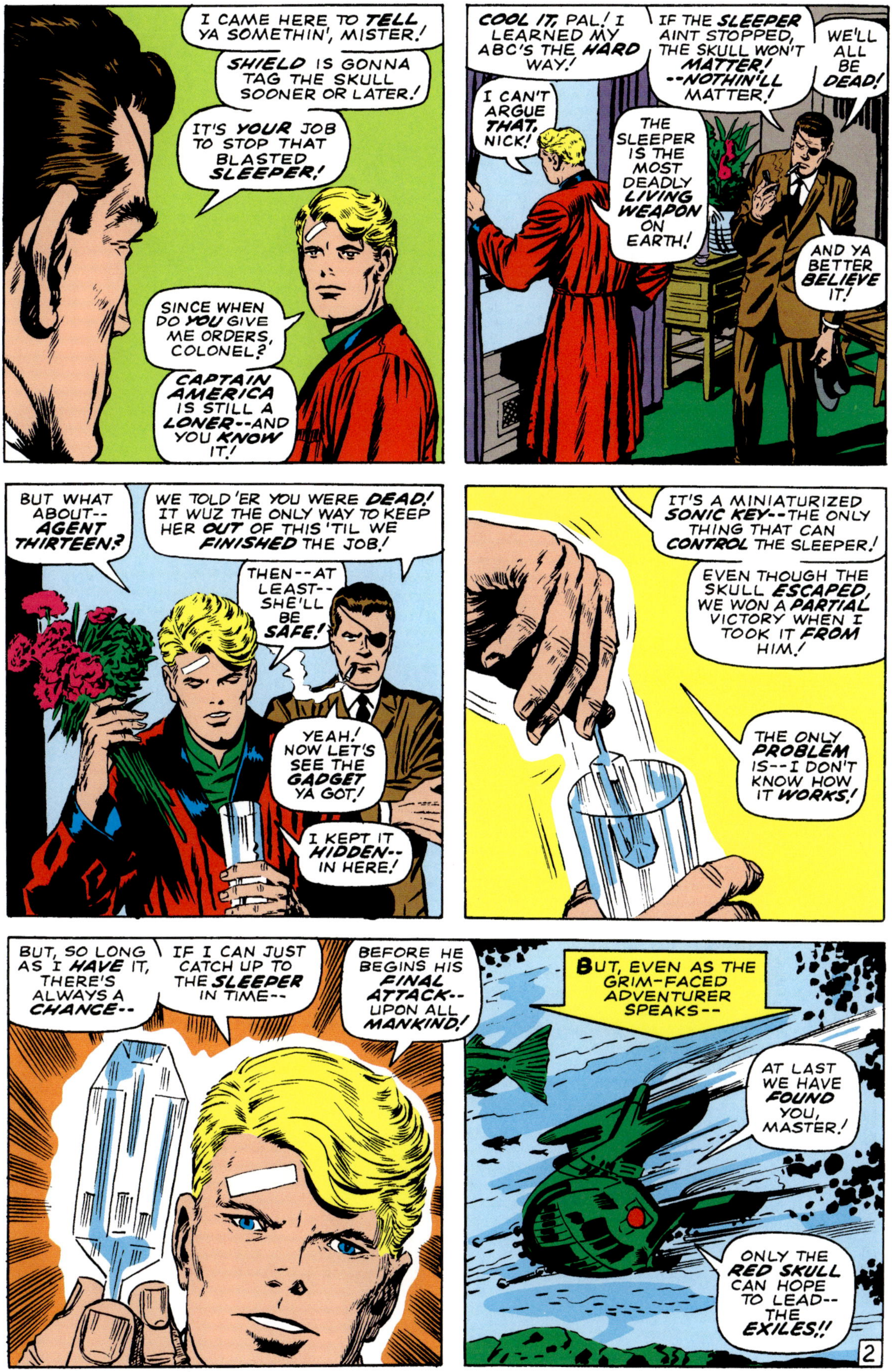
I CAME HERE TO TELL YA SOMETHIN', MISTER!
SHIELD IS GONNA TAG THE SKULL SOONER OR LATER!
IT'S YOUR JOB TO STOP THAT BLASTED SLEEPER!
SINCE WHEN DO YOU GIVE ME ORDERS, COLONEL?
CAPTAIN AMERICA IS STILL A LONER--AND YOU KNOW IT!
COOL IT, PAL! I LEARNED MY ABC'S THE HARD WAY!
IF THE SLEEPER AINT STOPPED, THE SKULL WON'T MATTER! --NOTHIN'LL MATTER!
WE'LL ALL BE DEAD!
I CAN'T ARGUE THAT, NICK!
THE SLEEPER IS THE MOST DEADLY LIVING WEAPON ON EARTH!
AND YA BETTER BELIEVE IT!
BUT WHAT ABOUT-- AGENT THIRTEEN?
WE TOLD 'ER YOU WERE DEAD! IT WUZ THE ONLY WAY TO KEEP HER OUT OF THIS 'TIL WE FINISHED THE JOB!
THEN--AT LEAST-- SHE'LL BE SAFE!
YEAH! NOW LET'S SEE THE GADGET YA GOT!
I KEPT IT HIDDEN-- IN HERE!
IT'S A MINIATURIZED SONIC KEY--THE ONLY THING THAT CAN CONTROL THE SLEEPER!
EVEN THOUGH THE SKULL ESCAPED, WE WON A PARTIAL VICTORY WHEN I TOOK IT FROM HIM!
THE ONLY PROBLEM IS--I DON'T KNOW HOW IT WORKS!
BUT, SO LONG AS I HAVE IT, THERE'S ALWAYS A CHANCE--
IF I CAN JUST CATCH UP TO THE SLEEPER IN TIME--
BEFORE HE BEGINS HIS FINAL ATTACK-- UPON ALL MANKIND!
BUT, EVEN AS THE GRIM-FACED ADVENTURER SPEAKS--
AT LAST WE HAVE FOUND YOU, MASTER!
ONLY THE RED SKULL CAN HOPE TO LEAD-- THE EXILES!!
2

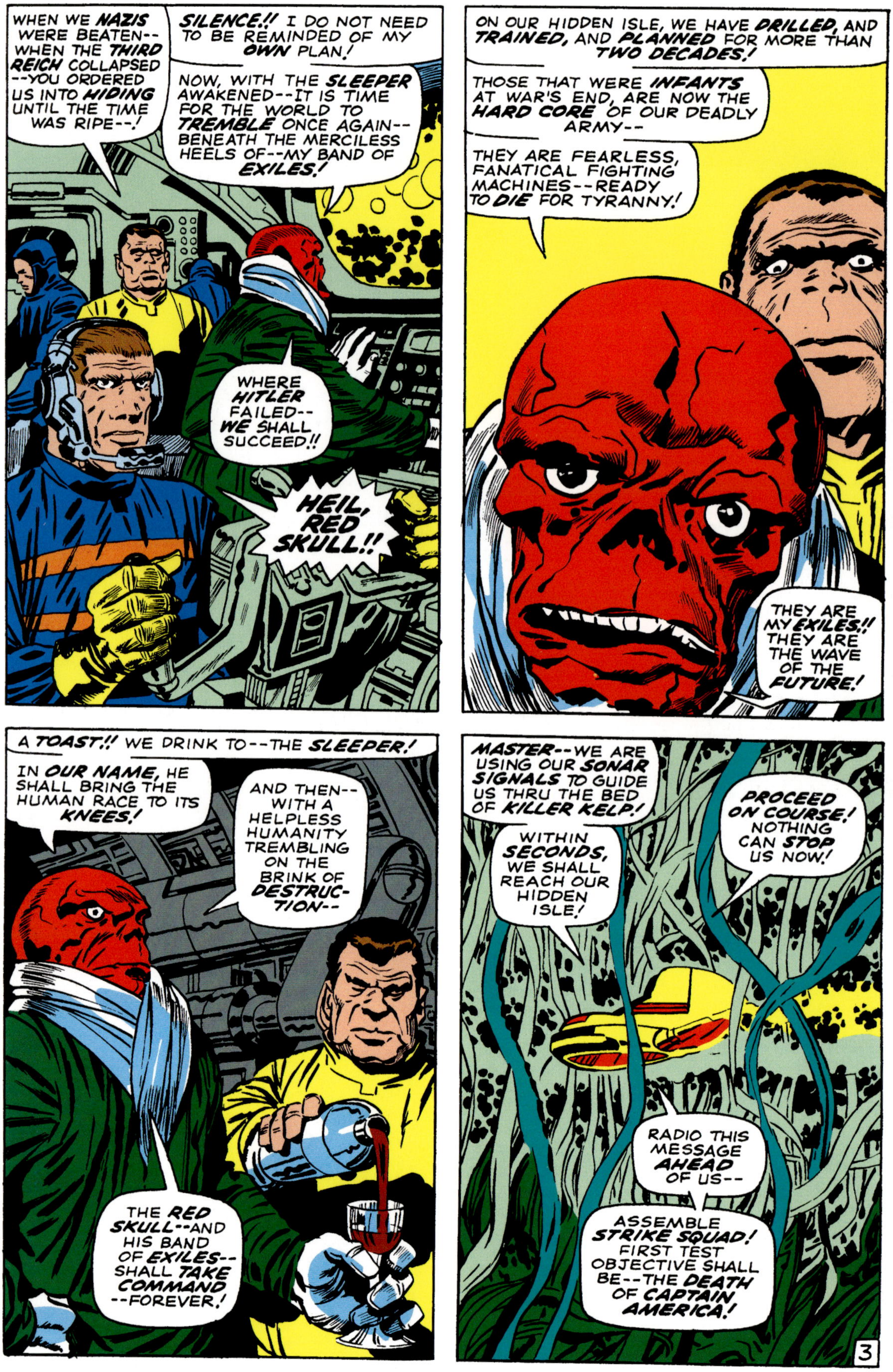
WHEN WE NAZIS WERE BEATEN-- WHEN THE THIRD REICH COLLAPSED --YOU ORDERED US INTO HIDING UNTIL THE TIME WAS RIPE--!
SILENCE!! I DO NOT NEED TO BE REMINDED OF MY OWN PLAN!
NOW, WITH THE SLEEPER AWAKENED--IT IS TIME FOR THE WORLD TO TREMBLE ONCE AGAIN-- BENEATH THE MERCILESS HEELS OF--MY BAND OF EXILES!
WHERE HITLER FAILED-- WE SHALL SUCCEED!!
HEIL, RED SKULL!!
ON OUR HIDDEN ISLE, WE HAVE DRILLED, AND TRAINED, AND PLANNED FOR MORE THAN TWO DECADES!
THOSE THAT WERE INFANTS AT WAR'S END, ARE NOW THE HARD CORE OF OUR DEADLY ARMY--
THEY ARE FEARLESS, FANATICAL FIGHTING MACHINES--READY TO DIE FOR TYRANNY!
THEY ARE MY EXILES!! THEY ARE THE WAVE OF THE FUTURE!
A TOAST!! WE DRINK TO--THE SLEEPER!
IN OUR NAME, HE SHALL BRING THE HUMAN RACE TO ITS KNEES!
AND THEN-- WITH A HELPLESS HUMANITY TREMBLING ON THE BRINK OF DESTRUCTION--
THE RED SKULL--AND HIS BAND OF EXILES-- SHALL TAKE COMMAND --FOREVER!
MASTER--WE ARE USING OUR SONAR SIGNALS TO GUIDE US THRU THE BED OF KILLER KELP!
WITHIN SECONDS, WE SHALL REACH OUR HIDDEN ISLE!
PROCEED ON COURSE! NOTHING CAN STOP US NOW!
RADIO THIS MESSAGE AHEAD OF US--
ASSEMBLE STRIKE SQUAD! FIRST TEST OBJECTIVE SHALL BE--THE DEATH OF CAPTAIN AMERICA!
3

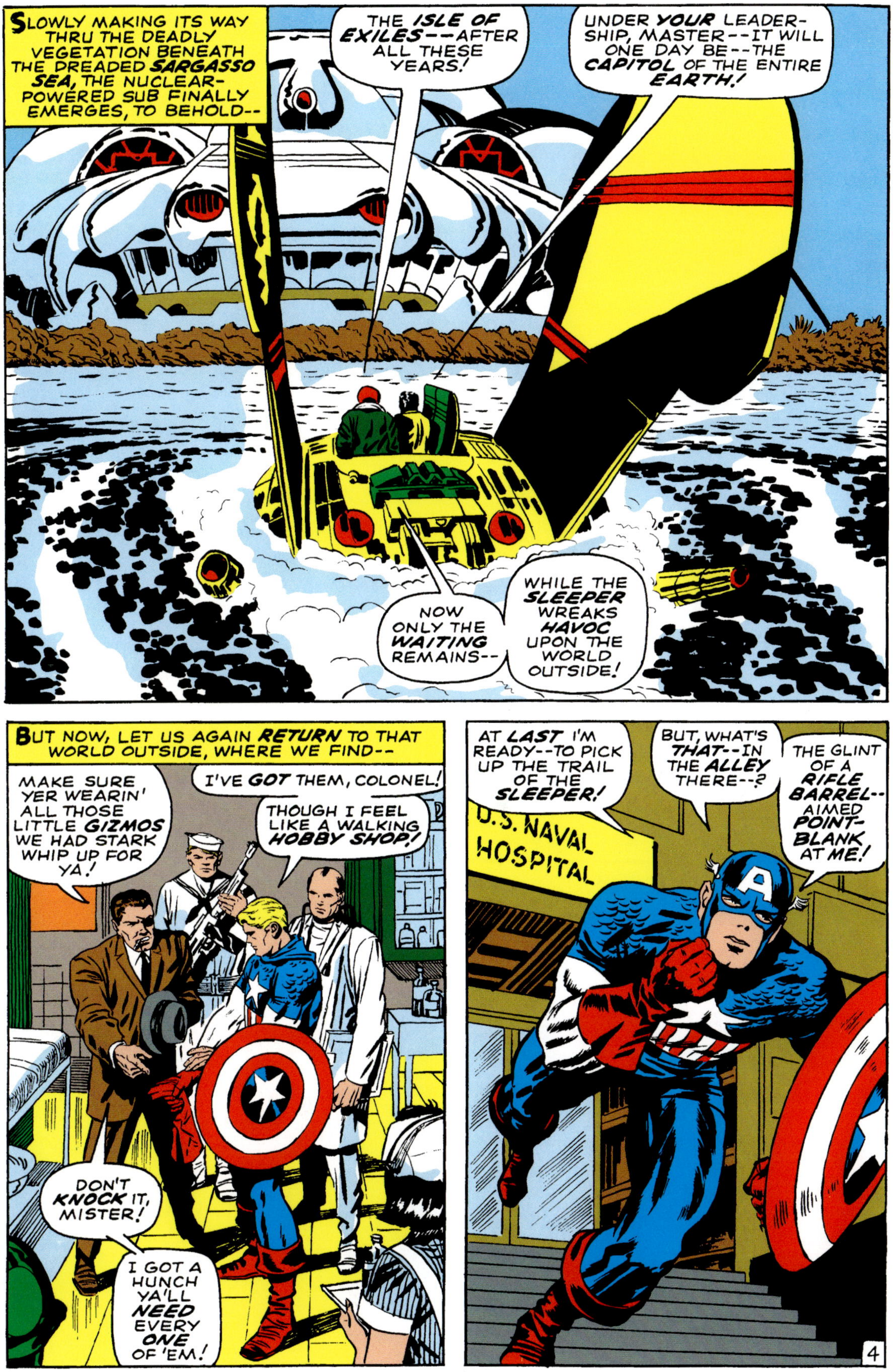
SLOWLY MAKING ITS WAY THRU THE DEADLY VEGETATION BENEATH THE DREADED SARGASSO SEA, THE NUCLEAR-POWERED SUB FINALLY EMERGES, TO BEHOLD--
THE ISLE OF EXILES--AFTER ALL THESE YEARS!
UNDER YOUR LEADERSHIP, MASTER--IT WILL ONE DAY BE--THE CAPITOL OF THE ENTIRE EARTH!
NOW ONLY THE WAITING REMAINS--
WHILE THE SLEEPER WREAKS HAVOC UPON THE WORLD OUTSIDE!
BUT NOW, LET US AGAIN RETURN TO THAT WORLD OUTSIDE, WHERE WE FIND--
MAKE SURE YER WEARIN' ALL THOSE LITTLE GIZMOS WE HAD STARK WHIP UP FOR YA!
I'VE GOT THEM, COLONEL!
THOUGH I FEEL LIKE A WALKING HOBBY SHOP!
DON'T KNOCK IT, MISTER!
I GOT A HUNCH YA'LL NEED EVERY ONE OF 'EM!
AT LAST I'M READY--TO PICK UP THE TRAIL OF THE SLEEPER!
BUT, WHAT'S THAT--IN THE ALLEY THERE--?
THE GLINT OF A RIFLE BARREL--AIMED POINT-BLANK AT ME!
U.S. NAVAL HOSPITAL
4

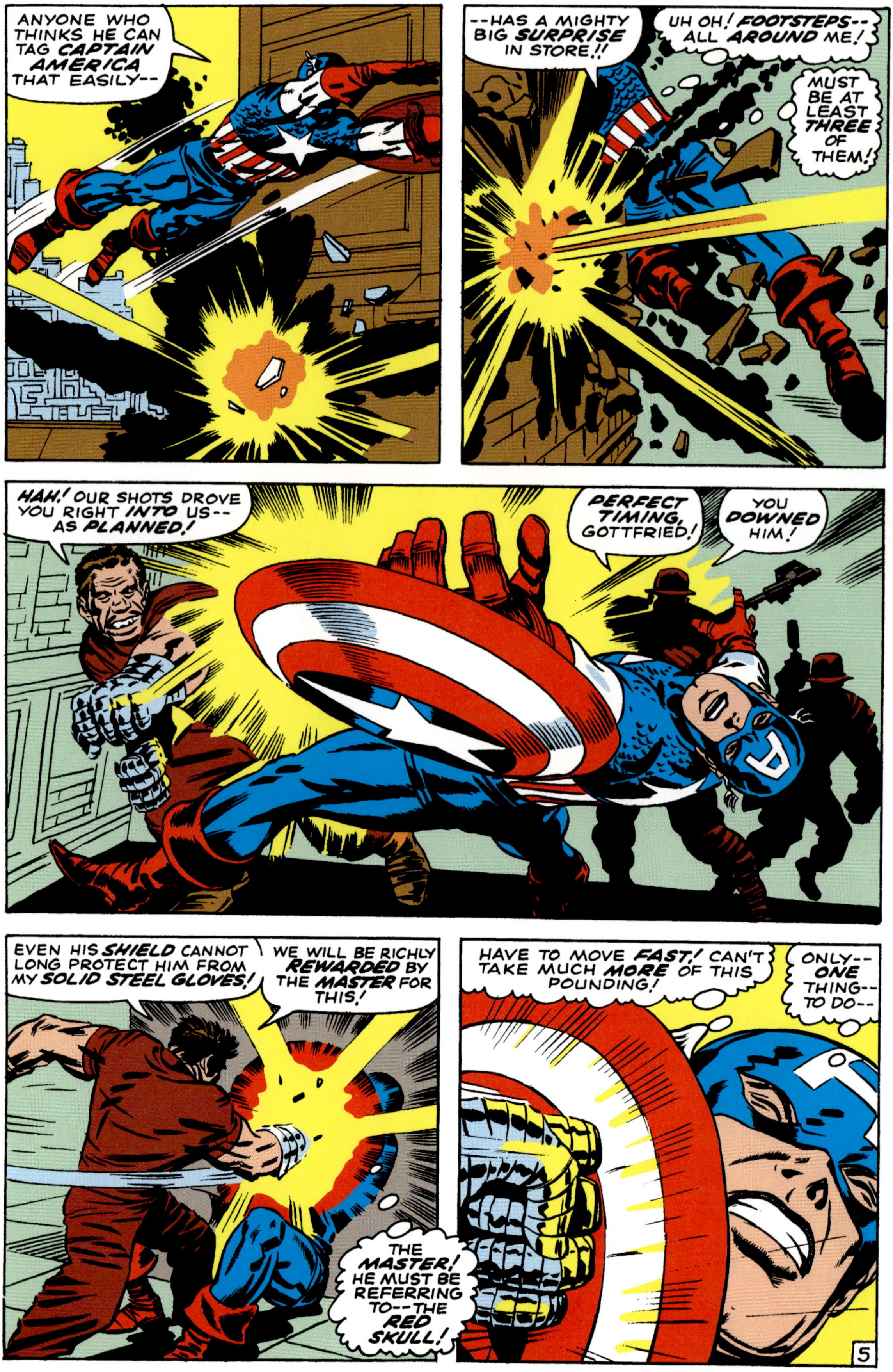
ANYONE WHO THINKS HE CAN TAG CAPTAIN AMERICA THAT EASILY--
--HAS A MIGHTY BIG SURPRISE IN STORE!!
UH OH! FOOTSTEPS-- ALL AROUND ME!
MUST BE AT LEAST THREE OF THEM!
HAH! OUR SHOTS DROVE YOU RIGHT INTO US-- AS PLANNED!
PERFECT TIMING, GOTTFRIED!
YOU DOWNED HIM!
EVEN HIS SHIELD CANNOT LONG PROTECT HIM FROM MY SOLID STEEL GLOVES!
WE WILL BE RICHLY REWARDED BY THE MASTER FOR THIS!
THE MASTER! HE MUST BE REFERRING TO--THE RED SKULL!
HAVE TO MOVE FAST! CAN'T TAKE MUCH MORE OF THIS POUNDING!
ONLY-- ONE THING-- TO DO--
5

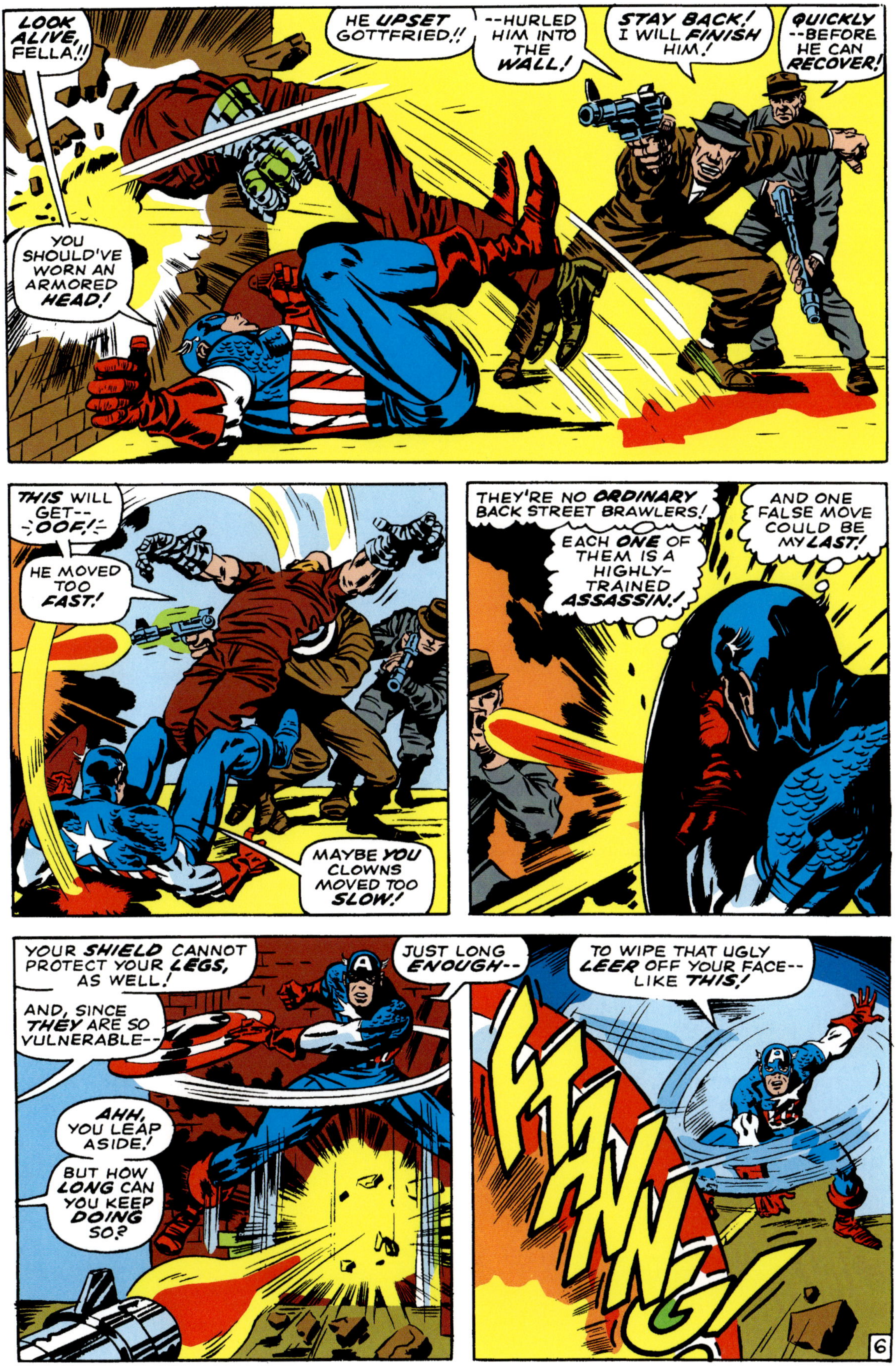
LOOK ALIVE, FELLA!!
YOU SHOULD'VE WORN AN ARMORED HEAD!
HE UPSET GOTTFRIED!!
--HURLED HIM INTO THE WALL!
STAY BACK! I WILL FINISH HIM!
QUICKLY --BEFORE HE CAN RECOVER!
THIS WILL GET-- -OOF!-
HE MOVED TOO FAST!
MAYBE YOU CLOWNS MOVED TOO SLOW!
THEY'RE NO ORDINARY BACK STREET BRAWLERS!
EACH ONE OF THEM IS A HIGHLY-TRAINED ASSASSIN!
AND ONE FALSE MOVE COULD BE MY LAST!
YOUR SHIELD CANNOT PROTECT YOUR LEGS, AS WELL!
AND, SINCE THEY ARE SO VULNERABLE--
JUST LONG ENOUGH--
AHH, YOU LEAP ASIDE!
BUT HOW LONG CAN YOU KEEP DOING SO?
TO WIPE THAT UGLY LEER OFF YOUR FACE-- LIKE THIS!
6

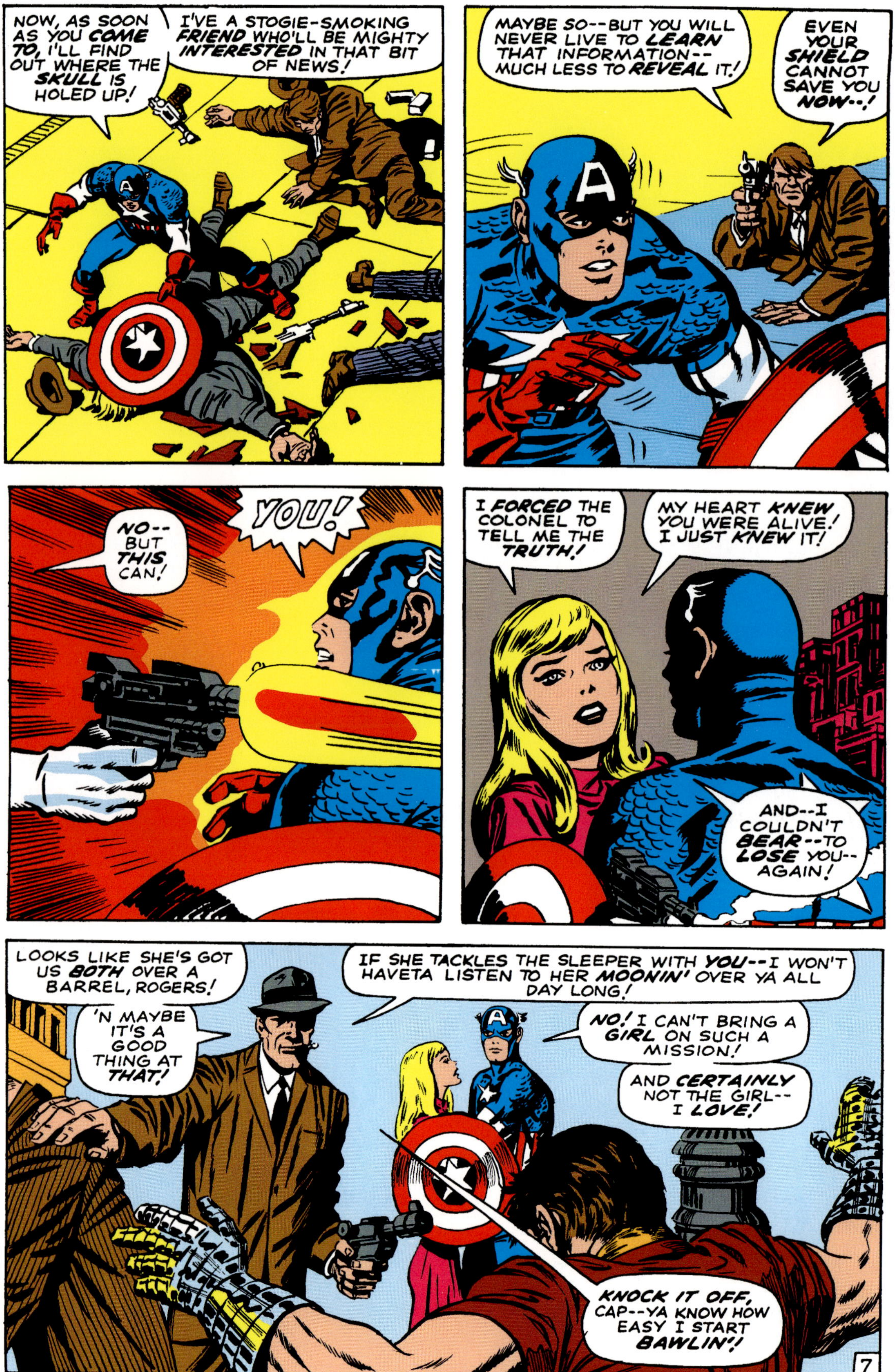
NOW, AS SOON AS YOU COME TO, I'LL FIND OUT WHERE THE SKULL IS HOLED UP!
I'VE A STOGIE-SMOKING FRIEND WHO'LL BE MIGHTY INTERESTED IN THAT BIT OF NEWS!
MAYBE SO--BUT YOU WILL NEVER LIVE TO LEARN THAT INFORMATION--MUCH LESS TO REVEAL IT!
EVEN YOUR SHIELD CANNOT SAVE YOU NOW--!
NO--BUT THIS CAN!
YOU!
I FORCED THE COLONEL TO TELL ME THE TRUTH!
MY HEART KNEW YOU WERE ALIVE! I JUST KNEW IT!
AND--I COULDN'T BEAR--TO LOSE YOU--AGAIN!
LOOKS LIKE SHE'S GOT US BOTH OVER A BARREL, ROGERS!
'N MAYBE IT'S A GOOD THING AT THAT!
IF SHE TACKLES THE SLEEPER WITH YOU--I WON'T HAVETA LISTEN TO HER MOONIN' OVER YA ALL DAY LONG!
NO! I CAN'T BRING A GIRL ON SUCH A MISSION!
AND CERTAINLY NOT THE GIRL--I LOVE!
KNOCK IT OFF, CAP--YA KNOW HOW EASY I START BAWLIN'!
7

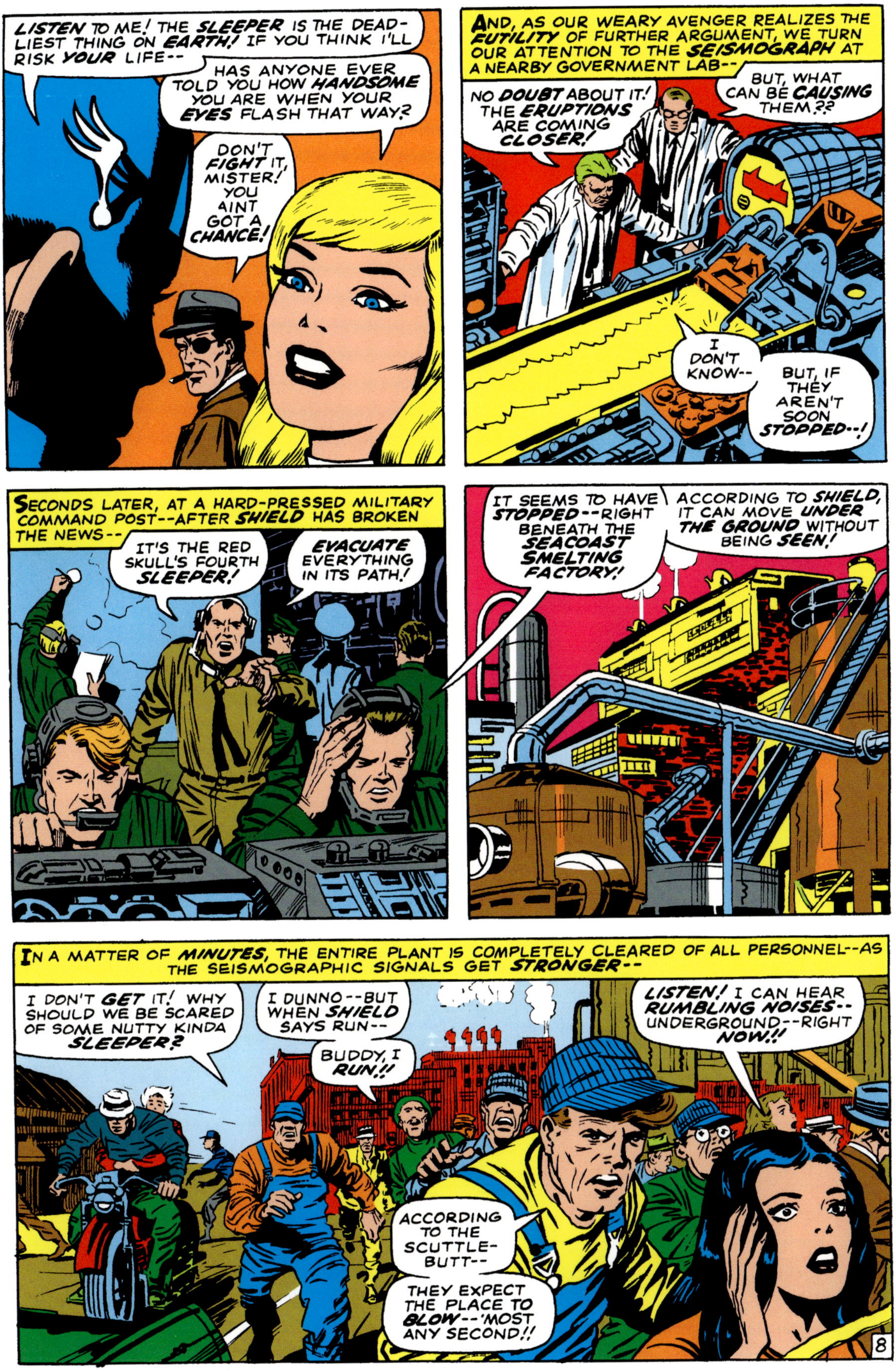
LISTEN TO ME! THE SLEEPER IS THE DEADLIEST THING ON EARTH! IF YOU THINK I'LL RISK YOUR LIFE--
HAS ANYONE EVER TOLD YOU HOW HANDSOME YOU ARE WHEN YOUR EYES FLASH THAT WAY?
DON'T FIGHT IT, MISTER! YOU AINT GOT A CHANCE!
AND, AS OUR WEARY AVENGER REALIZES THE FUTILITY OF FURTHER ARGUMENT, WE TURN OUR ATTENTION TO THE SEISMOGRAPH AT A NEARBY GOVERNMENT LAB--
NO DOUBT ABOUT IT! THE ERUPTIONS ARE COMING CLOSER!
BUT, WHAT CAN BE CAUSING THEM??
I DON'T KNOW--
BUT, IF THEY AREN'T SOON STOPPED--!
SECONDS LATER, AT A HARD-PRESSED MILITARY COMMAND POST--AFTER SHIELD HAS BROKEN THE NEWS--
IT'S THE RED SKULL'S FOURTH SLEEPER!
EVACUATE EVERYTHING IN ITS PATH!
IT SEEMS TO HAVE STOPPED--RIGHT BENEATH THE SEACOAST SMELTING FACTORY!
ACCORDING TO SHIELD, IT CAN MOVE UNDER THE GROUND WITHOUT BEING SEEN!
IN A MATTER OF MINUTES, THE ENTIRE PLANT IS COMPLETELY CLEARED OF ALL PERSONNEL--AS THE SEISMOGRAPHIC SIGNALS GET STRONGER--
I DON'T GET IT! WHY SHOULD WE BE SCARED OF SOME NUTTY KINDA SLEEPER?
I DUNNO--BUT WHEN SHIELD SAYS RUN--
BUDDY, I RUN!!
LISTEN! I CAN HEAR RUMBLING NOISES--UNDERGROUND--RIGHT NOW!!
ACCORDING TO THE SCUTTLE-BUTT--
THEY EXPECT THE PLACE TO BLOW--'MOST ANY SECOND!!
8

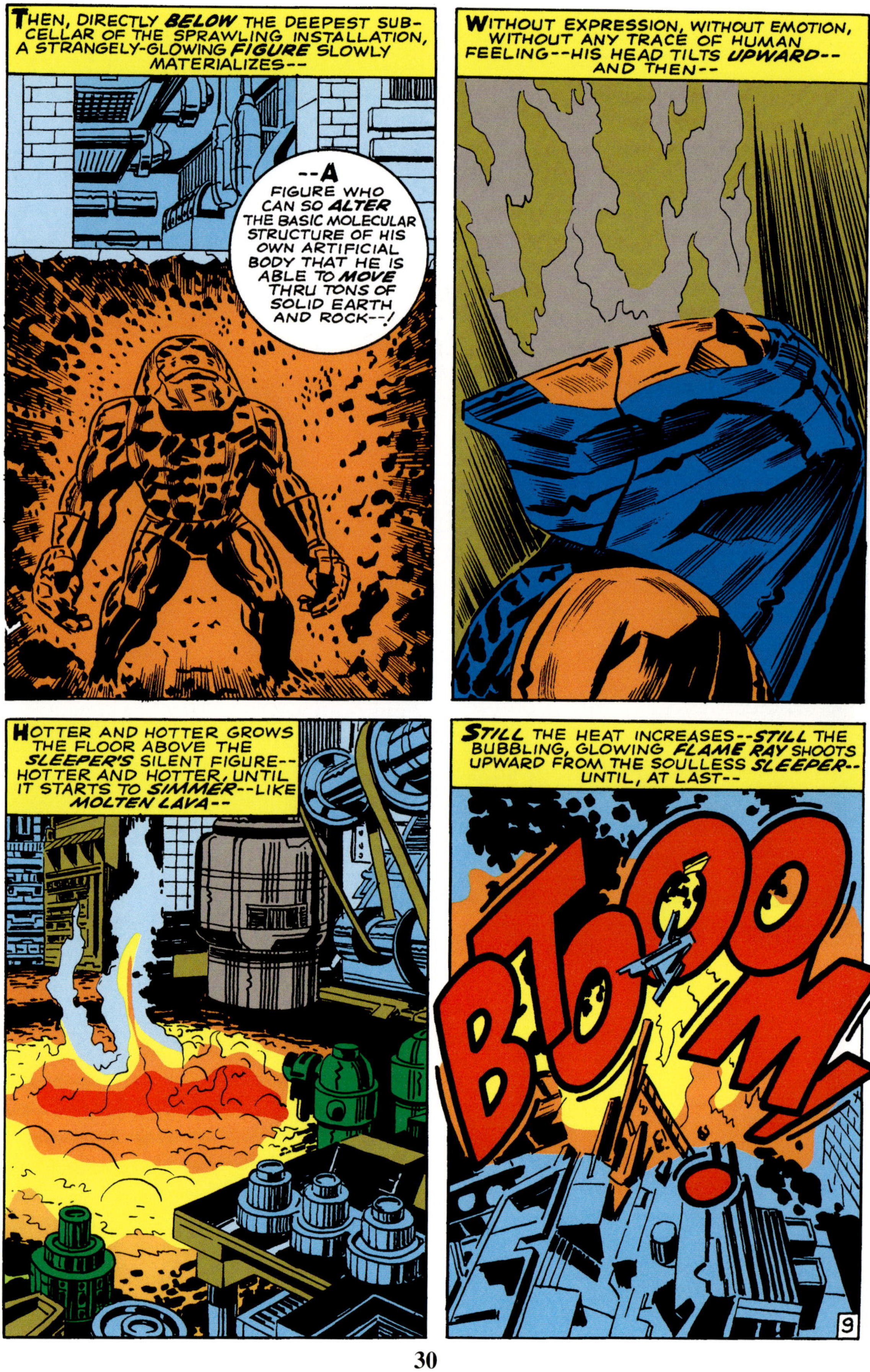
THEN, DIRECTLY BELOW THE DEEPEST SUB-CELLAR OF THE SPRAWLING INSTALLATION, A STRANGELY-GLOWING FIGURE SLOWLY MATERIALIZES--
--A FIGURE WHO CAN SO ALTER THE BASIC MOLECULAR STRUCTURE OF HIS OWN ARTIFICIAL BODY THAT HE IS ABLE TO MOVE THRU TONS OF SOLID EARTH AND ROCK--!
WITHOUT EXPRESSION, WITHOUT EMOTION, WITHOUT ANY TRACE OF HUMAN FEELING--HIS HEAD TILTS UPWARD--AND THEN--
HOTTER AND HOTTER GROWS THE FLOOR ABOVE THE SLEEPER'S SILENT FIGURE--HOTTER AND HOTTER, UNTIL IT STARTS TO SIMMER--LIKE MOLTEN LAVA--
STILL THE HEAT INCREASES--STILL THE BUBBLING, GLOWING FLAME RAY SHOOTS UPWARD FROM THE SOULLESS SLEEPER--UNTIL, AT LAST--
BTOOOM!
9

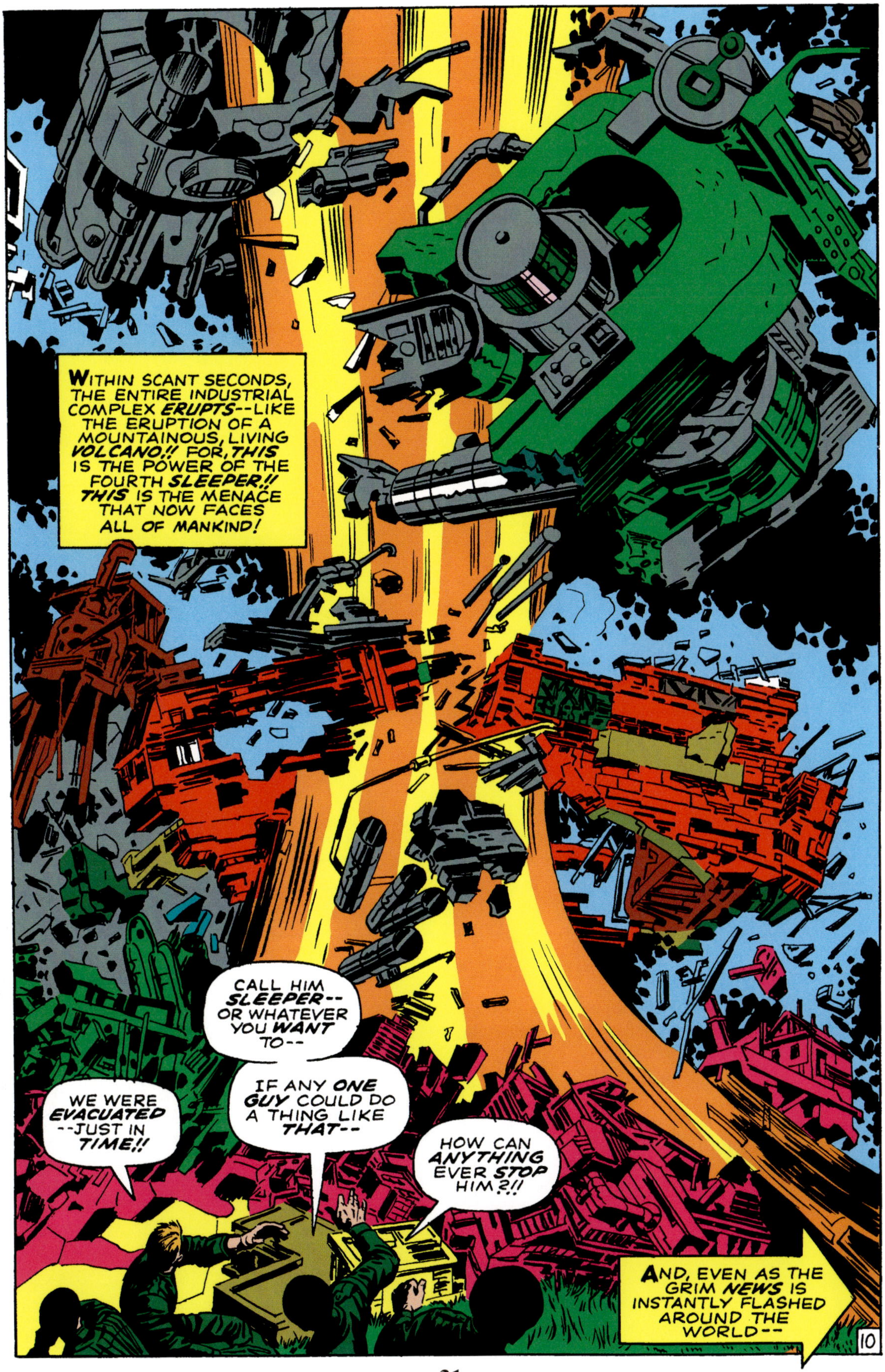
WITHIN SCANT SECONDS, THE ENTIRE INDUSTRIAL COMPLEX ERUPTS--LIKE THE ERUPTION OF A MOUNTAINOUS, LIVING VOLCANO!! FOR, THIS IS THE POWER OF THE FOURTH SLEEPER!! THIS IS THE MENACE THAT NOW FACES ALL OF MANKIND!
CALL HIM SLEEPER-- OR WHATEVER YOU WANT TO--
IF ANY ONE GUY COULD DO A THING LIKE THAT--
WE WERE EVACUATED --JUST IN TIME!!
HOW CAN ANYTHING EVER STOP HIM?!!
AND, EVEN AS THE GRIM NEWS IS INSTANTLY FLASHED AROUND THE WORLD--
10

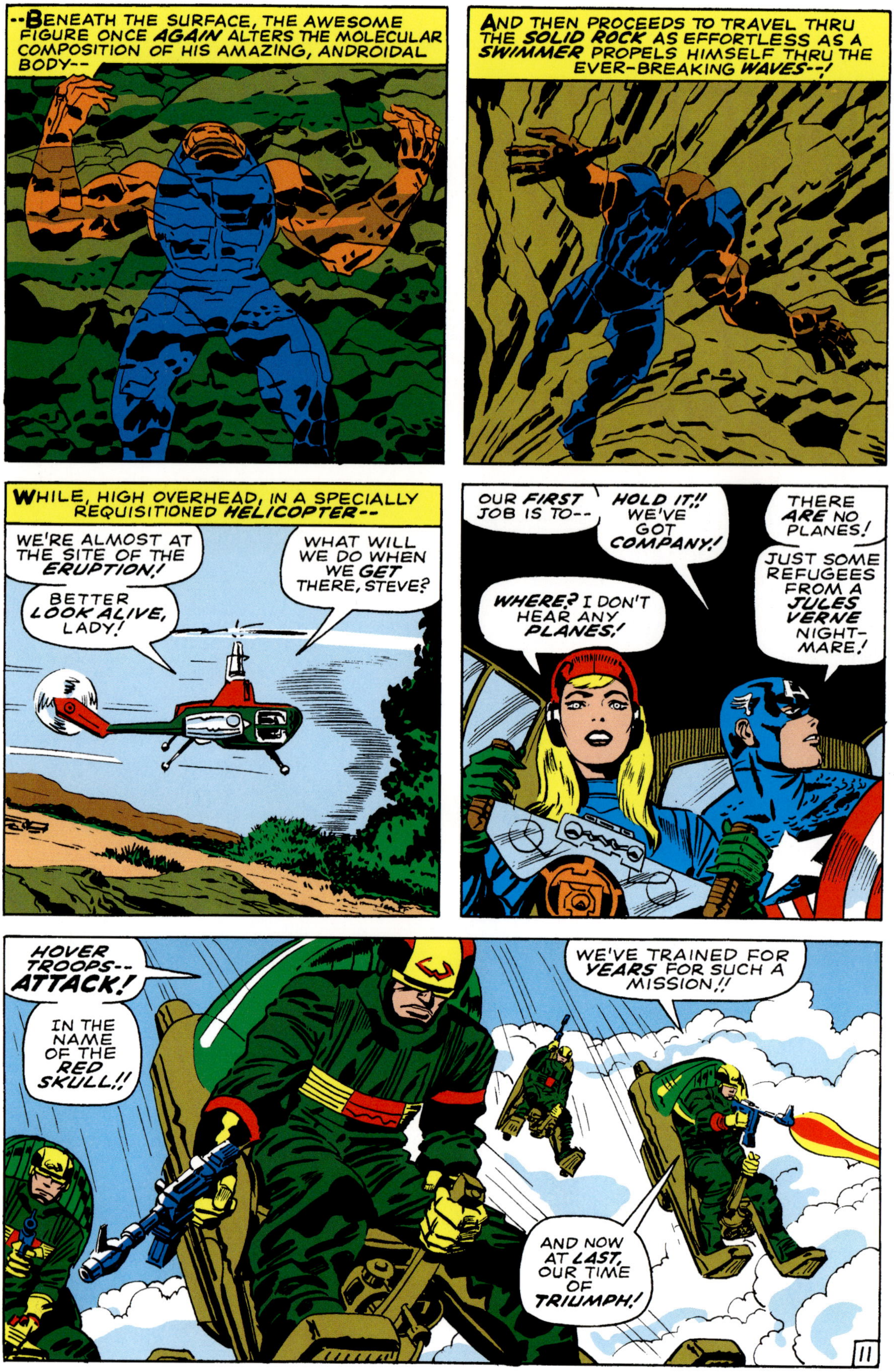
--BENEATH THE SURFACE, THE AWESOME FIGURE ONCE AGAIN ALTERS THE MOLECULAR COMPOSITION OF HIS AMAZING, ANDROIDAL BODY--
AND THEN PROCEEDS TO TRAVEL THRU THE SOLID ROCK AS EFFORTLESS AS A SWIMMER PROPELS HIMSELF THRU THE EVER-BREAKING WAVES--!
WHILE, HIGH OVERHEAD, IN A SPECIALLY REQUISITIONED HELICOPTER--
WE'RE ALMOST AT THE SITE OF THE ERUPTION!
BETTER LOOK ALIVE, LADY!
WHAT WILL WE DO WHEN WE GET THERE, STEVE?
OUR FIRST JOB IS TO--
HOLD IT!! WE'VE GOT COMPANY!
WHERE? I DON'T HEAR ANY PLANES!
THERE ARE NO PLANES!
JUST SOME REFUGEES FROM A JULES VERNE NIGHT-MARE!
HOVER TROOPS-- ATTACK!
IN THE NAME OF THE RED SKULL!!
WE'VE TRAINED FOR YEARS FOR SUCH A MISSION!!
AND NOW AT LAST, OUR TIME OF TRIUMPH!
11

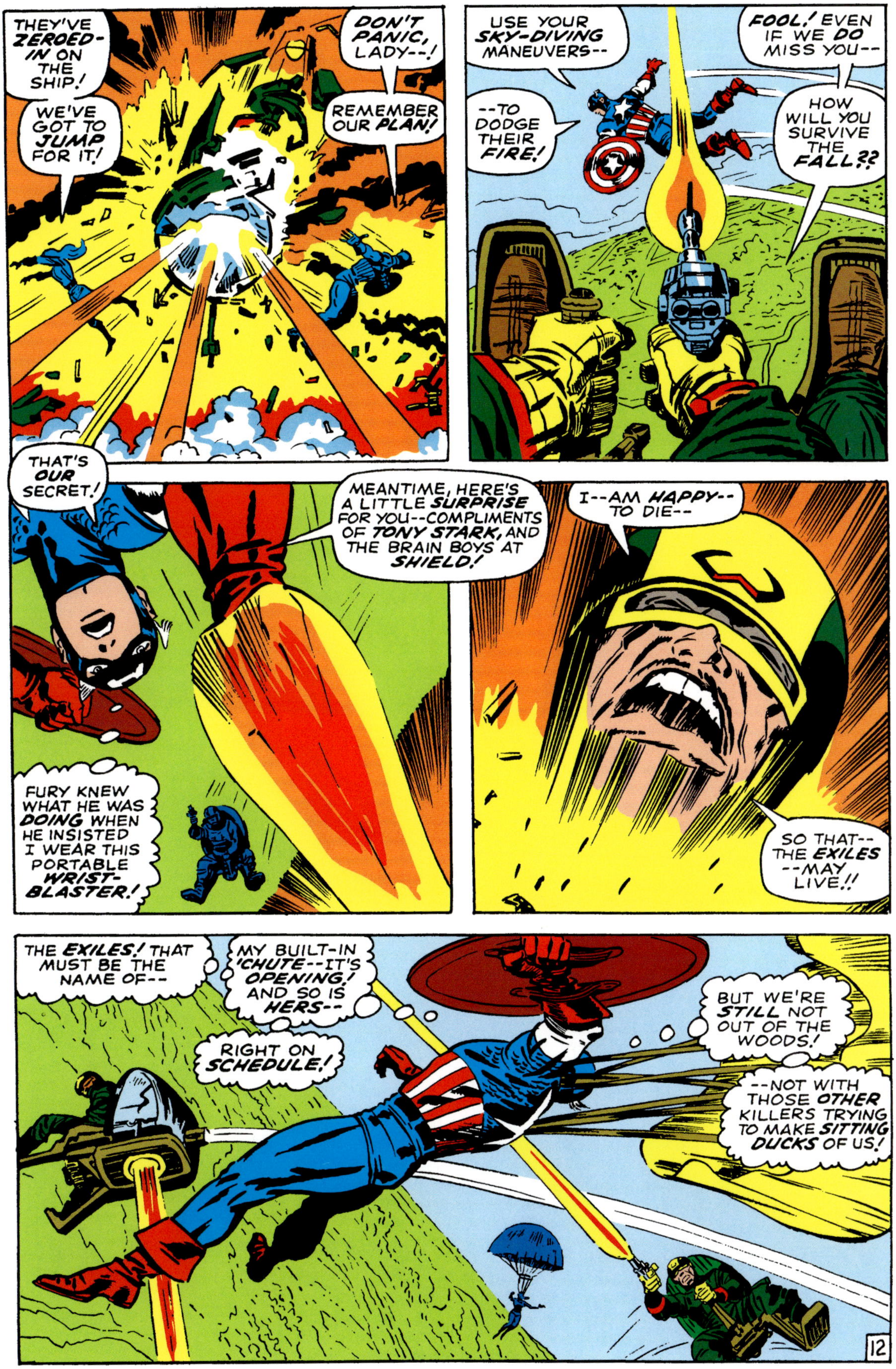
THEY'VE ZEROED-IN ON THE SHIP!
WE'VE GOT TO JUMP FOR IT!
DON'T PANIC, LADY--!
REMEMBER OUR PLAN!
USE YOUR SKY-DIVING MANEUVERS--
--TO DODGE THEIR FIRE!
FOOL! EVEN IF WE DO MISS YOU--
HOW WILL YOU SURVIVE THE FALL??
THAT'S OUR SECRET!
MEANTIME, HERE'S A LITTLE SURPRISE FOR YOU--COMPLIMENTS OF TONY STARK, AND THE BRAIN BOYS AT SHIELD!
FURY KNEW WHAT HE WAS DOING WHEN HE INSISTED I WEAR THIS PORTABLE WRIST-BLASTER!
I--AM HAPPY--TO DIE--
SO THAT--THE EXILES--MAY LIVE!!
THE EXILES! THAT MUST BE THE NAME OF--
MY BUILT-IN 'CHUTE--IT'S OPENING! AND SO IS HERS--
RIGHT ON SCHEDULE!
BUT WE'RE STILL NOT OUT OF THE WOODS!
--NOT WITH THOSE OTHER KILLERS TRYING TO MAKE SITTING DUCKS OF US!
12

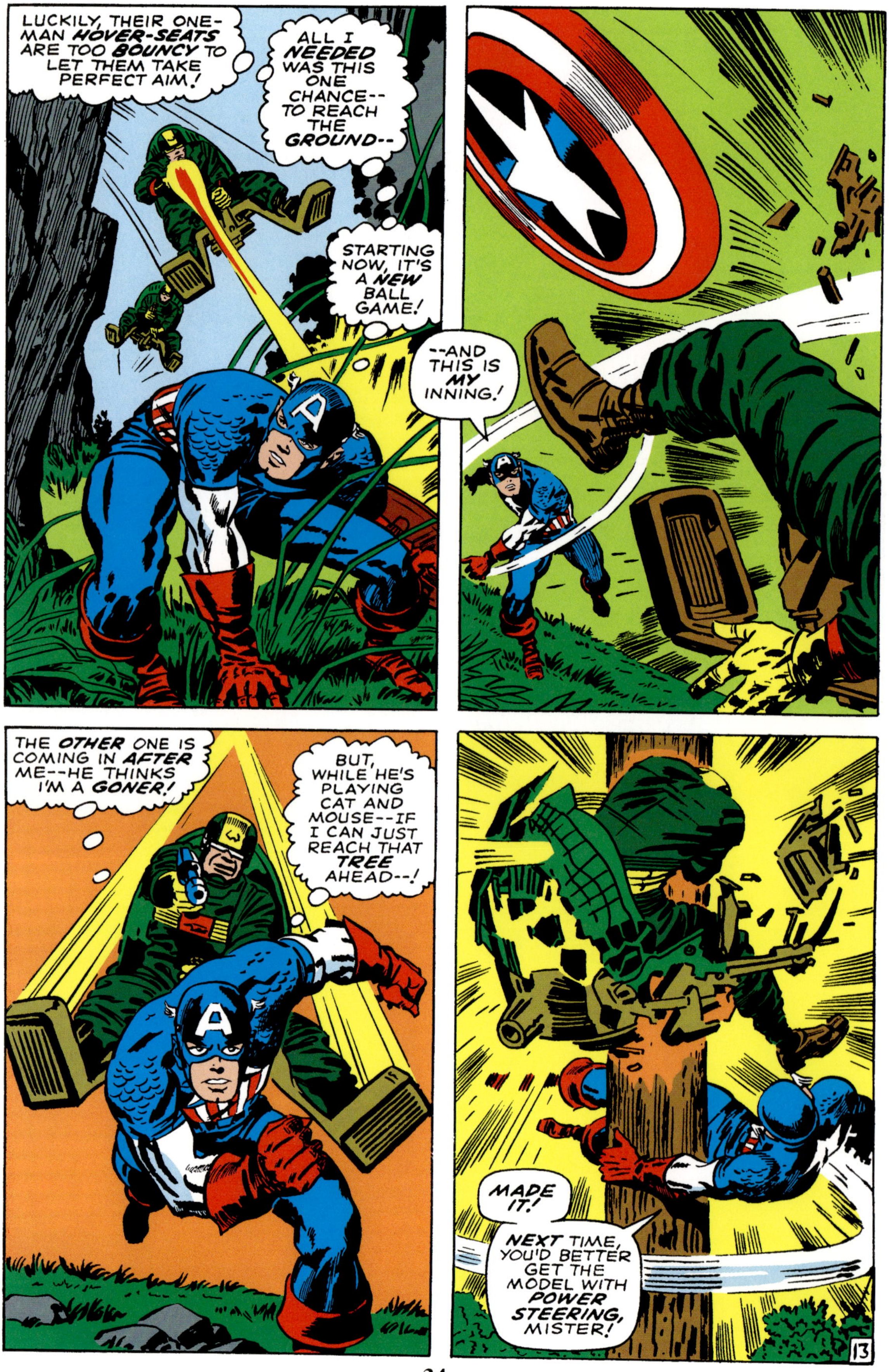
LUCKILY, THEIR ONE-MAN HOVER-SEATS ARE TOO BOUNCY TO LET THEM TAKE PERFECT AIM!
ALL I NEEDED WAS THIS ONE CHANCE-- TO REACH THE GROUND--
STARTING NOW, IT'S A NEW BALL GAME!
--AND THIS IS MY INNING!
THE OTHER ONE IS COMING IN AFTER ME--HE THINKS I'M A GONER!
BUT, WHILE HE'S PLAYING CAT AND MOUSE--IF I CAN JUST REACH THAT TREE AHEAD--!
MADE IT!
NEXT TIME, YOU'D BETTER GET THE MODEL WITH POWER STEERING, MISTER!
13

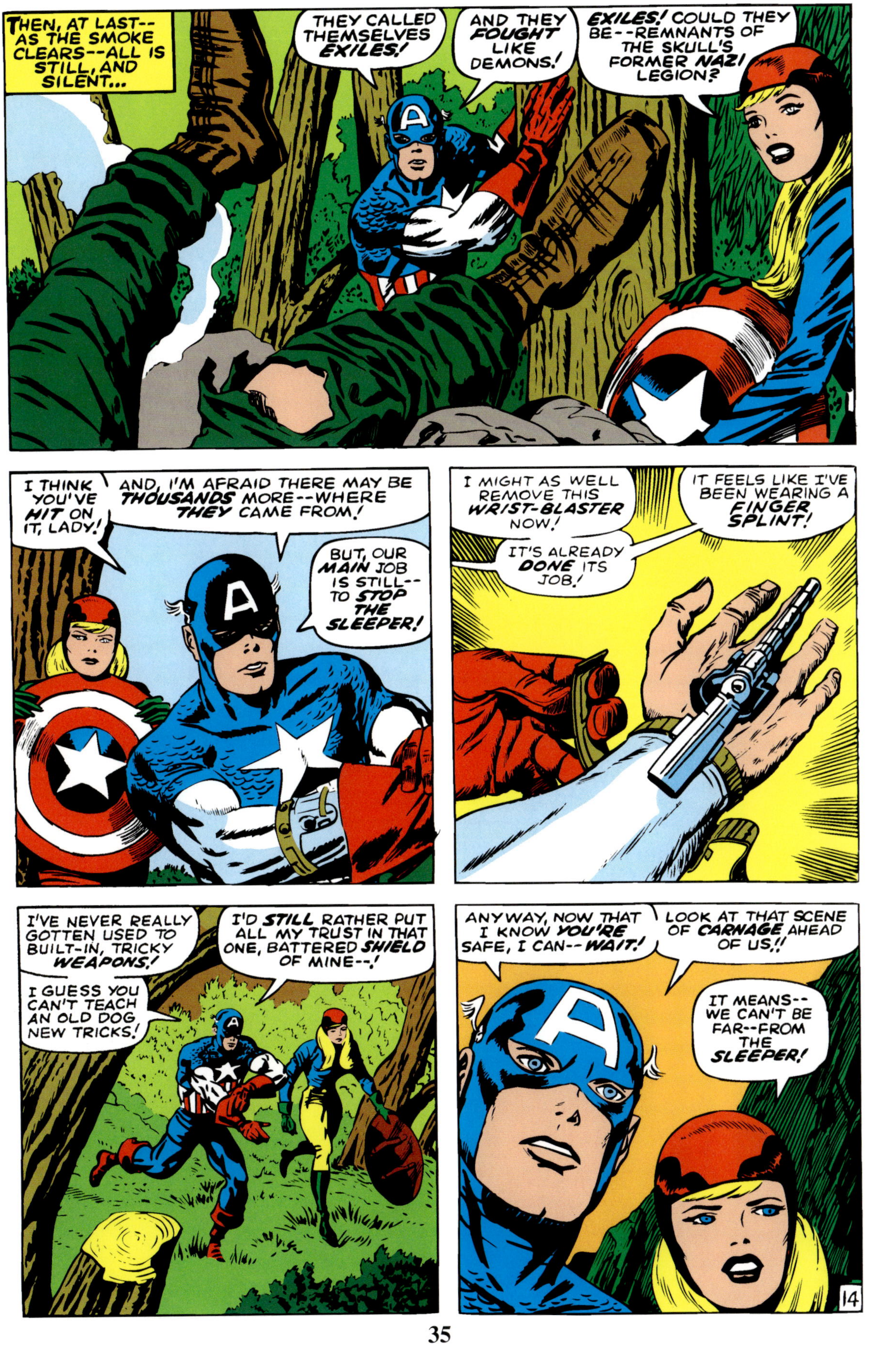
THEN, AT LAST-- AS THE SMOKE CLEARS--ALL IS STILL, AND SILENT...
THEY CALLED THEMSELVES EXILES!
AND THEY FOUGHT LIKE DEMONS!
EXILES! COULD THEY BE--REMNANTS OF THE SKULL'S FORMER NAZI LEGION?
I THINK YOU'VE HIT ON IT, LADY!
AND, I'M AFRAID THERE MAY BE THOUSANDS MORE--WHERE THEY CAME FROM!
BUT, OUR MAIN JOB IS STILL-- TO STOP THE SLEEPER!
I MIGHT AS WELL REMOVE THIS WRIST-BLASTER NOW!
IT FEELS LIKE I'VE BEEN WEARING A FINGER SPLINT!
IT'S ALREADY DONE ITS JOB!
I'VE NEVER REALLY GOTTEN USED TO BUILT-IN, TRICKY WEAPONS!
I GUESS YOU CAN'T TEACH AN OLD DOG NEW TRICKS!
I'D STILL RATHER PUT ALL MY TRUST IN THAT ONE, BATTERED SHIELD OF MINE--!
ANYWAY, NOW THAT I KNOW YOU'RE SAFE, I CAN--WAIT!
LOOK AT THAT SCENE OF CARNAGE AHEAD OF US!!
IT MEANS-- WE CAN'T BE FAR--FROM THE SLEEPER!
14

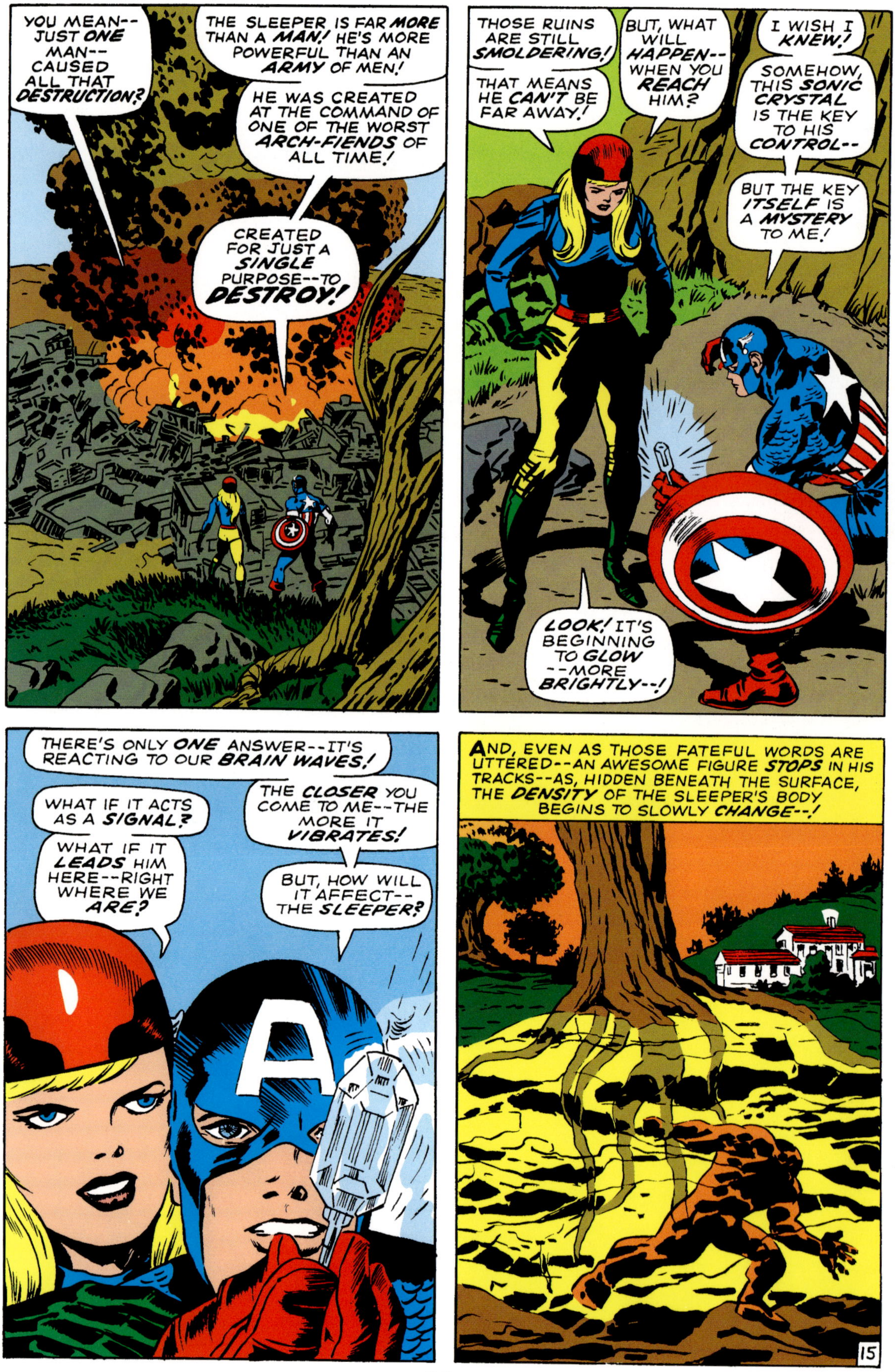
YOU MEAN-- JUST ONE MAN-- CAUSED ALL THAT DESTRUCTION?
THE SLEEPER IS FAR MORE THAN A MAN! HE'S MORE POWERFUL THAN AN ARMY OF MEN!
HE WAS CREATED AT THE COMMAND OF ONE OF THE WORST ARCH-FIENDS OF ALL TIME!
CREATED FOR JUST A SINGLE PURPOSE--TO DESTROY!
THOSE RUINS ARE STILL SMOLDERING!
THAT MEANS HE CAN'T BE FAR AWAY!
BUT, WHAT WILL HAPPEN-- WHEN YOU REACH HIM?
I WISH I KNEW!
SOMEHOW, THIS SONIC CRYSTAL IS THE KEY TO HIS CONTROL--
BUT THE KEY ITSELF IS A MYSTERY TO ME!
LOOK! IT'S BEGINNING TO GLOW --MORE BRIGHTLY--!
THERE'S ONLY ONE ANSWER--IT'S REACTING TO OUR BRAIN WAVES!
WHAT IF IT ACTS AS A SIGNAL?
WHAT IF IT LEADS HIM HERE--RIGHT WHERE WE ARE?
THE CLOSER YOU COME TO ME--THE MORE IT VIBRATES!
BUT, HOW WILL IT AFFECT-- THE SLEEPER?
AND, EVEN AS THOSE FATEFUL WORDS ARE UTTERED--AN AWESOME FIGURE STOPS IN HIS TRACKS--AS, HIDDEN BENEATH THE SURFACE, THE DENSITY OF THE SLEEPER'S BODY BEGINS TO SLOWLY CHANGE--!
15

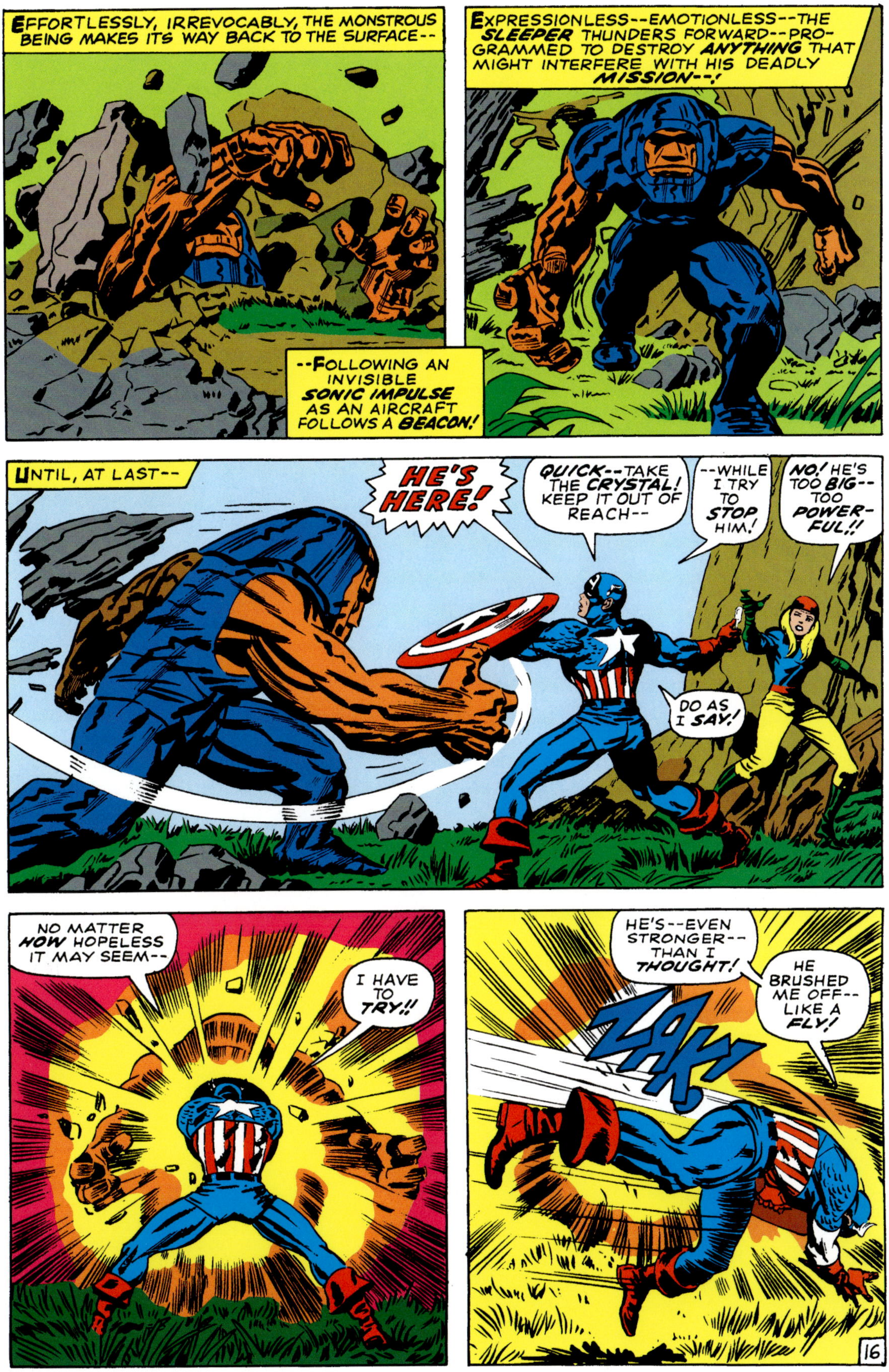
EFFORTLESSLY, IRREVOCABLY, THE MONSTROUS BEING MAKES ITS WAY BACK TO THE SURFACE--
EXPRESSIONLESS--EMOTIONLESS--THE SLEEPER THUNDERS FORWARD--PROGRAMMED TO DESTROY ANYTHING THAT MIGHT INTERFERE WITH HIS DEADLY MISSION--!
--FOLLOWING AN INVISIBLE SONIC IMPULSE AS AN AIRCRAFT FOLLOWS A BEACON!
UNTIL, AT LAST--
HE'S HERE!
QUICK--TAKE THE CRYSTAL! KEEP IT OUT OF REACH--
--WHILE I TRY TO STOP HIM!
NO! HE'S TOO BIG--TOO POWERFUL!!
DO AS I SAY!
NO MATTER HOW HOPELESS IT MAY SEEM--
I HAVE TO TRY!!
HE'S--EVEN STRONGER--THAN I THOUGHT!
HE BRUSHED ME OFF--LIKE A FLY!
ZAK!
16

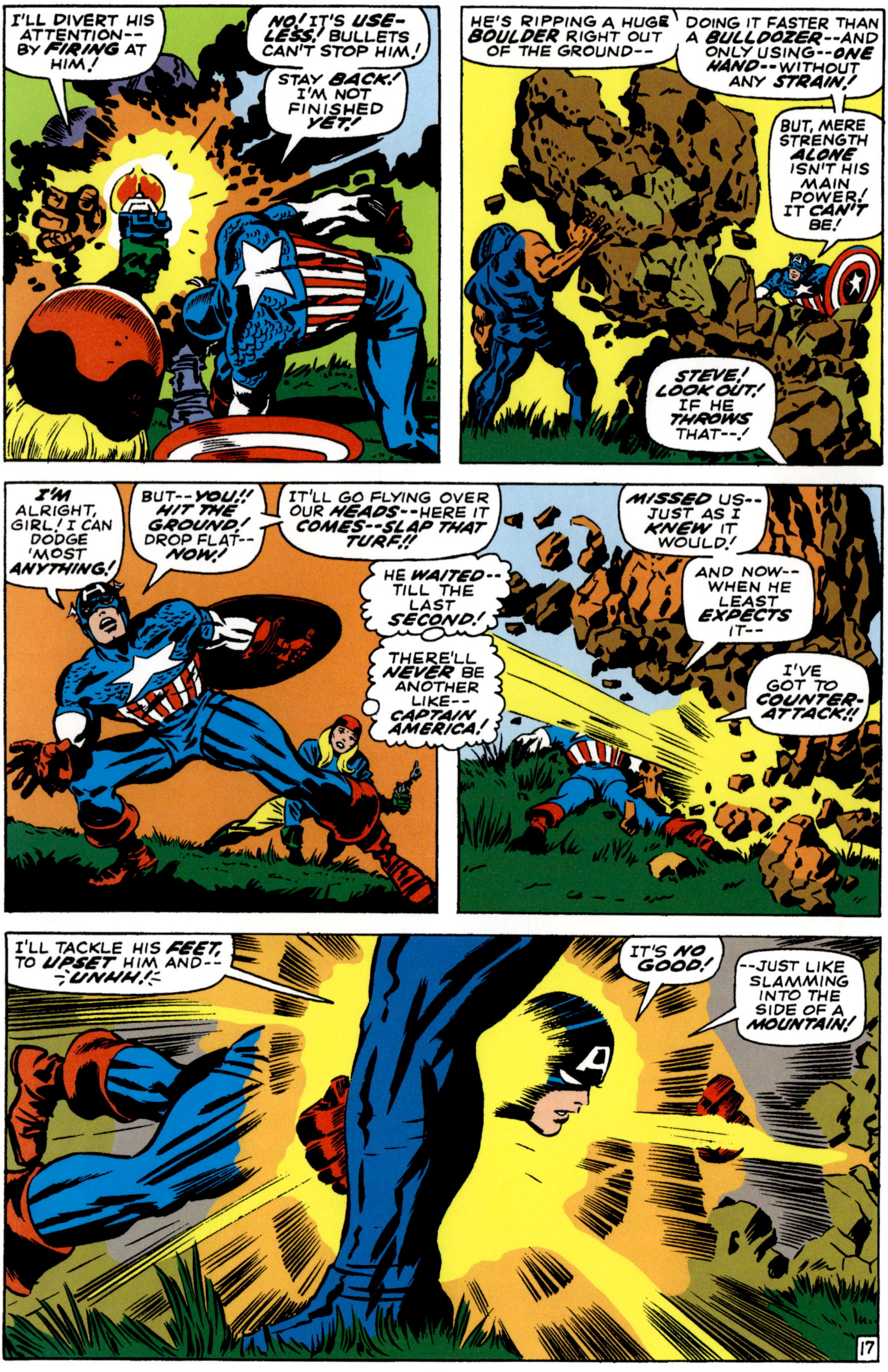
I'LL DIVERT HIS ATTENTION-- BY FIRING AT HIM!
NO! IT'S USELESS! BULLETS CAN'T STOP HIM!
STAY BACK! I'M NOT FINISHED YET!
HE'S RIPPING A HUGE BOULDER RIGHT OUT OF THE GROUND--
DOING IT FASTER THAN A BULLDOZER--AND ONLY USING--ONE HAND--WITHOUT ANY STRAIN!
BUT, MERE STRENGTH ALONE ISN'T HIS MAIN POWER! IT CAN'T BE!
STEVE! LOOK OUT! IF HE THROWS THAT--!
I'M ALRIGHT, GIRL! I CAN DODGE 'MOST ANYTHING!
BUT--YOU!! HIT THE GROUND! DROP FLAT-- NOW!
IT'LL GO FLYING OVER OUR HEADS--HERE IT COMES--SLAP THAT TURF!!
HE WAITED-- TILL THE LAST SECOND!
THERE'LL NEVER BE ANOTHER LIKE-- CAPTAIN AMERICA!
MISSED US-- JUST AS I KNEW IT WOULD!
AND NOW-- WHEN HE LEAST EXPECTS IT--
I'VE GOT TO COUNTER-ATTACK!!
I'LL TACKLE HIS FEET, TO UPSET HIM AND-- -UNHH!-
IT'S NO GOOD!
--JUST LIKE SLAMMING INTO THE SIDE OF A MOUNTAIN!
17

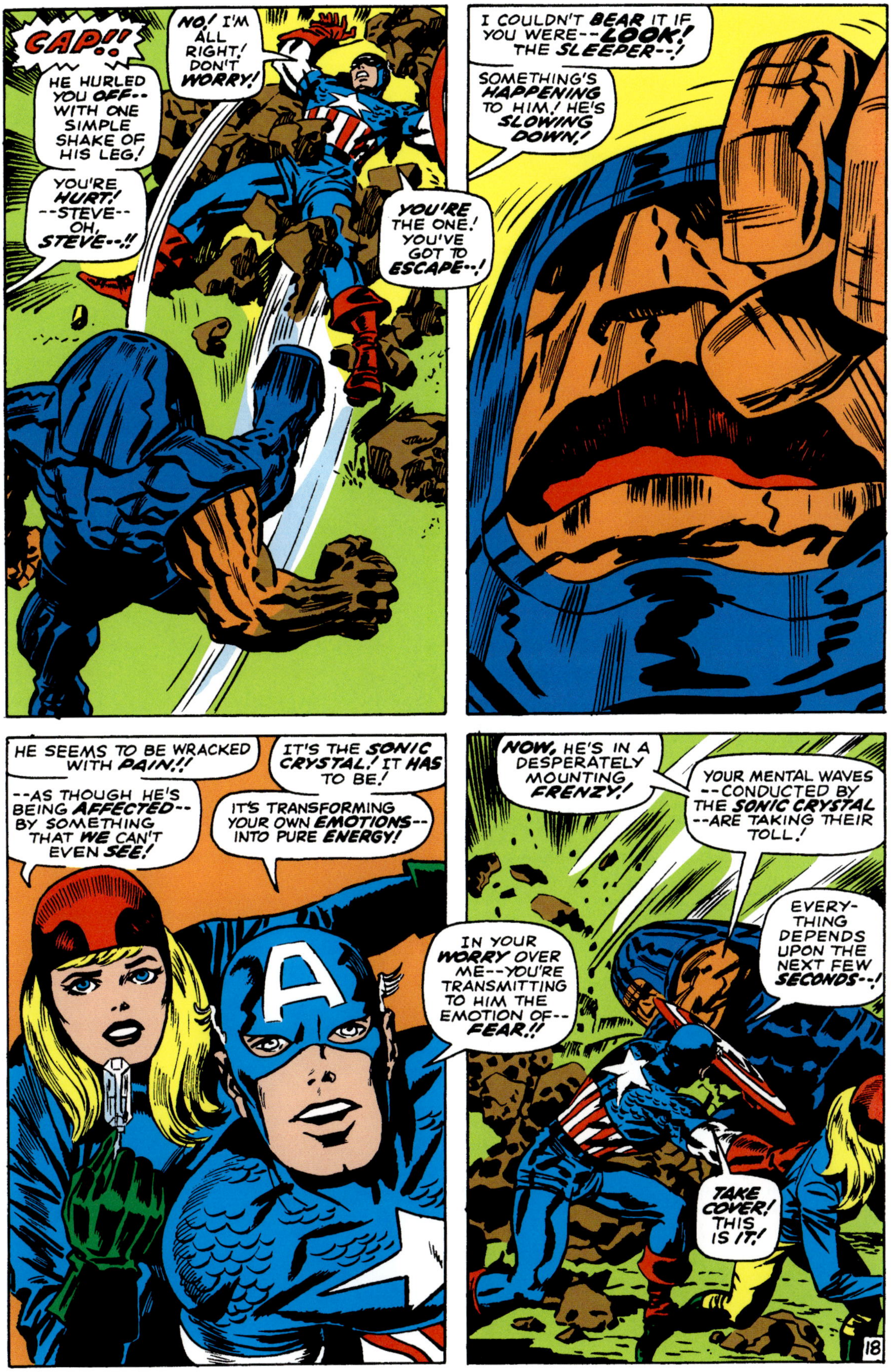
CAP!!
HE HURLED YOU OFF--WITH ONE SIMPLE SHAKE OF HIS LEG!
NO! I'M ALL RIGHT! DON'T WORRY!
YOU'RE HURT! --STEVE-- OH, STEVE--!!
YOU'RE THE ONE! YOU'VE GOT TO ESCAPE--!
I COULDN'T BEAR IT IF YOU WERE--LOOK! THE SLEEPER--!
SOMETHING'S HAPPENING TO HIM! HE'S SLOWING DOWN!
HE SEEMS TO BE WRACKED WITH PAIN!!
--AS THOUGH HE'S BEING AFFECTED--BY SOMETHING THAT WE CAN'T EVEN SEE!
IT'S THE SONIC CRYSTAL! IT HAS TO BE!
IT'S TRANSFORMING YOUR OWN EMOTIONS--INTO PURE ENERGY!
IN YOUR WORRY OVER ME--YOU'RE TRANSMITTING TO HIM THE EMOTION OF--FEAR!!
NOW, HE'S IN A DESPERATELY MOUNTING FRENZY!
YOUR MENTAL WAVES --CONDUCTED BY THE SONIC CRYSTAL --ARE TAKING THEIR TOLL!
EVERY-THING DEPENDS UPON THE NEXT FEW SECONDS--!
TAKE COVER! THIS IS IT!
18

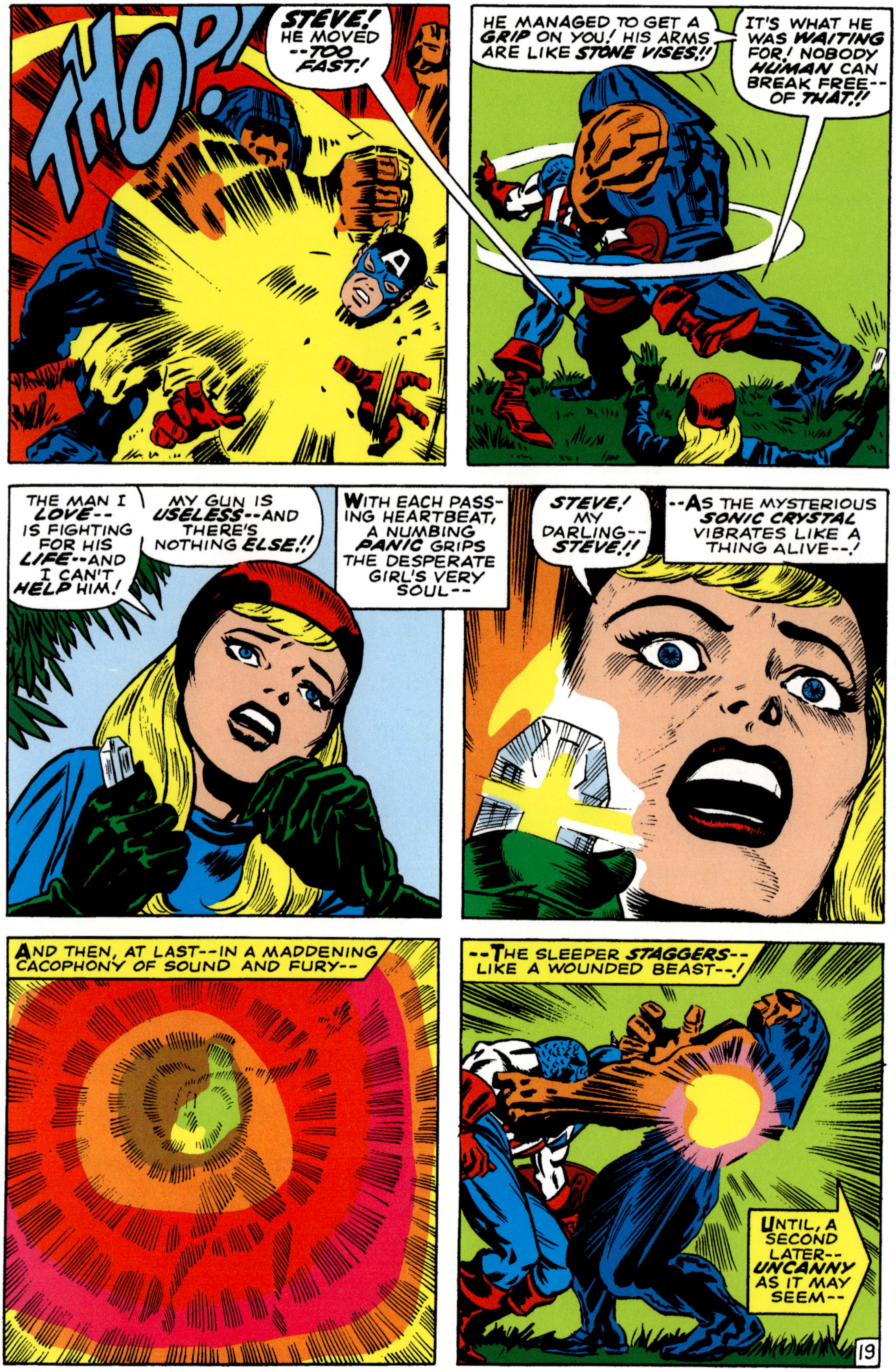
THOP!
STEVE! HE MOVED --TOO FAST!
HE MANAGED TO GET A GRIP ON YOU! HIS ARMS ARE LIKE STONE VISES!!
IT'S WHAT HE WAS WAITING FOR! NOBODY HUMAN CAN BREAK FREE-- OF THAT!!
THE MAN I LOVE-- IS FIGHTING FOR HIS LIFE--AND I CAN'T HELP HIM!
MY GUN IS USELESS--AND THERE'S NOTHING ELSE!!
WITH EACH PASSING HEARTBEAT, A NUMBING PANIC GRIPS THE DESPERATE GIRL'S VERY SOUL--
STEVE! MY DARLING-- STEVE!!
--AS THE MYSTERIOUS SONIC CRYSTAL VIBRATES LIKE A THING ALIVE--!
AND THEN, AT LAST--IN A MADDENING CACOPHONY OF SOUND AND FURY--
--THE SLEEPER STAGGERS-- LIKE A WOUNDED BEAST--!
UNTIL, A SECOND LATER-- UNCANNY AS IT MAY SEEM--
19

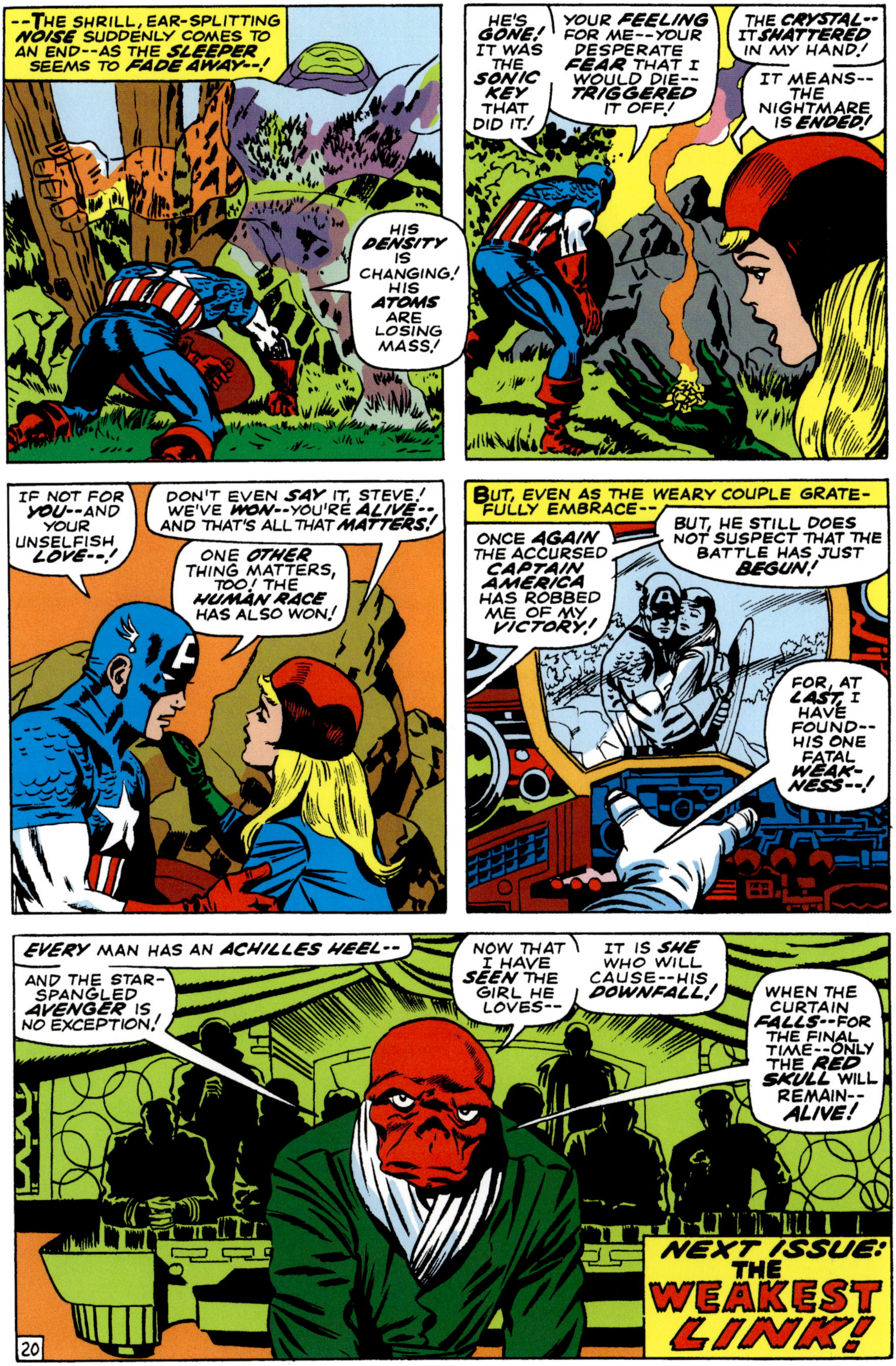
--THE SHRILL, EAR-SPLITTING NOISE SUDDENLY COMES TO AN END--AS THE SLEEPER SEEMS TO FADE AWAY--!
HIS DENSITY IS CHANGING! HIS ATOMS ARE LOSING MASS!
HE'S GONE! IT WAS THE SONIC KEY THAT DID IT!
YOUR FEELING FOR ME--YOUR DESPERATE FEAR THAT I WOULD DIE--TRIGGERED IT OFF!
THE CRYSTAL--IT SHATTERED IN MY HAND!
IT MEANS--THE NIGHTMARE IS ENDED!
IF NOT FOR YOU--AND YOUR UNSELFISH LOVE--!
DON'T EVEN SAY IT, STEVE! WE'VE WON--YOU'RE ALIVE--AND THAT'S ALL THAT MATTERS!
ONE OTHER THING MATTERS, TOO! THE HUMAN RACE HAS ALSO WON!
BUT, EVEN AS THE WEARY COUPLE GRATEFULLY EMBRACE--
ONCE AGAIN THE ACCURSED CAPTAIN AMERICA HAS ROBBED ME OF MY VICTORY!
BUT, HE STILL DOES NOT SUSPECT THAT THE BATTLE HAS JUST BEGUN!
FOR, AT LAST, I HAVE FOUND--HIS ONE FATAL WEAKNESS--!
EVERY MAN HAS AN ACHILLES HEEL--
AND THE STAR-SPANGLED AVENGER IS NO EXCEPTION!
NOW THAT I HAVE SEEN THE GIRL HE LOVES--
IT IS SHE WHO WILL CAUSE--HIS DOWNFALL!
WHEN THE CURTAIN FALLS--FOR THE FINAL TIME--ONLY THE RED SKULL WILL REMAIN--ALIVE!
NEXT ISSUE: THE WEAKEST LINK!
20

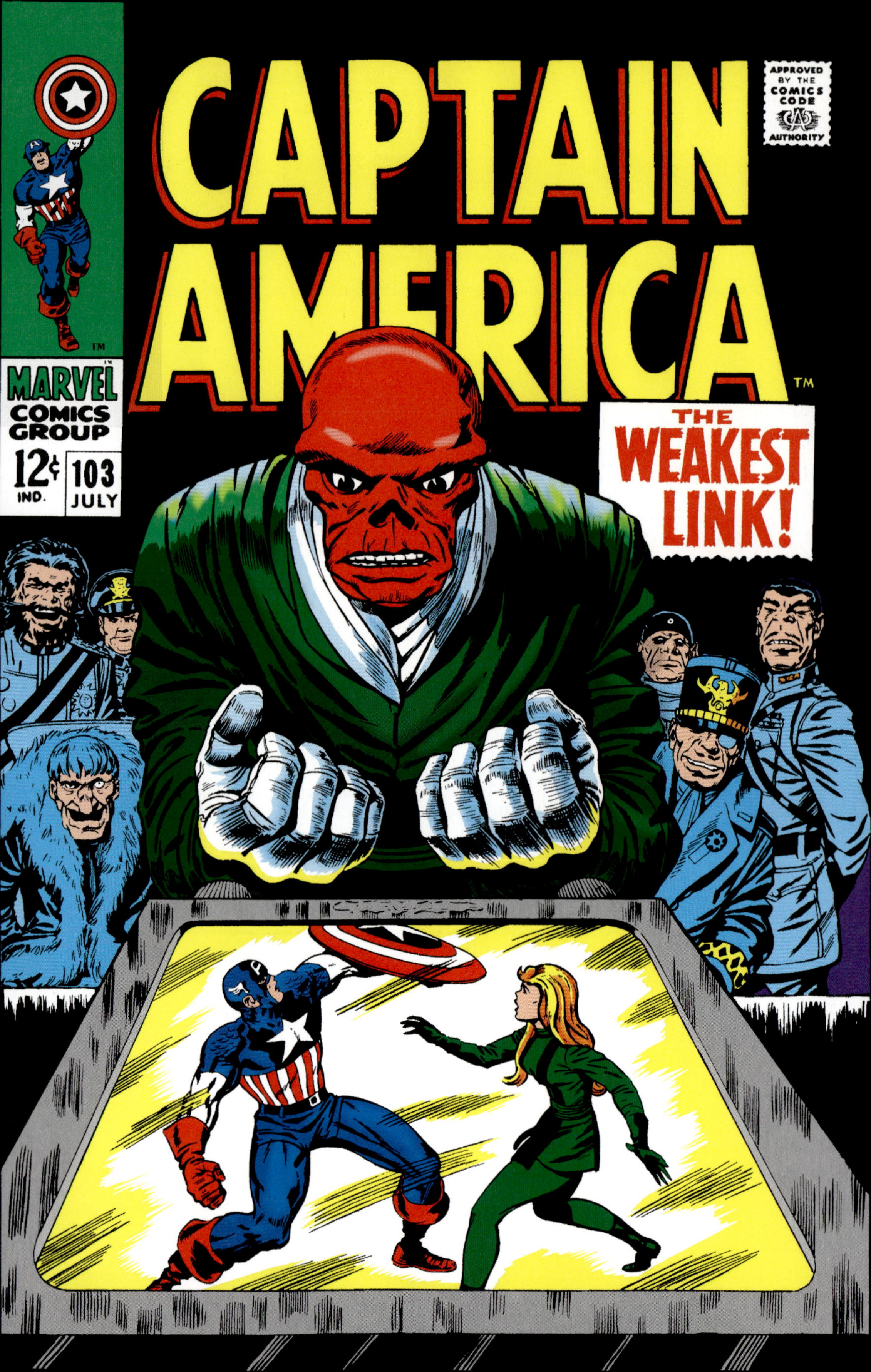

CAPTAIN AMERICA
MARVEL COMICS GROUP
12¢ IND.
103 JULY
APPROVED BY THE COMICS CODE AUTHORITY
THE WEAKEST LINK!

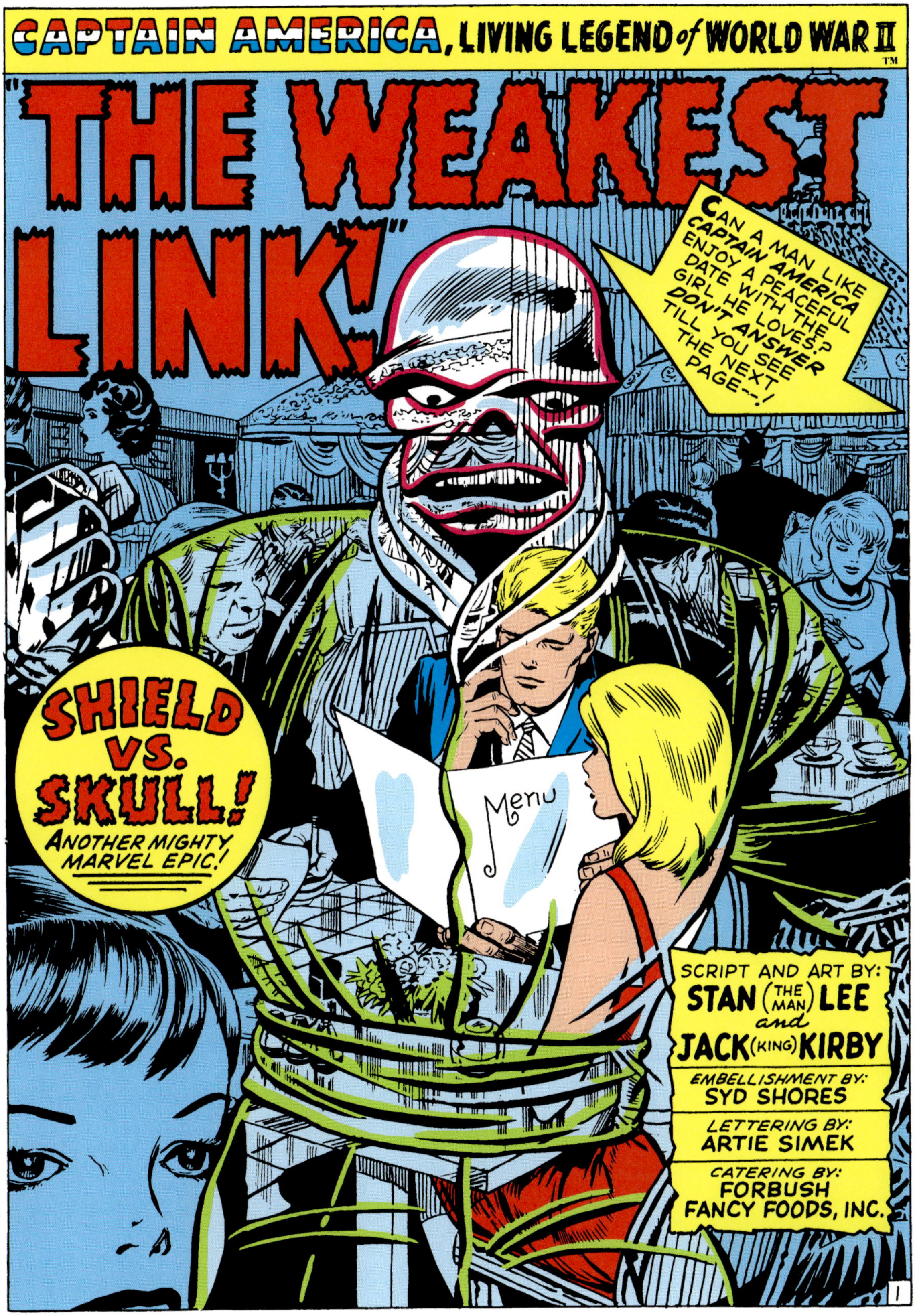
CAPTAIN AMERICA, LIVING LEGEND of WORLD WAR II
TM
"THE WEAKEST LINK!"
CAN A MAN LIKE CAPTAIN AMERICA ENJOY A PEACEFUL DATE WITH THE GIRL HE LOVES? DON'T ANSWER TILL YOU SEE THE NEXT PAGE--!
SHIELD VS. SKULL! ANOTHER MIGHTY MARVEL EPIC!
Menu
SCRIPT AND ART BY: STAN (THE MAN) LEE and JACK (KING) KIRBY
EMBELLISHMENT BY: SYD SHORES
LETTERING BY: ARTIE SIMEK
CATERING BY: FORBUSH FANCY FOODS, INC.
1

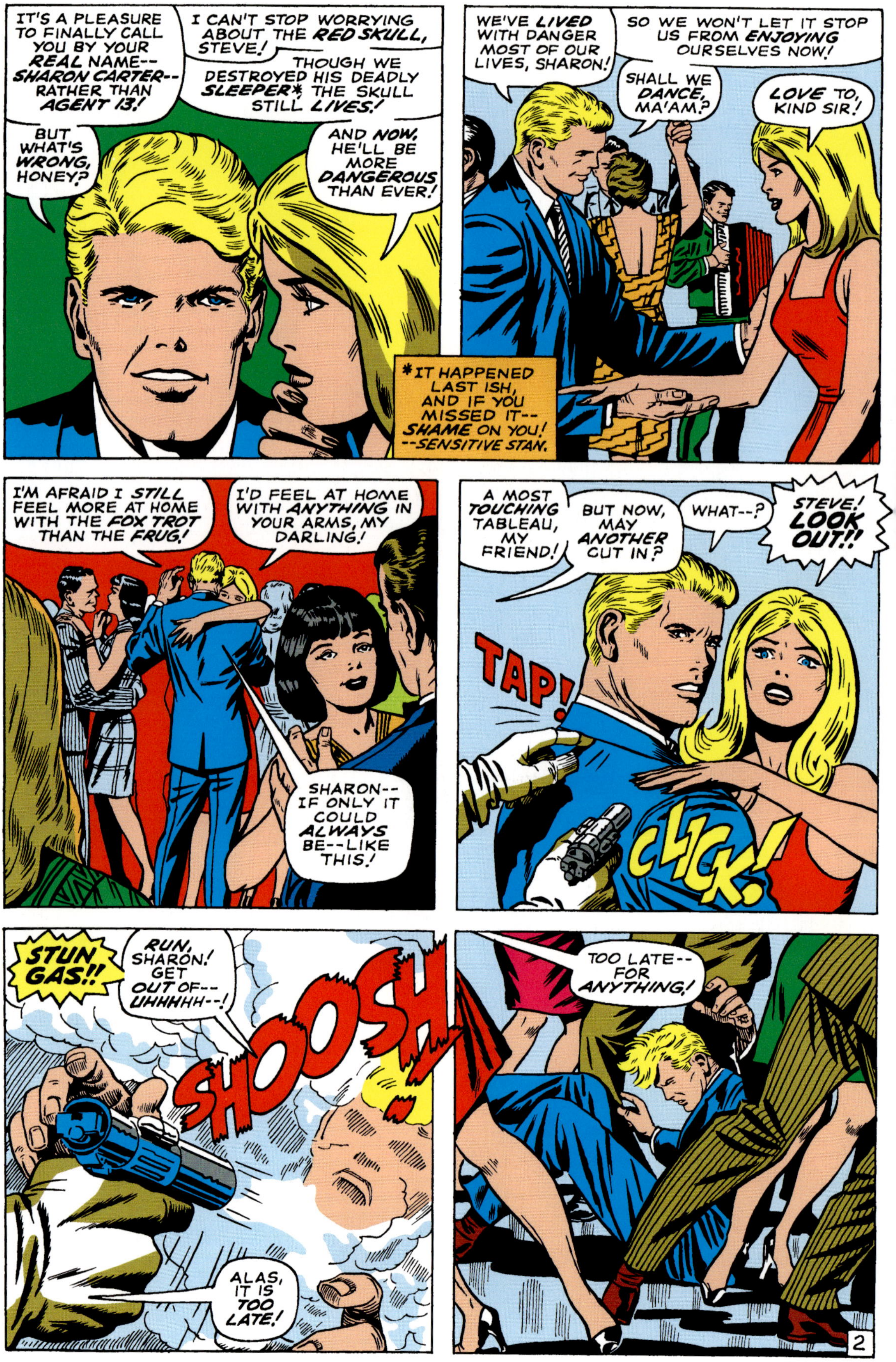
IT'S A PLEASURE TO FINALLY CALL YOU BY YOUR REAL NAME-- SHARON CARTER-- RATHER THAN AGENT 13!
I CAN'T STOP WORRYING ABOUT THE RED SKULL, STEVE!
THOUGH WE DESTROYED HIS DEADLY SLEEPER* THE SKULL STILL LIVES!
BUT WHAT'S WRONG, HONEY?
AND NOW, HE'LL BE MORE DANGEROUS THAN EVER!
*IT HAPPENED LAST ISH, AND IF YOU MISSED IT-- SHAME ON YOU! --SENSITIVE STAN.
WE'VE LIVED WITH DANGER MOST OF OUR LIVES, SHARON!
SO WE WON'T LET IT STOP US FROM ENJOYING OURSELVES NOW!
SHALL WE DANCE, MA'AM?
LOVE TO, KIND SIR!
I'M AFRAID I STILL FEEL MORE AT HOME WITH THE FOX TROT THAN THE FRUG!
I'D FEEL AT HOME WITH ANYTHING IN YOUR ARMS, MY DARLING!
SHARON-- IF ONLY IT COULD ALWAYS BE--LIKE THIS!
A MOST TOUCHING TABLEAU, MY FRIEND!
BUT NOW, MAY ANOTHER CUT IN?
WHAT--?
STEVE! LOOK OUT!!
TAP!
CLICK!
STUN GAS!!
RUN, SHARON! GET OUT OF-- UHHHHH--!
SHOOSH!
ALAS, IT IS TOO LATE!
TOO LATE-- FOR ANYTHING!
2

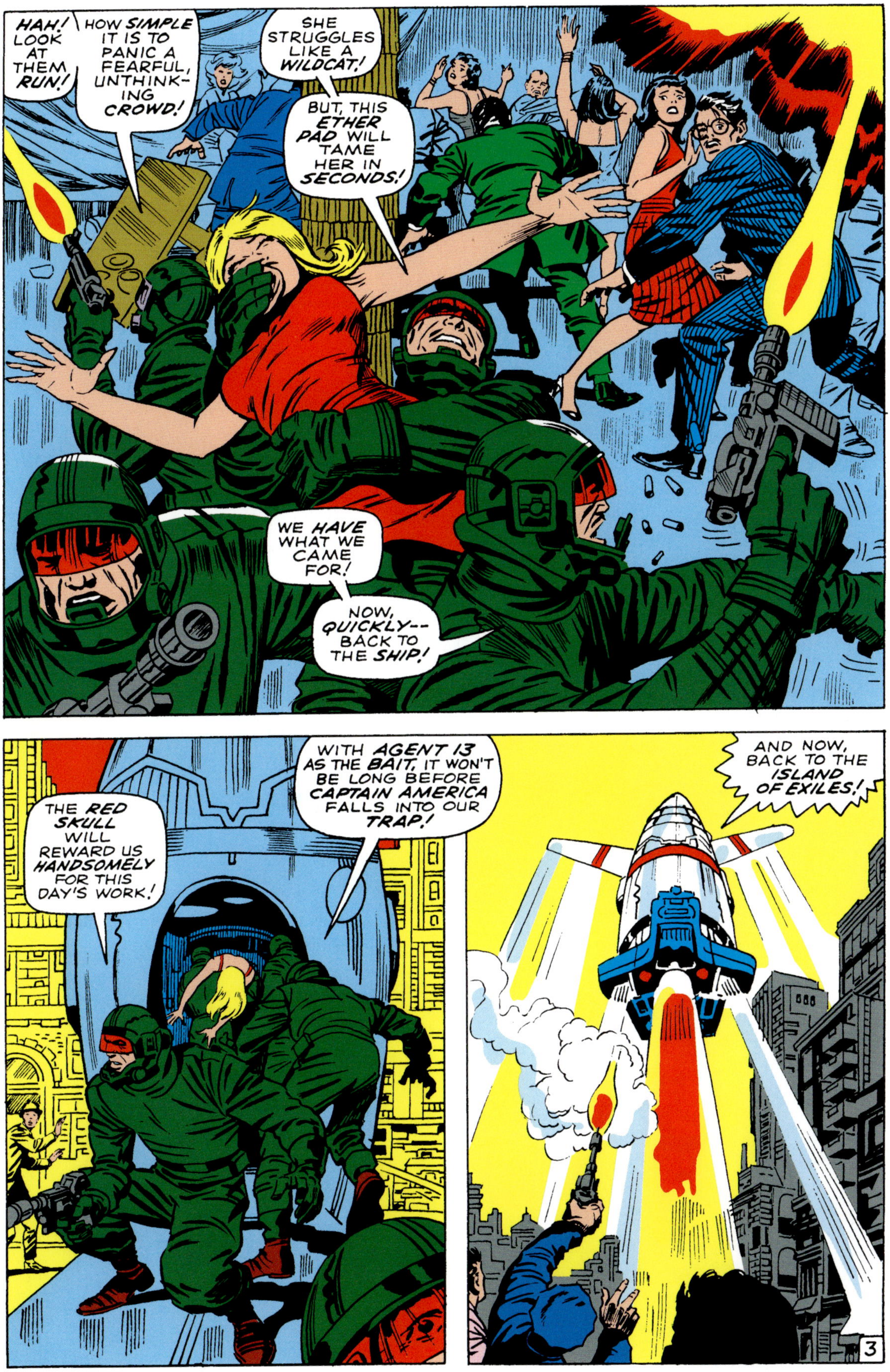
HAH! LOOK AT THEM RUN!
HOW SIMPLE IT IS TO PANIC A FEARFUL, UNTHINKING CROWD!
SHE STRUGGLES LIKE A WILDCAT!
BUT, THIS ETHER PAD WILL TAME HER IN SECONDS!
WE HAVE WHAT WE CAME FOR!
NOW, QUICKLY-- BACK TO THE SHIP!
THE RED SKULL WILL REWARD US HANDSOMELY FOR THIS DAY'S WORK!
WITH AGENT 13 AS THE BAIT, IT WON'T BE LONG BEFORE CAPTAIN AMERICA FALLS INTO OUR TRAP!
AND NOW, BACK TO THE ISLAND OF EXILES!
3

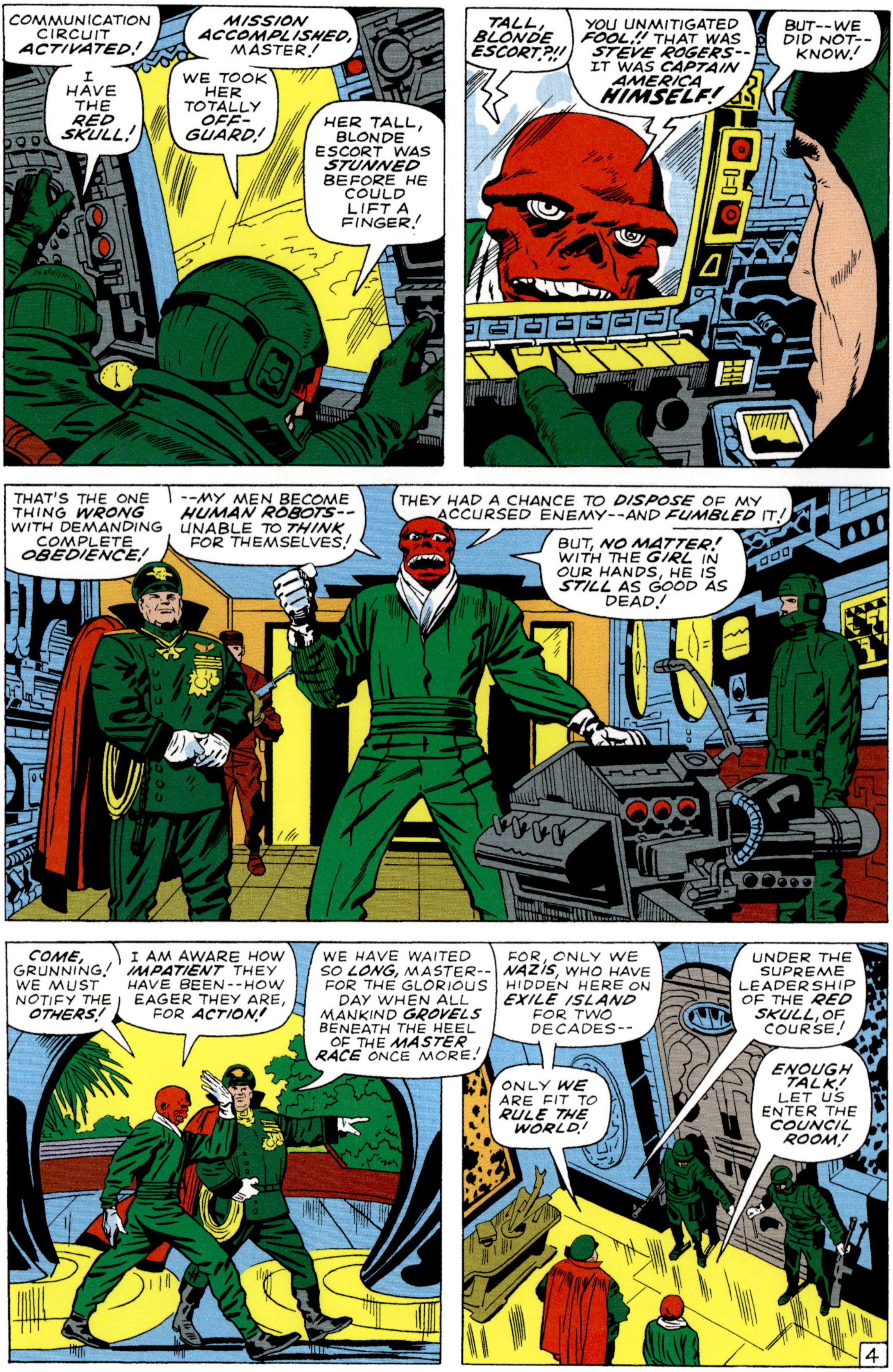
COMMUNICATION CIRCUIT ACTIVATED!
I HAVE THE RED SKULL!
MISSION ACCOMPLISHED, MASTER!
WE TOOK HER TOTALLY OFF-GUARD!
HER TALL, BLONDE ESCORT WAS STUNNED BEFORE HE COULD LIFT A FINGER!
TALL, BLONDE ESCORT?!!
YOU UNMITIGATED FOOL!! THAT WAS STEVE ROGERS-- IT WAS CAPTAIN AMERICA HIMSELF!
BUT--WE DID NOT-- KNOW!
THAT'S THE ONE THING WRONG WITH DEMANDING COMPLETE OBEDIENCE!
--MY MEN BECOME HUMAN ROBOTS-- UNABLE TO THINK FOR THEMSELVES!
THEY HAD A CHANCE TO DISPOSE OF MY ACCURSED ENEMY--AND FUMBLED IT!
BUT, NO MATTER! WITH THE GIRL IN OUR HANDS, HE IS STILL AS GOOD AS DEAD!
COME, GRUNNING! WE MUST NOTIFY THE OTHERS!
I AM AWARE HOW IMPATIENT THEY HAVE BEEN--HOW EAGER THEY ARE, FOR ACTION!
WE HAVE WAITED SO LONG, MASTER-- FOR THE GLORIOUS DAY WHEN ALL MANKIND GROVELS BENEATH THE HEEL OF THE MASTER RACE ONCE MORE!
FOR, ONLY WE NAZIS, WHO HAVE HIDDEN HERE ON EXILE ISLAND FOR TWO DECADES--
ONLY WE ARE FIT TO RULE THE WORLD!
UNDER THE SUPREME LEADERSHIP OF THE RED SKULL, OF COURSE!
ENOUGH TALK! LET US ENTER THE COUNCIL ROOM!
4

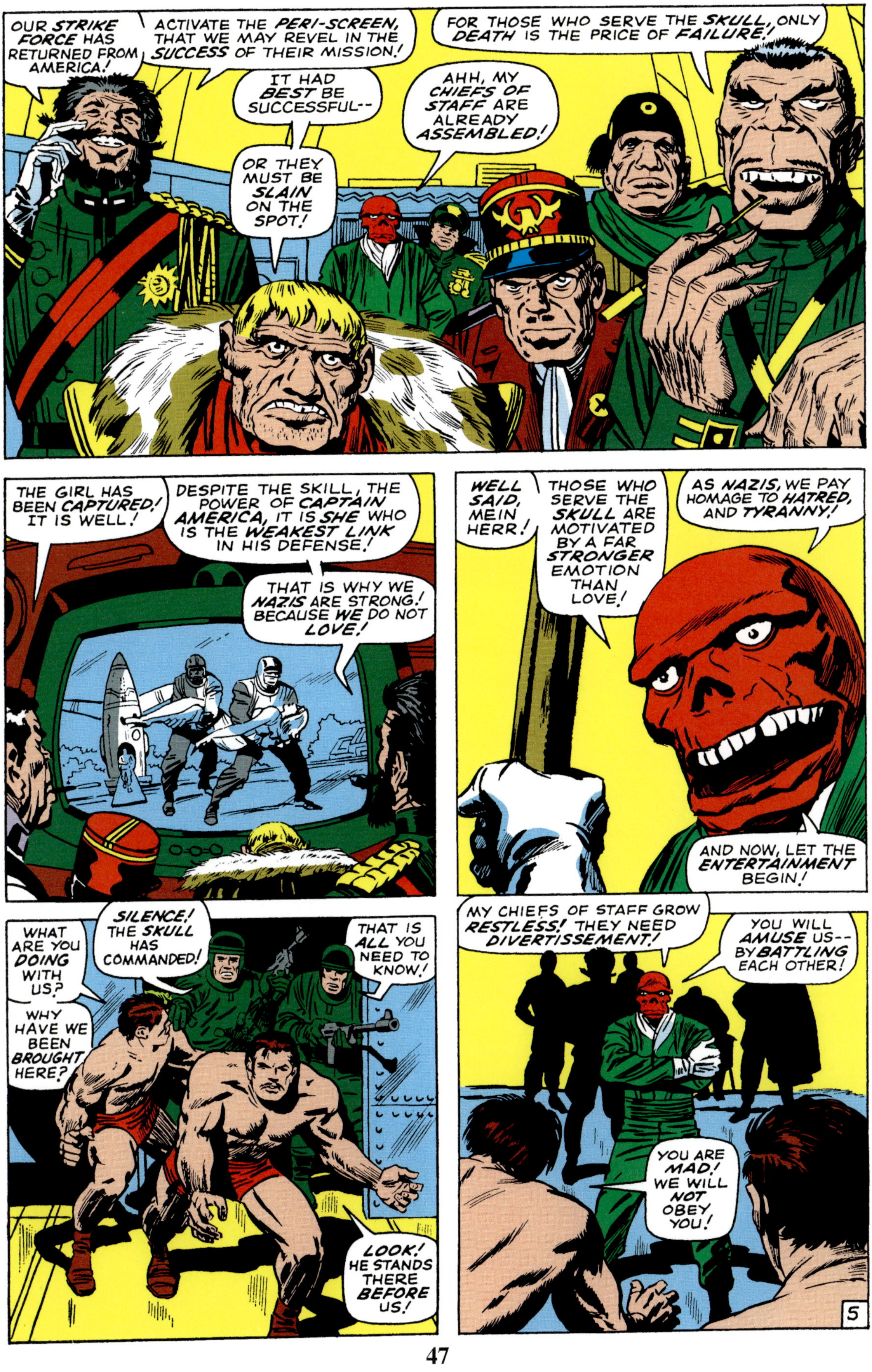
OUR STRIKE FORCE HAS RETURNED FROM AMERICA!
ACTIVATE THE PERI-SCREEN, THAT WE MAY REVEL IN THE SUCCESS OF THEIR MISSION!
IT HAD BEST BE SUCCESSFUL--
OR THEY MUST BE SLAIN ON THE SPOT!
AHH, MY CHIEFS OF STAFF ARE ALREADY ASSEMBLED!
FOR THOSE WHO SERVE THE SKULL, ONLY DEATH IS THE PRICE OF FAILURE!
THE GIRL HAS BEEN CAPTURED! IT IS WELL!
DESPITE THE SKILL, THE POWER OF CAPTAIN AMERICA, IT IS SHE WHO IS THE WEAKEST LINK IN HIS DEFENSE!
THAT IS WHY WE NAZIS ARE STRONG! BECAUSE WE DO NOT LOVE!
WELL SAID, MEIN HERR!
THOSE WHO SERVE THE SKULL ARE MOTIVATED BY A FAR STRONGER EMOTION THAN LOVE!
AS NAZIS, WE PAY HOMAGE TO HATRED, AND TYRANNY!
AND NOW, LET THE ENTERTAINMENT BEGIN!
WHAT ARE YOU DOING WITH US?
WHY HAVE WE BEEN BROUGHT HERE?
SILENCE! THE SKULL HAS COMMANDED!
THAT IS ALL YOU NEED TO KNOW!
LOOK! HE STANDS THERE BEFORE US!
MY CHIEFS OF STAFF GROW RESTLESS! THEY NEED DIVERTISSEMENT!
YOU WILL AMUSE US-- BY BATTLING EACH OTHER!
YOU ARE MAD! WE WILL NOT OBEY YOU!
5

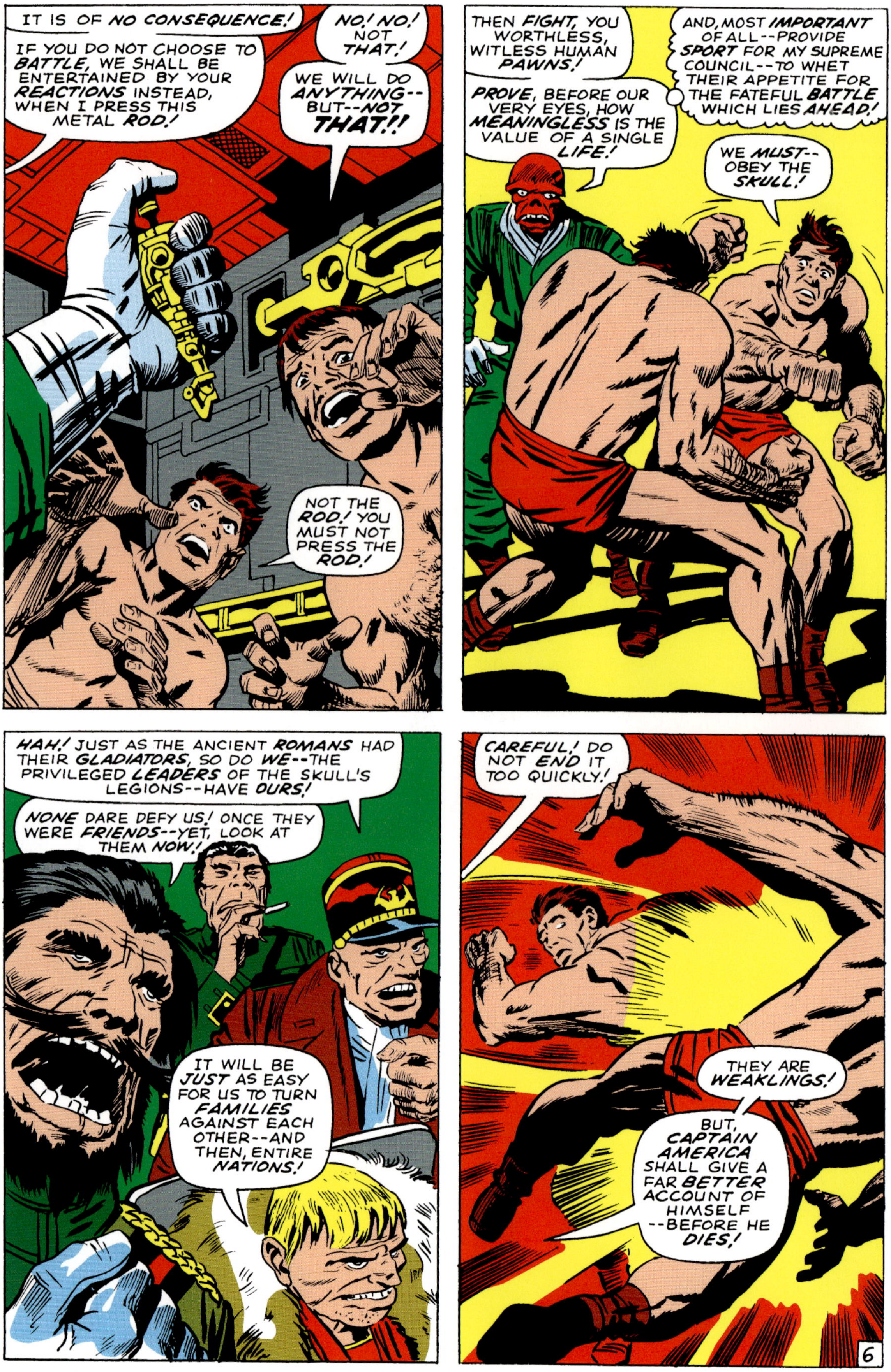
IT IS OF NO CONSEQUENCE!
IF YOU DO NOT CHOOSE TO BATTLE, WE SHALL BE ENTERTAINED BY YOUR REACTIONS INSTEAD, WHEN I PRESS THIS METAL ROD!
NO! NO! NOT THAT!
WE WILL DO ANYTHING-- BUT--NOT THAT!!
NOT THE ROD! YOU MUST NOT PRESS THE ROD!
THEN FIGHT, YOU WORTHLESS, WITLESS HUMAN PAWNS!
PROVE, BEFORE OUR VERY EYES, HOW MEANINGLESS IS THE VALUE OF A SINGLE LIFE!
AND, MOST IMPORTANT OF ALL--PROVIDE SPORT FOR MY SUPREME COUNCIL--TO WHET THEIR APPETITE FOR THE FATEFUL BATTLE WHICH LIES AHEAD!
WE MUST-- OBEY THE SKULL!
HAH! JUST AS THE ANCIENT ROMANS HAD THEIR GLADIATORS, SO DO WE--THE PRIVILEGED LEADERS OF THE SKULL'S LEGIONS--HAVE OURS!
NONE DARE DEFY US! ONCE THEY WERE FRIENDS--YET, LOOK AT THEM NOW!
IT WILL BE JUST AS EASY FOR US TO TURN FAMILIES AGAINST EACH OTHER--AND THEN, ENTIRE NATIONS!
CAREFUL! DO NOT END IT TOO QUICKLY!
THEY ARE WEAKLINGS!
BUT, CAPTAIN AMERICA SHALL GIVE A FAR BETTER ACCOUNT OF HIMSELF --BEFORE HE DIES!
6

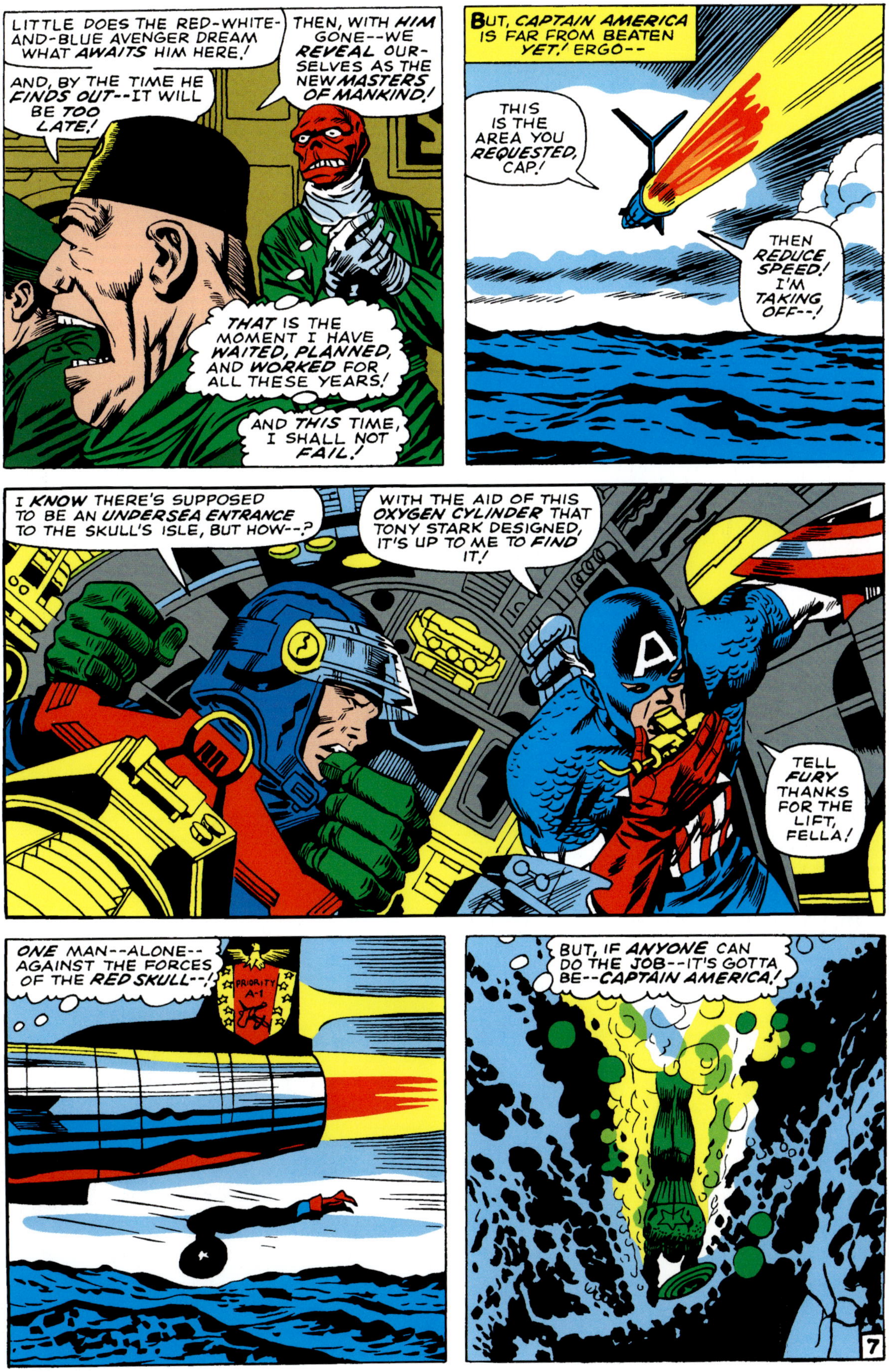
LITTLE DOES THE RED-WHITE-AND-BLUE AVENGER DREAM WHAT AWAITS HIM HERE!
AND, BY THE TIME HE FINDS OUT--IT WILL BE TOO LATE!
THEN, WITH HIM GONE--WE REVEAL OURSELVES AS THE NEW MASTERS OF MANKIND!
THAT IS THE MOMENT I HAVE WAITED, PLANNED, AND WORKED FOR ALL THESE YEARS!
AND THIS TIME, I SHALL NOT FAIL!
BUT, CAPTAIN AMERICA IS FAR FROM BEATEN YET! ERGO--
THIS IS THE AREA YOU REQUESTED, CAP!
THEN REDUCE SPEED! I'M TAKING OFF--!
I KNOW THERE'S SUPPOSED TO BE AN UNDERSEA ENTRANCE TO THE SKULL'S ISLE, BUT HOW--?
WITH THE AID OF THIS OXYGEN CYLINDER THAT TONY STARK DESIGNED, IT'S UP TO ME TO FIND IT!
TELL FURY THANKS FOR THE LIFT, FELLA!
ONE MAN--ALONE--AGAINST THE FORCES OF THE RED SKULL--!
PRIORITY A-1
BUT, IF ANYONE CAN DO THE JOB--IT'S GOTTA BE--CAPTAIN AMERICA!
7

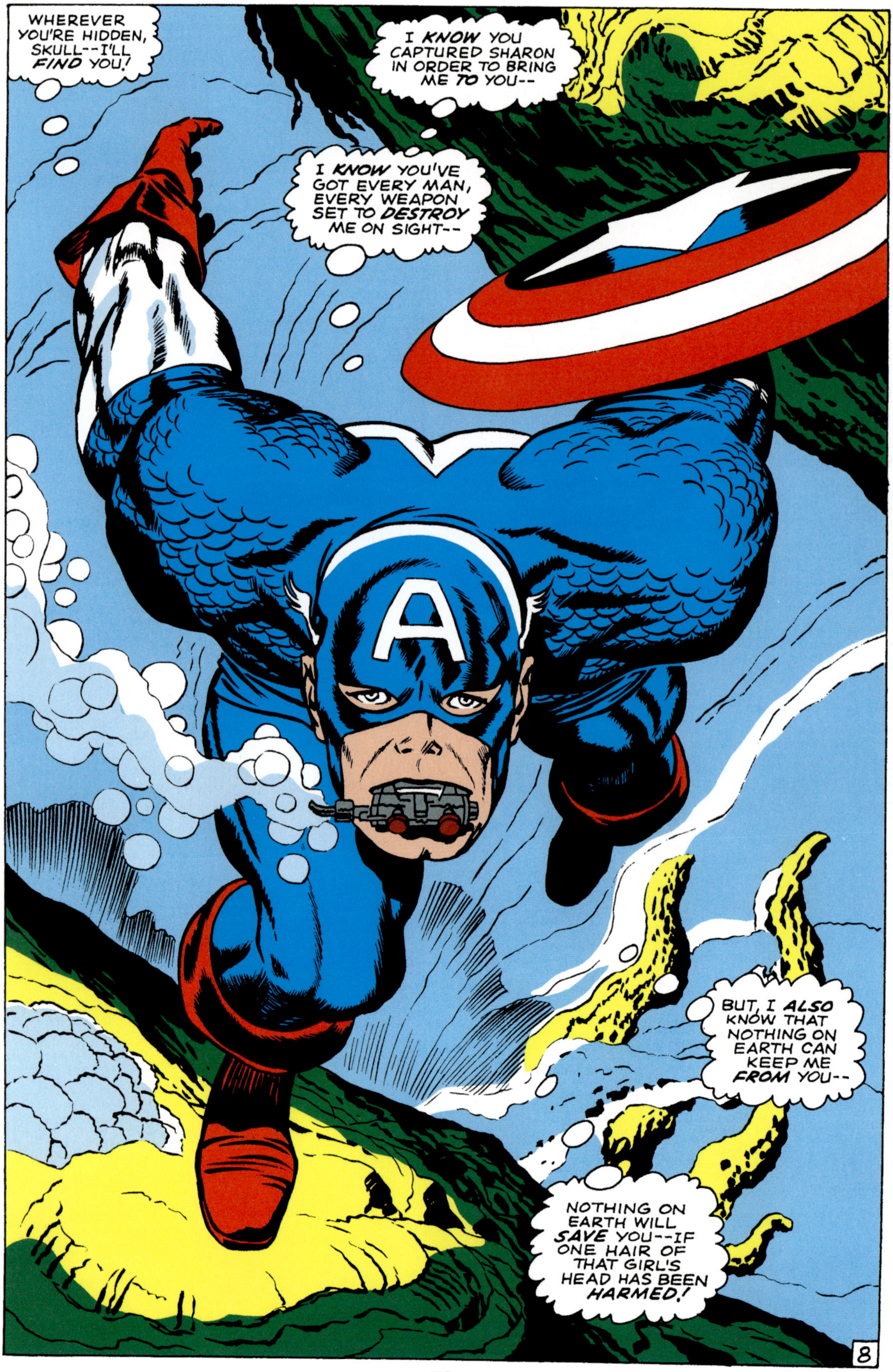
WHEREVER YOU'RE HIDDEN, SKULL--I'LL FIND YOU!
I KNOW YOU CAPTURED SHARON IN ORDER TO BRING ME TO YOU--
I KNOW YOU'VE GOT EVERY MAN, EVERY WEAPON SET TO DESTROY ME ON SIGHT--
BUT, I ALSO KNOW THAT NOTHING ON EARTH CAN KEEP ME FROM YOU--
NOTHING ON EARTH WILL SAVE YOU--IF ONE HAIR OF THAT GIRL'S HEAD HAS BEEN HARMED!
8

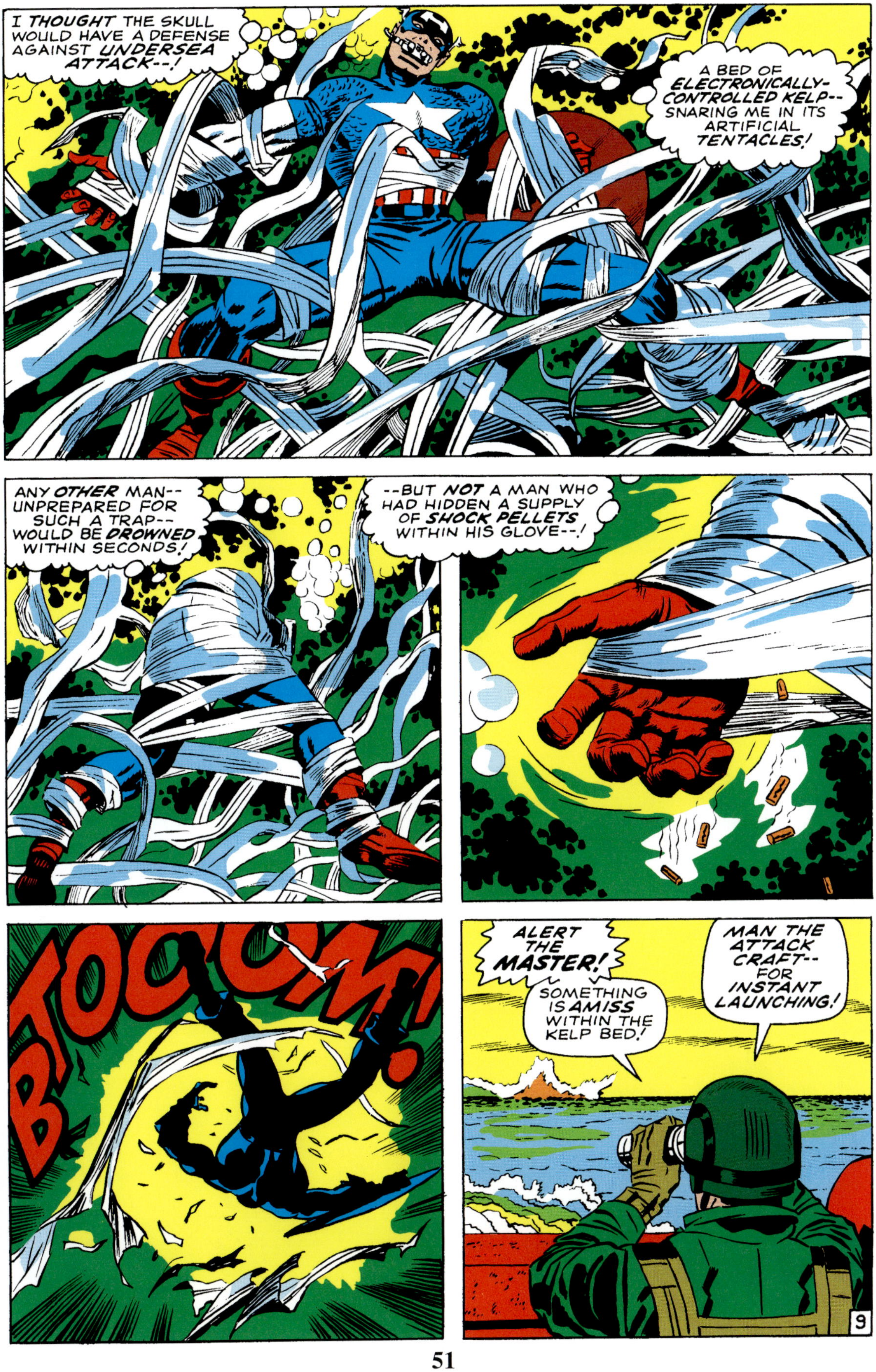
I THOUGHT THE SKULL WOULD HAVE A DEFENSE AGAINST UNDERSEA ATTACK--!
A BED OF ELECTRONICALLY-CONTROLLED KELP--SNARING ME IN ITS ARTIFICIAL TENTACLES!
ANY OTHER MAN--UNPREPARED FOR SUCH A TRAP--WOULD BE DROWNED WITHIN SECONDS!
--BUT NOT A MAN WHO HAD HIDDEN A SUPPLY OF SHOCK PELLETS WITHIN HIS GLOVE--!
BTOOOM!
ALERT THE MASTER!
SOMETHING IS AMISS WITHIN THE KELP BED!
MAN THE ATTACK CRAFT--FOR INSTANT LAUNCHING!
9

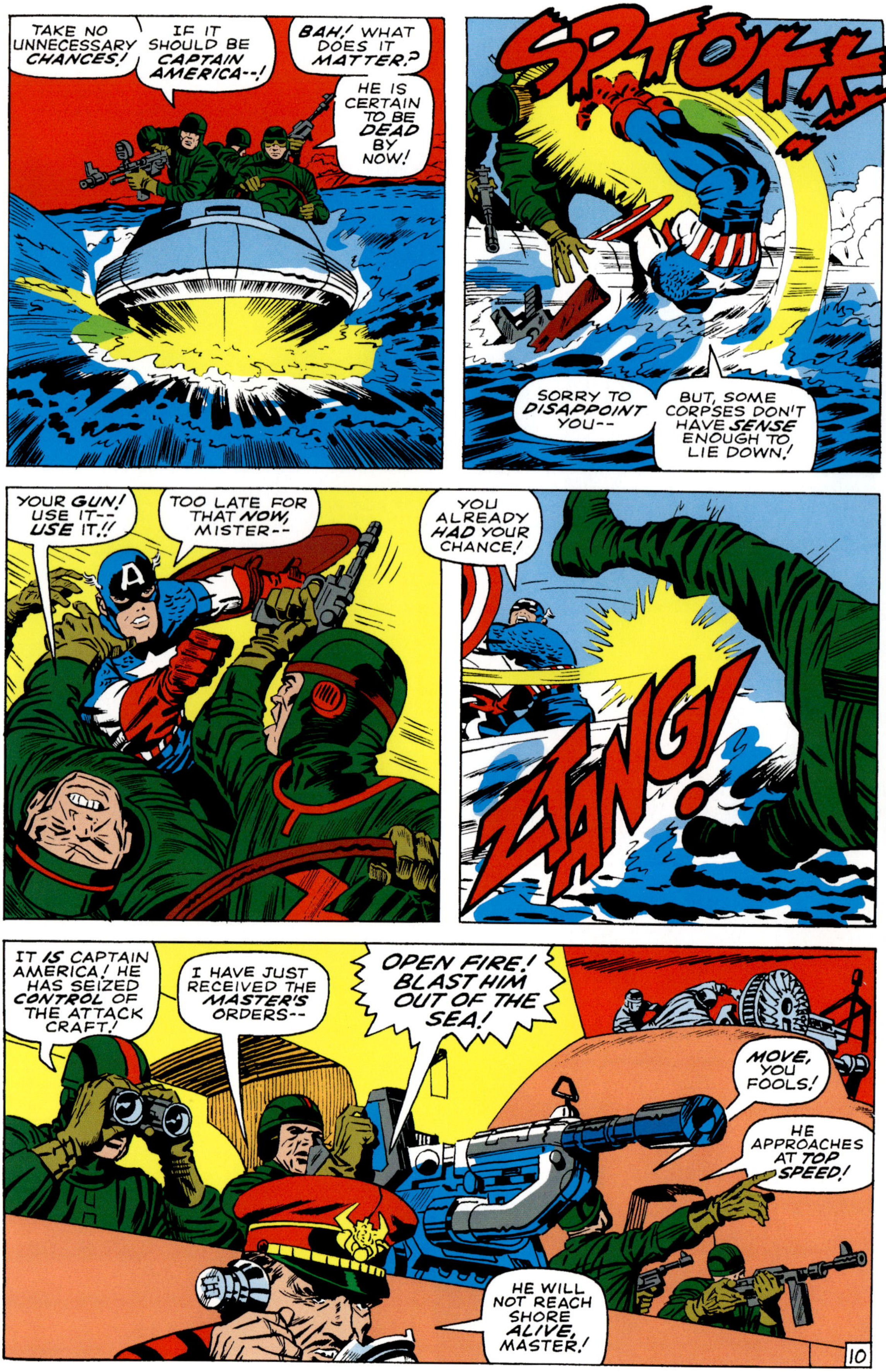

TAKE NO UNNECESSARY CHANCES!
IF IT SHOULD BE CAPTAIN AMERICA--!
BAH! WHAT DOES IT MATTER?
HE IS CERTAIN TO BE DEAD BY NOW!
SPTOKK
SORRY TO DISAPPOINT YOU--
BUT, SOME CORPSES DON'T HAVE SENSE ENOUGH TO LIE DOWN!
YOUR GUN! USE IT-- USE IT!!
TOO LATE FOR THAT NOW, MISTER--
YOU ALREADY HAD YOUR CHANCE!
ZTANG!
IT IS CAPTAIN AMERICA! HE HAS SEIZED CONTROL OF THE ATTACK CRAFT!
I HAVE JUST RECEIVED THE MASTER'S ORDERS--
OPEN FIRE! BLAST HIM OUT OF THE SEA!
MOVE, YOU FOOLS!
HE APPROACHES AT TOP SPEED!
HE WILL NOT REACH SHORE ALIVE, MASTER!
10

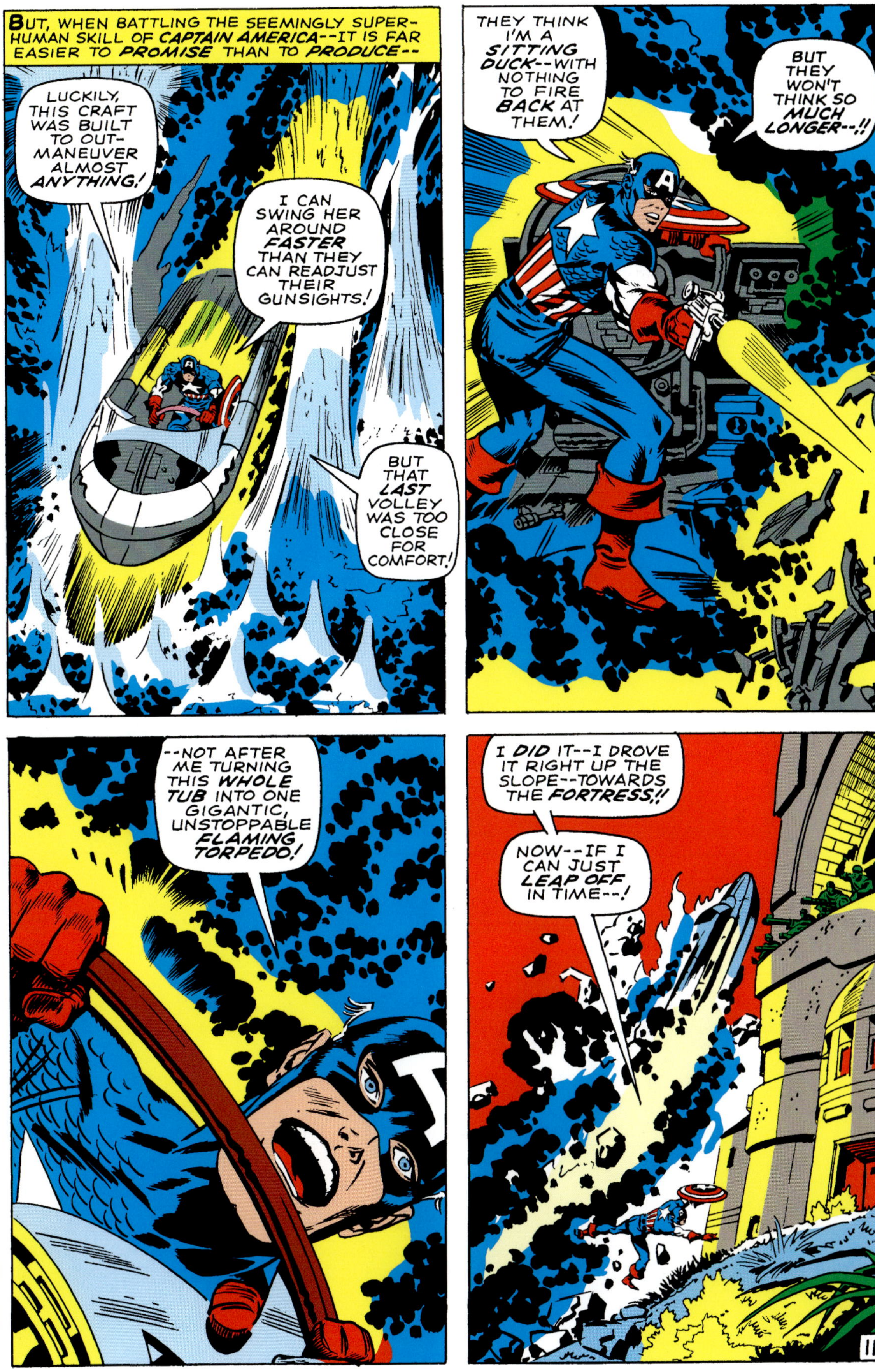
BUT, WHEN BATTLING THE SEEMINGLY SUPER-HUMAN SKILL OF CAPTAIN AMERICA--IT IS FAR EASIER TO PROMISE THAN TO PRODUCE--
LUCKILY, THIS CRAFT WAS BUILT TO OUT-MANEUVER ALMOST ANYTHING!
I CAN SWING HER AROUND FASTER THAN THEY CAN READJUST THEIR GUNSIGHTS!
BUT THAT LAST VOLLEY WAS TOO CLOSE FOR COMFORT!
THEY THINK I'M A SITTING DUCK--WITH NOTHING TO FIRE BACK AT THEM!
BUT THEY WON'T THINK SO MUCH LONGER--!!
--NOT AFTER ME TURNING THIS WHOLE TUB INTO ONE GIGANTIC, UNSTOPPABLE FLAMING TORPEDO!
I DID IT--I DROVE IT RIGHT UP THE SLOPE--TOWARDS THE FORTRESS!!
NOW--IF I CAN JUST LEAP OFF IN TIME--!
11

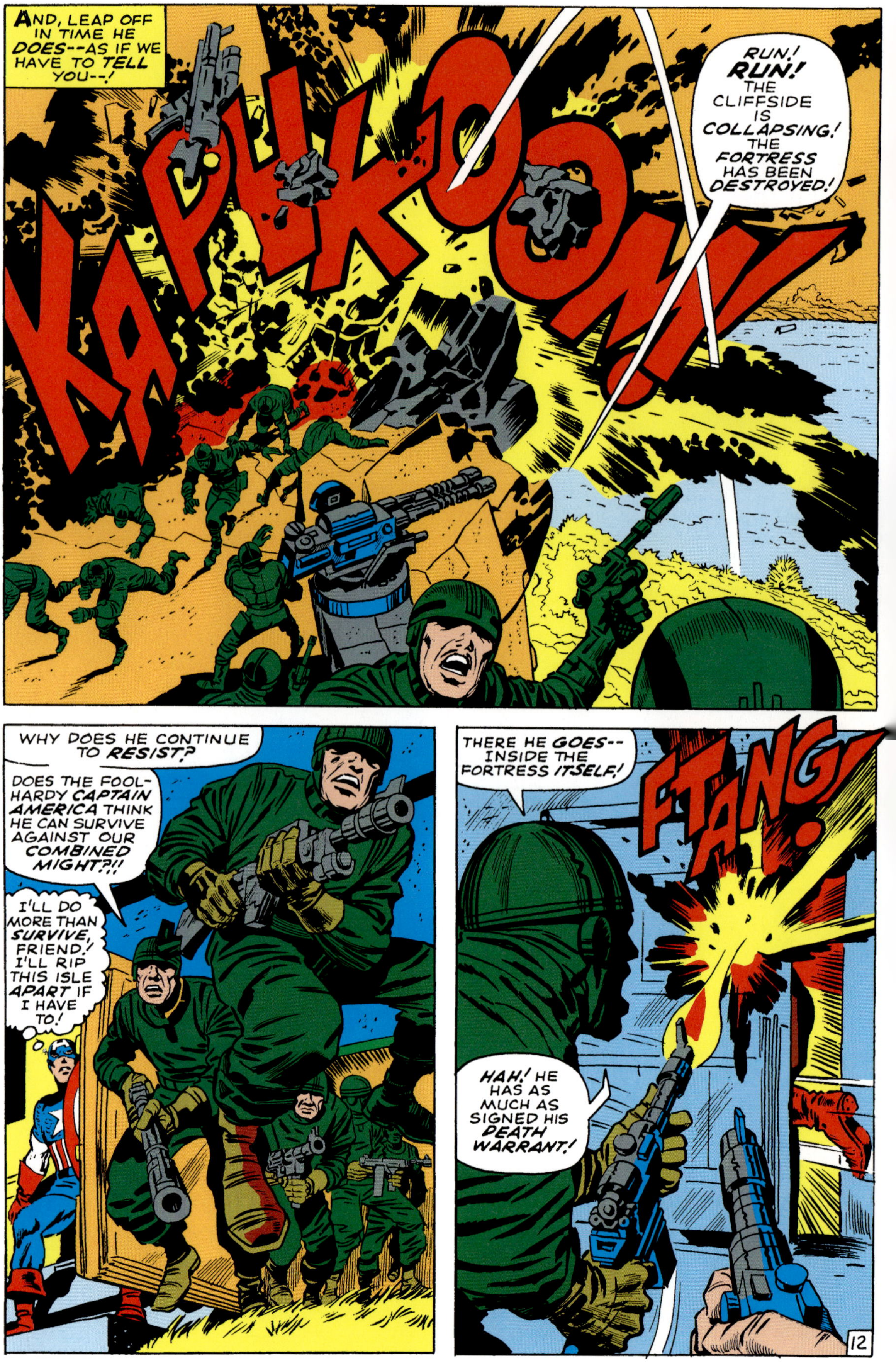
AND, LEAP OFF IN TIME HE DOES--AS IF WE HAVE TO TELL YOU--!
KAPUKOOM!
RUN! RUN! THE CLIFFSIDE IS COLLAPSING! THE FORTRESS HAS BEEN DESTROYED!
WHY DOES HE CONTINUE TO RESIST?
DOES THE FOOL-HARDY CAPTAIN AMERICA THINK HE CAN SURVIVE AGAINST OUR COMBINED MIGHT?!!
I'LL DO MORE THAN SURVIVE, FRIEND! I'LL RIP THIS ISLE APART IF I HAVE TO!
THERE HE GOES-- INSIDE THE FORTRESS ITSELF!
FTANG!
HAH! HE HAS AS MUCH AS SIGNED HIS DEATH WARRANT!
12

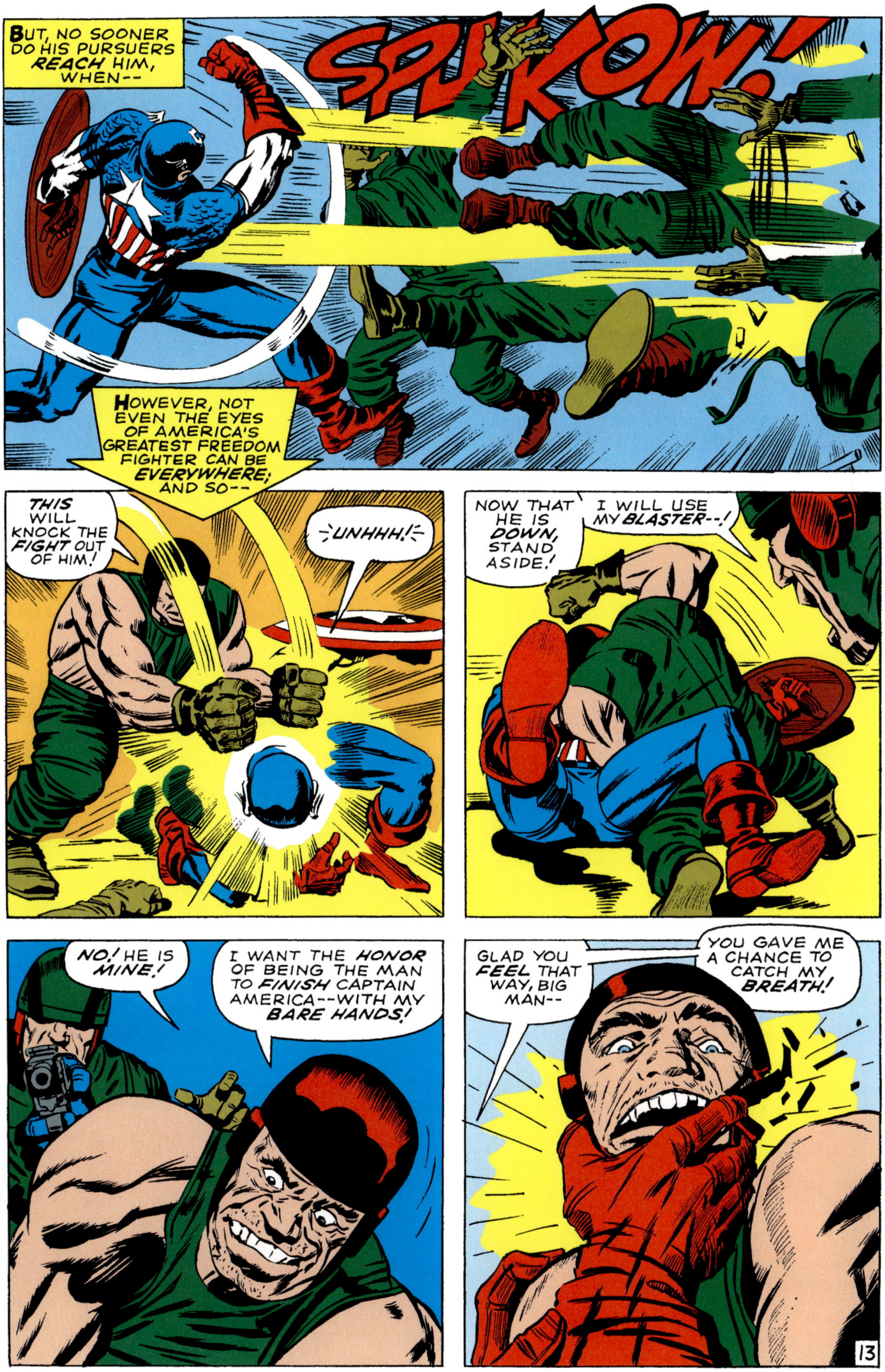
BUT, NO SOONER DO HIS PURSUERS REACH HIM, WHEN--
SPUKOW!
HOWEVER, NOT EVEN THE EYES OF AMERICA'S GREATEST FREEDOM FIGHTER CAN BE EVERYWHERE; AND SO--
THIS WILL KNOCK THE FIGHT OUT OF HIM!
UNHHH!
NOW THAT HE IS DOWN, STAND ASIDE!
I WILL USE MY BLASTER--!
NO! HE IS MINE!
I WANT THE HONOR OF BEING THE MAN TO FINISH CAPTAIN AMERICA--WITH MY BARE HANDS!
GLAD YOU FEEL THAT WAY, BIG MAN--
YOU GAVE ME A CHANCE TO CATCH MY BREATH!
13

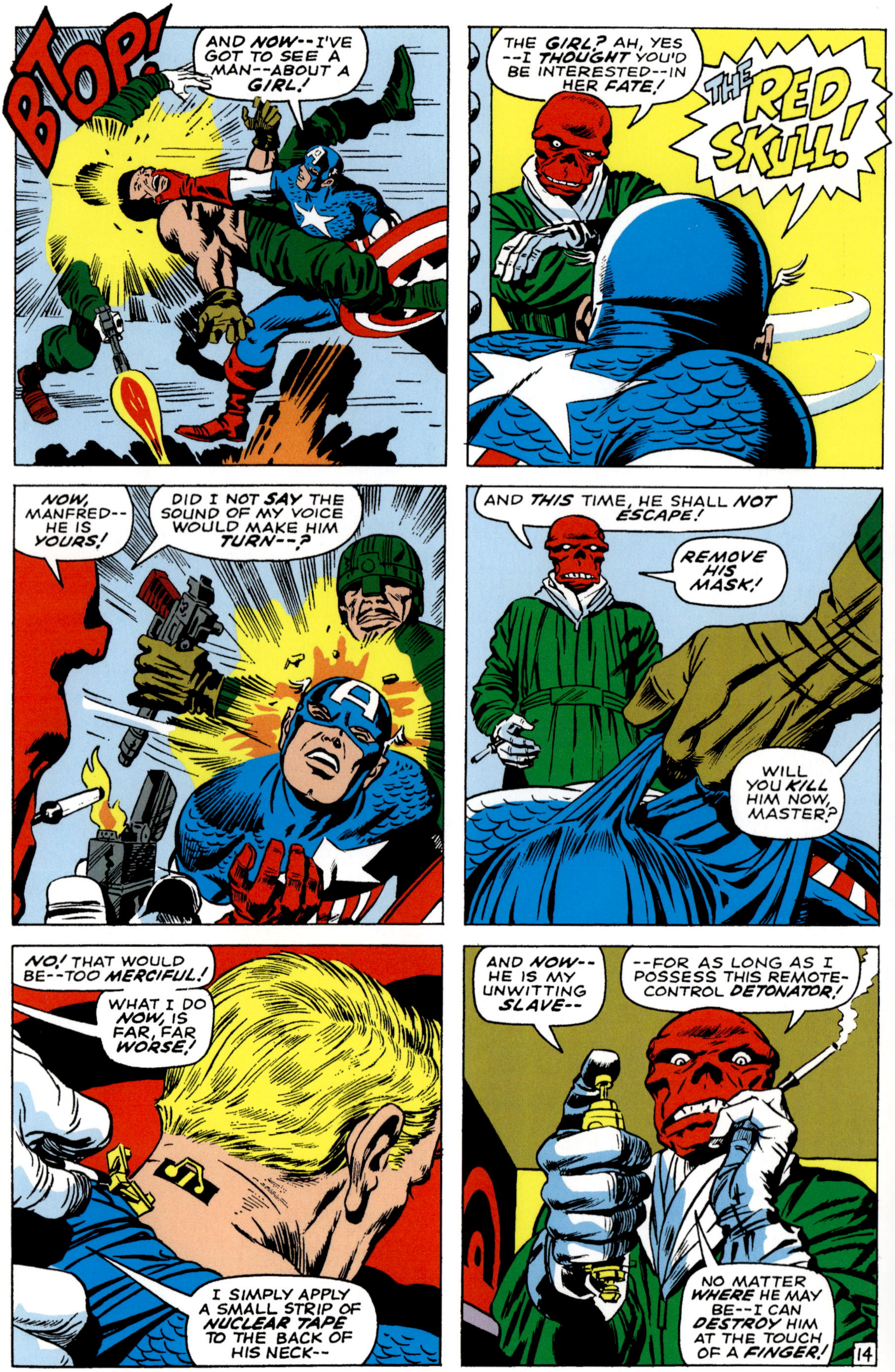
BTOP!
AND NOW--I'VE GOT TO SEE A MAN--ABOUT A GIRL!
THE GIRL? AH, YES--I THOUGHT YOU'D BE INTERESTED--IN HER FATE!
THE RED SKULL!
NOW, MANFRED--HE IS YOURS!
DID I NOT SAY THE SOUND OF MY VOICE WOULD MAKE HIM TURN--?
AND THIS TIME, HE SHALL NOT ESCAPE!
REMOVE HIS MASK!
WILL YOU KILL HIM NOW, MASTER?
NO! THAT WOULD BE--TOO MERCIFUL!
WHAT I DO NOW, IS FAR, FAR WORSE!
I SIMPLY APPLY A SMALL STRIP OF NUCLEAR TAPE TO THE BACK OF HIS NECK--
AND NOW--HE IS MY UNWITTING SLAVE--
--FOR AS LONG AS I POSSESS THIS REMOTE-CONTROL DETONATOR!
NO MATTER WHERE HE MAY BE--I CAN DESTROY HIM AT THE TOUCH OF A FINGER!
14

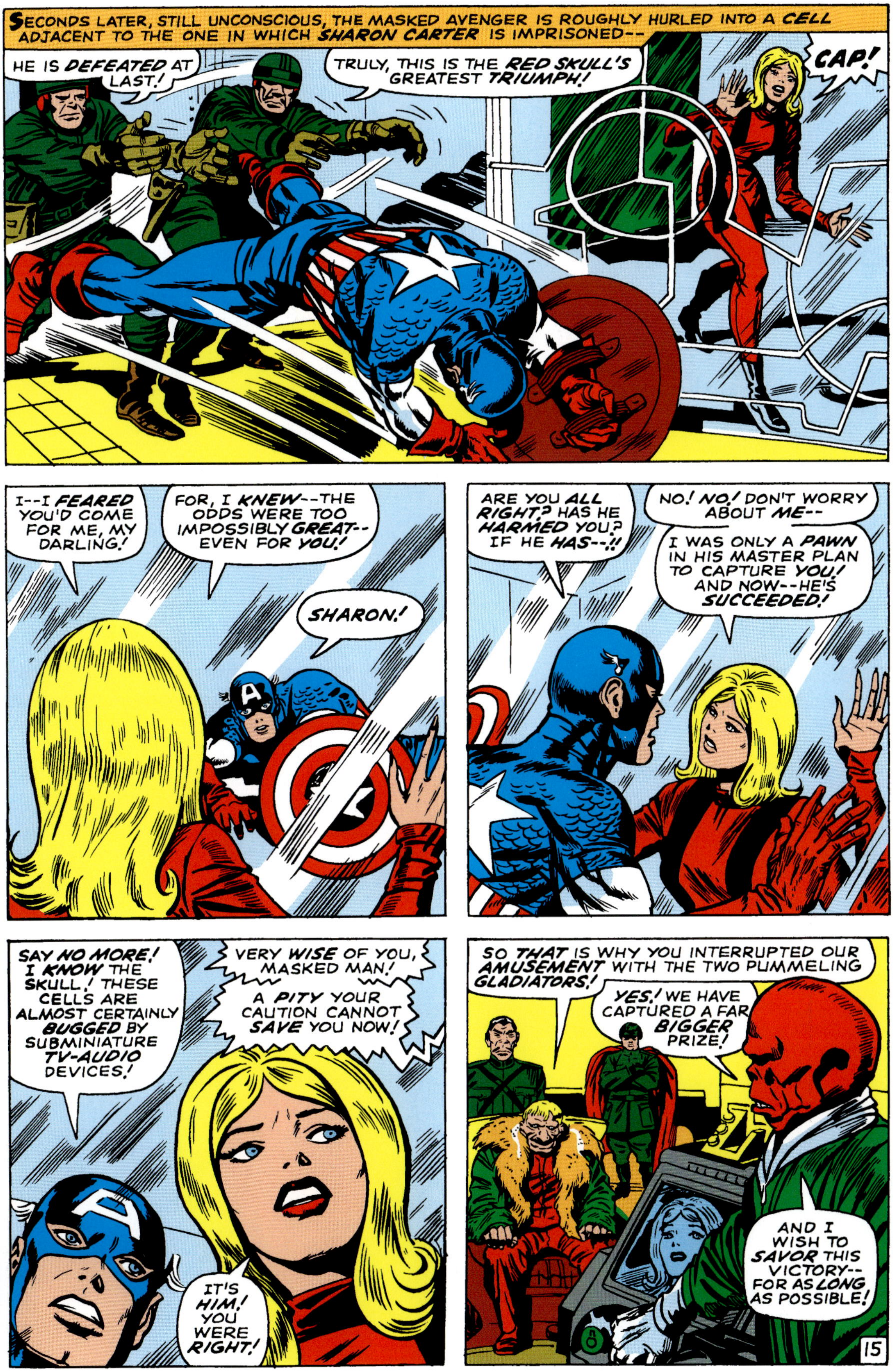
SECONDS LATER, STILL UNCONSCIOUS, THE MASKED AVENGER IS ROUGHLY HURLED INTO A CELL ADJACENT TO THE ONE IN WHICH SHARON CARTER IS IMPRISONED--
HE IS DEFEATED AT LAST!
TRULY, THIS IS THE RED SKULL'S GREATEST TRIUMPH!
CAP!
I--I FEARED YOU'D COME FOR ME, MY DARLING!
FOR, I KNEW--THE ODDS WERE TOO IMPOSSIBLY GREAT--EVEN FOR YOU!
SHARON!
ARE YOU ALL RIGHT? HAS HE HARMED YOU? IF HE HAS--!!
NO! NO! DON'T WORRY ABOUT ME--
I WAS ONLY A PAWN IN HIS MASTER PLAN TO CAPTURE YOU! AND NOW--HE'S SUCCEEDED!
SAY NO MORE! I KNOW THE SKULL! THESE CELLS ARE ALMOST CERTAINLY BUGGED BY SUBMINIATURE TV-AUDIO DEVICES!
VERY WISE OF YOU, MASKED MAN!
A PITY YOUR CAUTION CANNOT SAVE YOU NOW!
IT'S HIM! YOU WERE RIGHT!
SO THAT IS WHY YOU INTERRUPTED OUR AMUSEMENT WITH THE TWO PUMMELING GLADIATORS!
YES! WE HAVE CAPTURED A FAR BIGGER PRIZE!
AND I WISH TO SAVOR THIS VICTORY--FOR AS LONG AS POSSIBLE!
15

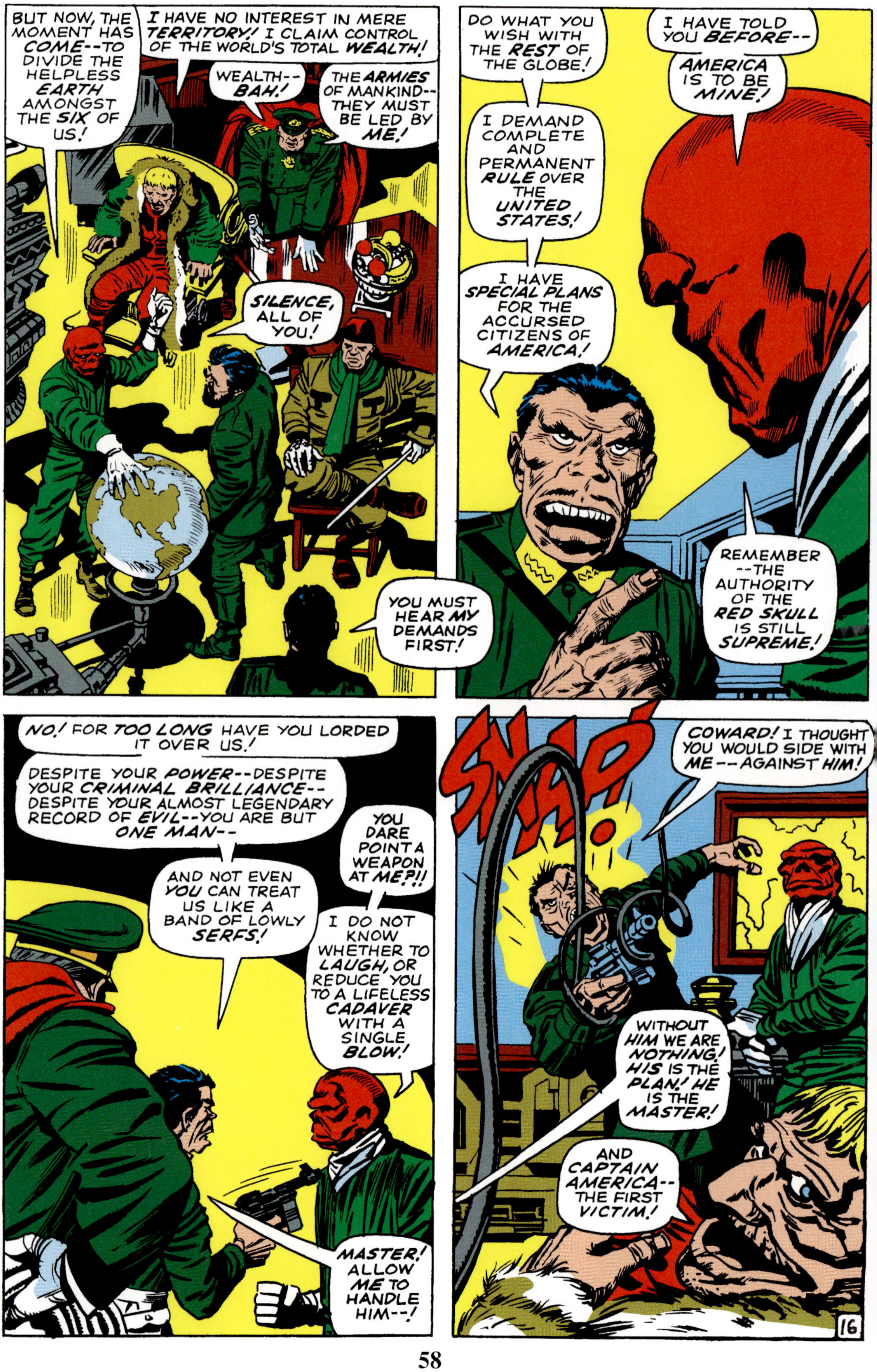
BUT NOW, THE MOMENT HAS COME--TO DIVIDE THE HELPLESS EARTH AMONGST THE SIX OF US!
I HAVE NO INTEREST IN MERE TERRITORY! I CLAIM CONTROL OF THE WORLD'S TOTAL WEALTH!
WEALTH--BAH!
THE ARMIES OF MANKIND--THEY MUST BE LED BY ME!
SILENCE, ALL OF YOU!
YOU MUST HEAR MY DEMANDS FIRST!
DO WHAT YOU WISH WITH THE REST OF THE GLOBE!
I DEMAND COMPLETE AND PERMANENT RULE OVER THE UNITED STATES!
I HAVE SPECIAL PLANS FOR THE ACCURSED CITIZENS OF AMERICA!
I HAVE TOLD YOU BEFORE--
AMERICA IS TO BE MINE!
REMEMBER--THE AUTHORITY OF THE RED SKULL IS STILL SUPREME!
NO! FOR TOO LONG HAVE YOU LORDED IT OVER US!
DESPITE YOUR POWER--DESPITE YOUR CRIMINAL BRILLIANCE--DESPITE YOUR ALMOST LEGENDARY RECORD OF EVIL--YOU ARE BUT ONE MAN--
AND NOT EVEN YOU CAN TREAT US LIKE A BAND OF LOWLY SERFS!
YOU DARE POINT A WEAPON AT ME?!!
I DO NOT KNOW WHETHER TO LAUGH, OR REDUCE YOU TO A LIFELESS CADAVER WITH A SINGLE BLOW!
MASTER! ALLOW ME TO HANDLE HIM--!
SNAP!
COWARD! I THOUGHT YOU WOULD SIDE WITH ME--AGAINST HIM!
WITHOUT HIM WE ARE NOTHING! HIS IS THE PLAN! HE IS THE MASTER!
AND CAPTAIN AMERICA--THE FIRST VICTIM!
16

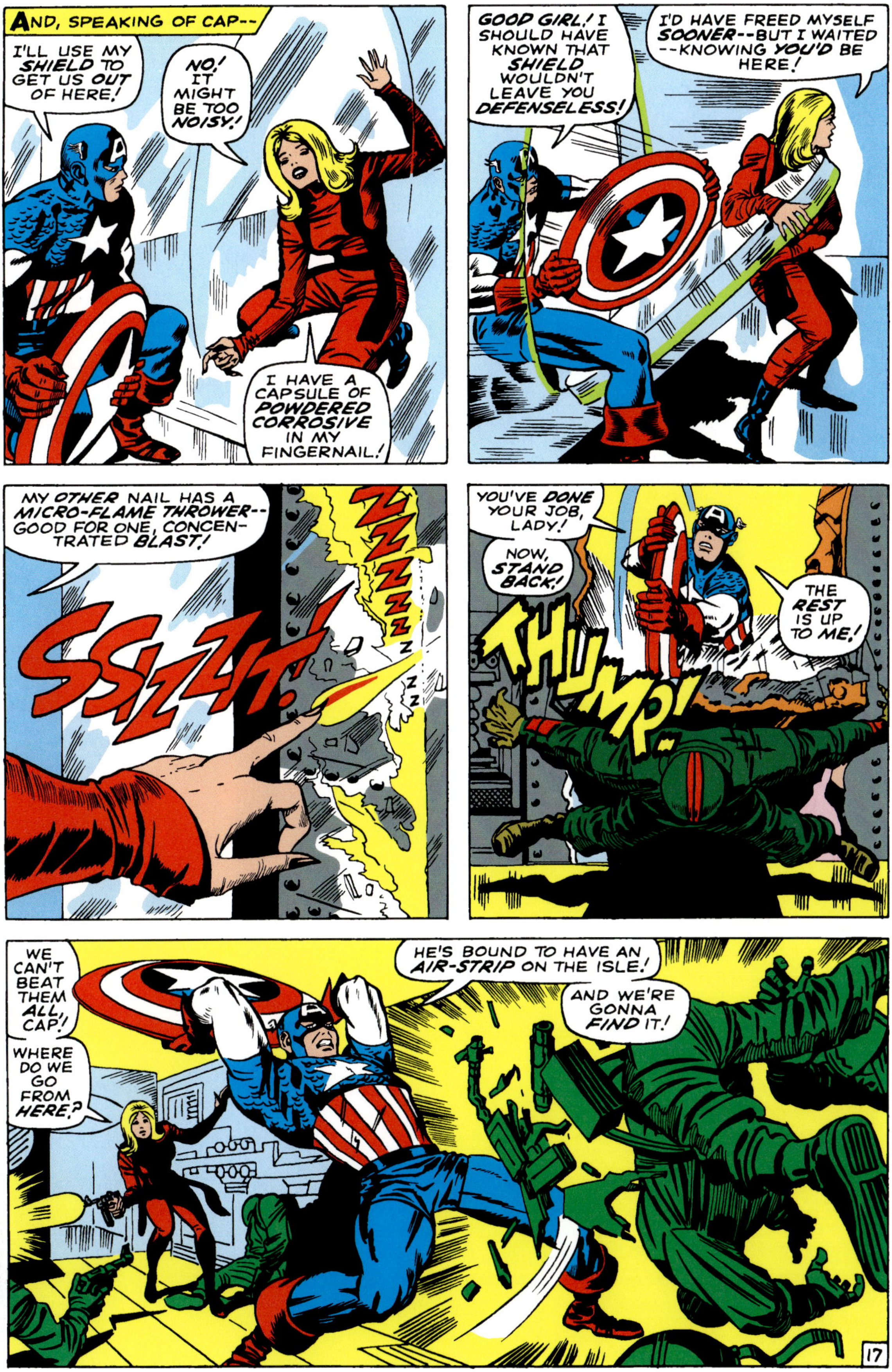

AND, SPEAKING OF CAP--
I'LL USE MY SHIELD TO GET US OUT OF HERE!
NO! IT MIGHT BE TOO NOISY!
I HAVE A CAPSULE OF POWDERED CORROSIVE IN MY FINGERNAIL!
GOOD GIRL! I SHOULD HAVE KNOWN THAT SHIELD WOULDN'T LEAVE YOU DEFENSELESS!
I'D HAVE FREED MYSELF SOONER--BUT I WAITED --KNOWING YOU'D BE HERE!
MY OTHER NAIL HAS A MICRO-FLAME THROWER-- GOOD FOR ONE, CONCENTRATED BLAST!
SSIZZZIT!
ZZZZZ
YOU'VE DONE YOUR JOB, LADY!
NOW, STAND BACK!
THE REST IS UP TO ME!
THUMP!
WE CAN'T BEAT THEM ALL, CAP!
WHERE DO WE GO FROM HERE?
HE'S BOUND TO HAVE AN AIR-STRIP ON THE ISLE!
AND WE'RE GONNA FIND IT!
17

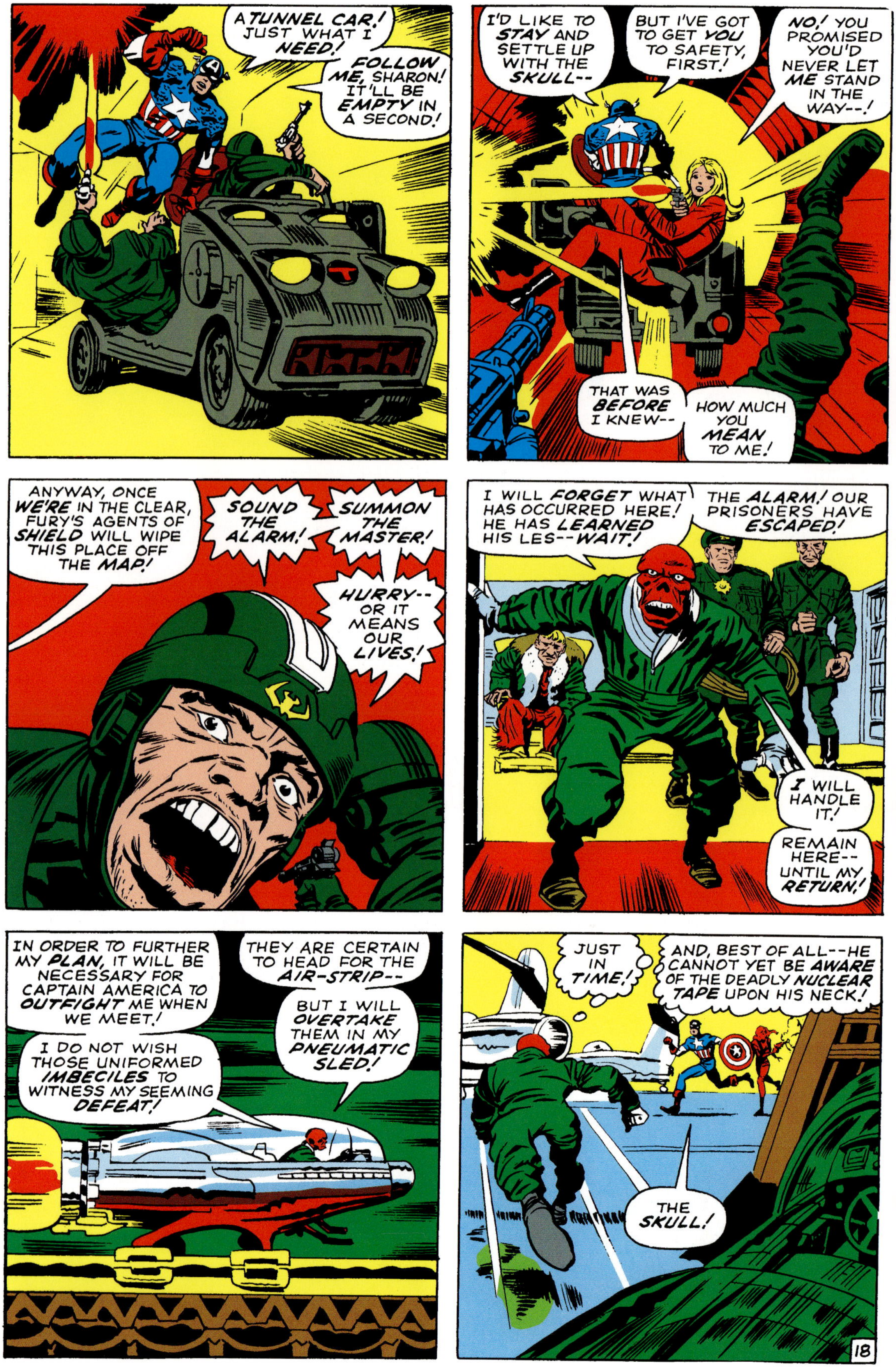
A TUNNEL CAR! JUST WHAT I NEED!
FOLLOW ME, SHARON! IT'LL BE EMPTY IN A SECOND!
I'D LIKE TO STAY AND SETTLE UP WITH THE SKULL--
BUT I'VE GOT TO GET YOU TO SAFETY, FIRST!
NO! YOU PROMISED YOU'D NEVER LET ME STAND IN THE WAY--!
THAT WAS BEFORE I KNEW--
HOW MUCH YOU MEAN TO ME!
ANYWAY, ONCE WE'RE IN THE CLEAR, FURY'S AGENTS OF SHIELD WILL WIPE THIS PLACE OFF THE MAP!
SOUND THE ALARM!
SUMMON THE MASTER!
HURRY--OR IT MEANS OUR LIVES!
I WILL FORGET WHAT HAS OCCURRED HERE! HE HAS LEARNED HIS LES--WAIT!
THE ALARM! OUR PRISONERS HAVE ESCAPED!
I WILL HANDLE IT!
REMAIN HERE--UNTIL MY RETURN!
IN ORDER TO FURTHER MY PLAN, IT WILL BE NECESSARY FOR CAPTAIN AMERICA TO OUTFIGHT ME WHEN WE MEET!
I DO NOT WISH THOSE UNIFORMED IMBECILES TO WITNESS MY SEEMING DEFEAT!
THEY ARE CERTAIN TO HEAD FOR THE AIR-STRIP--
BUT I WILL OVERTAKE THEM IN MY PNEUMATIC SLED!
JUST IN TIME!
AND, BEST OF ALL--HE CANNOT YET BE AWARE OF THE DEADLY NUCLEAR TAPE UPON HIS NECK!
THE SKULL!
18

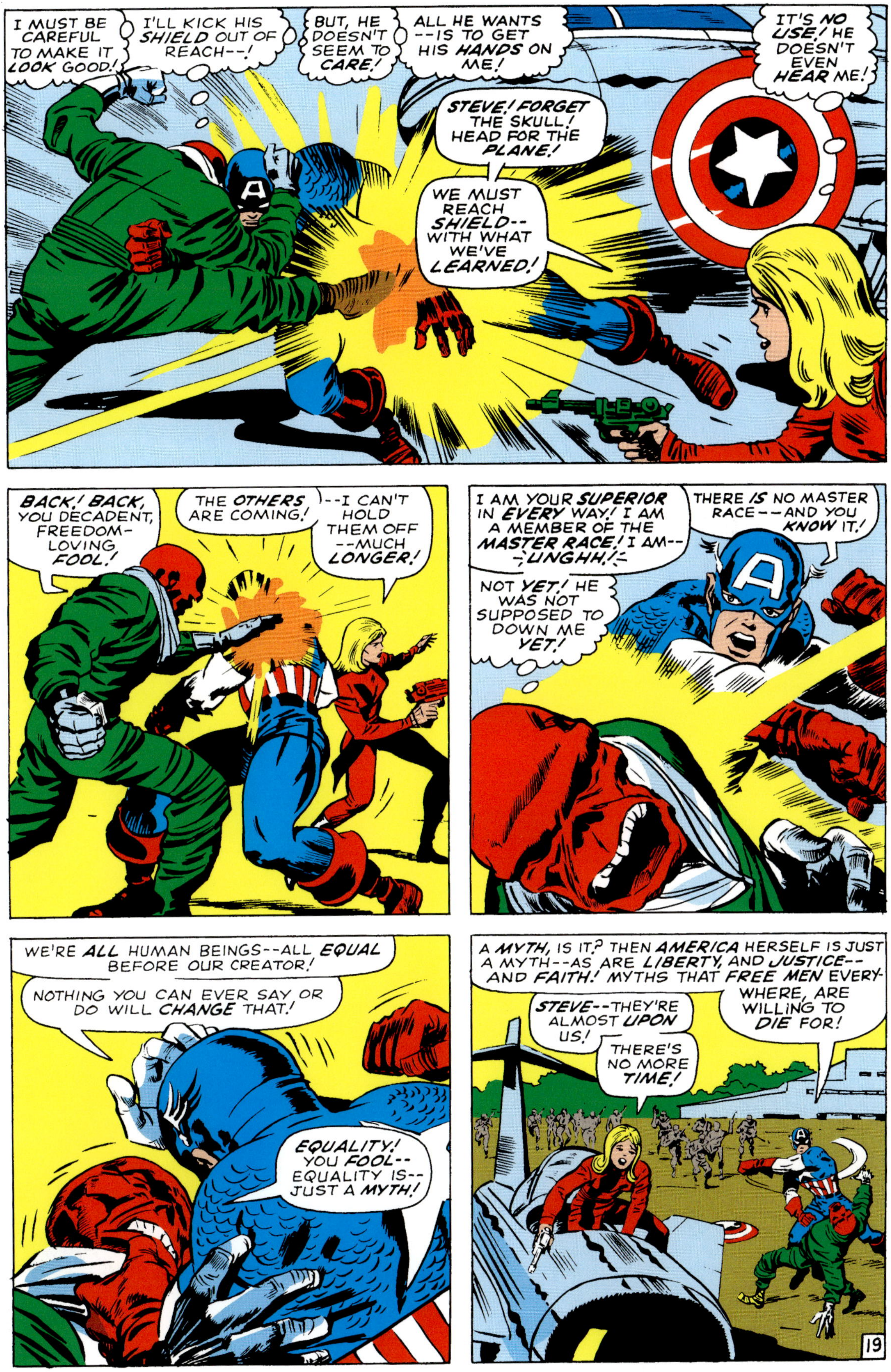
I MUST BE CAREFUL TO MAKE IT LOOK GOOD!
I'LL KICK HIS SHIELD OUT OF REACH--!
BUT, HE DOESN'T SEEM TO CARE!
ALL HE WANTS --IS TO GET HIS HANDS ON ME!
IT'S NO USE! HE DOESN'T EVEN HEAR ME!
STEVE! FORGET THE SKULL! HEAD FOR THE PLANE!
WE MUST REACH SHIELD-- WITH WHAT WE'VE LEARNED!
BACK! BACK, YOU DECADENT, FREEDOM-LOVING FOOL!
THE OTHERS ARE COMING!
--I CAN'T HOLD THEM OFF --MUCH LONGER!
I AM YOUR SUPERIOR IN EVERY WAY! I AM A MEMBER OF THE MASTER RACE! I AM-- UNGHH!
THERE IS NO MASTER RACE--AND YOU KNOW IT!
NOT YET! HE WAS NOT SUPPOSED TO DOWN ME YET!
WE'RE ALL HUMAN BEINGS--ALL EQUAL BEFORE OUR CREATOR!
NOTHING YOU CAN EVER SAY OR DO WILL CHANGE THAT!
EQUALITY! YOU FOOL-- EQUALITY IS-- JUST A MYTH!
A MYTH, IS IT? THEN AMERICA HERSELF IS JUST A MYTH--AS ARE LIBERTY, AND JUSTICE-- AND FAITH! MYTHS THAT FREE MEN EVERY-WHERE, ARE WILLING TO DIE FOR!
STEVE--THEY'RE ALMOST UPON US!
THERE'S NO MORE TIME!
19

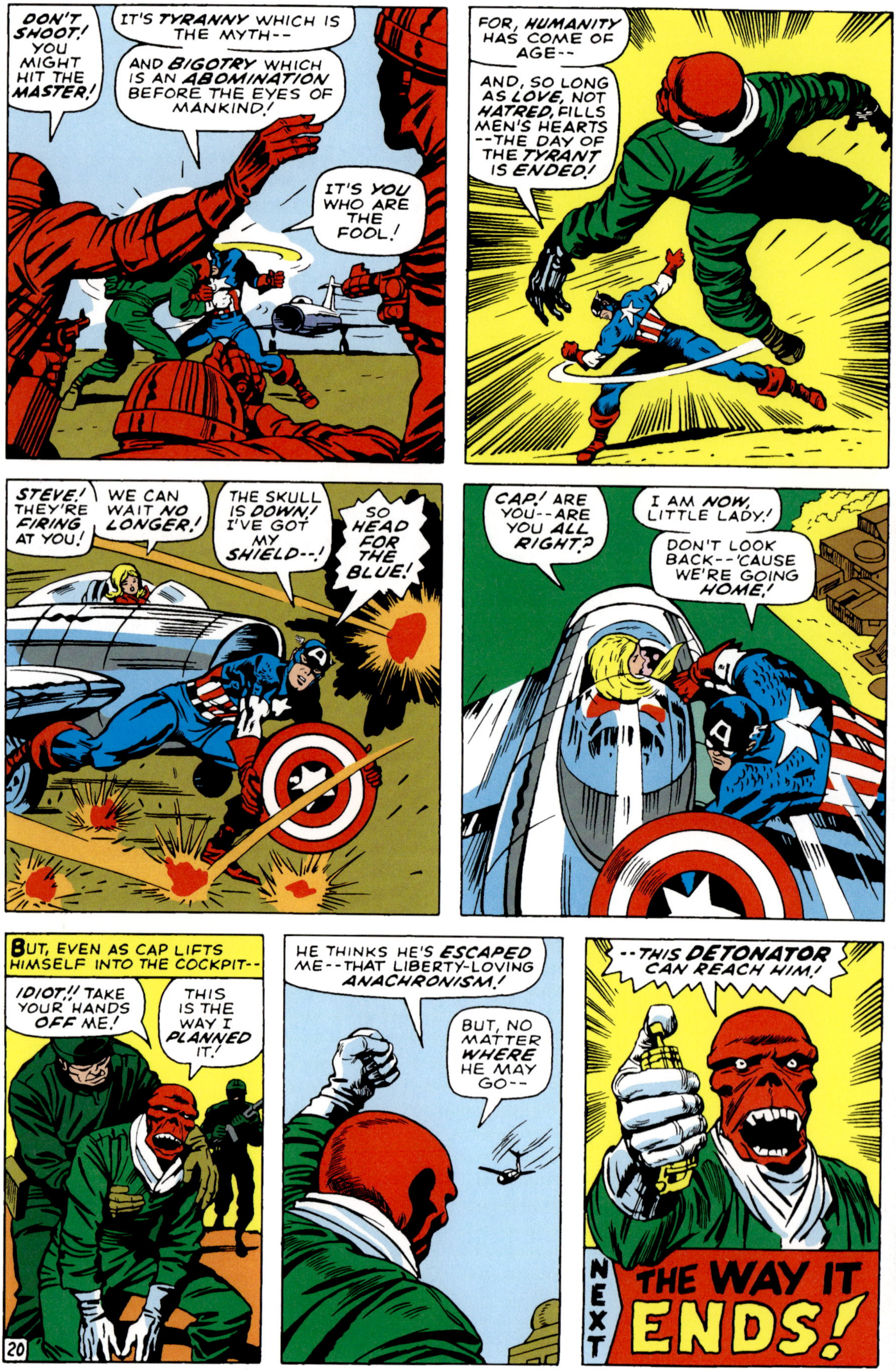
DON'T SHOOT! YOU MIGHT HIT THE MASTER!
IT'S TYRANNY WHICH IS THE MYTH--
AND BIGOTRY WHICH IS AN ABOMINATION BEFORE THE EYES OF MANKIND!
IT'S YOU WHO ARE THE FOOL!
FOR, HUMANITY HAS COME OF AGE--
AND, SO LONG AS LOVE, NOT HATRED, FILLS MEN'S HEARTS --THE DAY OF THE TYRANT IS ENDED!
STEVE! THEY'RE FIRING AT YOU!
WE CAN WAIT NO LONGER!
THE SKULL IS DOWN! I'VE GOT MY SHIELD--!
SO HEAD FOR THE BLUE!
CAP! ARE YOU--ARE YOU ALL RIGHT?
I AM NOW, LITTLE LADY!
DON'T LOOK BACK--'CAUSE WE'RE GOING HOME!
BUT, EVEN AS CAP LIFTS HIMSELF INTO THE COCKPIT--
IDIOT!! TAKE YOUR HANDS OFF ME!
THIS IS THE WAY I PLANNED IT!
20
HE THINKS HE'S ESCAPED ME--THAT LIBERTY-LOVING ANACHRONISM!
BUT, NO MATTER WHERE HE MAY GO--
--THIS DETONATOR CAN REACH HIM!
NEXT
THE WAY IT ENDS!

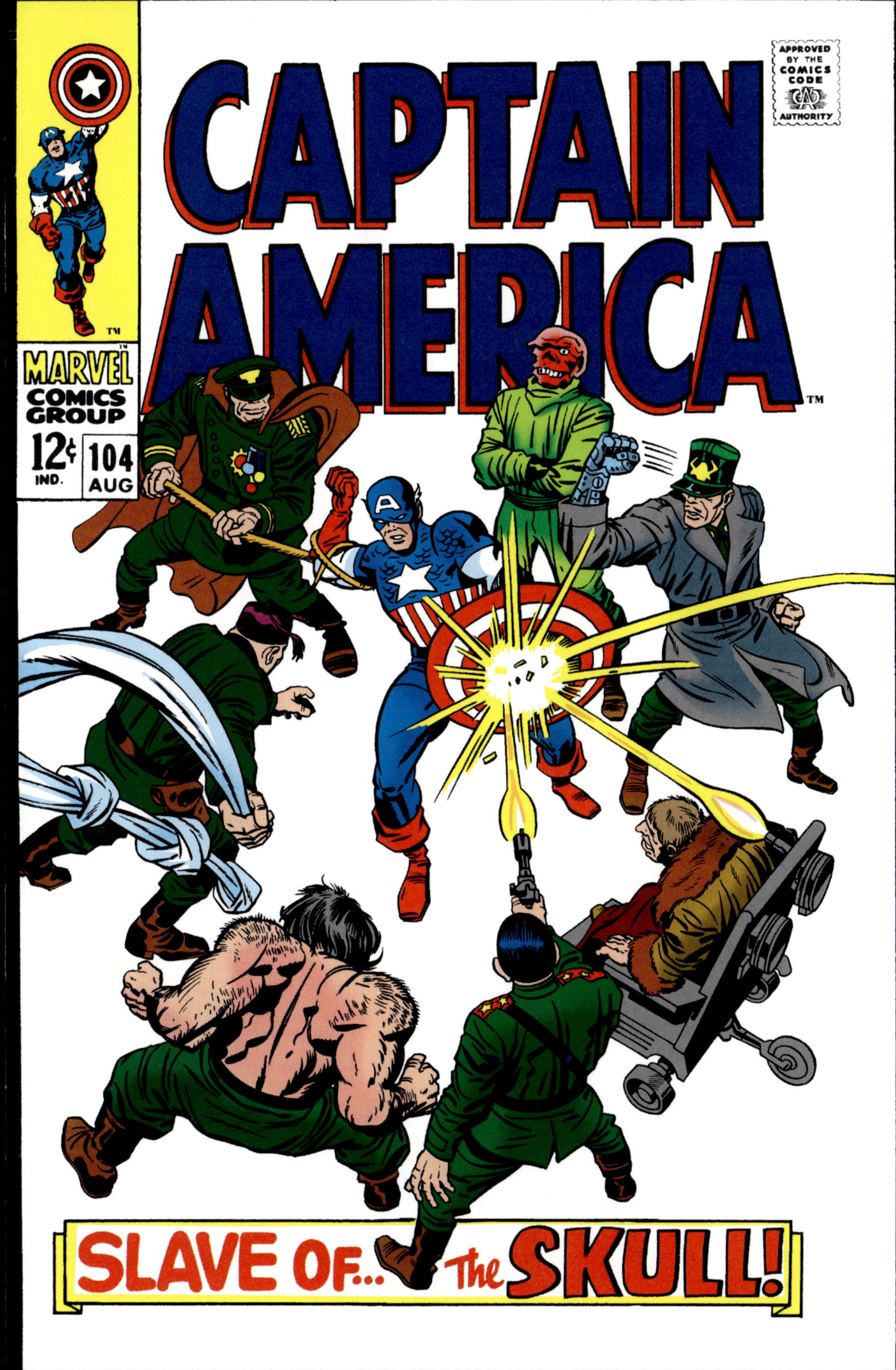
CAPTAIN AMERICA™
TM
MARVEL™ COMICS GROUP
12¢ IND.
104 AUG
APPROVED BY THE COMICS CODE AUTHORITY
SLAVE OF... the SKULL!

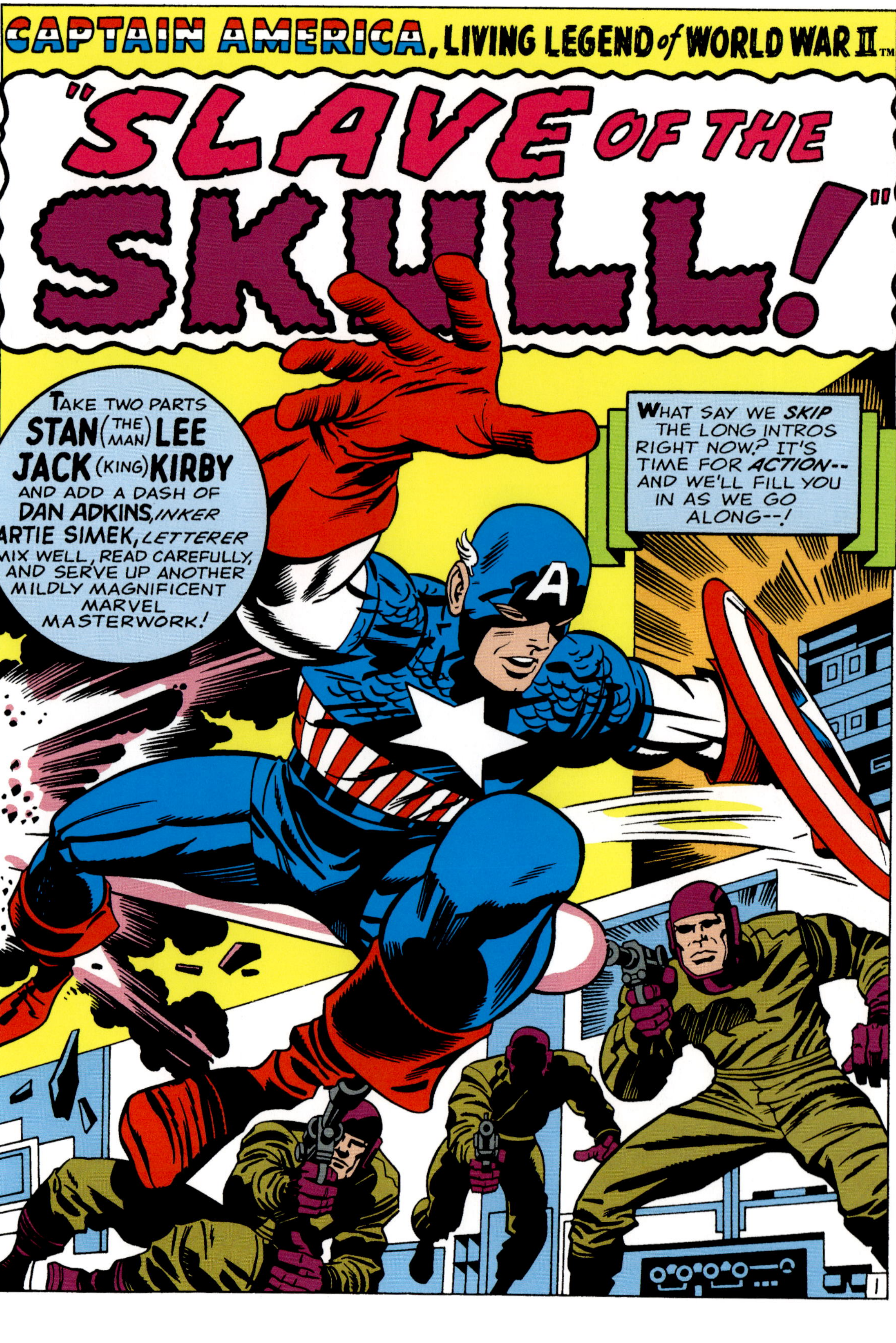
CAPTAIN AMERICA, LIVING LEGEND of WORLD WAR II TM
"SLAVE OF THE SKULL!"
TAKE TWO PARTS STAN (THE MAN) LEE JACK (KING) KIRBY AND ADD A DASH OF DAN ADKINS, INKER ARTIE SIMEK, LETTERER MIX WELL, READ CAREFULLY, AND SERVE UP ANOTHER MILDLY MAGNIFICENT MARVEL MASTERWORK!
WHAT SAY WE SKIP THE LONG INTROS RIGHT NOW? IT'S TIME FOR ACTION-- AND WE'LL FILL YOU IN AS WE GO ALONG--!
1

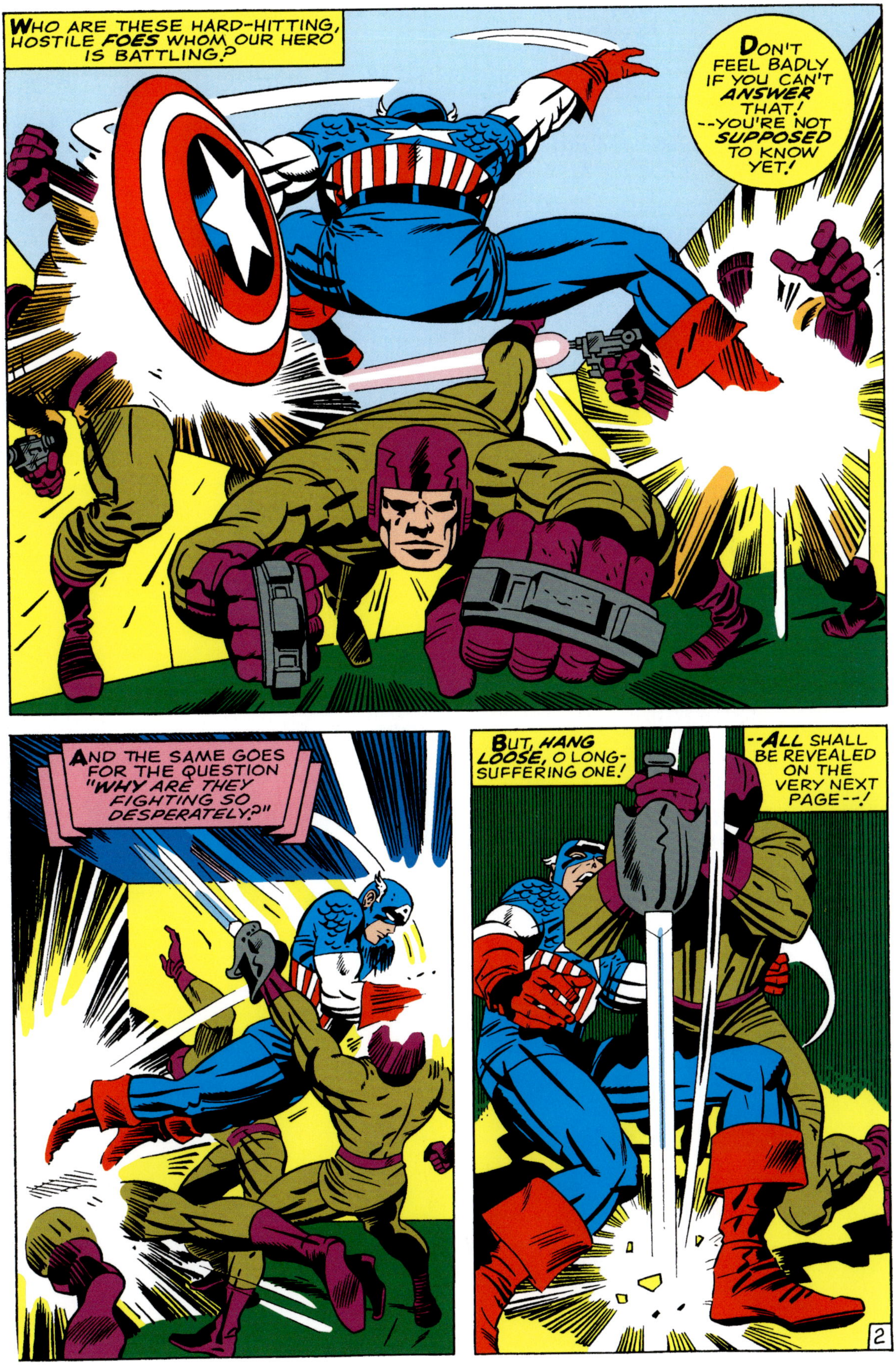
WHO ARE THESE HARD-HITTING, HOSTILE FOES WHOM OUR HERO IS BATTLING?
DON'T FEEL BADLY IF YOU CAN'T ANSWER THAT! --YOU'RE NOT SUPPOSED TO KNOW YET!
AND THE SAME GOES FOR THE QUESTION "WHY ARE THEY FIGHTING SO DESPERATELY?"
BUT, HANG LOOSE, O LONG-SUFFERING ONE!
--ALL SHALL BE REVEALED ON THE VERY NEXT PAGE--!
2

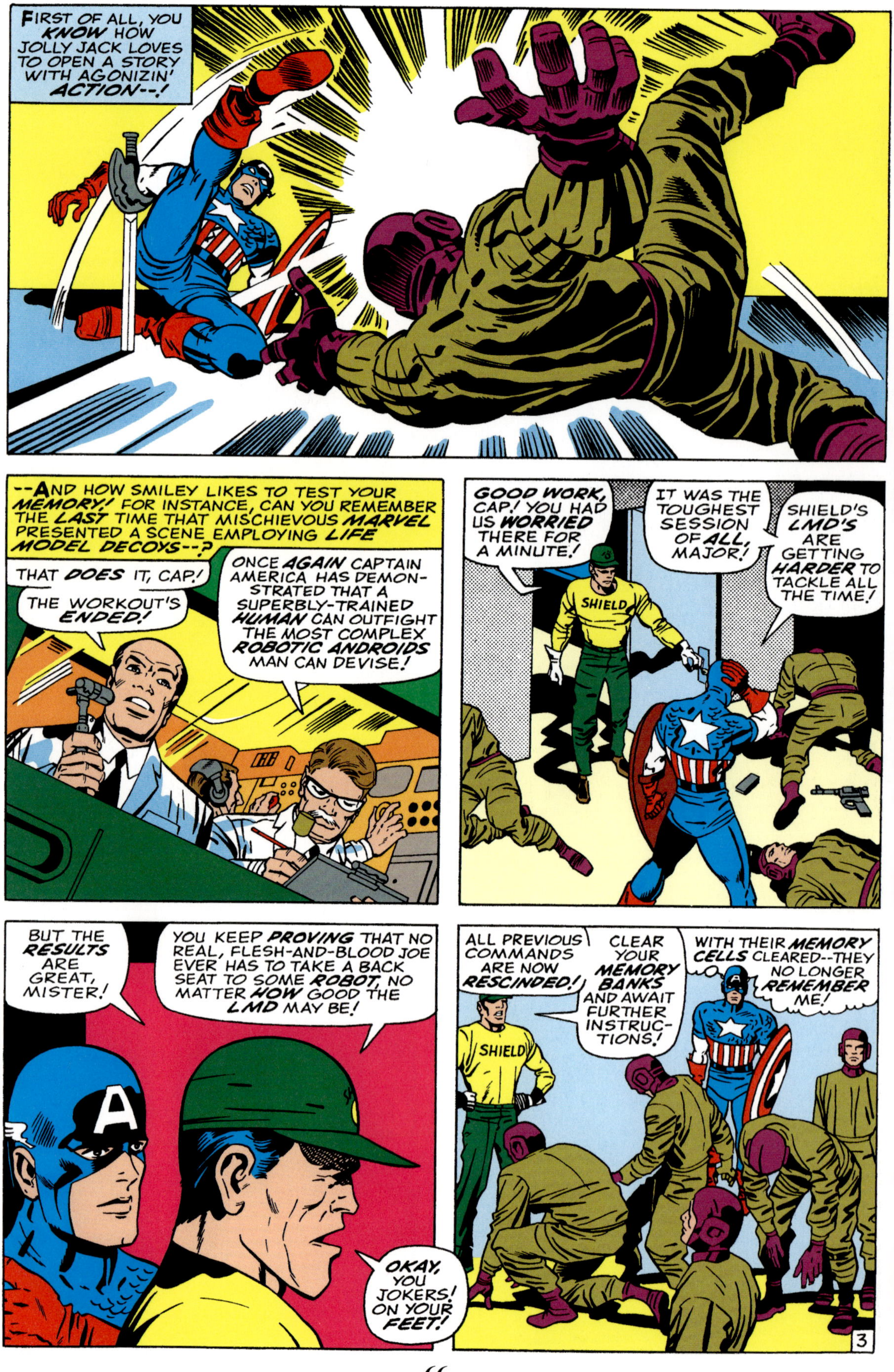
FIRST OF ALL, YOU KNOW HOW JOLLY JACK LOVES TO OPEN A STORY WITH AGONIZIN' ACTION--!
--AND HOW SMILEY LIKES TO TEST YOUR MEMORY! FOR INSTANCE, CAN YOU REMEMBER THE LAST TIME THAT MISCHIEVOUS MARVEL PRESENTED A SCENE EMPLOYING LIFE MODEL DECOYS--?
THAT DOES IT, CAP!
THE WORKOUT'S ENDED!
ONCE AGAIN CAPTAIN AMERICA HAS DEMONSTRATED THAT A SUPERBLY-TRAINED HUMAN CAN OUTFIGHT THE MOST COMPLEX ROBOTIC ANDROIDS MAN CAN DEVISE!
GOOD WORK, CAP! YOU HAD US WORRIED THERE FOR A MINUTE!
IT WAS THE TOUGHEST SESSION OF ALL, MAJOR!
SHIELD'S LMD'S ARE GETTING HARDER TO TACKLE ALL THE TIME!
SHIELD
BUT THE RESULTS ARE GREAT, MISTER!
YOU KEEP PROVING THAT NO REAL, FLESH-AND-BLOOD JOE EVER HAS TO TAKE A BACK SEAT TO SOME ROBOT, NO MATTER HOW GOOD THE LMD MAY BE!
OKAY, YOU JOKERS! ON YOUR FEET!
ALL PREVIOUS COMMANDS ARE NOW RESCINDED!
CLEAR YOUR MEMORY BANKS AND AWAIT FURTHER INSTRUCTIONS!
WITH THEIR MEMORY CELLS CLEARED--THEY NO LONGER REMEMBER ME!
SHIELD
3

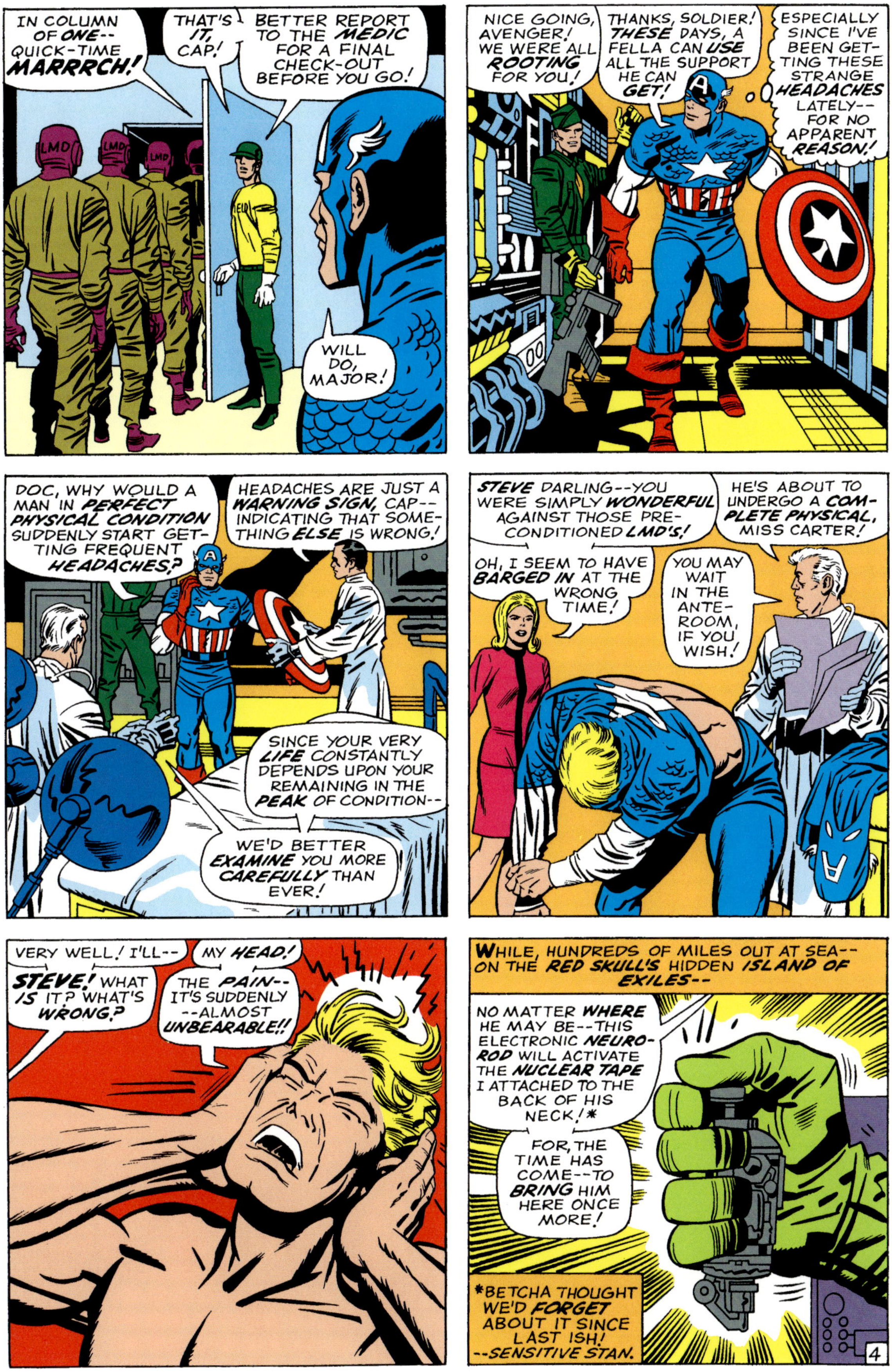
IN COLUMN OF ONE-- QUICK-TIME MARRRCH!
THAT'S IT, CAP!
BETTER REPORT TO THE MEDIC FOR A FINAL CHECK-OUT BEFORE YOU GO!
WILL DO, MAJOR!
NICE GOING, AVENGER! WE WERE ALL ROOTING FOR YOU!
THANKS, SOLDIER! THESE DAYS, A FELLA CAN USE ALL THE SUPPORT HE CAN GET!
ESPECIALLY SINCE I'VE BEEN GETTING THESE STRANGE HEADACHES LATELY-- FOR NO APPARENT REASON!
DOC, WHY WOULD A MAN IN PERFECT PHYSICAL CONDITION SUDDENLY START GETTING FREQUENT HEADACHES?
HEADACHES ARE JUST A WARNING SIGN, CAP-- INDICATING THAT SOMETHING ELSE IS WRONG!
SINCE YOUR VERY LIFE CONSTANTLY DEPENDS UPON YOUR REMAINING IN THE PEAK OF CONDITION--
WE'D BETTER EXAMINE YOU MORE CAREFULLY THAN EVER!
STEVE DARLING--YOU WERE SIMPLY WONDERFUL AGAINST THOSE PRE-CONDITIONED LMD'S!
HE'S ABOUT TO UNDERGO A COMPLETE PHYSICAL, MISS CARTER!
OH, I SEEM TO HAVE BARGED IN AT THE WRONG TIME!
YOU MAY WAIT IN THE ANTE-ROOM, IF YOU WISH!
VERY WELL! I'LL--
MY HEAD!
STEVE! WHAT IS IT? WHAT'S WRONG?
THE PAIN-- IT'S SUDDENLY --ALMOST UNBEARABLE!!
WHILE, HUNDREDS OF MILES OUT AT SEA-- ON THE RED SKULL'S HIDDEN ISLAND OF EXILES--
NO MATTER WHERE HE MAY BE--THIS ELECTRONIC NEURO-ROD WILL ACTIVATE THE NUCLEAR TAPE I ATTACHED TO THE BACK OF HIS NECK!*
FOR, THE TIME HAS COME--TO BRING HIM HERE ONCE MORE!
*BETCHA THOUGHT WE'D FORGET ABOUT IT SINCE LAST ISH! --SENSITIVE STAN.
4

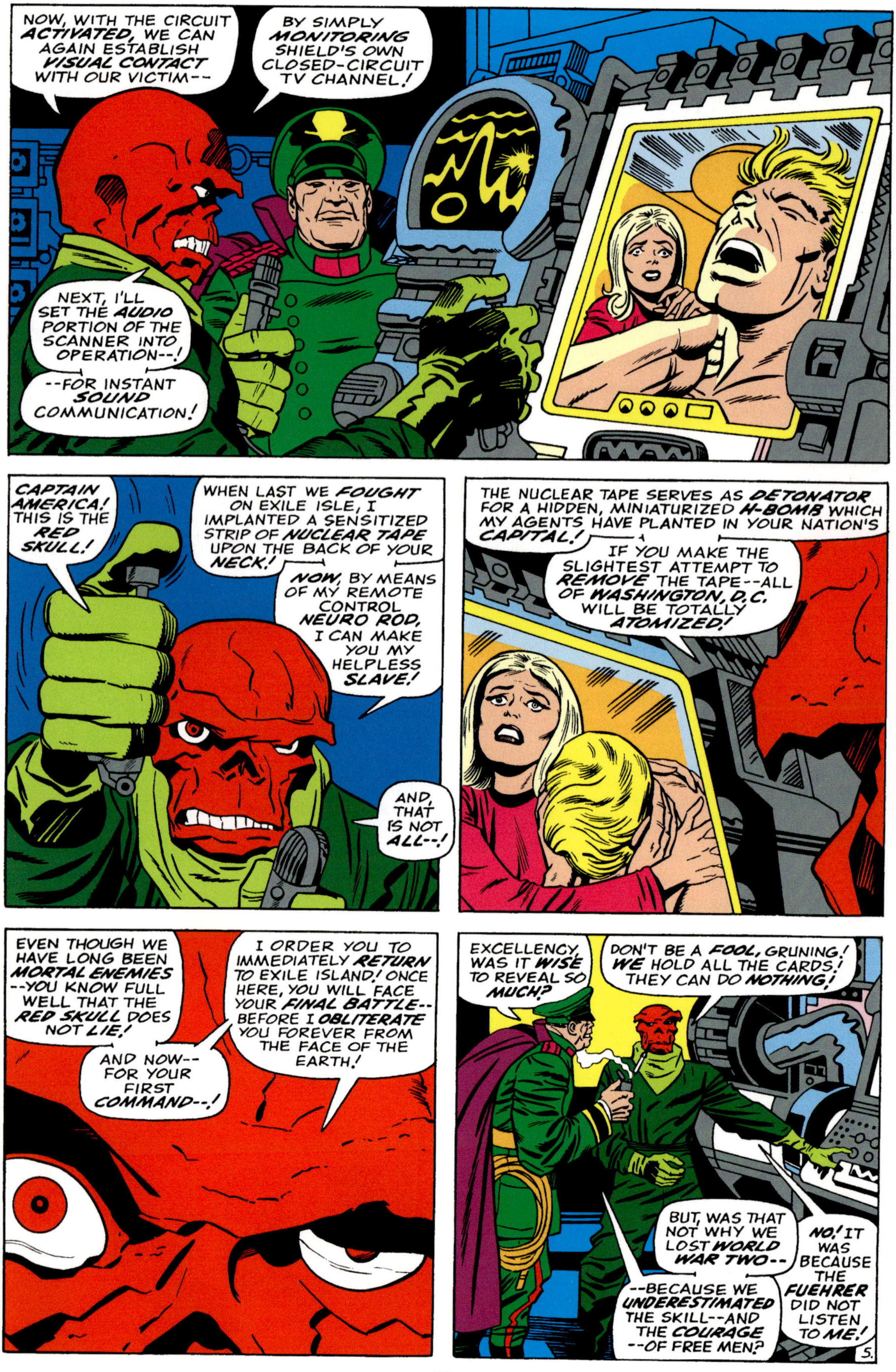
NOW, WITH THE CIRCUIT ACTIVATED, WE CAN AGAIN ESTABLISH VISUAL CONTACT WITH OUR VICTIM--
BY SIMPLY MONITORING SHIELD'S OWN CLOSED-CIRCUIT TV CHANNEL!
NEXT, I'LL SET THE AUDIO PORTION OF THE SCANNER INTO OPERATION--!
--FOR INSTANT SOUND COMMUNICATION!
CAPTAIN AMERICA! THIS IS THE RED SKULL!
WHEN LAST WE FOUGHT ON EXILE ISLE, I IMPLANTED A SENSITIZED STRIP OF NUCLEAR TAPE UPON THE BACK OF YOUR NECK!
NOW, BY MEANS OF MY REMOTE CONTROL NEURO ROD, I CAN MAKE YOU MY HELPLESS SLAVE!
AND, THAT IS NOT ALL--!
THE NUCLEAR TAPE SERVES AS DETONATOR FOR A HIDDEN, MINIATURIZED H-BOMB WHICH MY AGENTS HAVE PLANTED IN YOUR NATION'S CAPITAL!
IF YOU MAKE THE SLIGHTEST ATTEMPT TO REMOVE THE TAPE--ALL OF WASHINGTON, D.C. WILL BE TOTALLY ATOMIZED!
EVEN THOUGH WE HAVE LONG BEEN MORTAL ENEMIES --YOU KNOW FULL WELL THAT THE RED SKULL DOES NOT LIE!
AND NOW-- FOR YOUR FIRST COMMAND--!
I ORDER YOU TO IMMEDIATELY RETURN TO EXILE ISLAND! ONCE HERE, YOU WILL FACE YOUR FINAL BATTLE-- BEFORE I OBLITERATE YOU FOREVER FROM THE FACE OF THE EARTH!
EXCELLENCY, WAS IT WISE TO REVEAL SO MUCH?
DON'T BE A FOOL, GRUNING! WE HOLD ALL THE CARDS! THEY CAN DO NOTHING!
BUT, WAS THAT NOT WHY WE LOST WORLD WAR TWO--
--BECAUSE WE UNDERESTIMATED THE SKILL--AND THE COURAGE --OF FREE MEN?
NO! IT WAS BECAUSE THE FUEHRER DID NOT LISTEN TO ME!
5.

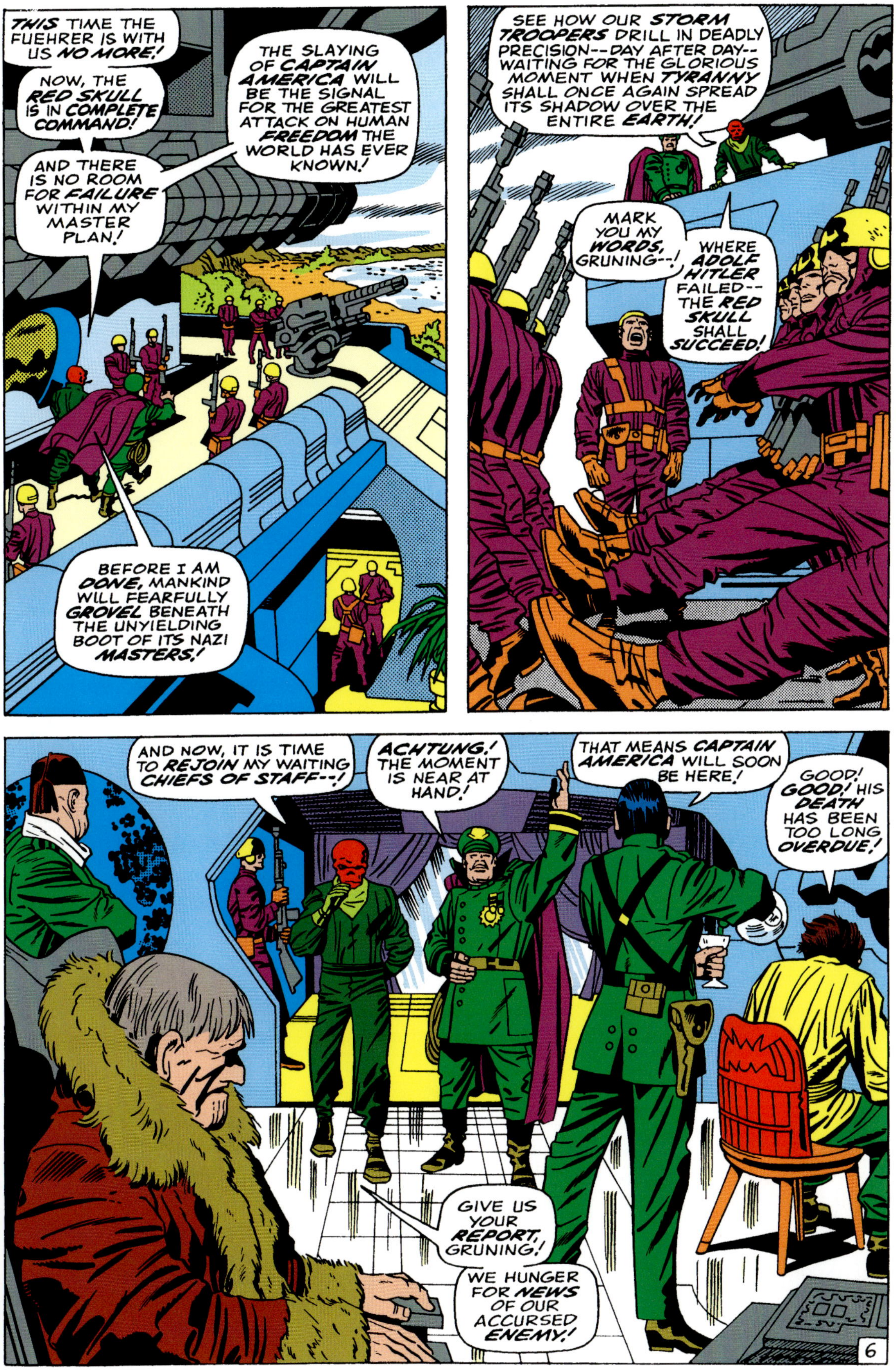
THIS TIME THE FUEHRER IS WITH US NO MORE!
NOW, THE RED SKULL IS IN COMPLETE COMMAND!
AND THERE IS NO ROOM FOR FAILURE WITHIN MY MASTER PLAN!
THE SLAYING OF CAPTAIN AMERICA WILL BE THE SIGNAL FOR THE GREATEST ATTACK ON HUMAN FREEDOM THE WORLD HAS EVER KNOWN!
BEFORE I AM DONE, MANKIND WILL FEARFULLY GROVEL BENEATH THE UNYIELDING BOOT OF ITS NAZI MASTERS!
SEE HOW OUR STORM TROOPERS DRILL IN DEADLY PRECISION--DAY AFTER DAY--WAITING FOR THE GLORIOUS MOMENT WHEN TYRANNY SHALL ONCE AGAIN SPREAD ITS SHADOW OVER THE ENTIRE EARTH!
MARK YOU MY WORDS, GRUNING--!
WHERE ADOLF HITLER FAILED--THE RED SKULL SHALL SUCCEED!
AND NOW, IT IS TIME TO REJOIN MY WAITING CHIEFS OF STAFF--!
ACHTUNG! THE MOMENT IS NEAR AT HAND!
THAT MEANS CAPTAIN AMERICA WILL SOON BE HERE!
GOOD! GOOD! HIS DEATH HAS BEEN TOO LONG OVERDUE!
GIVE US YOUR REPORT, GRUNING!
WE HUNGER FOR NEWS OF OUR ACCURSED ENEMY!
6

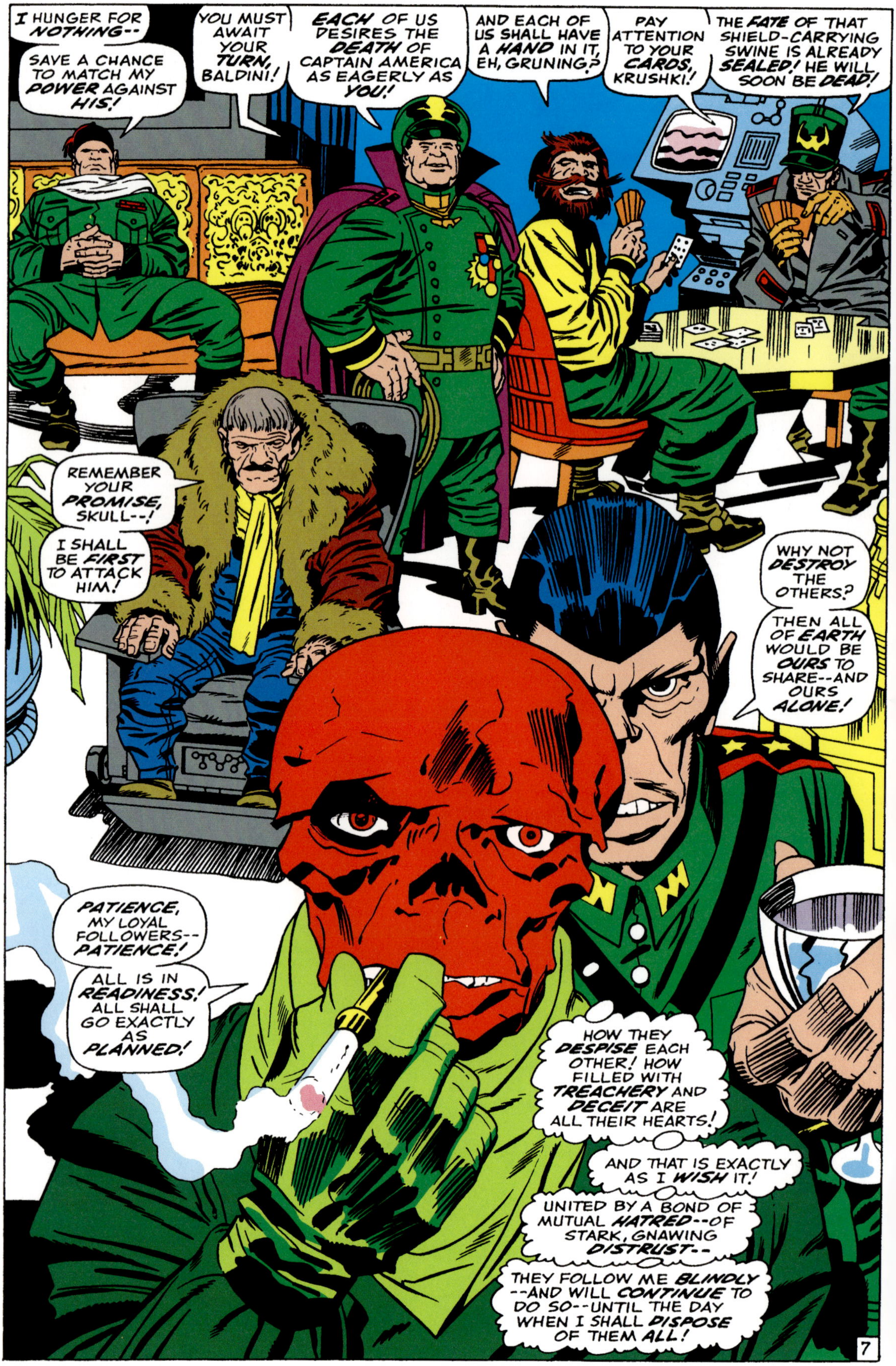
I HUNGER FOR NOTHING--
SAVE A CHANCE TO MATCH MY POWER AGAINST HIS!
YOU MUST AWAIT YOUR TURN, BALDINI!
EACH OF US DESIRES THE DEATH OF CAPTAIN AMERICA AS EAGERLY AS YOU!
AND EACH OF US SHALL HAVE A HAND IN IT, EH, GRUNING?
PAY ATTENTION TO YOUR CARDS, KRUSHKI!
THE FATE OF THAT SHIELD-CARRYING SWINE IS ALREADY SEALED! HE WILL SOON BE DEAD!
REMEMBER YOUR PROMISE, SKULL--!
I SHALL BE FIRST TO ATTACK HIM!
WHY NOT DESTROY THE OTHERS?
THEN ALL OF EARTH WOULD BE OURS TO SHARE--AND OURS ALONE!
PATIENCE, MY LOYAL FOLLOWERS--PATIENCE!
ALL IS IN READINESS! ALL SHALL GO EXACTLY AS PLANNED!
HOW THEY DESPISE EACH OTHER! HOW FILLED WITH TREACHERY AND DECEIT ARE ALL THEIR HEARTS!
AND THAT IS EXACTLY AS I WISH IT!
UNITED BY A BOND OF MUTUAL HATRED--OF STARK, GNAWING DISTRUST--
THEY FOLLOW ME BLINDLY--AND WILL CONTINUE TO DO SO--UNTIL THE DAY WHEN I SHALL DISPOSE OF THEM ALL!
7

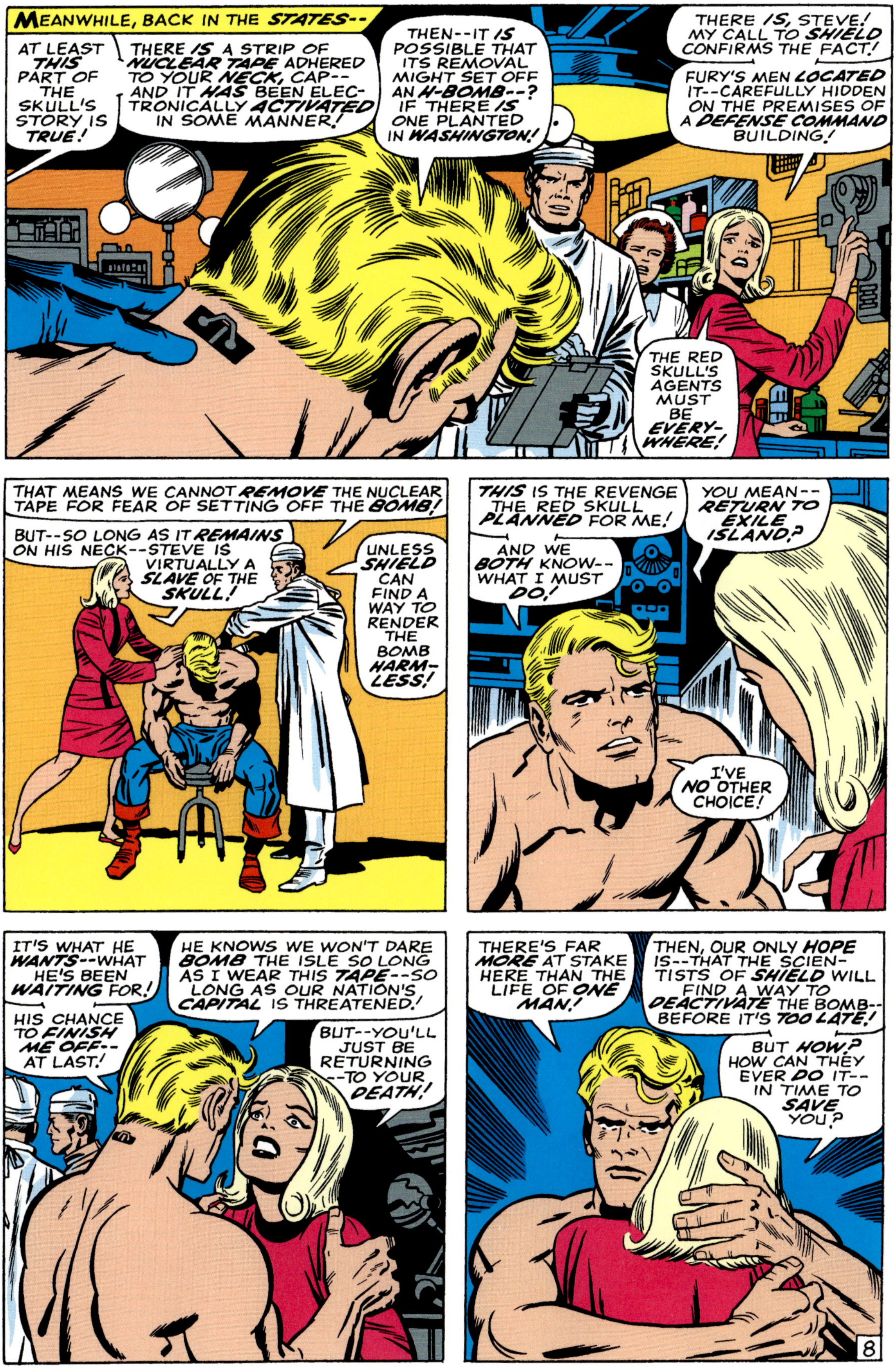
MEANWHILE, BACK IN THE STATES--
AT LEAST THIS PART OF THE SKULL'S STORY IS TRUE!
THERE IS A STRIP OF NUCLEAR TAPE ADHERED TO YOUR NECK, CAP-- AND IT HAS BEEN ELECTRONICALLY ACTIVATED IN SOME MANNER!
THEN--IT IS POSSIBLE THAT ITS REMOVAL MIGHT SET OFF AN H-BOMB--? IF THERE IS ONE PLANTED IN WASHINGTON!
THERE IS, STEVE! MY CALL TO SHIELD CONFIRMS THE FACT!
FURY'S MEN LOCATED IT--CAREFULLY HIDDEN ON THE PREMISES OF A DEFENSE COMMAND BUILDING!
THE RED SKULL'S AGENTS MUST BE EVERYWHERE!
THAT MEANS WE CANNOT REMOVE THE NUCLEAR TAPE FOR FEAR OF SETTING OFF THE BOMB!
BUT--SO LONG AS IT REMAINS ON HIS NECK--STEVE IS VIRTUALLY A SLAVE OF THE SKULL!
UNLESS SHIELD CAN FIND A WAY TO RENDER THE BOMB HARMLESS!
THIS IS THE REVENGE THE RED SKULL PLANNED FOR ME!
AND WE BOTH KNOW-- WHAT I MUST DO!
YOU MEAN-- RETURN TO EXILE ISLAND?
I'VE NO OTHER CHOICE!
IT'S WHAT HE WANTS--WHAT HE'S BEEN WAITING FOR!
HIS CHANCE TO FINISH ME OFF-- AT LAST!
HE KNOWS WE WON'T DARE BOMB THE ISLE SO LONG AS I WEAR THIS TAPE--SO LONG AS OUR NATION'S CAPITAL IS THREATENED!
BUT--YOU'LL JUST BE RETURNING --TO YOUR DEATH!
THERE'S FAR MORE AT STAKE HERE THAN THE LIFE OF ONE MAN!
THEN, OUR ONLY HOPE IS--THAT THE SCIENTISTS OF SHIELD WILL FIND A WAY TO DEACTIVATE THE BOMB-- BEFORE IT'S TOO LATE!
BUT HOW? HOW CAN THEY EVER DO IT-- IN TIME TO SAVE YOU?
8

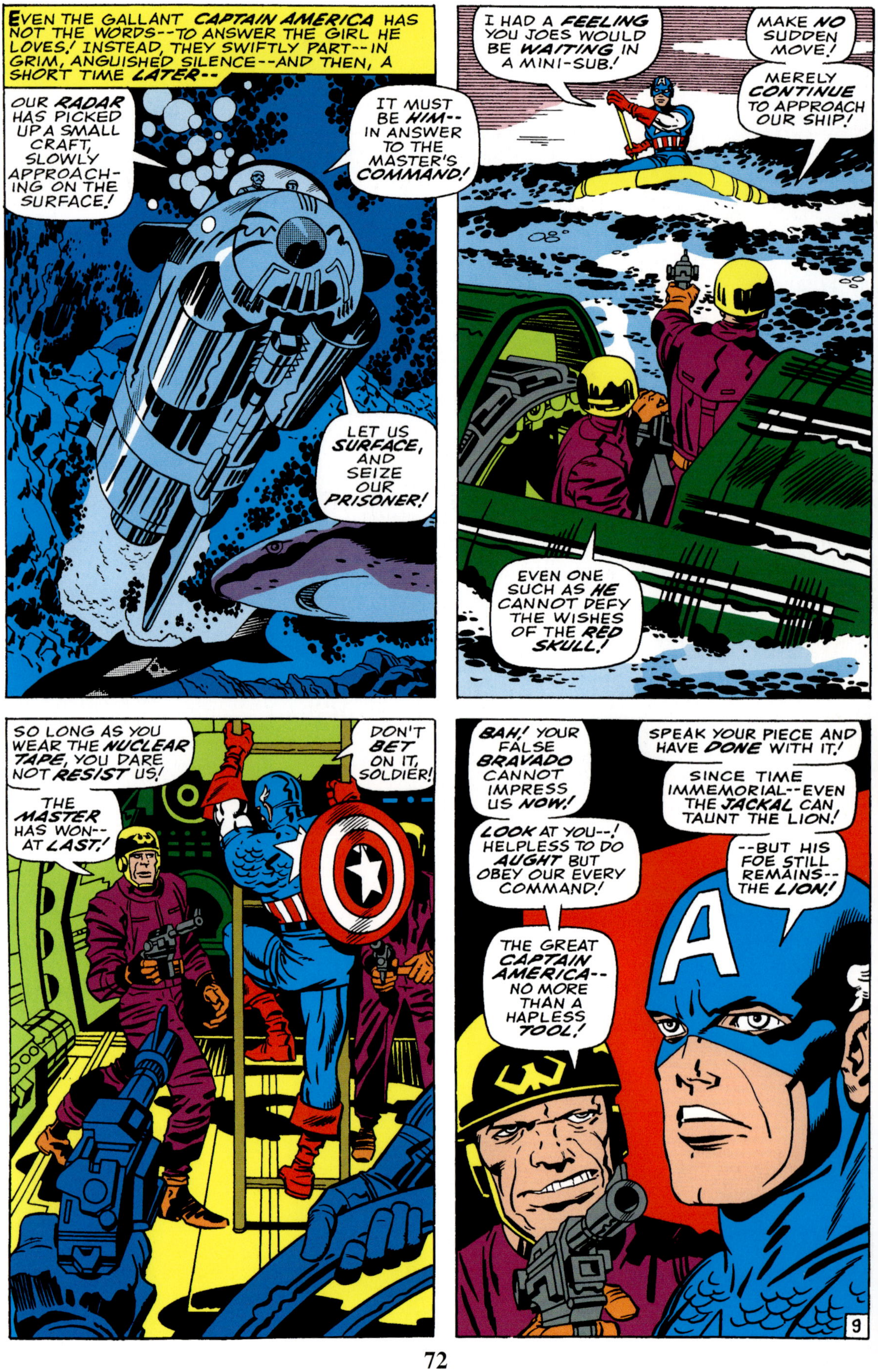
EVEN THE GALLANT CAPTAIN AMERICA HAS NOT THE WORDS--TO ANSWER THE GIRL HE LOVES! INSTEAD, THEY SWIFTLY PART--IN GRIM, ANGUISHED SILENCE--AND THEN, A SHORT TIME LATER--
OUR RADAR HAS PICKED UP A SMALL CRAFT, SLOWLY APPROACHING ON THE SURFACE!
IT MUST BE HIM--IN ANSWER TO THE MASTER'S COMMAND!
LET US SURFACE, AND SEIZE OUR PRISONER!
I HAD A FEELING YOU JOES WOULD BE WAITING IN A MINI-SUB!
MAKE NO SUDDEN MOVE!
MERELY CONTINUE TO APPROACH OUR SHIP!
EVEN ONE SUCH AS HE CANNOT DEFY THE WISHES OF THE RED SKULL!
SO LONG AS YOU WEAR THE NUCLEAR TAPE, YOU DARE NOT RESIST US!
THE MASTER HAS WON--AT LAST!
DON'T BET ON IT, SOLDIER!
BAH! YOUR FALSE BRAVADO CANNOT IMPRESS US NOW!
LOOK AT YOU--! HELPLESS TO DO AUGHT BUT OBEY OUR EVERY COMMAND!
THE GREAT CAPTAIN AMERICA--NO MORE THAN A HAPLESS TOOL!
SPEAK YOUR PIECE AND HAVE DONE WITH IT!
SINCE TIME IMMEMORIAL--EVEN THE JACKAL CAN TAUNT THE LION!
--BUT HIS FOE STILL REMAINS--THE LION!
9

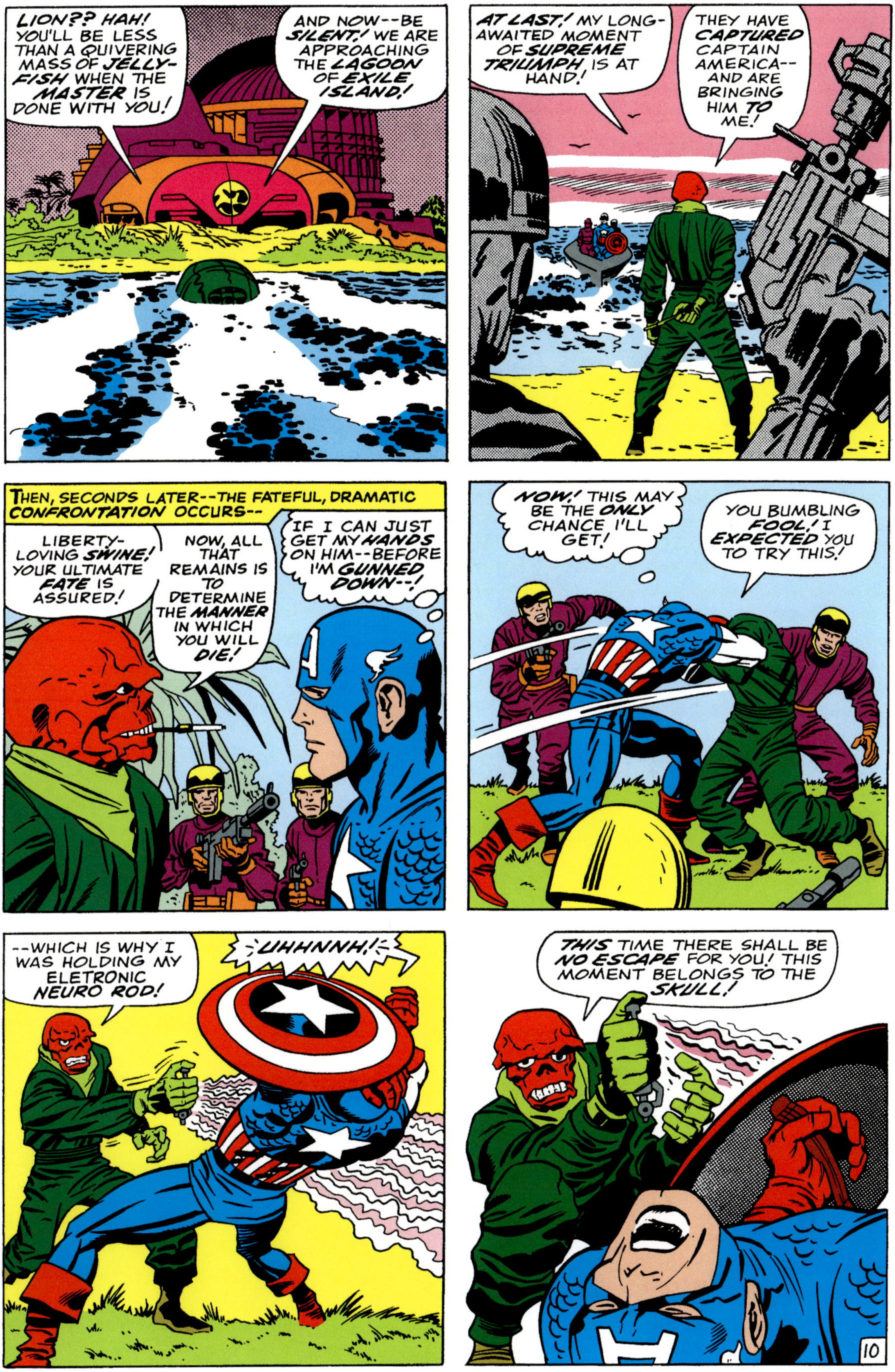
LION?? HAH! YOU'LL BE LESS THAN A QUIVERING MASS OF JELLY-FISH WHEN THE MASTER IS DONE WITH YOU!
AND NOW--BE SILENT! WE ARE APPROACHING THE LAGOON OF EXILE ISLAND!
AT LAST! MY LONG-AWAITED MOMENT OF SUPREME TRIUMPH IS AT HAND!
THEY HAVE CAPTURED CAPTAIN AMERICA--AND ARE BRINGING HIM TO ME!
THEN, SECONDS LATER--THE FATEFUL, DRAMATIC CONFRONTATION OCCURS--
LIBERTY-LOVING SWINE! YOUR ULTIMATE FATE IS ASSURED!
NOW, ALL THAT REMAINS IS TO DETERMINE THE MANNER IN WHICH YOU WILL DIE!
IF I CAN JUST GET MY HANDS ON HIM--BEFORE I'M GUNNED DOWN--!
NOW! THIS MAY BE THE ONLY CHANCE I'LL GET!
YOU BUMBLING FOOL! I EXPECTED YOU TO TRY THIS!
--WHICH IS WHY I WAS HOLDING MY ELETRONIC NEURO ROD!
UHHNNH!
THIS TIME THERE SHALL BE NO ESCAPE FOR YOU! THIS MOMENT BELONGS TO THE SKULL!
10

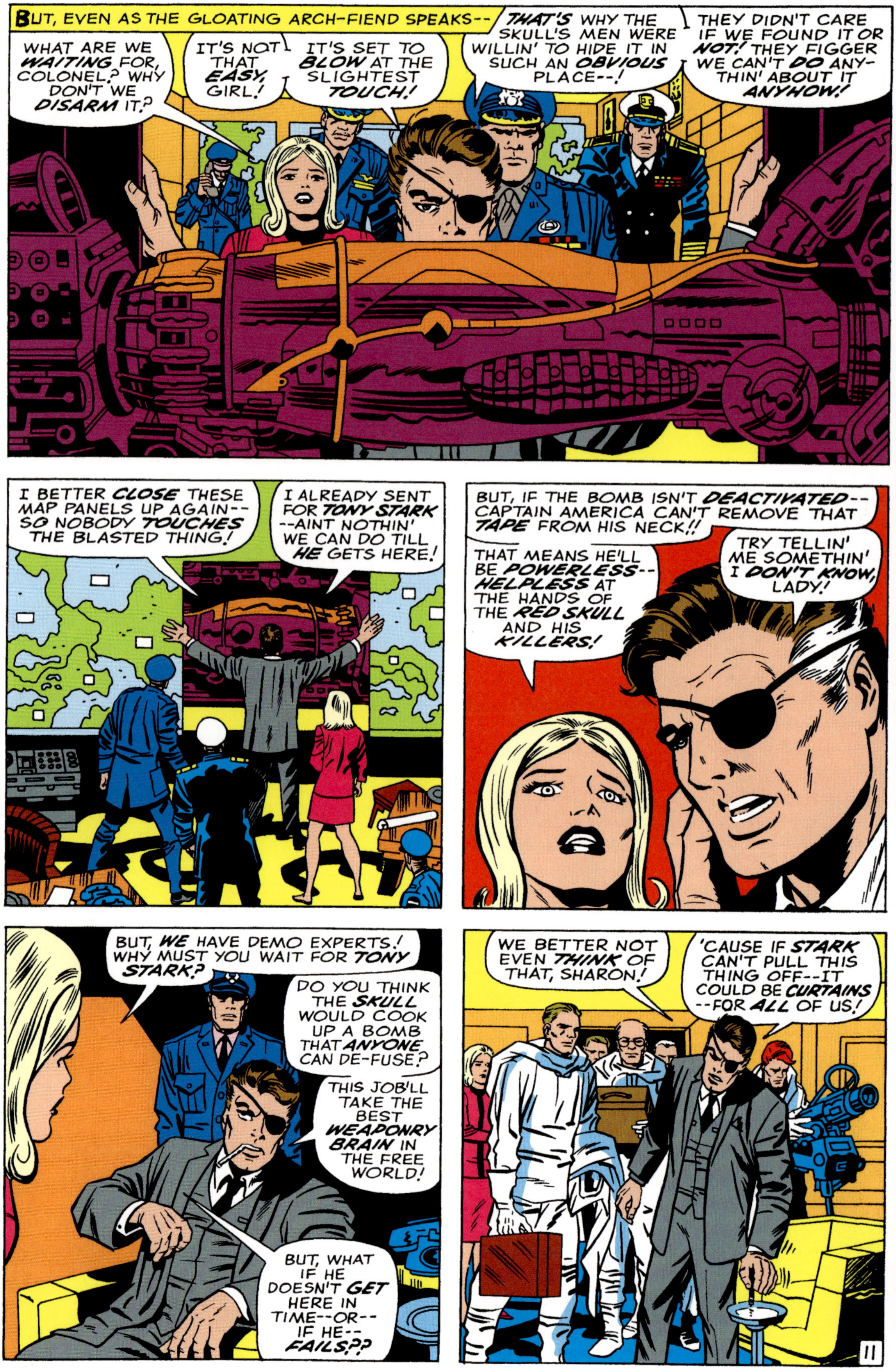
BUT, EVEN AS THE GLOATING ARCH-FIEND SPEAKS--
WHAT ARE WE WAITING FOR, COLONEL? WHY DON'T WE DISARM IT?
IT'S NOT THAT EASY, GIRL!
IT'S SET TO BLOW AT THE SLIGHTEST TOUCH!
THAT'S WHY THE SKULL'S MEN WERE WILLIN' TO HIDE IT IN SUCH AN OBVIOUS PLACE--!
THEY DIDN'T CARE IF WE FOUND IT OR NOT! THEY FIGGER WE CAN'T DO ANY-THIN' ABOUT IT ANYHOW!
I BETTER CLOSE THESE MAP PANELS UP AGAIN--SO NOBODY TOUCHES THE BLASTED THING!
I ALREADY SENT FOR TONY STARK --AINT NOTHIN' WE CAN DO TILL HE GETS HERE!
BUT, IF THE BOMB ISN'T DEACTIVATED--CAPTAIN AMERICA CAN'T REMOVE THAT TAPE FROM HIS NECK!!
THAT MEANS HE'LL BE POWERLESS--HELPLESS AT THE HANDS OF THE RED SKULL AND HIS KILLERS!
TRY TELLIN' ME SOMETHIN' I DON'T KNOW, LADY!
BUT, WE HAVE DEMO EXPERTS! WHY MUST YOU WAIT FOR TONY STARK?
DO YOU THINK THE SKULL WOULD COOK UP A BOMB THAT ANYONE CAN DE-FUSE?
THIS JOB'LL TAKE THE BEST WEAPONRY BRAIN IN THE FREE WORLD!
BUT, WHAT IF HE DOESN'T GET HERE IN TIME--OR--IF HE--FAILS??
WE BETTER NOT EVEN THINK OF THAT, SHARON!
'CAUSE IF STARK CAN'T PULL THIS THING OFF--IT COULD BE CURTAINS--FOR ALL OF US!
11

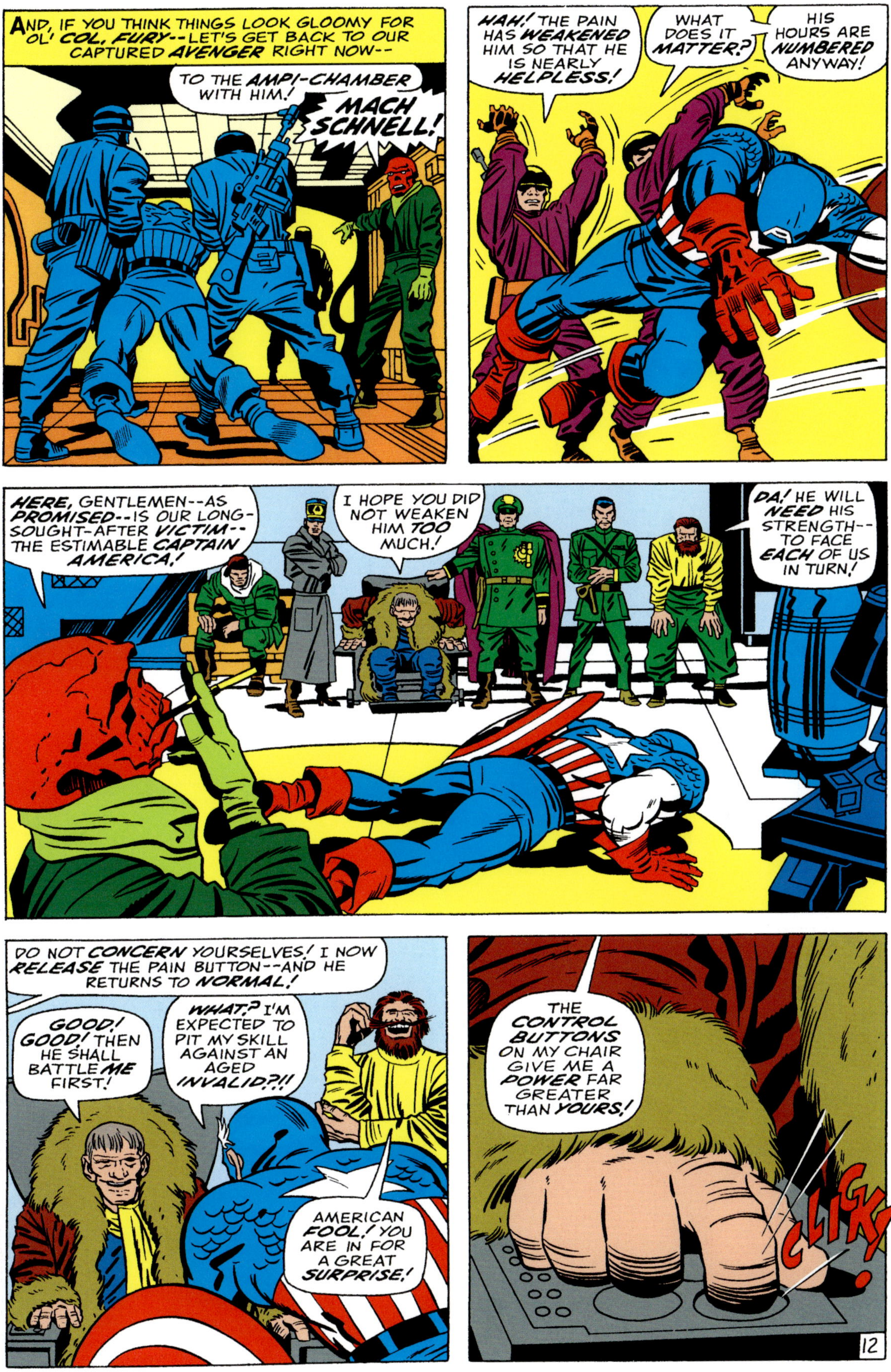

AND, IF YOU THINK THINGS LOOK GLOOMY FOR OL' COL. FURY--LET'S GET BACK TO OUR CAPTURED AVENGER RIGHT NOW--
TO THE AMPI-CHAMBER WITH HIM!
MACH SCHNELL!
HAH! THE PAIN HAS WEAKENED HIM SO THAT HE IS NEARLY HELPLESS!
WHAT DOES IT MATTER?
HIS HOURS ARE NUMBERED ANYWAY!
HERE, GENTLEMEN--AS PROMISED--IS OUR LONG-SOUGHT-AFTER VICTIM--THE ESTIMABLE CAPTAIN AMERICA!
I HOPE YOU DID NOT WEAKEN HIM TOO MUCH!
DA! HE WILL NEED HIS STRENGTH--TO FACE EACH OF US IN TURN!
DO NOT CONCERN YOURSELVES! I NOW RELEASE THE PAIN BUTTON--AND HE RETURNS TO NORMAL!
GOOD! GOOD! THEN HE SHALL BATTLE ME FIRST!
WHAT? I'M EXPECTED TO PIT MY SKILL AGAINST AN AGED INVALID?!!
AMERICAN FOOL! YOU ARE IN FOR A GREAT SURPRISE!
THE CONTROL BUTTONS ON MY CHAIR GIVE ME A POWER FAR GREATER THAN YOURS!
CLICK!
12

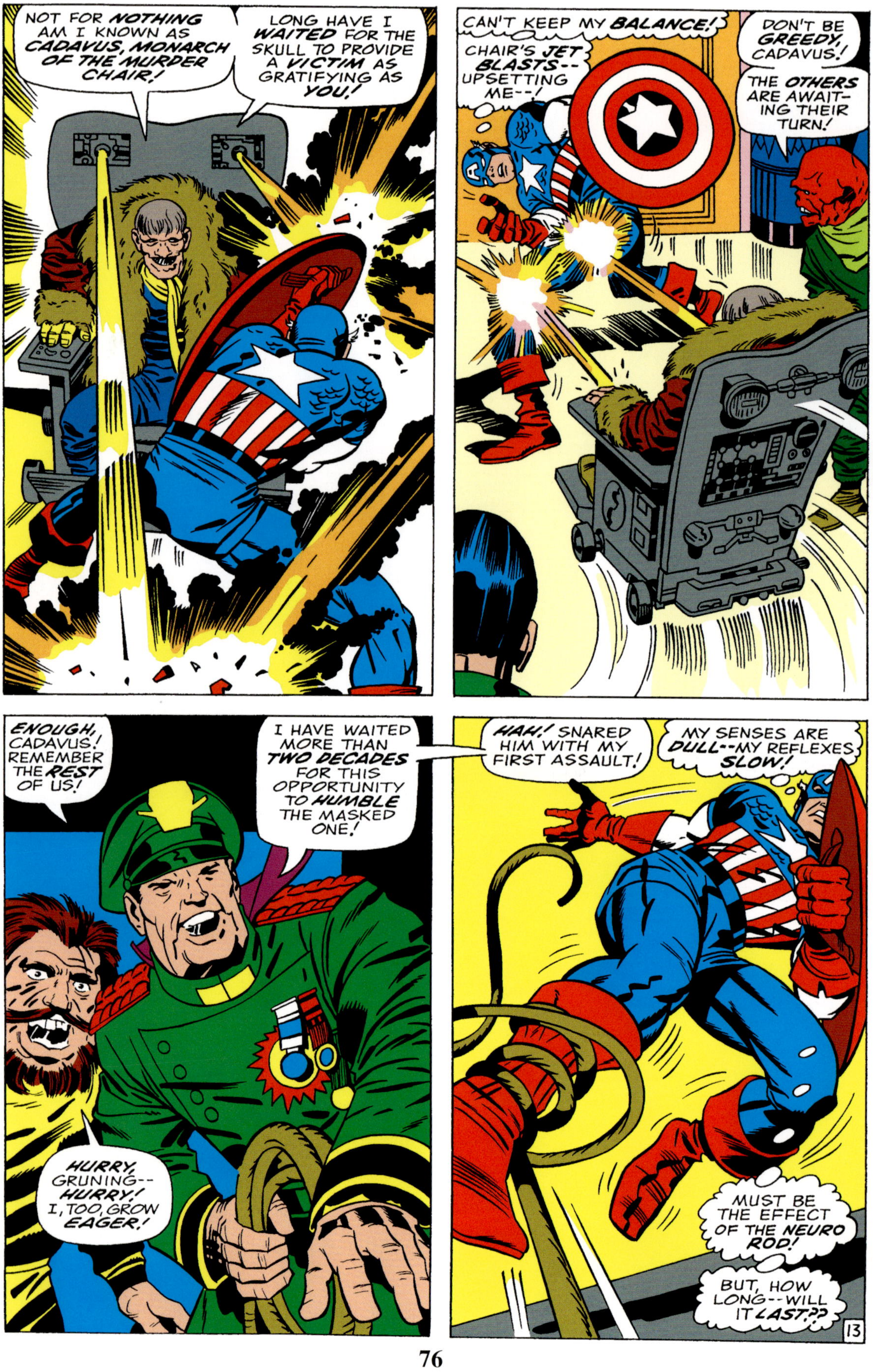
NOT FOR NOTHING AM I KNOWN AS CADAVUS, MONARCH OF THE MURDER CHAIR!
LONG HAVE I WAITED FOR THE SKULL TO PROVIDE A VICTIM AS GRATIFYING AS YOU!
CAN'T KEEP MY BALANCE!
CHAIR'S JET BLASTS-- UPSETTING ME--!
DON'T BE GREEDY, CADAVUS!
THE OTHERS ARE AWAITING THEIR TURN!
ENOUGH, CADAVUS! REMEMBER THE REST OF US!
I HAVE WAITED MORE THAN TWO DECADES FOR THIS OPPORTUNITY TO HUMBLE THE MASKED ONE!
HURRY, GRUNING-- HURRY! I, TOO, GROW EAGER!
HAH! SNARED HIM WITH MY FIRST ASSAULT!
MY SENSES ARE DULL--MY REFLEXES SLOW!
MUST BE THE EFFECT OF THE NEURO ROD!
BUT, HOW LONG--WILL IT LAST??
13

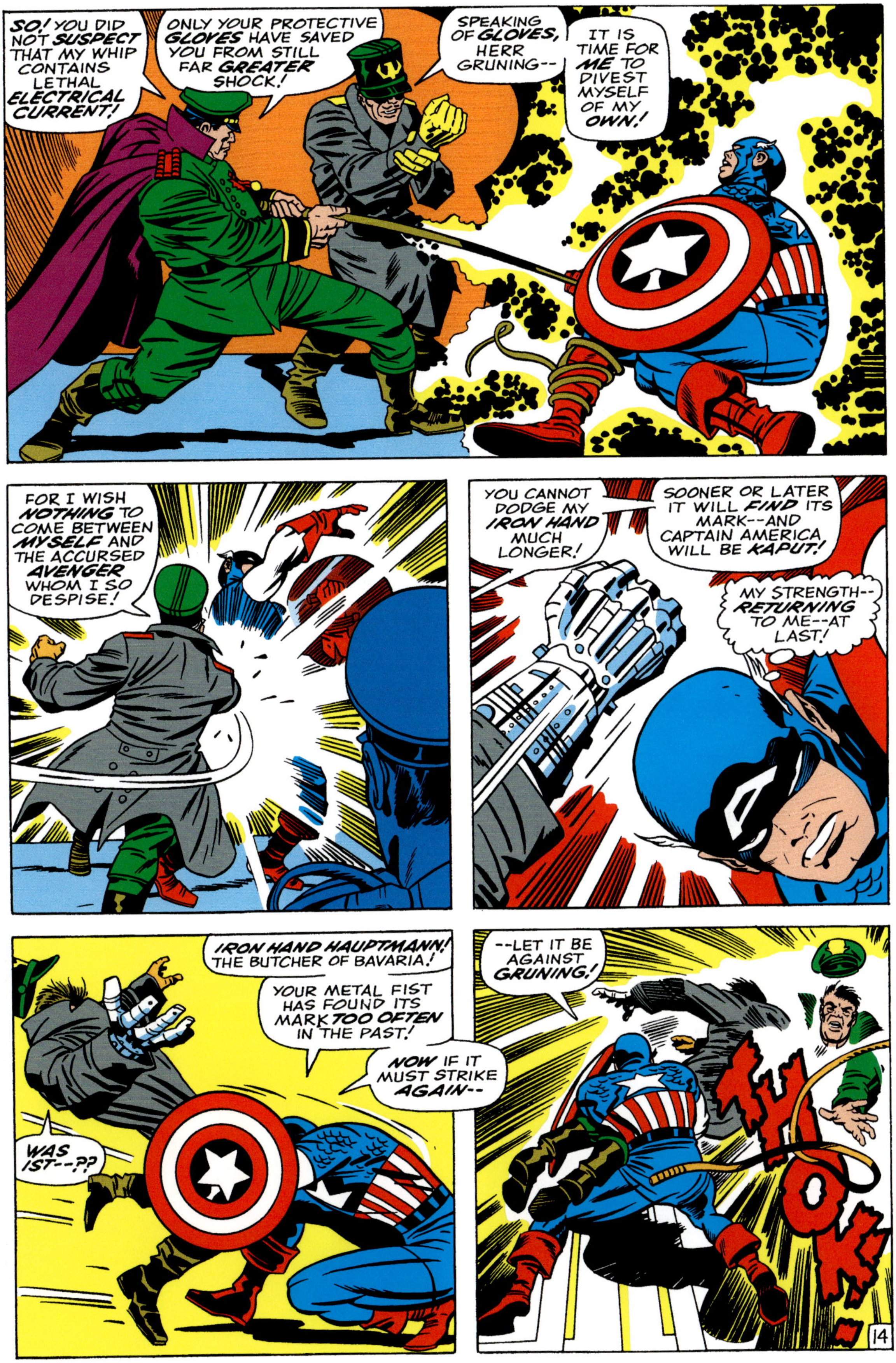

SO! YOU DID NOT SUSPECT THAT MY WHIP CONTAINS LETHAL ELECTRICAL CURRENT!
ONLY YOUR PROTECTIVE GLOVES HAVE SAVED YOU FROM STILL FAR GREATER SHOCK!
SPEAKING OF GLOVES, HERR GRUNING--
IT IS TIME FOR ME TO DIVEST MYSELF OF MY OWN!
FOR I WISH NOTHING TO COME BETWEEN MYSELF AND THE ACCURSED AVENGER WHOM I SO DESPISE!
YOU CANNOT DODGE MY IRON HAND MUCH LONGER!
SOONER OR LATER IT WILL FIND ITS MARK--AND CAPTAIN AMERICA WILL BE KAPUT!
MY STRENGTH--RETURNING TO ME--AT LAST!
IRON HAND HAUPTMANN! THE BUTCHER OF BAVARIA!
YOUR METAL FIST HAS FOUND ITS MARK TOO OFTEN IN THE PAST!
NOW IF IT MUST STRIKE AGAIN--
WAS IST--??
--LET IT BE AGAINST GRUNING!
THOK!
14

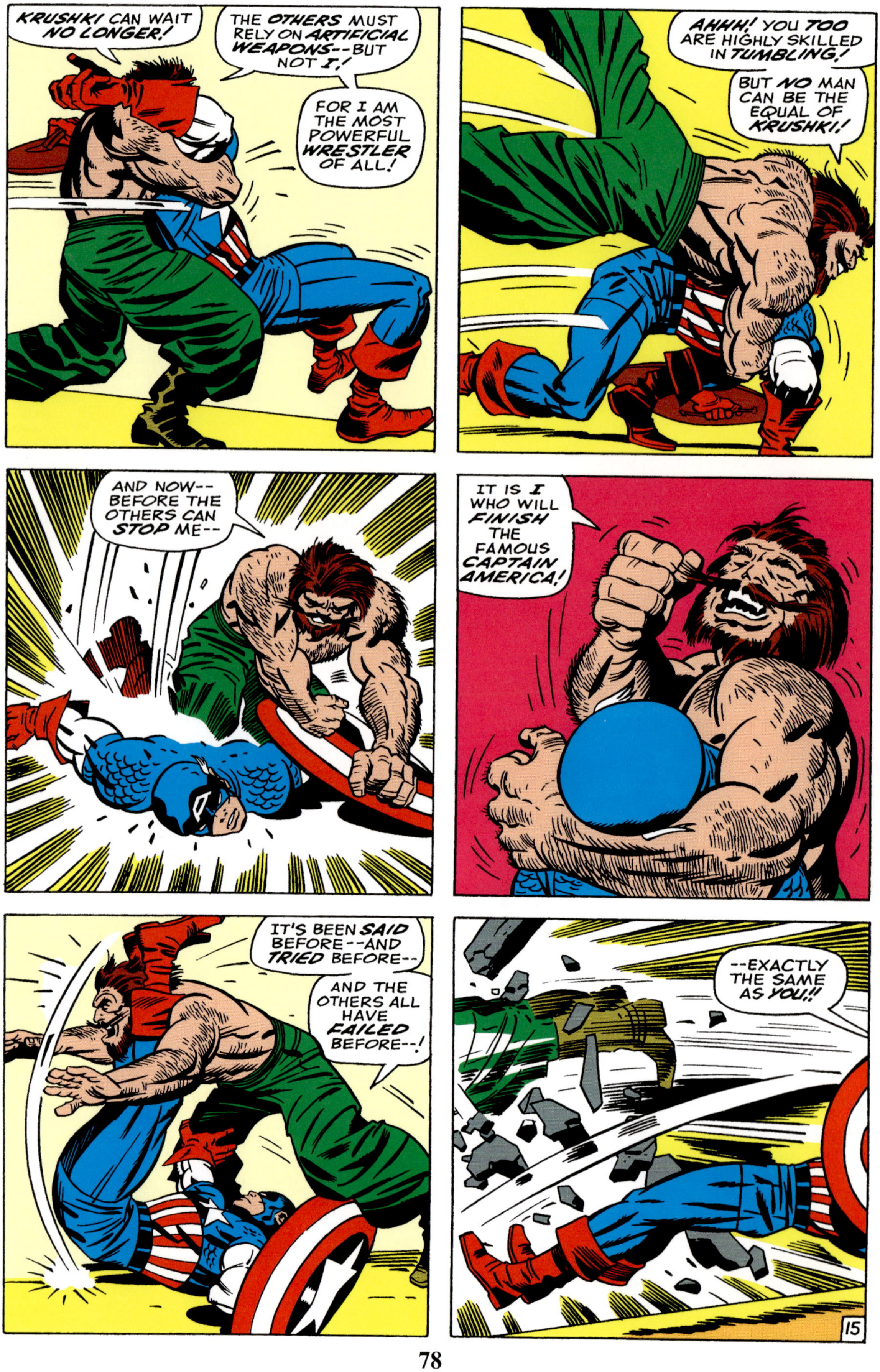
KRUSHKI CAN WAIT NO LONGER!
THE OTHERS MUST RELY ON ARTIFICIAL WEAPONS--BUT NOT I.!
FOR I AM THE MOST POWERFUL WRESTLER OF ALL!
AHHH! YOU TOO ARE HIGHLY SKILLED IN TUMBLING!
BUT NO MAN CAN BE THE EQUAL OF KRUSHKI!
AND NOW-- BEFORE THE OTHERS CAN STOP ME--
IT IS I WHO WILL FINISH THE FAMOUS CAPTAIN AMERICA!
IT'S BEEN SAID BEFORE--AND TRIED BEFORE--
AND THE OTHERS ALL HAVE FAILED BEFORE--!
--EXACTLY THE SAME AS YOU!!
15

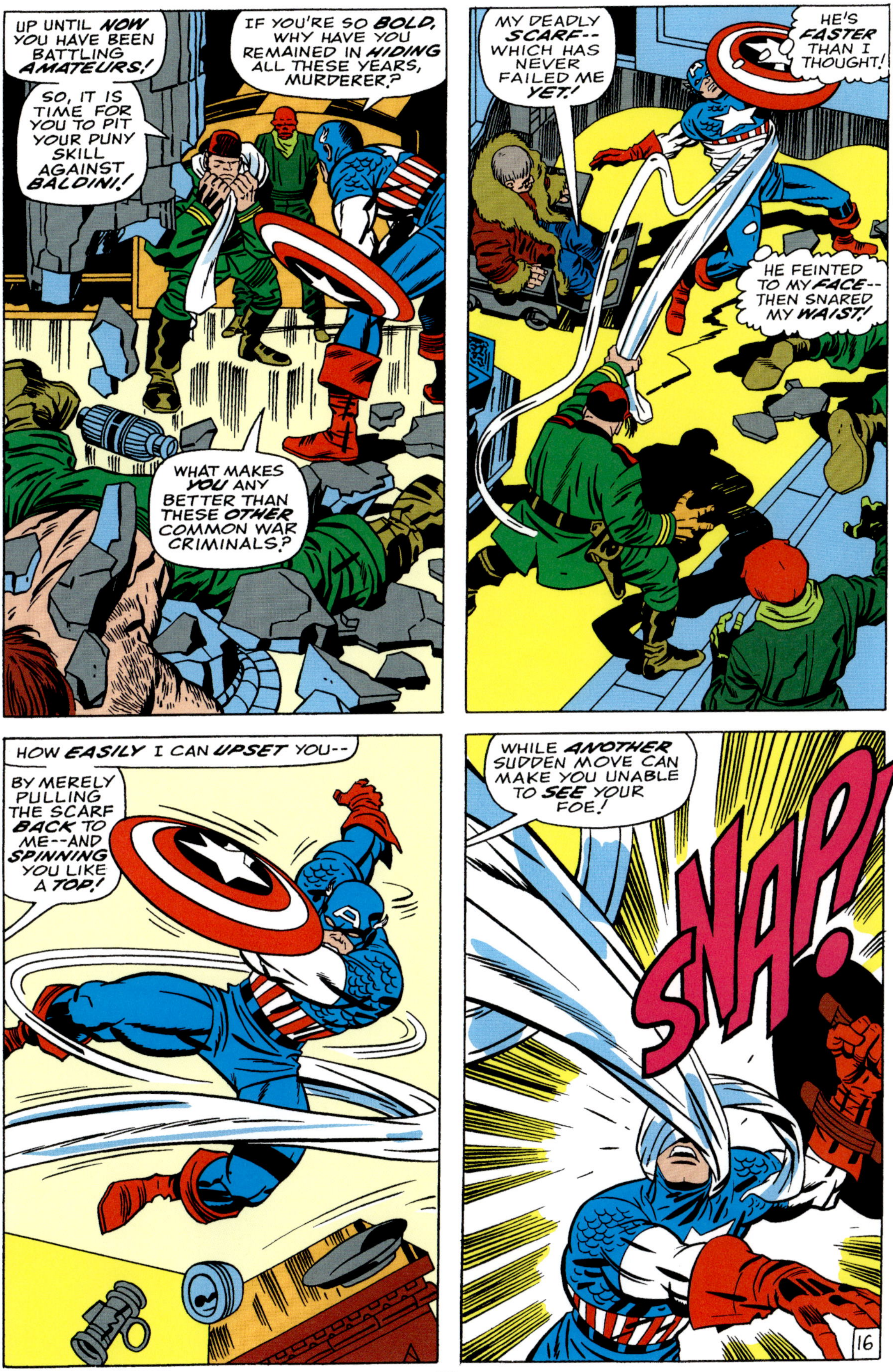
UP UNTIL NOW YOU HAVE BEEN BATTLING AMATEURS!
SO, IT IS TIME FOR YOU TO PIT YOUR PUNY SKILL AGAINST BALDINI!
IF YOU'RE SO BOLD, WHY HAVE YOU REMAINED IN HIDING ALL THESE YEARS, MURDERER?
WHAT MAKES YOU ANY BETTER THAN THESE OTHER COMMON WAR CRIMINALS?
MY DEADLY SCARF-- WHICH HAS NEVER FAILED ME YET!
HE'S FASTER THAN I THOUGHT!
HE FEINTED TO MY FACE-- THEN SNARED MY WAIST!
HOW EASILY I CAN UPSET YOU--
BY MERELY PULLING THE SCARF BACK TO ME--AND SPINNING YOU LIKE A TOP!
WHILE ANOTHER SUDDEN MOVE CAN MAKE YOU UNABLE TO SEE YOUR FOE!
SNAP!
16

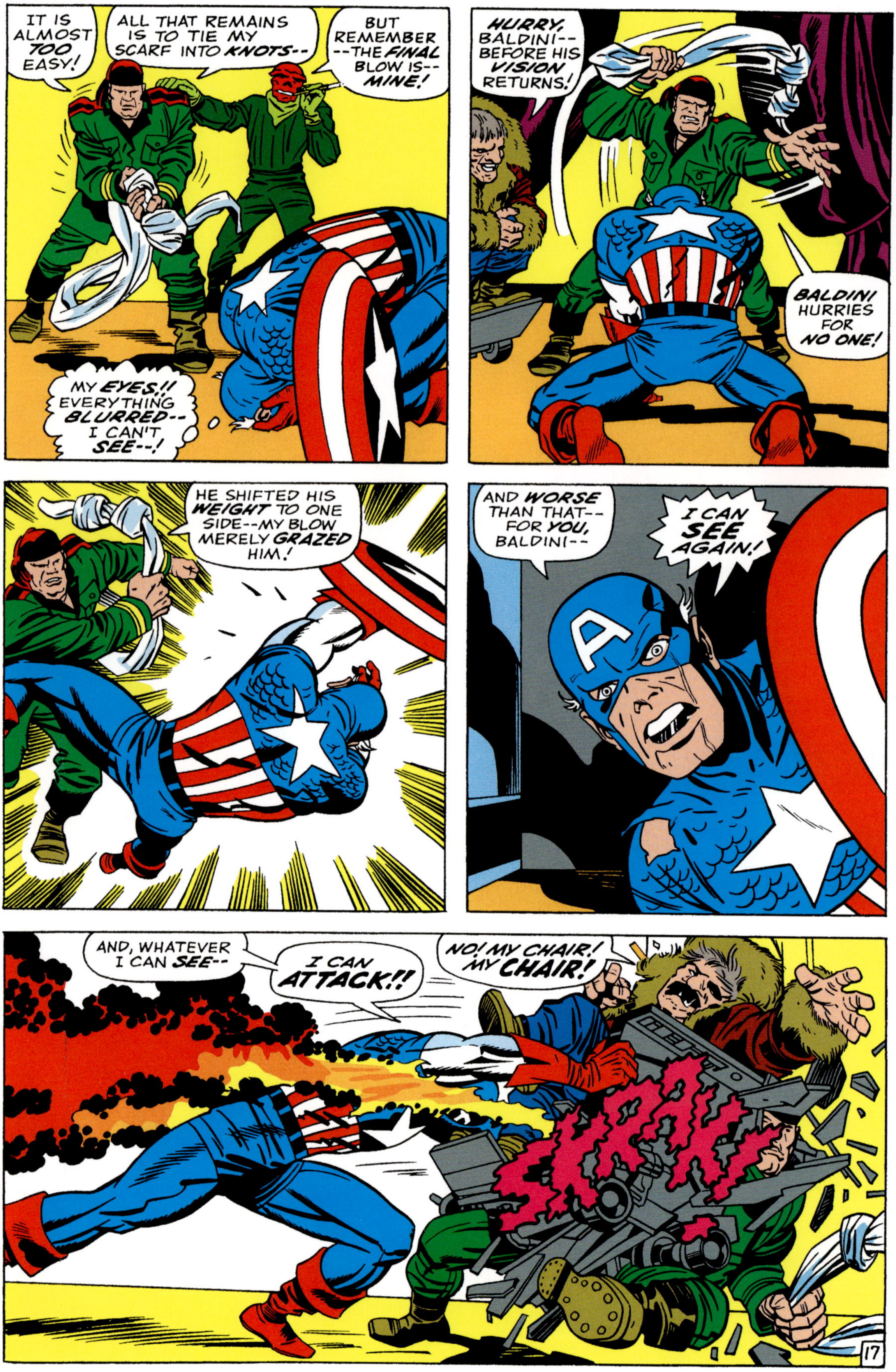
IT IS ALMOST TOO EASY!
ALL THAT REMAINS IS TO TIE MY SCARF INTO KNOTS--
BUT REMEMBER --THE FINAL BLOW IS-- MINE!
MY EYES!! EVERYTHING BLURRED-- I CAN'T SEE--!
HURRY, BALDINI-- BEFORE HIS VISION RETURNS!
BALDINI HURRIES FOR NO ONE!
HE SHIFTED HIS WEIGHT TO ONE SIDE--MY BLOW MERELY GRAZED HIM!
AND WORSE THAN THAT-- FOR YOU, BALDINI--
I CAN SEE AGAIN!
AND, WHATEVER I CAN SEE--
I CAN ATTACK!!
NO! MY CHAIR! MY CHAIR!
SKRAK!
17

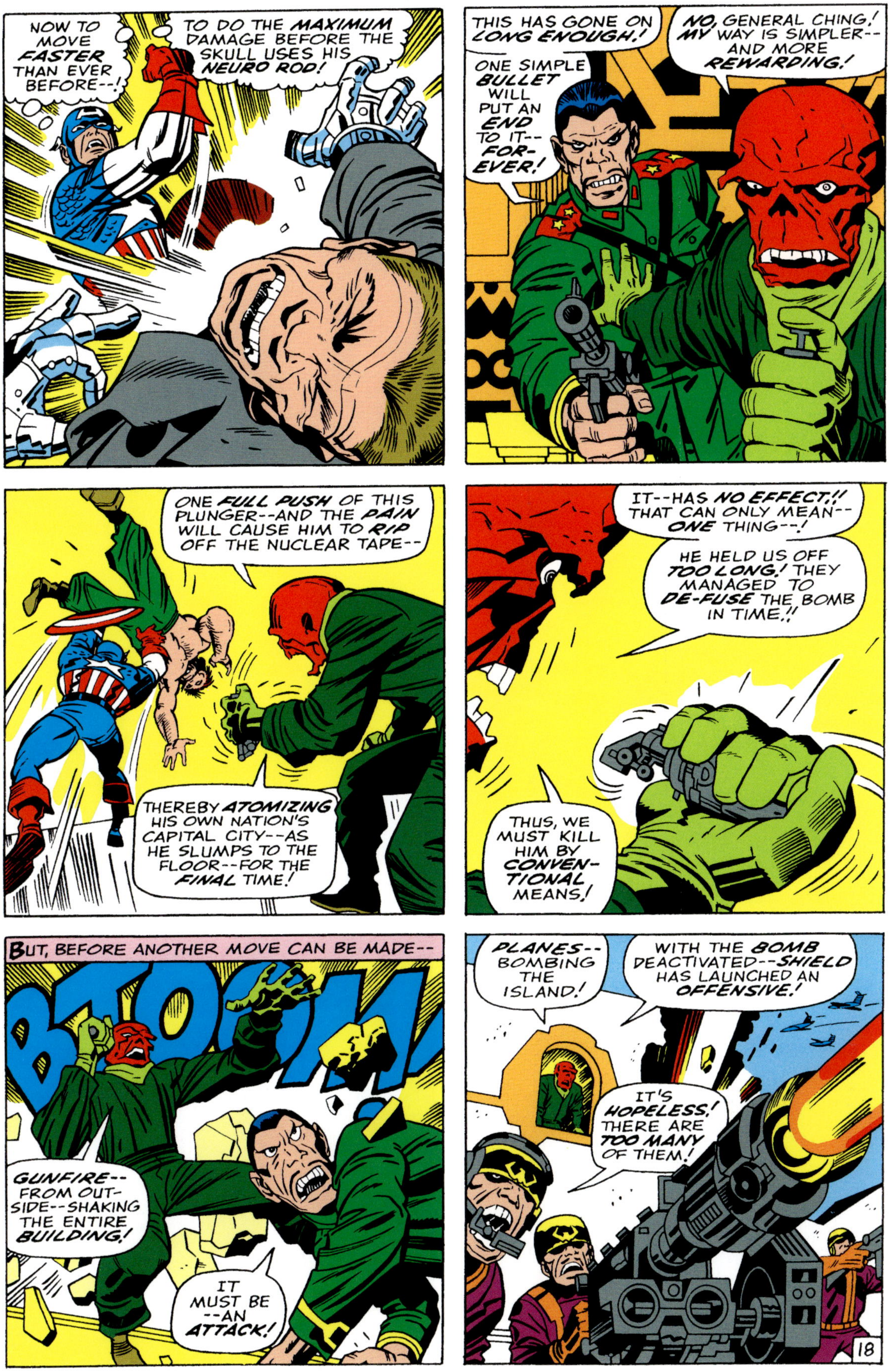
NOW TO MOVE FASTER THAN EVER BEFORE--!
TO DO THE MAXIMUM DAMAGE BEFORE THE SKULL USES HIS NEURO ROD!
THIS HAS GONE ON LONG ENOUGH!
ONE SIMPLE BULLET WILL PUT AN END TO IT--FOR-EVER!
NO, GENERAL CHING! MY WAY IS SIMPLER--AND MORE REWARDING!
ONE FULL PUSH OF THIS PLUNGER--AND THE PAIN WILL CAUSE HIM TO RIP OFF THE NUCLEAR TAPE--
THEREBY ATOMIZING HIS OWN NATION'S CAPITAL CITY--AS HE SLUMPS TO THE FLOOR--FOR THE FINAL TIME!
IT--HAS NO EFFECT!! THAT CAN ONLY MEAN--ONE THING--!
HE HELD US OFF TOO LONG! THEY MANAGED TO DE-FUSE THE BOMB IN TIME!!
THUS, WE MUST KILL HIM BY CONVEN-TIONAL MEANS!
BUT, BEFORE ANOTHER MOVE CAN BE MADE--
BTOOM
GUNFIRE--FROM OUT-SIDE--SHAKING THE ENTIRE BUILDING!
IT MUST BE--AN ATTACK!
PLANES--BOMBING THE ISLAND!
WITH THE BOMB DEACTIVATED--SHIELD HAS LAUNCHED AN OFFENSIVE!
IT'S HOPELESS! THERE ARE TOO MANY OF THEM!
18

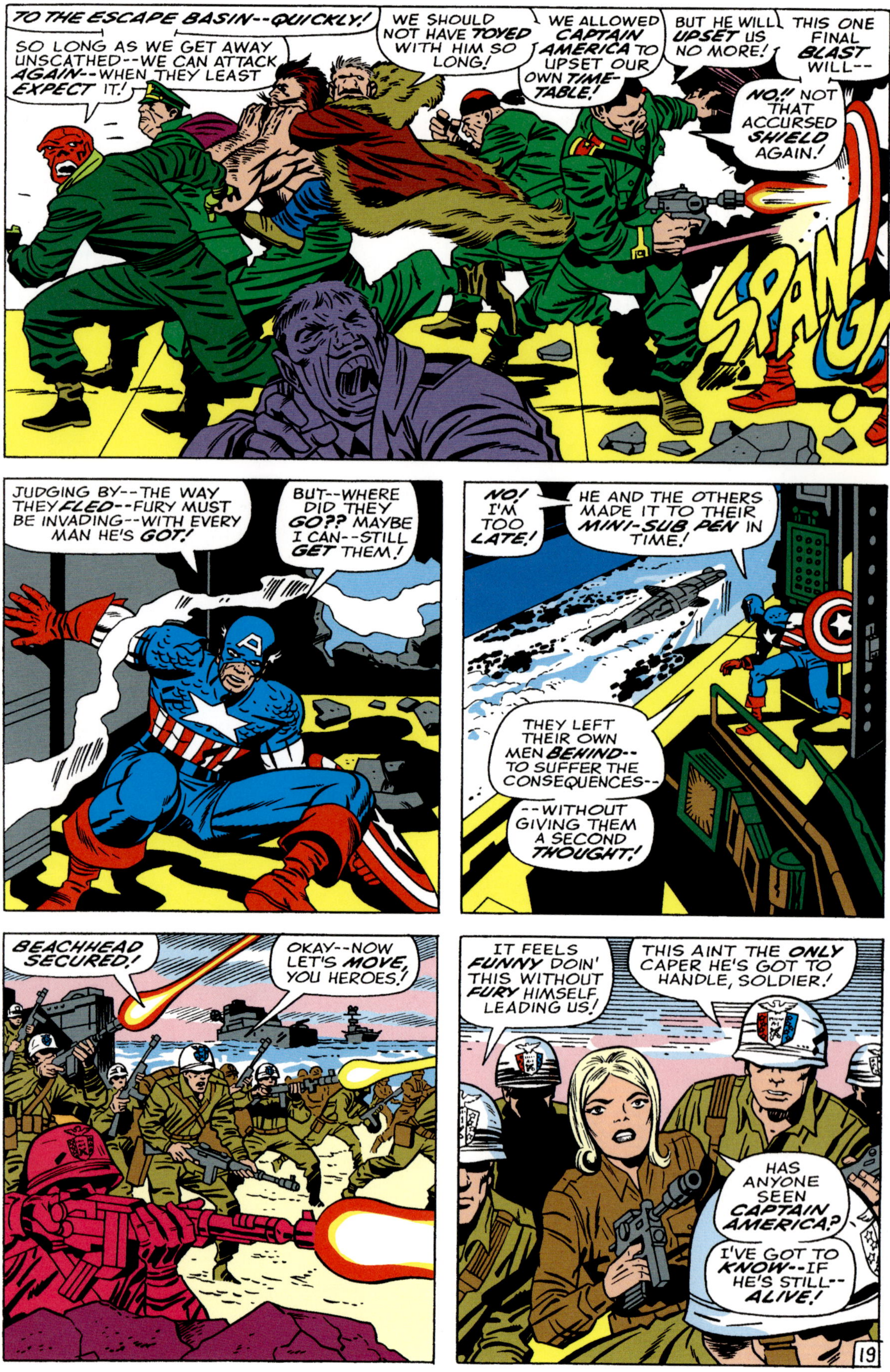
TO THE ESCAPE BASIN--QUICKLY!
SO LONG AS WE GET AWAY UNSCATHED--WE CAN ATTACK AGAIN--WHEN THEY LEAST EXPECT IT!
WE SHOULD NOT HAVE TOYED WITH HIM SO LONG!
WE ALLOWED CAPTAIN AMERICA TO UPSET OUR OWN TIME-TABLE!
BUT HE WILL UPSET US NO MORE!
THIS ONE FINAL BLAST WILL--
NO!! NOT THAT ACCURSED SHIELD AGAIN!
SPANG!
JUDGING BY--THE WAY THEY FLED--FURY MUST BE INVADING--WITH EVERY MAN HE'S GOT!
BUT--WHERE DID THEY GO?? MAYBE I CAN--STILL GET THEM!
NO! I'M TOO LATE!
HE AND THE OTHERS MADE IT TO THEIR MINI-SUB PEN IN TIME!
THEY LEFT THEIR OWN MEN BEHIND--TO SUFFER THE CONSEQUENCES--
--WITHOUT GIVING THEM A SECOND THOUGHT!
BEACHHEAD SECURED!
OKAY--NOW LET'S MOVE, YOU HEROES!
IT FEELS FUNNY DOIN' THIS WITHOUT FURY HIMSELF LEADING US!
THIS AINT THE ONLY CAPER HE'S GOT TO HANDLE, SOLDIER!
HAS ANYONE SEEN CAPTAIN AMERICA?
I'VE GOT TO KNOW--IF HE'S STILL--ALIVE!
19

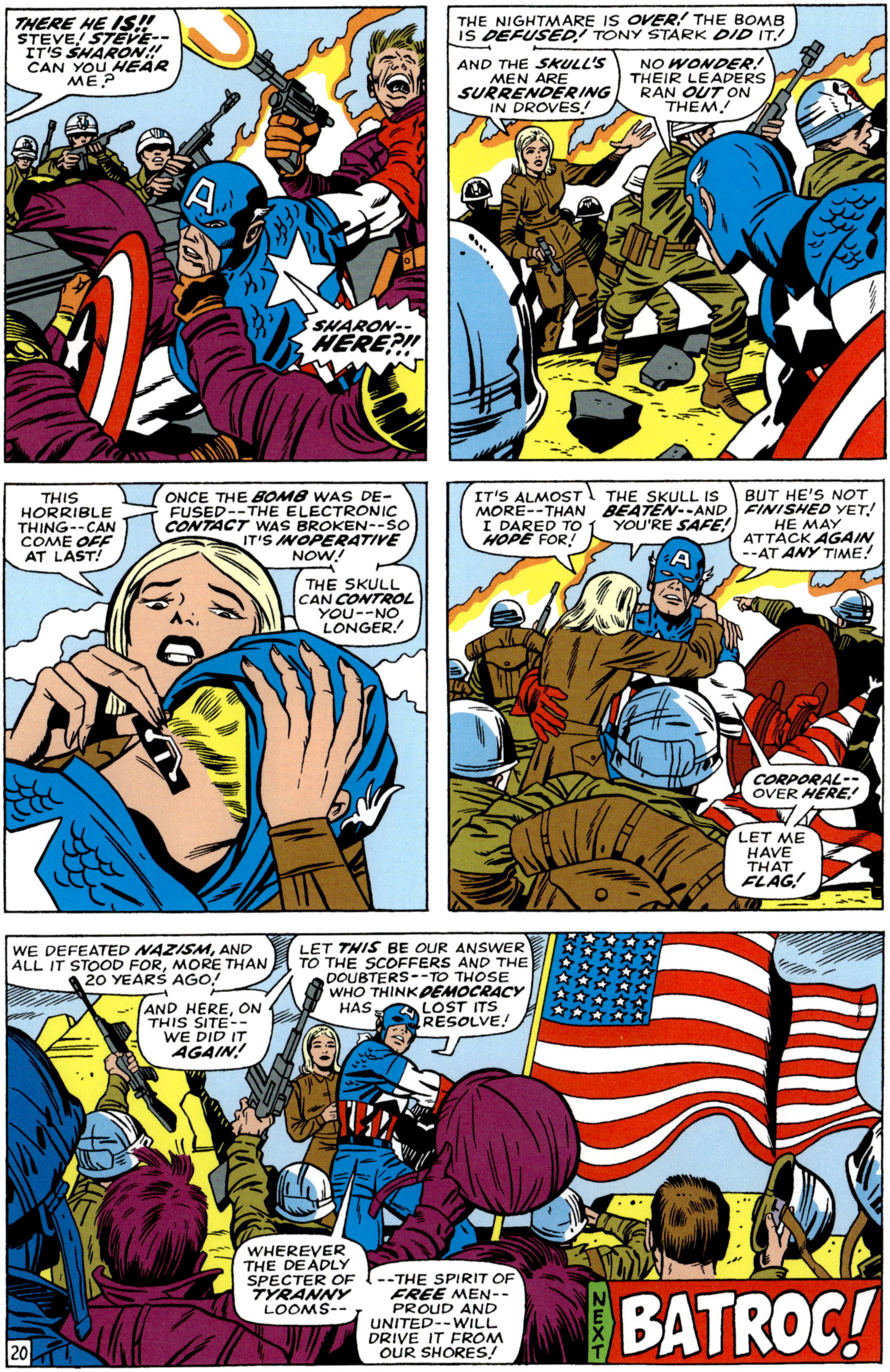
THERE HE IS!! STEVE! STEVE-- IT'S SHARON!! CAN YOU HEAR ME?
SHARON-- HERE?!!
THE NIGHTMARE IS OVER! THE BOMB IS DEFUSED! TONY STARK DID IT.!
AND THE SKULL'S MEN ARE SURRENDERING IN DROVES!
NO WONDER! THEIR LEADERS RAN OUT ON THEM.!
THIS HORRIBLE THING--CAN COME OFF AT LAST!
ONCE THE BOMB WAS DE-FUSED--THE ELECTRONIC CONTACT WAS BROKEN--SO IT'S INOPERATIVE NOW.!
THE SKULL CAN CONTROL YOU--NO LONGER.!
IT'S ALMOST MORE--THAN I DARED TO HOPE FOR!
THE SKULL IS BEATEN--AND YOU'RE SAFE!
BUT HE'S NOT FINISHED YET! HE MAY ATTACK AGAIN --AT ANY TIME!
CORPORAL-- OVER HERE!
LET ME HAVE THAT FLAG!
WE DEFEATED NAZISM, AND ALL IT STOOD FOR, MORE THAN 20 YEARS AGO!
AND HERE, ON THIS SITE-- WE DID IT AGAIN!
LET THIS BE OUR ANSWER TO THE SCOFFERS AND THE DOUBTERS--TO THOSE WHO THINK DEMOCRACY HAS LOST ITS RESOLVE.!
WHEREVER THE DEADLY SPECTER OF TYRANNY LOOMS--
--THE SPIRIT OF FREE MEN-- PROUD AND UNITED--WILL DRIVE IT FROM OUR SHORES.!
NEXT
BATROC!
20

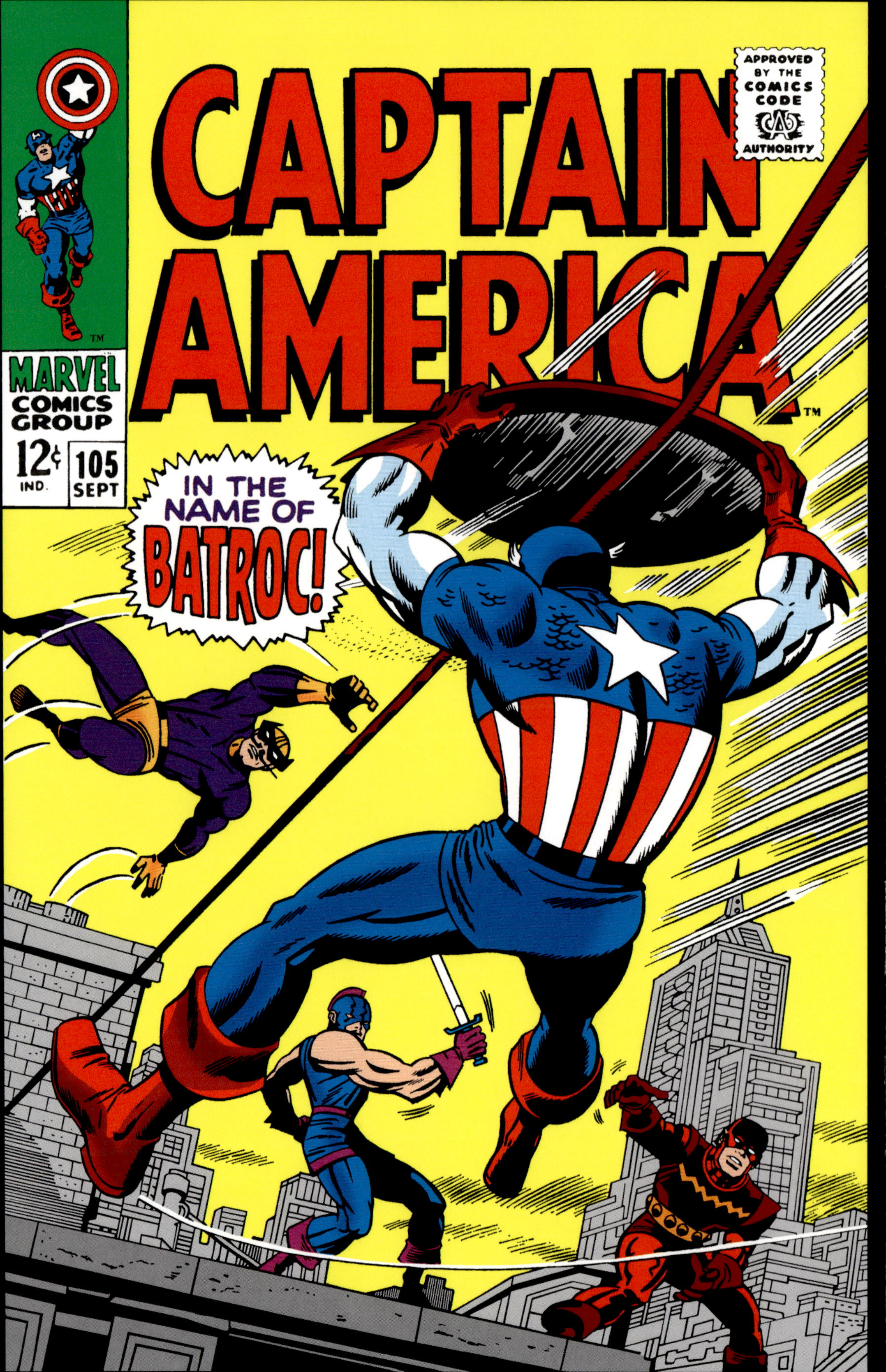
CAPTAIN AMERICA
MARVEL COMICS GROUP
12¢ IND.
105 SEPT
APPROVED BY THE COMICS CODE AUTHORITY
IN THE NAME OF BATROC!

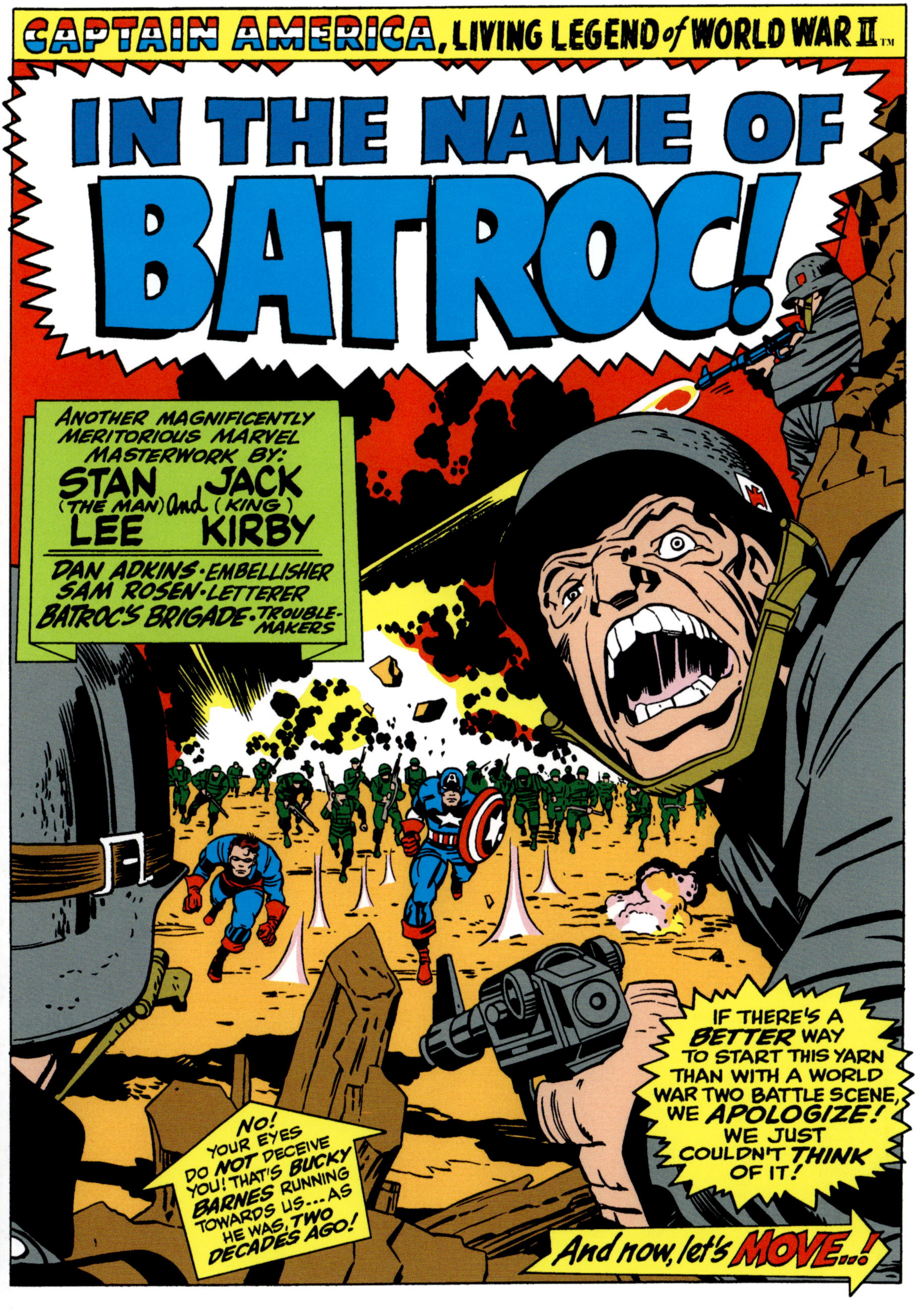

CAPTAIN AMERICA, LIVING LEGEND of WORLD WAR II TM
IN THE NAME OF BATROC!
ANOTHER MAGNIFICENTLY MERITORIOUS MARVEL MASTERWORK BY: STAN (THE MAN) LEE and JACK (KING) KIRBY
DAN ADKINS · EMBELLISHER
SAM ROSEN · LETTERER
BATROC'S BRIGADE · TROUBLE-MAKERS
IF THERE'S A BETTER WAY TO START THIS YARN THAN WITH A WORLD WAR TWO BATTLE SCENE, WE APOLOGIZE! WE JUST COULDN'T THINK OF IT!
NO! YOUR EYES DO NOT DECEIVE YOU! THAT'S BUCKY BARNES RUNNING TOWARDS US... AS HE WAS, TWO DECADES AGO!
And now, let's MOVE..!

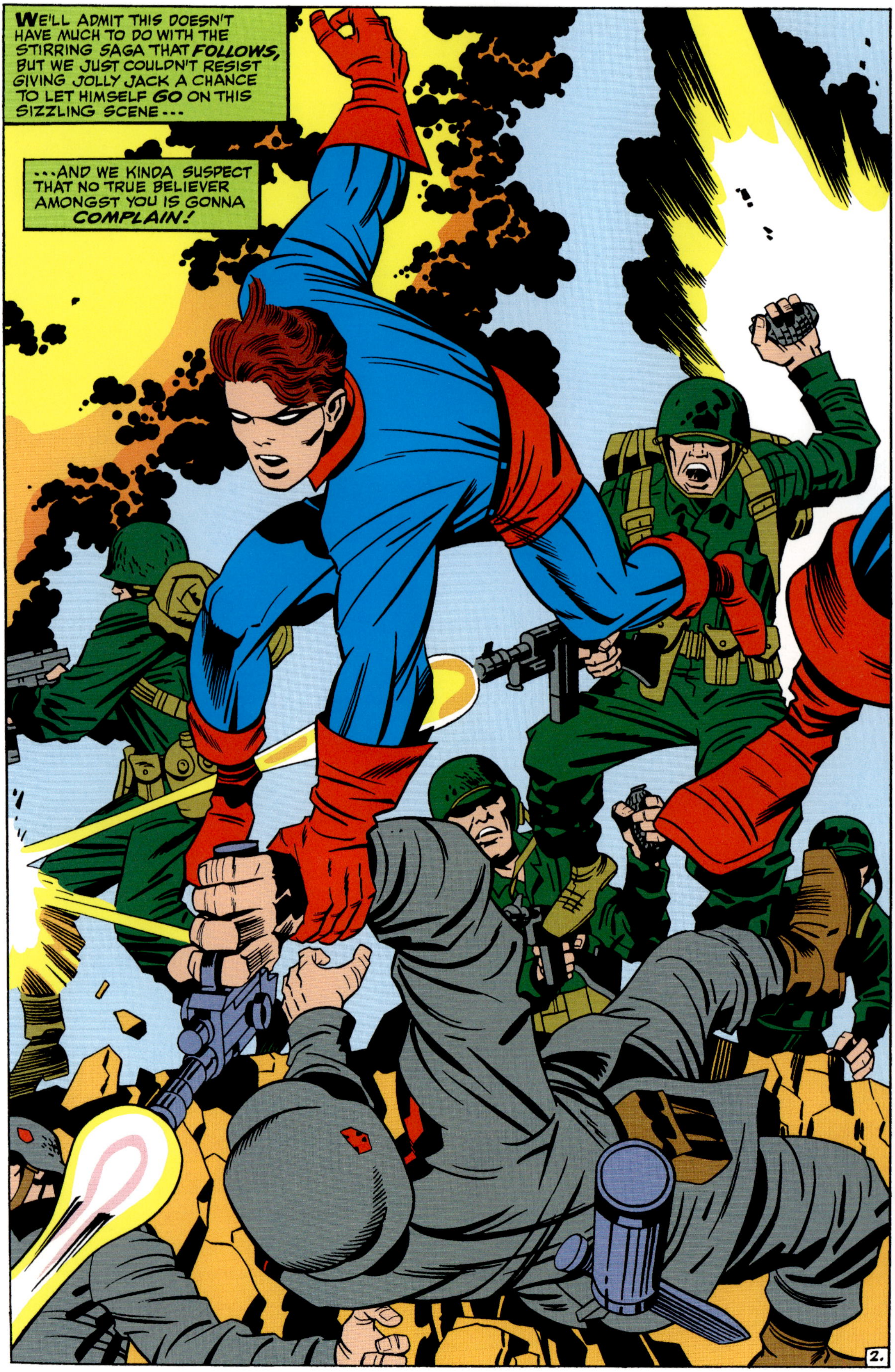

WE'LL ADMIT THIS DOESN'T HAVE MUCH TO DO WITH THE STIRRING SAGA THAT FOLLOWS, BUT WE JUST COULDN'T RESIST GIVING JOLLY JACK A CHANCE TO LET HIMSELF GO ON THIS SIZZLING SCENE...
...AND WE KINDA SUSPECT THAT NO TRUE BELIEVER AMONGST YOU IS GONNA COMPLAIN!
2.

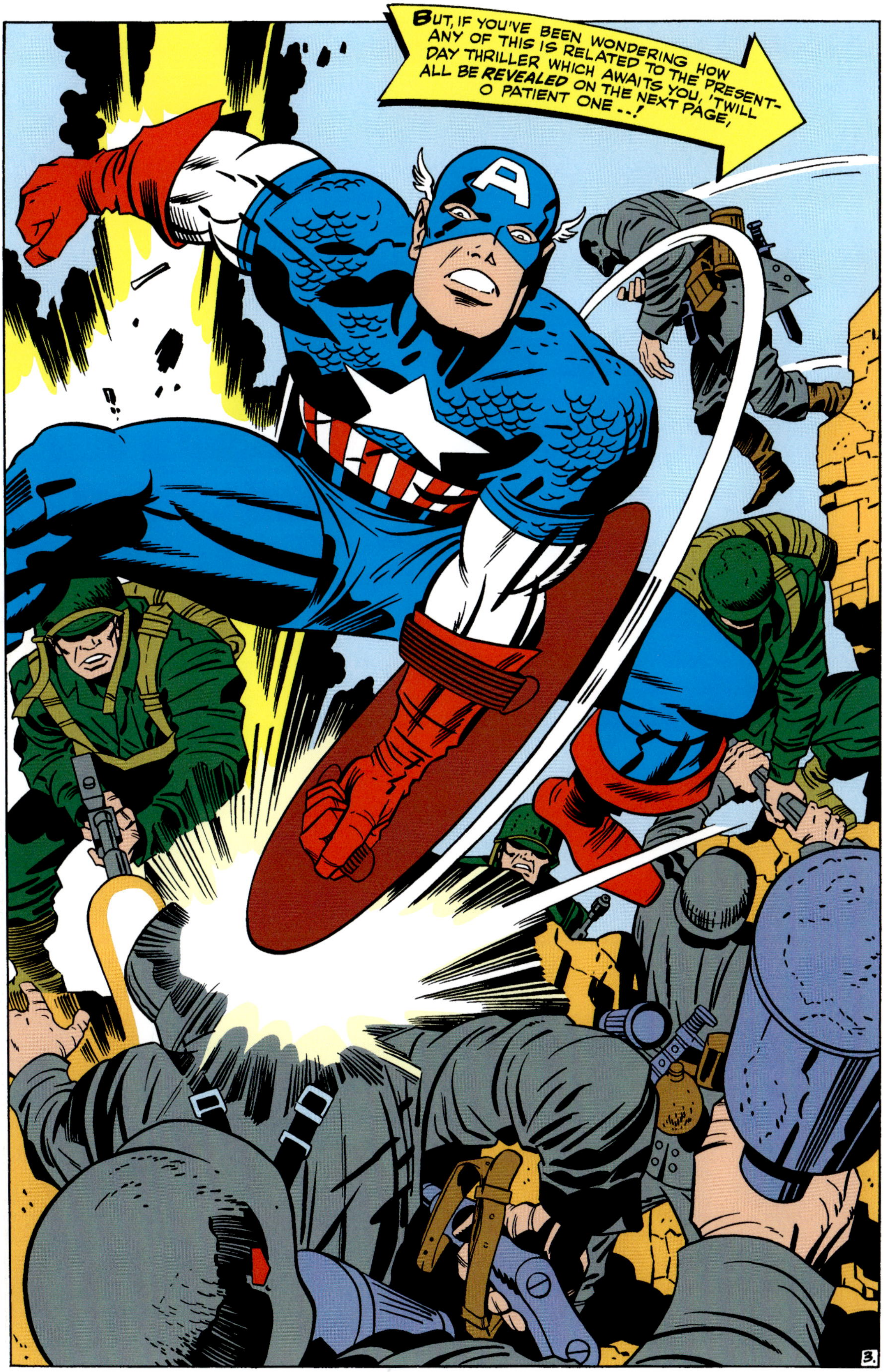
BUT, IF YOU'VE BEEN WONDERING HOW ANY OF THIS IS RELATED TO THE PRESENT-DAY THRILLER WHICH AWAITS YOU, 'TWILL ALL BE REVEALED ON THE NEXT PAGE, O PATIENT ONE..!
3.

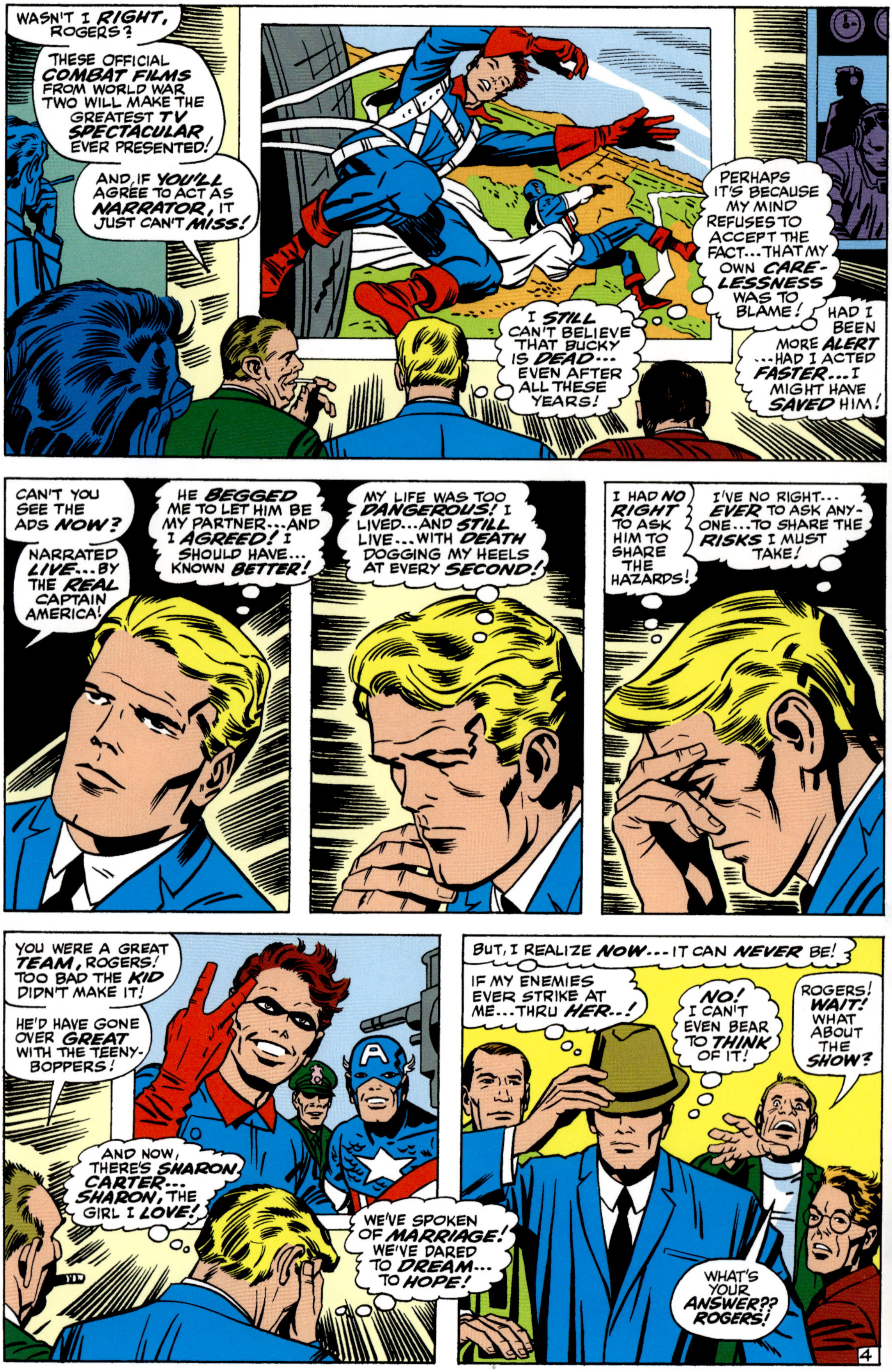
WASN'T I RIGHT, ROGERS?
THESE OFFICIAL COMBAT FILMS FROM WORLD WAR TWO WILL MAKE THE GREATEST TV SPECTACULAR EVER PRESENTED!
AND, IF YOU'LL AGREE TO ACT AS NARRATOR, IT JUST CAN'T MISS!
I STILL CAN'T BELIEVE THAT BUCKY IS DEAD... EVEN AFTER ALL THESE YEARS!
PERHAPS IT'S BECAUSE MY MIND REFUSES TO ACCEPT THE FACT... THAT MY OWN CARELESSNESS WAS TO BLAME!
HAD I BEEN MORE ALERT ...HAD I ACTED FASTER... I MIGHT HAVE SAVED HIM!
CAN'T YOU SEE THE ADS NOW?
NARRATED LIVE... BY THE REAL CAPTAIN AMERICA!
HE BEGGED ME TO LET HIM BE MY PARTNER... AND I AGREED! I SHOULD HAVE... KNOWN BETTER!
MY LIFE WAS TOO DANGEROUS! I LIVED... AND STILL LIVE... WITH DEATH DOGGING MY HEELS AT EVERY SECOND!
I HAD NO RIGHT TO ASK HIM TO SHARE THE HAZARDS!
I'VE NO RIGHT... EVER TO ASK ANYONE... TO SHARE THE RISKS I MUST TAKE!
YOU WERE A GREAT TEAM, ROGERS! TOO BAD THE KID DIDN'T MAKE IT!
HE'D HAVE GONE OVER GREAT WITH THE TEENY-BOPPERS!
AND NOW, THERE'S SHARON CARTER... SHARON, THE GIRL I LOVE!
WE'VE SPOKEN OF MARRIAGE! WE'VE DARED TO DREAM... TO HOPE!
BUT, I REALIZE NOW... IT CAN NEVER BE!
IF MY ENEMIES EVER STRIKE AT ME... THRU HER...!
NO! I CAN'T EVEN BEAR TO THINK OF IT!
ROGERS! WAIT! WHAT ABOUT THE SHOW?
WHAT'S YOUR ANSWER?? ROGERS!
4

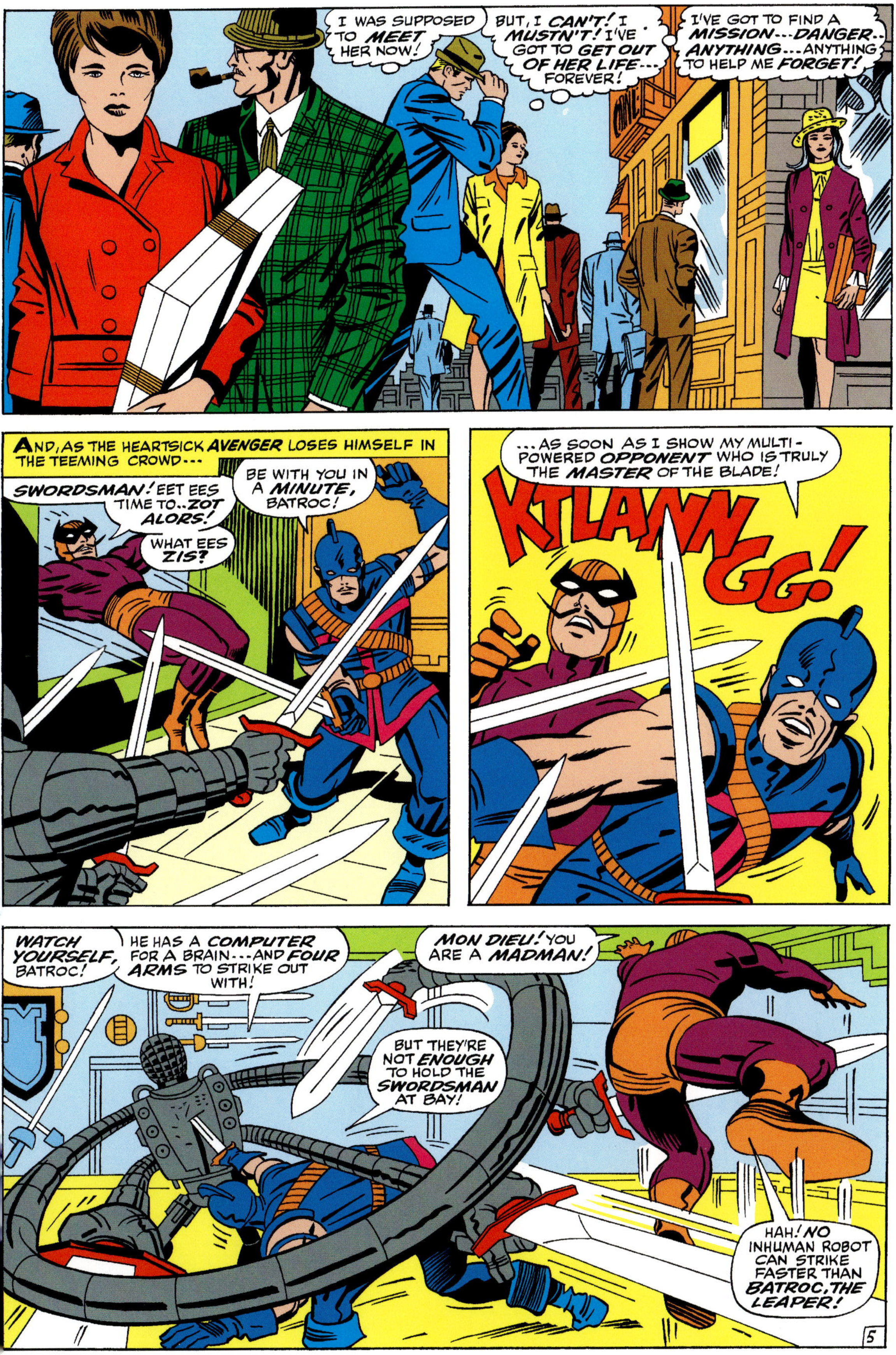

I WAS SUPPOSED TO MEET HER NOW!
BUT, I CAN'T! I MUSTN'T! I'VE GOT TO GET OUT OF HER LIFE--- FOREVER!
I'VE GOT TO FIND A MISSION---DANGER-- ANYTHING---ANYTHING TO HELP ME FORGET!
AND, AS THE HEARTSICK AVENGER LOSES HIMSELF IN THE TEEMING CROWD---
SWORDSMAN! EET EES TIME TO..ZOT ALORS!
WHAT EES ZIS?
BE WITH YOU IN A MINUTE, BATROC!
...AS SOON AS I SHOW MY MULTI-POWERED OPPONENT WHO IS TRULY THE MASTER OF THE BLADE!
KTLANNGG!
WATCH YOURSELF, BATROC!
HE HAS A COMPUTER FOR A BRAIN---AND FOUR ARMS TO STRIKE OUT WITH!
MON DIEU! YOU ARE A MADMAN!
BUT THEY'RE NOT ENOUGH TO HOLD THE SWORDSMAN AT BAY!
HAH! NO INHUMAN ROBOT CAN STRIKE FASTER THAN BATROC, THE LEAPER!
5

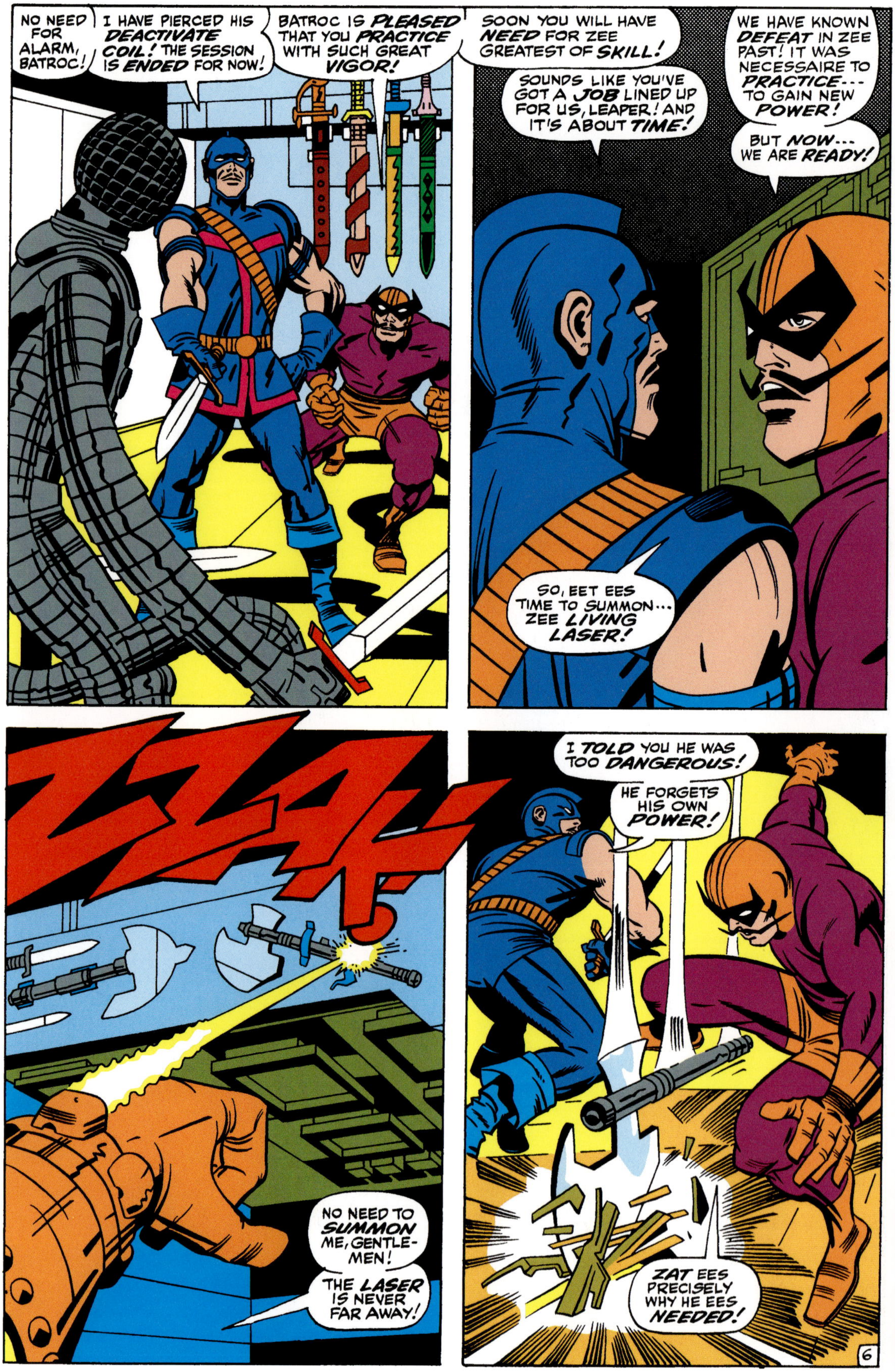
NO NEED FOR ALARM, BATROC!
I HAVE PIERCED HIS DEACTIVATE COIL! THE SESSION IS ENDED FOR NOW!
BATROC IS PLEASED THAT YOU PRACTICE WITH SUCH GREAT VIGOR!
SOON YOU WILL HAVE NEED FOR ZEE GREATEST OF SKILL!
SOUNDS LIKE YOU'VE GOT A JOB LINED UP FOR US, LEAPER! AND IT'S ABOUT TIME!
WE HAVE KNOWN DEFEAT IN ZEE PAST! IT WAS NECESSAIRE TO PRACTICE--- TO GAIN NEW POWER!
BUT NOW... WE ARE READY!
SO, EET EES TIME TO SUMMON... ZEE LIVING LASER!
ZZAK!
NO NEED TO SUMMON ME, GENTLE-MEN!
THE LASER IS NEVER FAR AWAY!
I TOLD YOU HE WAS TOO DANGEROUS!
HE FORGETS HIS OWN POWER!
ZAT EES PRECISELY WHY HE EES NEEDED!
6

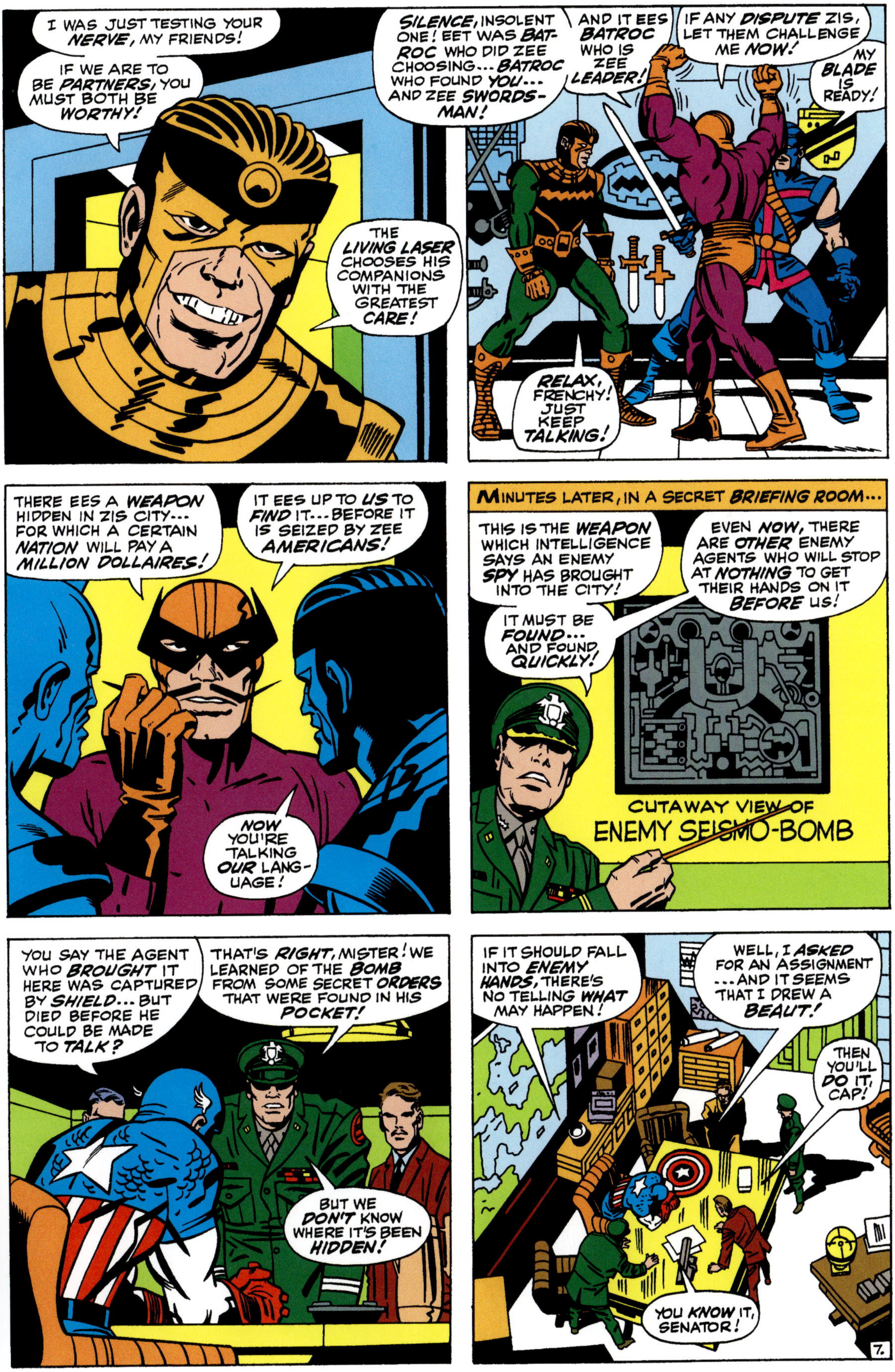
I WAS JUST TESTING YOUR NERVE, MY FRIENDS!
IF WE ARE TO BE PARTNERS, YOU MUST BOTH BE WORTHY!
THE LIVING LASER CHOOSES HIS COMPANIONS WITH THE GREATEST CARE!
SILENCE, INSOLENT ONE! EET WAS BATROC WHO DID ZEE CHOOSING... BATROC WHO FOUND YOU... AND ZEE SWORDSMAN!
AND IT EES BATROC WHO IS ZEE LEADER!
IF ANY DISPUTE ZIS, LET THEM CHALLENGE ME NOW!
MY BLADE IS READY!
RELAX, FRENCHY! JUST KEEP TALKING!
THERE EES A WEAPON HIDDEN IN ZIS CITY... FOR WHICH A CERTAIN NATION WILL PAY A MILLION DOLLAIRES!
IT EES UP TO US TO FIND IT... BEFORE IT IS SEIZED BY ZEE AMERICANS!
NOW YOU'RE TALKING OUR LANGUAGE!
MINUTES LATER, IN A SECRET BRIEFING ROOM...
THIS IS THE WEAPON WHICH INTELLIGENCE SAYS AN ENEMY SPY HAS BROUGHT INTO THE CITY!
EVEN NOW, THERE ARE OTHER ENEMY AGENTS WHO WILL STOP AT NOTHING TO GET THEIR HANDS ON IT BEFORE US!
IT MUST BE FOUND... AND FOUND QUICKLY!
CUTAWAY VIEW OF
ENEMY SEISMO-BOMB
YOU SAY THE AGENT WHO BROUGHT IT HERE WAS CAPTURED BY SHIELD... BUT DIED BEFORE HE COULD BE MADE TO TALK?
THAT'S RIGHT, MISTER! WE LEARNED OF THE BOMB FROM SOME SECRET ORDERS THAT WERE FOUND IN HIS POCKET!
BUT WE DON'T KNOW WHERE IT'S BEEN HIDDEN!
IF IT SHOULD FALL INTO ENEMY HANDS, THERE'S NO TELLING WHAT MAY HAPPEN!
WELL, I ASKED FOR AN ASSIGNMENT ...AND IT SEEMS THAT I DREW A BEAUT!
THEN YOU'LL DO IT, CAP!
YOU KNOW IT, SENATOR!
7.

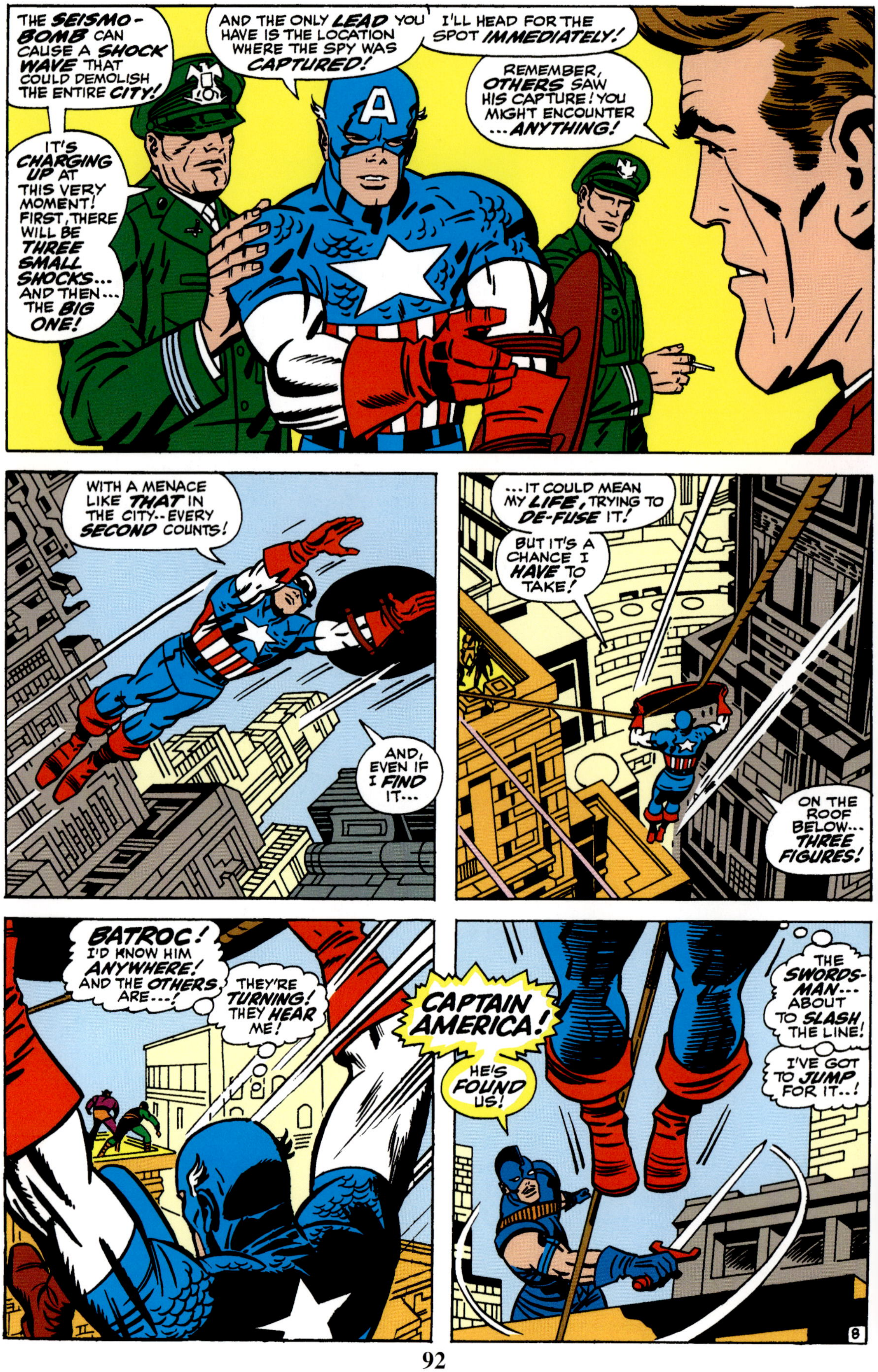
THE SEISMO-BOMB CAN CAUSE A SHOCK WAVE THAT COULD DEMOLISH THE ENTIRE CITY!
IT'S CHARGING UP AT THIS VERY MOMENT! FIRST, THERE WILL BE THREE SMALL SHOCKS... AND THEN... THE BIG ONE!
AND THE ONLY LEAD YOU HAVE IS THE LOCATION WHERE THE SPY WAS CAPTURED!
I'LL HEAD FOR THE SPOT IMMEDIATELY!
REMEMBER, OTHERS SAW HIS CAPTURE! YOU MIGHT ENCOUNTER ...ANYTHING!
WITH A MENACE LIKE THAT IN THE CITY--EVERY SECOND COUNTS!
AND, EVEN IF I FIND IT...
...IT COULD MEAN MY LIFE, TRYING TO DE-FUSE IT!
BUT IT'S A CHANCE I HAVE TO TAKE!
ON THE ROOF BELOW... THREE FIGURES!
BATROC! I'D KNOW HIM ANYWHERE! AND THE OTHERS ARE...!
THEY'RE TURNING! THEY HEAR ME!
CAPTAIN AMERICA!
HE'S FOUND US!
THE SWORDSMAN... ABOUT TO SLASH THE LINE!
I'VE GOT TO JUMP FOR IT..!
8

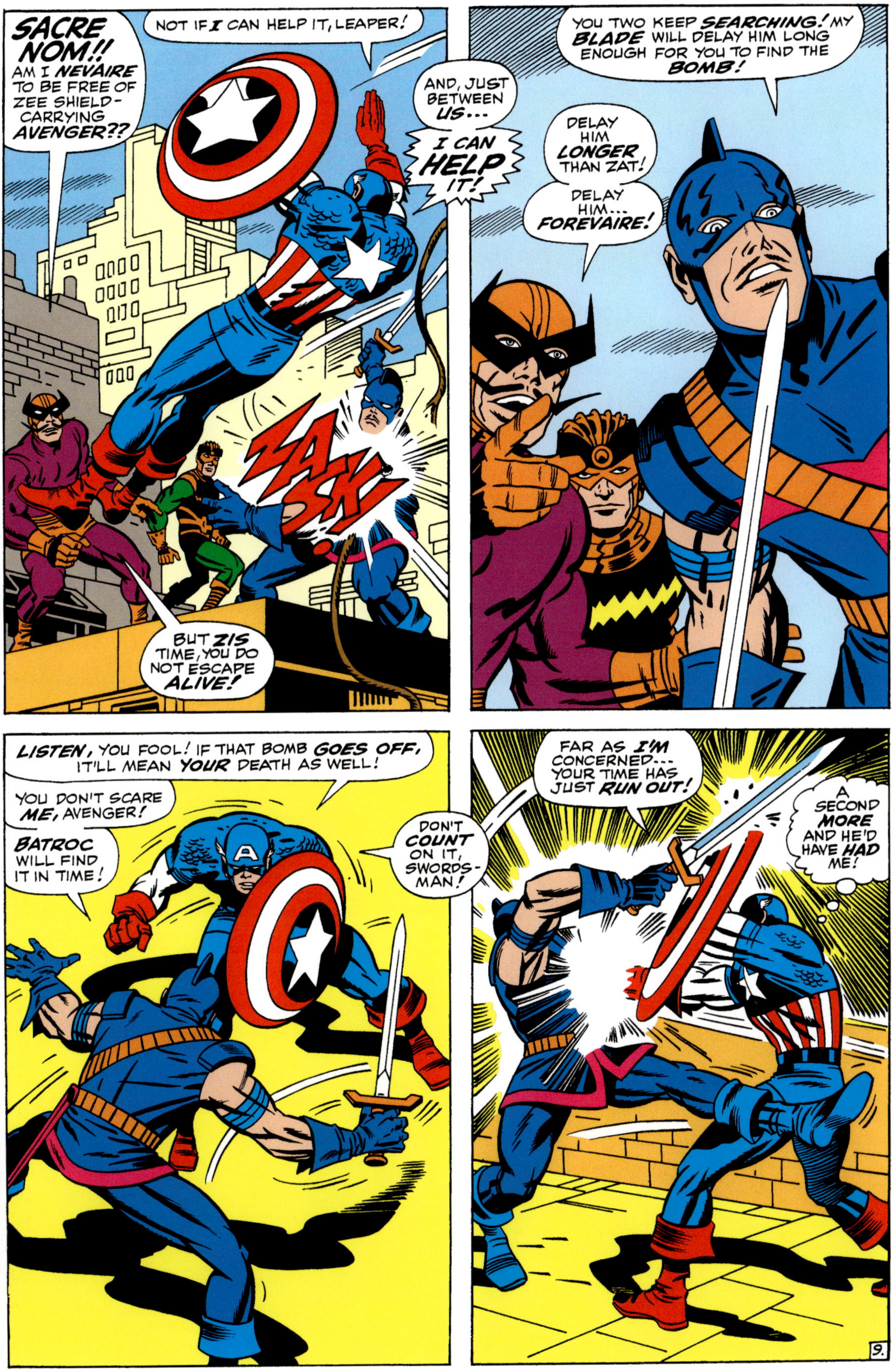
SACRE NOM!! AM I NEVAIRE TO BE FREE OF ZEE SHIELD-CARRYING AVENGER??
NOT IF I CAN HELP IT, LEAPER!
AND, JUST BETWEEN US...
I CAN HELP IT!
ZAK!
BUT ZIS TIME, YOU DO NOT ESCAPE ALIVE!
YOU TWO KEEP SEARCHING! MY BLADE WILL DELAY HIM LONG ENOUGH FOR YOU TO FIND THE BOMB!
DELAY HIM LONGER THAN ZAT!
DELAY HIM... FOREVAIRE!
LISTEN, YOU FOOL! IF THAT BOMB GOES OFF, IT'LL MEAN YOUR DEATH AS WELL!
YOU DON'T SCARE ME, AVENGER!
BATROC WILL FIND IT IN TIME!
DON'T COUNT ON IT, SWORDS-MAN!
FAR AS I'M CONCERNED... YOUR TIME HAS JUST RUN OUT!
A SECOND MORE AND HE'D HAVE HAD ME!
9.

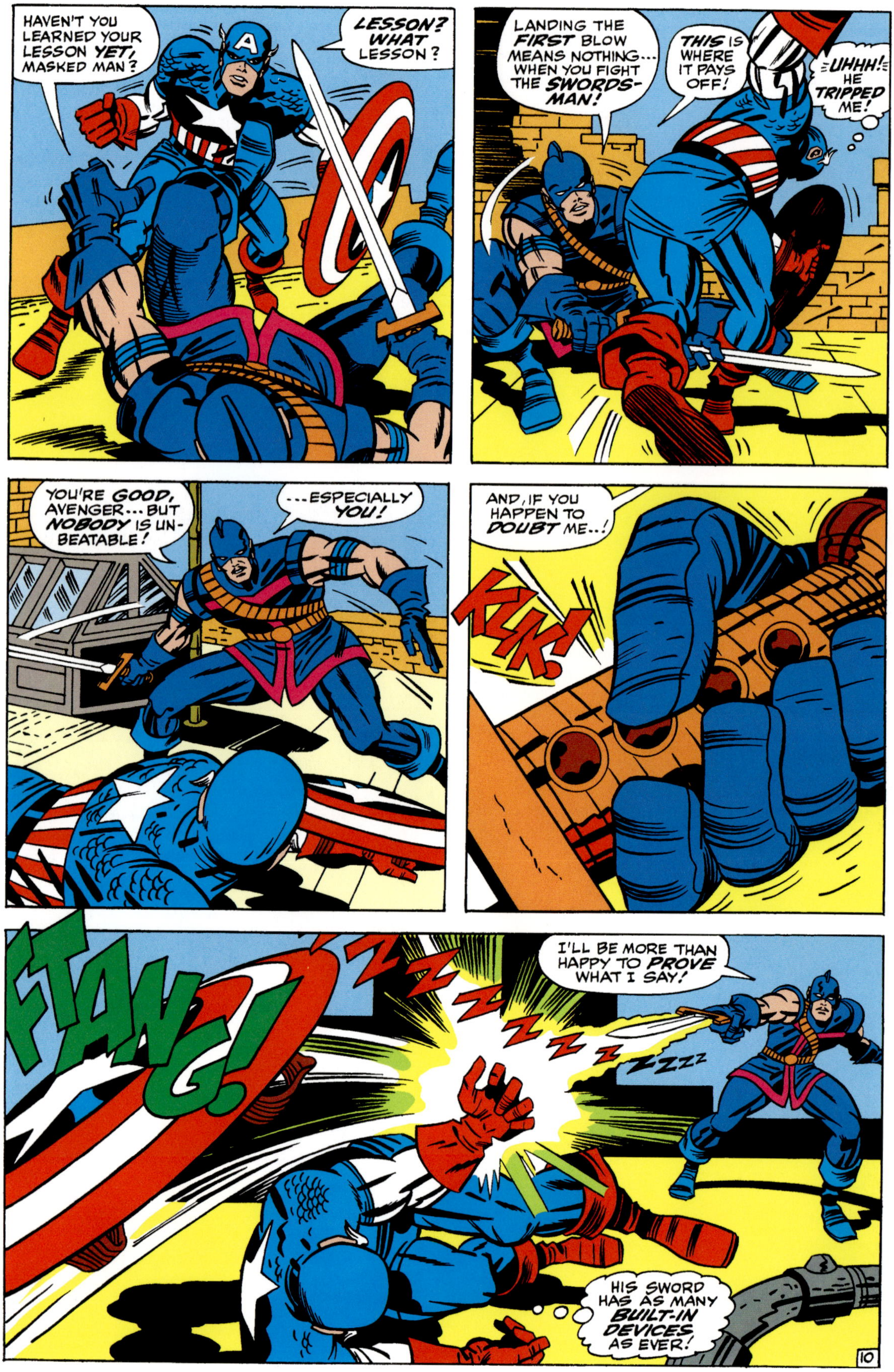
HAVEN'T YOU LEARNED YOUR LESSON YET, MASKED MAN?
LESSON? WHAT LESSON?
LANDING THE FIRST BLOW MEANS NOTHING... WHEN YOU FIGHT THE SWORDS-MAN!
THIS IS WHERE IT PAYS OFF!
UHHH! HE TRIPPED ME!
YOU'RE GOOD, AVENGER... BUT NOBODY IS UN-BEATABLE!
...ESPECIALLY YOU!
AND, IF YOU HAPPEN TO DOUBT ME..!
KLIK!
I'LL BE MORE THAN HAPPY TO PROVE WHAT I SAY!
TANG!
ZZZZZZZZZZ
HIS SWORD HAS AS MANY BUILT-IN DEVICES AS EVER!
10

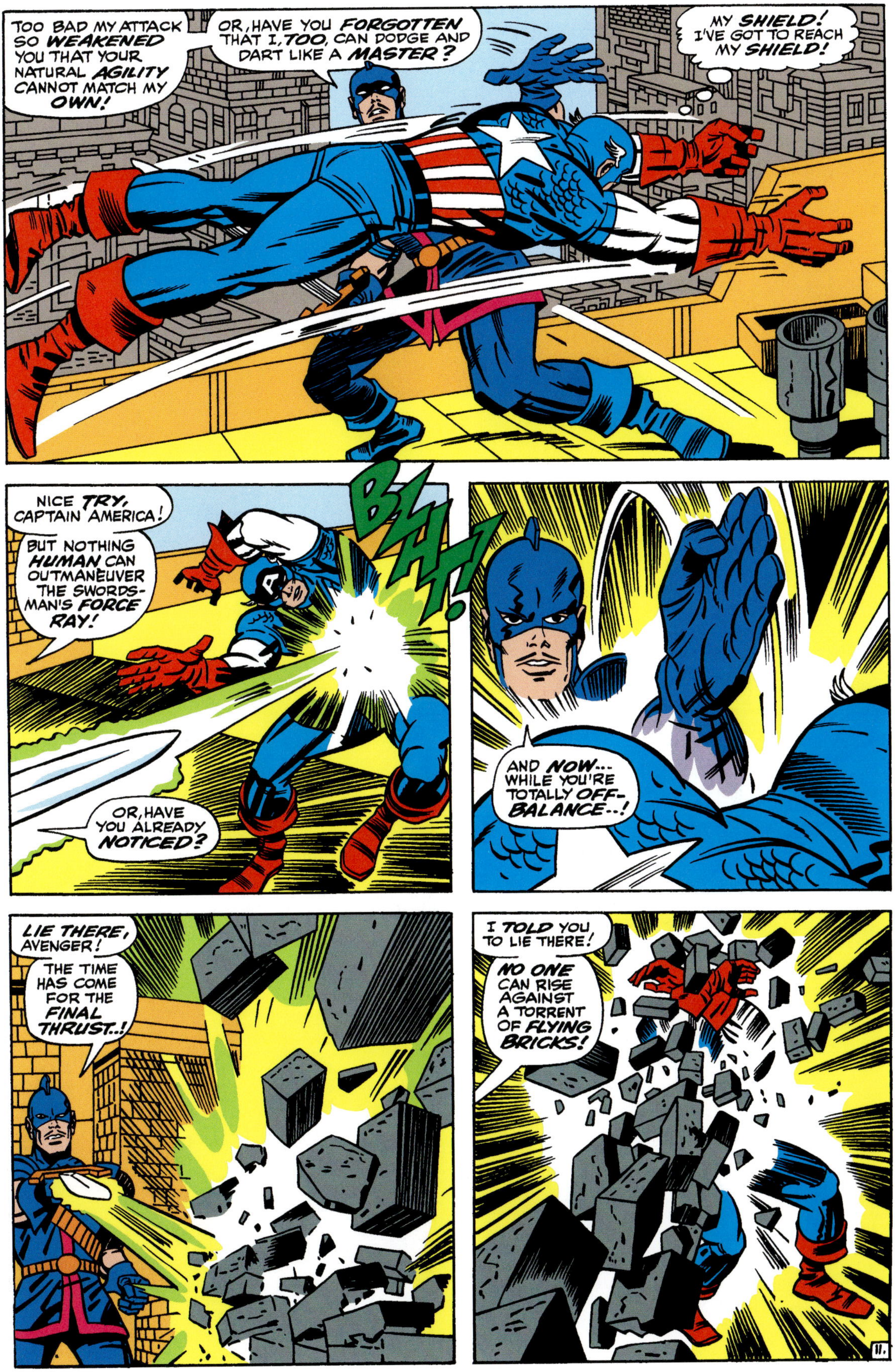

TOO BAD MY ATTACK SO WEAKENED YOU THAT YOUR NATURAL AGILITY CANNOT MATCH MY OWN!
OR, HAVE YOU FORGOTTEN THAT I, TOO, CAN DODGE AND DART LIKE A MASTER?
MY SHIELD! I'VE GOT TO REACH MY SHIELD!
NICE TRY, CAPTAIN AMERICA!
BUT NOTHING HUMAN CAN OUTMANEUVER THE SWORDS-MAN'S FORCE RAY!
BZAK!
OR, HAVE YOU ALREADY NOTICED?
AND NOW... WHILE YOU'RE TOTALLY OFF-BALANCE..!
LIE THERE, AVENGER!
THE TIME HAS COME FOR THE FINAL THRUST..!
I TOLD YOU TO LIE THERE!
NO ONE CAN RISE AGAINST A TORRENT OF FLYING BRICKS!
11.

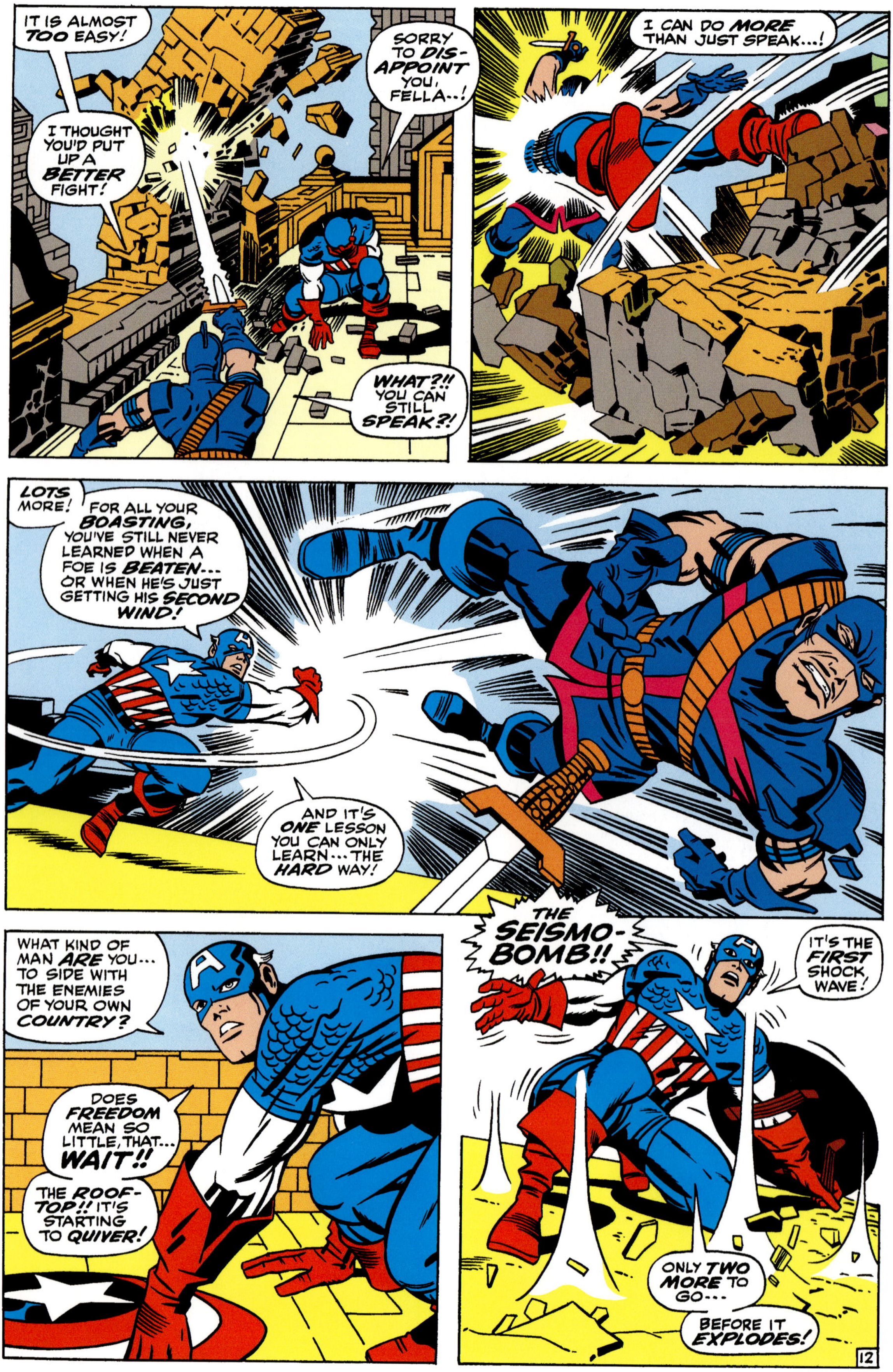
IT IS ALMOST TOO EASY!
I THOUGHT YOU'D PUT UP A BETTER FIGHT!
SORRY TO DIS-APPOINT YOU, FELLA..!
WHAT?!! YOU CAN STILL SPEAK?!
I CAN DO MORE THAN JUST SPEAK...!
LOTS MORE!
FOR ALL YOUR BOASTING, YOU'VE STILL NEVER LEARNED WHEN A FOE IS BEATEN... OR WHEN HE'S JUST GETTING HIS SECOND WIND!
AND IT'S ONE LESSON YOU CAN ONLY LEARN... THE HARD WAY!
WHAT KIND OF MAN ARE YOU... TO SIDE WITH THE ENEMIES OF YOUR OWN COUNTRY?
DOES FREEDOM MEAN SO LITTLE, THAT... WAIT!!
THE ROOF-TOP!! IT'S STARTING TO QUIVER!
THE SEISMO-BOMB!!
IT'S THE FIRST SHOCK WAVE!
ONLY TWO MORE TO GO...
BEFORE IT EXPLODES!
12

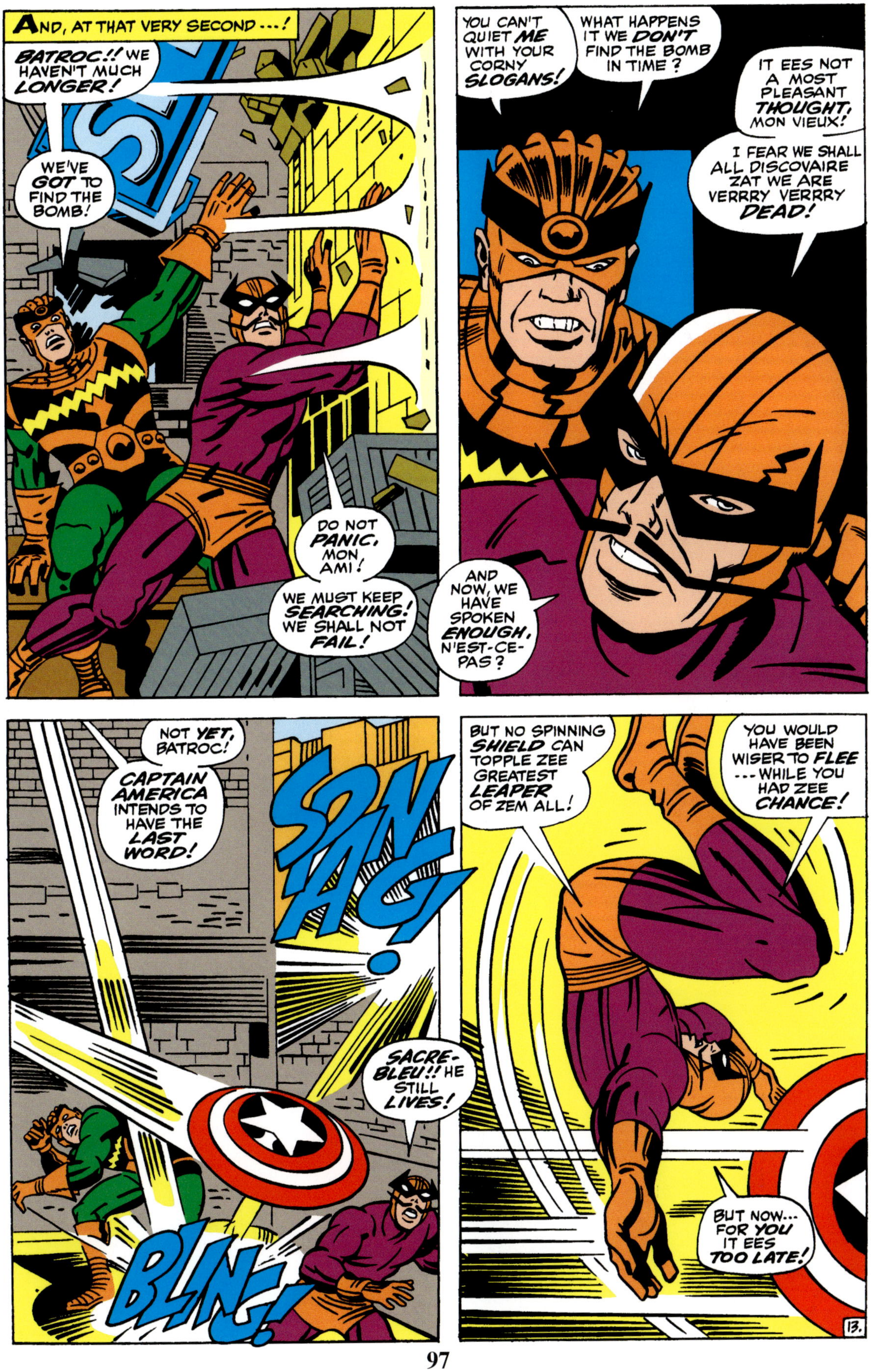
AND, AT THAT VERY SECOND ---!
BATROC!! WE HAVEN'T MUCH LONGER!
WE'VE GOT TO FIND THE BOMB!
DO NOT PANIC, MON AMI!
WE MUST KEEP SEARCHING! WE SHALL NOT FAIL!
YOU CAN'T QUIET ME WITH YOUR CORNY SLOGANS!
WHAT HAPPENS IT WE DON'T FIND THE BOMB IN TIME?
IT EES NOT A MOST PLEASANT THOUGHT, MON VIEUX!
I FEAR WE SHALL ALL DISCOVAIRE ZAT WE ARE VERRRY VERRRY DEAD!
AND NOW, WE HAVE SPOKEN ENOUGH, N'EST-CE-PAS?
NOT YET, BATROC!
CAPTAIN AMERICA INTENDS TO HAVE THE LAST WORD!
SPANG!
SACRE-BLEU!! HE STILL LIVES!
BLING!
BUT NO SPINNING SHIELD CAN TOPPLE ZEE GREATEST LEAPER OF ZEM ALL!
YOU WOULD HAVE BEEN WISER TO FLEE --- WHILE YOU HAD ZEE CHANCE!
BUT NOW... FOR YOU IT EES TOO LATE!
13.

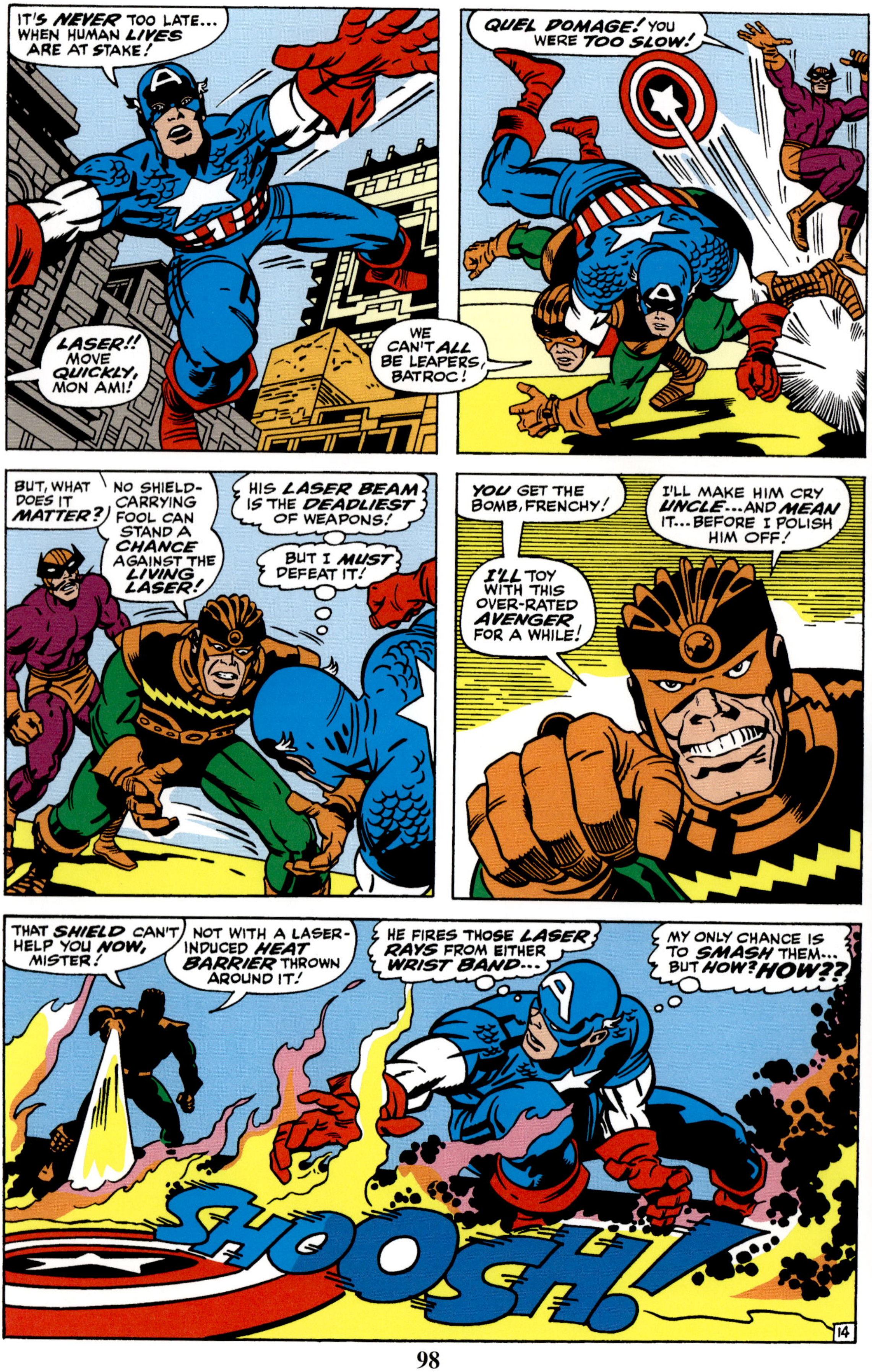

IT'S NEVER TOO LATE... WHEN HUMAN LIVES ARE AT STAKE!
LASER!! MOVE QUICKLY, MON AMI!
WE CAN'T ALL BE LEAPERS, BATROC!
QUEL DOMAGE! YOU WERE TOO SLOW!
BUT, WHAT DOES IT MATTER?
NO SHIELD-CARRYING FOOL CAN STAND A CHANCE AGAINST THE LIVING LASER!
HIS LASER BEAM IS THE DEADLIEST OF WEAPONS!
BUT I MUST DEFEAT IT!
YOU GET THE BOMB, FRENCHY!
I'LL TOY WITH THIS OVER-RATED AVENGER FOR A WHILE!
I'LL MAKE HIM CRY UNCLE...AND MEAN IT...BEFORE I POLISH HIM OFF!
THAT SHIELD CAN'T HELP YOU NOW, MISTER!
NOT WITH A LASER-INDUCED HEAT BARRIER THROWN AROUND IT!
HE FIRES THOSE LASER RAYS FROM EITHER WRIST BAND...
MY ONLY CHANCE IS TO SMASH THEM... BUT HOW? HOW??
SHOOSH!
14

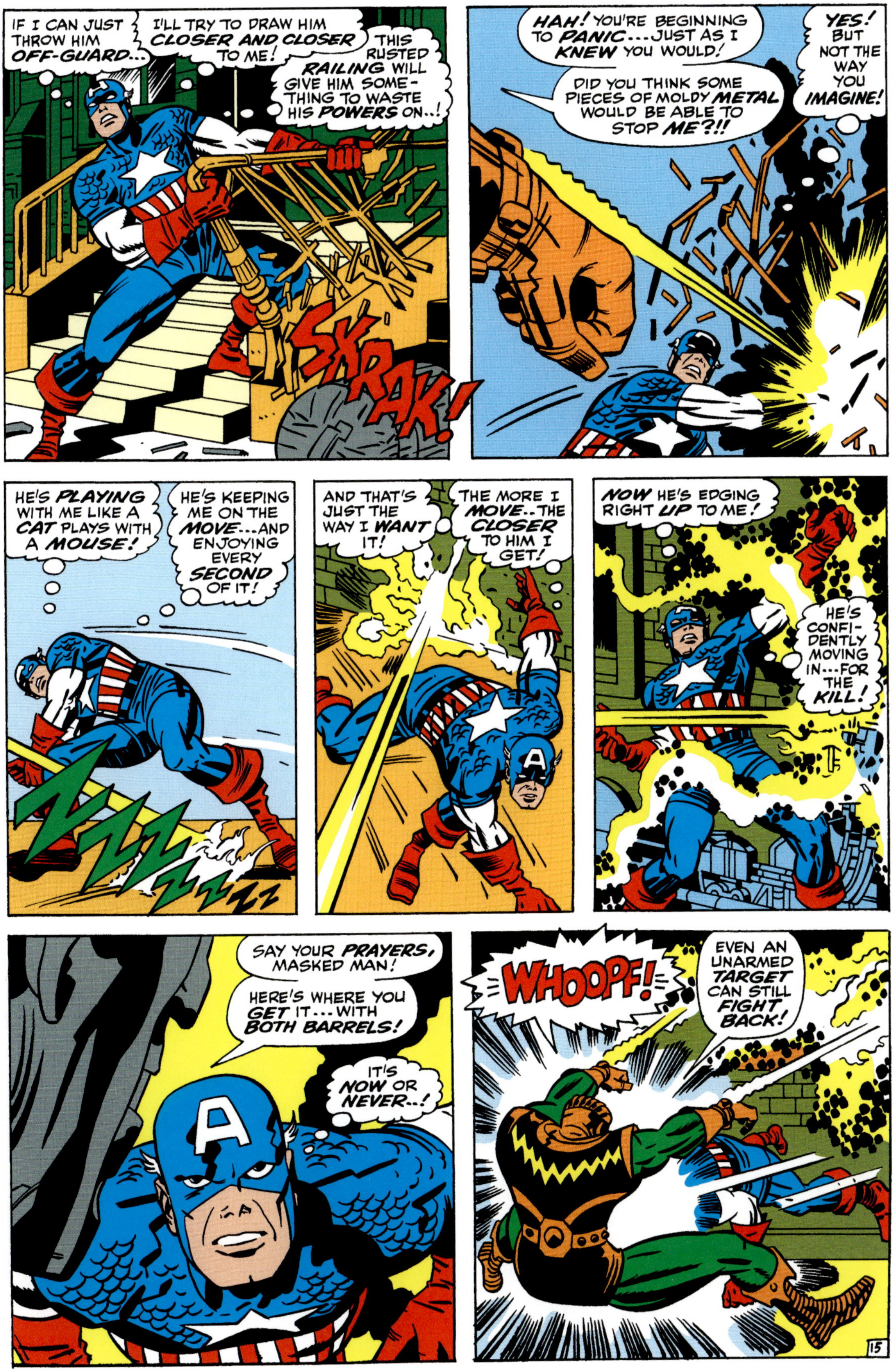
IF I CAN JUST THROW HIM OFF-GUARD...
I'LL TRY TO DRAW HIM CLOSER AND CLOSER TO ME!
THIS RUSTED RAILING WILL GIVE HIM SOMETHING TO WASTE HIS POWERS ON..!
SKRAK!
HAH! YOU'RE BEGINNING TO PANIC...JUST AS I KNEW YOU WOULD!
DID YOU THINK SOME PIECES OF MOLDY METAL WOULD BE ABLE TO STOP ME?!!
YES! BUT NOT THE WAY YOU IMAGINE!
HE'S PLAYING WITH ME LIKE A CAT PLAYS WITH A MOUSE!
HE'S KEEPING ME ON THE MOVE...AND ENJOYING EVERY SECOND OF IT!
AND THAT'S JUST THE WAY I WANT IT!
THE MORE I MOVE..THE CLOSER TO HIM I GET!
NOW HE'S EDGING RIGHT UP TO ME!
HE'S CONFIDENTLY MOVING IN...FOR THE KILL!
SAY YOUR PRAYERS, MASKED MAN!
HERE'S WHERE YOU GET IT...WITH BOTH BARRELS!
IT'S NOW OR NEVER..!
WHOOPF!
EVEN AN UNARMED TARGET CAN STILL FIGHT BACK!
15

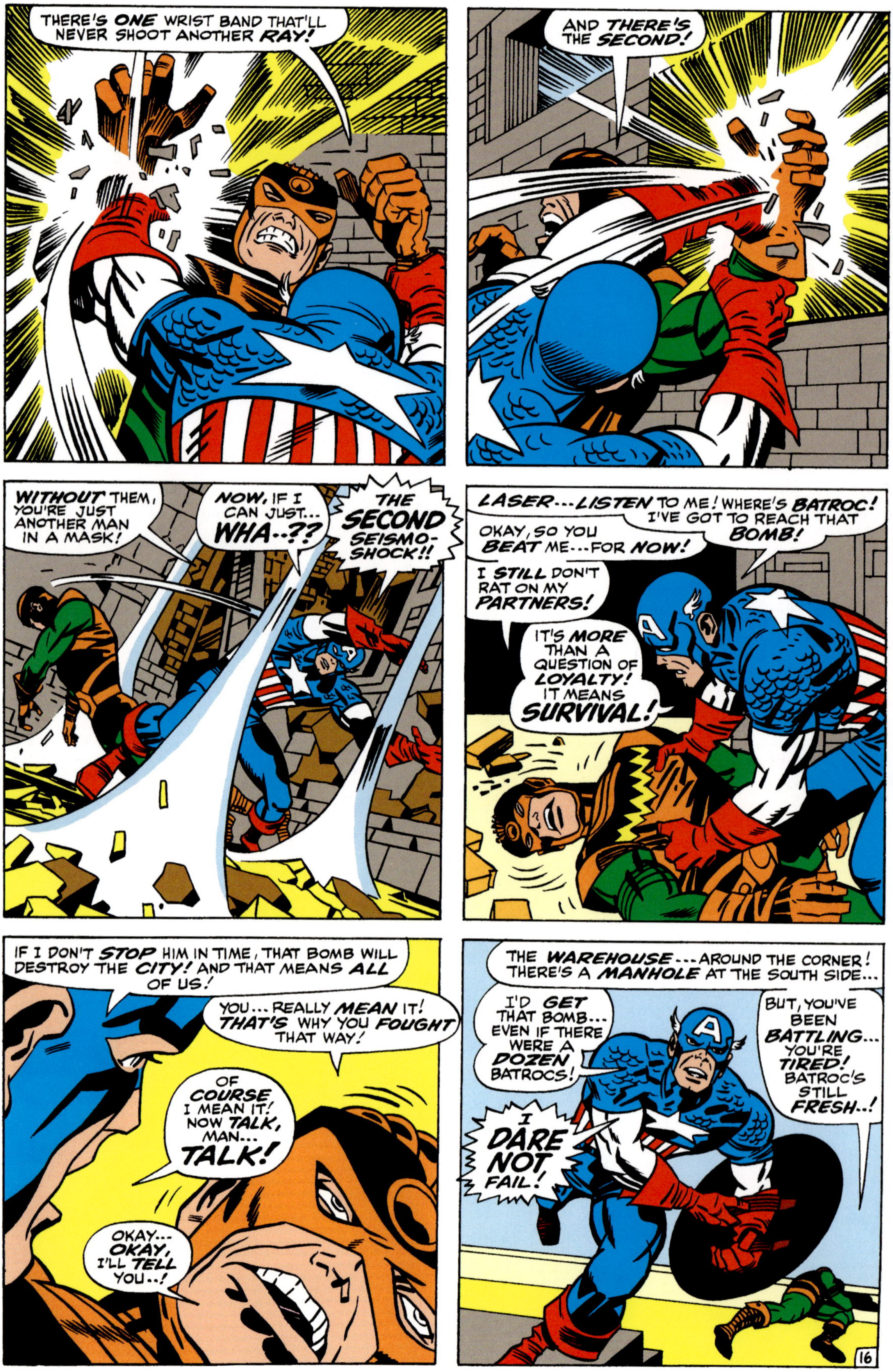
THERE'S ONE WRIST BAND THAT'LL NEVER SHOOT ANOTHER RAY!
AND THERE'S THE SECOND!
WITHOUT THEM, YOU'RE JUST ANOTHER MAN IN A MASK!
NOW, IF I CAN JUST... WHA--??
THE SECOND SEISMO-SHOCK!!
LASER...LISTEN TO ME! WHERE'S BATROC! I'VE GOT TO REACH THAT BOMB!
OKAY, SO YOU BEAT ME...FOR NOW!
I STILL DON'T RAT ON MY PARTNERS!
IT'S MORE THAN A QUESTION OF LOYALTY! IT MEANS SURVIVAL!
IF I DON'T STOP HIM IN TIME, THAT BOMB WILL DESTROY THE CITY! AND THAT MEANS ALL OF US!
YOU... REALLY MEAN IT! THAT'S WHY YOU FOUGHT THAT WAY!
OF COURSE I MEAN IT! NOW TALK, MAN... TALK!
OKAY... OKAY, I'LL TELL YOU..!
THE WAREHOUSE...AROUND THE CORNER! THERE'S A MANHOLE AT THE SOUTH SIDE...
I'D GET THAT BOMB... EVEN IF THERE WERE A DOZEN BATROCS!
BUT, YOU'VE BEEN BATTLING... YOU'RE TIRED! BATROC'S STILL FRESH..!
I DARE NOT FAIL!
16

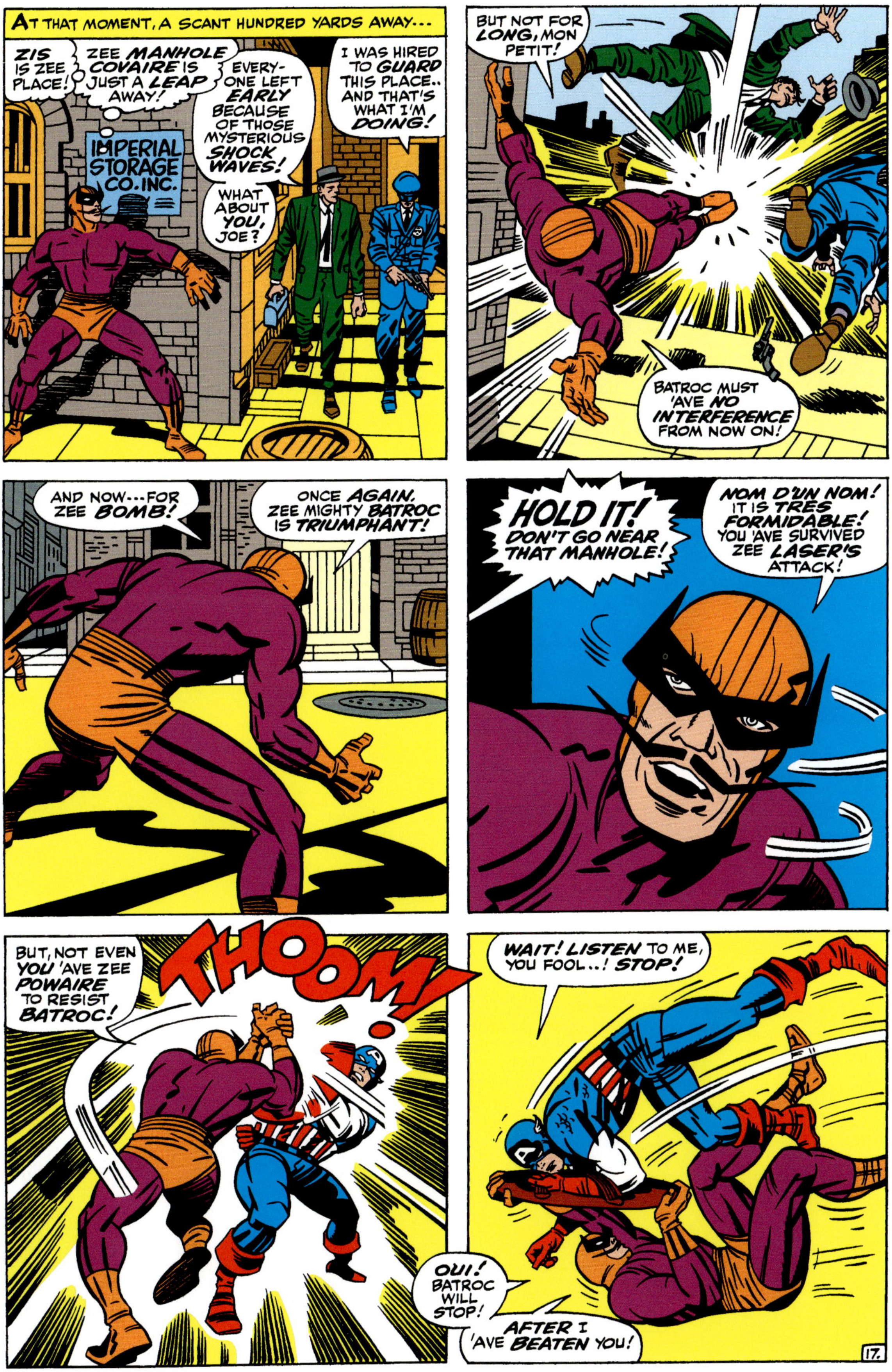
AT THAT MOMENT, A SCANT HUNDRED YARDS AWAY...
ZIS IS ZEE PLACE!
ZEE MANHOLE COVAIRE IS JUST A LEAP AWAY!
IMPERIAL STORAGE CO. INC.
EVERY-ONE LEFT EARLY BECAUSE OF THOSE MYSTERIOUS SHOCK WAVES!
WHAT ABOUT YOU, JOE?
I WAS HIRED TO GUARD THIS PLACE.. AND THAT'S WHAT I'M DOING!
BUT NOT FOR LONG, MON PETIT!
BATROC MUST 'AVE NO INTERFERENCE FROM NOW ON!
AND NOW...FOR ZEE BOMB!
ONCE AGAIN, ZEE MIGHTY BATROC IS TRIUMPHANT!
HOLD IT! DON'T GO NEAR THAT MANHOLE!
NOM D'UN NOM! IT IS TRES FORMIDABLE! YOU 'AVE SURVIVED ZEE LASER'S ATTACK!
BUT, NOT EVEN YOU 'AVE ZEE POWAIRE TO RESIST BATROC!
THOOM!
WAIT! LISTEN TO ME, YOU FOOL..! STOP!
OUI! BATROC WILL STOP!
AFTER I 'AVE BEATEN YOU!
17.

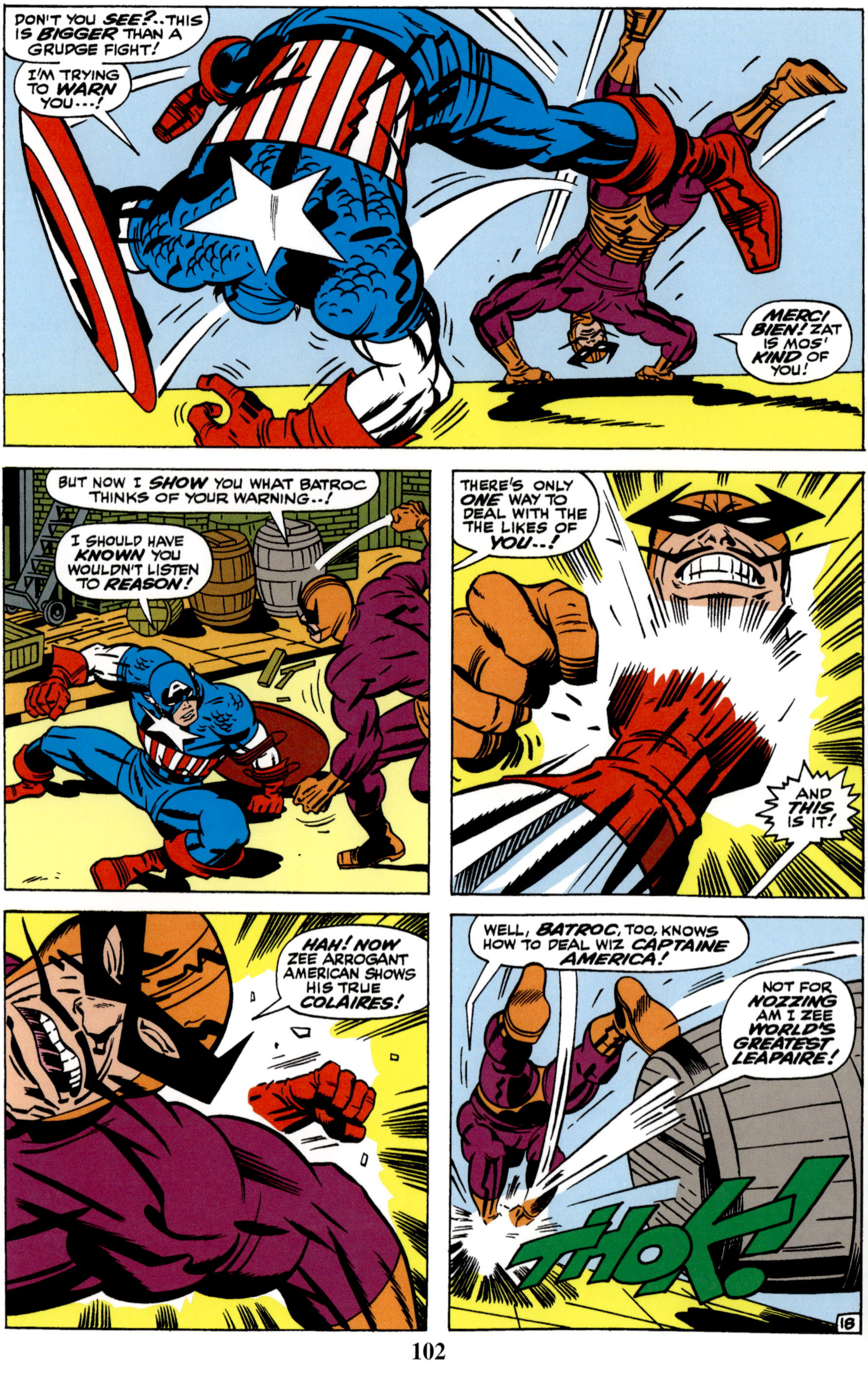
DON'T YOU SEE?..THIS IS BIGGER THAN A GRUDGE FIGHT!
I'M TRYING TO WARN YOU...!
MERCI BIEN! ZAT IS MOS' KIND OF YOU!
BUT NOW I SHOW YOU WHAT BATROC THINKS OF YOUR WARNING..!
I SHOULD HAVE KNOWN YOU WOULDN'T LISTEN TO REASON!
THERE'S ONLY ONE WAY TO DEAL WITH THE THE LIKES OF YOU..!
AND THIS IS IT!
HAH! NOW ZEE ARROGANT AMERICAN SHOWS HIS TRUE COLAIRES!
WELL, BATROC, TOO, KNOWS HOW TO DEAL WIZ CAPTAINE AMERICA!
NOT FOR NOZZING AM I ZEE WORLD'S GREATEST LEAPAIRE!
THOK!
18

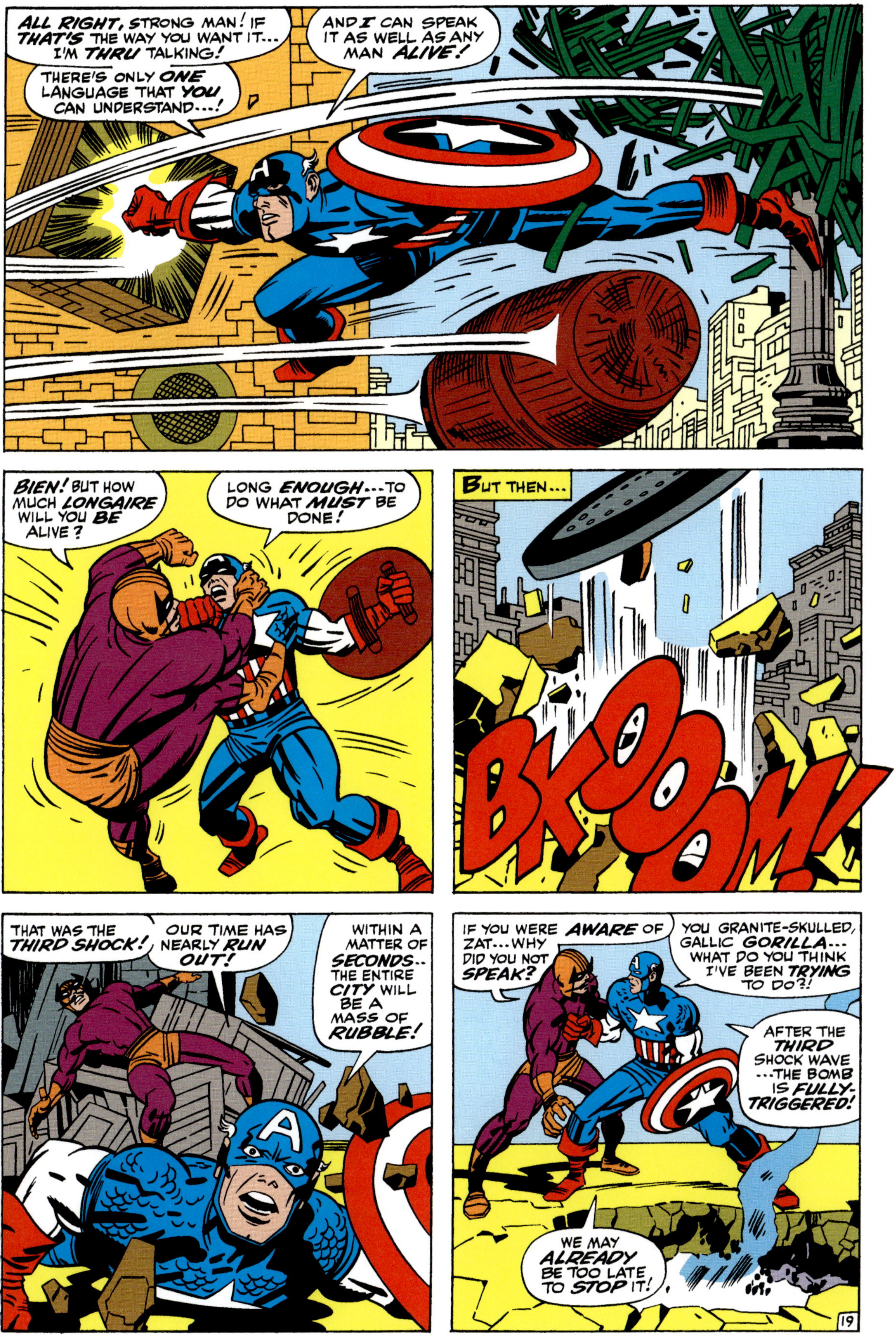
ALL RIGHT, STRONG MAN! IF THAT'S THE WAY YOU WANT IT... I'M THRU TALKING!
THERE'S ONLY ONE LANGUAGE THAT YOU CAN UNDERSTAND...!
AND I CAN SPEAK IT AS WELL AS ANY MAN ALIVE!
BIEN! BUT HOW MUCH LONGAIRE WILL YOU BE ALIVE?
LONG ENOUGH...TO DO WHAT MUST BE DONE!
BUT THEN...
BKOOOOM!
THAT WAS THE THIRD SHOCK!
OUR TIME HAS NEARLY RUN OUT!
WITHIN A MATTER OF SECONDS.. THE ENTIRE CITY WILL BE A MASS OF RUBBLE!
IF YOU WERE AWARE OF ZAT...WHY DID YOU NOT SPEAK?
YOU GRANITE-SKULLED, GALLIC GORILLA... WHAT DO YOU THINK I'VE BEEN TRYING TO DO?!
AFTER THE THIRD SHOCK WAVE ...THE BOMB IS FULLY-TRIGGERED!
WE MAY ALREADY BE TOO LATE TO STOP IT!
19

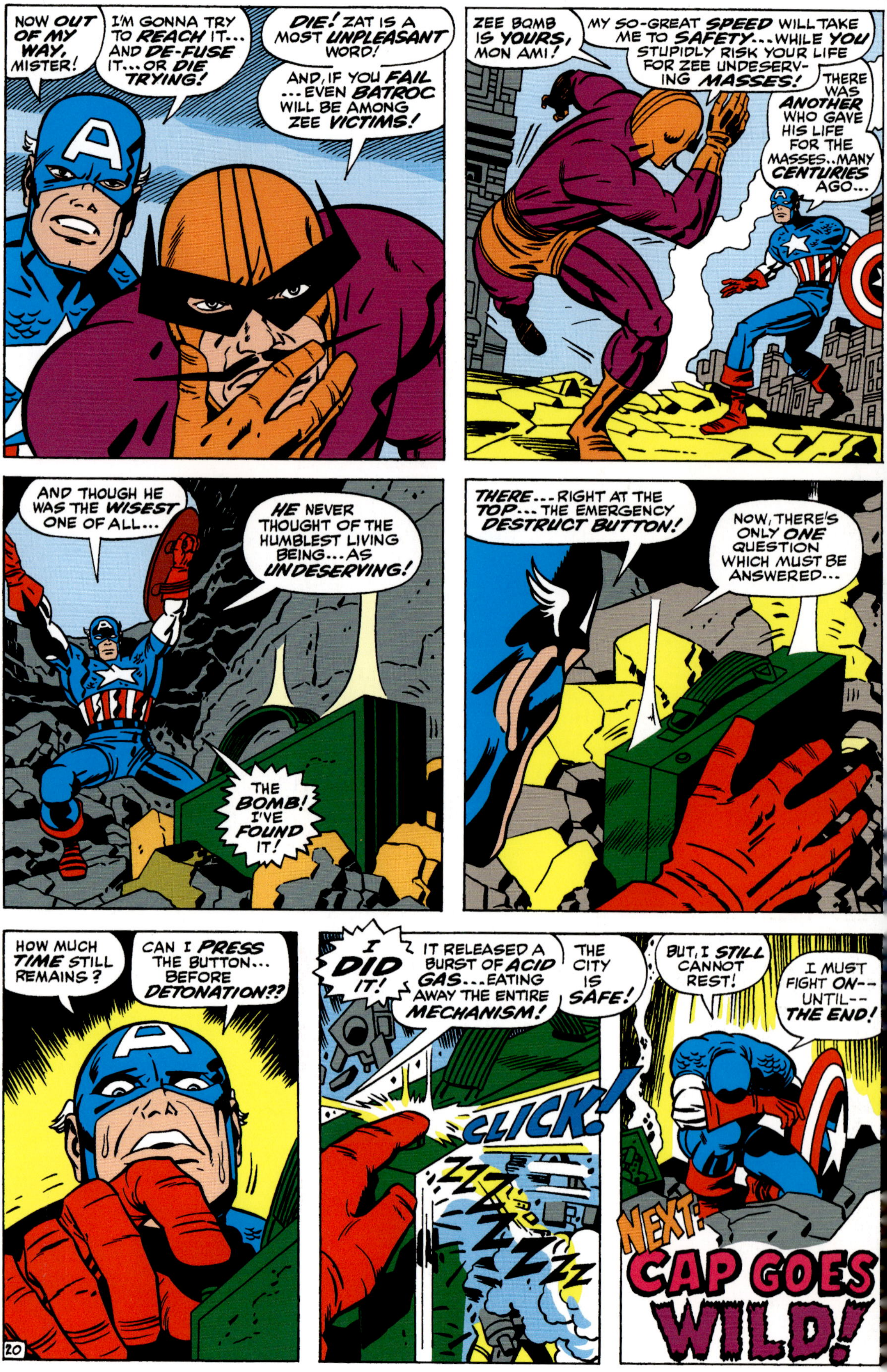
NOW OUT OF MY WAY, MISTER!
I'M GONNA TRY TO REACH IT... AND DE-FUSE IT...OR DIE TRYING!
DIE! ZAT IS A MOST UNPLEASANT WORD!
AND, IF YOU FAIL ...EVEN BATROC WILL BE AMONG ZEE VICTIMS!
ZEE BOMB IS YOURS, MON AMI!
MY SO-GREAT SPEED WILL TAKE ME TO SAFETY...WHILE YOU STUPIDLY RISK YOUR LIFE FOR ZEE UNDESERV-ING MASSES!
THERE WAS ANOTHER WHO GAVE HIS LIFE FOR THE MASSES..MANY CENTURIES AGO...
AND THOUGH HE WAS THE WISEST ONE OF ALL...
HE NEVER THOUGHT OF THE HUMBLEST LIVING BEING...AS UNDESERVING!
THE BOMB! I'VE FOUND IT!
THERE...RIGHT AT THE TOP...THE EMERGENCY DESTRUCT BUTTON!
NOW, THERE'S ONLY ONE QUESTION WHICH MUST BE ANSWERED...
HOW MUCH TIME STILL REMAINS?
CAN I PRESS THE BUTTON... BEFORE DETONATION??
20
I DID IT!
IT RELEASED A BURST OF ACID GAS...EATING AWAY THE ENTIRE MECHANISM!
THE CITY IS SAFE!
CLICK!
ZZZZZZ
BUT, I STILL CANNOT REST!
I MUST FIGHT ON--UNTIL--THE END!
NEXT: CAP GOES WILD!

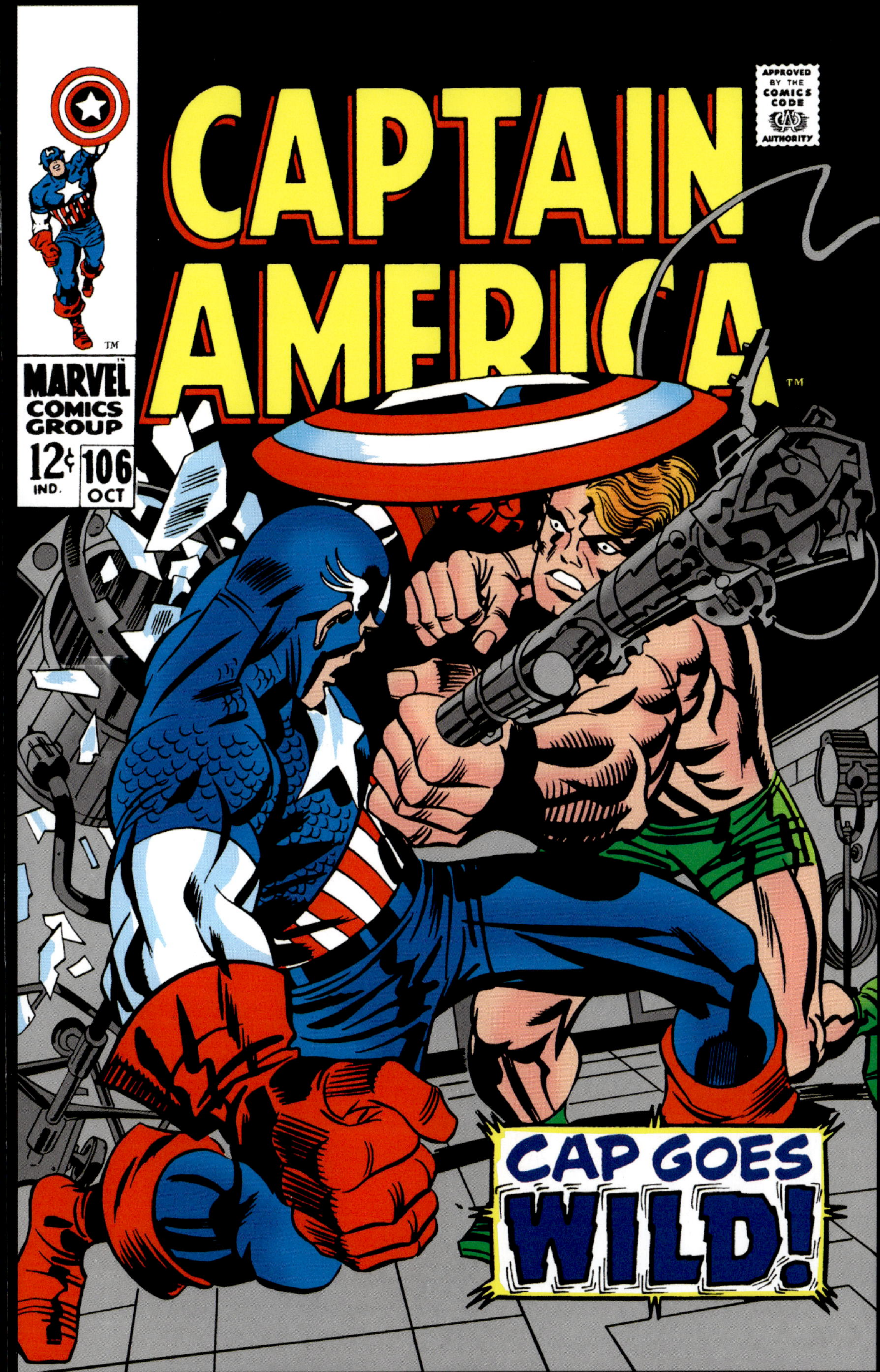

CAPTAIN AMERICA
MARVEL COMICS GROUP
12¢ IND.
106 OCT
APPROVED BY THE COMICS CODE AUTHORITY
CAP GOES WILD!

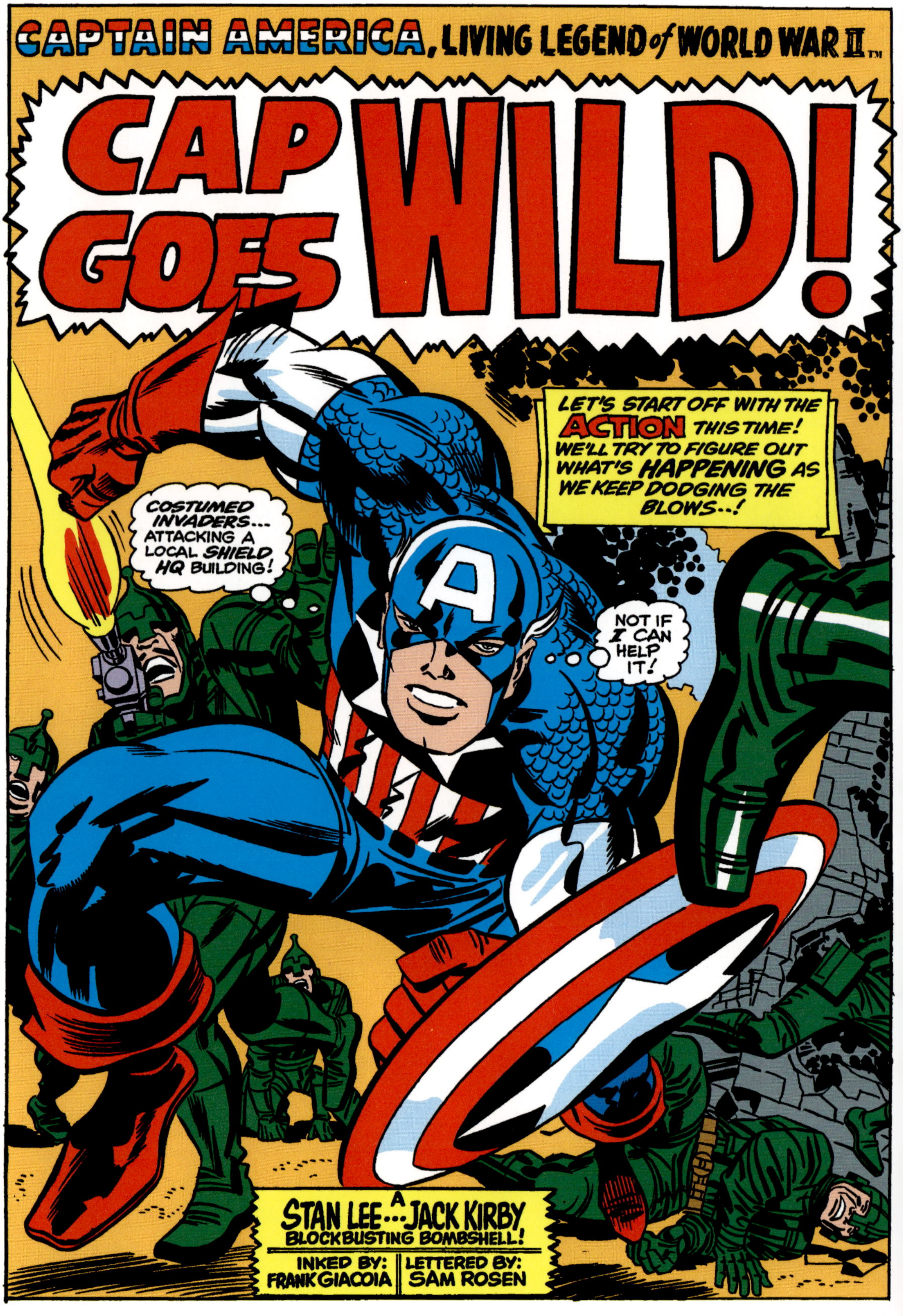
CAPTAIN AMERICA, LIVING LEGEND of WORLD WAR II™
CAP GOES WILD!
LET'S START OFF WITH THE ACTION THIS TIME! WE'LL TRY TO FIGURE OUT WHAT'S HAPPENING AS WE KEEP DODGING THE BLOWS..!
COSTUMED INVADERS... ATTACKING A LOCAL SHIELD HQ BUILDING!
NOT IF I CAN HELP IT!
STAN LEE...A JACK KIRBY BLOCKBUSTING BOMBSHELL!
INKED BY: FRANK GIACOIA
LETTERED BY: SAM ROSEN

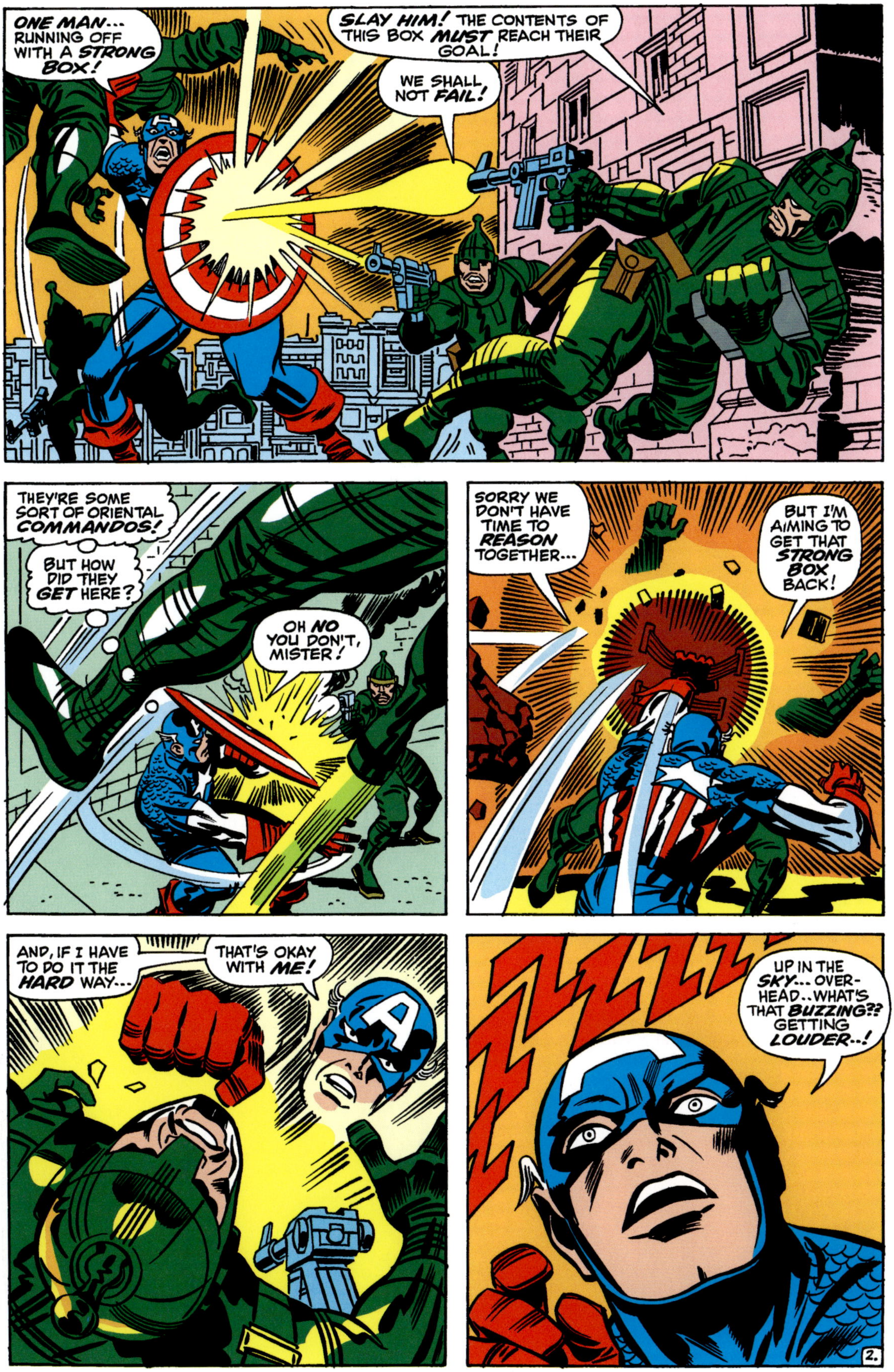
ONE MAN... RUNNING OFF WITH A STRONG BOX!
SLAY HIM! THE CONTENTS OF THIS BOX MUST REACH THEIR GOAL!
WE SHALL NOT FAIL!
THEY'RE SOME SORT OF ORIENTAL COMMANDOS!
BUT HOW DID THEY GET HERE?
OH NO YOU DON'T, MISTER!
SORRY WE DON'T HAVE TIME TO REASON TOGETHER...
BUT I'M AIMING TO GET THAT STRONG BOX BACK!
AND, IF I HAVE TO DO IT THE HARD WAY...
THAT'S OKAY WITH ME!
ZZZZZZ
UP IN THE SKY... OVER-HEAD.. WHAT'S THAT BUZZING?? GETTING LOUDER..!
2.

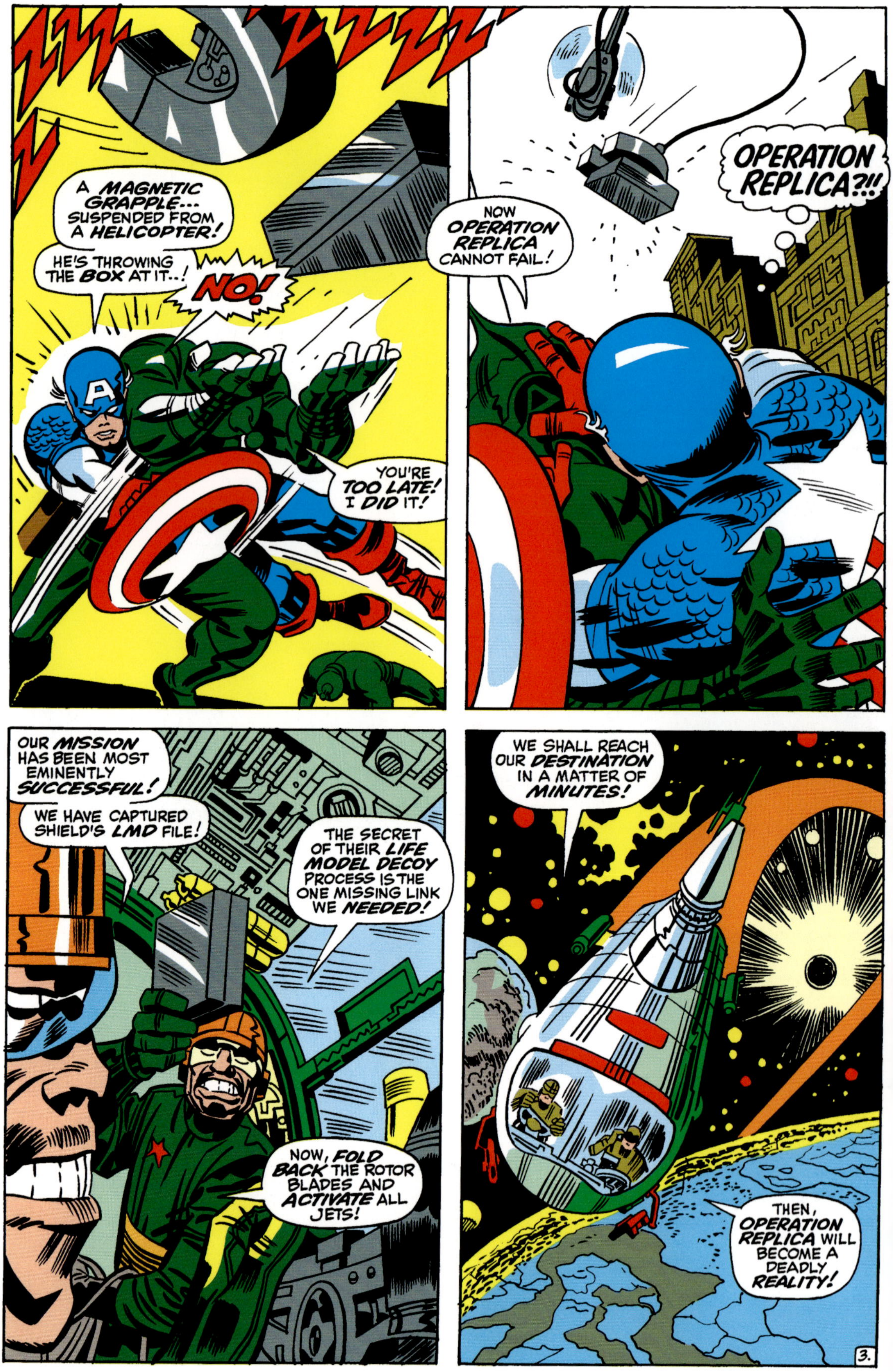
ZZZZZZZZZZ
A MAGNETIC GRAPPLE... SUSPENDED FROM A HELICOPTER!
HE'S THROWING THE BOX AT IT..!
NO!
YOU'RE TOO LATE! I DID IT!
NOW OPERATION REPLICA CANNOT FAIL!
OPERATION REPLICA?!!
OUR MISSION HAS BEEN MOST EMINENTLY SUCCESSFUL!
WE HAVE CAPTURED SHIELD'S LMD FILE!
THE SECRET OF THEIR LIFE MODEL DECOY PROCESS IS THE ONE MISSING LINK WE NEEDED!
NOW, FOLD BACK THE ROTOR BLADES AND ACTIVATE ALL JETS!
WE SHALL REACH OUR DESTINATION IN A MATTER OF MINUTES!
THEN, OPERATION REPLICA WILL BECOME A DEADLY REALITY!
3.

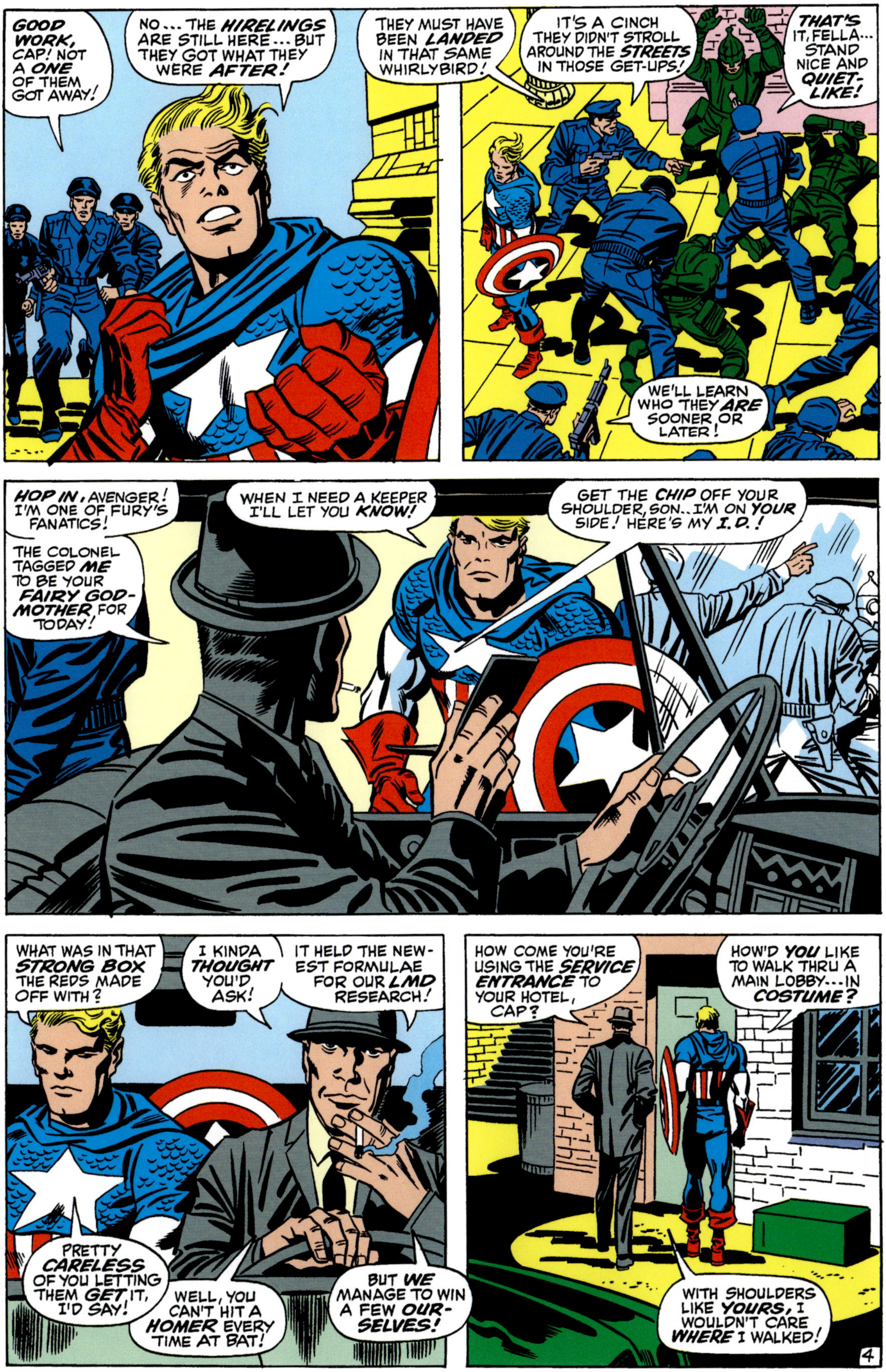
GOOD WORK, CAP! NOT A ONE OF THEM GOT AWAY!
NO... THE HIRELINGS ARE STILL HERE... BUT THEY GOT WHAT THEY WERE AFTER!
THEY MUST HAVE BEEN LANDED IN THAT SAME WHIRLYBIRD!
IT'S A CINCH THEY DIDN'T STROLL AROUND THE STREETS IN THOSE GET-UPS!
THAT'S IT, FELLA... STAND NICE AND QUIET-LIKE!
WE'LL LEARN WHO THEY ARE SOONER OR LATER!
HOP IN, AVENGER! I'M ONE OF FURY'S FANATICS!
THE COLONEL TAGGED ME TO BE YOUR FAIRY GOD-MOTHER FOR TODAY!
WHEN I NEED A KEEPER I'LL LET YOU KNOW!
GET THE CHIP OFF YOUR SHOULDER, SON.. I'M ON YOUR SIDE! HERE'S MY I.D.!
WHAT WAS IN THAT STRONG BOX THE REDS MADE OFF WITH?
I KINDA THOUGHT YOU'D ASK!
IT HELD THE NEW-EST FORMULAE FOR OUR LMD RESEARCH!
PRETTY CARELESS OF YOU LETTING THEM GET IT, I'D SAY!
WELL, YOU CAN'T HIT A HOMER EVERY TIME AT BAT!
BUT WE MANAGE TO WIN A FEW OUR-SELVES!
HOW COME YOU'RE USING THE SERVICE ENTRANCE TO YOUR HOTEL, CAP?
HOW'D YOU LIKE TO WALK THRU A MAIN LOBBY... IN COSTUME?
WITH SHOULDERS LIKE YOURS, I WOULDN'T CARE WHERE I WALKED!
4

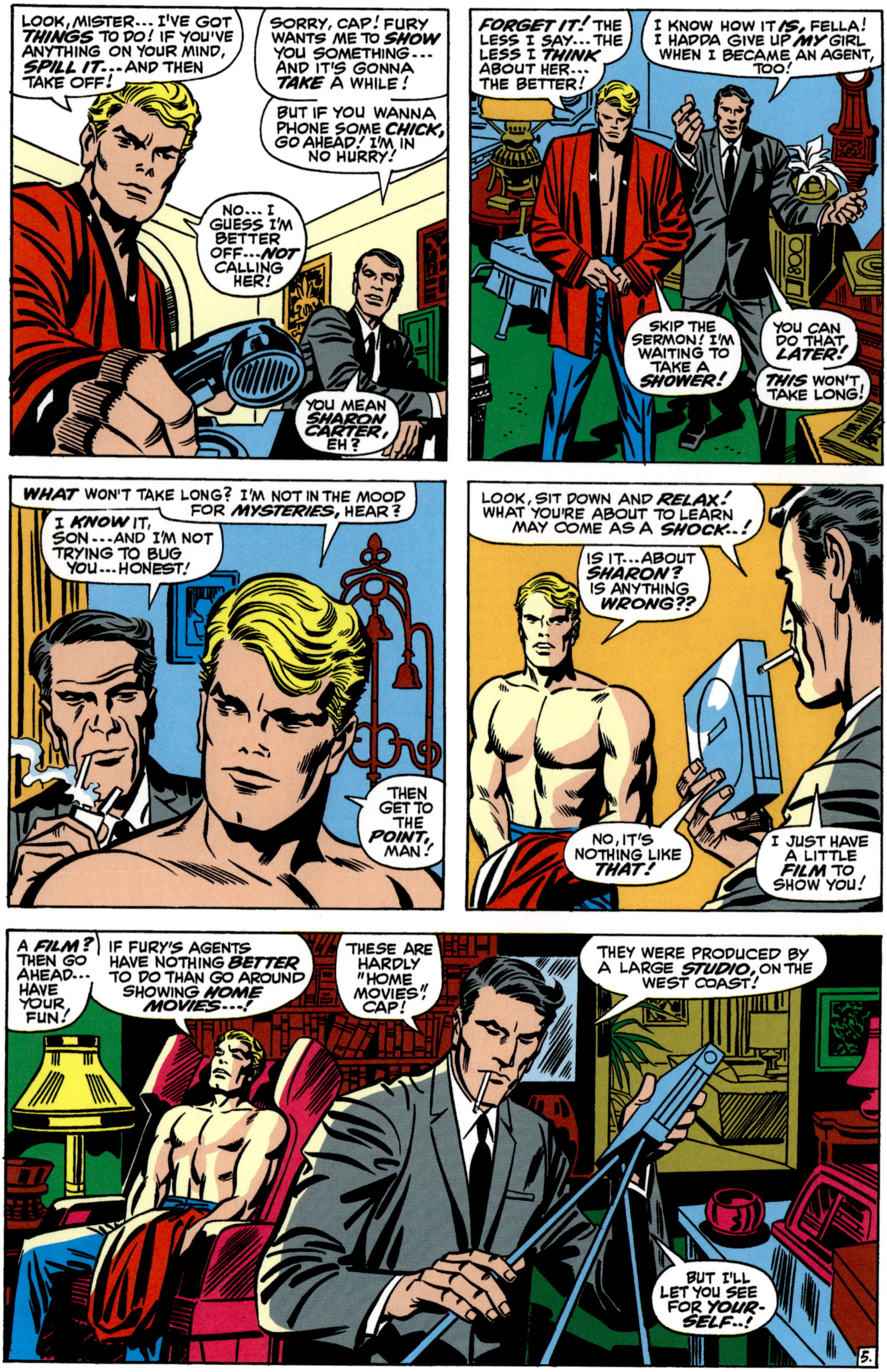
LOOK, MISTER... I'VE GOT THINGS TO DO! IF YOU'VE ANYTHING ON YOUR MIND, SPILL IT... AND THEN TAKE OFF!
SORRY, CAP! FURY WANTS ME TO SHOW YOU SOMETHING... AND IT'S GONNA TAKE A WHILE!
BUT IF YOU WANNA PHONE SOME CHICK, GO AHEAD! I'M IN NO HURRY!
NO... I GUESS I'M BETTER OFF... NOT CALLING HER!
YOU MEAN SHARON CARTER, EH?
FORGET IT! THE LESS I SAY... THE LESS I THINK ABOUT HER... THE BETTER!
I KNOW HOW IT IS, FELLA! I HADDA GIVE UP MY GIRL WHEN I BECAME AN AGENT, TOO!
SKIP THE SERMON! I'M WAITING TO TAKE A SHOWER!
YOU CAN DO THAT LATER!
THIS WON'T TAKE LONG!
WHAT WON'T TAKE LONG? I'M NOT IN THE MOOD FOR MYSTERIES, HEAR?
I KNOW IT, SON... AND I'M NOT TRYING TO BUG YOU... HONEST!
THEN GET TO THE POINT, MAN!
LOOK, SIT DOWN AND RELAX! WHAT YOU'RE ABOUT TO LEARN MAY COME AS A SHOCK..!
IS IT... ABOUT SHARON? IS ANYTHING WRONG??
NO, IT'S NOTHING LIKE THAT!
I JUST HAVE A LITTLE FILM TO SHOW YOU!
A FILM? THEN GO AHEAD... HAVE YOUR FUN!
IF FURY'S AGENTS HAVE NOTHING BETTER TO DO THAN GO AROUND SHOWING HOME MOVIES...!
THESE ARE HARDLY "HOME MOVIES," CAP!
THEY WERE PRODUCED BY A LARGE STUDIO, ON THE WEST COAST!
BUT I'LL LET YOU SEE FOR YOURSELF..!
5.

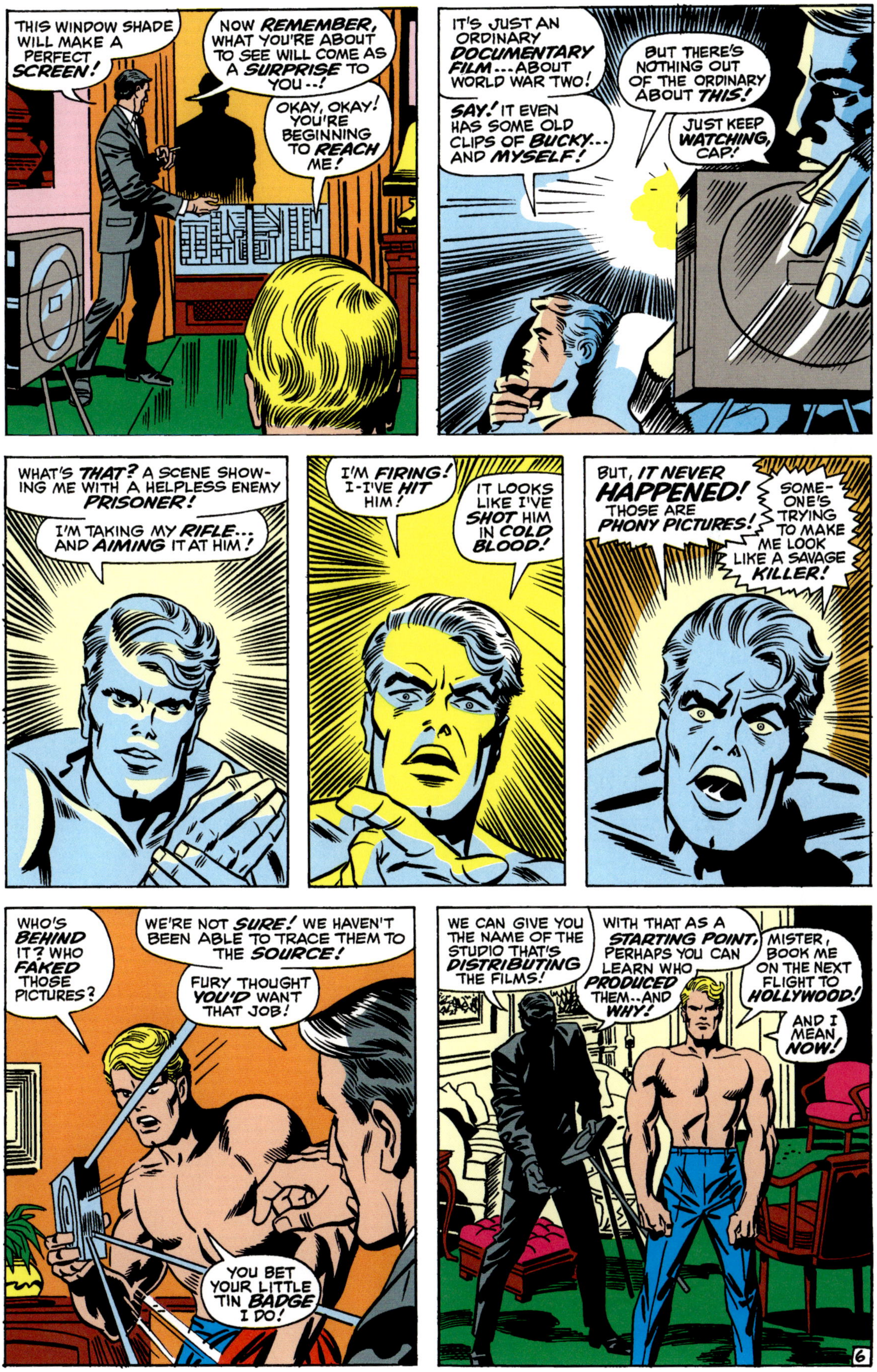
THIS WINDOW SHADE WILL MAKE A PERFECT SCREEN!
NOW REMEMBER, WHAT YOU'RE ABOUT TO SEE WILL COME AS A SURPRISE TO YOU--!
OKAY, OKAY! YOU'RE BEGINNING TO REACH ME!
IT'S JUST AN ORDINARY DOCUMENTARY FILM...ABOUT WORLD WAR TWO!
SAY! IT EVEN HAS SOME OLD CLIPS OF BUCKY... AND MYSELF!
BUT THERE'S NOTHING OUT OF THE ORDINARY ABOUT THIS!
JUST KEEP WATCHING, CAP!
WHAT'S THAT? A SCENE SHOWING ME WITH A HELPLESS ENEMY PRISONER!
I'M TAKING MY RIFLE... AND AIMING IT AT HIM!
I'M FIRING! I-I'VE HIT HIM!
IT LOOKS LIKE I'VE SHOT HIM IN COLD BLOOD!
BUT, IT NEVER HAPPENED! THOSE ARE PHONY PICTURES!
SOMEONE'S TRYING TO MAKE ME LOOK LIKE A SAVAGE KILLER!
WHO'S BEHIND IT? WHO FAKED THOSE PICTURES?
WE'RE NOT SURE! WE HAVEN'T BEEN ABLE TO TRACE THEM TO THE SOURCE!
FURY THOUGHT YOU'D WANT THAT JOB!
YOU BET YOUR LITTLE TIN BADGE I DO!
WE CAN GIVE YOU THE NAME OF THE STUDIO THAT'S DISTRIBUTING THE FILMS!
WITH THAT AS A STARTING POINT, PERHAPS YOU CAN LEARN WHO PRODUCED THEM..AND WHY!
MISTER, BOOK ME ON THE NEXT FLIGHT TO HOLLYWOOD!
AND I MEAN NOW!
6

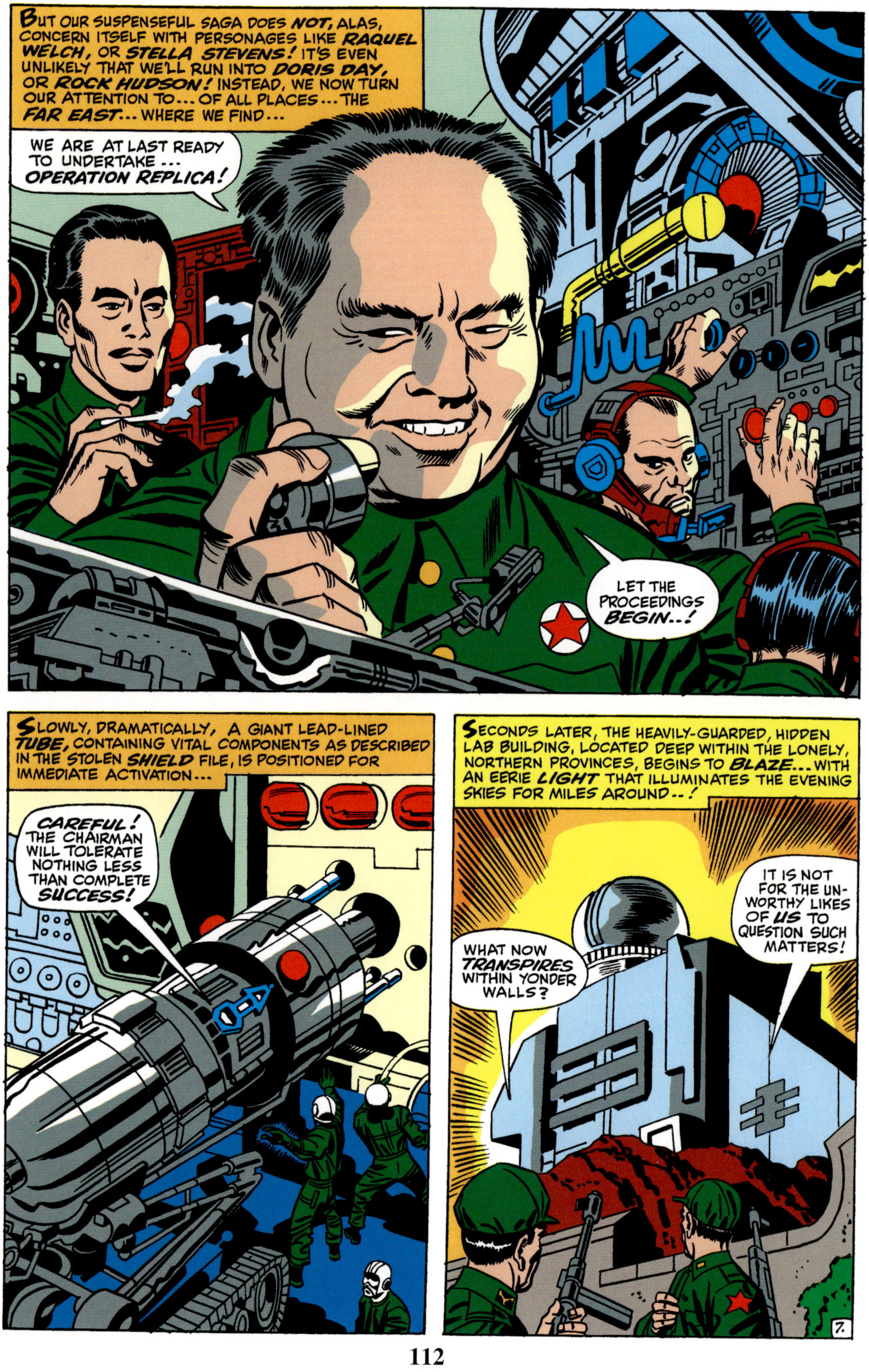

BUT OUR SUSPENSEFUL SAGA DOES NOT, ALAS, CONCERN ITSELF WITH PERSONAGES LIKE RAQUEL WELCH, OR STELLA STEVENS! IT'S EVEN UNLIKELY THAT WE'LL RUN INTO DORIS DAY, OR ROCK HUDSON! INSTEAD, WE NOW TURN OUR ATTENTION TO... OF ALL PLACES... THE FAR EAST... WHERE WE FIND...
WE ARE AT LAST READY TO UNDERTAKE... OPERATION REPLICA!
LET THE PROCEEDINGS BEGIN..!
SLOWLY, DRAMATICALLY, A GIANT LEAD-LINED TUBE, CONTAINING VITAL COMPONENTS AS DESCRIBED IN THE STOLEN SHIELD FILE, IS POSITIONED FOR IMMEDIATE ACTIVATION...
CAREFUL! THE CHAIRMAN WILL TOLERATE NOTHING LESS THAN COMPLETE SUCCESS!
SECONDS LATER, THE HEAVILY-GUARDED, HIDDEN LAB BUILDING, LOCATED DEEP WITHIN THE LONELY, NORTHERN PROVINCES, BEGINS TO BLAZE... WITH AN EERIE LIGHT THAT ILLUMINATES THE EVENING SKIES FOR MILES AROUND..!
WHAT NOW TRANSPIRES WITHIN YONDER WALLS?
IT IS NOT FOR THE UNWORTHY LIKES OF US TO QUESTION SUCH MATTERS!
7.

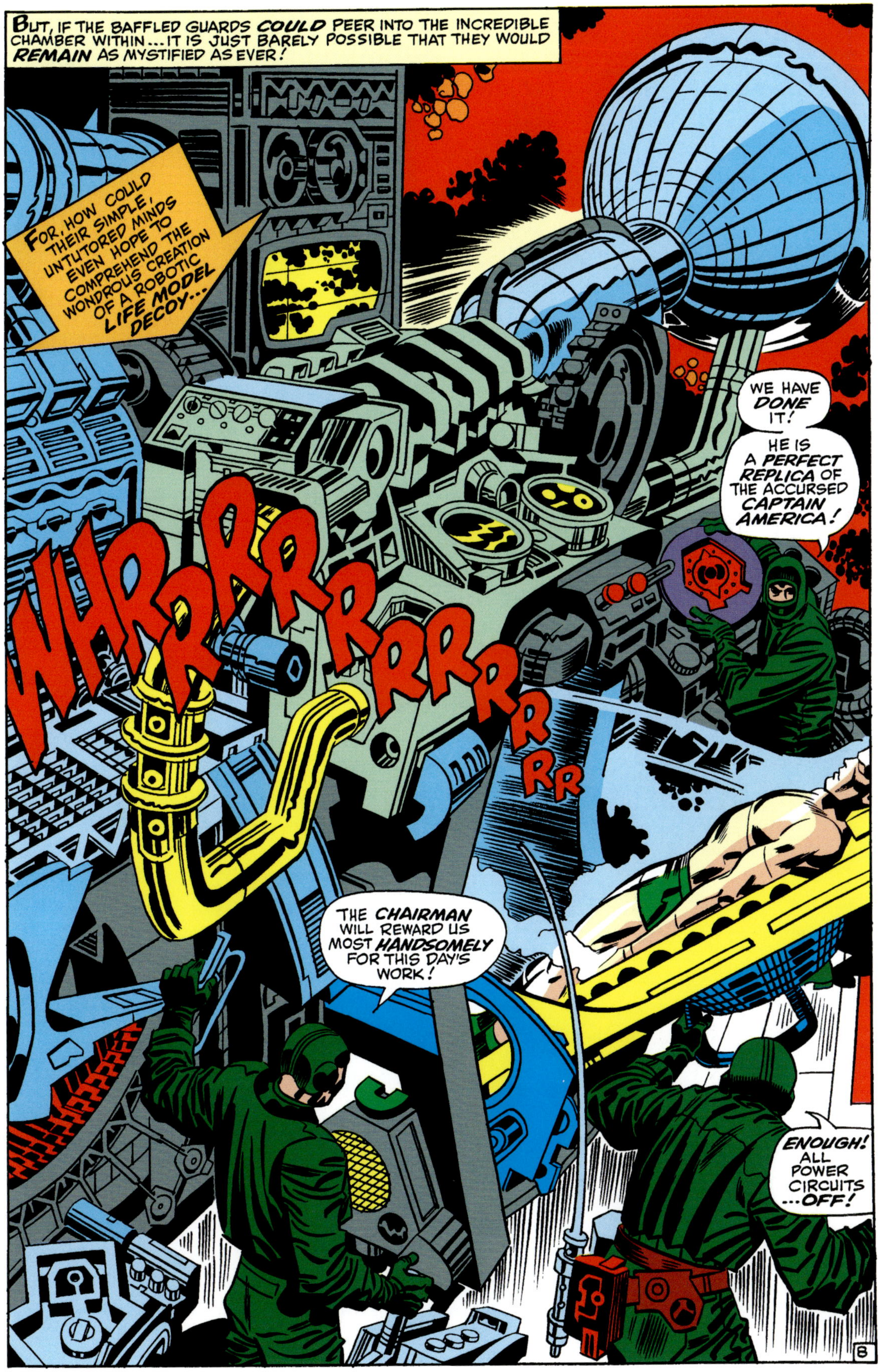
BUT, IF THE BAFFLED GUARDS COULD PEER INTO THE INCREDIBLE CHAMBER WITHIN... IT IS JUST BARELY POSSIBLE THAT THEY WOULD REMAIN AS MYSTIFIED AS EVER!
FOR, HOW COULD THEIR SIMPLE, UNTUTORED MINDS EVEN HOPE TO COMPREHEND THE WONDROUS CREATION OF A ROBOTIC LIFE MODEL DECOY...
WE HAVE DONE IT!
HE IS A PERFECT REPLICA OF THE ACCURSED CAPTAIN AMERICA!
WHRRRRRRRRRRR
THE CHAIRMAN WILL REWARD US MOST HANDSOMELY FOR THIS DAY'S WORK!
ENOUGH! ALL POWER CIRCUITS ...OFF!
8

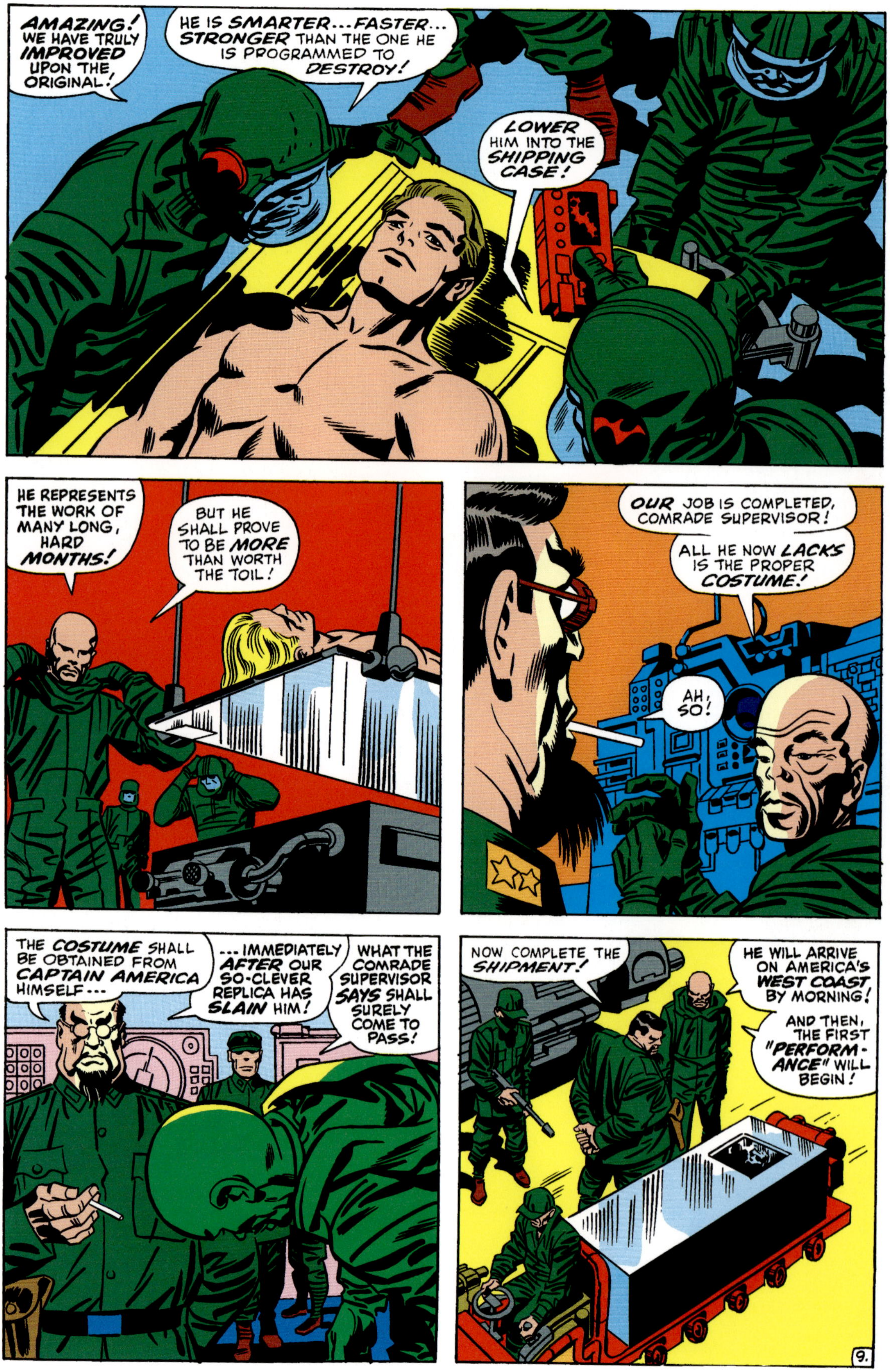
AMAZING! WE HAVE TRULY IMPROVED UPON THE ORIGINAL!
HE IS SMARTER...FASTER... STRONGER THAN THE ONE HE IS PROGRAMMED TO DESTROY!
LOWER HIM INTO THE SHIPPING CASE!
HE REPRESENTS THE WORK OF MANY LONG, HARD MONTHS!
BUT HE SHALL PROVE TO BE MORE THAN WORTH THE TOIL!
OUR JOB IS COMPLETED, COMRADE SUPERVISOR!
ALL HE NOW LACKS IS THE PROPER COSTUME!
AH, SO!
THE COSTUME SHALL BE OBTAINED FROM CAPTAIN AMERICA HIMSELF---
---IMMEDIATELY AFTER OUR SO-CLEVER REPLICA HAS SLAIN HIM!
WHAT THE COMRADE SUPERVISOR SAYS SHALL SURELY COME TO PASS!
NOW COMPLETE THE SHIPMENT!
HE WILL ARRIVE ON AMERICA'S WEST COAST BY MORNING!
AND THEN, THE FIRST "PERFORM-ANCE" WILL BEGIN!
9.

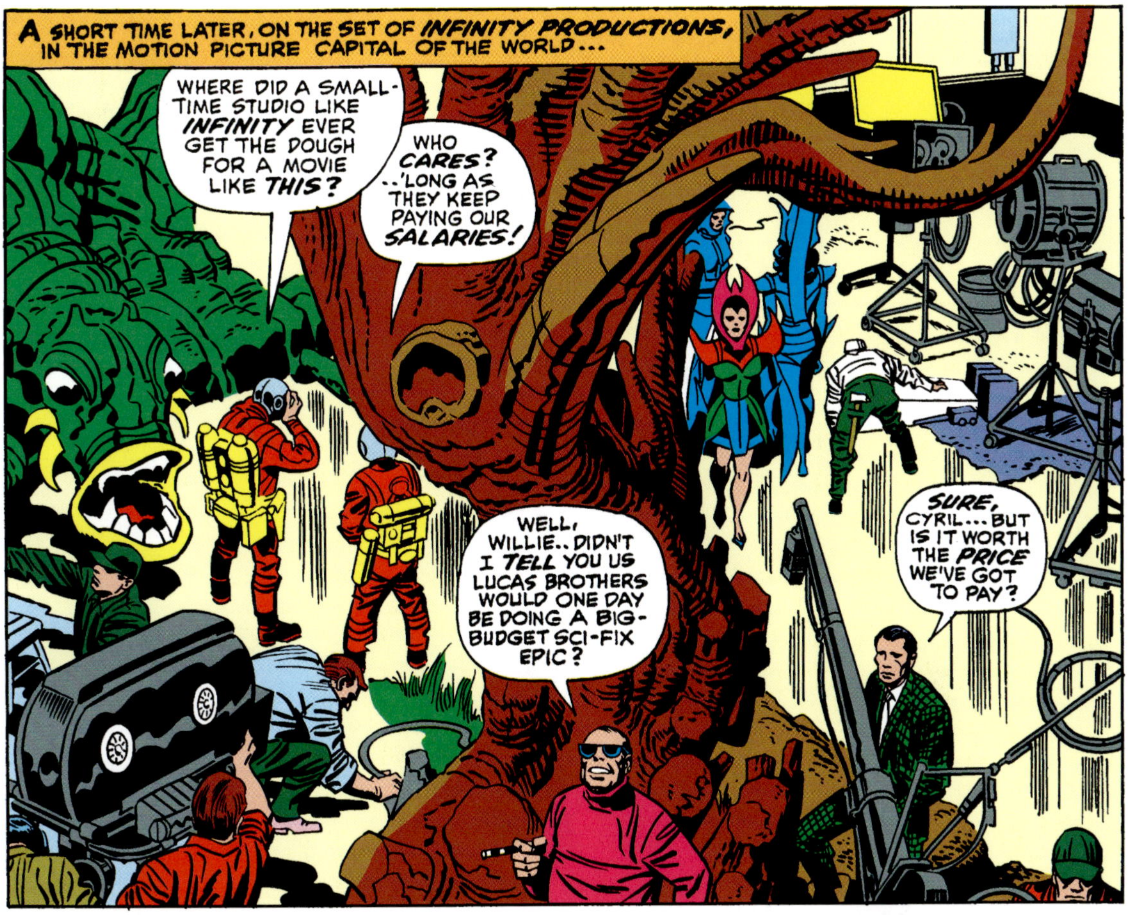
A SHORT TIME LATER, ON THE SET OF INFINITY PRODUCTIONS, IN THE MOTION PICTURE CAPITAL OF THE WORLD...
WHERE DID A SMALL-TIME STUDIO LIKE INFINITY EVER GET THE DOUGH FOR A MOVIE LIKE THIS?
WHO CARES? ..'LONG AS THEY KEEP PAYING OUR SALARIES!
WELL, WILLIE.. DIDN'T I TELL YOU US LUCAS BROTHERS WOULD ONE DAY BE DOING A BIG-BUDGET SCI-FIX EPIC?
SURE, CYRIL... BUT IS IT WORTH THE PRICE WE'VE GOT TO PAY?

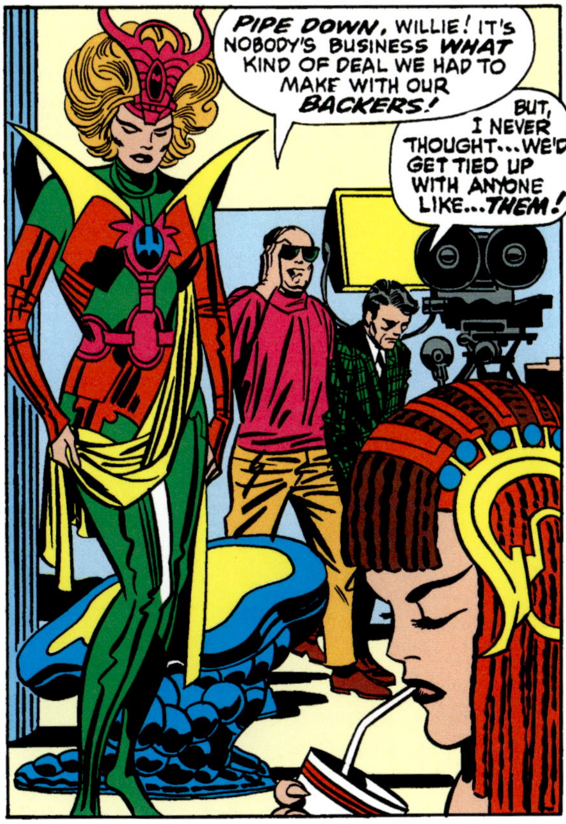
PIPE DOWN, WILLIE! IT'S NOBODY'S BUSINESS WHAT KIND OF DEAL WE HAD TO MAKE WITH OUR BACKERS!
BUT, I NEVER THOUGHT... WE'D GET TIED UP WITH ANYONE LIKE... THEM!

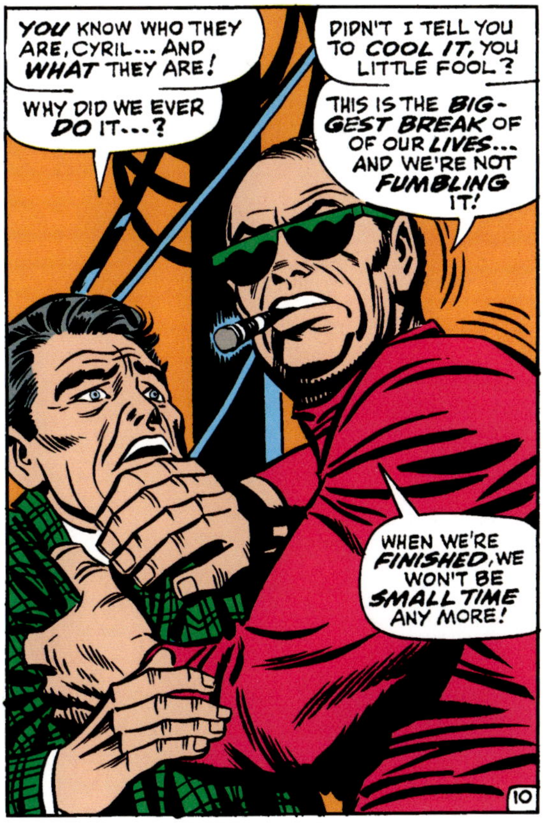
YOU KNOW WHO THEY ARE, CYRIL... AND WHAT THEY ARE!
WHY DID WE EVER DO IT...?
DIDN'T I TELL YOU TO COOL IT, YOU LITTLE FOOL?
THIS IS THE BIGGEST BREAK OF OF OUR LIVES... AND WE'RE NOT FUMBLING IT!
WHEN WE'RE FINISHED, WE WON'T BE SMALL TIME ANY MORE!
10

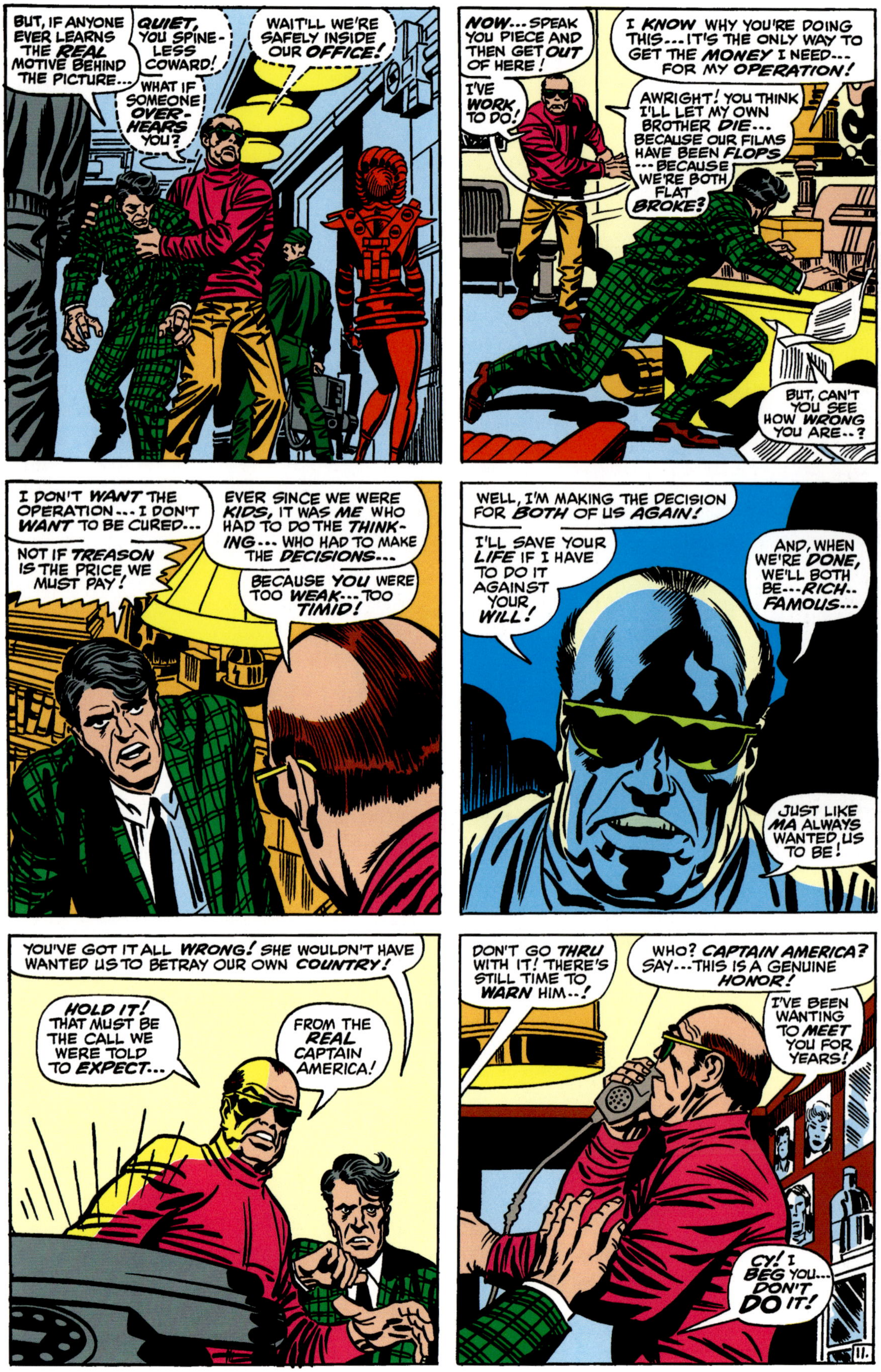

BUT, IF ANYONE EVER LEARNS THE REAL MOTIVE BEHIND THE PICTURE...
QUIET, YOU SPINELESS COWARD!
WHAT IF SOMEONE OVERHEARS YOU?
WAIT'LL WE'RE SAFELY INSIDE OUR OFFICE!
NOW... SPEAK YOU PIECE AND THEN GET OUT OF HERE!
I'VE WORK TO DO!
I KNOW WHY YOU'RE DOING THIS... IT'S THE ONLY WAY TO GET THE MONEY I NEED... FOR MY OPERATION!
AWRIGHT! YOU THINK I'LL LET MY OWN BROTHER DIE... BECAUSE OUR FILMS HAVE BEEN FLOPS --- BECAUSE WE'RE BOTH FLAT BROKE?
BUT, CAN'T YOU SEE HOW WRONG YOU ARE..?
I DON'T WANT THE OPERATION... I DON'T WANT TO BE CURED...
NOT IF TREASON IS THE PRICE WE MUST PAY!
EVER SINCE WE WERE KIDS, IT WAS ME WHO HAD TO DO THE THINKING... WHO HAD TO MAKE THE DECISIONS...
BECAUSE YOU WERE TOO WEAK... TOO TIMID!
WELL, I'M MAKING THE DECISION FOR BOTH OF US AGAIN!
I'LL SAVE YOUR LIFE IF I HAVE TO DO IT AGAINST YOUR WILL!
AND, WHEN WE'RE DONE, WE'LL BOTH BE---RICH.. FAMOUS...
JUST LIKE MA ALWAYS WANTED US TO BE!
YOU'VE GOT IT ALL WRONG! SHE WOULDN'T HAVE WANTED US TO BETRAY OUR OWN COUNTRY!
HOLD IT! THAT MUST BE THE CALL WE WERE TOLD TO EXPECT...
FROM THE REAL CAPTAIN AMERICA!
DON'T GO THRU WITH IT! THERE'S STILL TIME TO WARN HIM..!
WHO? CAPTAIN AMERICA? SAY---THIS IS A GENUINE HONOR!
I'VE BEEN WANTING TO MEET YOU FOR YEARS!
CY! I BEG YOU... DON'T DO IT!
11.

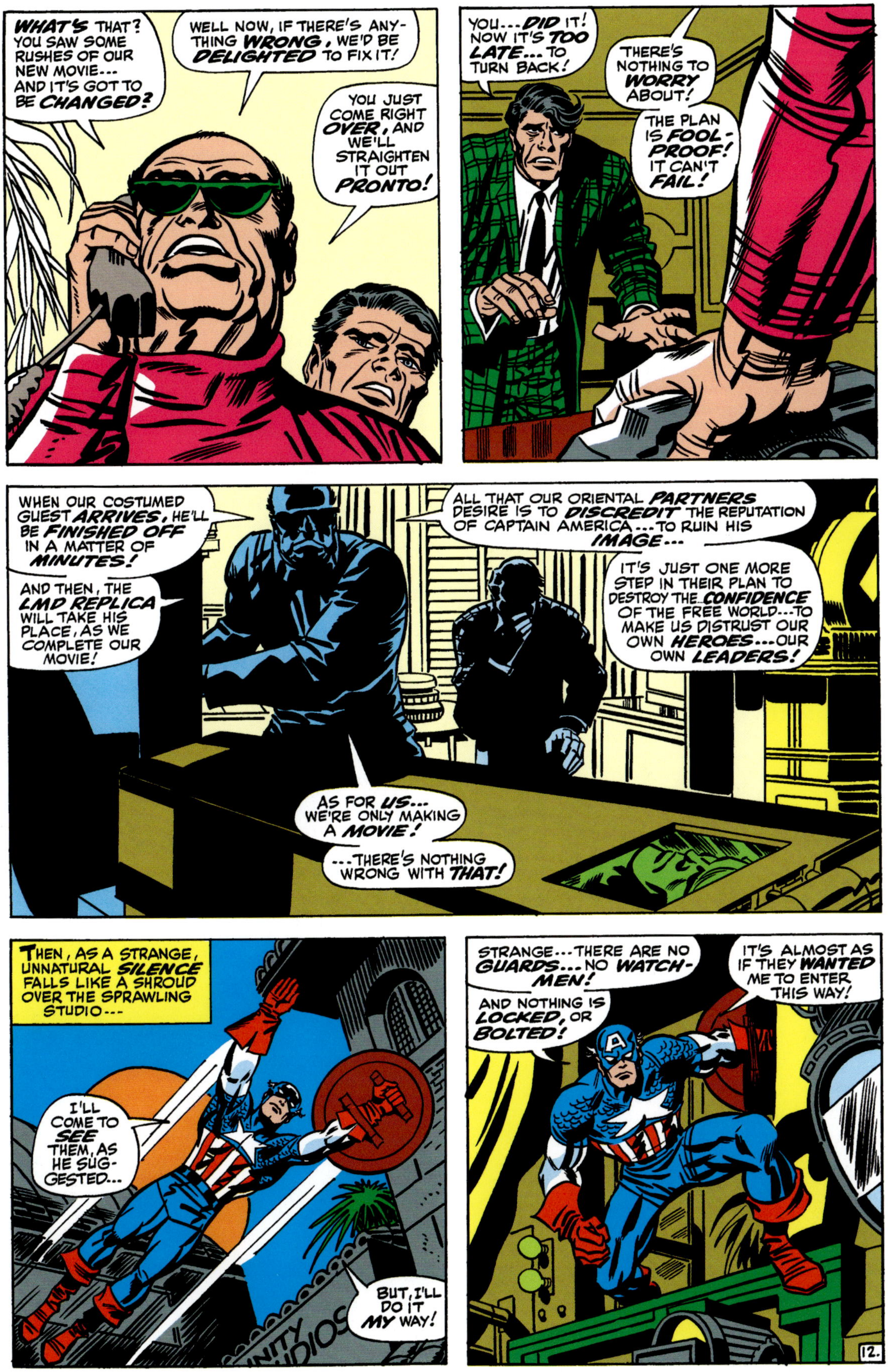
WHAT'S THAT? YOU SAW SOME RUSHES OF OUR NEW MOVIE--- AND IT'S GOT TO BE CHANGED?
WELL NOW, IF THERE'S ANYTHING WRONG, WE'D BE DELIGHTED TO FIX IT!
YOU JUST COME RIGHT OVER, AND WE'LL STRAIGHTEN IT OUT PRONTO!
YOU---DID IT! NOW IT'S TOO LATE---TO TURN BACK!
THERE'S NOTHING TO WORRY ABOUT!
THE PLAN IS FOOL-PROOF! IT CAN'T FAIL!
WHEN OUR COSTUMED GUEST ARRIVES, HE'LL BE FINISHED OFF IN A MATTER OF MINUTES!
AND THEN, THE LMD REPLICA WILL TAKE HIS PLACE, AS WE COMPLETE OUR MOVIE!
ALL THAT OUR ORIENTAL PARTNERS DESIRE IS TO DISCREDIT THE REPUTATION OF CAPTAIN AMERICA---TO RUIN HIS IMAGE---
IT'S JUST ONE MORE STEP IN THEIR PLAN TO DESTROY THE CONFIDENCE OF THE FREE WORLD---TO MAKE US DISTRUST OUR OWN HEROES---OUR OWN LEADERS!
AS FOR US--- WE'RE ONLY MAKING A MOVIE!
---THERE'S NOTHING WRONG WITH THAT!
THEN, AS A STRANGE, UNNATURAL SILENCE FALLS LIKE A SHROUD OVER THE SPRAWLING STUDIO---
I'LL COME TO SEE THEM, AS HE SUGGESTED---
BUT, I'LL DO IT MY WAY!
STRANGE---THERE ARE NO GUARDS---NO WATCHMEN!
AND NOTHING IS LOCKED, OR BOLTED!
IT'S ALMOST AS IF THEY WANTED ME TO ENTER THIS WAY!
12.

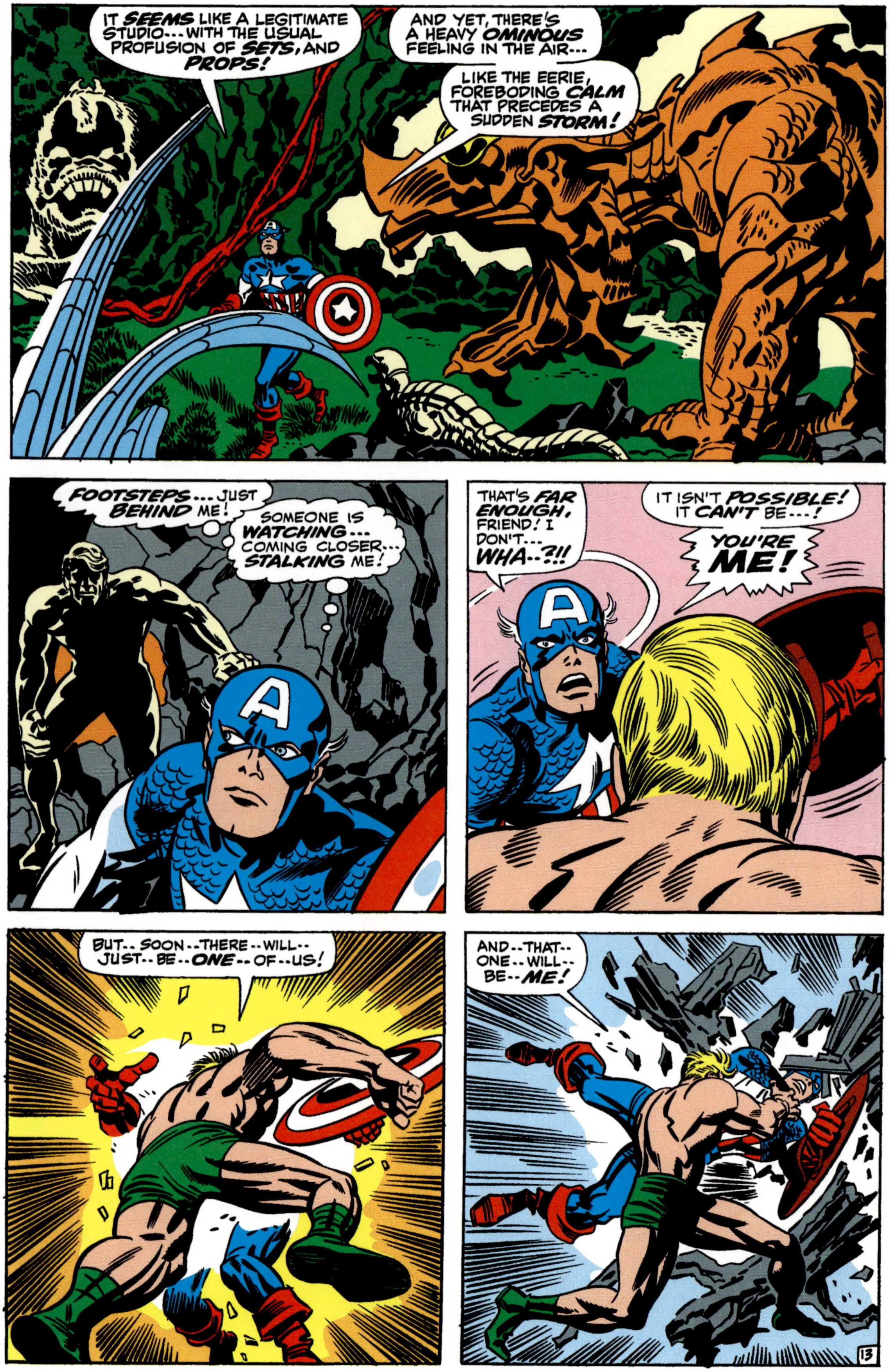
IT SEEMS LIKE A LEGITIMATE STUDIO... WITH THE USUAL PROFUSION OF SETS, AND PROPS!
AND YET, THERE'S A HEAVY OMINOUS FEELING IN THE AIR...
LIKE THE EERIE, FOREBODING CALM THAT PRECEDES A SUDDEN STORM!
FOOTSTEPS... JUST BEHIND ME!
SOMEONE IS WATCHING... COMING CLOSER... STALKING ME!
THAT'S FAR ENOUGH, FRIEND! I DON'T... WHA--?!!
IT ISN'T POSSIBLE! IT CAN'T BE...!
YOU'RE ME!
BUT.. SOON.. THERE.. WILL.. JUST.. BE.. ONE.. OF.. US!
AND.. THAT.. ONE.. WILL.. BE.. ME!
13

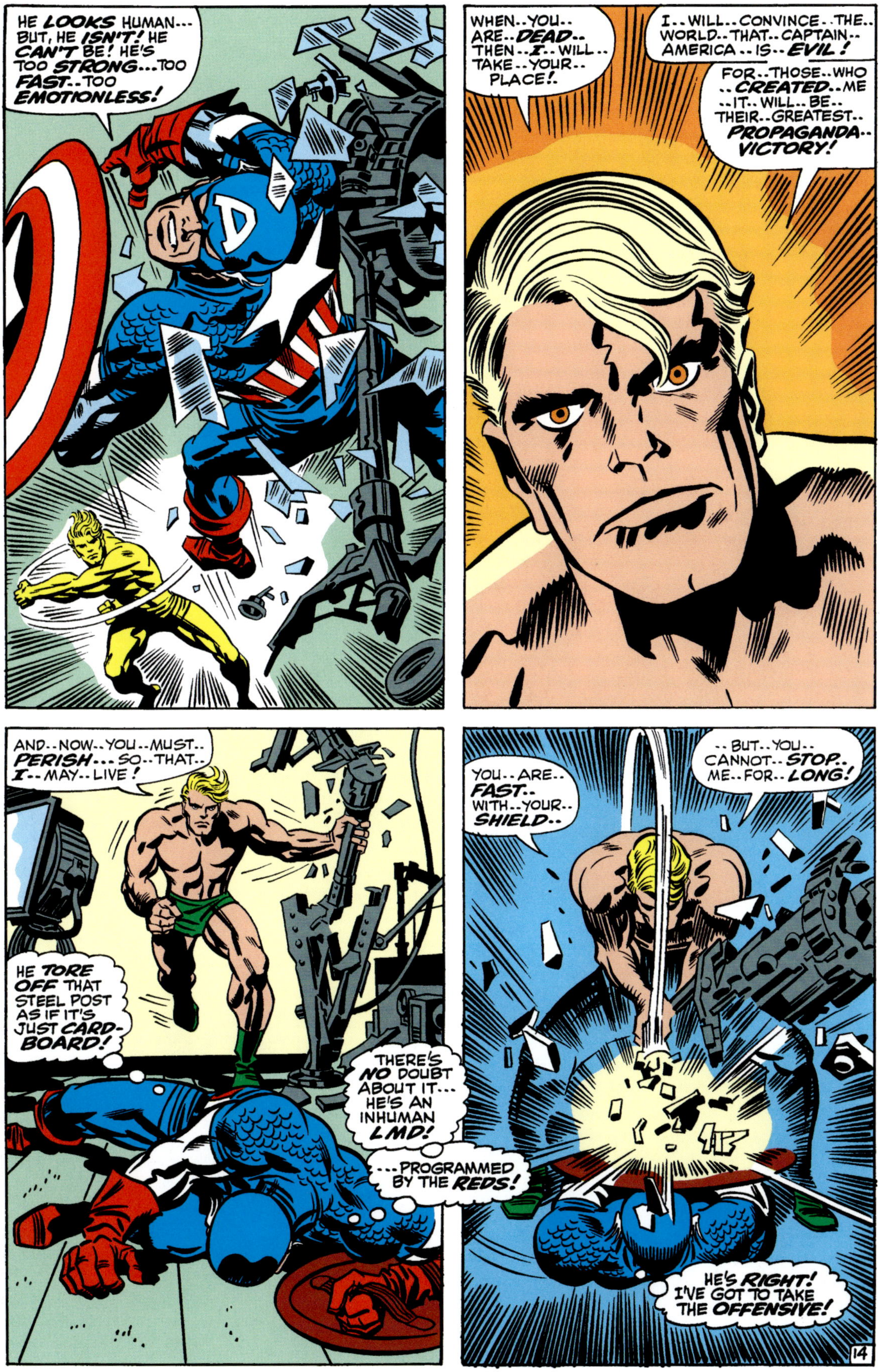
HE LOOKS HUMAN--BUT, HE ISN'T! HE CAN'T BE! HE'S TOO STRONG...TOO FAST--TOO EMOTIONLESS!
WHEN--YOU--ARE--DEAD--THEN--I--WILL--TAKE--YOUR--PLACE!.
I--WILL--CONVINCE--THE--WORLD--THAT--CAPTAIN--AMERICA--IS--EVIL!
FOR--THOSE--WHO--CREATED--ME--IT--WILL--BE--THEIR--GREATEST--PROPAGANDA--VICTORY!
AND--NOW--YOU--MUST--PERISH...SO--THAT--I--MAY--LIVE!
HE TORE OFF THAT STEEL POST AS IF IT'S JUST CARD-BOARD!
THERE'S NO DOUBT ABOUT IT...HE'S AN INHUMAN LMD!
...PROGRAMMED BY THE REDS!
YOU--ARE--FAST--WITH--YOUR--SHIELD--
--BUT--YOU--CANNOT--STOP--ME--FOR--LONG!
HE'S RIGHT! I'VE GOT TO TAKE THE OFFENSIVE!
14

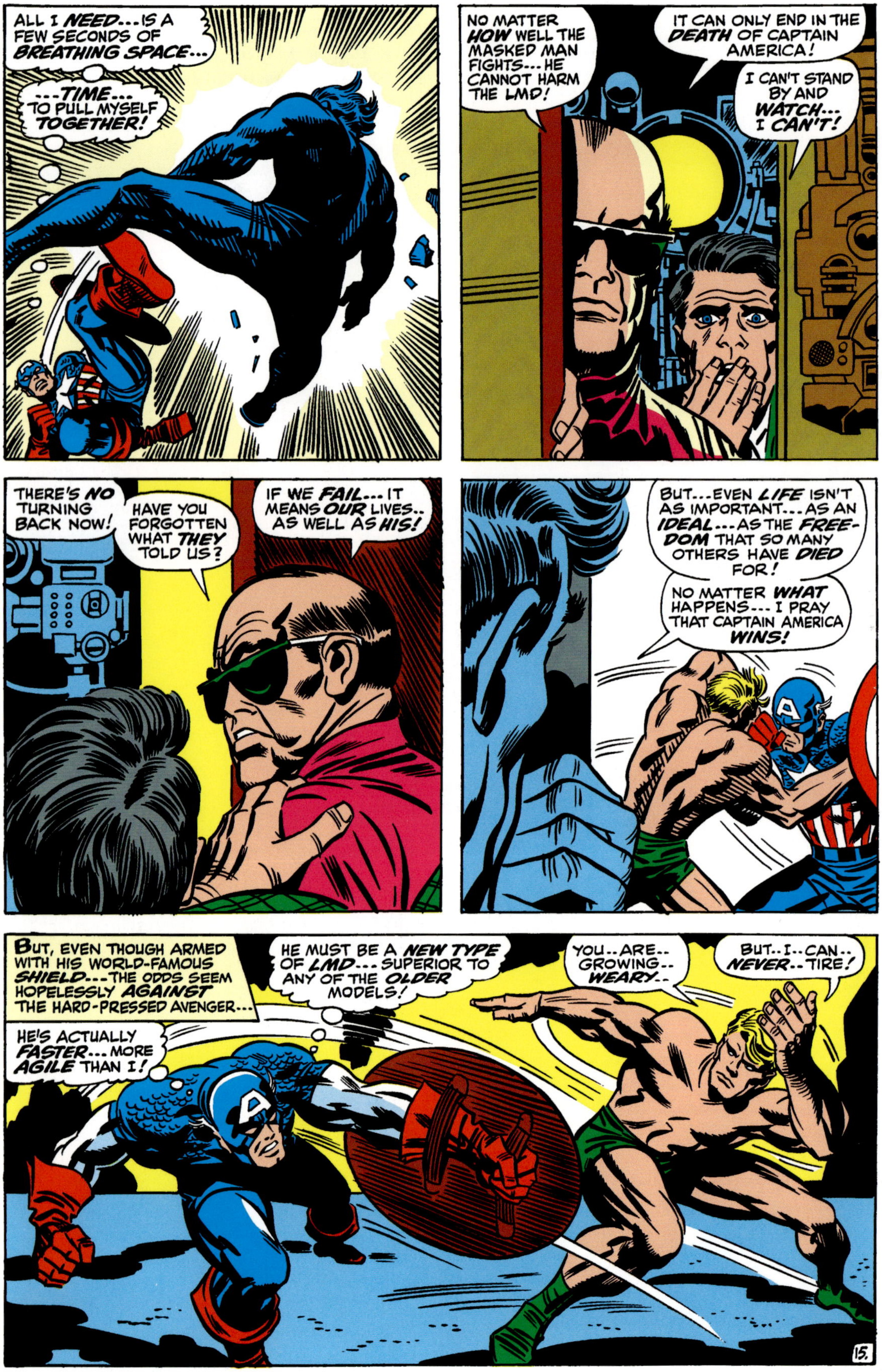
ALL I NEED... IS A FEW SECONDS OF BREATHING SPACE...
...TIME... TO PULL MYSELF TOGETHER!
NO MATTER HOW WELL THE MASKED MAN FIGHTS... HE CANNOT HARM THE LMD!
IT CAN ONLY END IN THE DEATH OF CAPTAIN AMERICA!
I CAN'T STAND BY AND WATCH... I CAN'T!
THERE'S NO TURNING BACK NOW!
HAVE YOU FORGOTTEN WHAT THEY TOLD US?
IF WE FAIL... IT MEANS OUR LIVES.. AS WELL AS HIS!
BUT... EVEN LIFE ISN'T AS IMPORTANT... AS AN IDEAL... AS THE FREE-DOM THAT SO MANY OTHERS HAVE DIED FOR!
NO MATTER WHAT HAPPENS... I PRAY THAT CAPTAIN AMERICA WINS!
BUT, EVEN THOUGH ARMED WITH HIS WORLD-FAMOUS SHIELD... THE ODDS SEEM HOPELESSLY AGAINST THE HARD-PRESSED AVENGER...
HE MUST BE A NEW TYPE OF LMD... SUPERIOR TO ANY OF THE OLDER MODELS!
HE'S ACTUALLY FASTER... MORE AGILE THAN I!
YOU.. ARE.. GROWING.. WEARY..
BUT.. I.. CAN.. NEVER.. TIRE!
15.

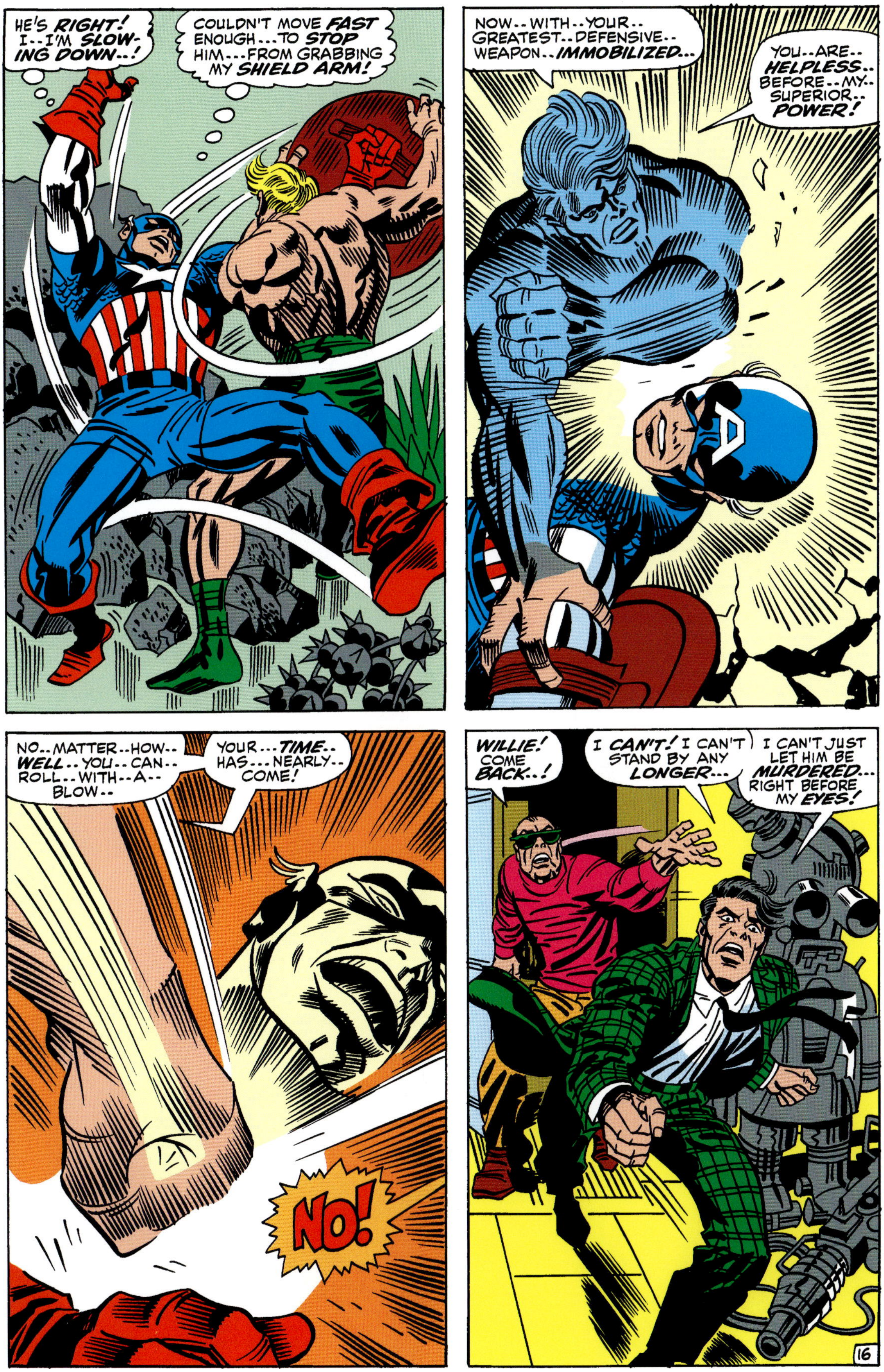

HE'S RIGHT! I--I'M SLOWING DOWN--!
COULDN'T MOVE FAST ENOUGH...TO STOP HIM...FROM GRABBING MY SHIELD ARM!
NOW--WITH--YOUR--GREATEST--DEFENSIVE--WEAPON--IMMOBILIZED...
YOU--ARE--HELPLESS--BEFORE--MY--SUPERIOR--POWER!
NO--MATTER--HOW--WELL--YOU--CAN--ROLL--WITH--A--BLOW--
YOUR...TIME--HAS...NEARLY--COME!
NO!
WILLIE! COME BACK--!
I CAN'T! I CAN'T STAND BY ANY LONGER...
I CAN'T JUST LET HIM BE MURDERED... RIGHT BEFORE MY EYES!
16

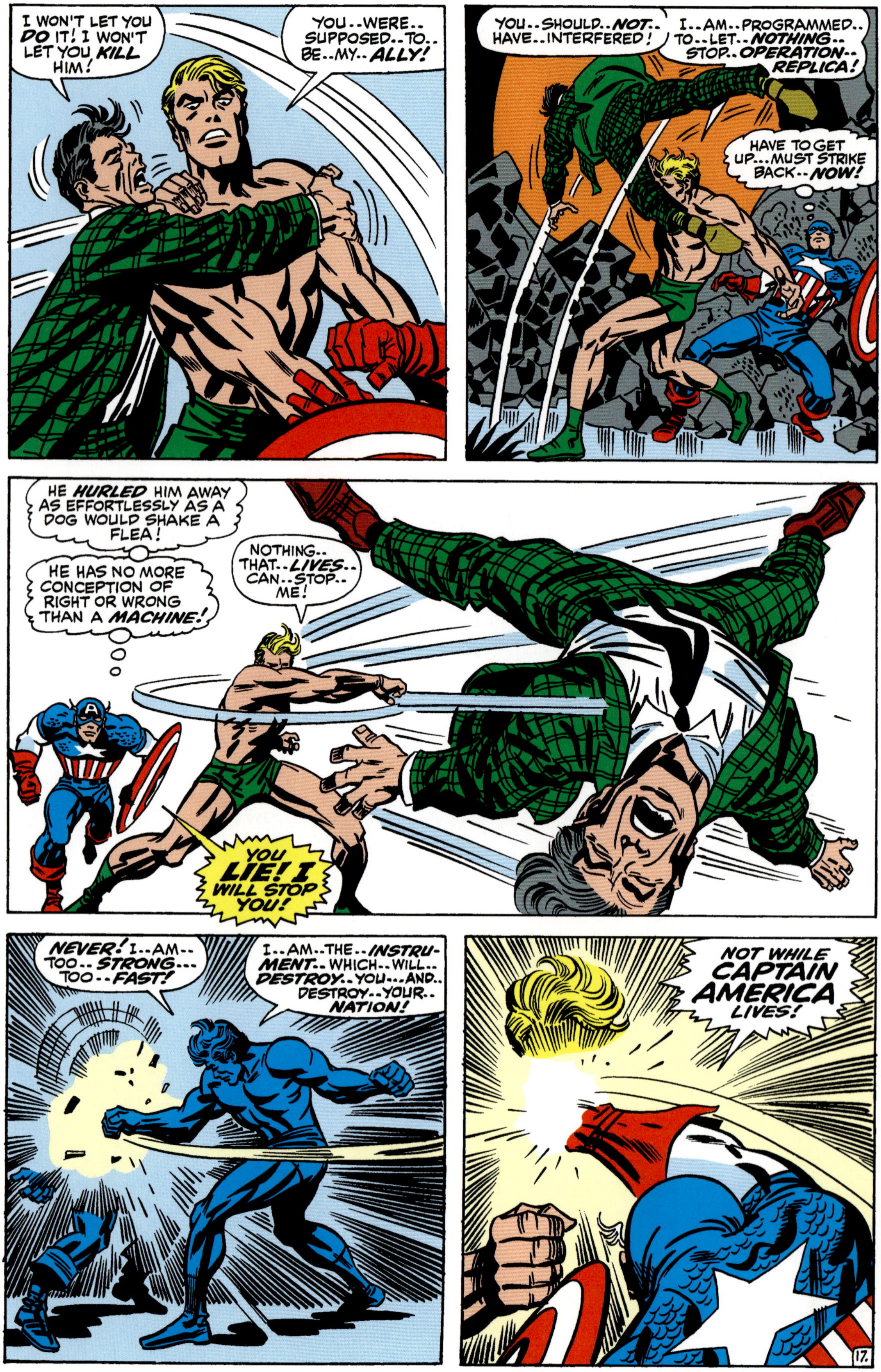
I WON'T LET YOU DO IT! I WON'T LET YOU KILL HIM!
YOU..WERE.. SUPPOSED..TO.. BE..MY..ALLY!
YOU..SHOULD..NOT.. HAVE..INTERFERED!
I..AM..PROGRAMMED.. TO..LET..NOTHING.. STOP..OPERATION.. REPLICA!
HAVE TO GET UP...MUST STRIKE BACK..NOW!
HE HURLED HIM AWAY AS EFFORTLESSLY AS A DOG WOULD SHAKE A FLEA!
HE HAS NO MORE CONCEPTION OF RIGHT OR WRONG THAN A MACHINE!
NOTHING.. THAT..LIVES.. CAN..STOP.. ME!
YOU LIE! I WILL STOP YOU!
NEVER! I..AM.. TOO..STRONG... TOO..FAST!
I..AM..THE..INSTRUMENT..WHICH..WILL.. DESTROY..YOU...AND.. DESTROY..YOUR.. NATION!
NOT WHILE CAPTAIN AMERICA LIVES!
17.

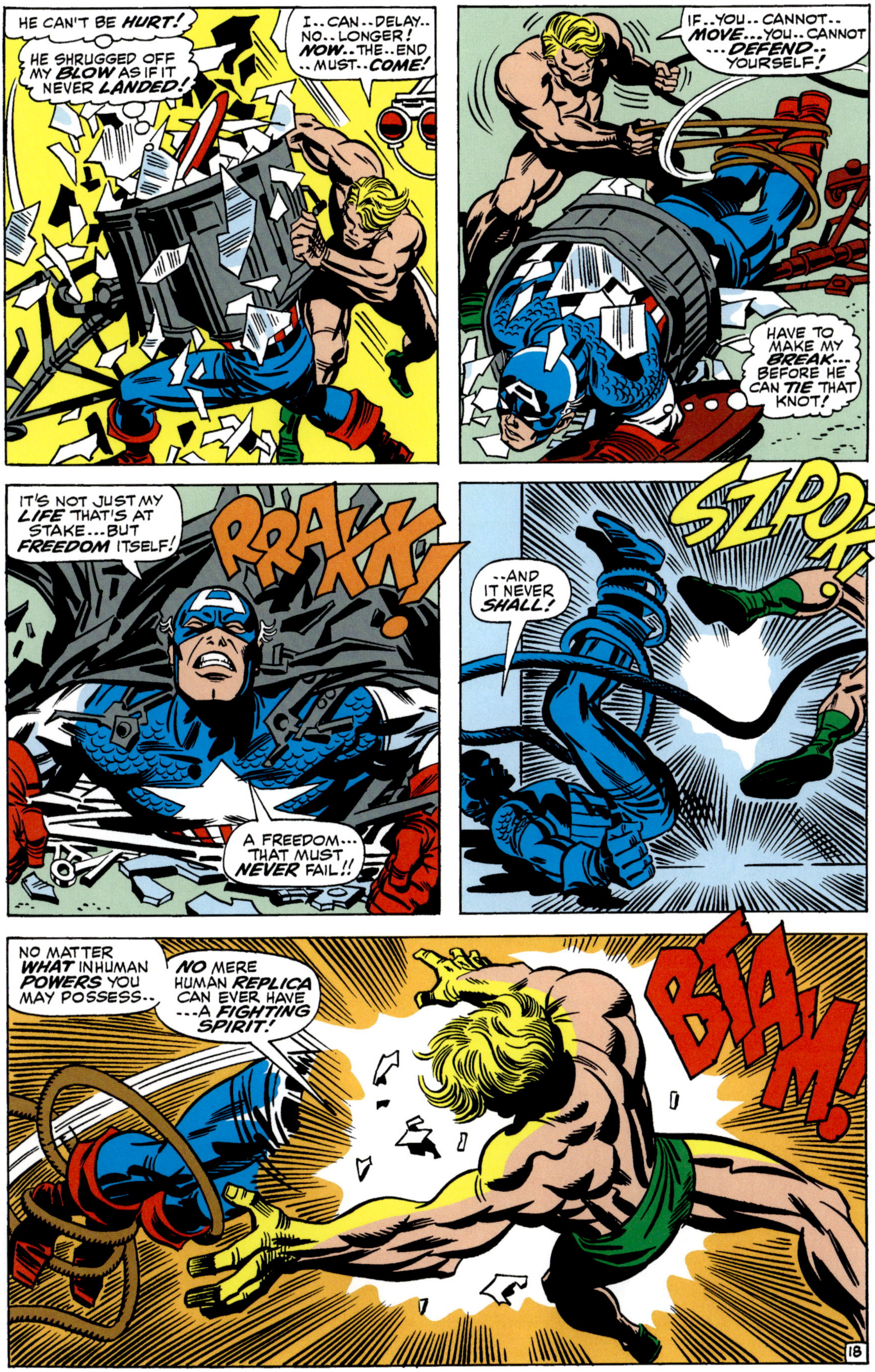
HE CAN'T BE HURT!
HE SHRUGGED OFF MY BLOW AS IF IT NEVER LANDED!
I.. CAN.. DELAY.. NO.. LONGER! NOW.. THE.. END.. MUST.. COME!
IF.. YOU.. CANNOT.. MOVE... YOU.. CANNOT ...DEFEND.. YOURSELF!
HAVE TO MAKE MY BREAK... BEFORE HE CAN TIE THAT KNOT!
IT'S NOT JUST MY LIFE THAT'S AT STAKE... BUT FREEDOM ITSELF!
RRAKK!
A FREEDOM... THAT MUST NEVER FAIL!!
SZPOK!
--AND IT NEVER SHALL!
NO MATTER WHAT INHUMAN POWERS YOU MAY POSSESS..
NO MERE HUMAN REPLICA CAN EVER HAVE ---A FIGHTING SPIRIT!
BTAM!
18

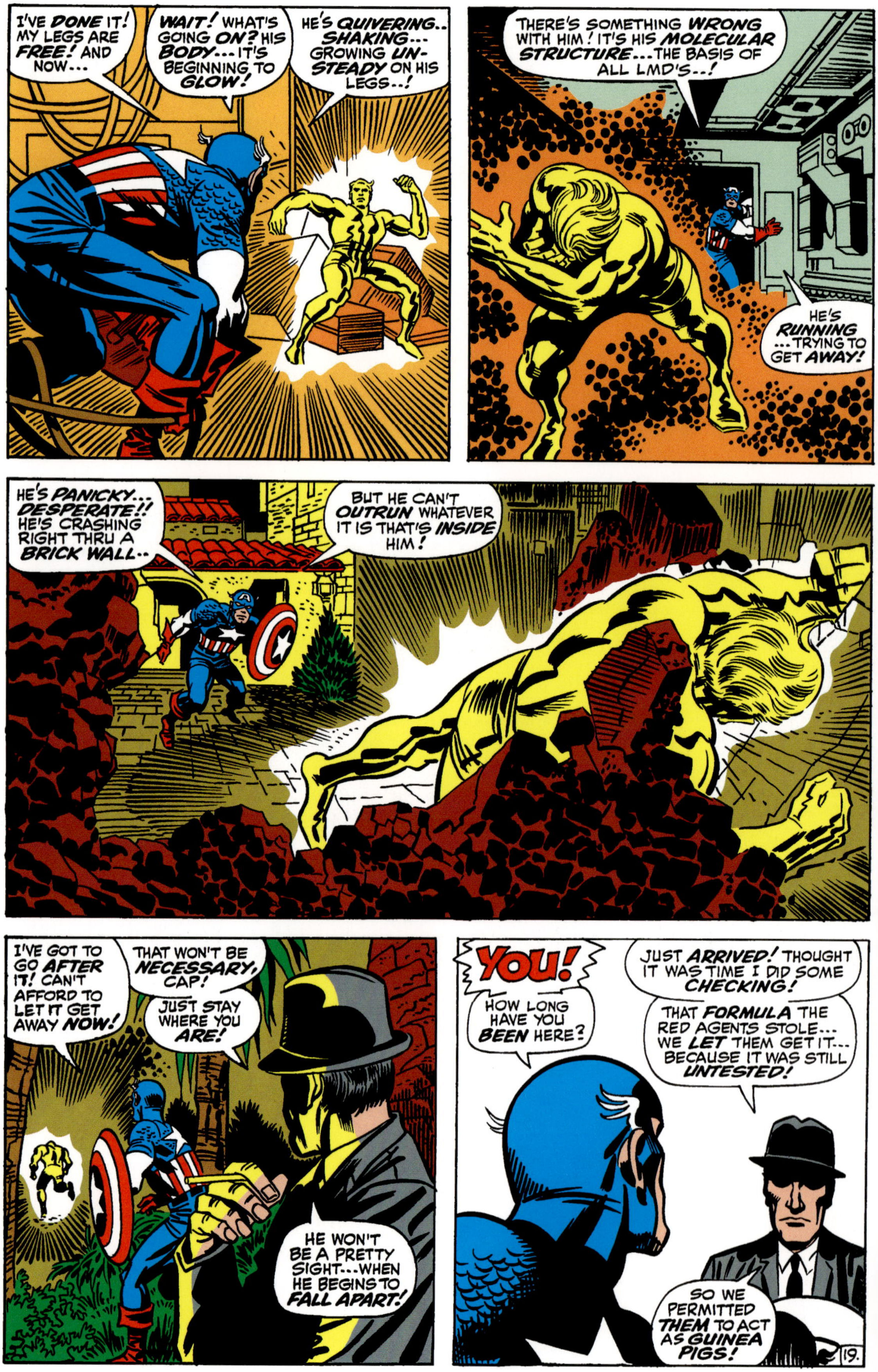
I'VE DONE IT! MY LEGS ARE FREE! AND NOW...
WAIT! WHAT'S GOING ON? HIS BODY...IT'S BEGINNING TO GLOW!
HE'S QUIVERING.. SHAKING... GROWING UNSTEADY ON HIS LEGS..!
THERE'S SOMETHING WRONG WITH HIM! IT'S HIS MOLECULAR STRUCTURE...THE BASIS OF ALL LMD'S..!
HE'S RUNNING ...TRYING TO GET AWAY!
HE'S PANICKY... DESPERATE!! HE'S CRASHING RIGHT THRU A BRICK WALL..
BUT HE CAN'T OUTRUN WHATEVER IT IS THAT'S INSIDE HIM!
I'VE GOT TO GO AFTER IT! CAN'T AFFORD TO LET IT GET AWAY NOW!
THAT WON'T BE NECESSARY, CAP!
JUST STAY WHERE YOU ARE!
HE WON'T BE A PRETTY SIGHT...WHEN HE BEGINS TO FALL APART!
YOU!
HOW LONG HAVE YOU BEEN HERE?
JUST ARRIVED! THOUGHT IT WAS TIME I DID SOME CHECKING!
THAT FORMULA THE RED AGENTS STOLE... WE LET THEM GET IT... BECAUSE IT WAS STILL UNTESTED!
SO WE PERMITTED THEM TO ACT AS GUINEA PIGS!
19.

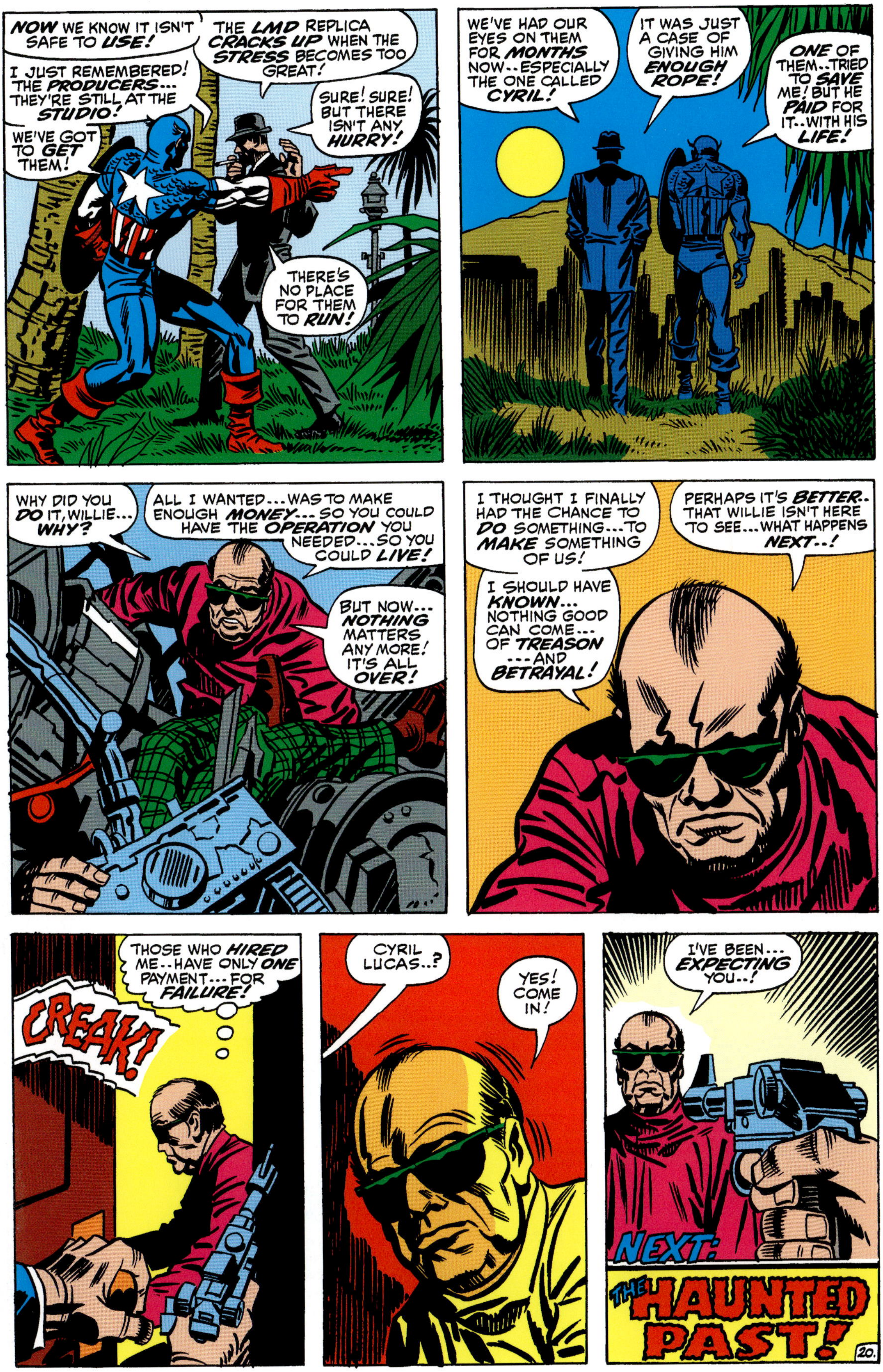
NOW WE KNOW IT ISN'T SAFE TO USE!
THE LMD REPLICA CRACKS UP WHEN THE STRESS BECOMES TOO GREAT!
I JUST REMEMBERED! THE PRODUCERS... THEY'RE STILL AT THE STUDIO!
WE'VE GOT TO GET THEM!
SURE! SURE! BUT THERE ISN'T ANY HURRY!
THERE'S NO PLACE FOR THEM TO RUN!
WE'VE HAD OUR EYES ON THEM FOR MONTHS NOW..ESPECIALLY THE ONE CALLED CYRIL!
IT WAS JUST A CASE OF GIVING HIM ENOUGH ROPE!
ONE OF THEM..TRIED TO SAVE ME! BUT HE PAID FOR IT..WITH HIS LIFE!
WHY DID YOU DO IT, WILLIE... WHY?
ALL I WANTED...WAS TO MAKE ENOUGH MONEY... SO YOU COULD HAVE THE OPERATION YOU NEEDED...SO YOU COULD LIVE!
BUT NOW... NOTHING MATTERS ANY MORE! IT'S ALL OVER!
I THOUGHT I FINALLY HAD THE CHANCE TO DO SOMETHING...TO MAKE SOMETHING OF US!
I SHOULD HAVE KNOWN... NOTHING GOOD CAN COME... OF TREASON ...AND BETRAYAL!
PERHAPS IT'S BETTER.. THAT WILLIE ISN'T HERE TO SEE...WHAT HAPPENS NEXT..!
THOSE WHO HIRED ME..HAVE ONLY ONE PAYMENT... FOR FAILURE!
CREAK!
CYRIL LUCAS..?
YES! COME IN!
I'VE BEEN... EXPECTING YOU..!
NEXT:
THE HAUNTED PAST!
20.

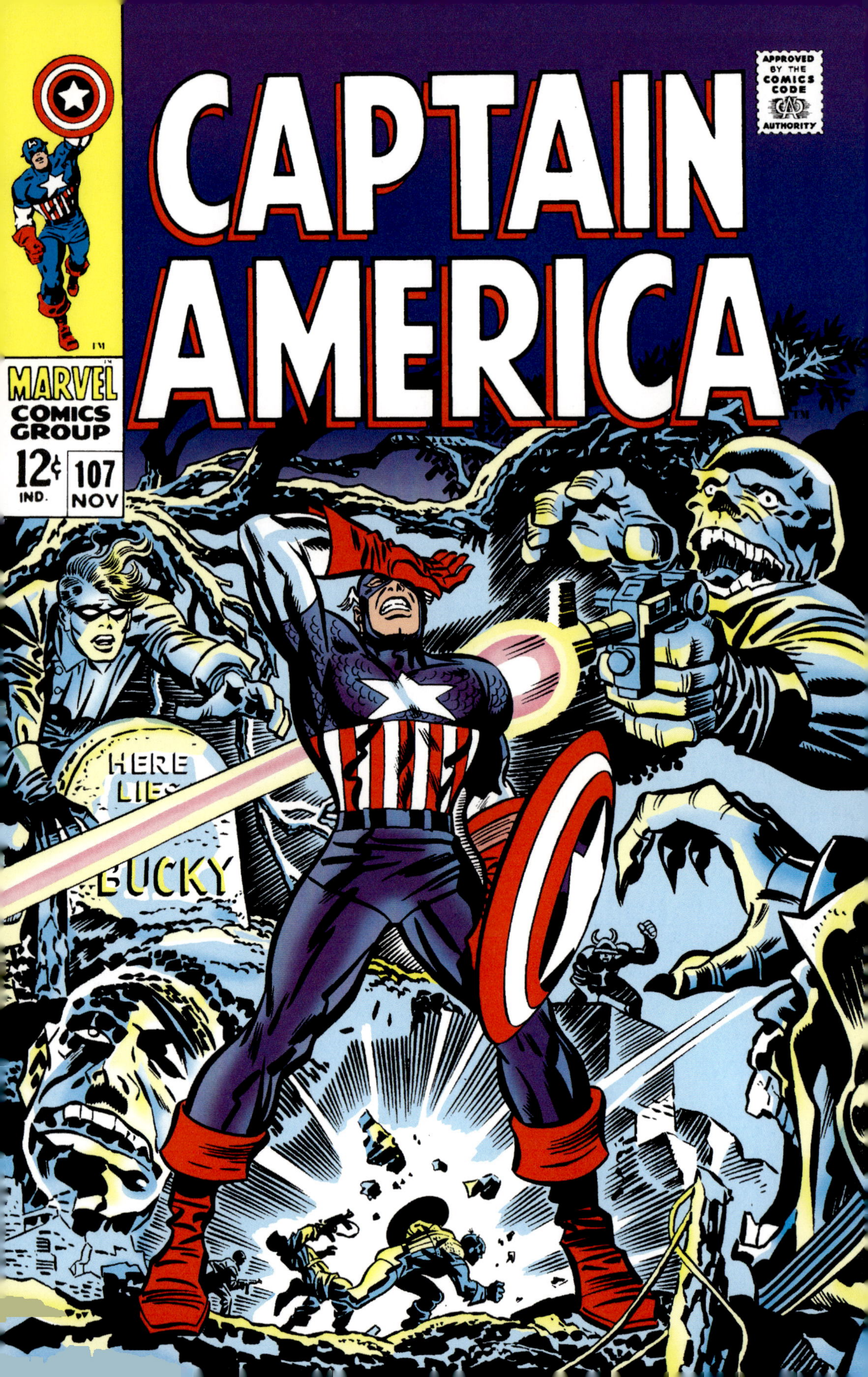

CAPTAIN AMERICA
MARVEL COMICS GROUP
12¢ IND.
107 NOV
APPROVED BY THE COMICS CODE AUTHORITY
HERE LIES BUCKY

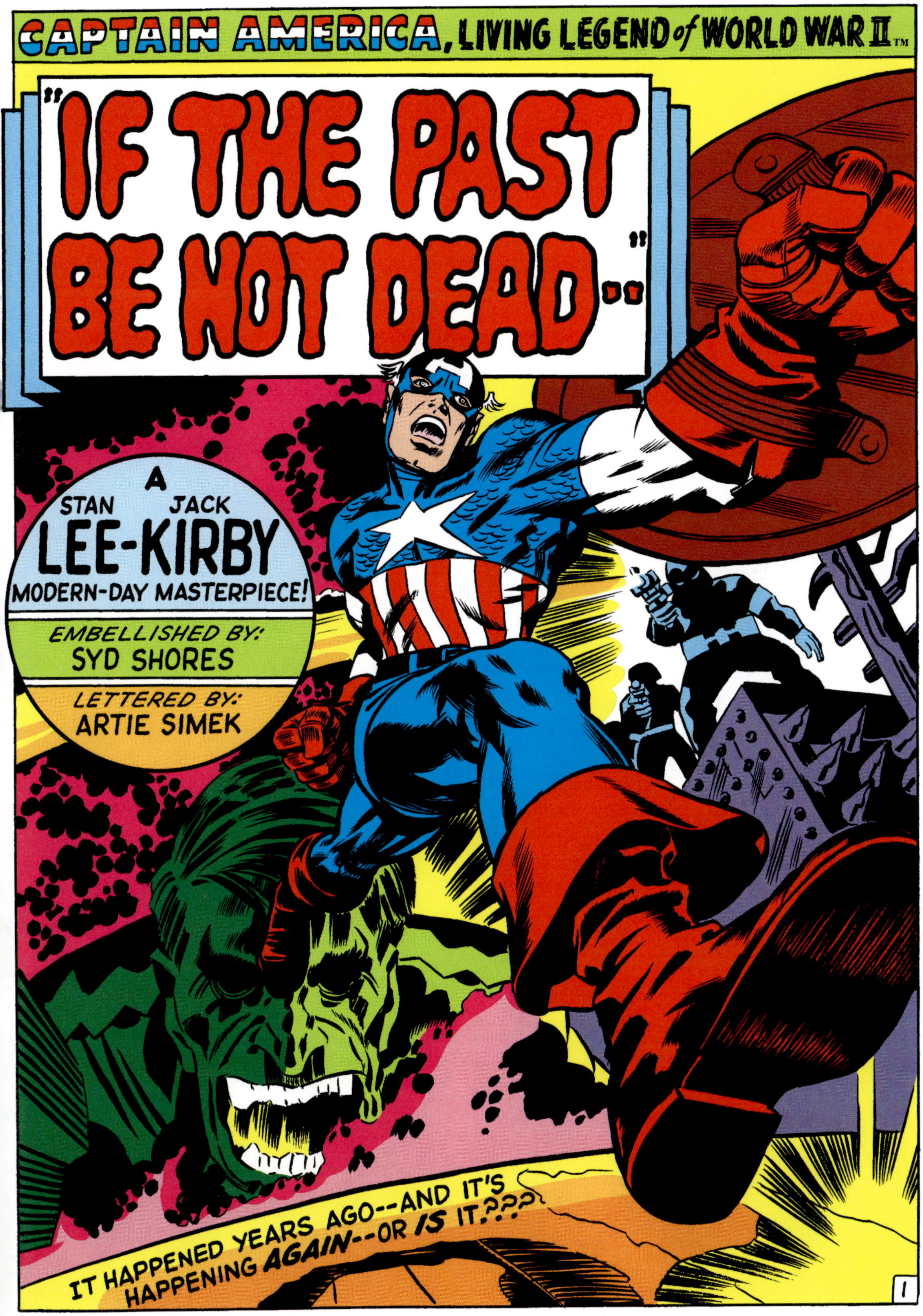
CAPTAIN AMERICA, LIVING LEGEND of WORLD WAR II ™
"IF THE PAST BE NOT DEAD--"
A STAN JACK LEE-KIRBY MODERN-DAY MASTERPIECE!
EMBELLISHED BY: SYD SHORES
LETTERED BY: ARTIE SIMEK
IT HAPPENED YEARS AGO--AND IT'S HAPPENING AGAIN--OR IS IT???
1

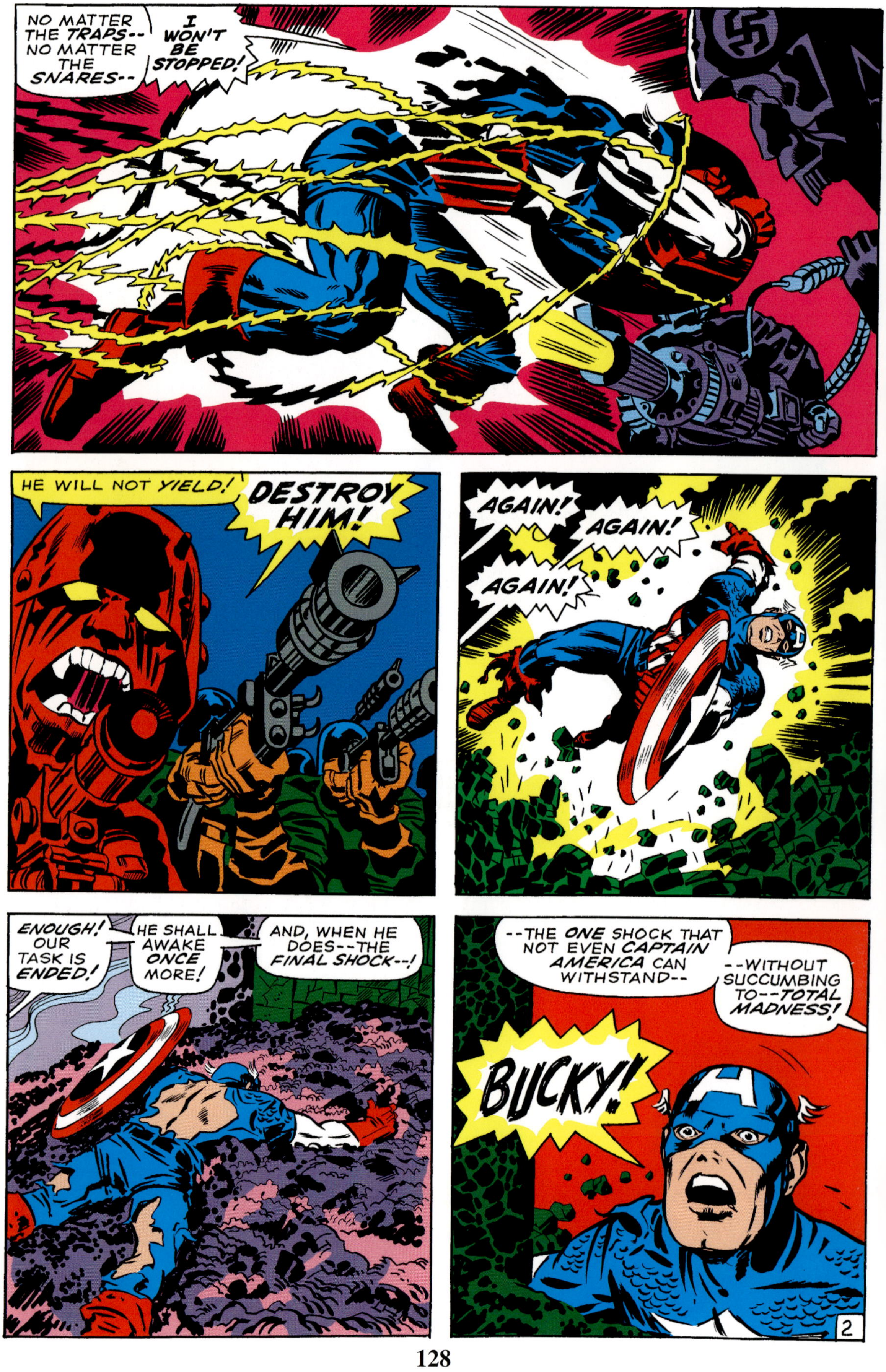
NO MATTER THE TRAPS-- NO MATTER THE SNARES--
I WON'T BE STOPPED!
HE WILL NOT YIELD!
DESTROY HIM!
AGAIN!
AGAIN!
AGAIN!
ENOUGH! OUR TASK IS ENDED!
HE SHALL AWAKE ONCE MORE!
AND, WHEN HE DOES--THE FINAL SHOCK--!
--THE ONE SHOCK THAT NOT EVEN CAPTAIN AMERICA CAN WITHSTAND--
--WITHOUT SUCCUMBING TO--TOTAL MADNESS!
BUCKY!
2

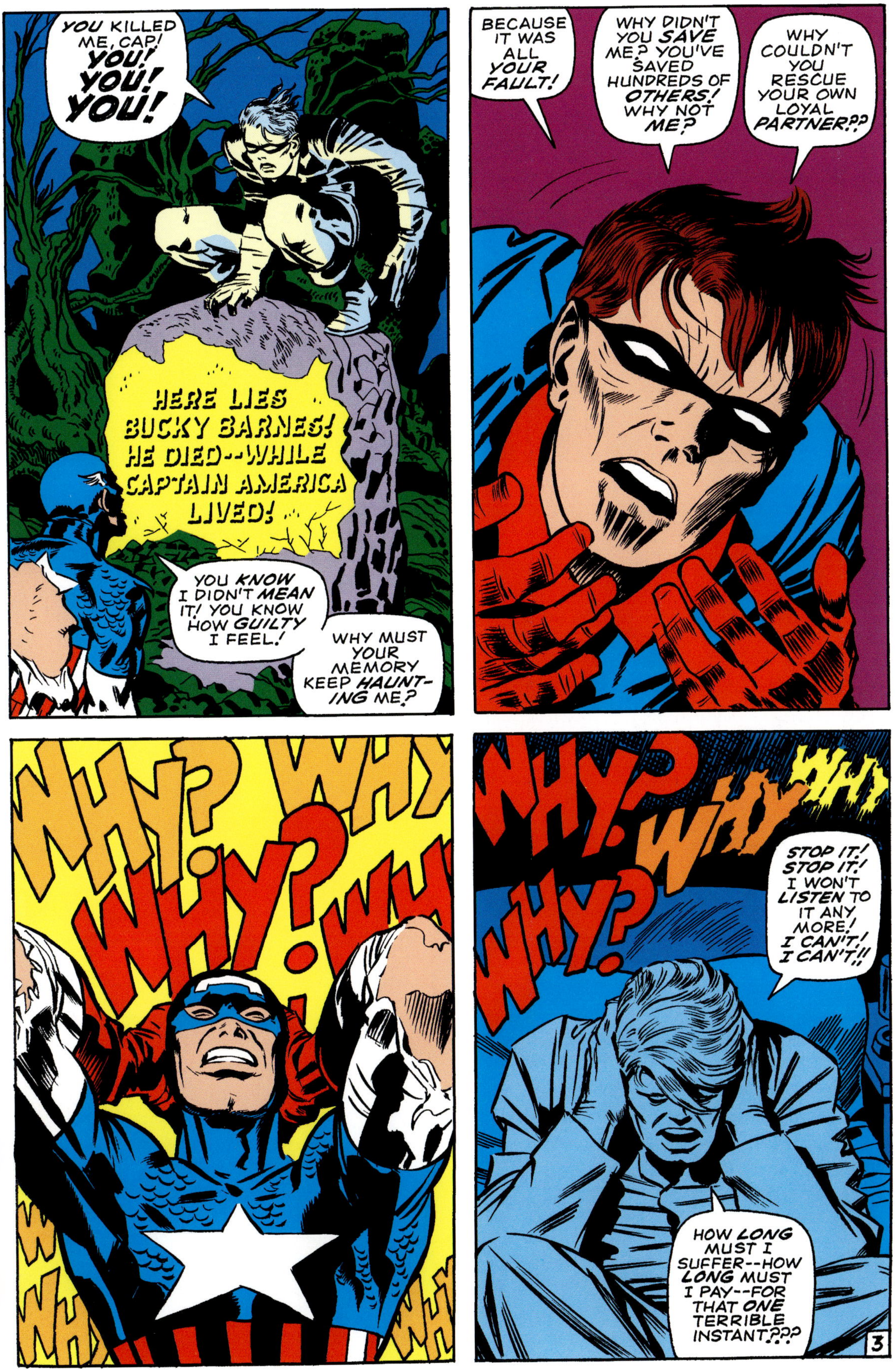
YOU KILLED ME, CAP! YOU! YOU! YOU!
HERE LIES BUCKY BARNES! HE DIED--WHILE CAPTAIN AMERICA LIVED!
YOU KNOW I DIDN'T MEAN IT! YOU KNOW HOW GUILTY I FEEL!
WHY MUST YOUR MEMORY KEEP HAUNTING ME?
BECAUSE IT WAS ALL YOUR FAULT!
WHY DIDN'T YOU SAVE ME? YOU'VE SAVED HUNDREDS OF OTHERS! WHY NOT ME?
WHY COULDN'T YOU RESCUE YOUR OWN LOYAL PARTNER??
WHY? WHY WHY? WHY? WH
WHY? WHY? WHY WHY
STOP IT! STOP IT! I WON'T LISTEN TO IT ANY MORE! I CAN'T! I CAN'T!!
HOW LONG MUST I SUFFER--HOW LONG MUST I PAY--FOR THAT ONE TERRIBLE INSTANT???
3

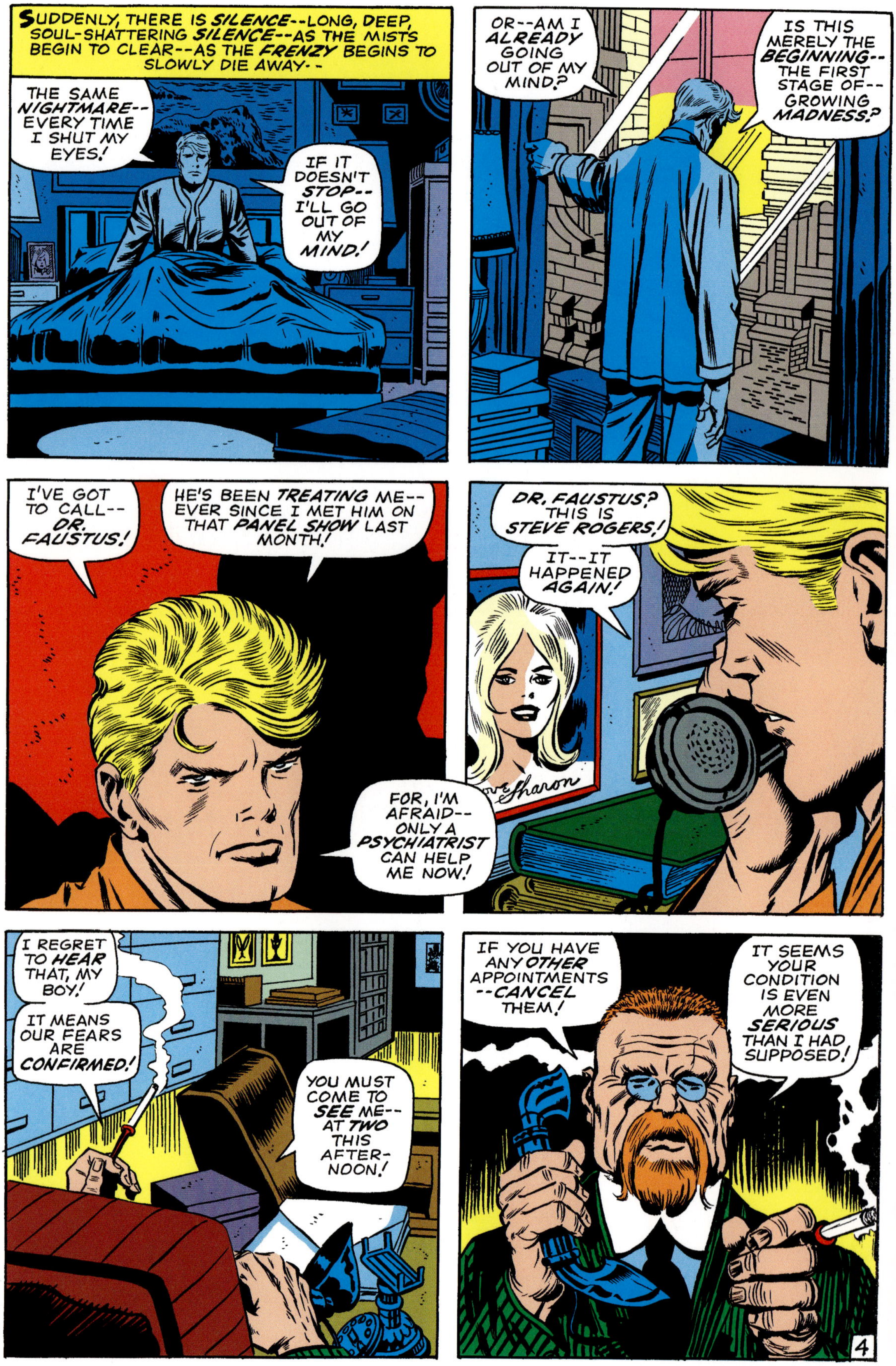
SUDDENLY, THERE IS SILENCE--LONG, DEEP, SOUL-SHATTERING SILENCE--AS THE MISTS BEGIN TO CLEAR--AS THE FRENZY BEGINS TO SLOWLY DIE AWAY--
THE SAME NIGHTMARE--EVERY TIME I SHUT MY EYES!
IF IT DOESN'T STOP--I'LL GO OUT OF MY MIND!
OR--AM I ALREADY GOING OUT OF MY MIND?
IS THIS MERELY THE BEGINNING--THE FIRST STAGE OF--GROWING MADNESS?
I'VE GOT TO CALL--DR. FAUSTUS!
HE'S BEEN TREATING ME--EVER SINCE I MET HIM ON THAT PANEL SHOW LAST MONTH!
FOR, I'M AFRAID--ONLY A PSYCHIATRIST CAN HELP ME NOW!
DR. FAUSTUS? THIS IS STEVE ROGERS!
IT--IT HAPPENED AGAIN!
Love Sharon
I REGRET TO HEAR THAT, MY BOY!
IT MEANS OUR FEARS ARE CONFIRMED!
YOU MUST COME TO SEE ME--AT TWO THIS AFTER-NOON!
IF YOU HAVE ANY OTHER APPOINTMENTS --CANCEL THEM!
IT SEEMS YOUR CONDITION IS EVEN MORE SERIOUS THAN I HAD SUPPOSED!
4

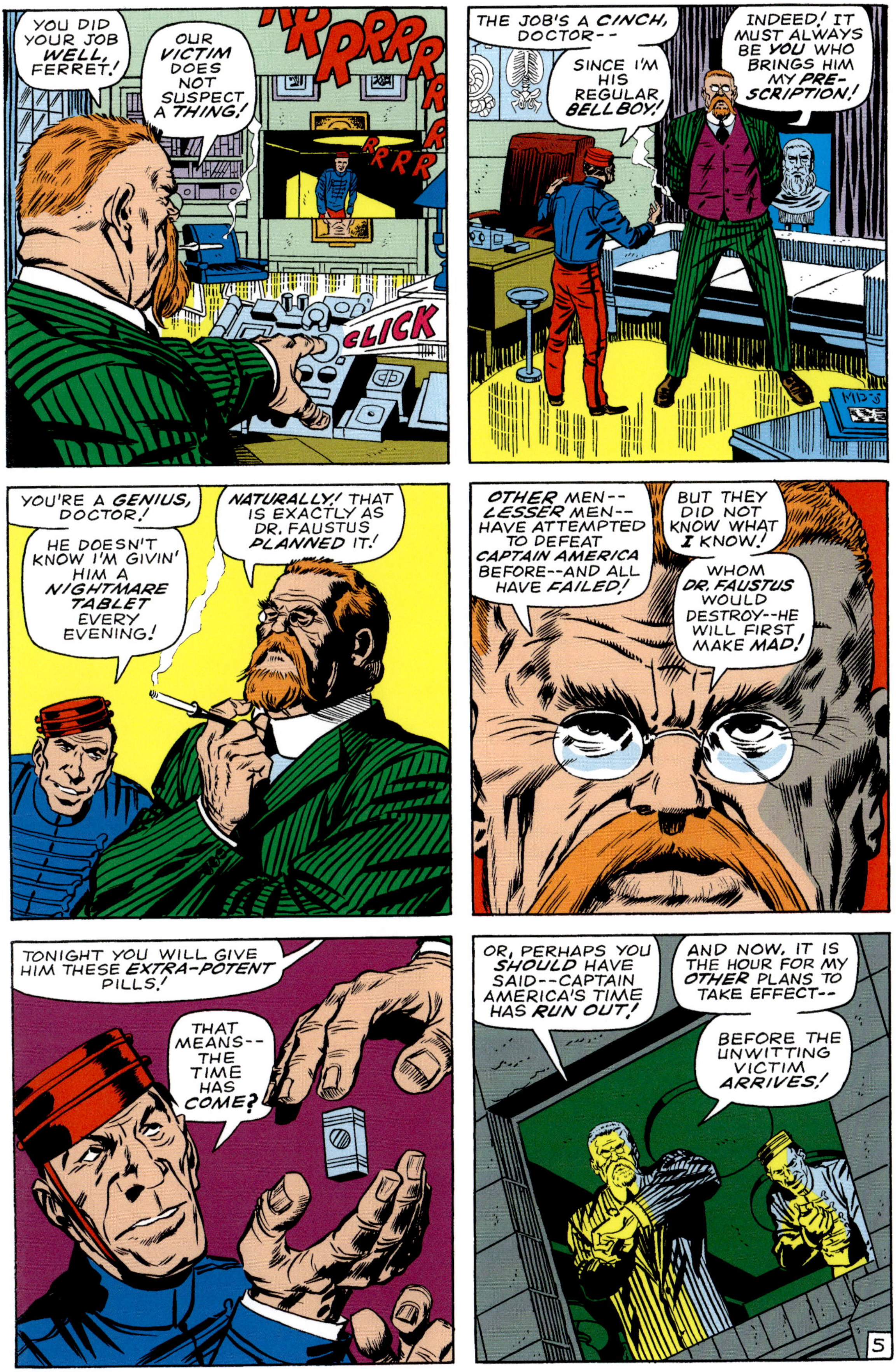

YOU DID YOUR JOB WELL, FERRET!
OUR VICTIM DOES NOT SUSPECT A THING!
RRRRRRRR
RRRR
CLICK
THE JOB'S A CINCH, DOCTOR--
SINCE I'M HIS REGULAR BELLBOY!
INDEED! IT MUST ALWAYS BE YOU WHO BRINGS HIM MY PRE-SCRIPTION!
YOU'RE A GENIUS, DOCTOR!
HE DOESN'T KNOW I'M GIVIN' HIM A NIGHTMARE TABLET EVERY EVENING!
NATURALLY! THAT IS EXACTLY AS DR. FAUSTUS PLANNED IT!
OTHER MEN--LESSER MEN--HAVE ATTEMPTED TO DEFEAT CAPTAIN AMERICA BEFORE--AND ALL HAVE FAILED!
BUT THEY DID NOT KNOW WHAT I KNOW!
WHOM DR. FAUSTUS WOULD DESTROY--HE WILL FIRST MAKE MAD!
TONIGHT YOU WILL GIVE HIM THESE EXTRA-POTENT PILLS!
THAT MEANS--THE TIME HAS COME?
OR, PERHAPS YOU SHOULD HAVE SAID--CAPTAIN AMERICA'S TIME HAS RUN OUT!
AND NOW, IT IS THE HOUR FOR MY OTHER PLANS TO TAKE EFFECT--
BEFORE THE UNWITTING VICTIM ARRIVES!
5

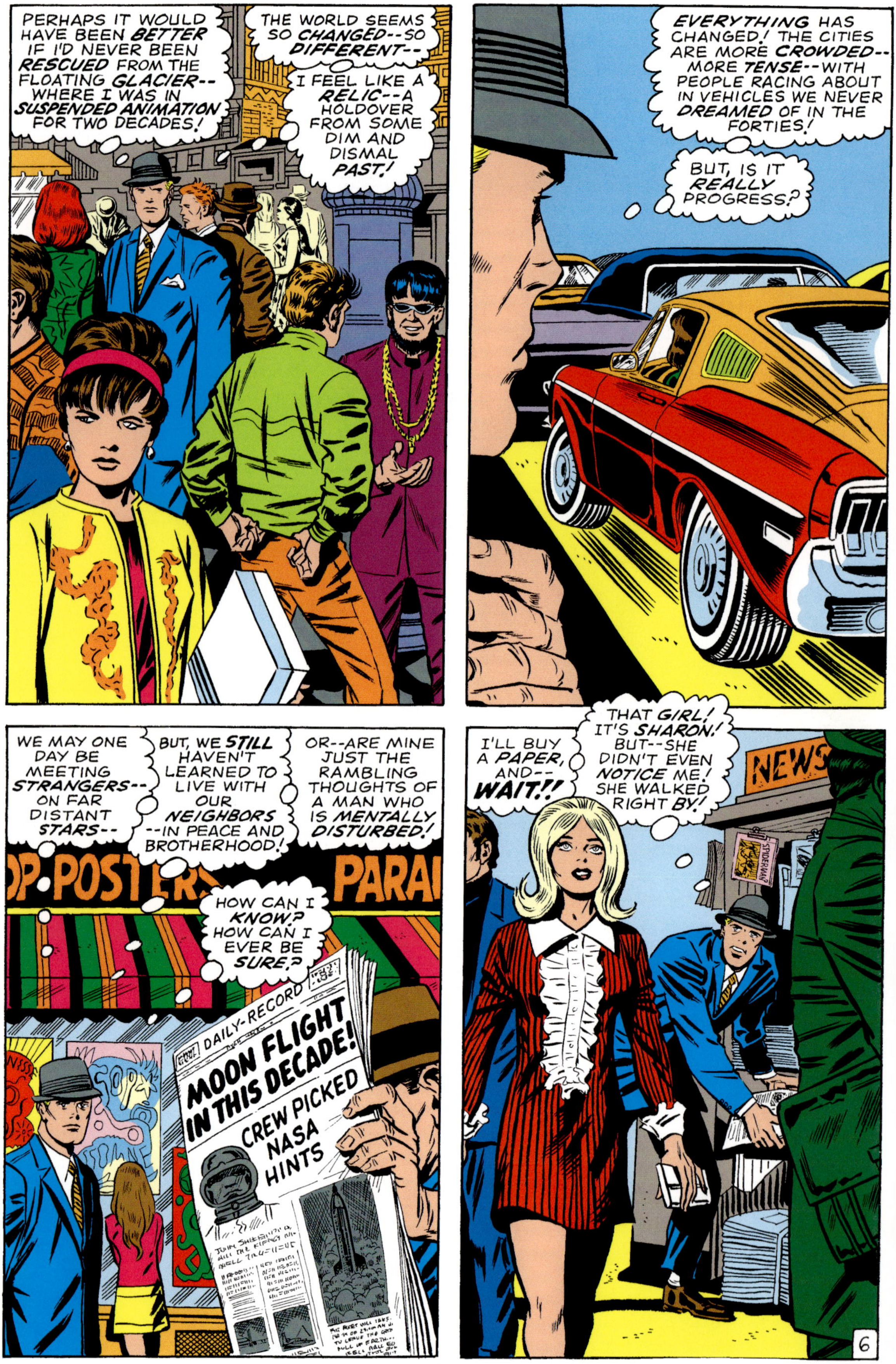
PERHAPS IT WOULD HAVE BEEN BETTER IF I'D NEVER BEEN RESCUED FROM THE FLOATING GLACIER--WHERE I WAS IN SUSPENDED ANIMATION FOR TWO DECADES!
THE WORLD SEEMS SO CHANGED--SO DIFFERENT--
I FEEL LIKE A RELIC--A HOLDOVER FROM SOME DIM AND DISMAL PAST!
EVERYTHING HAS CHANGED! THE CITIES ARE MORE CROWDED--MORE TENSE--WITH PEOPLE RACING ABOUT IN VEHICLES WE NEVER DREAMED OF IN THE FORTIES!
BUT, IS IT REALLY PROGRESS?
WE MAY ONE DAY BE MEETING STRANGERS--ON FAR DISTANT STARS--
BUT, WE STILL HAVEN'T LEARNED TO LIVE WITH OUR NEIGHBORS--IN PEACE AND BROTHERHOOD!
OR--ARE MINE JUST THE RAMBLING THOUGHTS OF A MAN WHO IS MENTALLY DISTURBED!
POSTERS
HOW CAN I KNOW? HOW CAN I EVER BE SURE?
DAILY-RECORD
MOON FLIGHT IN THIS DECADE!
CREW PICKED NASA HINTS
I'LL BUY A PAPER, AND--WAIT!!
THAT GIRL! IT'S SHARON! BUT--SHE DIDN'T EVEN NOTICE ME! SHE WALKED RIGHT BY!
NEWS
6

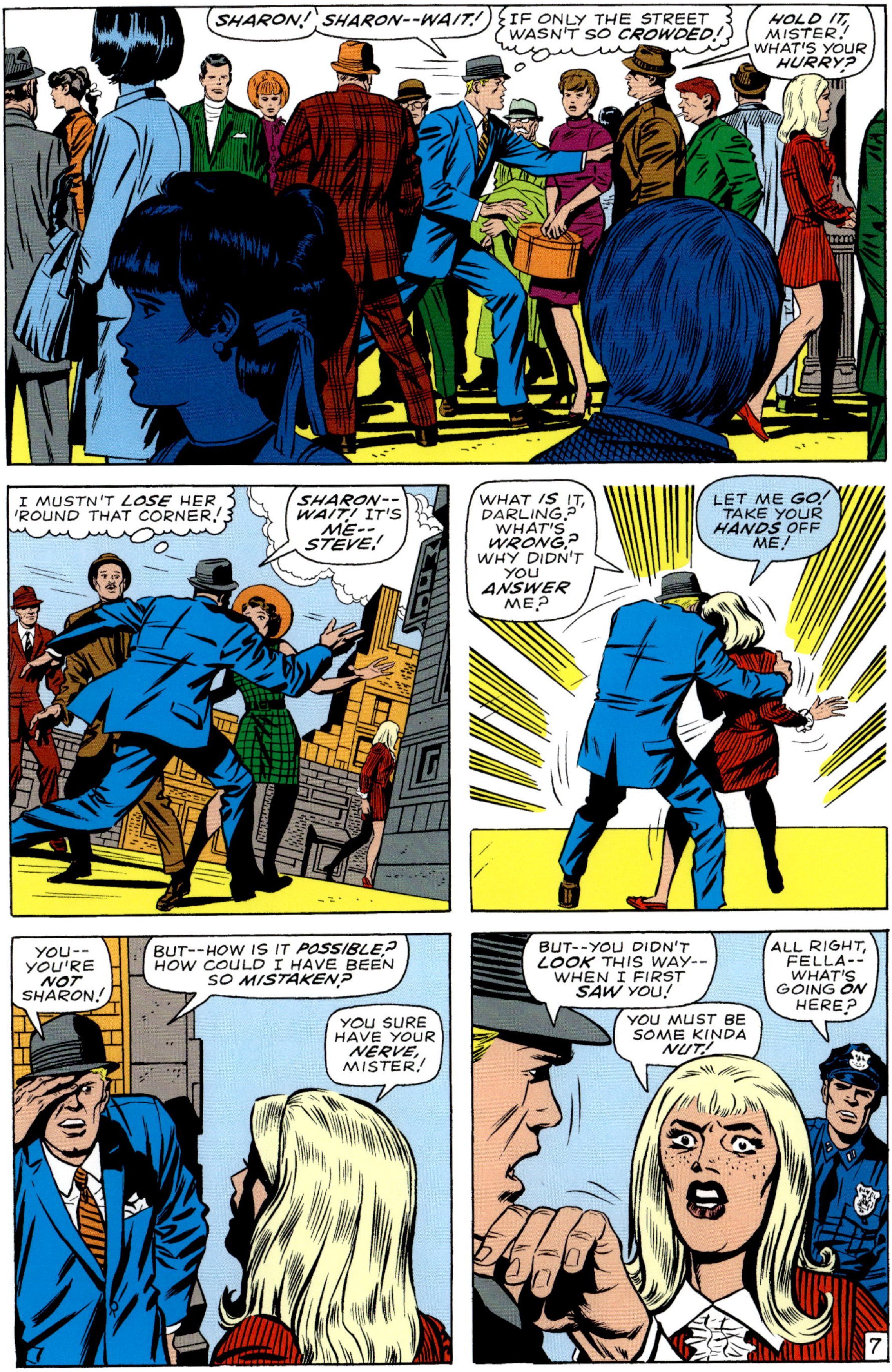
SHARON! SHARON--WAIT!
IF ONLY THE STREET WASN'T SO CROWDED!
HOLD IT, MISTER! WHAT'S YOUR HURRY?
I MUSTN'T LOSE HER 'ROUND THAT CORNER!
SHARON--WAIT! IT'S ME--STEVE!
WHAT IS IT, DARLING? WHAT'S WRONG? WHY DIDN'T YOU ANSWER ME?
LET ME GO! TAKE YOUR HANDS OFF ME!
YOU--YOU'RE NOT SHARON!
BUT--HOW IS IT POSSIBLE? HOW COULD I HAVE BEEN SO MISTAKEN?
YOU SURE HAVE YOUR NERVE, MISTER!
BUT--YOU DIDN'T LOOK THIS WAY--WHEN I FIRST SAW YOU!
YOU MUST BE SOME KINDA NUT!
ALL RIGHT, FELLA--WHAT'S GOING ON HERE?
7

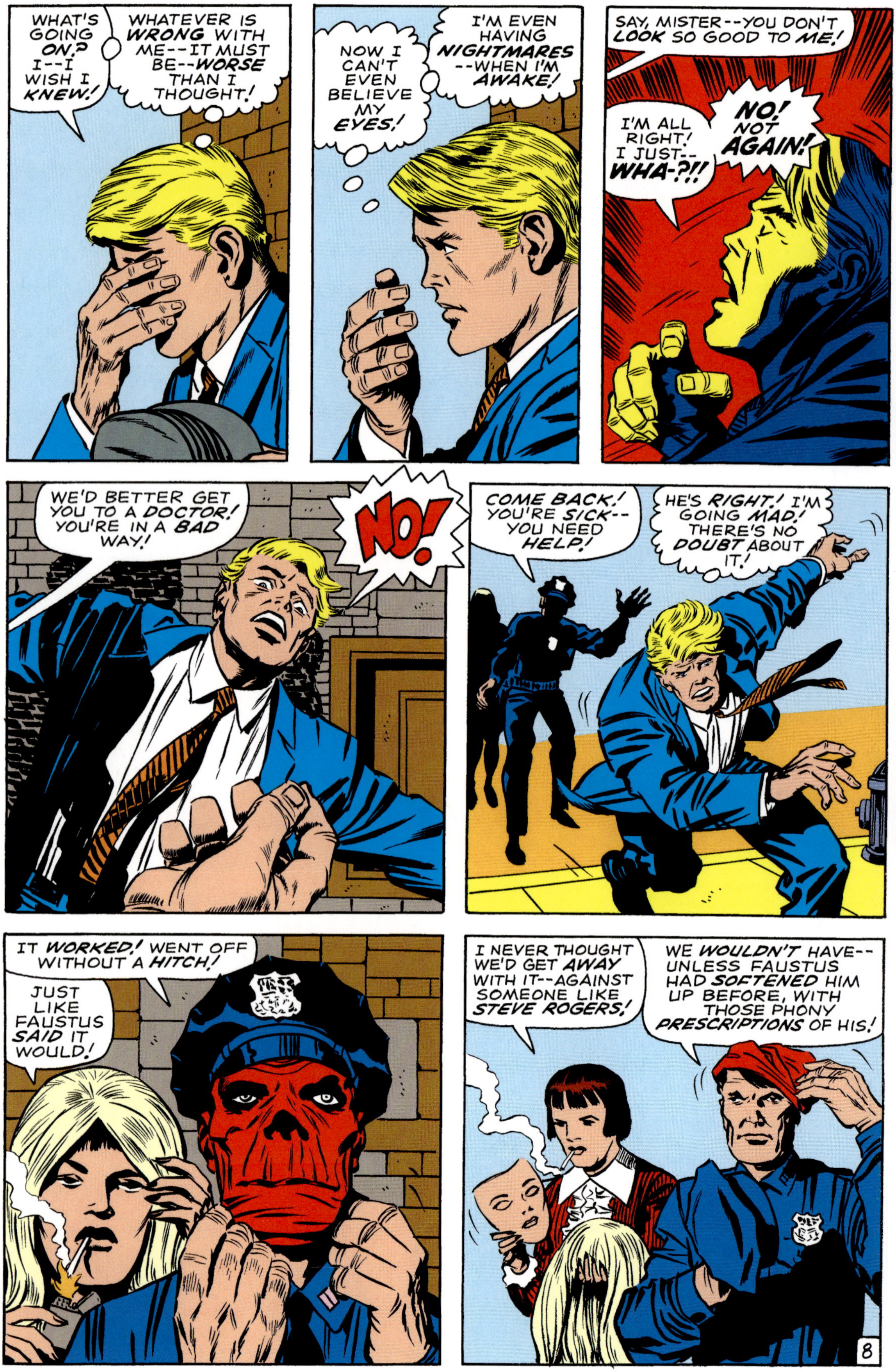
WHAT'S GOING ON? I--I WISH I KNEW!
WHATEVER IS WRONG WITH ME--IT MUST BE--WORSE THAN I THOUGHT!
NOW I CAN'T EVEN BELIEVE MY EYES!
I'M EVEN HAVING NIGHTMARES --WHEN I'M AWAKE!
SAY, MISTER--YOU DON'T LOOK SO GOOD TO ME!
I'M ALL RIGHT! I JUST-- WHA-?!!
NO! NOT AGAIN!
WE'D BETTER GET YOU TO A DOCTOR! YOU'RE IN A BAD WAY!
NO!
COME BACK! YOU'RE SICK-- YOU NEED HELP!
HE'S RIGHT! I'M GOING MAD! THERE'S NO DOUBT ABOUT IT!
IT WORKED! WENT OFF WITHOUT A HITCH!
JUST LIKE FAUSTUS SAID IT WOULD!
I NEVER THOUGHT WE'D GET AWAY WITH IT--AGAINST SOMEONE LIKE STEVE ROGERS!
WE WOULDN'T HAVE-- UNLESS FAUSTUS HAD SOFTENED HIM UP BEFORE, WITH THOSE PHONY PRESCRIPTIONS OF HIS!
8

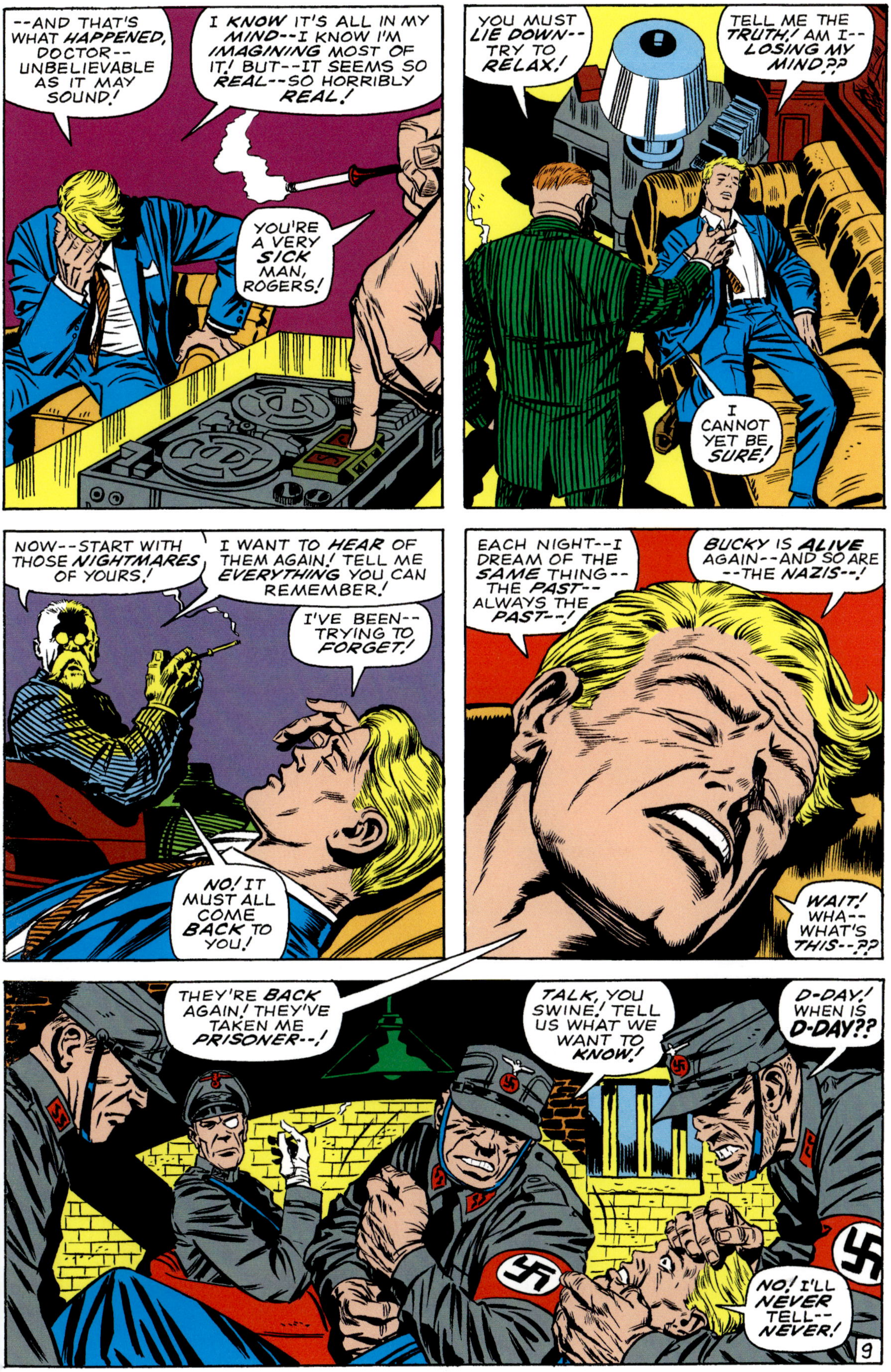
--AND THAT'S WHAT HAPPENED, DOCTOR-- UNBELIEVABLE AS IT MAY SOUND!
I KNOW IT'S ALL IN MY MIND--I KNOW I'M IMAGINING MOST OF IT! BUT--IT SEEMS SO REAL--SO HORRIBLY REAL!
YOU'RE A VERY SICK MAN, ROGERS!
YOU MUST LIE DOWN--TRY TO RELAX!
TELL ME THE TRUTH! AM I--LOSING MY MIND??
I CANNOT YET BE SURE!
NOW--START WITH THOSE NIGHTMARES OF YOURS!
I WANT TO HEAR OF THEM AGAIN! TELL ME EVERYTHING YOU CAN REMEMBER!
I'VE BEEN--TRYING TO FORGET!
NO! IT MUST ALL COME BACK TO YOU!
EACH NIGHT--I DREAM OF THE SAME THING--THE PAST--ALWAYS THE PAST--!
BUCKY IS ALIVE AGAIN--AND SO ARE--THE NAZIS--!
WAIT! WHA--WHAT'S THIS--??
THEY'RE BACK AGAIN! THEY'VE TAKEN ME PRISONER--!
TALK, YOU SWINE! TELL US WHAT WE WANT TO KNOW!
D-DAY! WHEN IS D-DAY??
NO! I'LL NEVER TELL--NEVER!
9

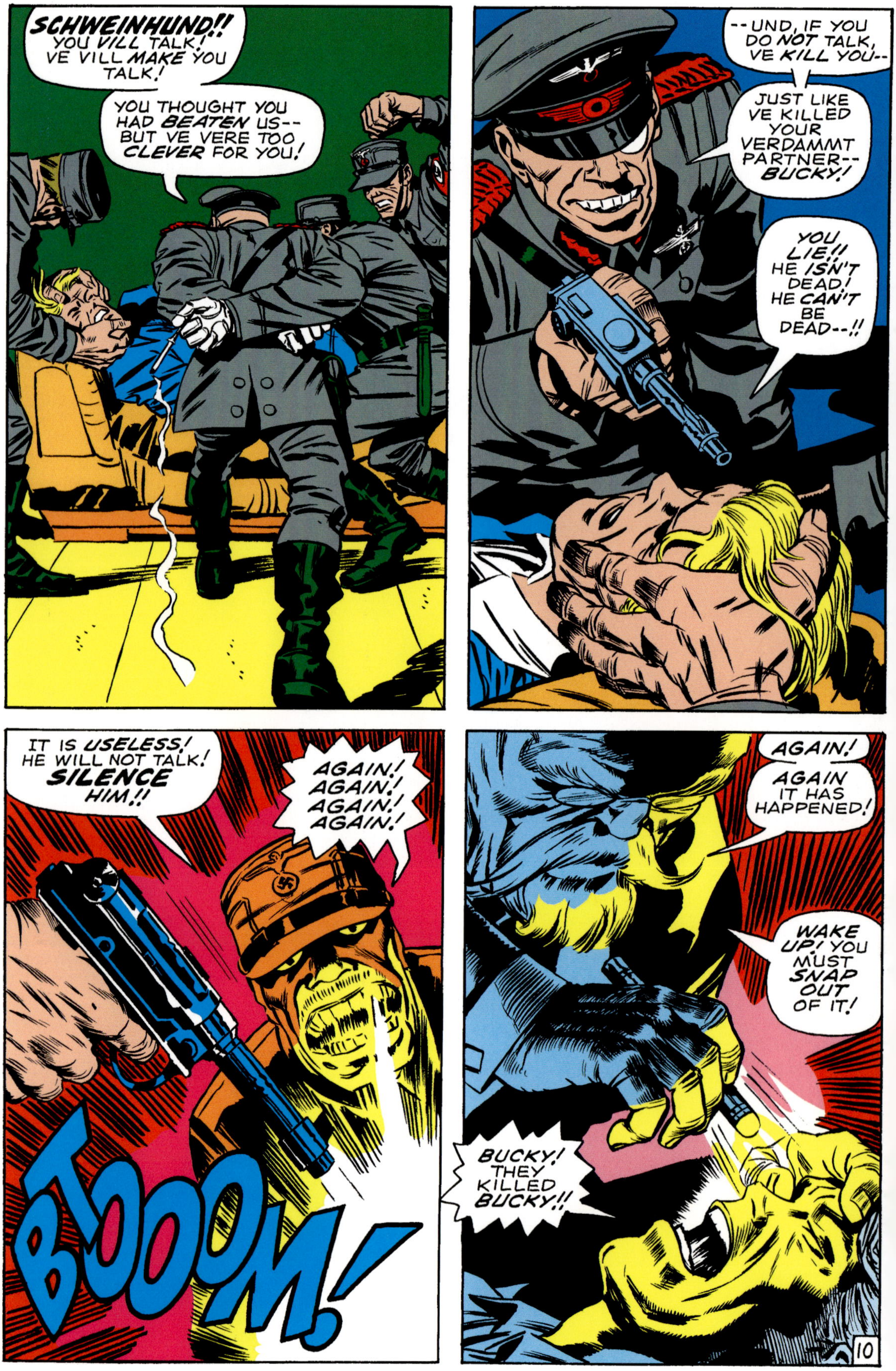
SCHWEINHUND!! YOU VILL TALK! VE VILL MAKE YOU TALK!
YOU THOUGHT YOU HAD BEATEN US-- BUT VE VERE TOO CLEVER FOR YOU!
--UND, IF YOU DO NOT TALK, VE KILL YOU--
JUST LIKE VE KILLED YOUR VERDAMMT PARTNER-- BUCKY!
YOU LIE!! HE ISN'T DEAD! HE CAN'T BE DEAD--!!
IT IS USELESS! HE WILL NOT TALK! SILENCE HIM!!
AGAIN! AGAIN! AGAIN! AGAIN!
BLOOOM!
AGAIN!
AGAIN IT HAS HAPPENED!
WAKE UP! YOU MUST SNAP OUT OF IT!
BUCKY! THEY KILLED BUCKY!!
10

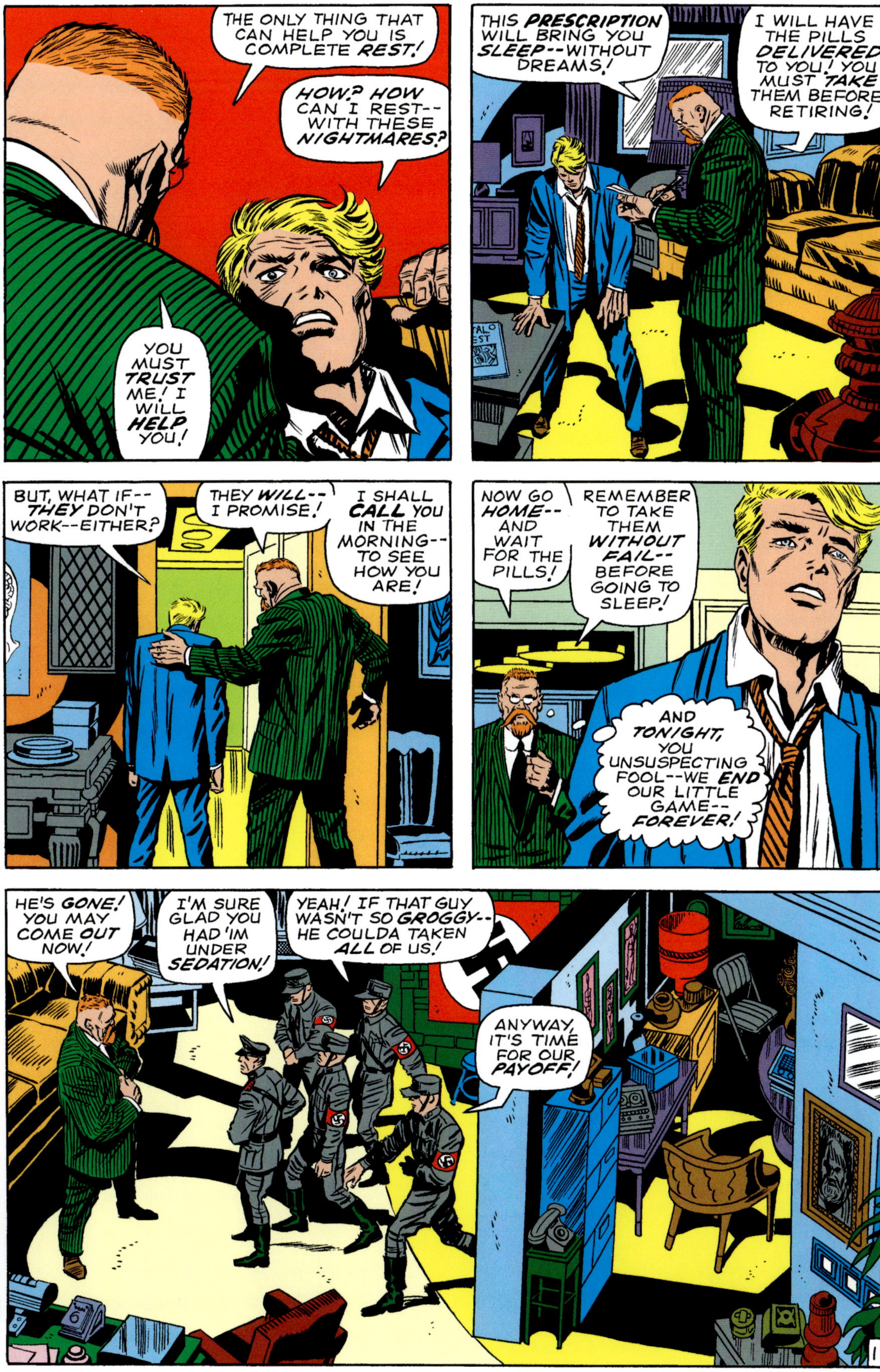
THE ONLY THING THAT CAN HELP YOU IS COMPLETE REST!
HOW? HOW CAN I REST-- WITH THESE NIGHTMARES?
YOU MUST TRUST ME! I WILL HELP YOU!
THIS PRESCRIPTION WILL BRING YOU SLEEP--WITHOUT DREAMS!
I WILL HAVE THE PILLS DELIVERED TO YOU! YOU MUST TAKE THEM BEFORE RETIRING!
BUT, WHAT IF-- THEY DON'T WORK--EITHER?
THEY WILL-- I PROMISE!
I SHALL CALL YOU IN THE MORNING-- TO SEE HOW YOU ARE!
NOW GO HOME-- AND WAIT FOR THE PILLS!
REMEMBER TO TAKE THEM WITHOUT FAIL-- BEFORE GOING TO SLEEP!
AND TONIGHT, YOU UNSUSPECTING FOOL--WE END OUR LITTLE GAME-- FOREVER!
HE'S GONE! YOU MAY COME OUT NOW!
I'M SURE GLAD YOU HAD 'IM UNDER SEDATION!
YEAH! IF THAT GUY WASN'T SO GROGGY-- HE COULDA TAKEN ALL OF US!
ANYWAY, IT'S TIME FOR OUR PAYOFF!
11

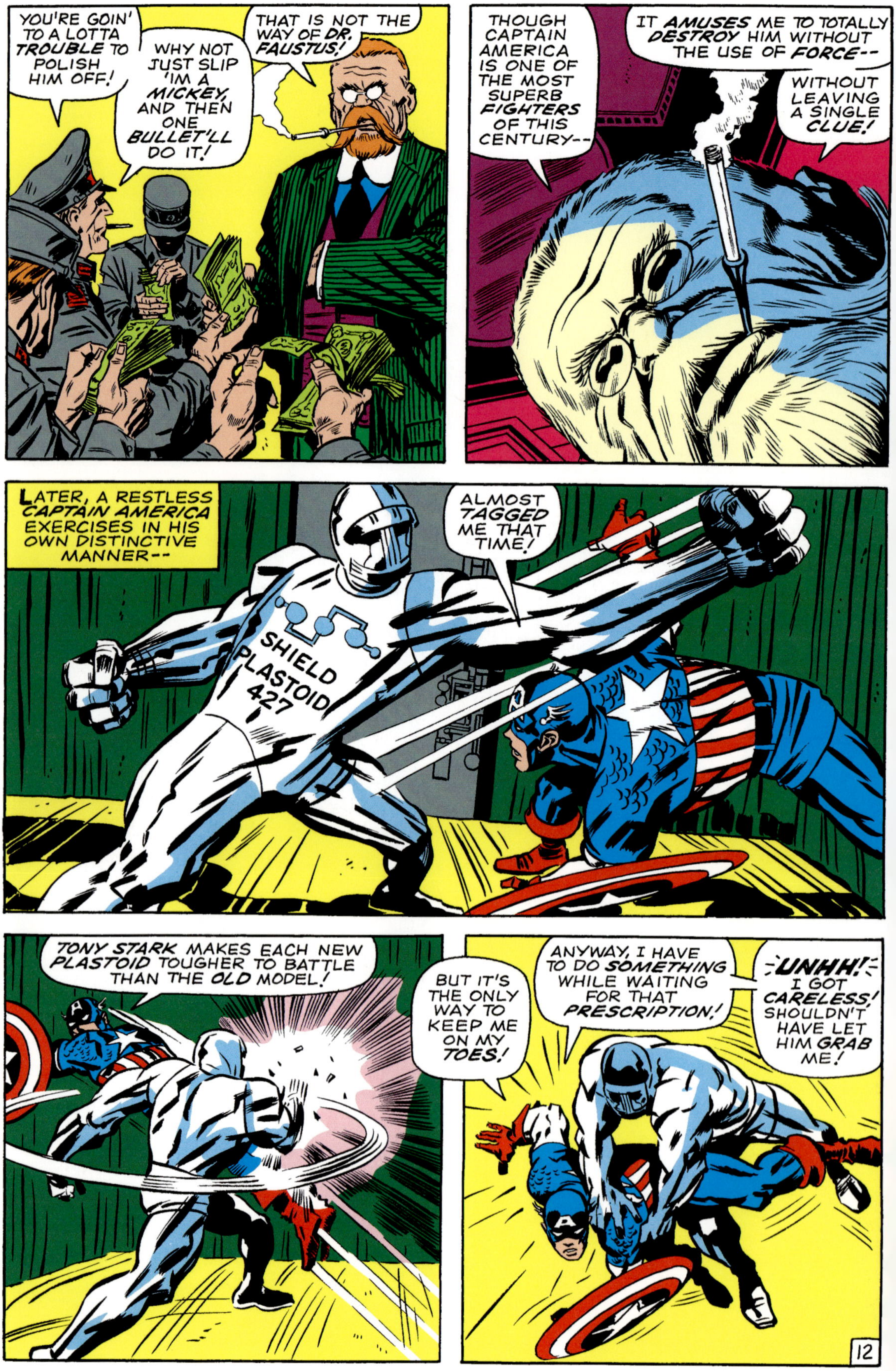
YOU'RE GOIN' TO A LOTTA TROUBLE TO POLISH HIM OFF!
WHY NOT JUST SLIP 'IM A MICKEY, AND THEN ONE BULLET'LL DO IT!
THAT IS NOT THE WAY OF DR. FAUSTUS!
THOUGH CAPTAIN AMERICA IS ONE OF THE MOST SUPERB FIGHTERS OF THIS CENTURY--
IT AMUSES ME TO TOTALLY DESTROY HIM WITHOUT THE USE OF FORCE--
WITHOUT LEAVING A SINGLE CLUE!
LATER, A RESTLESS CAPTAIN AMERICA EXERCISES IN HIS OWN DISTINCTIVE MANNER--
ALMOST TAGGED ME THAT TIME!
SHIELD PLASTOID 427
TONY STARK MAKES EACH NEW PLASTOID TOUGHER TO BATTLE THAN THE OLD MODEL!
BUT IT'S THE ONLY WAY TO KEEP ME ON MY TOES!
ANYWAY, I HAVE TO DO SOMETHING WHILE WAITING FOR THAT PRESCRIPTION!
UNHH! I GOT CARELESS! SHOULDN'T HAVE LET HIM GRAB ME!
12

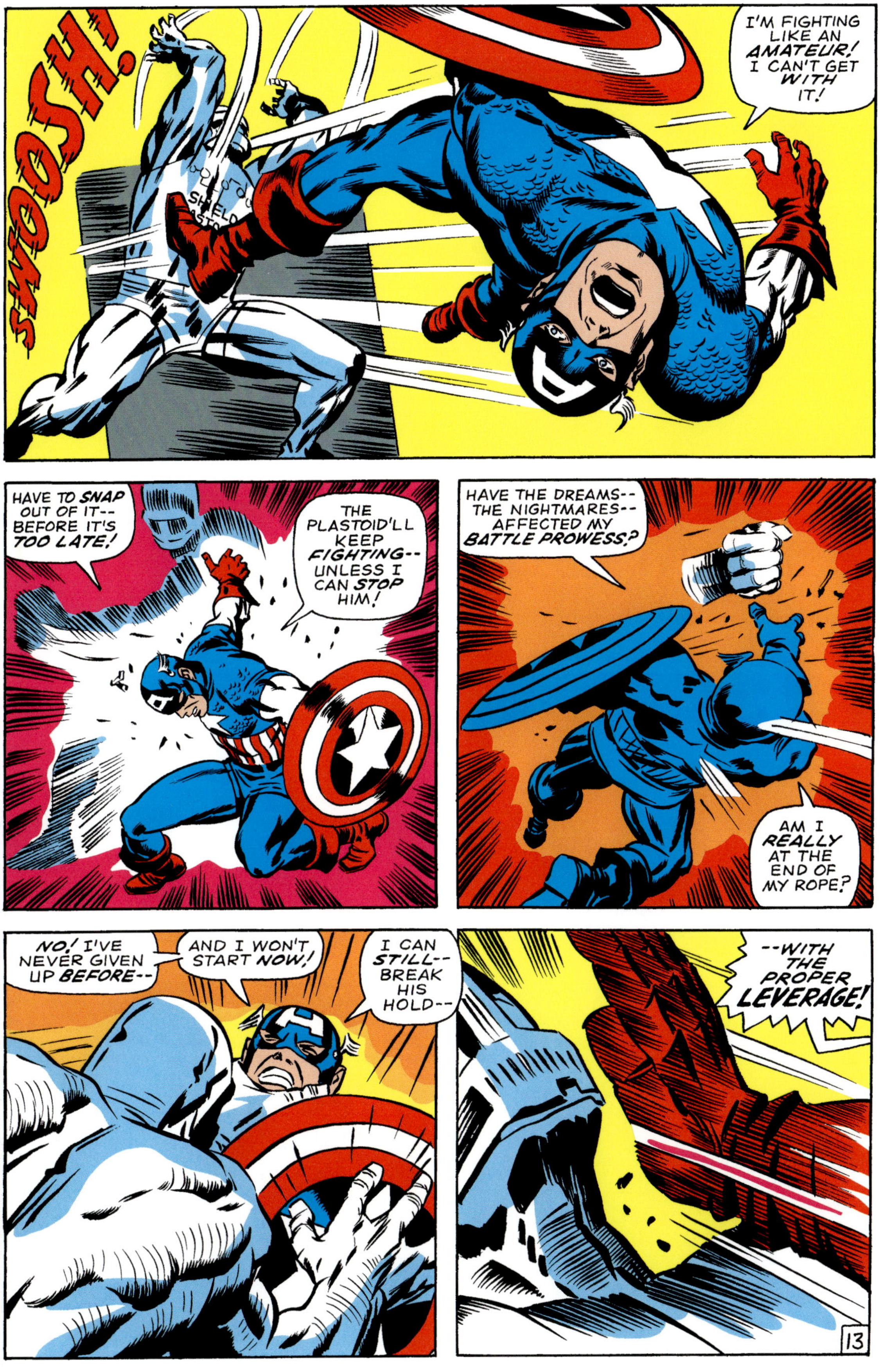
SWOOSH!
I'M FIGHTING LIKE AN AMATEUR! I CAN'T GET WITH IT!
HAVE TO SNAP OUT OF IT-- BEFORE IT'S TOO LATE!
THE PLASTOID'LL KEEP FIGHTING-- UNLESS I CAN STOP HIM!
HAVE THE DREAMS-- THE NIGHTMARES-- AFFECTED MY BATTLE PROWESS?
AM I REALLY AT THE END OF MY ROPE?
NO! I'VE NEVER GIVEN UP BEFORE--
AND I WON'T START NOW!
I CAN STILL-- BREAK HIS HOLD--
--WITH THE PROPER LEVERAGE!
13

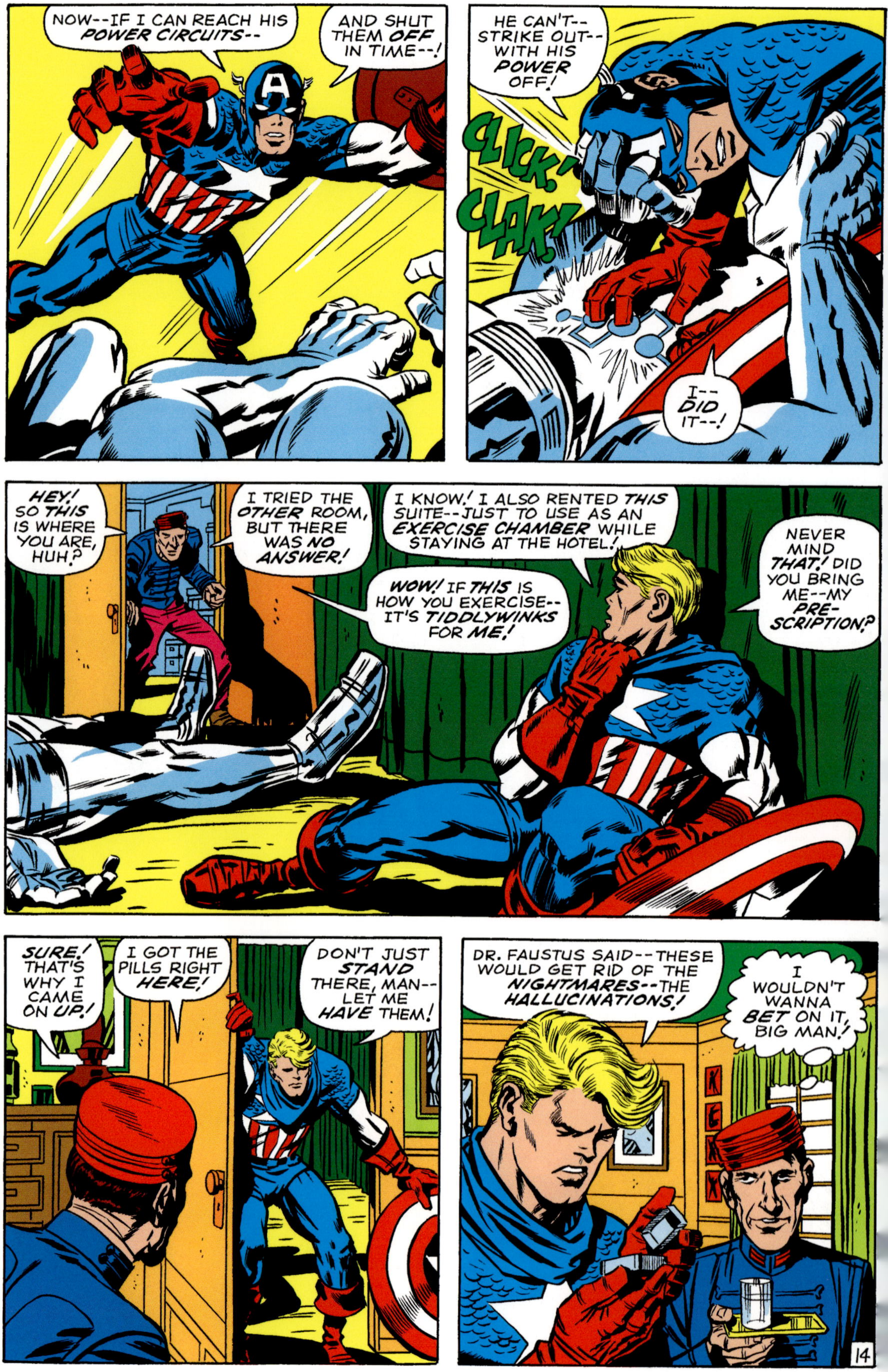
NOW--IF I CAN REACH HIS POWER CIRCUITS--
AND SHUT THEM OFF IN TIME--!
HE CAN'T--STRIKE OUT--WITH HIS POWER OFF!
CLICK! CLAK!
I--DID IT--!
HEY! SO THIS IS WHERE YOU ARE, HUH?
I TRIED THE OTHER ROOM, BUT THERE WAS NO ANSWER!
I KNOW! I ALSO RENTED THIS SUITE--JUST TO USE AS AN EXERCISE CHAMBER WHILE STAYING AT THE HOTEL!
WOW! IF THIS IS HOW YOU EXERCISE--IT'S TIDDLYWINKS FOR ME!
NEVER MIND THAT! DID YOU BRING ME--MY PRE-SCRIPTION?
SURE! THAT'S WHY I CAME ON UP!
I GOT THE PILLS RIGHT HERE!
DON'T JUST STAND THERE, MAN--LET ME HAVE THEM!
DR. FAUSTUS SAID--THESE WOULD GET RID OF THE NIGHTMARES--THE HALLUCINATIONS!
I WOULDN'T WANNA BET ON IT, BIG MAN!
14

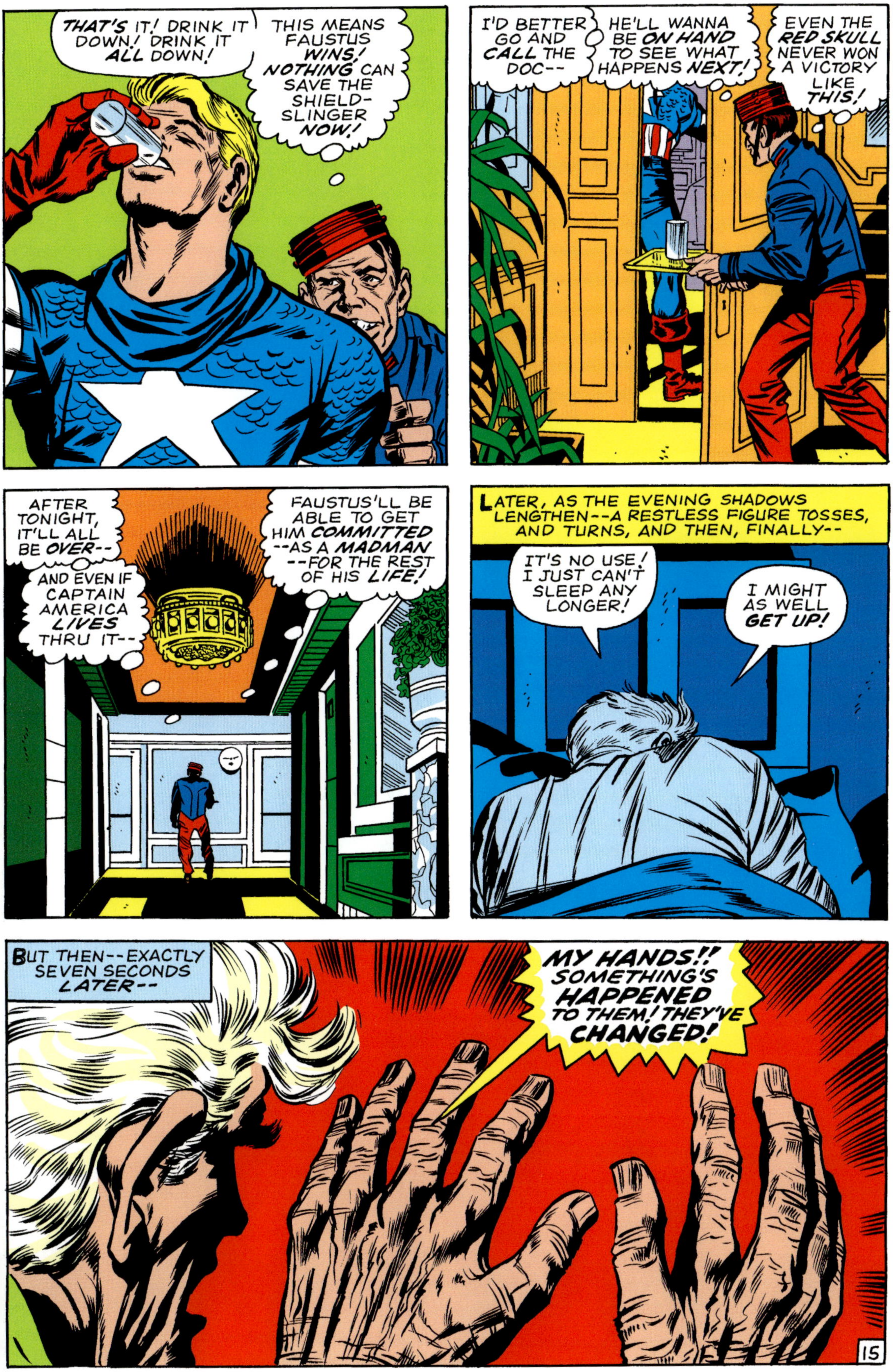
THAT'S IT! DRINK IT DOWN! DRINK IT ALL DOWN!
THIS MEANS FAUSTUS WINS! NOTHING CAN SAVE THE SHIELD-SLINGER NOW!
I'D BETTER GO AND CALL THE DOC--
HE'LL WANNA BE ON HAND TO SEE WHAT HAPPENS NEXT!
EVEN THE RED SKULL NEVER WON A VICTORY LIKE THIS!
AFTER TONIGHT, IT'LL ALL BE OVER--
AND EVEN IF CAPTAIN AMERICA LIVES THRU IT--
FAUSTUS'LL BE ABLE TO GET HIM COMMITTED --AS A MADMAN --FOR THE REST OF HIS LIFE!
LATER, AS THE EVENING SHADOWS LENGTHEN--A RESTLESS FIGURE TOSSES, AND TURNS, AND THEN, FINALLY--
IT'S NO USE! I JUST CAN'T SLEEP ANY LONGER!
I MIGHT AS WELL GET UP!
BUT THEN--EXACTLY SEVEN SECONDS LATER--
MY HANDS!! SOMETHING'S HAPPENED TO THEM! THEY'VE CHANGED!
15

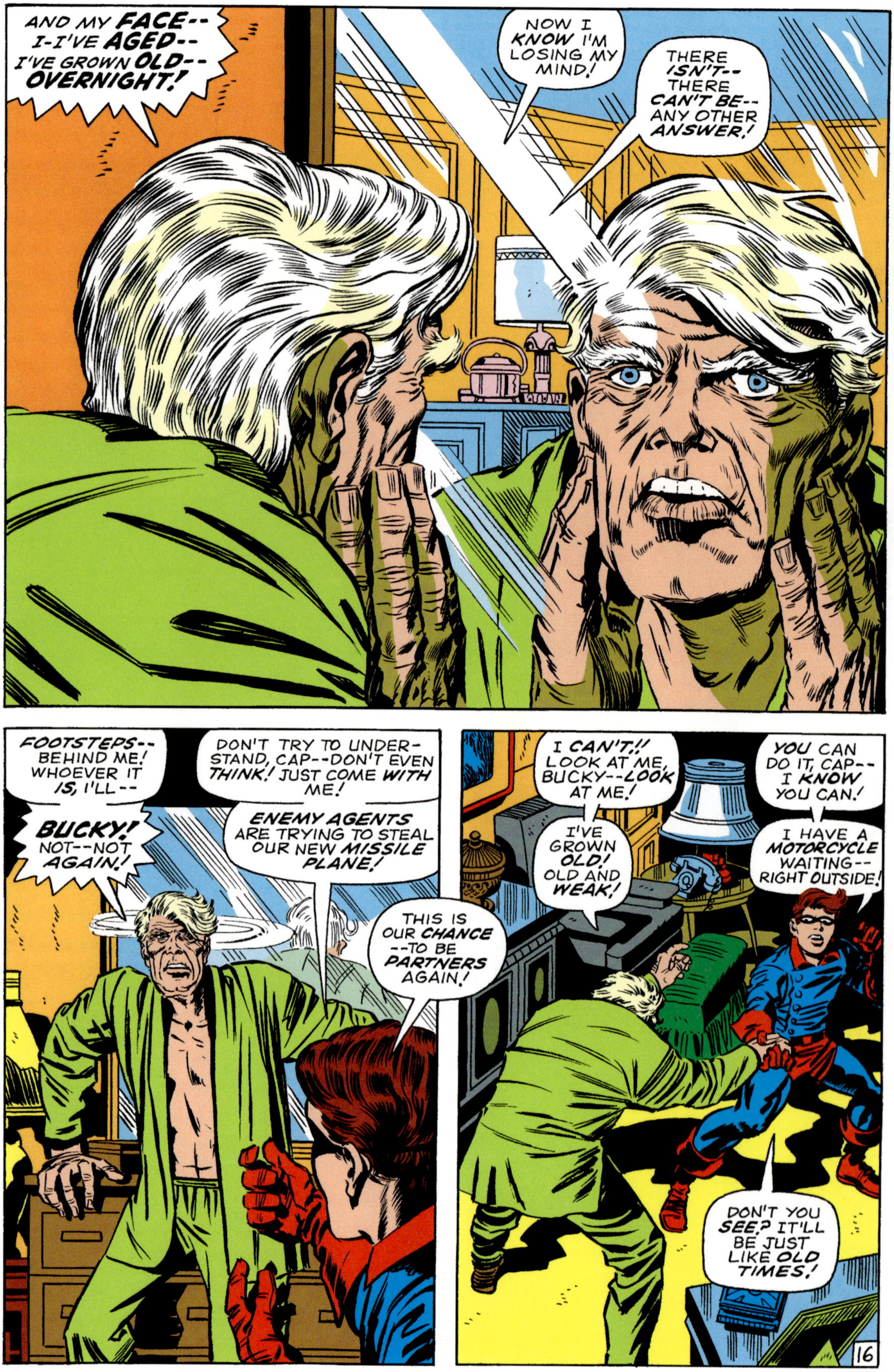
AND MY FACE-- I-I'VE AGED-- I'VE GROWN OLD-- OVERNIGHT!
NOW I KNOW I'M LOSING MY MIND!
THERE ISN'T-- THERE CAN'T BE-- ANY OTHER ANSWER!
FOOTSTEPS-- BEHIND ME! WHOEVER IT IS, I'LL--
BUCKY! NOT--NOT AGAIN!
DON'T TRY TO UNDERSTAND, CAP--DON'T EVEN THINK! JUST COME WITH ME!
ENEMY AGENTS ARE TRYING TO STEAL OUR NEW MISSILE PLANE!
THIS IS OUR CHANCE --TO BE PARTNERS AGAIN!
I CAN'T!! LOOK AT ME, BUCKY--LOOK AT ME!
I'VE GROWN OLD! OLD AND WEAK!
YOU CAN DO IT, CAP-- I KNOW YOU CAN!
I HAVE A MOTORCYCLE WAITING-- RIGHT OUTSIDE!
DON'T YOU SEE? IT'LL BE JUST LIKE OLD TIMES!
16

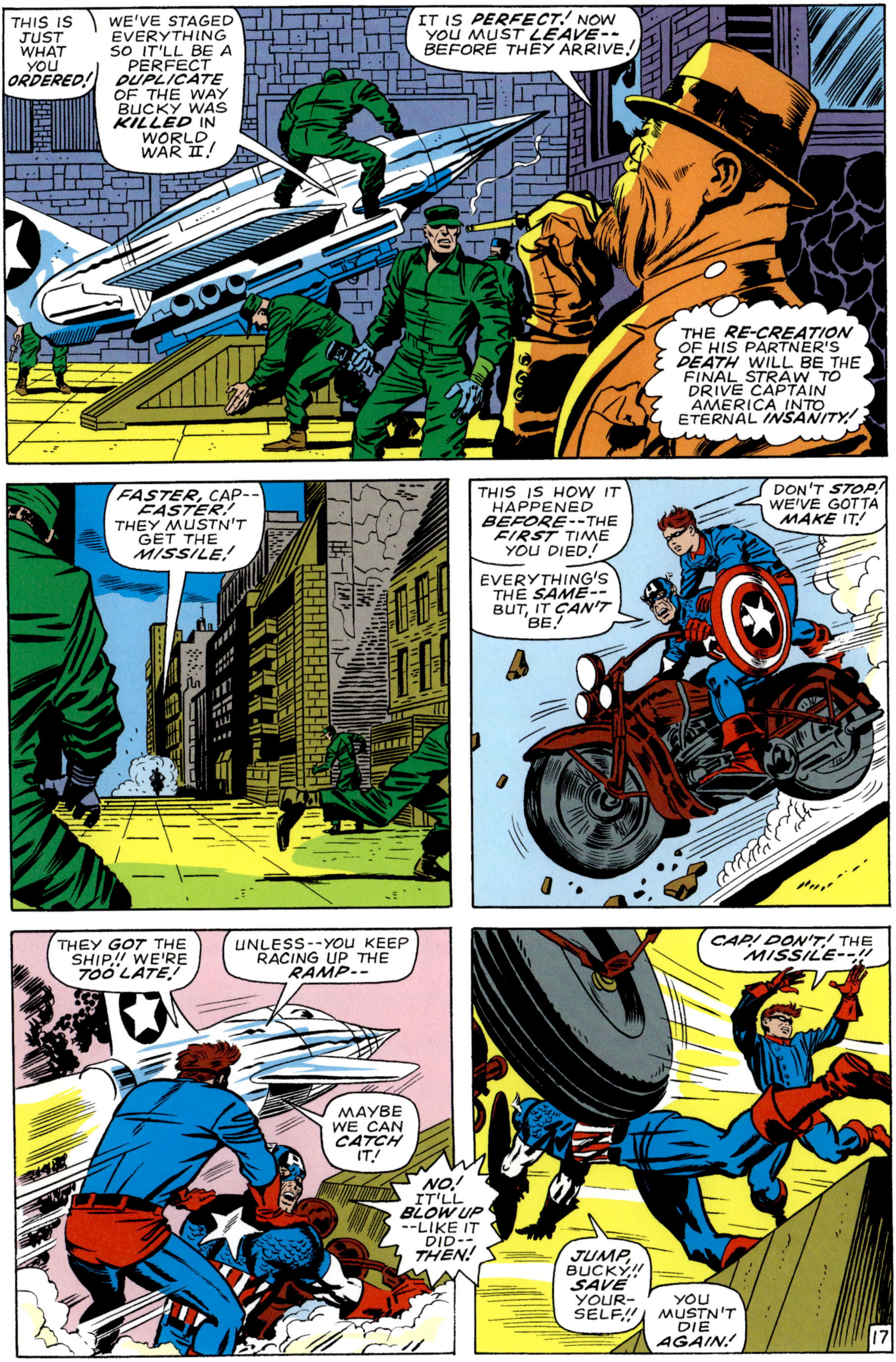
THIS IS JUST WHAT YOU ORDERED!
WE'VE STAGED EVERYTHING SO IT'LL BE A PERFECT DUPLICATE OF THE WAY BUCKY WAS KILLED IN WORLD WAR II!
IT IS PERFECT! NOW YOU MUST LEAVE-- BEFORE THEY ARRIVE!
THE RE-CREATION OF HIS PARTNER'S DEATH WILL BE THE FINAL STRAW TO DRIVE CAPTAIN AMERICA INTO ETERNAL INSANITY!
FASTER, CAP-- FASTER! THEY MUSTN'T GET THE MISSILE!
THIS IS HOW IT HAPPENED BEFORE--THE FIRST TIME YOU DIED!
EVERYTHING'S THE SAME-- BUT, IT CAN'T BE!
DON'T STOP! WE'VE GOTTA MAKE IT!
THEY GOT THE SHIP!! WE'RE TOO LATE!
UNLESS--YOU KEEP RACING UP THE RAMP--
MAYBE WE CAN CATCH IT!
NO! IT'LL BLOW UP --LIKE IT DID-- THEN!
CAP! DON'T! THE MISSILE--!!
JUMP, BUCKY!! SAVE YOUR-SELF!!
YOU MUSTN'T DIE AGAIN!
17

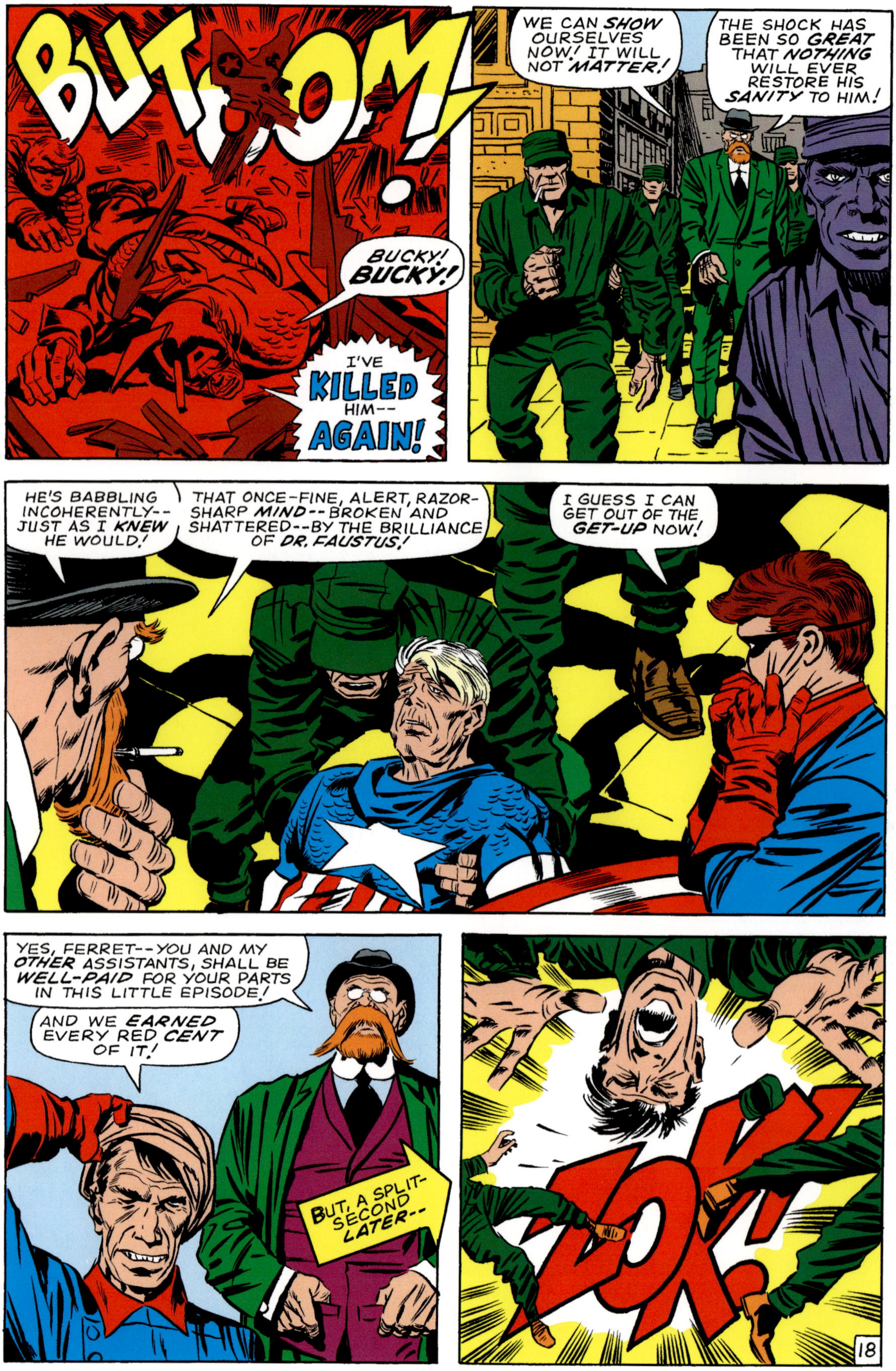
BUT-OOM!
BUCKY! BUCKY!
I'VE KILLED HIM-- AGAIN!
WE CAN SHOW OURSELVES NOW! IT WILL NOT MATTER!
THE SHOCK HAS BEEN SO GREAT THAT NOTHING WILL EVER RESTORE HIS SANITY TO HIM!
HE'S BABBLING INCOHERENTLY-- JUST AS I KNEW HE WOULD!
THAT ONCE-FINE, ALERT, RAZOR-SHARP MIND--BROKEN AND SHATTERED--BY THE BRILLIANCE OF DR. FAUSTUS!
I GUESS I CAN GET OUT OF THE GET-UP NOW!
YES, FERRET--YOU AND MY OTHER ASSISTANTS, SHALL BE WELL-PAID FOR YOUR PARTS IN THIS LITTLE EPISODE!
AND WE EARNED EVERY RED CENT OF IT!
BUT, A SPLIT-SECOND LATER--
ZOK!
18

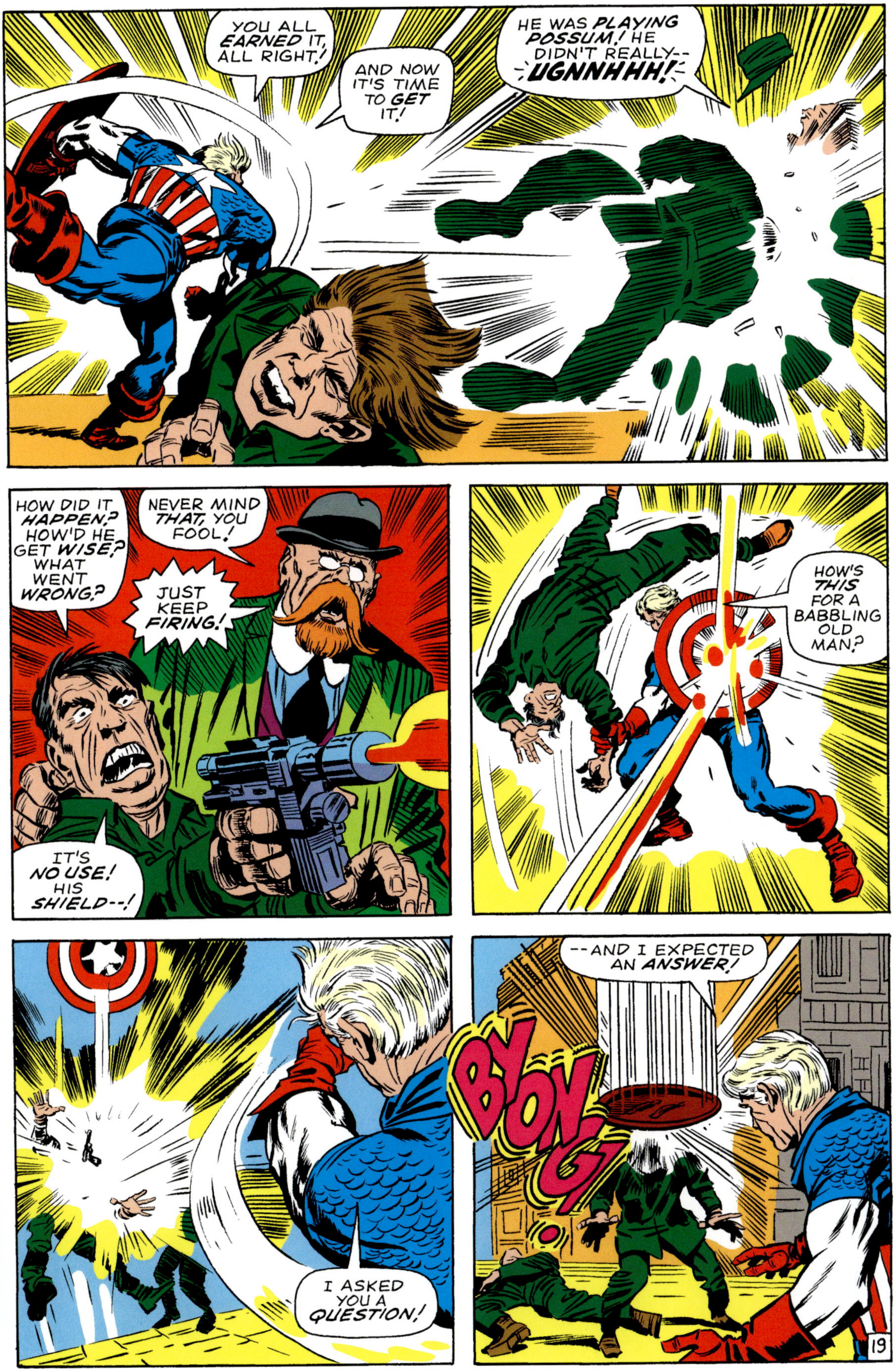
YOU ALL EARNED IT, ALL RIGHT!
AND NOW IT'S TIME TO GET IT!
HE WAS PLAYING POSSUM! HE DIDN'T REALLY-- UGNNHHH!
HOW DID IT HAPPEN? HOW'D HE GET WISE? WHAT WENT WRONG?
NEVER MIND THAT, YOU FOOL!
JUST KEEP FIRING!
IT'S NO USE! HIS SHIELD--!
HOW'S THIS FOR A BABBLING OLD MAN?
I ASKED YOU A QUESTION!
BYONG!
--AND I EXPECTED AN ANSWER!
19

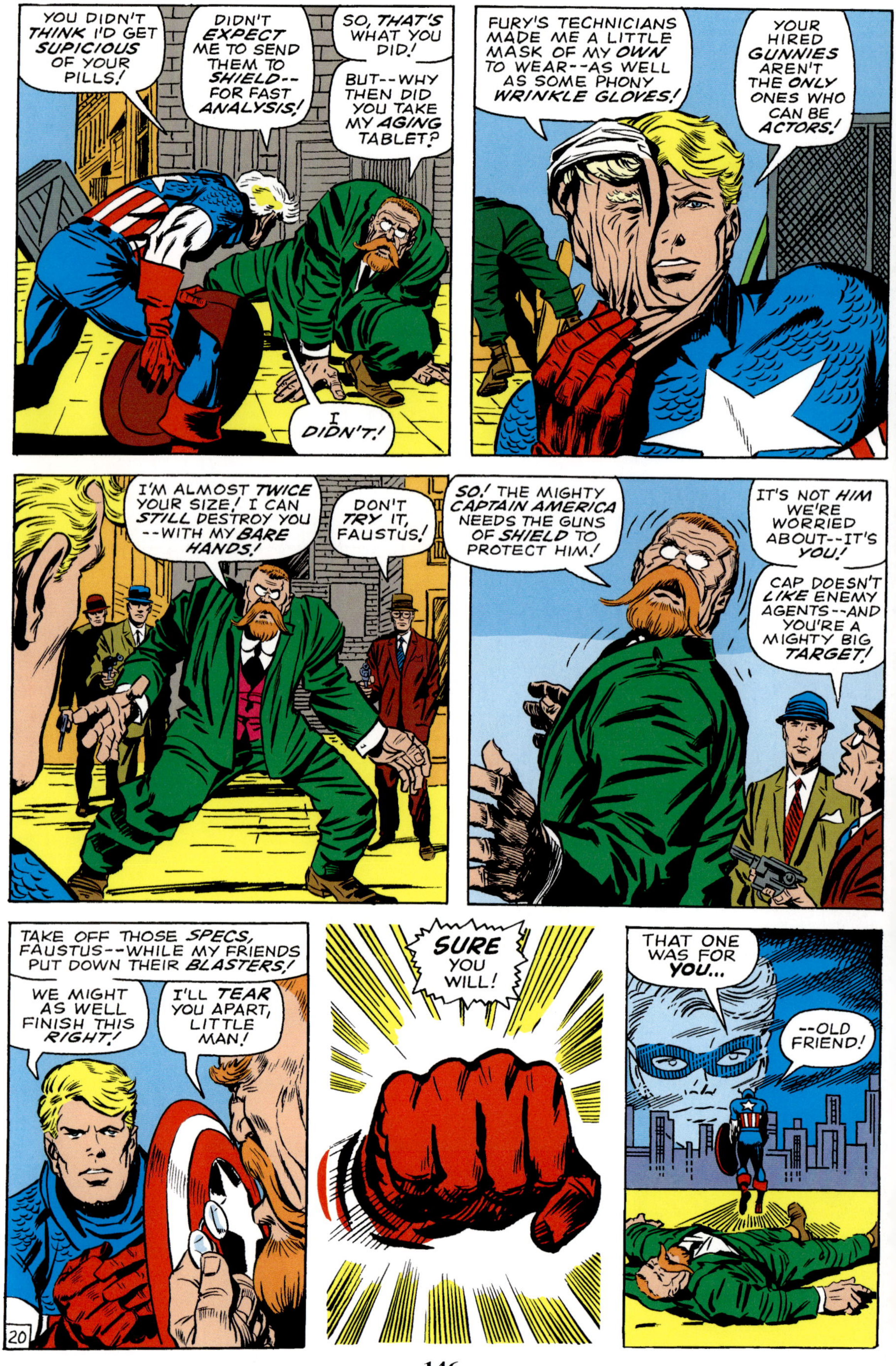

YOU DIDN'T THINK I'D GET SUPICIOUS OF YOUR PILLS!
DIDN'T EXPECT ME TO SEND THEM TO SHIELD-- FOR FAST ANALYSIS!
SO, THAT'S WHAT YOU DID!
BUT--WHY THEN DID YOU TAKE MY AGING TABLET?
I DIDN'T!
FURY'S TECHNICIANS MADE ME A LITTLE MASK OF MY OWN TO WEAR--AS WELL AS SOME PHONY WRINKLE GLOVES!
YOUR HIRED GUNNIES AREN'T THE ONLY ONES WHO CAN BE ACTORS!
I'M ALMOST TWICE YOUR SIZE! I CAN STILL DESTROY YOU --WITH MY BARE HANDS!
DON'T TRY IT, FAUSTUS!
SO! THE MIGHTY CAPTAIN AMERICA NEEDS THE GUNS OF SHIELD TO PROTECT HIM!
IT'S NOT HIM WE'RE WORRIED ABOUT--IT'S YOU!
CAP DOESN'T LIKE ENEMY AGENTS--AND YOU'RE A MIGHTY BIG TARGET!
TAKE OFF THOSE SPECS, FAUSTUS--WHILE MY FRIENDS PUT DOWN THEIR BLASTERS!
WE MIGHT AS WELL FINISH THIS RIGHT!
I'LL TEAR YOU APART, LITTLE MAN!
20
SURE YOU WILL!
THAT ONE WAS FOR YOU...
--OLD FRIEND!

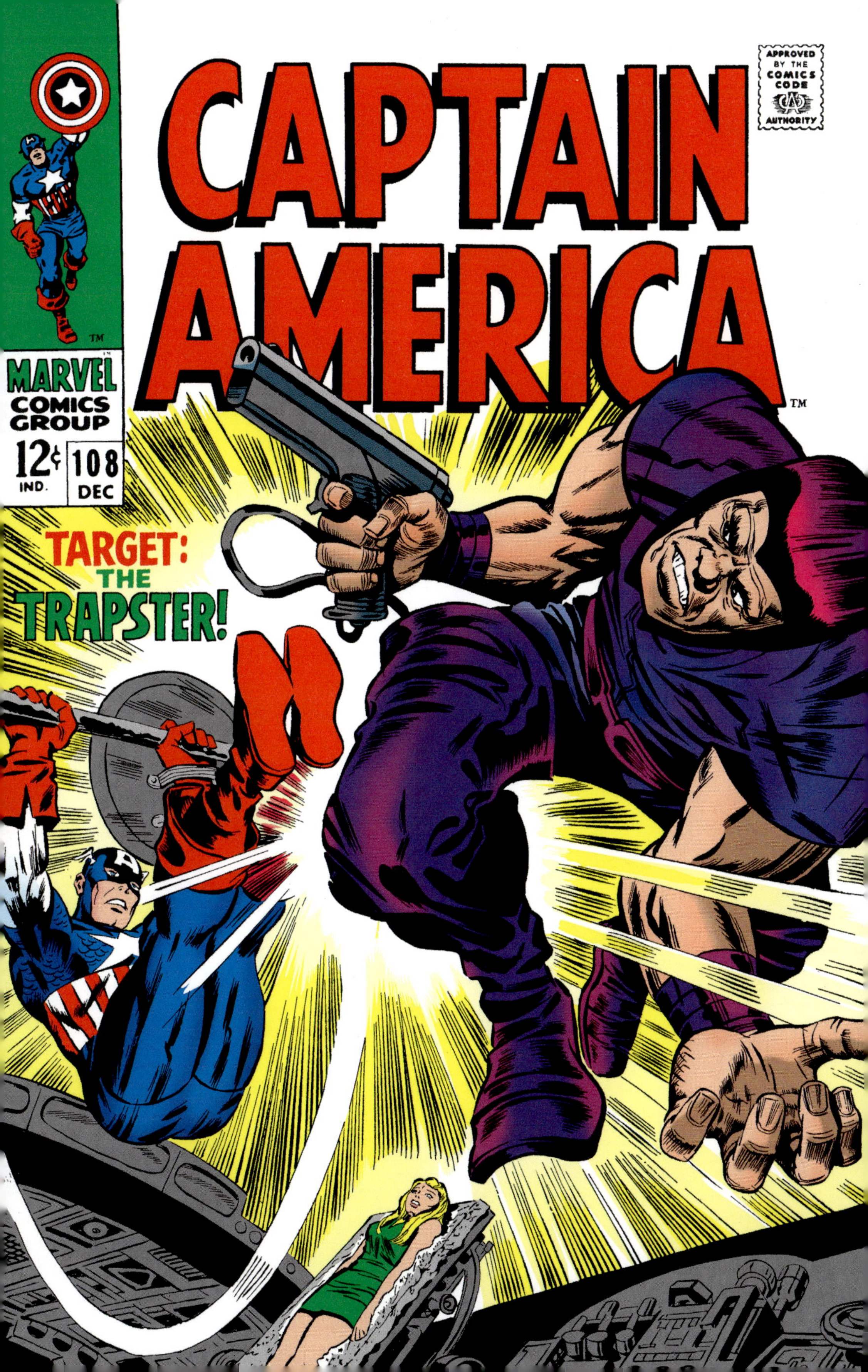

CAPTAIN AMERICA
MARVEL COMICS GROUP
12¢ IND.
108 DEC
APPROVED BY THE COMICS CODE AUTHORITY
TARGET: THE TRAPSTER!

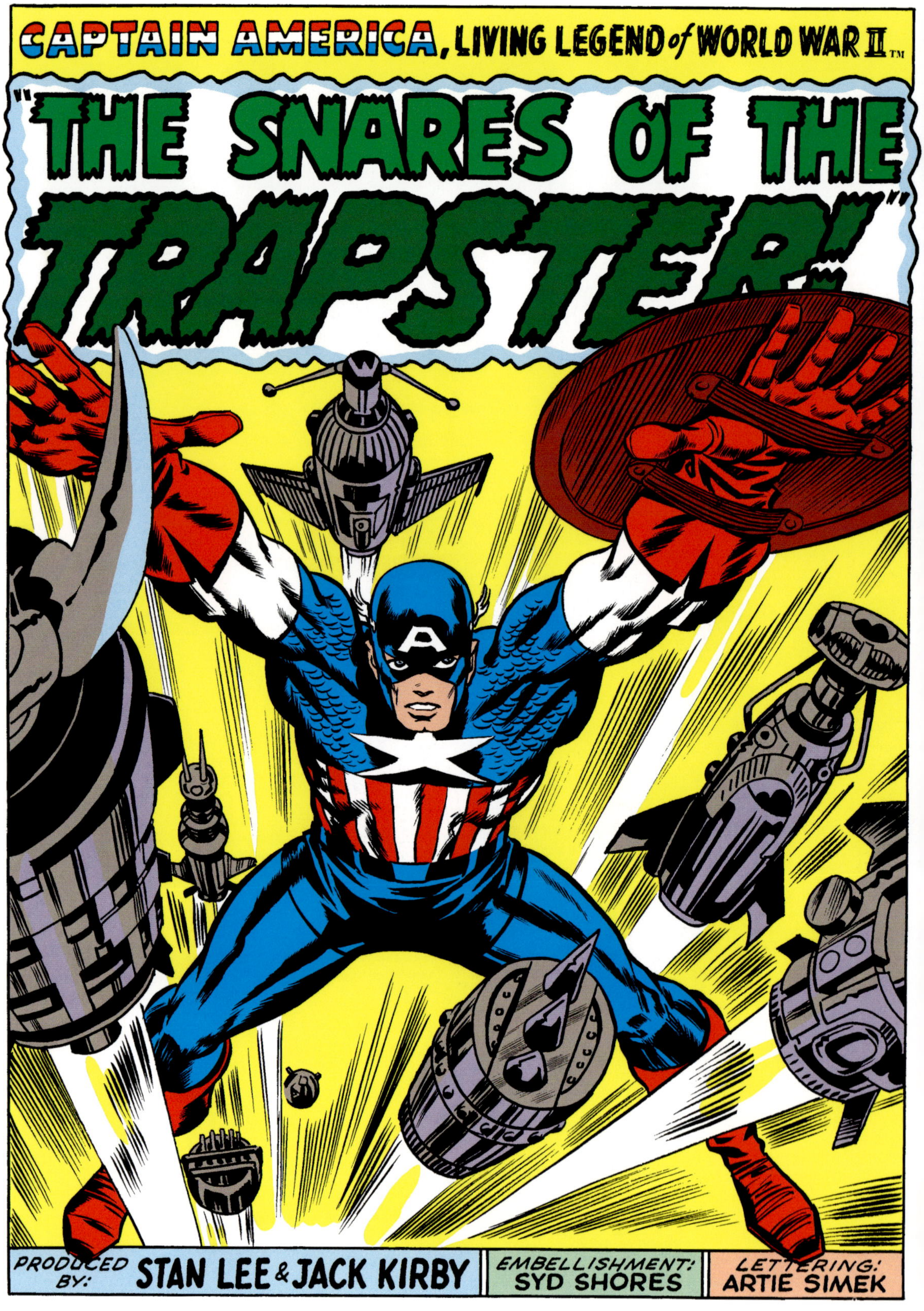
CAPTAIN AMERICA, LIVING LEGEND of WORLD WAR II ™
"THE SNARES OF THE TRAPSTER!"
PRODUCED BY: STAN LEE & JACK KIRBY
EMBELLISHMENT: SYD SHORES
LETTERING: ARTIE SIMEK

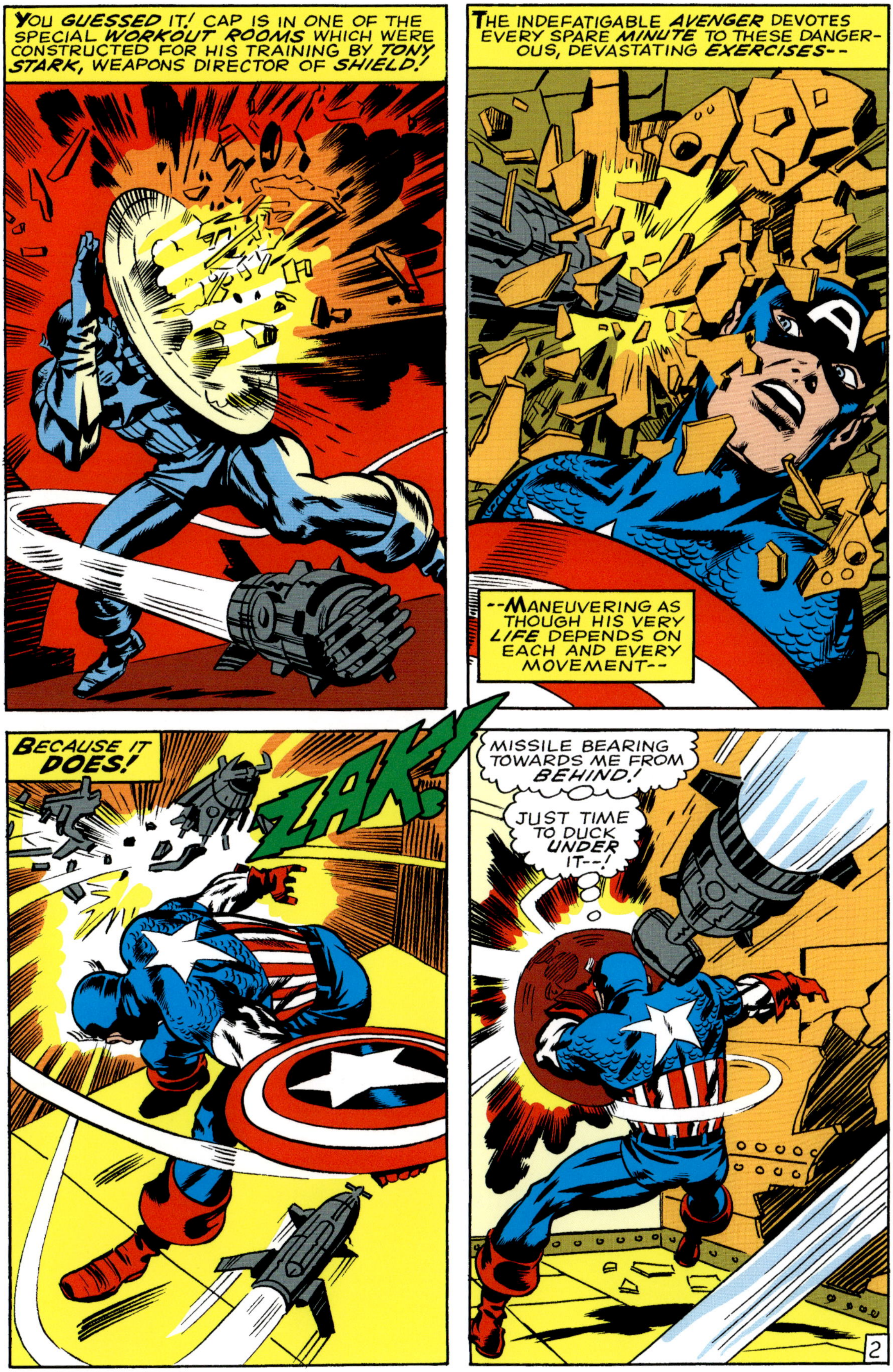
YOU GUESSED IT! CAP IS IN ONE OF THE SPECIAL WORKOUT ROOMS WHICH WERE CONSTRUCTED FOR HIS TRAINING BY TONY STARK, WEAPONS DIRECTOR OF SHIELD!
THE INDEFATIGABLE AVENGER DEVOTES EVERY SPARE MINUTE TO THESE DANGEROUS, DEVASTATING EXERCISES--
--MANEUVERING AS THOUGH HIS VERY LIFE DEPENDS ON EACH AND EVERY MOVEMENT--
BECAUSE IT DOES!
ZAK!
MISSILE BEARING TOWARDS ME FROM BEHIND!
JUST TIME TO DUCK UNDER IT--!
2

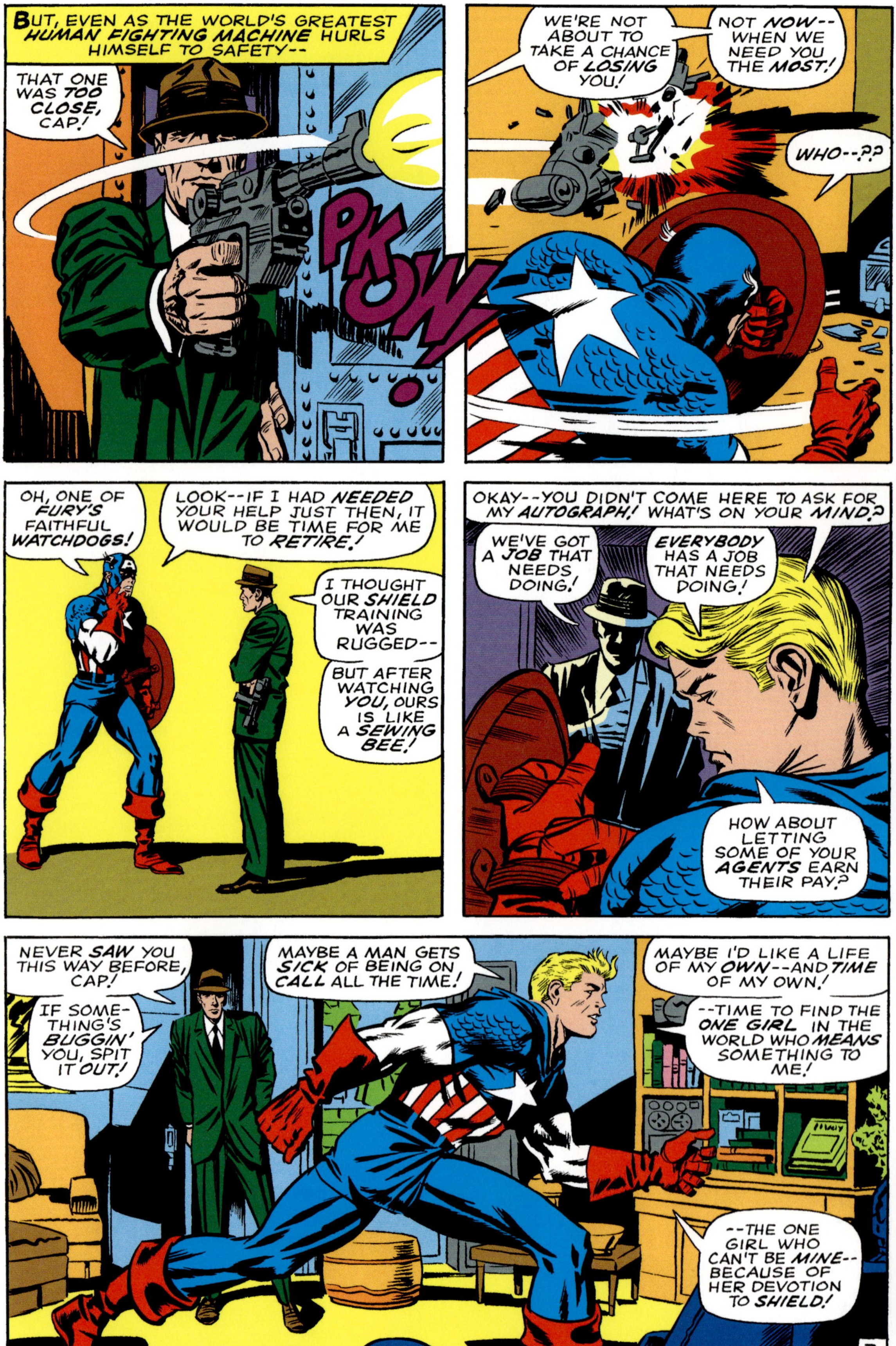

BUT, EVEN AS THE WORLD'S GREATEST HUMAN FIGHTING MACHINE HURLS HIMSELF TO SAFETY--
THAT ONE WAS TOO CLOSE, CAP!
PKOW!
WE'RE NOT ABOUT TO TAKE A CHANCE OF LOSING YOU!
NOT NOW--WHEN WE NEED YOU THE MOST!
WHO--??
OH, ONE OF FURY'S FAITHFUL WATCHDOGS!
LOOK--IF I HAD NEEDED YOUR HELP JUST THEN, IT WOULD BE TIME FOR ME TO RETIRE!
I THOUGHT OUR SHIELD TRAINING WAS RUGGED--
BUT AFTER WATCHING YOU, OURS IS LIKE A SEWING BEE!
OKAY--YOU DIDN'T COME HERE TO ASK FOR MY AUTOGRAPH! WHAT'S ON YOUR MIND?
WE'VE GOT A JOB THAT NEEDS DOING!
EVERYBODY HAS A JOB THAT NEEDS DOING!
HOW ABOUT LETTING SOME OF YOUR AGENTS EARN THEIR PAY?
NEVER SAW YOU THIS WAY BEFORE, CAP!
IF SOME-THING'S BUGGIN' YOU, SPIT IT OUT!
MAYBE A MAN GETS SICK OF BEING ON CALL ALL THE TIME!
MAYBE I'D LIKE A LIFE OF MY OWN--AND TIME OF MY OWN!
--TIME TO FIND THE ONE GIRL IN THE WORLD WHO MEANS SOMETHING TO ME!
--THE ONE GIRL WHO CAN'T BE MINE--BECAUSE OF HER DEVOTION TO SHIELD!
3

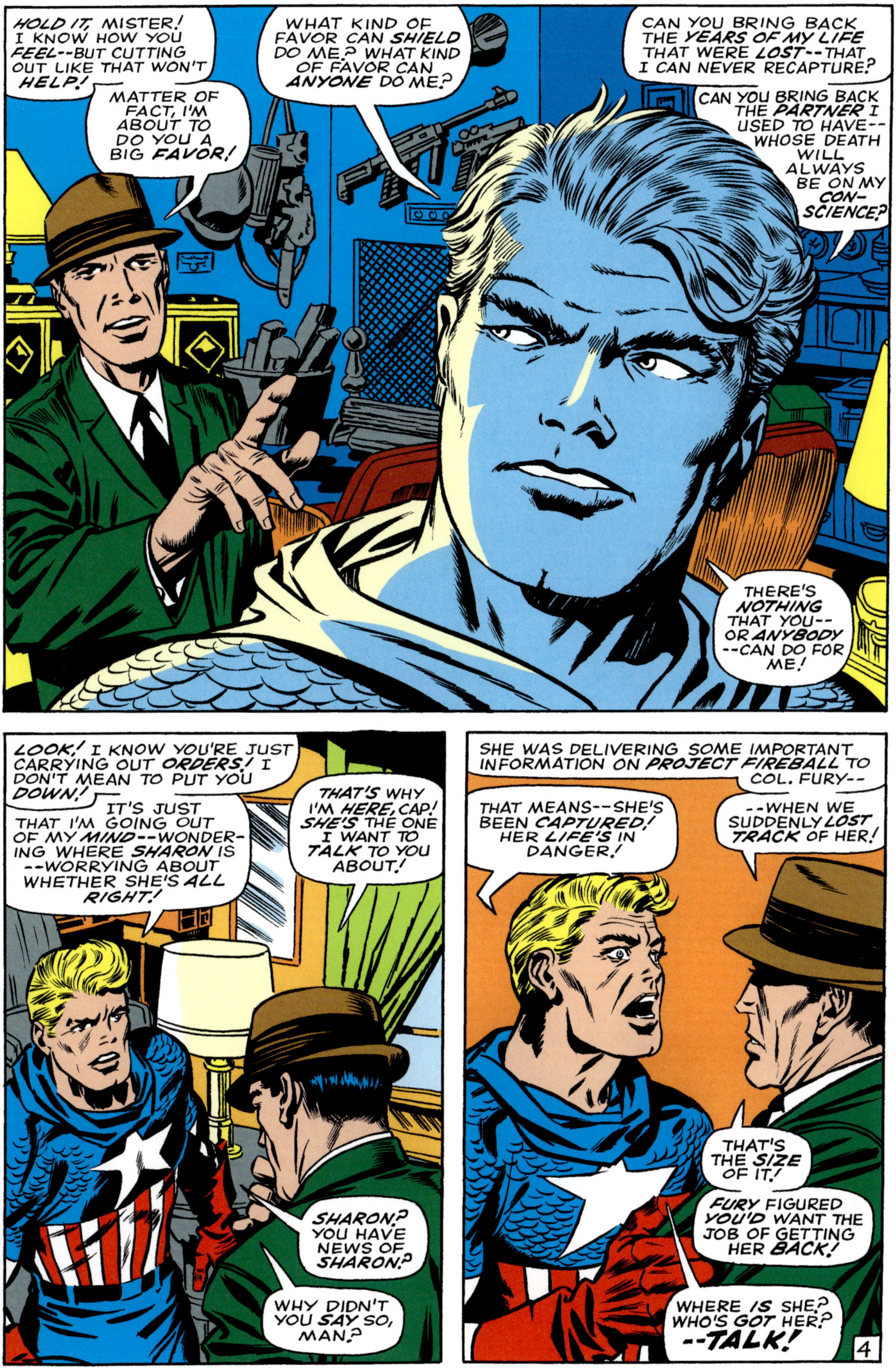
HOLD IT, MISTER! I KNOW HOW YOU FEEL--BUT CUTTING OUT LIKE THAT WON'T HELP!
MATTER OF FACT, I'M ABOUT TO DO YOU A BIG FAVOR!
WHAT KIND OF FAVOR CAN SHIELD DO ME? WHAT KIND OF FAVOR CAN ANYONE DO ME?
CAN YOU BRING BACK THE YEARS OF MY LIFE THAT WERE LOST--THAT I CAN NEVER RECAPTURE?
CAN YOU BRING BACK THE PARTNER I USED TO HAVE--WHOSE DEATH WILL ALWAYS BE ON MY CON-SCIENCE?
THERE'S NOTHING THAT YOU--OR ANYBODY--CAN DO FOR ME!
LOOK! I KNOW YOU'RE JUST CARRYING OUT ORDERS! I DON'T MEAN TO PUT YOU DOWN!
IT'S JUST THAT I'M GOING OUT OF MY MIND--WONDER-ING WHERE SHARON IS--WORRYING ABOUT WHETHER SHE'S ALL RIGHT!
THAT'S WHY I'M HERE, CAP! SHE'S THE ONE I WANT TO TALK TO YOU ABOUT!
SHARON? YOU HAVE NEWS OF SHARON?
WHY DIDN'T YOU SAY SO, MAN?
SHE WAS DELIVERING SOME IMPORTANT INFORMATION ON PROJECT FIREBALL TO COL. FURY--
--WHEN WE SUDDENLY LOST TRACK OF HER!
THAT MEANS--SHE'S BEEN CAPTURED! HER LIFE'S IN DANGER!
THAT'S THE SIZE OF IT!
FURY FIGURED YOU'D WANT THE JOB OF GETTING HER BACK!
WHERE IS SHE? WHO'S GOT HER? --TALK!
4

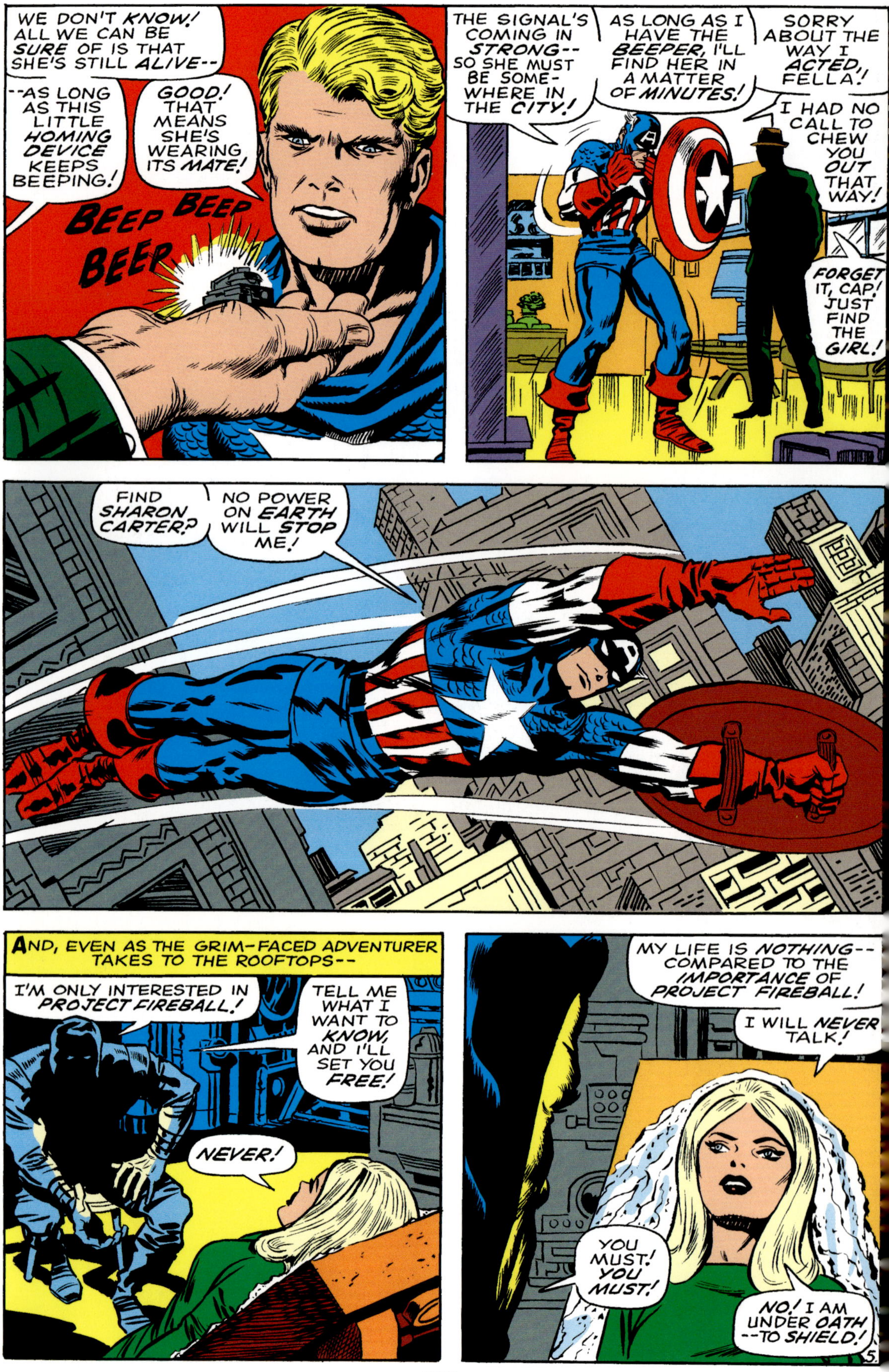
WE DON'T KNOW! ALL WE CAN BE SURE OF IS THAT SHE'S STILL ALIVE--
--AS LONG AS THIS LITTLE HOMING DEVICE KEEPS BEEPING!
GOOD! THAT MEANS SHE'S WEARING ITS MATE!
BEEP BEEP BEEP
THE SIGNAL'S COMING IN STRONG-- SO SHE MUST BE SOME-WHERE IN THE CITY!
AS LONG AS I HAVE THE BEEPER, I'LL FIND HER IN A MATTER OF MINUTES!
SORRY ABOUT THE WAY I ACTED, FELLA!
I HAD NO CALL TO CHEW YOU OUT THAT WAY!
FORGET IT, CAP! JUST FIND THE GIRL!
FIND SHARON CARTER?
NO POWER ON EARTH WILL STOP ME!
AND, EVEN AS THE GRIM-FACED ADVENTURER TAKES TO THE ROOFTOPS--
I'M ONLY INTERESTED IN PROJECT FIREBALL!
TELL ME WHAT I WANT TO KNOW, AND I'LL SET YOU FREE!
NEVER!
MY LIFE IS NOTHING-- COMPARED TO THE IMPORTANCE OF PROJECT FIREBALL!
I WILL NEVER TALK!
YOU MUST! YOU MUST!
NO! I AM UNDER OATH --TO SHIELD!
5.

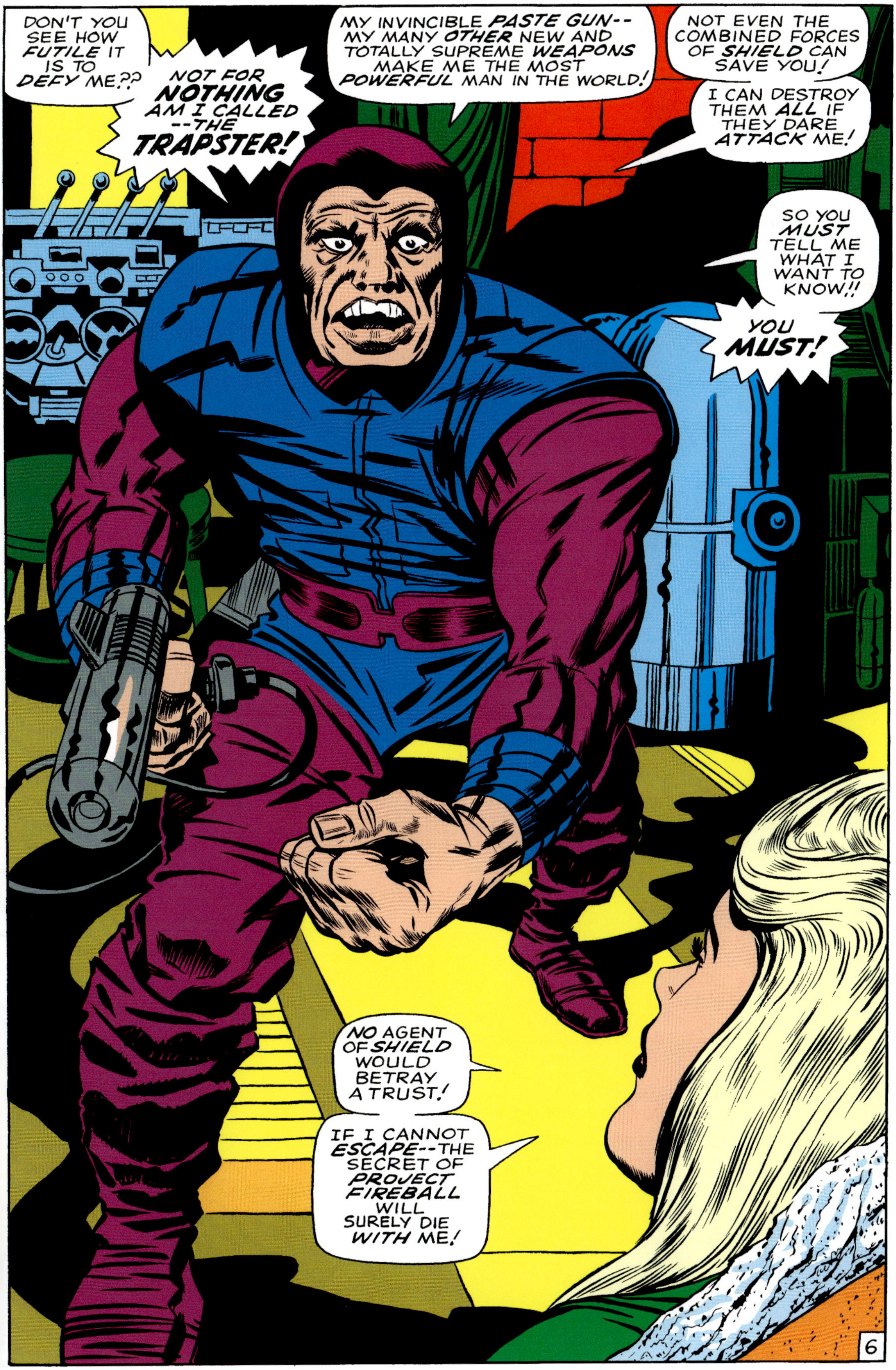
DON'T YOU SEE HOW FUTILE IT IS TO DEFY ME??
NOT FOR NOTHING AM I CALLED --THE TRAPSTER!
MY INVINCIBLE PASTE GUN-- MY MANY OTHER NEW AND TOTALLY SUPREME WEAPONS MAKE ME THE MOST POWERFUL MAN IN THE WORLD!
NOT EVEN THE COMBINED FORCES OF SHIELD CAN SAVE YOU!
I CAN DESTROY THEM ALL IF THEY DARE ATTACK ME!
SO YOU MUST TELL ME WHAT I WANT TO KNOW!!
YOU MUST!
NO AGENT OF SHIELD WOULD BETRAY A TRUST!
IF I CANNOT ESCAPE--THE SECRET OF PROJECT FIREBALL WILL SURELY DIE WITH ME!
6

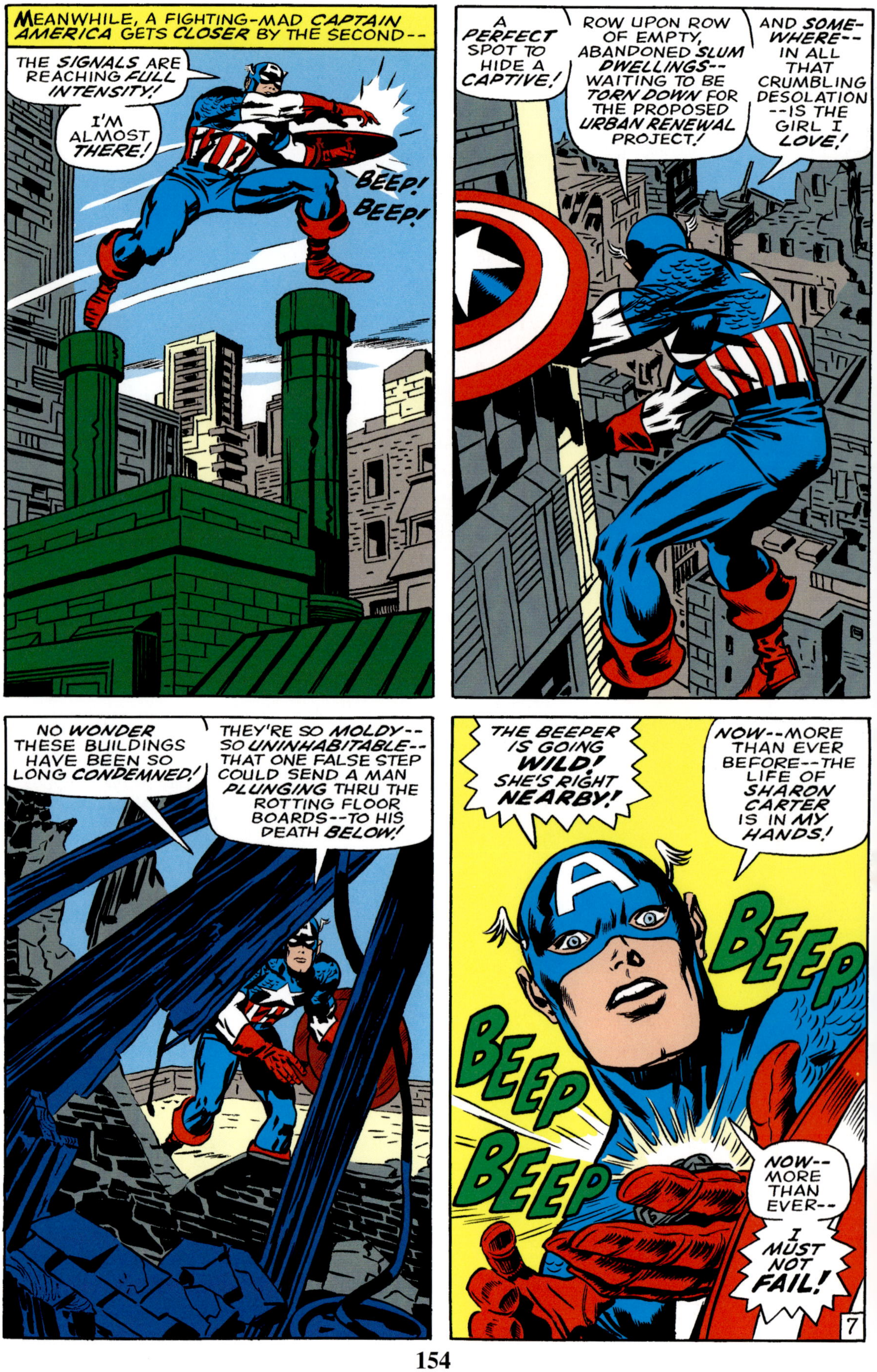
MEANWHILE, A FIGHTING-MAD CAPTAIN AMERICA GETS CLOSER BY THE SECOND--
THE SIGNALS ARE REACHING FULL INTENSITY!
I'M ALMOST THERE!
BEEP! BEEP!
A PERFECT SPOT TO HIDE A CAPTIVE!
ROW UPON ROW OF EMPTY, ABANDONED SLUM DWELLINGS-- WAITING TO BE TORN DOWN FOR THE PROPOSED URBAN RENEWAL PROJECT!
AND SOME-WHERE-- IN ALL THAT CRUMBLING DESOLATION --IS THE GIRL I LOVE!
NO WONDER THESE BUILDINGS HAVE BEEN SO LONG CONDEMNED!
THEY'RE SO MOLDY-- SO UNINHABITABLE-- THAT ONE FALSE STEP COULD SEND A MAN PLUNGING THRU THE ROTTING FLOOR BOARDS--TO HIS DEATH BELOW!
THE BEEPER IS GOING WILD! SHE'S RIGHT NEARBY!
NOW--MORE THAN EVER BEFORE--THE LIFE OF SHARON CARTER IS IN MY HANDS!
BEEP
BEEP
BEEP
NOW-- MORE THAN EVER-- I MUST NOT FAIL!
7

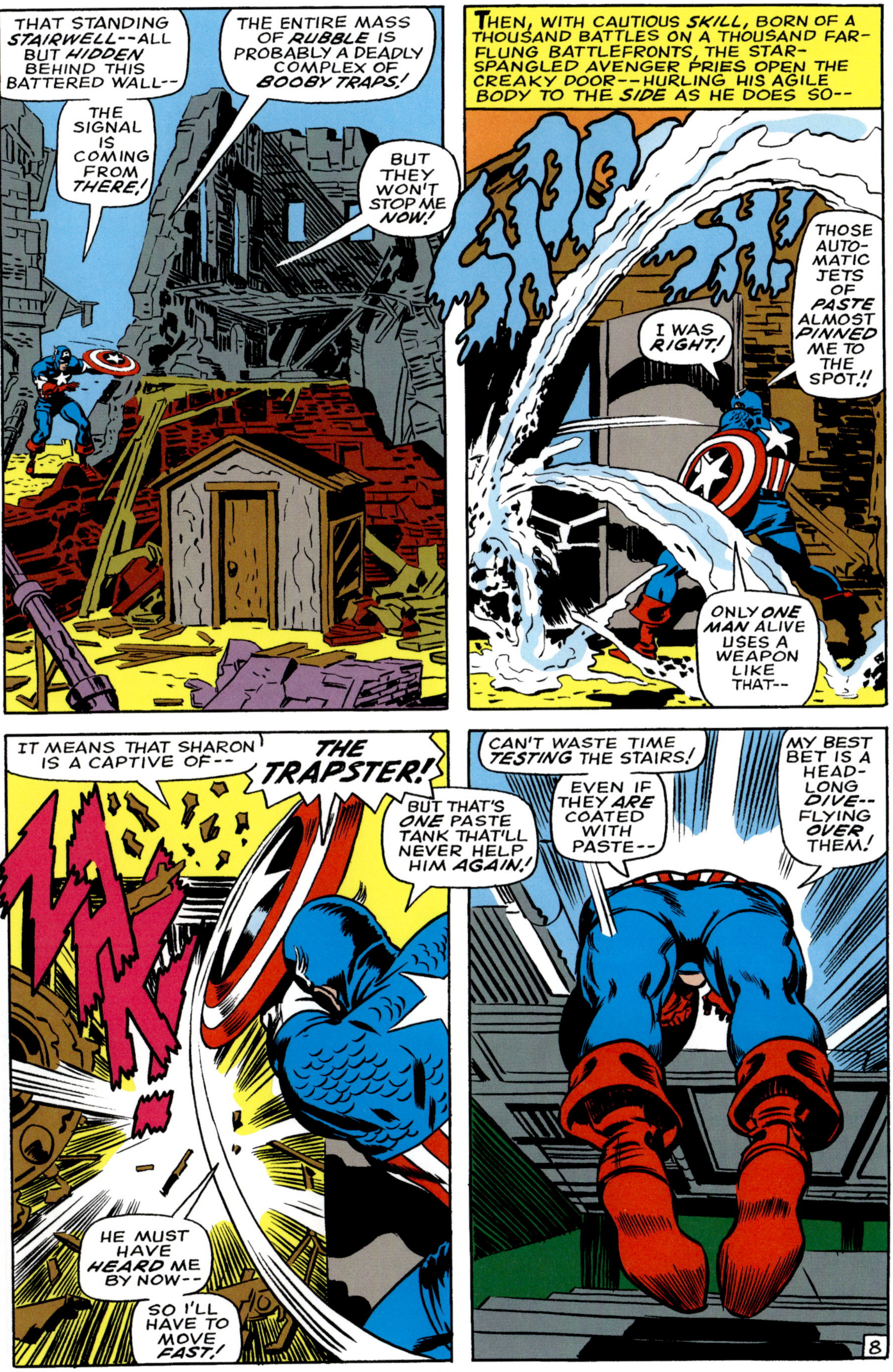
THAT STANDING STAIRWELL--ALL BUT HIDDEN BEHIND THIS BATTERED WALL--
THE ENTIRE MASS OF RUBBLE IS PROBABLY A DEADLY COMPLEX OF BOOBY TRAPS!
THE SIGNAL IS COMING FROM THERE!
BUT THEY WON'T STOP ME NOW!
THEN, WITH CAUTIOUS SKILL, BORN OF A THOUSAND BATTLES ON A THOUSAND FAR-FLUNG BATTLEFRONTS, THE STAR-SPANGLED AVENGER PRIES OPEN THE CREAKY DOOR--HURLING HIS AGILE BODY TO THE SIDE AS HE DOES SO--
SPOOSH
THOSE AUTOMATIC JETS OF PASTE ALMOST PINNED ME TO THE SPOT!!
I WAS RIGHT!
ONLY ONE MAN ALIVE USES A WEAPON LIKE THAT--
IT MEANS THAT SHARON IS A CAPTIVE OF--
THE TRAPSTER!
BUT THAT'S ONE PASTE TANK THAT'LL NEVER HELP HIM AGAIN!
ZAK
HE MUST HAVE HEARD ME BY NOW--
SO I'LL HAVE TO MOVE FAST!
CAN'T WASTE TIME TESTING THE STAIRS!
EVEN IF THEY ARE COATED WITH PASTE--
MY BEST BET IS A HEAD-LONG DIVE--FLYING OVER THEM!
8

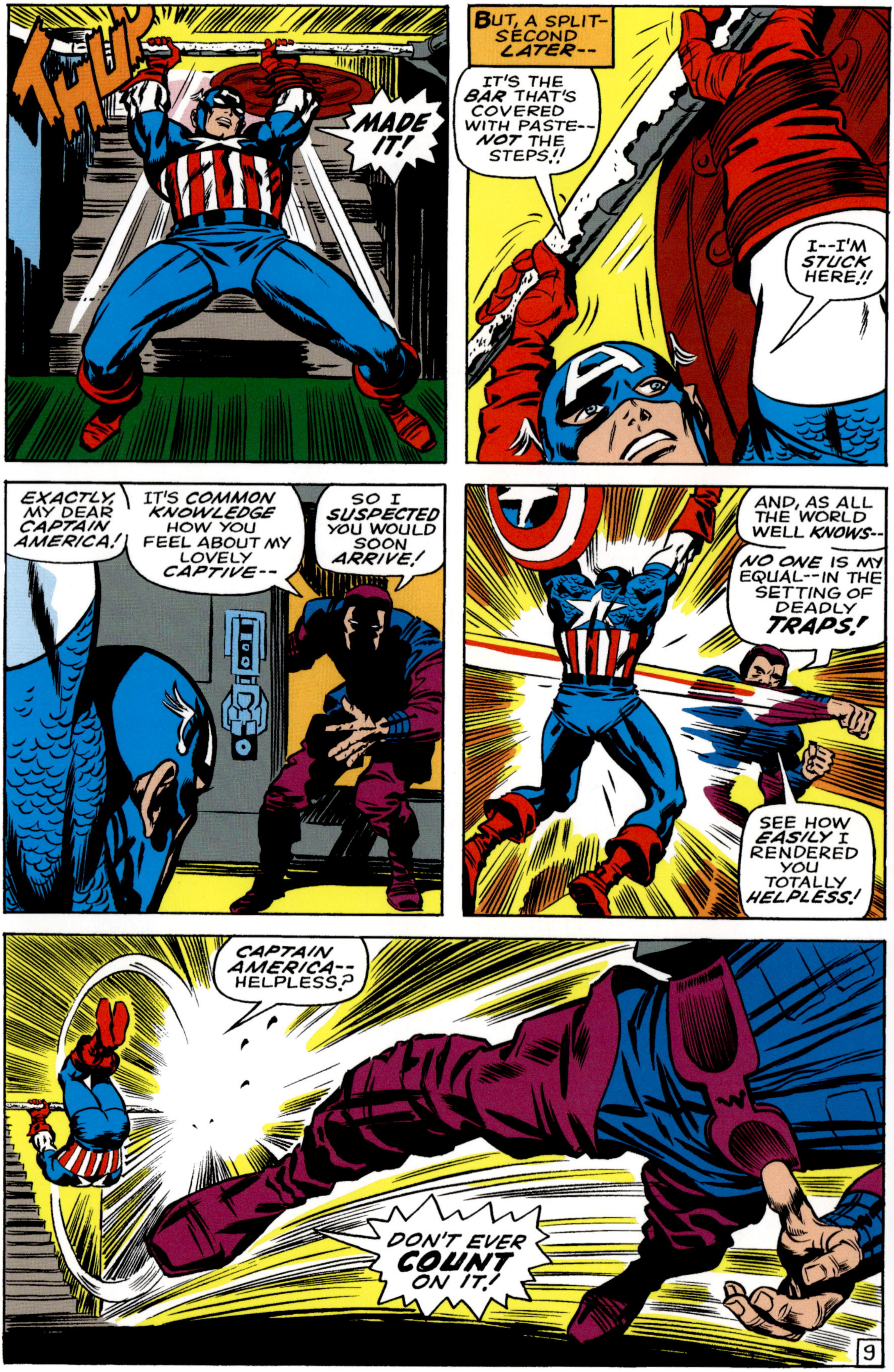
THUD
MADE IT!
BUT, A SPLIT-SECOND LATER--
IT'S THE BAR THAT'S COVERED WITH PASTE-- NOT THE STEPS!!
I--I'M STUCK HERE!!
EXACTLY, MY DEAR CAPTAIN AMERICA!
IT'S COMMON KNOWLEDGE HOW YOU FEEL ABOUT MY LOVELY CAPTIVE--
SO I SUSPECTED YOU WOULD SOON ARRIVE!
AND, AS ALL THE WORLD WELL KNOWS--
NO ONE IS MY EQUAL--IN THE SETTING OF DEADLY TRAPS!
SEE HOW EASILY I RENDERED YOU TOTALLY HELPLESS!
CAPTAIN AMERICA-- HELPLESS?
DON'T EVER COUNT ON IT!
9

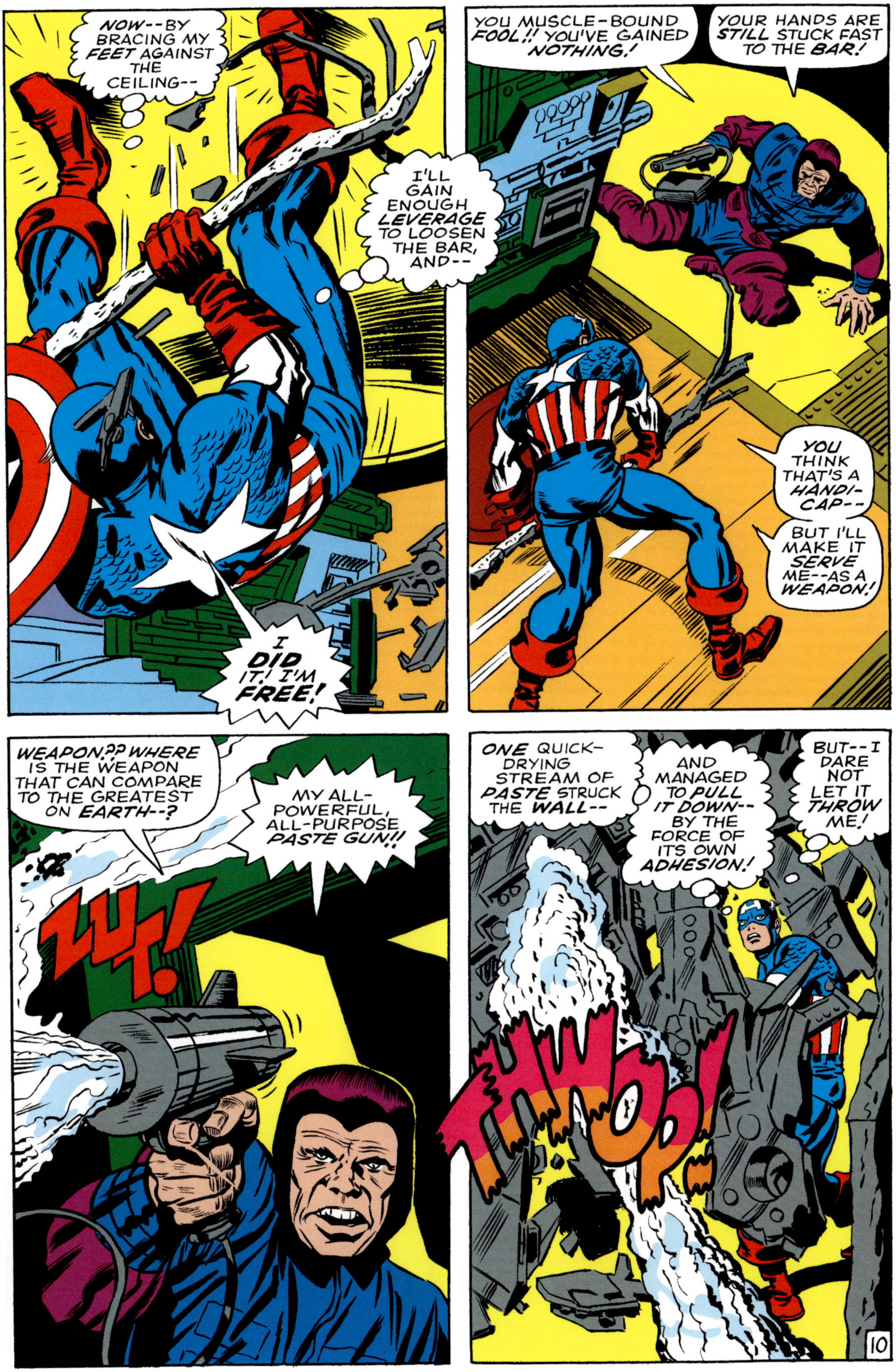
NOW--BY BRACING MY FEET AGAINST THE CEILING--
I'LL GAIN ENOUGH LEVERAGE TO LOOSEN THE BAR, AND--
I DID IT! I'M FREE!
YOU MUSCLE-BOUND FOOL!! YOU'VE GAINED NOTHING!
YOUR HANDS ARE STILL STUCK FAST TO THE BAR!
YOU THINK THAT'S A HANDI-CAP--
BUT I'LL MAKE IT SERVE ME--AS A WEAPON!
WEAPON?? WHERE IS THE WEAPON THAT CAN COMPARE TO THE GREATEST ON EARTH--?
MY ALL-POWERFUL, ALL-PURPOSE PASTE GUN!!
ZUT!
ONE QUICK-DRYING STREAM OF PASTE STRUCK THE WALL--
AND MANAGED TO PULL IT DOWN-- BY THE FORCE OF ITS OWN ADHESION!
BUT--I DARE NOT LET IT THROW ME!
THWOP!
10

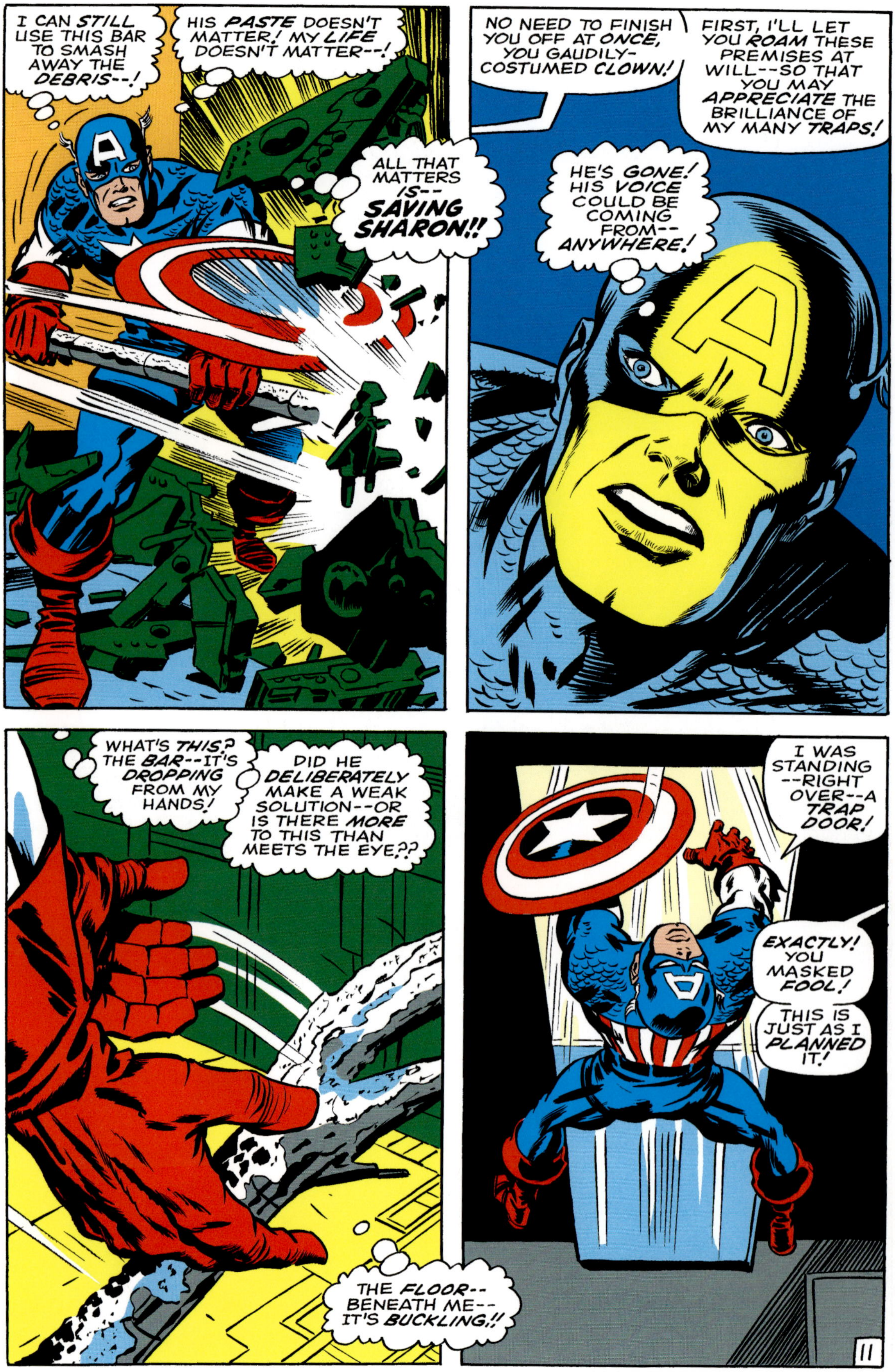
I CAN STILL USE THIS BAR TO SMASH AWAY THE DEBRIS--!
HIS PASTE DOESN'T MATTER! MY LIFE DOESN'T MATTER--!
ALL THAT MATTERS IS-- SAVING SHARON!!
NO NEED TO FINISH YOU OFF AT ONCE, YOU GAUDILY-COSTUMED CLOWN!
FIRST, I'LL LET YOU ROAM THESE PREMISES AT WILL--SO THAT YOU MAY APPRECIATE THE BRILLIANCE OF MY MANY TRAPS!
HE'S GONE! HIS VOICE COULD BE COMING FROM-- ANYWHERE!
WHAT'S THIS? THE BAR--IT'S DROPPING FROM MY HANDS!
DID HE DELIBERATELY MAKE A WEAK SOLUTION--OR IS THERE MORE TO THIS THAN MEETS THE EYE??
THE FLOOR-- BENEATH ME-- IT'S BUCKLING!!
I WAS STANDING --RIGHT OVER--A TRAP DOOR!
EXACTLY! YOU MASKED FOOL!
THIS IS JUST AS I PLANNED IT!
11

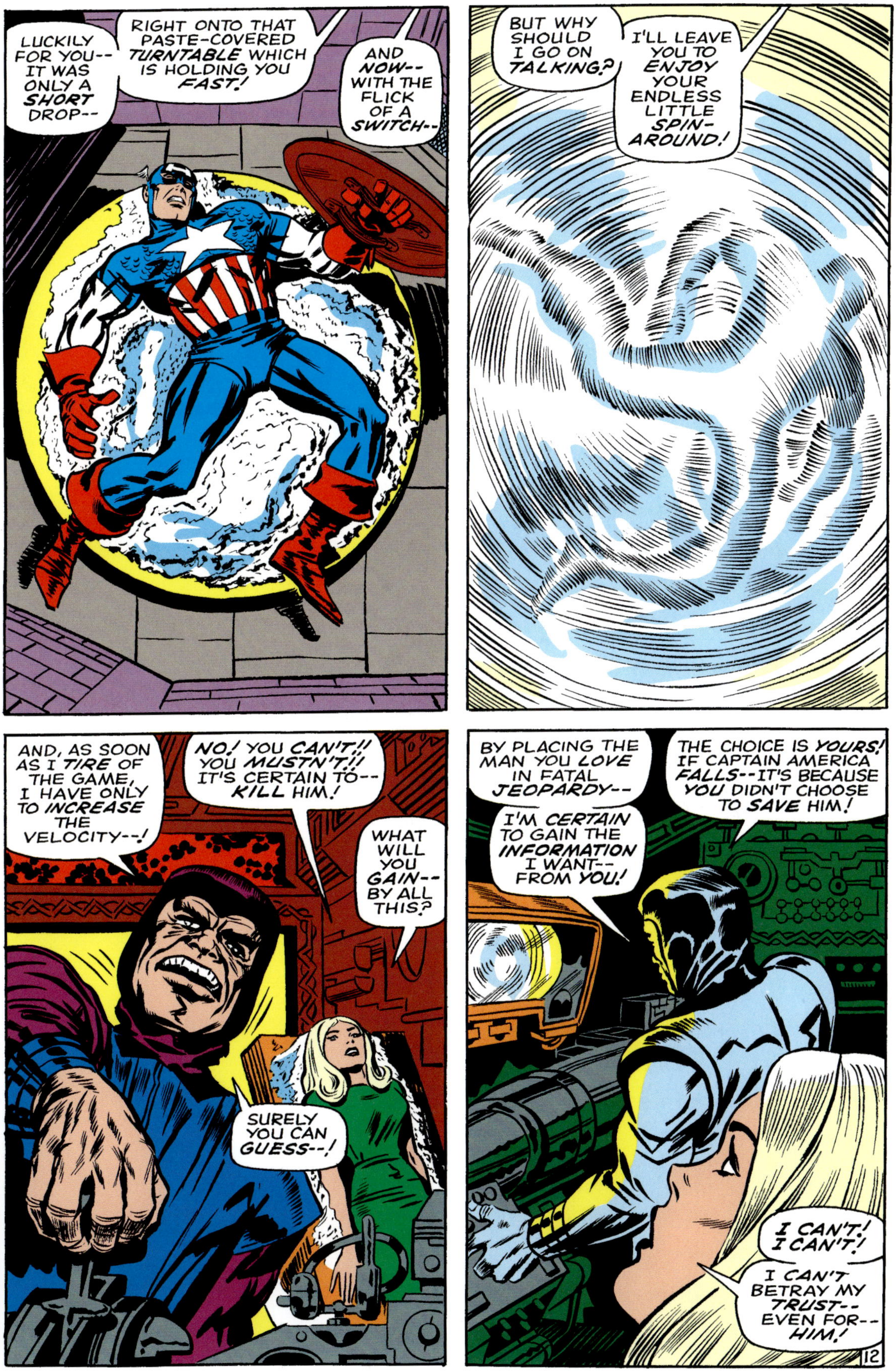
LUCKILY FOR YOU-- IT WAS ONLY A SHORT DROP--
RIGHT ONTO THAT PASTE-COVERED TURNTABLE WHICH IS HOLDING YOU FAST!
AND NOW-- WITH THE FLICK OF A SWITCH--
BUT WHY SHOULD I GO ON TALKING?
I'LL LEAVE YOU TO ENJOY YOUR ENDLESS LITTLE SPIN-AROUND!
AND, AS SOON AS I TIRE OF THE GAME, I HAVE ONLY TO INCREASE THE VELOCITY--!
NO! YOU CAN'T!! YOU MUSTN'T!! IT'S CERTAIN TO-- KILL HIM!
WHAT WILL YOU GAIN-- BY ALL THIS?
SURELY YOU CAN GUESS--!
BY PLACING THE MAN YOU LOVE IN FATAL JEOPARDY--
I'M CERTAIN TO GAIN THE INFORMATION I WANT-- FROM YOU!
THE CHOICE IS YOURS! IF CAPTAIN AMERICA FALLS--IT'S BECAUSE YOU DIDN'T CHOOSE TO SAVE HIM!
I CAN'T! I CAN'T!
I CAN'T BETRAY MY TRUST-- EVEN FOR-- HIM!
12

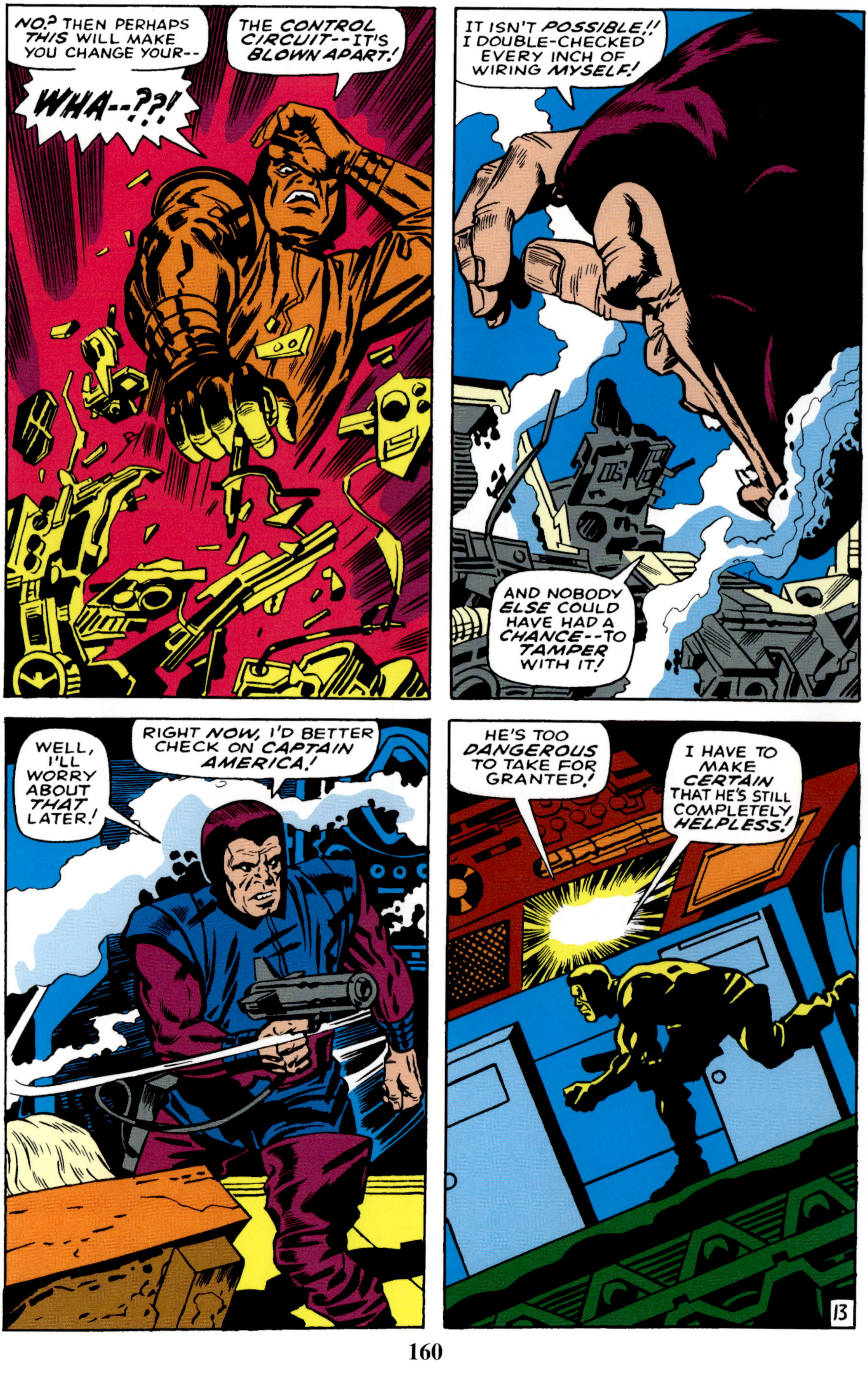
NO? THEN PERHAPS THIS WILL MAKE YOU CHANGE YOUR--
WHA--??!
THE CONTROL CIRCUIT--IT'S BLOWN APART!
IT ISN'T POSSIBLE!! I DOUBLE-CHECKED EVERY INCH OF WIRING MYSELF!
AND NOBODY ELSE COULD HAVE HAD A CHANCE--TO TAMPER WITH IT!
WELL, I'LL WORRY ABOUT THAT LATER!
RIGHT NOW, I'D BETTER CHECK ON CAPTAIN AMERICA!
HE'S TOO DANGEROUS TO TAKE FOR GRANTED!
I HAVE TO MAKE CERTAIN THAT HE'S STILL COMPLETELY HELPLESS!
13

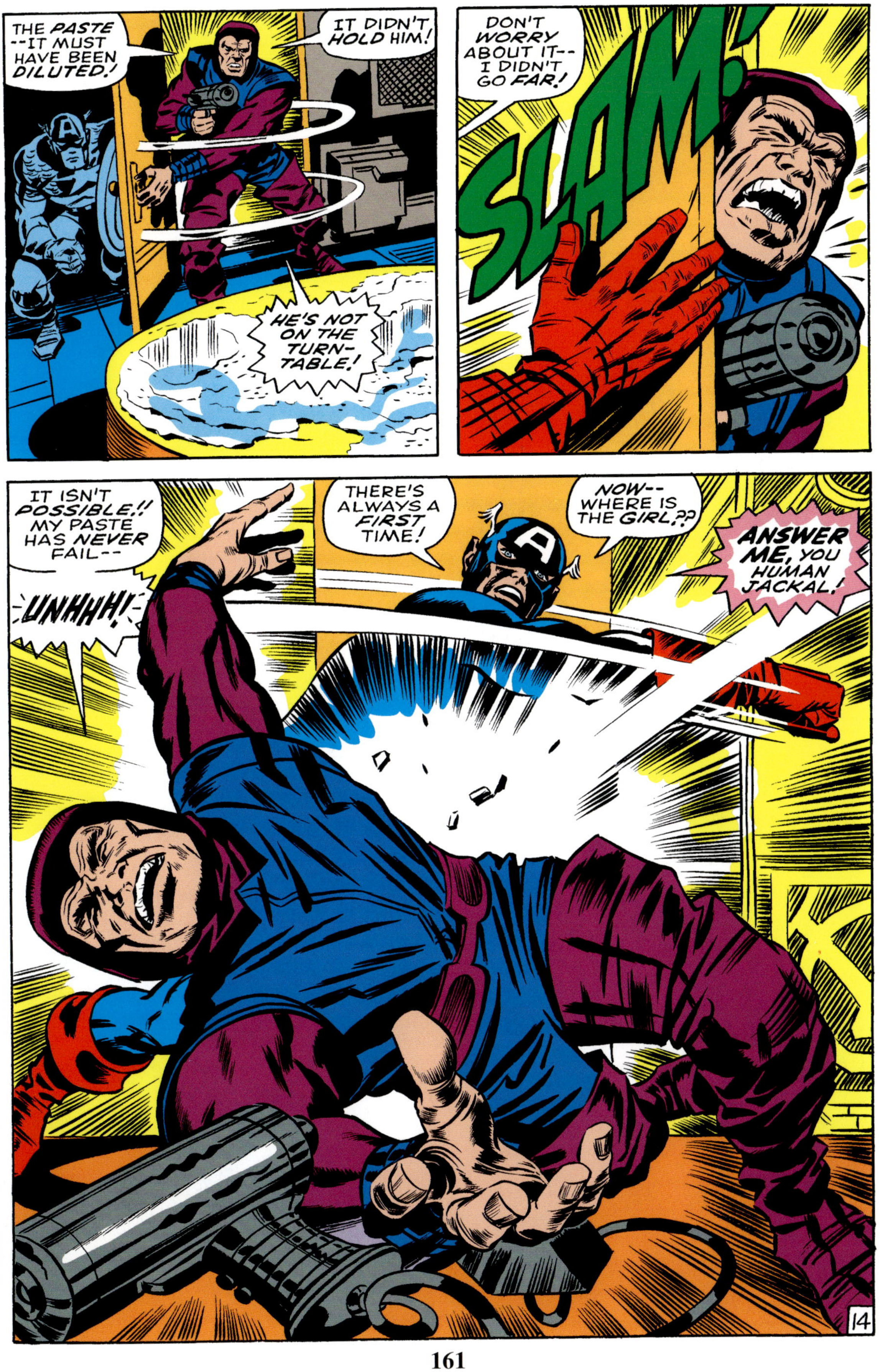
THE PASTE --IT MUST HAVE BEEN DILUTED!
IT DIDN'T HOLD HIM!
HE'S NOT ON THE TURN-TABLE!
DON'T WORRY ABOUT IT-- I DIDN'T GO FAR!
SLAM!
IT ISN'T POSSIBLE!! MY PASTE HAS NEVER FAIL--
UNHHH!
THERE'S ALWAYS A FIRST TIME!
NOW-- WHERE IS THE GIRL??
ANSWER ME, YOU HUMAN JACKAL!
14

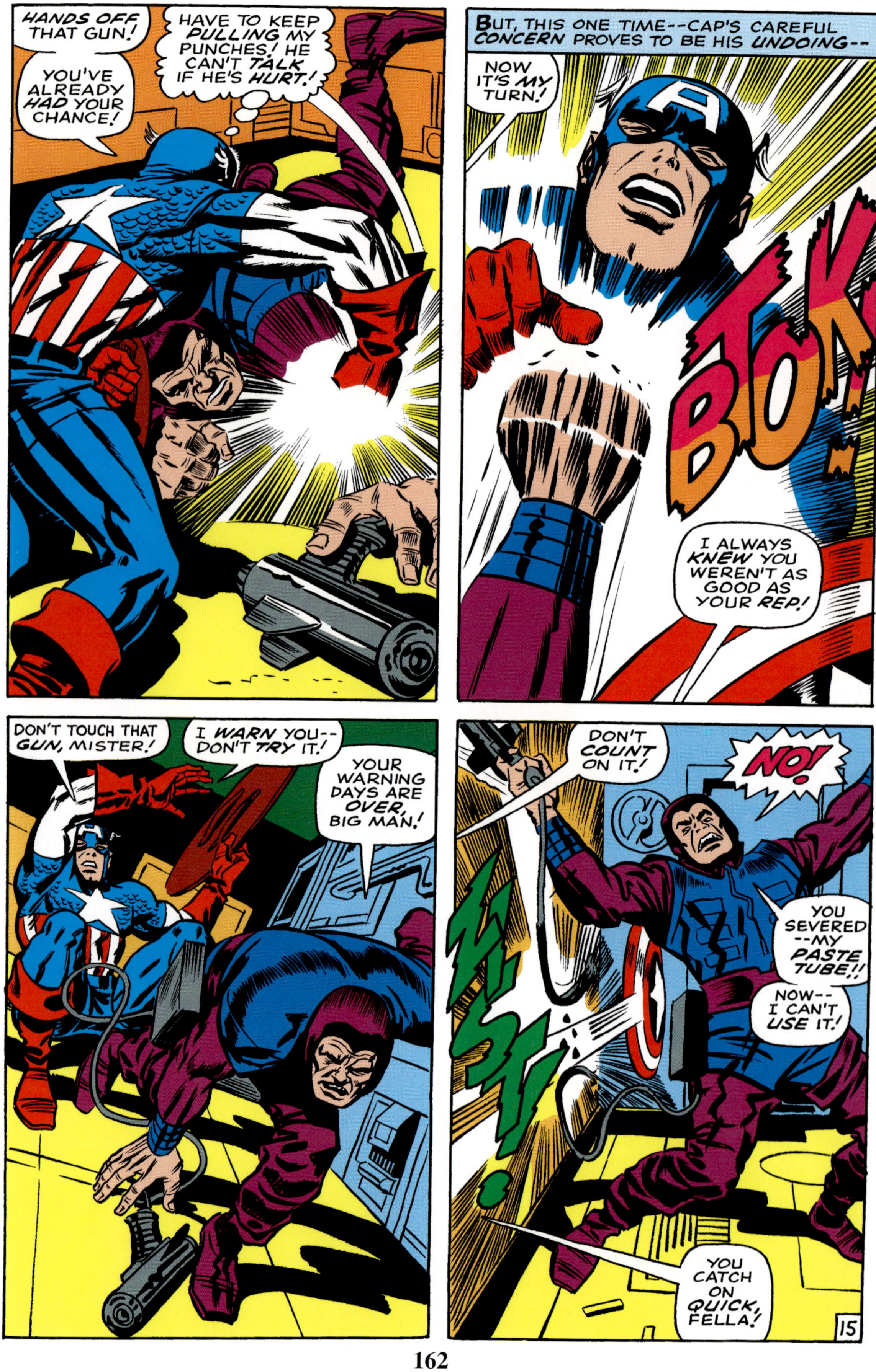
HANDS OFF THAT GUN!
YOU'VE ALREADY HAD YOUR CHANCE!
HAVE TO KEEP PULLING MY PUNCHES! HE CAN'T TALK IF HE'S HURT!
BUT, THIS ONE TIME--CAP'S CAREFUL CONCERN PROVES TO BE HIS UNDOING--
NOW IT'S MY TURN!
BTOK!
I ALWAYS KNEW YOU WEREN'T AS GOOD AS YOUR REP!
DON'T TOUCH THAT GUN, MISTER!
I WARN YOU--DON'T TRY IT!
YOUR WARNING DAYS ARE OVER, BIG MAN!
DON'T COUNT ON IT!
NO!
YOU SEVERED --MY PASTE TUBE!!
NOW-- I CAN'T USE IT!
YOU CATCH ON QUICK, FELLA!
15

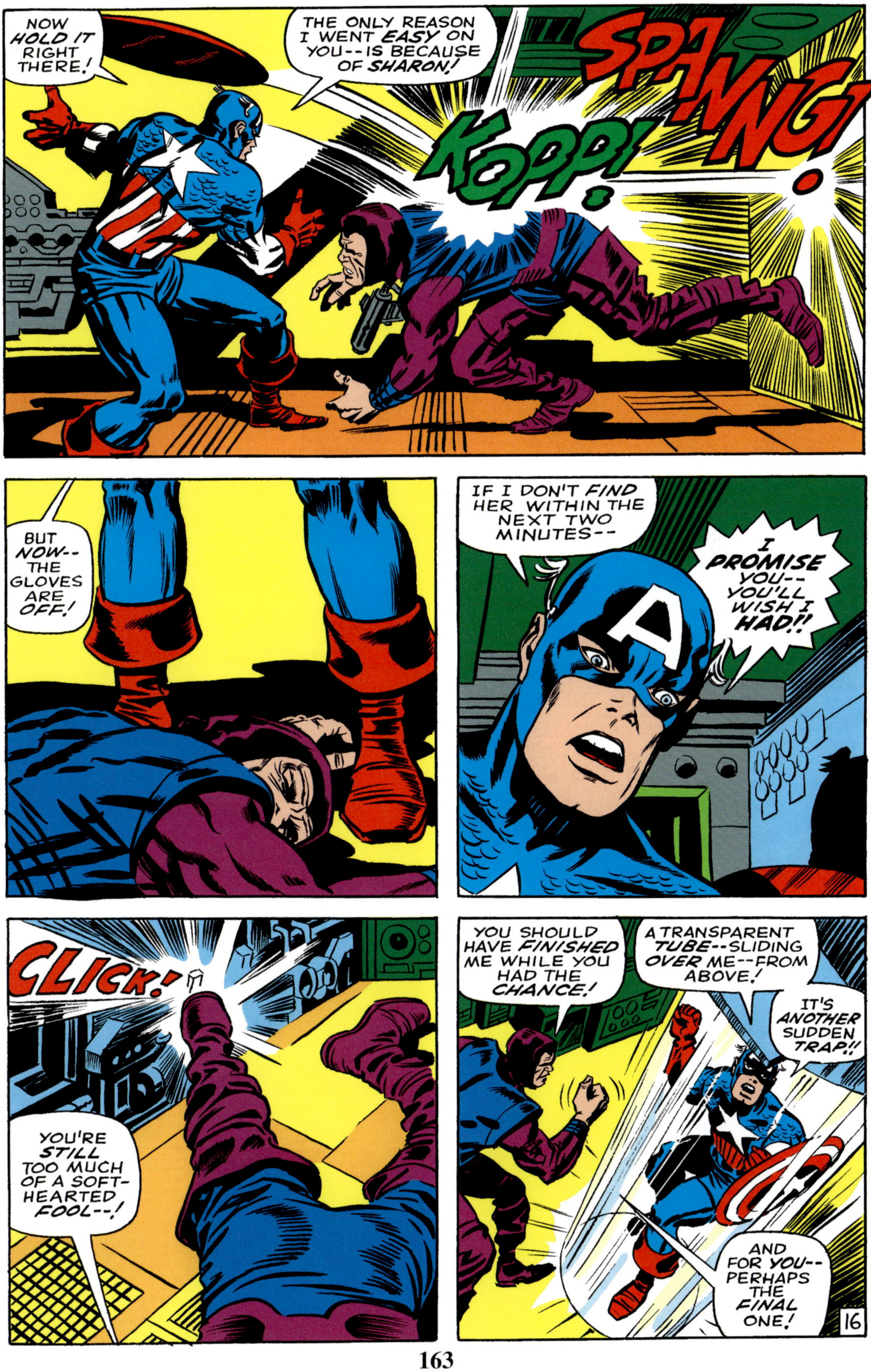
NOW HOLD IT RIGHT THERE!
THE ONLY REASON I WENT EASY ON YOU--IS BECAUSE OF SHARON!
SPANNG!
KOPP!
BUT NOW--THE GLOVES ARE OFF!
IF I DON'T FIND HER WITHIN THE NEXT TWO MINUTES--
I PROMISE YOU--YOU'LL WISH I HAD!!
CLICK!
YOU'RE STILL TOO MUCH OF A SOFT-HEARTED FOOL--!
YOU SHOULD HAVE FINISHED ME WHILE YOU HAD THE CHANCE!
A TRANSPARENT TUBE--SLIDING OVER ME--FROM ABOVE!
IT'S ANOTHER SUDDEN TRAP!!
AND FOR YOU--PERHAPS THE FINAL ONE!
16

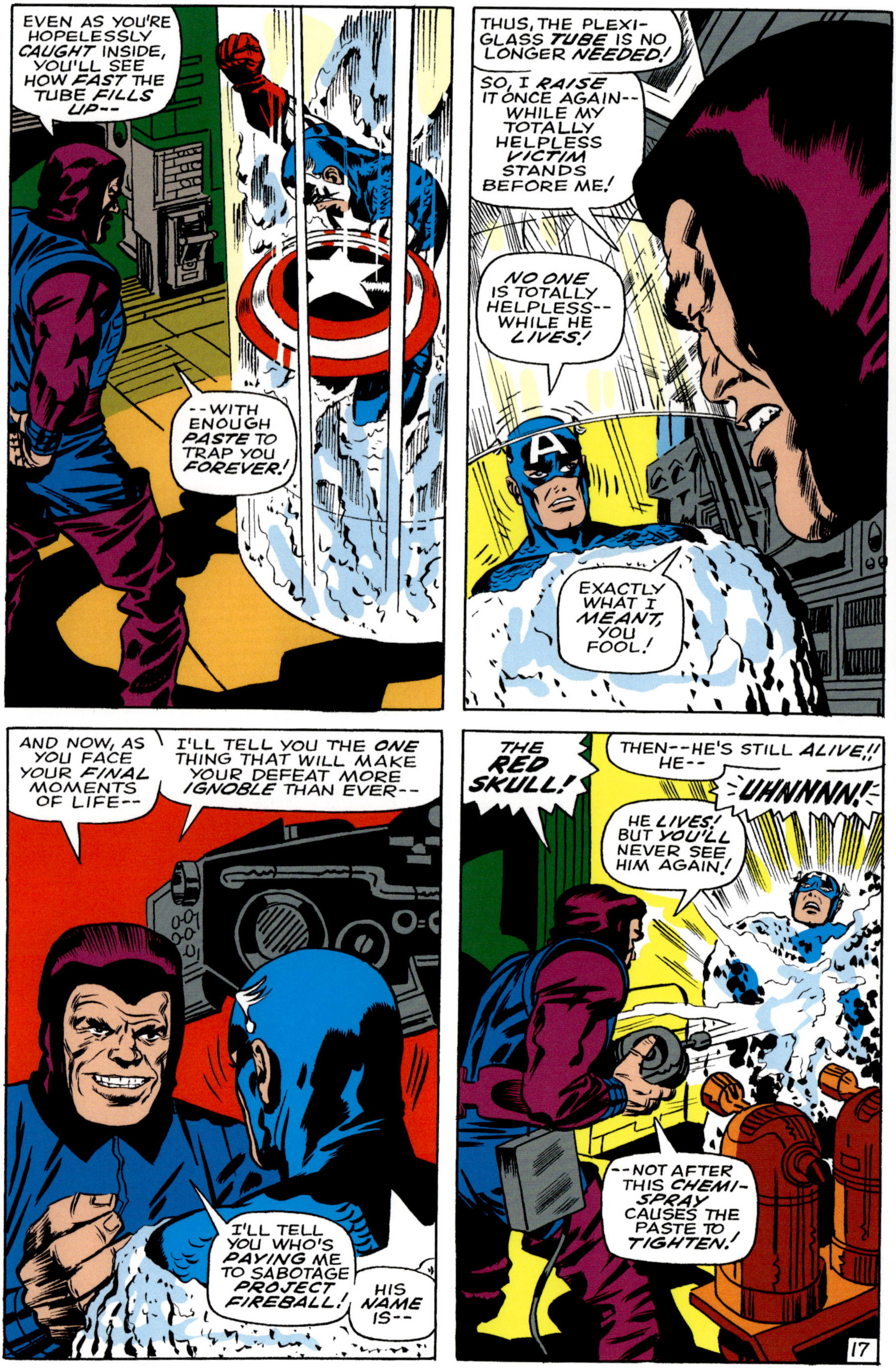
EVEN AS YOU'RE HOPELESSLY CAUGHT INSIDE, YOU'LL SEE HOW FAST THE TUBE FILLS UP--
--WITH ENOUGH PASTE TO TRAP YOU FOREVER!
THUS, THE PLEXIGLASS TUBE IS NO LONGER NEEDED!
SO, I RAISE IT ONCE AGAIN--WHILE MY TOTALLY HELPLESS VICTIM STANDS BEFORE ME!
NO ONE IS TOTALLY HELPLESS--WHILE HE LIVES!
EXACTLY WHAT I MEANT, YOU FOOL!
AND NOW, AS YOU FACE YOUR FINAL MOMENTS OF LIFE--
I'LL TELL YOU THE ONE THING THAT WILL MAKE YOUR DEFEAT MORE IGNOBLE THAN EVER--
I'LL TELL YOU WHO'S PAYING ME TO SABOTAGE PROJECT FIREBALL!
HIS NAME IS--
THE RED SKULL!
THEN--HE'S STILL ALIVE!! HE--
UHNNNN!
HE LIVES! BUT YOU'LL NEVER SEE HIM AGAIN!
--NOT AFTER THIS CHEMI-SPRAY CAUSES THE PASTE TO TIGHTEN!
17

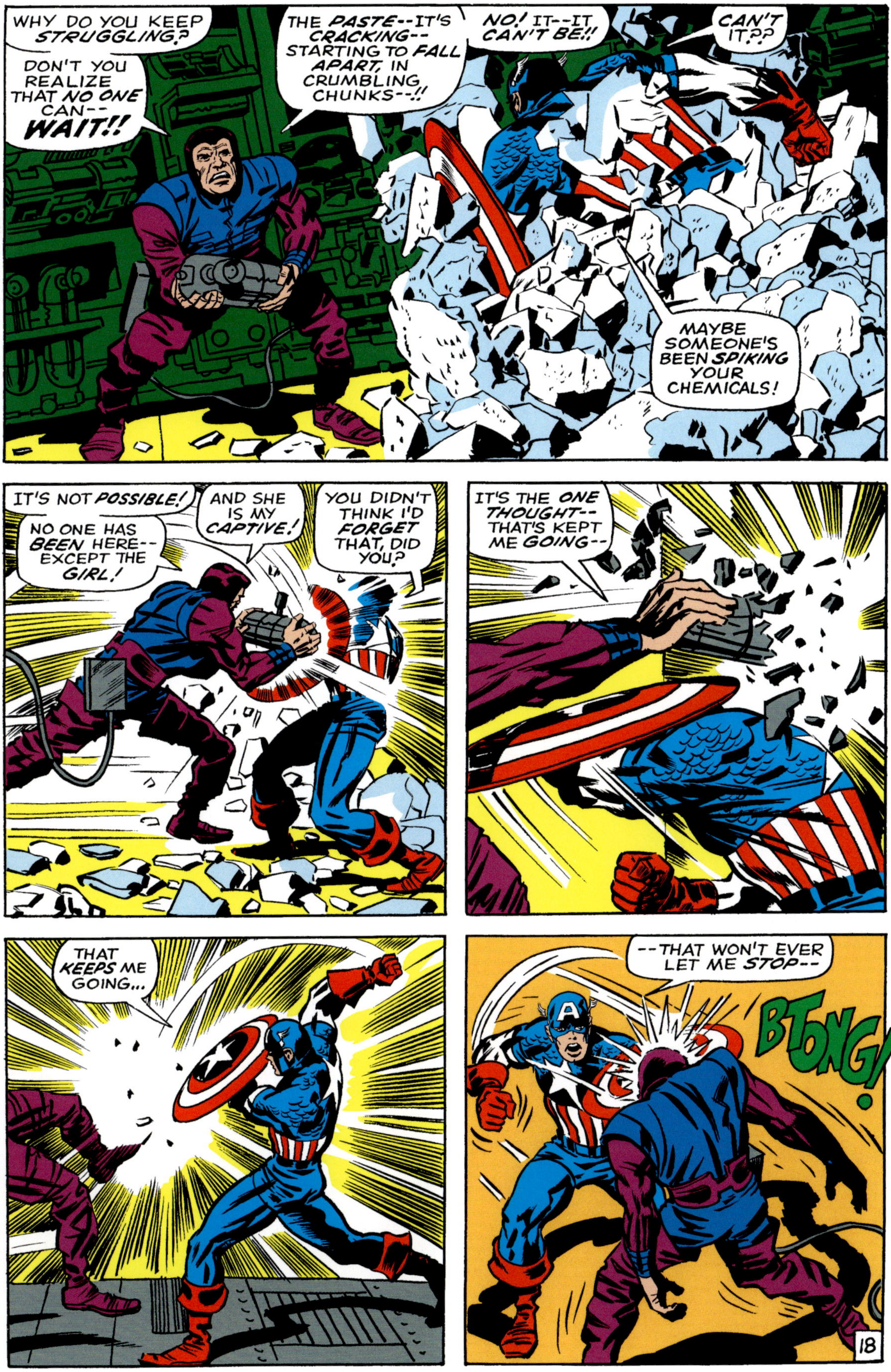
WHY DO YOU KEEP STRUGGLING?
DON'T YOU REALIZE THAT NO ONE CAN--
WAIT!!
THE PASTE--IT'S CRACKING--STARTING TO FALL APART, IN CRUMBLING CHUNKS--!!
NO! IT--IT CAN'T BE!!
CAN'T IT??
MAYBE SOMEONE'S BEEN SPIKING YOUR CHEMICALS!
IT'S NOT POSSIBLE!
NO ONE HAS BEEN HERE--EXCEPT THE GIRL!
AND SHE IS MY CAPTIVE!
YOU DIDN'T THINK I'D FORGET THAT, DID YOU?
IT'S THE ONE THOUGHT--THAT'S KEPT ME GOING--
THAT KEEPS ME GOING...
--THAT WON'T EVER LET ME STOP--
BTONG!
18

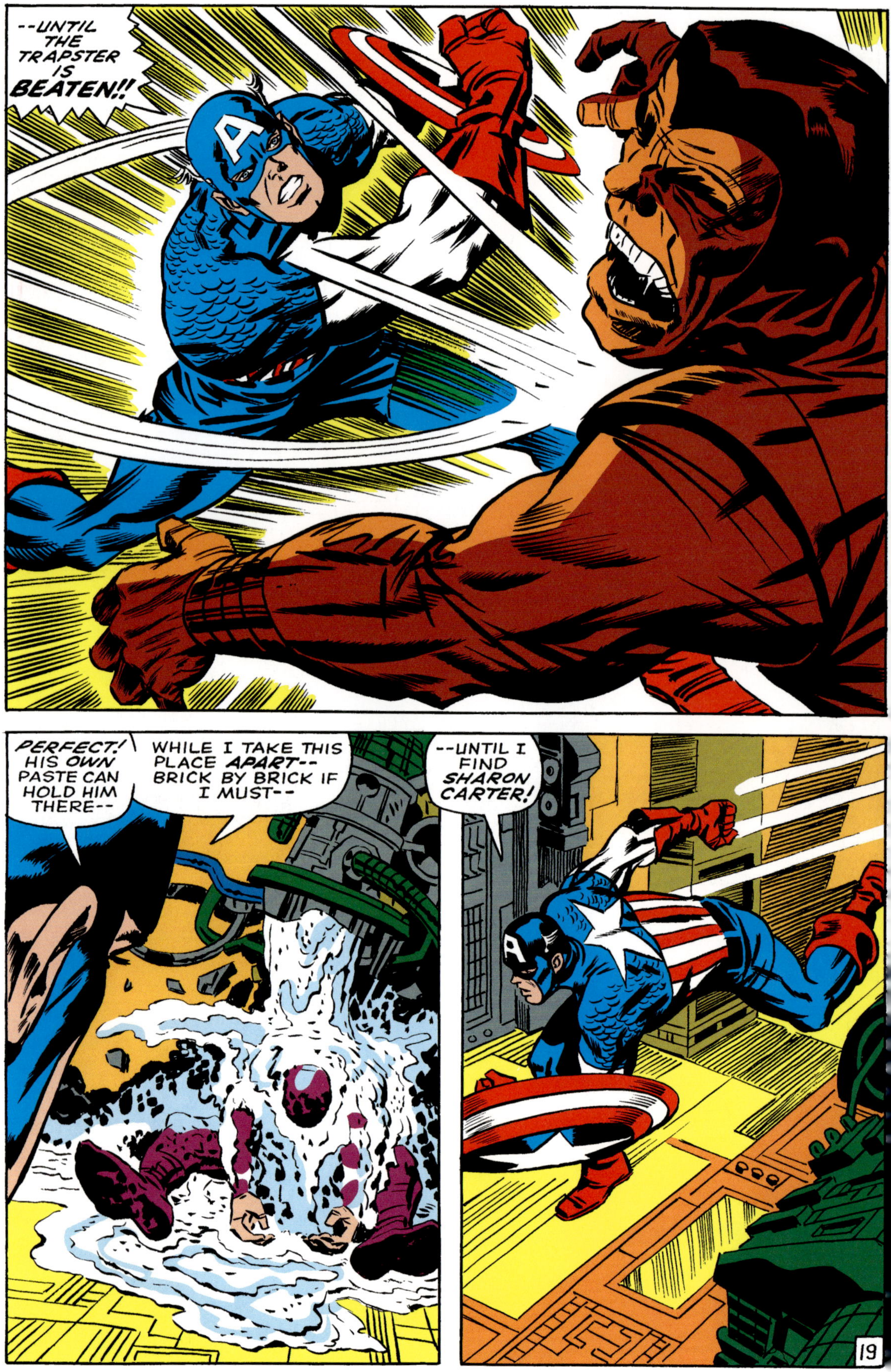
--UNTIL THE TRAPSTER IS BEATEN!!
PERFECT! HIS OWN PASTE CAN HOLD HIM THERE--
WHILE I TAKE THIS PLACE APART-- BRICK BY BRICK IF I MUST--
--UNTIL I FIND SHARON CARTER!
19

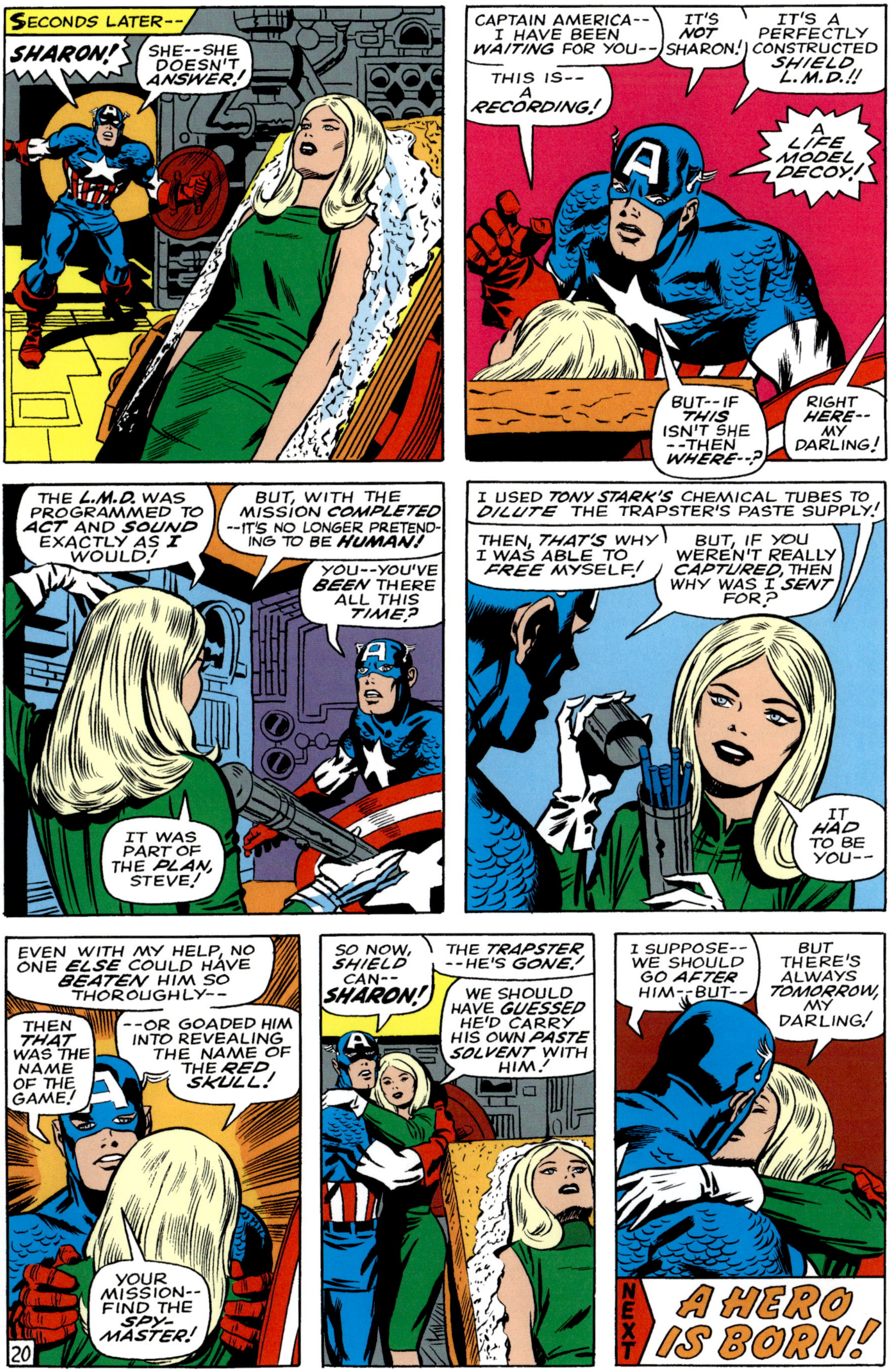

SECONDS LATER--
SHARON!
SHE--SHE DOESN'T ANSWER!
CAPTAIN AMERICA-- I HAVE BEEN WAITING FOR YOU--
THIS IS-- A RECORDING!
IT'S NOT SHARON!
IT'S A PERFECTLY CONSTRUCTED SHIELD L.M.D.!!
A LIFE MODEL DECOY!
BUT--IF THIS ISN'T SHE --THEN WHERE--?
RIGHT HERE-- MY DARLING!
THE L.M.D. WAS PROGRAMMED TO ACT AND SOUND EXACTLY AS I WOULD!
BUT, WITH THE MISSION COMPLETED --IT'S NO LONGER PRETENDING TO BE HUMAN!
YOU--YOU'VE BEEN THERE ALL THIS TIME?
IT WAS PART OF THE PLAN, STEVE!
I USED TONY STARK'S CHEMICAL TUBES TO DILUTE THE TRAPSTER'S PASTE SUPPLY!
THEN, THAT'S WHY I WAS ABLE TO FREE MYSELF!
BUT, IF YOU WEREN'T REALLY CAPTURED, THEN WHY WAS I SENT FOR?
IT HAD TO BE YOU--
EVEN WITH MY HELP, NO ONE ELSE COULD HAVE BEATEN HIM SO THOROUGHLY--
--OR GOADED HIM INTO REVEALING THE NAME OF THE RED SKULL!
THEN THAT WAS THE NAME OF THE GAME!
YOUR MISSION-- FIND THE SPY-MASTER!
20
SO NOW, SHIELD CAN-- SHARON!
THE TRAPSTER --HE'S GONE!
WE SHOULD HAVE GUESSED HE'D CARRY HIS OWN PASTE SOLVENT WITH HIM!
I SUPPOSE-- WE SHOULD GO AFTER HIM--BUT--
BUT THERE'S ALWAYS TOMORROW, MY DARLING!
NEXT
A HERO IS BORN!

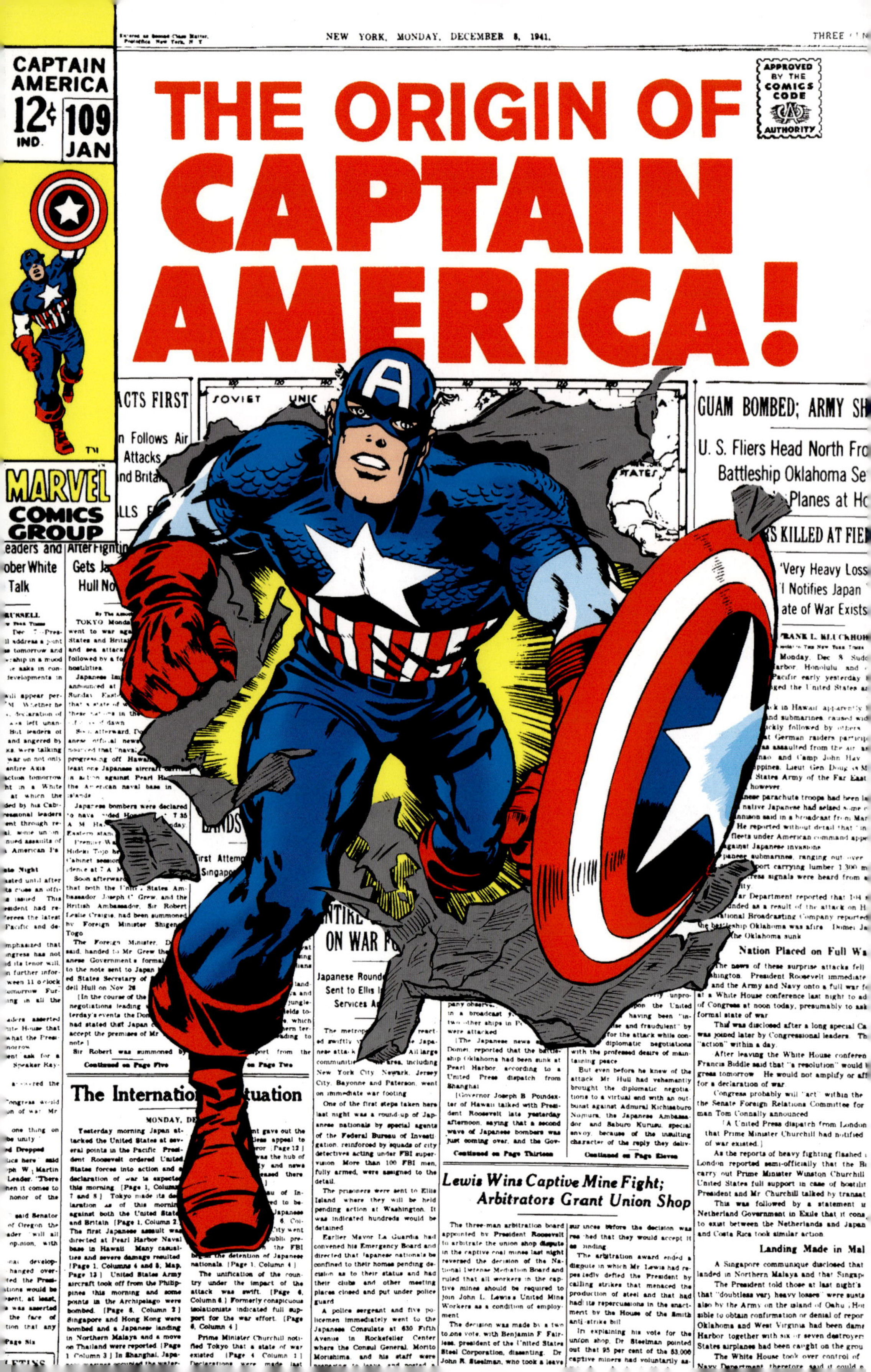
NEW YORK, MONDAY, DECEMBER 8, 1941.
CAPTAIN AMERICA
12¢
IND.
109
JAN
MARVEL COMICS GROUP
APPROVED BY THE COMICS CODE AUTHORITY
THE ORIGIN OF CAPTAIN AMERICA!
GUAM BOMBED; ARMY SH
U. S. Fliers Head North Fro
Battleship Oklahoma Se
Planes at Ho
The International Situation
Lewis Wins Captive Mine Fight;
Arbitrators Grant Union Shop
Nation Placed on Full Wa
Landing Made in Mal

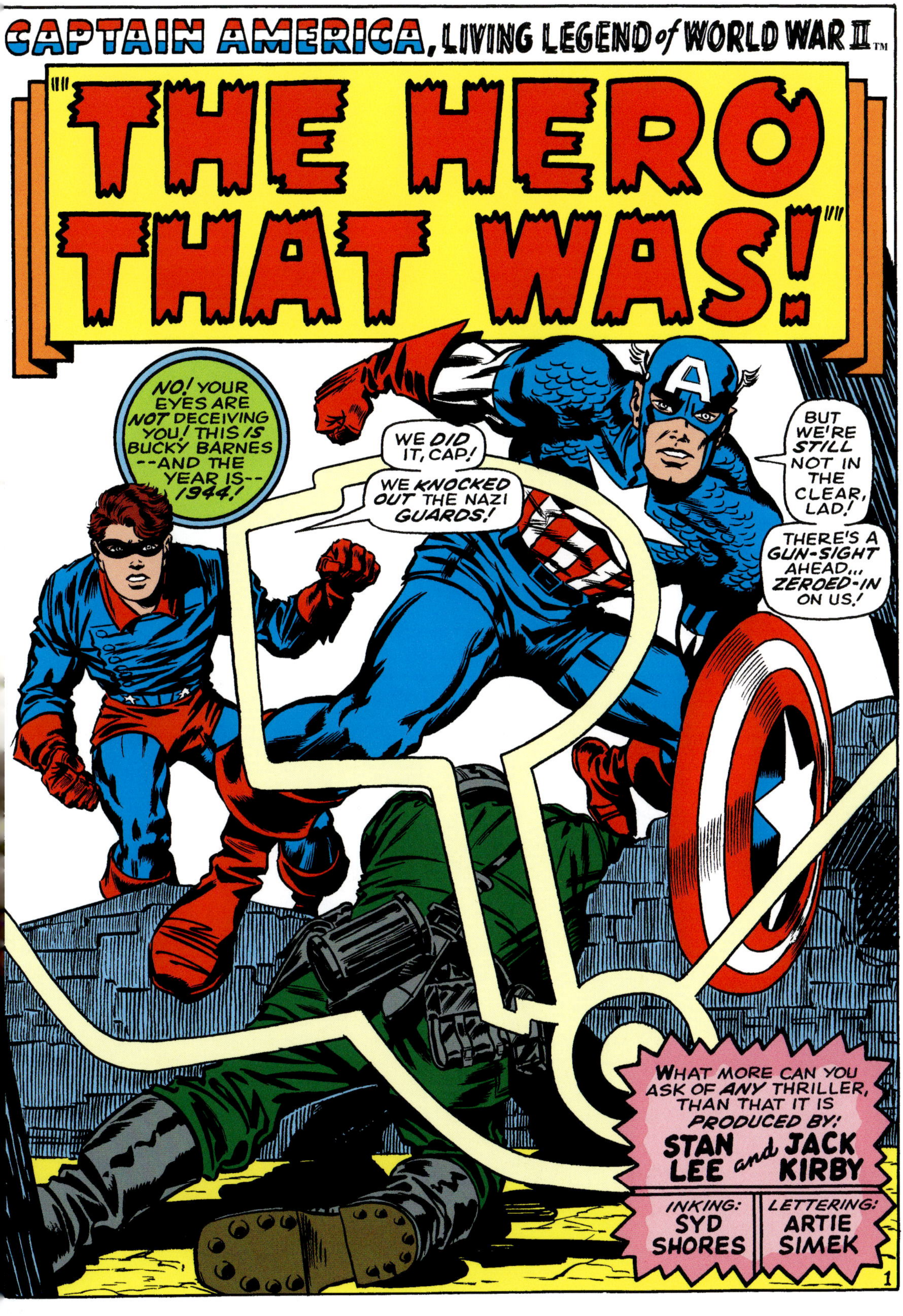
CAPTAIN AMERICA, LIVING LEGEND of WORLD WAR II TM
"THE HERO THAT WAS!"
NO! YOUR EYES ARE NOT DECEIVING YOU! THIS IS BUCKY BARNES --AND THE YEAR IS-- 1944!
WE DID IT, CAP!
WE KNOCKED OUT THE NAZI GUARDS!
BUT WE'RE STILL NOT IN THE CLEAR, LAD!
THERE'S A GUN-SIGHT AHEAD... ZEROED-IN ON US!
WHAT MORE CAN YOU ASK OF ANY THRILLER, THAN THAT IT IS PRODUCED BY: STAN LEE and JACK KIRBY
INKING: SYD SHORES
LETTERING: ARTIE SIMEK
1

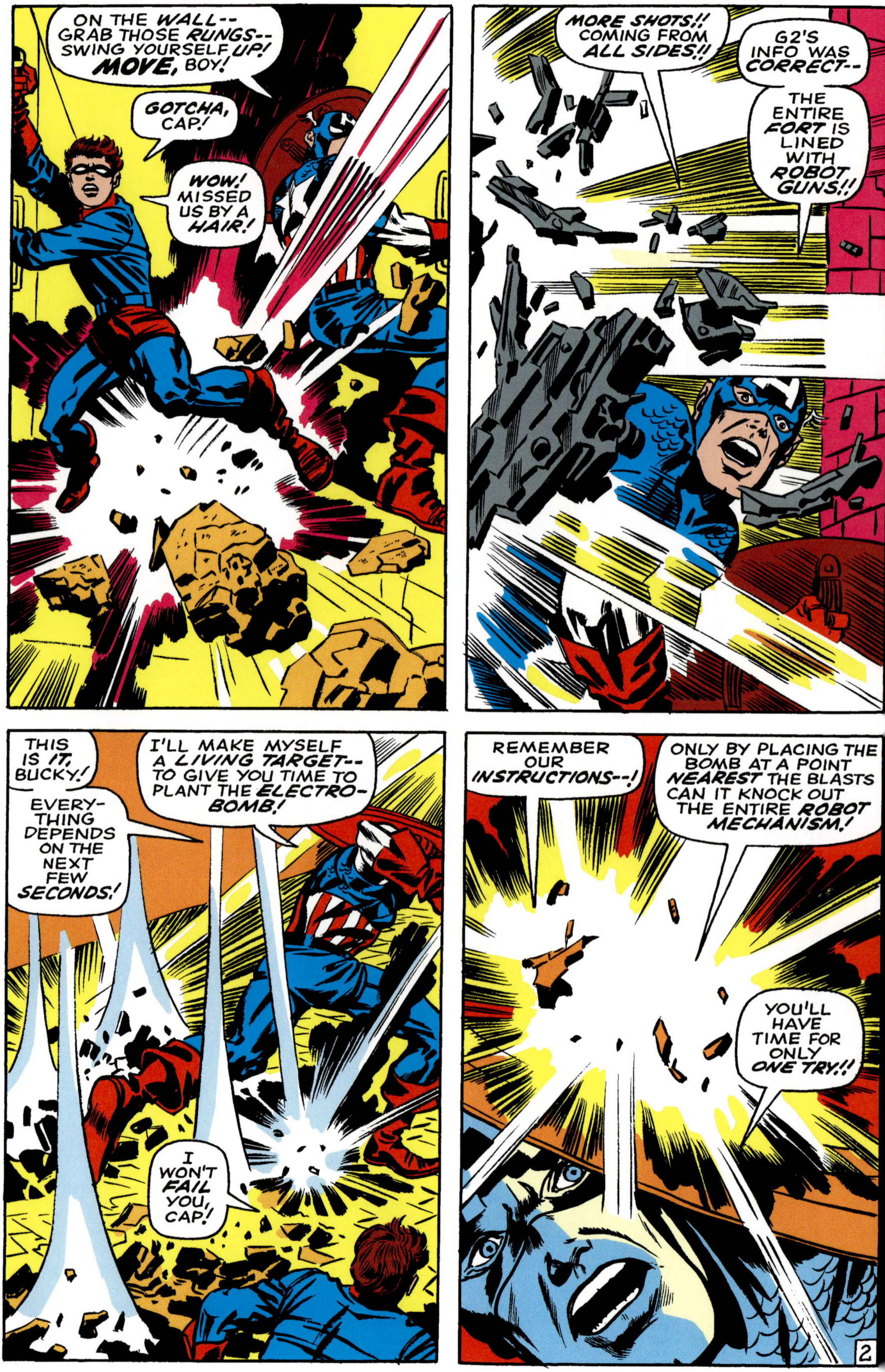
ON THE WALL-- GRAB THOSE RUNGS-- SWING YOURSELF UP! MOVE, BOY!
GOTCHA, CAP!
WOW! MISSED US BY A HAIR!
MORE SHOTS!! COMING FROM ALL SIDES!!
G2'S INFO WAS CORRECT--
THE ENTIRE FORT IS LINED WITH ROBOT GUNS!!
THIS IS IT, BUCKY!
EVERY-THING DEPENDS ON THE NEXT FEW SECONDS!
I'LL MAKE MYSELF A LIVING TARGET-- TO GIVE YOU TIME TO PLANT THE ELECTRO-BOMB!
I WON'T FAIL YOU, CAP!
REMEMBER OUR INSTRUCTIONS--!
ONLY BY PLACING THE BOMB AT A POINT NEAREST THE BLASTS CAN IT KNOCK OUT THE ENTIRE ROBOT MECHANISM!
YOU'LL HAVE TIME FOR ONLY ONE TRY!!
2

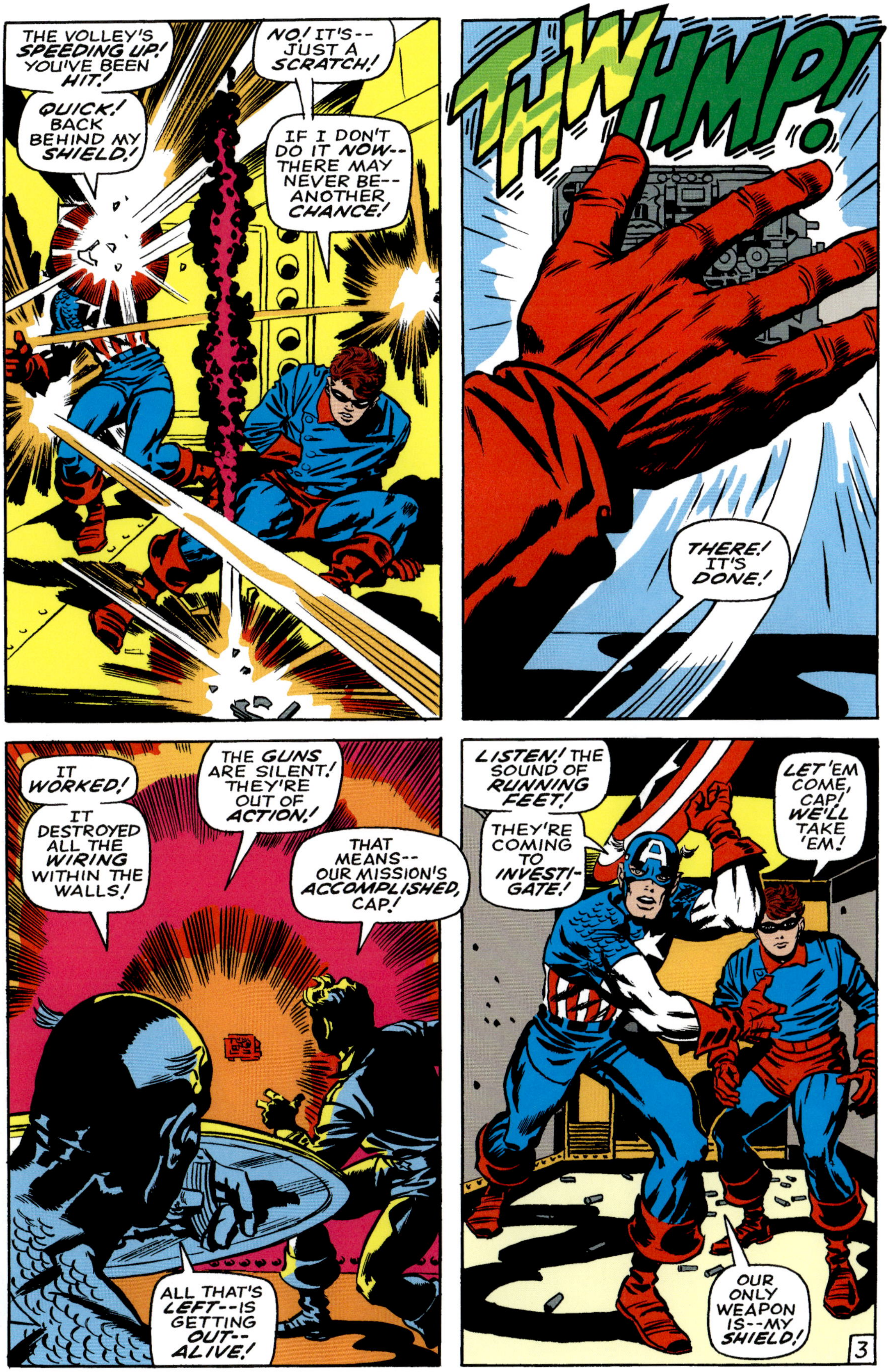
THE VOLLEY'S SPEEDING UP! YOU'VE BEEN HIT!
QUICK! BACK BEHIND MY SHIELD!
NO! IT'S-- JUST A SCRATCH!
IF I DON'T DO IT NOW-- THERE MAY NEVER BE-- ANOTHER CHANCE!
THWHMP!
THERE! IT'S DONE!
IT WORKED!
IT DESTROYED ALL THE WIRING WITHIN THE WALLS!
THE GUNS ARE SILENT! THEY'RE OUT OF ACTION!
THAT MEANS-- OUR MISSION'S ACCOMPLISHED, CAP!
ALL THAT'S LEFT--IS GETTING OUT-- ALIVE!
LISTEN! THE SOUND OF RUNNING FEET!
THEY'RE COMING TO INVESTI-GATE!
LET 'EM COME, CAP! WE'LL TAKE 'EM!
OUR ONLY WEAPON IS--MY SHIELD!
3

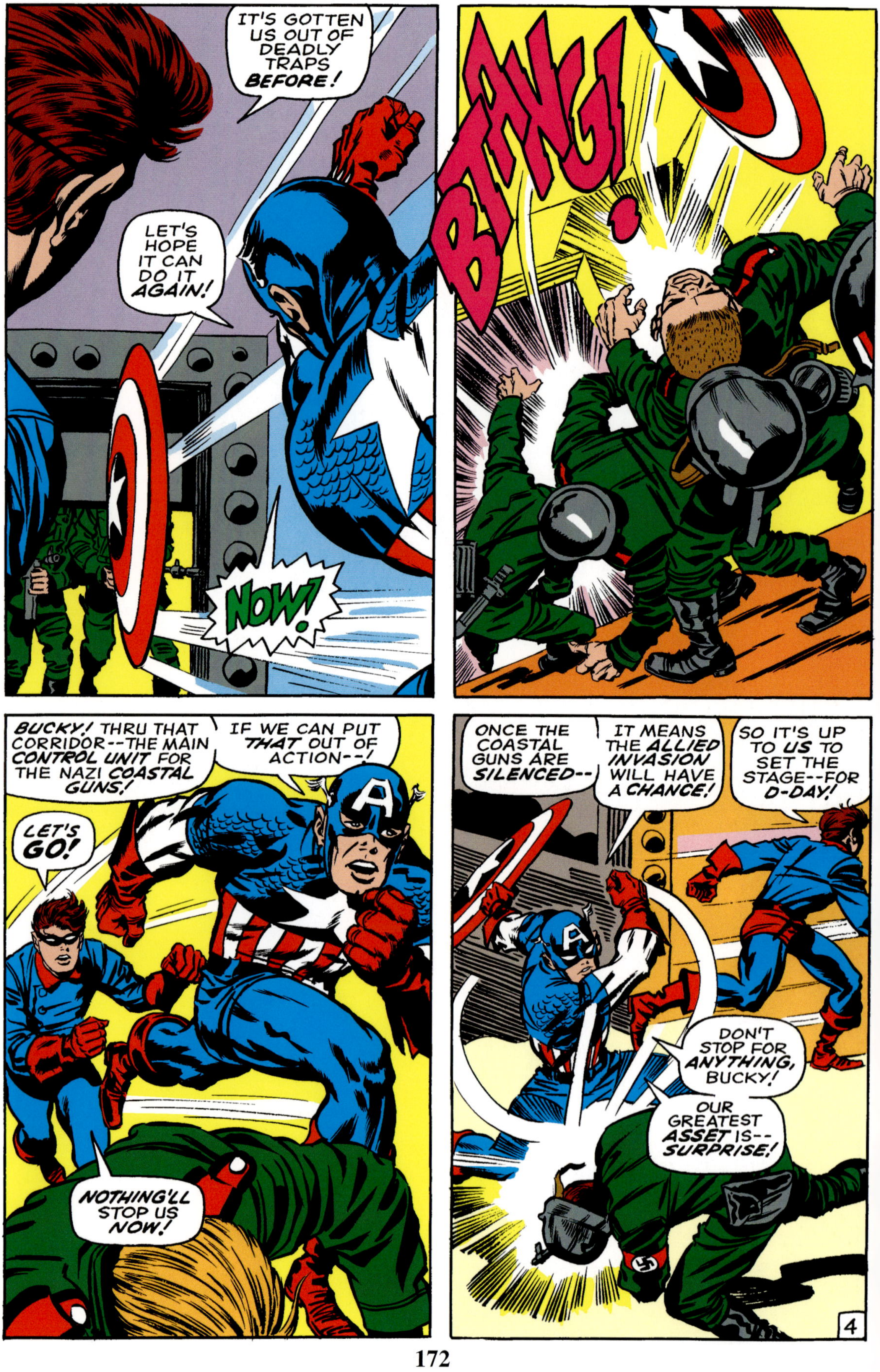

IT'S GOTTEN US OUT OF DEADLY TRAPS BEFORE!
LET'S HOPE IT CAN DO IT AGAIN!
NOW!
BTANG!
BUCKY! THRU THAT CORRIDOR--THE MAIN CONTROL UNIT FOR THE NAZI COASTAL GUNS!
IF WE CAN PUT THAT OUT OF ACTION--!
LET'S GO!
NOTHING'LL STOP US NOW!
ONCE THE COASTAL GUNS ARE SILENCED--
IT MEANS THE ALLIED INVASION WILL HAVE A CHANCE!
SO IT'S UP TO US TO SET THE STAGE--FOR D-DAY!
DON'T STOP FOR ANYTHING, BUCKY!
OUR GREATEST ASSET IS--SURPRISE!
4

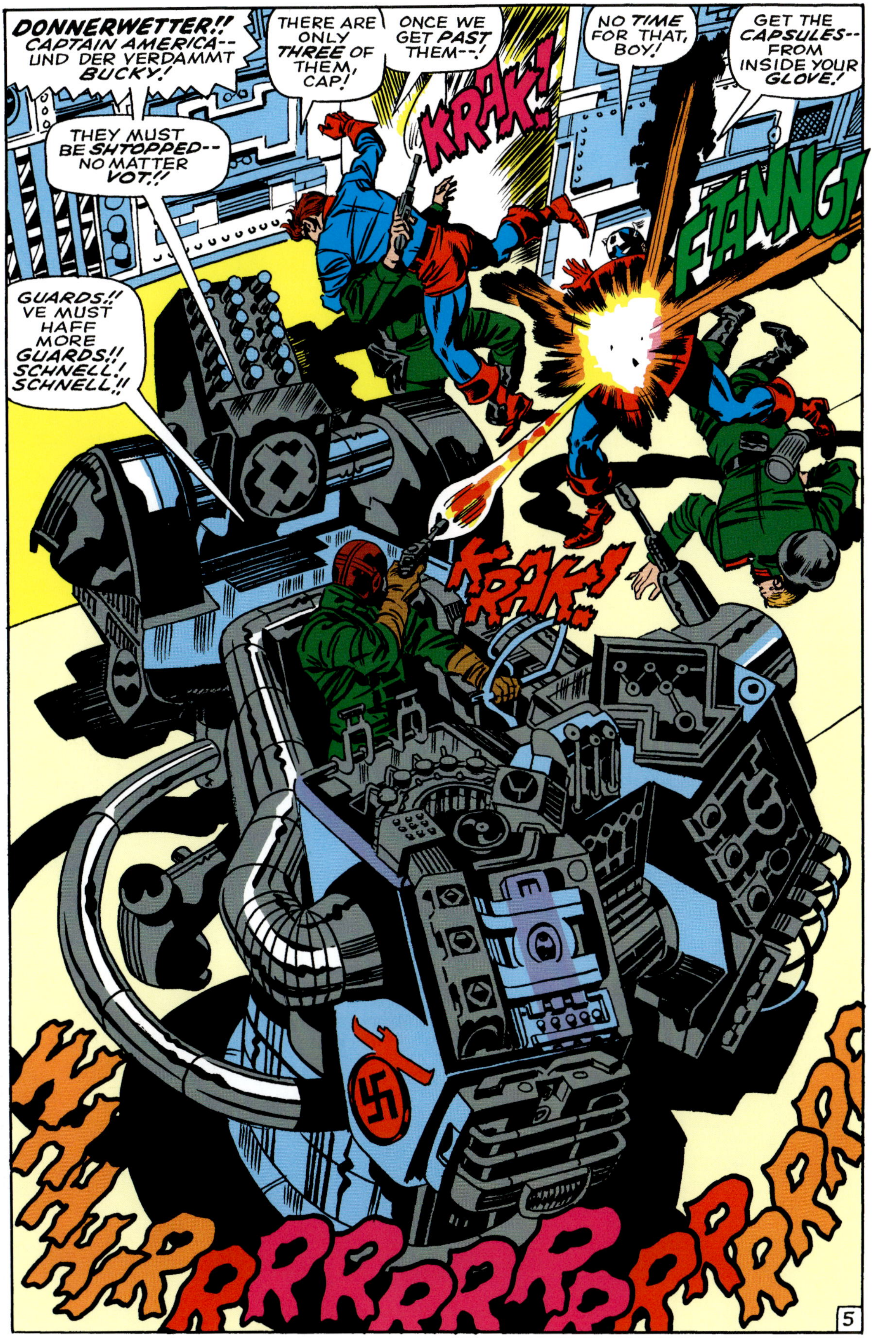
DONNERWETTER!! CAPTAIN AMERICA-- UND DER VERDAMMT BUCKY!
THEY MUST BE SHTOPPED-- NO MATTER VOT!!
THERE ARE ONLY THREE OF THEM, CAP!
ONCE WE GET PAST THEM--!
KRAK!
NO TIME FOR THAT, BOY!
GET THE CAPSULES-- FROM INSIDE YOUR GLOVE!
FTANNG!
GUARDS!! VE MUST HAFF MORE GUARDS!! SCHNELL! SCHNELL!!
KRAK!
WHIRRRRRRRRRRRRR
5

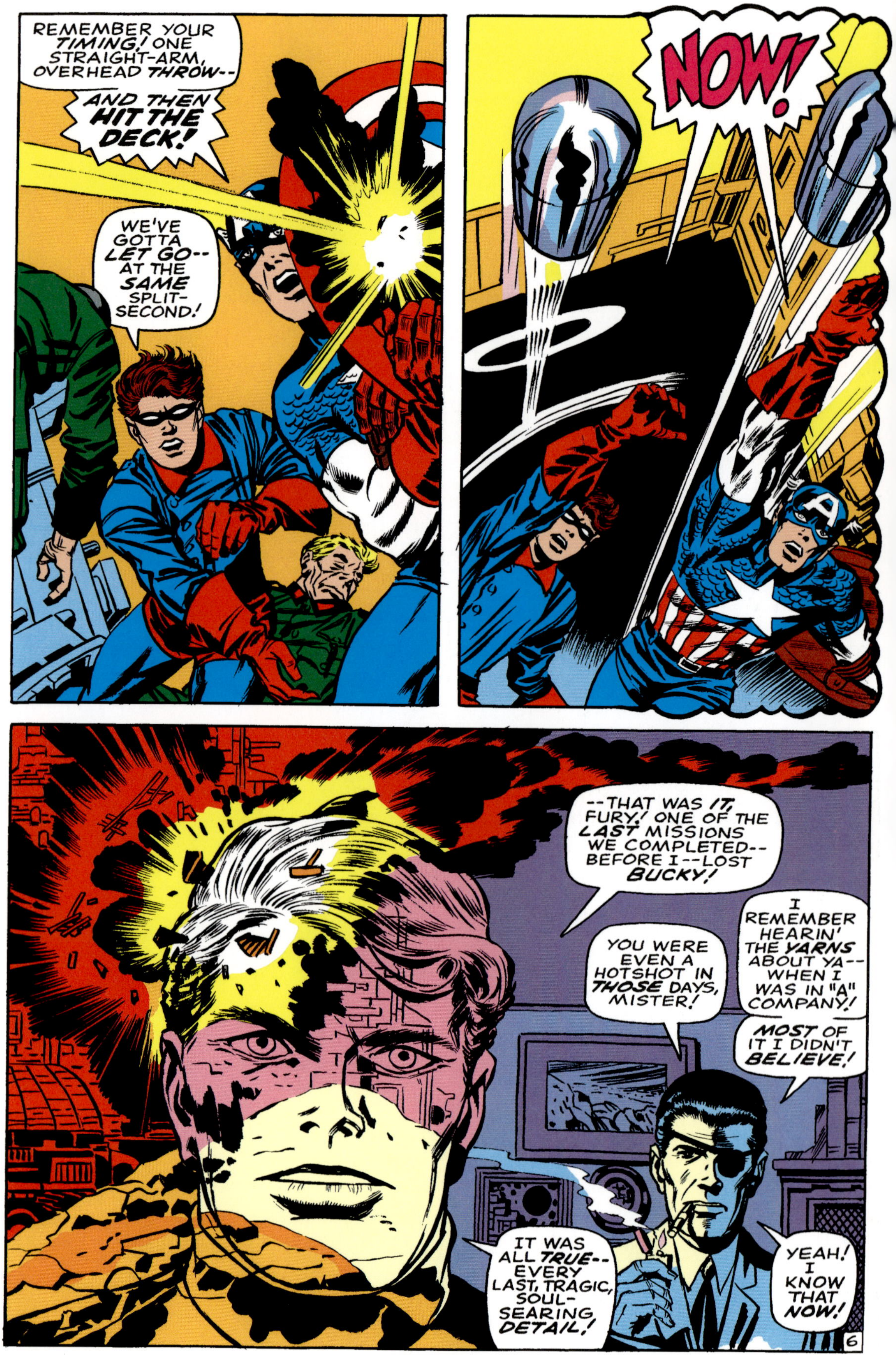
REMEMBER YOUR TIMING! ONE STRAIGHT-ARM, OVERHEAD THROW--
AND THEN HIT THE DECK!
WE'VE GOTTA LET GO--AT THE SAME SPLIT-SECOND!
NOW!
--THAT WAS IT, FURY! ONE OF THE LAST MISSIONS WE COMPLETED--BEFORE I--LOST BUCKY!
YOU WERE EVEN A HOTSHOT IN THOSE DAYS, MISTER!
I REMEMBER HEARIN' THE YARNS ABOUT YA--WHEN I WAS IN "A" COMPANY!
MOST OF IT I DIDN'T BELIEVE!
IT WAS ALL TRUE--EVERY LAST, TRAGIC, SOUL-SEARING DETAIL!
YEAH! I KNOW THAT NOW!
6

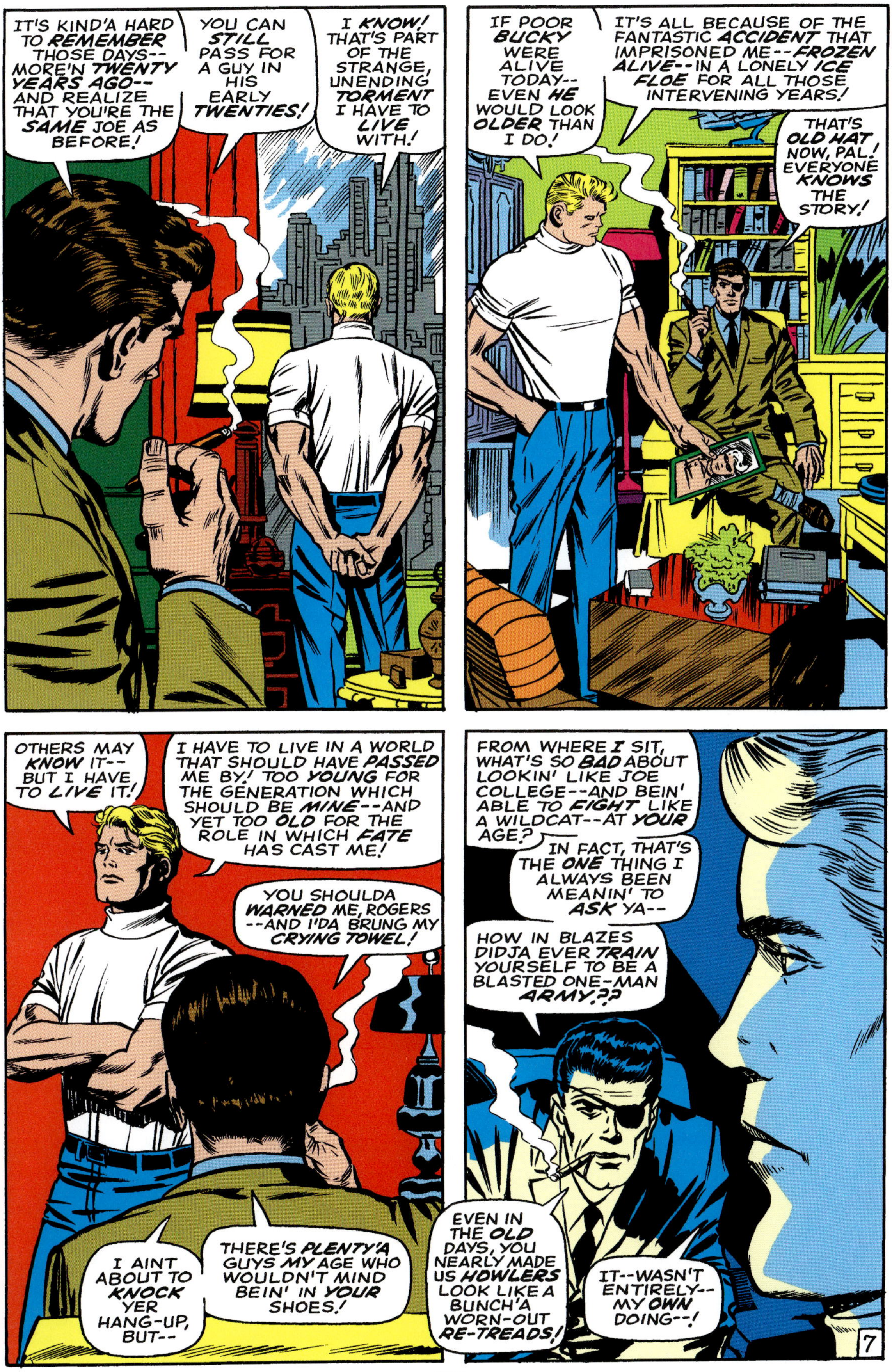
IT'S KIND'A HARD TO REMEMBER THOSE DAYS-- MORE'N TWENTY YEARS AGO-- AND REALIZE THAT YOU'RE THE SAME JOE AS BEFORE!
YOU CAN STILL PASS FOR A GUY IN HIS EARLY TWENTIES!
I KNOW! THAT'S PART OF THE STRANGE, UNENDING TORMENT I HAVE TO LIVE WITH!
IF POOR BUCKY WERE ALIVE TODAY-- EVEN HE WOULD LOOK OLDER THAN I DO!
IT'S ALL BECAUSE OF THE FANTASTIC ACCIDENT THAT IMPRISONED ME--FROZEN ALIVE--IN A LONELY ICE FLOE FOR ALL THOSE INTERVENING YEARS!
THAT'S OLD HAT NOW, PAL! EVERYONE KNOWS THE STORY!
OTHERS MAY KNOW IT-- BUT I HAVE TO LIVE IT!
I HAVE TO LIVE IN A WORLD THAT SHOULD HAVE PASSED ME BY! TOO YOUNG FOR THE GENERATION WHICH SHOULD BE MINE--AND YET TOO OLD FOR THE ROLE IN WHICH FATE HAS CAST ME!
YOU SHOULDA WARNED ME, ROGERS --AND I'DA BRUNG MY CRYING TOWEL!
I AINT ABOUT TO KNOCK YER HANG-UP, BUT--
THERE'S PLENTY'A GUYS MY AGE WHO WOULDN'T MIND BEIN' IN YOUR SHOES!
FROM WHERE I SIT, WHAT'S SO BAD ABOUT LOOKIN' LIKE JOE COLLEGE--AND BEIN' ABLE TO FIGHT LIKE A WILDCAT--AT YOUR AGE?
IN FACT, THAT'S THE ONE THING I ALWAYS BEEN MEANIN' TO ASK YA--
HOW IN BLAZES DIDJA EVER TRAIN YOURSELF TO BE A BLASTED ONE-MAN ARMY??
EVEN IN THE OLD DAYS, YOU NEARLY MADE US HOWLERS LOOK LIKE A BUNCH'A WORN-OUT RE-TREADS!
IT--WASN'T ENTIRELY-- MY OWN DOING--!
7

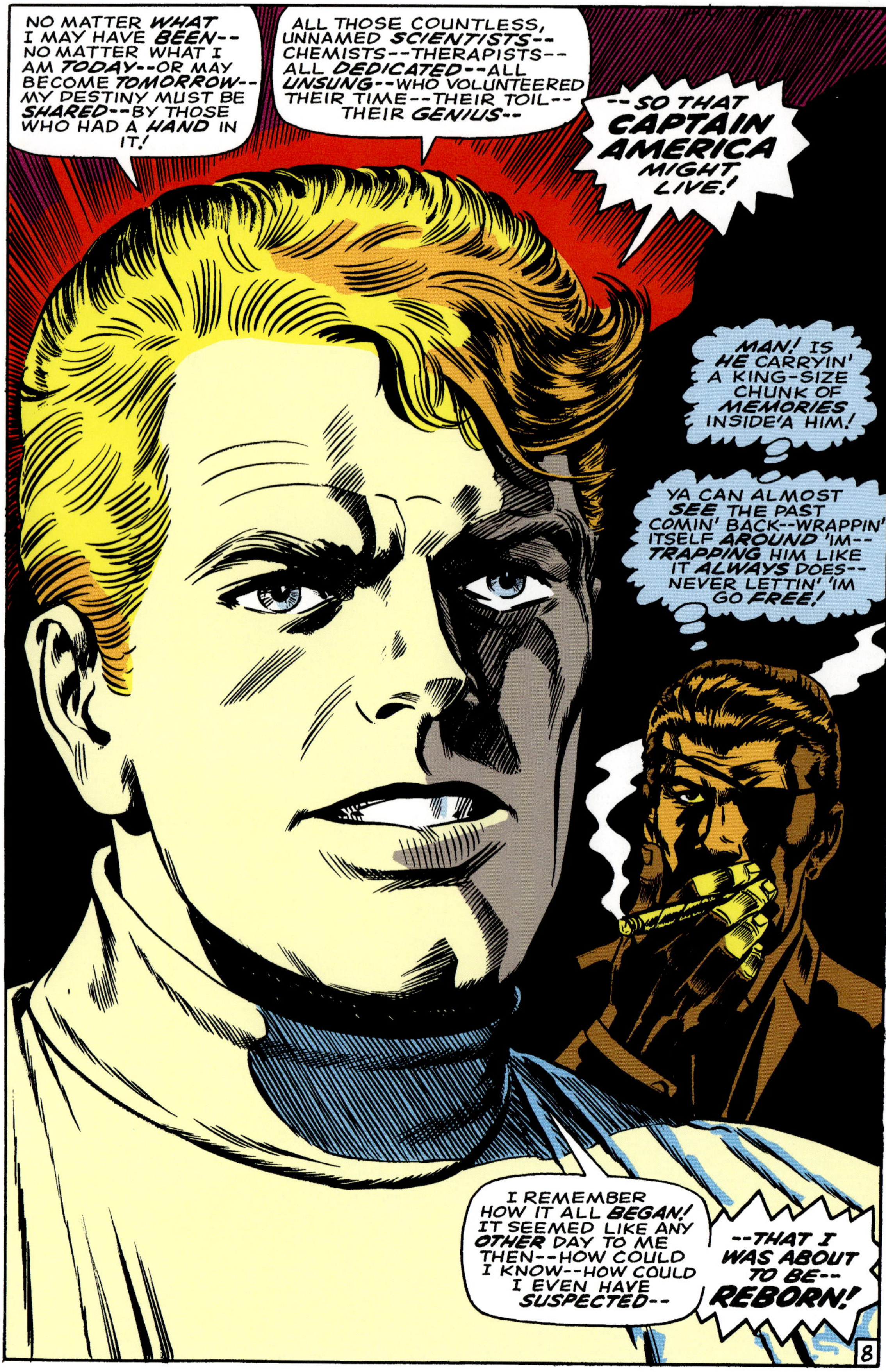
NO MATTER WHAT I MAY HAVE BEEN-- NO MATTER WHAT I AM TODAY--OR MAY BECOME TOMORROW-- MY DESTINY MUST BE SHARED--BY THOSE WHO HAD A HAND IN IT!
ALL THOSE COUNTLESS, UNNAMED SCIENTISTS-- CHEMISTS--THERAPISTS-- ALL DEDICATED--ALL UNSUNG--WHO VOLUNTEERED THEIR TIME--THEIR TOIL-- THEIR GENIUS--
--SO THAT CAPTAIN AMERICA MIGHT LIVE!
MAN! IS HE CARRYIN' A KING-SIZE CHUNK OF MEMORIES INSIDE'A HIM!
YA CAN ALMOST SEE THE PAST COMIN' BACK--WRAPPIN' ITSELF AROUND 'IM-- TRAPPING HIM LIKE IT ALWAYS DOES-- NEVER LETTIN' 'IM GO FREE!
I REMEMBER HOW IT ALL BEGAN! IT SEEMED LIKE ANY OTHER DAY TO ME THEN--HOW COULD I KNOW--HOW COULD I EVEN HAVE SUSPECTED--
--THAT I WAS ABOUT TO BE-- REBORN!
8

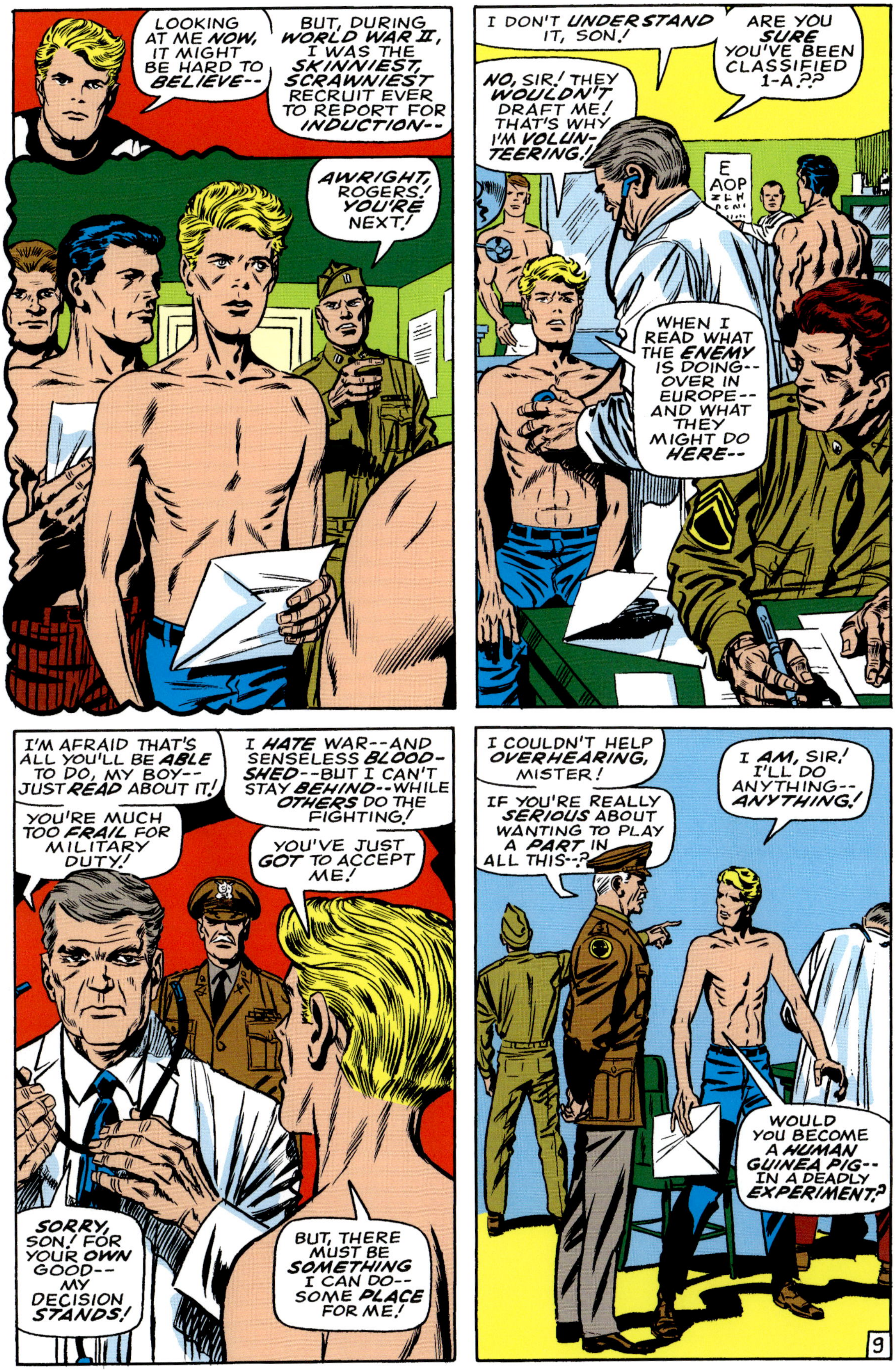

LOOKING AT ME NOW, IT MIGHT BE HARD TO BELIEVE--
BUT, DURING WORLD WAR II, I WAS THE SKINNIEST, SCRAWNIEST RECRUIT EVER TO REPORT FOR INDUCTION--
AWRIGHT, ROGERS! YOU'RE NEXT!
I DON'T UNDERSTAND IT, SON!
ARE YOU SURE YOU'VE BEEN CLASSIFIED 1-A??
NO, SIR! THEY WOULDN'T DRAFT ME! THAT'S WHY I'M VOLUNTEERING!
E
AOP
WHEN I READ WHAT THE ENEMY IS DOING-- OVER IN EUROPE-- AND WHAT THEY MIGHT DO HERE--
I'M AFRAID THAT'S ALL YOU'LL BE ABLE TO DO, MY BOY-- JUST READ ABOUT IT!
YOU'RE MUCH TOO FRAIL FOR MILITARY DUTY!
I HATE WAR--AND SENSELESS BLOODSHED--BUT I CAN'T STAY BEHIND--WHILE OTHERS DO THE FIGHTING!
YOU'VE JUST GOT TO ACCEPT ME!
SORRY, SON! FOR YOUR OWN GOOD-- MY DECISION STANDS!
BUT, THERE MUST BE SOMETHING I CAN DO-- SOME PLACE FOR ME!
I COULDN'T HELP OVERHEARING, MISTER!
IF YOU'RE REALLY SERIOUS ABOUT WANTING TO PLAY A PART IN ALL THIS--?
I AM, SIR! I'LL DO ANYTHING-- ANYTHING!
WOULD YOU BECOME A HUMAN GUINEA PIG-- IN A DEADLY EXPERIMENT?
9

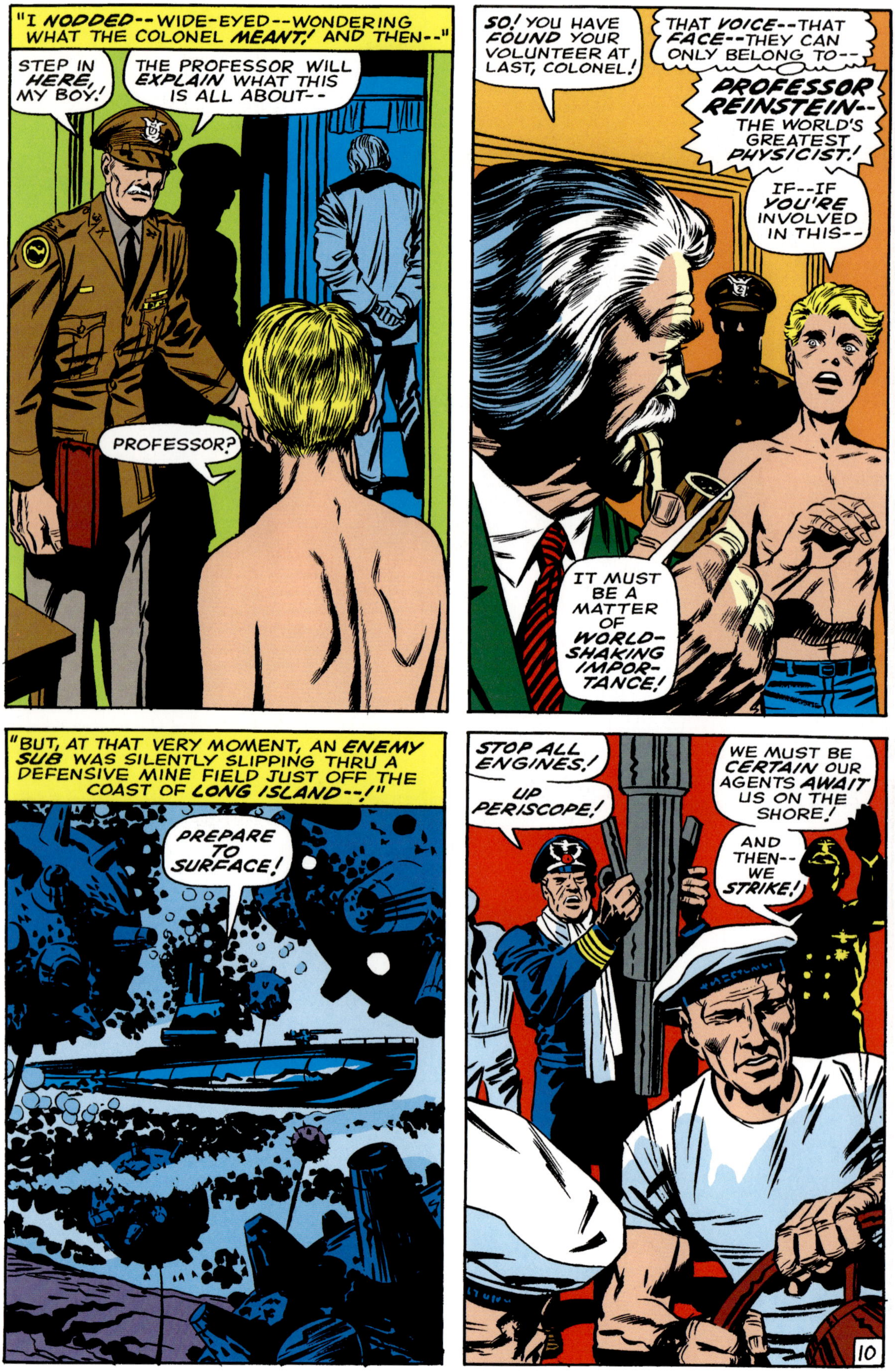
"I NODDED--WIDE-EYED--WONDERING WHAT THE COLONEL MEANT! AND THEN--"
STEP IN HERE, MY BOY!
THE PROFESSOR WILL EXPLAIN WHAT THIS IS ALL ABOUT--
PROFESSOR?
SO! YOU HAVE FOUND YOUR VOLUNTEER AT LAST, COLONEL!
THAT VOICE--THAT FACE--THEY CAN ONLY BELONG TO--
PROFESSOR REINSTEIN--THE WORLD'S GREATEST PHYSICIST!
IF--IF YOU'RE INVOLVED IN THIS--
IT MUST BE A MATTER OF WORLD-SHAKING IMPORTANCE!
"BUT, AT THAT VERY MOMENT, AN ENEMY SUB WAS SILENTLY SLIPPING THRU A DEFENSIVE MINE FIELD JUST OFF THE COAST OF LONG ISLAND--!"
PREPARE TO SURFACE!
STOP ALL ENGINES!
UP PERISCOPE!
WE MUST BE CERTAIN OUR AGENTS AWAIT US ON THE SHORE!
AND THEN--WE STRIKE!
10

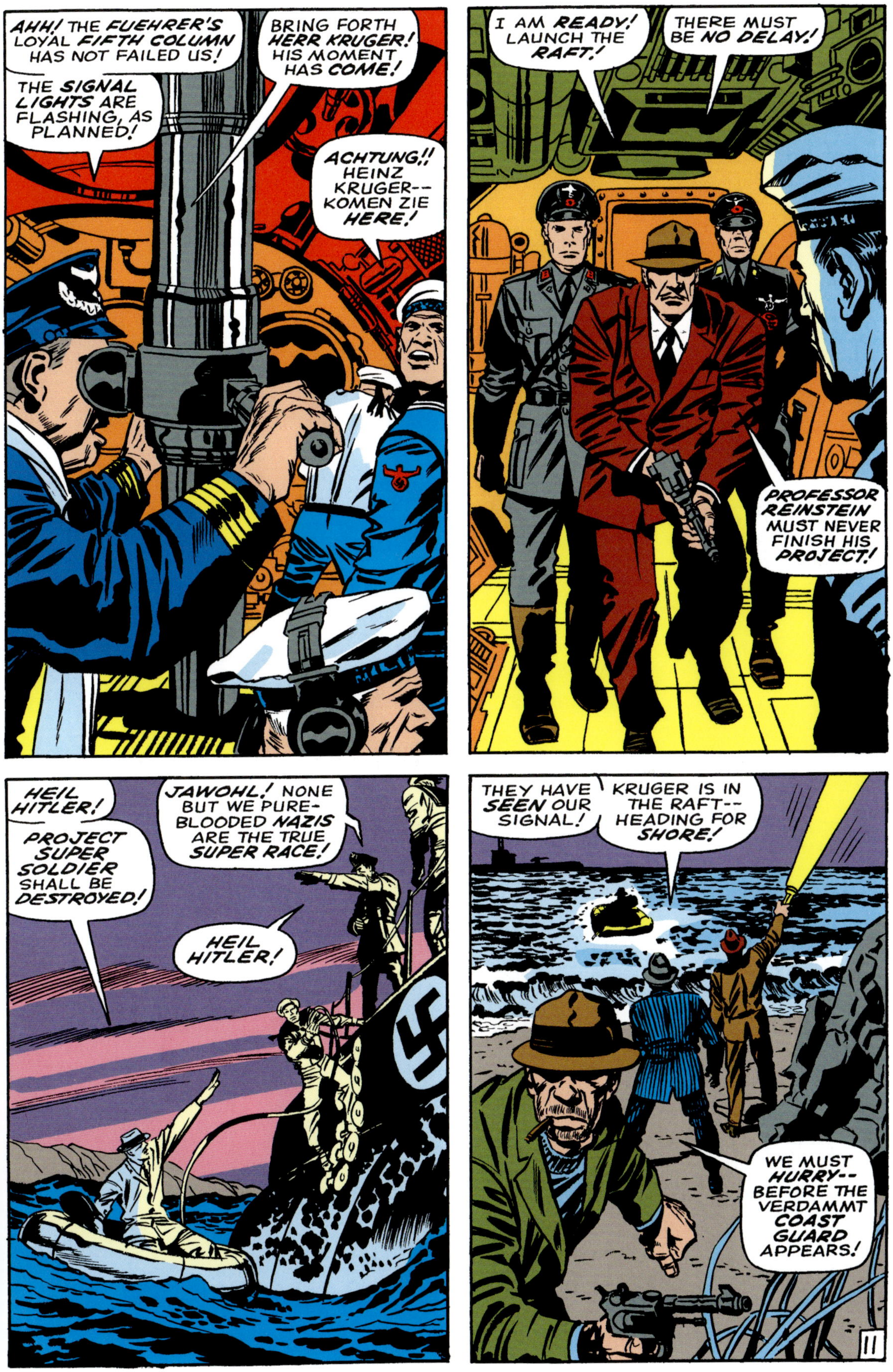
AHH! THE FUEHRER'S LOYAL FIFTH COLUMN HAS NOT FAILED US!
THE SIGNAL LIGHTS ARE FLASHING, AS PLANNED!
BRING FORTH HERR KRUGER! HIS MOMENT HAS COME!
ACHTUNG!! HEINZ KRUGER-- KOMEN ZIE HERE!
I AM READY! LAUNCH THE RAFT!
THERE MUST BE NO DELAY!
PROFESSOR REINSTEIN MUST NEVER FINISH HIS PROJECT!
HEIL HITLER!
PROJECT SUPER SOLDIER SHALL BE DESTROYED!
JAWOHL! NONE BUT WE PURE-BLOODED NAZIS ARE THE TRUE SUPER RACE!
HEIL HITLER!
THEY HAVE SEEN OUR SIGNAL!
KRUGER IS IN THE RAFT-- HEADING FOR SHORE!
WE MUST HURRY-- BEFORE THE VERDAMMT COAST GUARD APPEARS!
11

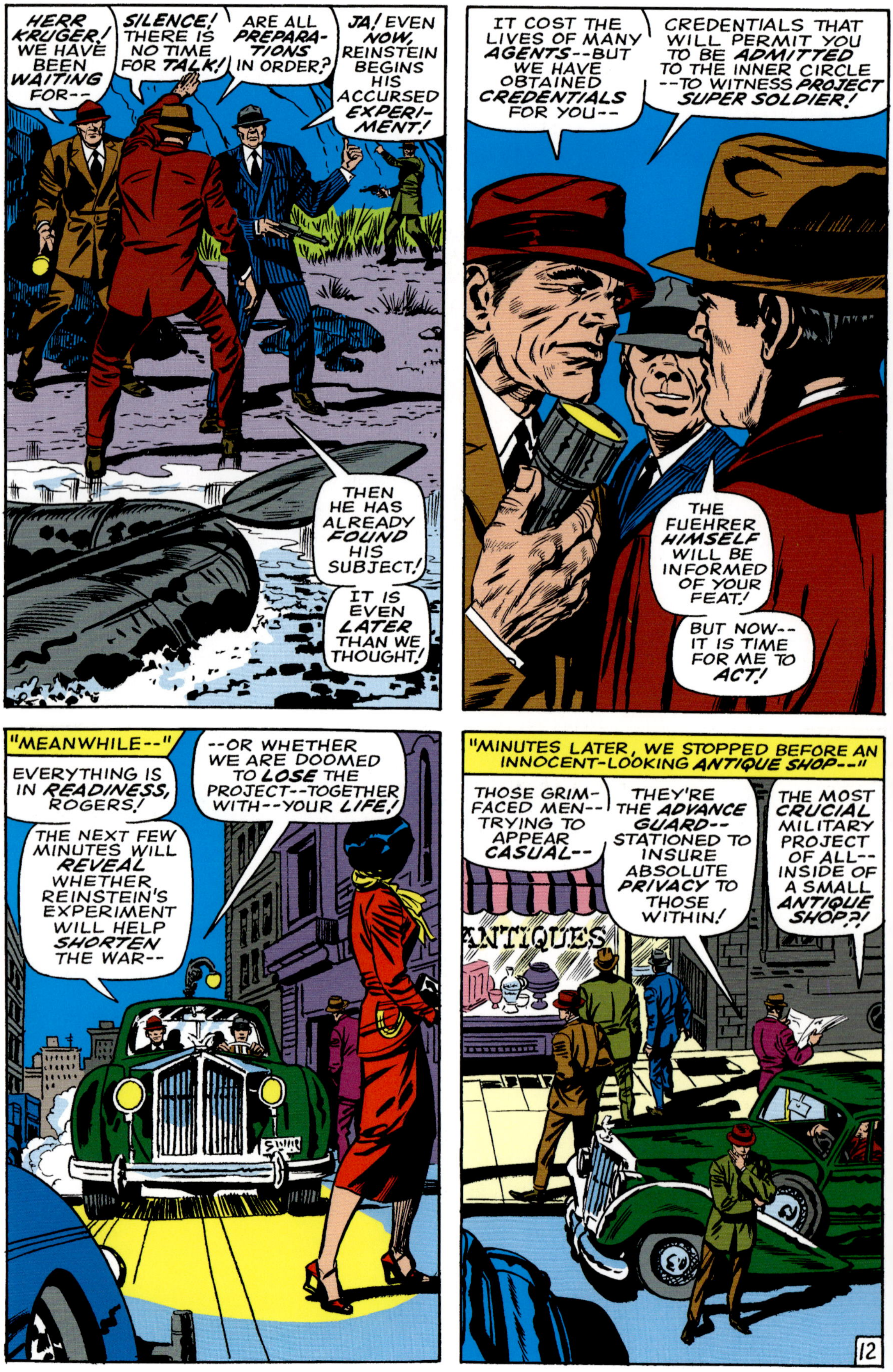
HERR KRUGER! WE HAVE BEEN WAITING FOR--
SILENCE! THERE IS NO TIME FOR TALK!
ARE ALL PREPARATIONS IN ORDER?
JA! EVEN NOW, REINSTEIN BEGINS HIS ACCURSED EXPERIMENT!
THEN HE HAS ALREADY FOUND HIS SUBJECT!
IT IS EVEN LATER THAN WE THOUGHT!
IT COST THE LIVES OF MANY AGENTS--BUT WE HAVE OBTAINED CREDENTIALS FOR YOU--
CREDENTIALS THAT WILL PERMIT YOU TO BE ADMITTED TO THE INNER CIRCLE --TO WITNESS PROJECT SUPER SOLDIER!
THE FUEHRER HIMSELF WILL BE INFORMED OF YOUR FEAT!
BUT NOW-- IT IS TIME FOR ME TO ACT!
"MEANWHILE--"
EVERYTHING IS IN READINESS, ROGERS!
THE NEXT FEW MINUTES WILL REVEAL WHETHER REINSTEIN'S EXPERIMENT WILL HELP SHORTEN THE WAR--
--OR WHETHER WE ARE DOOMED TO LOSE THE PROJECT--TOGETHER WITH--YOUR LIFE!
"MINUTES LATER, WE STOPPED BEFORE AN INNOCENT-LOOKING ANTIQUE SHOP--"
THOSE GRIM-FACED MEN--TRYING TO APPEAR CASUAL--
THEY'RE THE ADVANCE GUARD--STATIONED TO INSURE ABSOLUTE PRIVACY TO THOSE WITHIN!
THE MOST CRUCIAL MILITARY PROJECT OF ALL--INSIDE OF A SMALL ANTIQUE SHOP?!
ANTIQUES
12

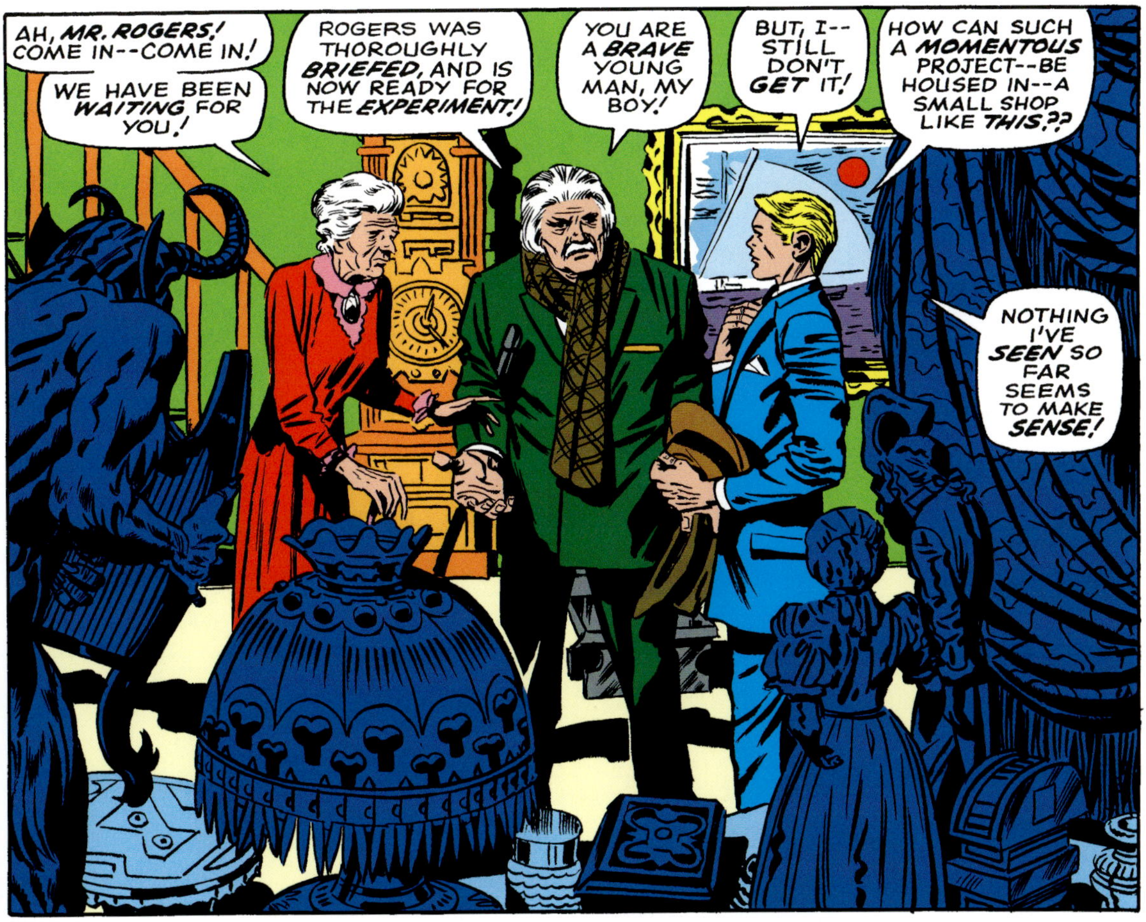
AH, MR. ROGERS! COME IN--COME IN!
WE HAVE BEEN WAITING FOR YOU!
ROGERS WAS THOROUGHLY BRIEFED, AND IS NOW READY FOR THE EXPERIMENT!
YOU ARE A BRAVE YOUNG MAN, MY BOY!
BUT, I-- STILL DON'T GET IT!
HOW CAN SUCH A MOMENTOUS PROJECT--BE HOUSED IN--A SMALL SHOP LIKE THIS??
NOTHING I'VE SEEN SO FAR SEEMS TO MAKE SENSE!

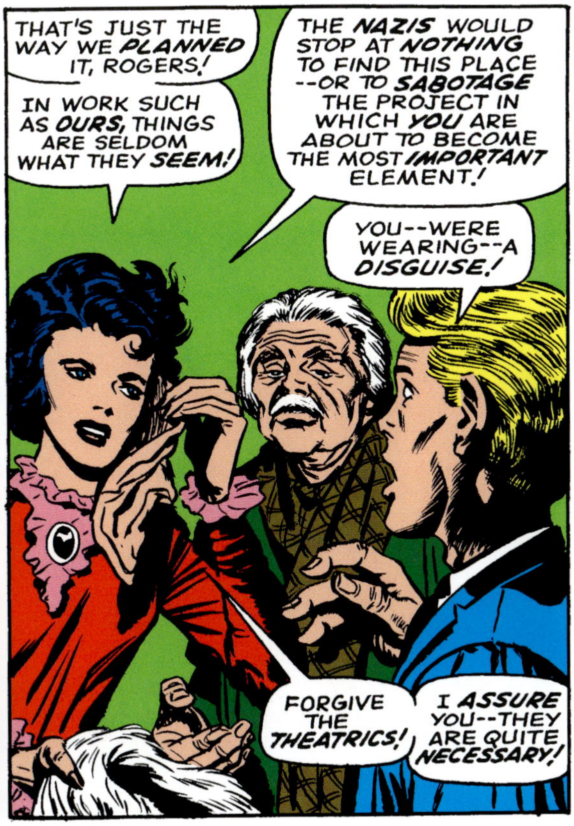
THAT'S JUST THE WAY WE PLANNED IT, ROGERS!
IN WORK SUCH AS OURS, THINGS ARE SELDOM WHAT THEY SEEM!
THE NAZIS WOULD STOP AT NOTHING TO FIND THIS PLACE --OR TO SABOTAGE THE PROJECT IN WHICH YOU ARE ABOUT TO BECOME THE MOST IMPORTANT ELEMENT!
YOU--WERE WEARING--A DISGUISE!
FORGIVE THE THEATRICS!
I ASSURE YOU--THEY ARE QUITE NECESSARY!

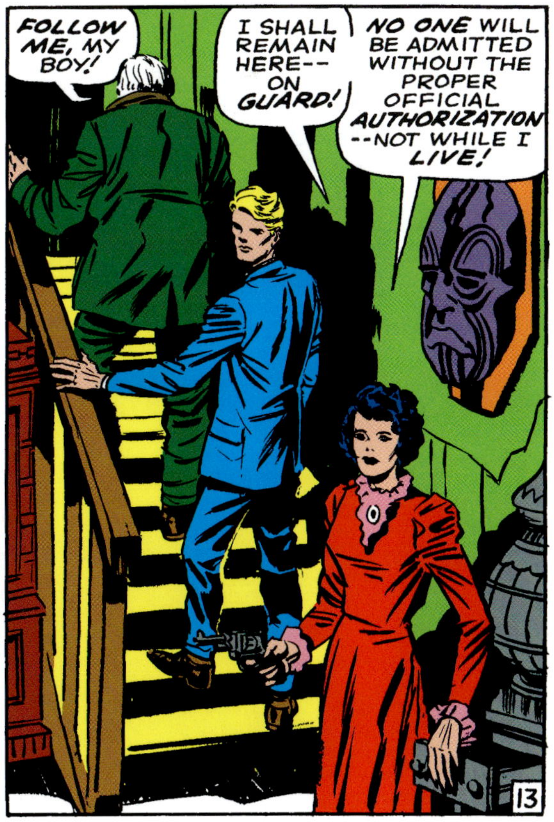
FOLLOW ME, MY BOY!
I SHALL REMAIN HERE-- ON GUARD!
NO ONE WILL BE ADMITTED WITHOUT THE PROPER OFFICIAL AUTHORIZATION --NOT WHILE I LIVE!
13

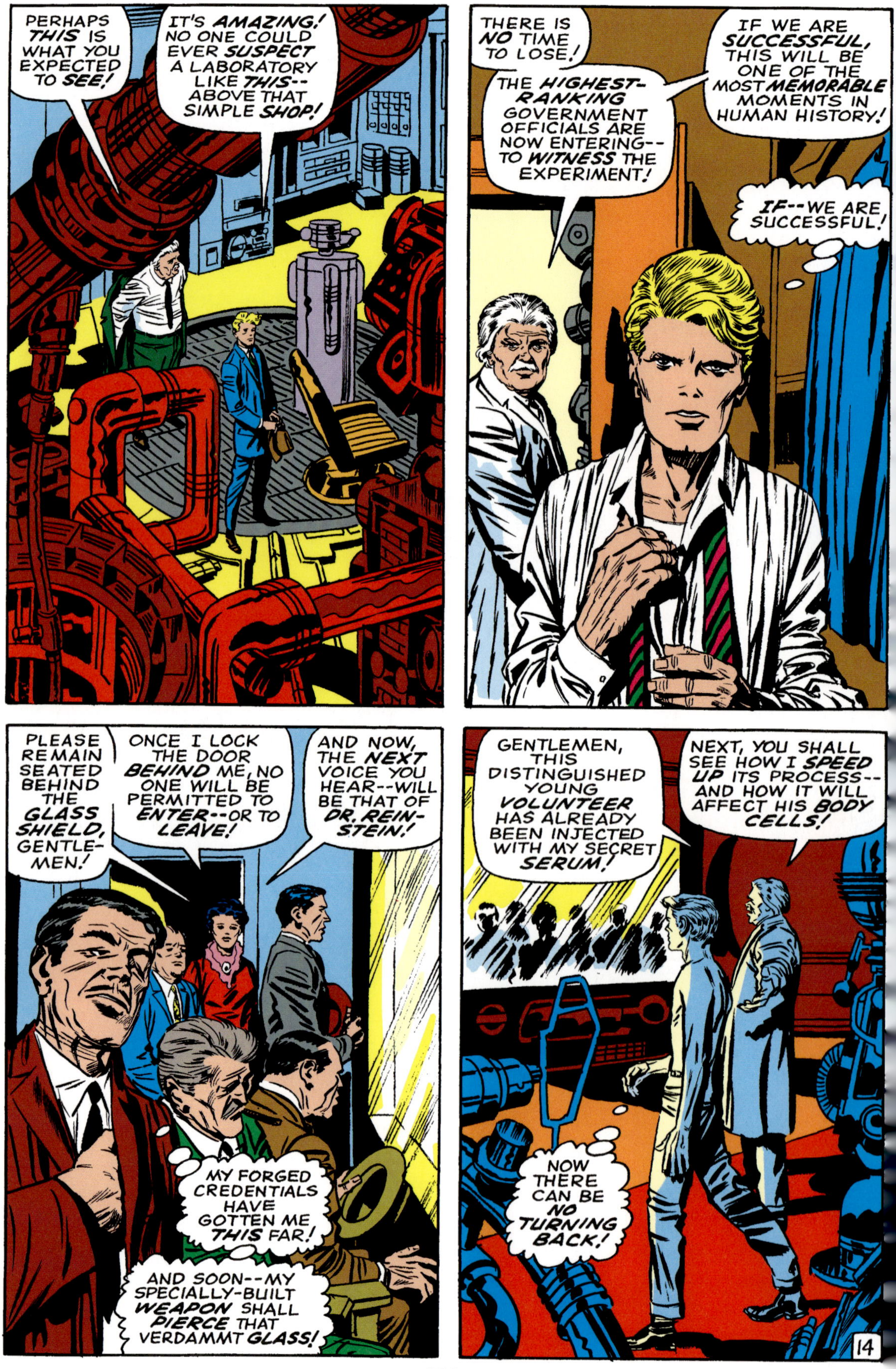
PERHAPS THIS IS WHAT YOU EXPECTED TO SEE!
IT'S AMAZING! NO ONE COULD EVER SUSPECT A LABORATORY LIKE THIS-- ABOVE THAT SIMPLE SHOP!
THERE IS NO TIME TO LOSE!
THE HIGHEST-RANKING GOVERNMENT OFFICIALS ARE NOW ENTERING-- TO WITNESS THE EXPERIMENT!
IF WE ARE SUCCESSFUL, THIS WILL BE ONE OF THE MOST MEMORABLE MOMENTS IN HUMAN HISTORY!
IF--WE ARE SUCCESSFUL!
PLEASE REMAIN SEATED BEHIND THE GLASS SHIELD, GENTLE-MEN!
ONCE I LOCK THE DOOR BEHIND ME, NO ONE WILL BE PERMITTED TO ENTER--OR TO LEAVE!
AND NOW, THE NEXT VOICE YOU HEAR--WILL BE THAT OF DR. REIN-STEIN!
MY FORGED CREDENTIALS HAVE GOTTEN ME THIS FAR!
AND SOON--MY SPECIALLY-BUILT WEAPON SHALL PIERCE THAT VERDAMMT GLASS!
GENTLEMEN, THIS DISTINGUISHED YOUNG VOLUNTEER HAS ALREADY BEEN INJECTED WITH MY SECRET SERUM!
NEXT, YOU SHALL SEE HOW I SPEED UP ITS PROCESS-- AND HOW IT WILL AFFECT HIS BODY CELLS!
NOW THERE CAN BE NO TURNING BACK!
14

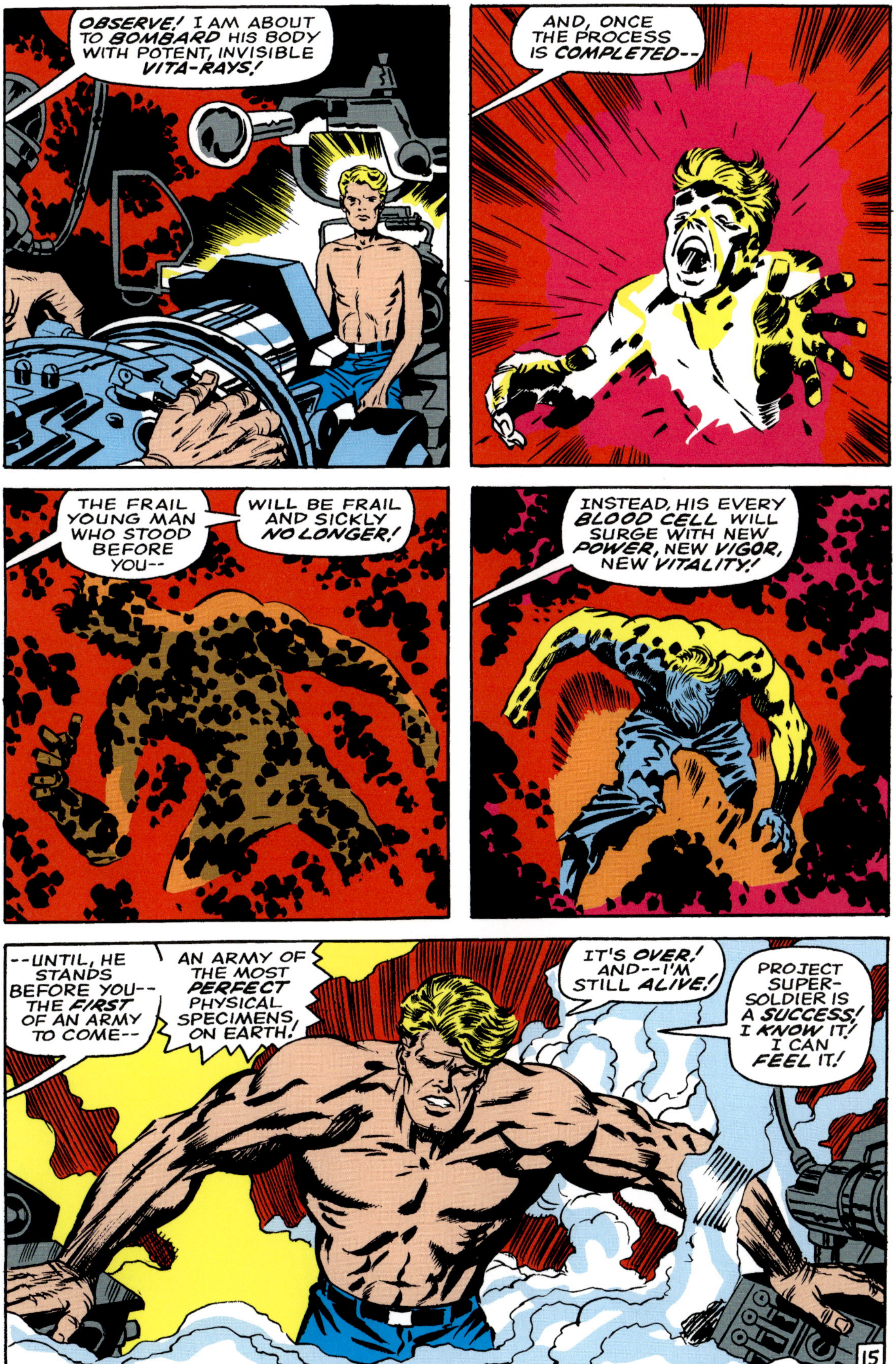
OBSERVE! I AM ABOUT TO BOMBARD HIS BODY WITH POTENT, INVISIBLE VITA-RAYS!
AND, ONCE THE PROCESS IS COMPLETED--
THE FRAIL YOUNG MAN WHO STOOD BEFORE YOU--
WILL BE FRAIL AND SICKLY NO LONGER!
INSTEAD, HIS EVERY BLOOD CELL WILL SURGE WITH NEW POWER, NEW VIGOR, NEW VITALITY!
--UNTIL, HE STANDS BEFORE YOU--THE FIRST OF AN ARMY TO COME--
AN ARMY OF THE MOST PERFECT PHYSICAL SPECIMENS ON EARTH!
IT'S OVER! AND--I'M STILL ALIVE!
PROJECT SUPER-SOLDIER IS A SUCCESS! I KNOW IT! I CAN FEEL IT!
15

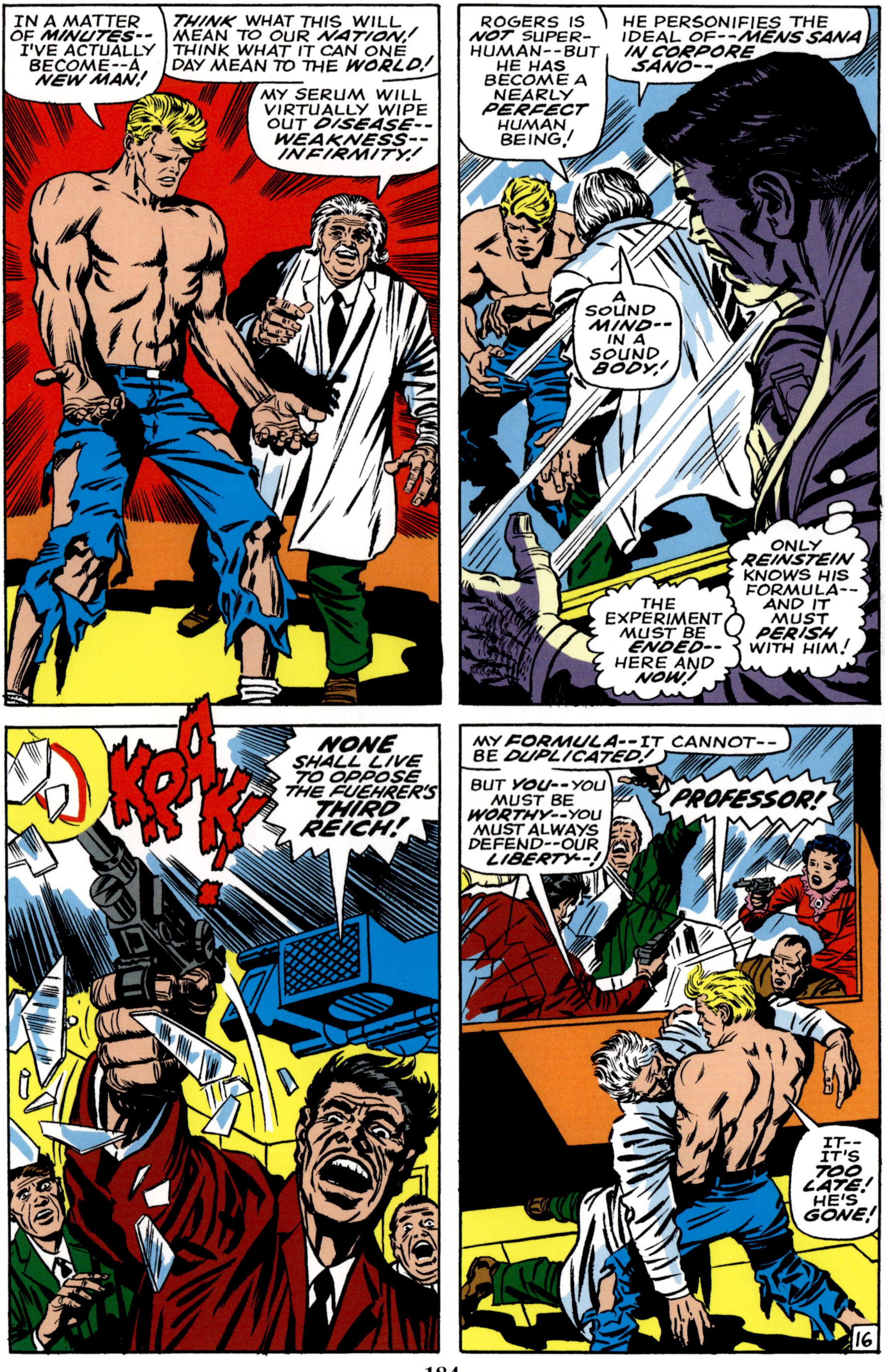

IN A MATTER OF MINUTES-- I'VE ACTUALLY BECOME--A NEW MAN!
THINK WHAT THIS WILL MEAN TO OUR NATION! THINK WHAT IT CAN ONE DAY MEAN TO THE WORLD!
MY SERUM WILL VIRTUALLY WIPE OUT DISEASE-- WEAKNESS-- INFIRMITY!
ROGERS IS NOT SUPER-HUMAN--BUT HE HAS BECOME A NEARLY PERFECT HUMAN BEING!
HE PERSONIFIES THE IDEAL OF--MENS SANA IN CORPORE SANO--
A SOUND MIND-- IN A SOUND BODY!
THE EXPERIMENT MUST BE ENDED-- HERE AND NOW!
ONLY REINSTEIN KNOWS HIS FORMULA-- AND IT MUST PERISH WITH HIM!
KRAK!
NONE SHALL LIVE TO OPPOSE THE FUEHRER'S THIRD REICH!
MY FORMULA--IT CANNOT-- BE DUPLICATED!
BUT YOU--YOU MUST BE WORTHY--YOU MUST ALWAYS DEFEND--OUR LIBERTY--!
PROFESSOR!
IT-- IT'S TOO LATE! HE'S GONE!
16

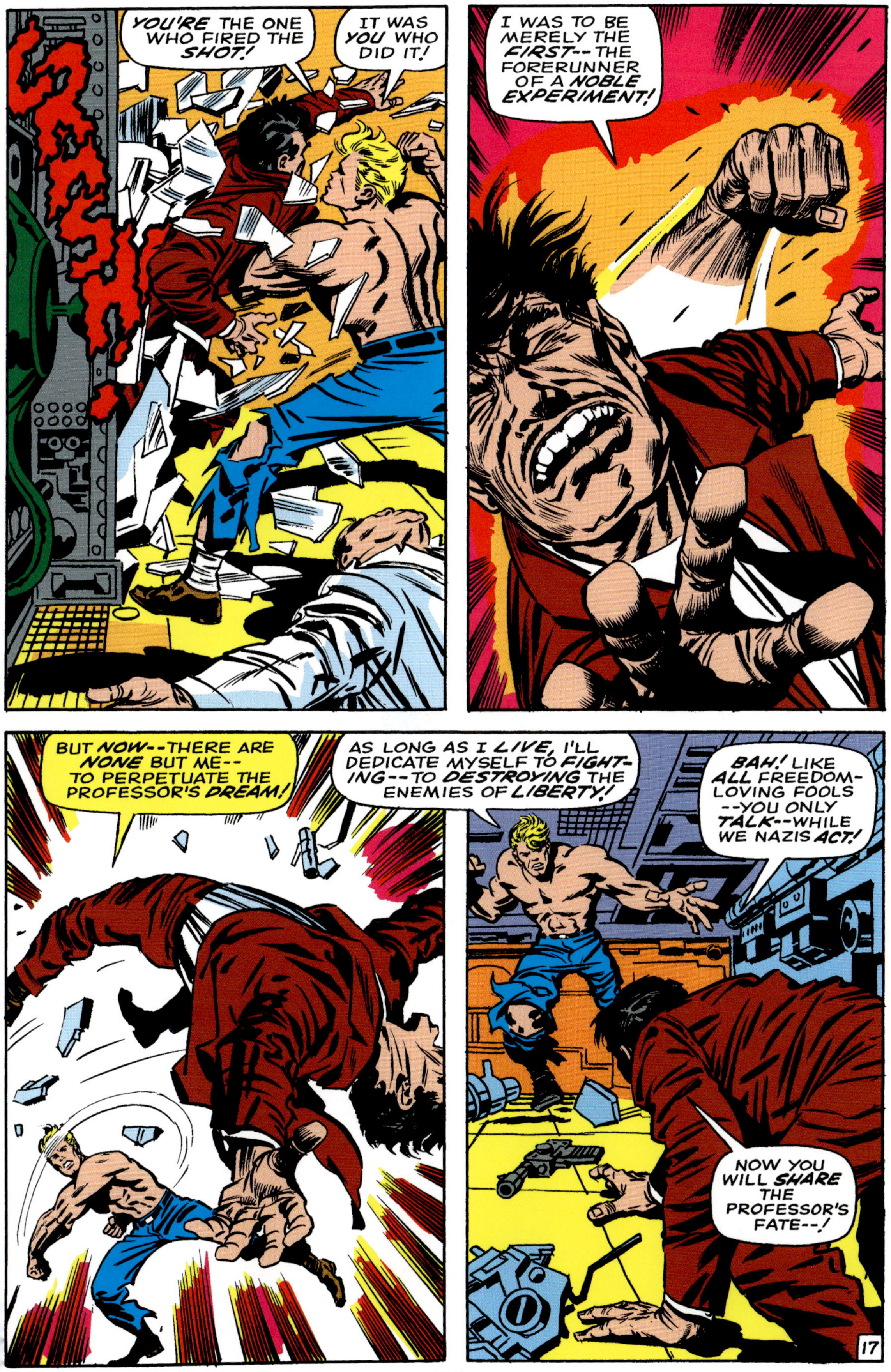
CRASH
YOU'RE THE ONE WHO FIRED THE SHOT!
IT WAS YOU WHO DID IT!
I WAS TO BE MERELY THE FIRST-- THE FORERUNNER OF A NOBLE EXPERIMENT!
BUT NOW--THERE ARE NONE BUT ME-- TO PERPETUATE THE PROFESSOR'S DREAM!
AS LONG AS I LIVE, I'LL DEDICATE MYSELF TO FIGHT-ING--TO DESTROYING THE ENEMIES OF LIBERTY!
BAH! LIKE ALL FREEDOM-LOVING FOOLS --YOU ONLY TALK--WHILE WE NAZIS ACT!
NOW YOU WILL SHARE THE PROFESSOR'S FATE--!
17

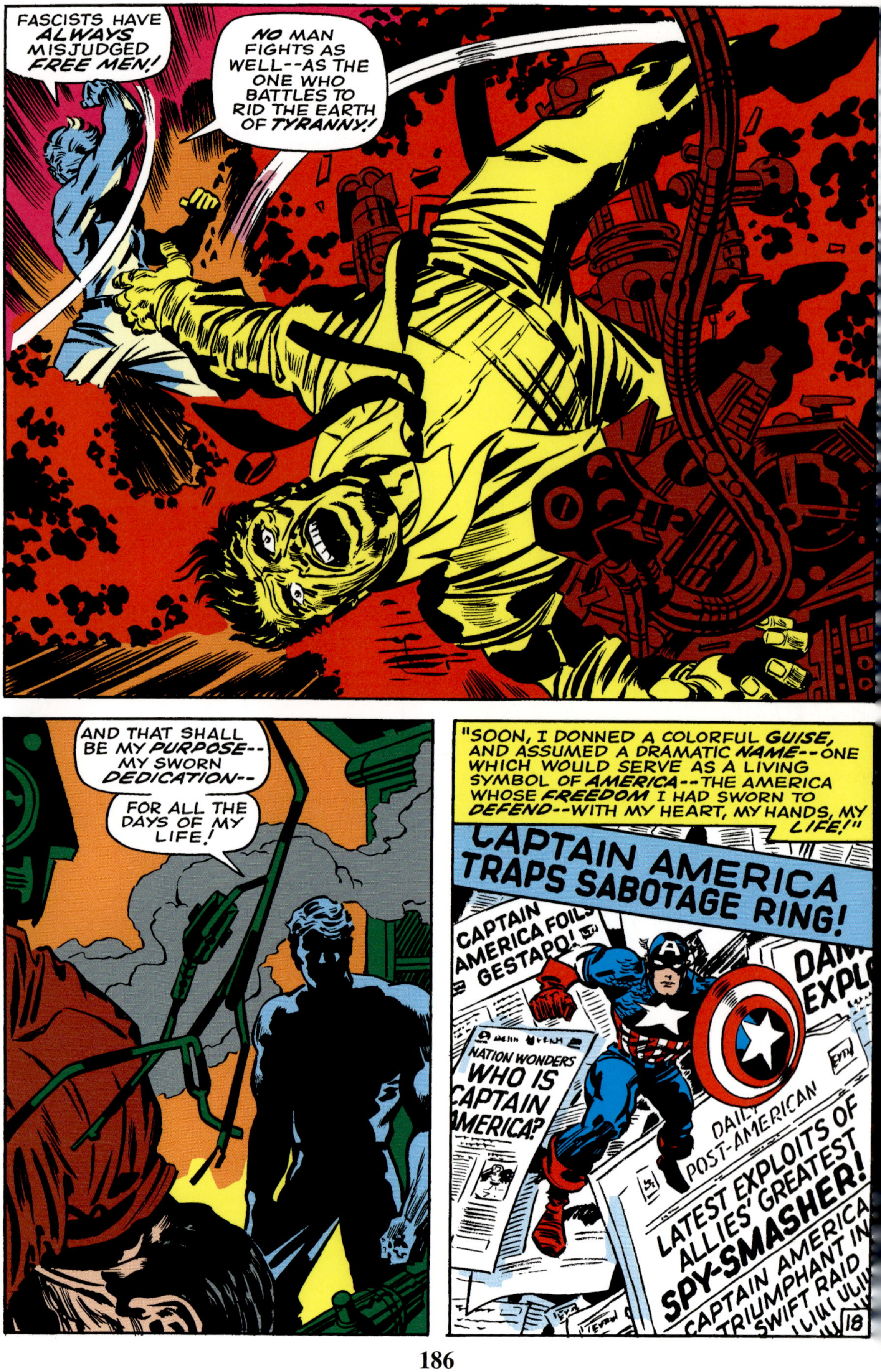

FASCISTS HAVE ALWAYS MISJUDGED FREE MEN!
NO MAN FIGHTS AS WELL--AS THE ONE WHO BATTLES TO RID THE EARTH OF TYRANNY!
AND THAT SHALL BE MY PURPOSE-- MY SWORN DEDICATION--
FOR ALL THE DAYS OF MY LIFE!
"SOON, I DONNED A COLORFUL GUISE, AND ASSUMED A DRAMATIC NAME--ONE WHICH WOULD SERVE AS A LIVING SYMBOL OF AMERICA--THE AMERICA WHOSE FREEDOM I HAD SWORN TO DEFEND--WITH MY HEART, MY HANDS, MY LIFE!"
CAPTAIN AMERICA TRAPS SABOTAGE RING!
CAPTAIN AMERICA FOILS GESTAPO!
NATION WONDERS WHO IS CAPTAIN AMERICA?
DAILY POST-AMERICAN
LATEST EXPLOITS OF ALLIES' GREATEST SPY-SMASHER!
CAPTAIN AMERICA TRIUMPHANT IN SWIFT RAID
18

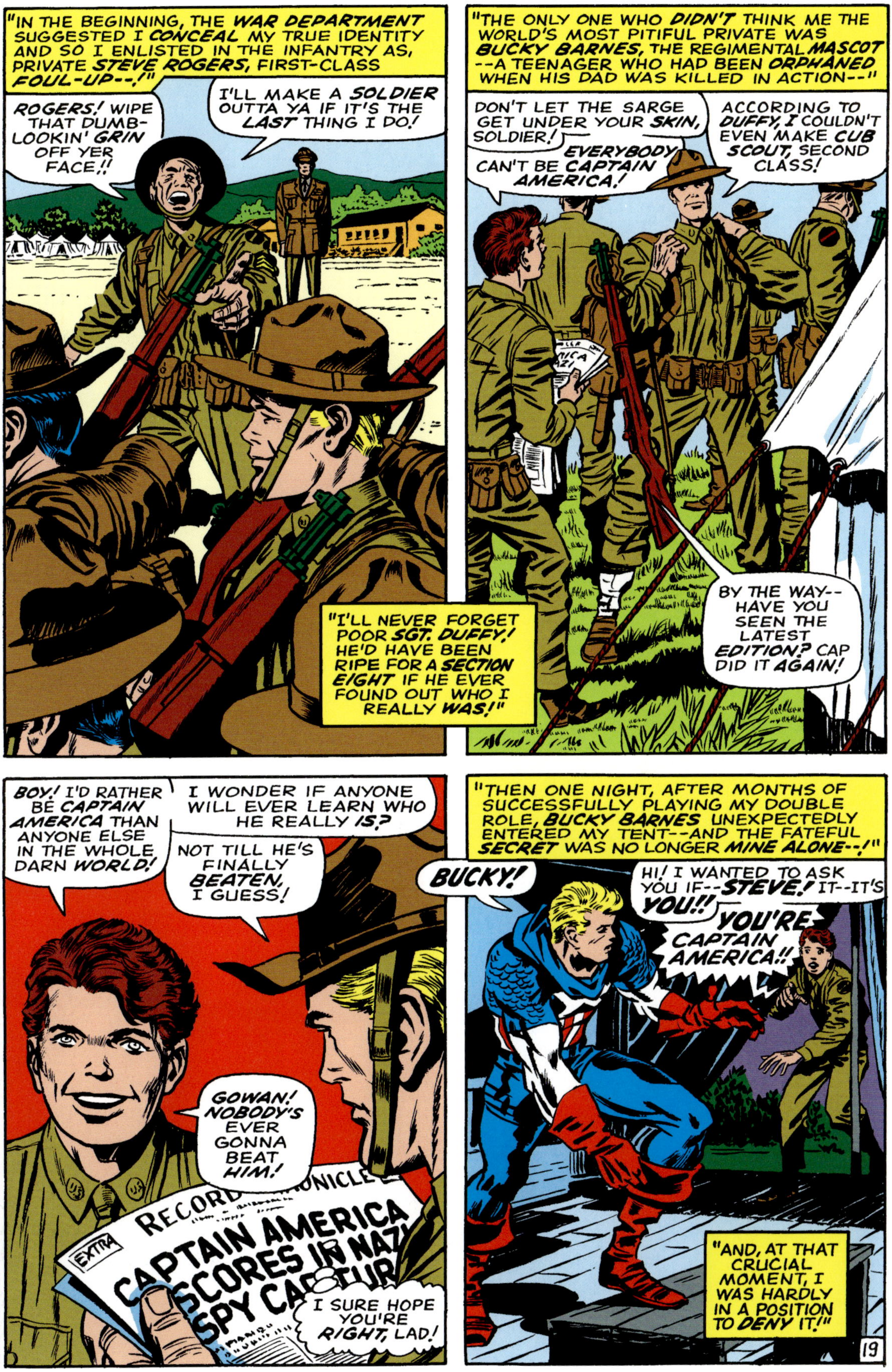
"IN THE BEGINNING, THE WAR DEPARTMENT SUGGESTED I CONCEAL MY TRUE IDENTITY AND SO I ENLISTED IN THE INFANTRY AS, PRIVATE STEVE ROGERS, FIRST-CLASS FOUL-UP--!"
ROGERS! WIPE THAT DUMB-LOOKIN' GRIN OFF YER FACE!!
I'LL MAKE A SOLDIER OUTTA YA IF IT'S THE LAST THING I DO!
"I'LL NEVER FORGET POOR SGT. DUFFY! HE'D HAVE BEEN RIPE FOR A SECTION EIGHT IF HE EVER FOUND OUT WHO I REALLY WAS!"
"THE ONLY ONE WHO DIDN'T THINK ME THE WORLD'S MOST PITIFUL PRIVATE WAS BUCKY BARNES, THE REGIMENTAL MASCOT --A TEENAGER WHO HAD BEEN ORPHANED WHEN HIS DAD WAS KILLED IN ACTION--"
DON'T LET THE SARGE GET UNDER YOUR SKIN, SOLDIER! EVERYBODY CAN'T BE CAPTAIN AMERICA!
ACCORDING TO DUFFY, I COULDN'T EVEN MAKE CUB SCOUT, SECOND CLASS!
BY THE WAY-- HAVE YOU SEEN THE LATEST EDITION? CAP DID IT AGAIN!
BOY! I'D RATHER BE CAPTAIN AMERICA THAN ANYONE ELSE IN THE WHOLE DARN WORLD!
I WONDER IF ANYONE WILL EVER LEARN WHO HE REALLY IS?
NOT TILL HE'S FINALLY BEATEN, I GUESS!
GOWAN! NOBODY'S EVER GONNA BEAT HIM!
RECORD CHRONICLE
EXTRA
CAPTAIN AMERICA SCORES IN NAZI SPY CAPTURE
I SURE HOPE YOU'RE RIGHT, LAD!
"THEN ONE NIGHT, AFTER MONTHS OF SUCCESSFULLY PLAYING MY DOUBLE ROLE, BUCKY BARNES UNEXPECTEDLY ENTERED MY TENT--AND THE FATEFUL SECRET WAS NO LONGER MINE ALONE--!"
BUCKY!
HI! I WANTED TO ASK YOU IF--STEVE! IT--IT'S YOU!!
YOU'RE CAPTAIN AMERICA!!
"AND, AT THAT CRUCIAL MOMENT, I WAS HARDLY IN A POSITION TO DENY IT!"
19

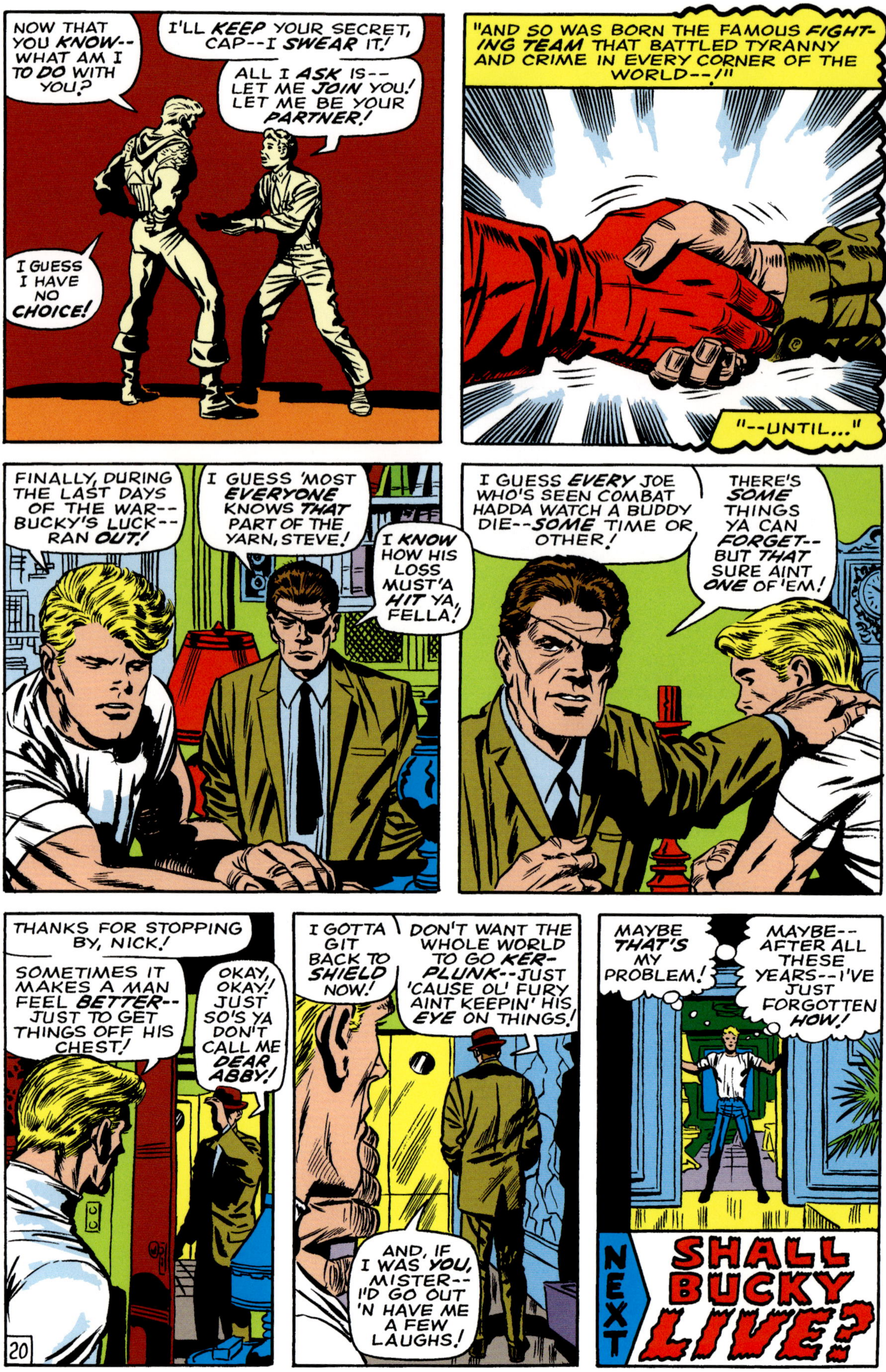
NOW THAT YOU KNOW-- WHAT AM I TO DO WITH YOU?
I'LL KEEP YOUR SECRET, CAP--I SWEAR IT!
ALL I ASK IS-- LET ME JOIN YOU! LET ME BE YOUR PARTNER!
I GUESS I HAVE NO CHOICE!
"AND SO WAS BORN THE FAMOUS FIGHTING TEAM THAT BATTLED TYRANNY AND CRIME IN EVERY CORNER OF THE WORLD--!"
"--UNTIL..."
FINALLY, DURING THE LAST DAYS OF THE WAR-- BUCKY'S LUCK-- RAN OUT!
I GUESS 'MOST EVERYONE KNOWS THAT PART OF THE YARN, STEVE!
I KNOW HOW HIS LOSS MUST'A HIT YA, FELLA!
I GUESS EVERY JOE WHO'S SEEN COMBAT HADDA WATCH A BUDDY DIE--SOME TIME OR OTHER!
THERE'S SOME THINGS YA CAN FORGET-- BUT THAT SURE AINT ONE OF 'EM!
THANKS FOR STOPPING BY, NICK!
SOMETIMES IT MAKES A MAN FEEL BETTER-- JUST TO GET THINGS OFF HIS CHEST!
OKAY, OKAY! JUST SO'S YA DON'T CALL ME DEAR ABBY!
20
I GOTTA GIT BACK TO SHIELD NOW!
DON'T WANT THE WHOLE WORLD TO GO KER-PLUNK--JUST 'CAUSE OL' FURY AINT KEEPIN' HIS EYE ON THINGS!
AND, IF I WAS YOU, MISTER-- I'D GO OUT 'N HAVE ME A FEW LAUGHS!
MAYBE THAT'S MY PROBLEM!
MAYBE-- AFTER ALL THESE YEARS--I'VE JUST FORGOTTEN HOW!
NEXT
SHALL BUCKY LIVE?

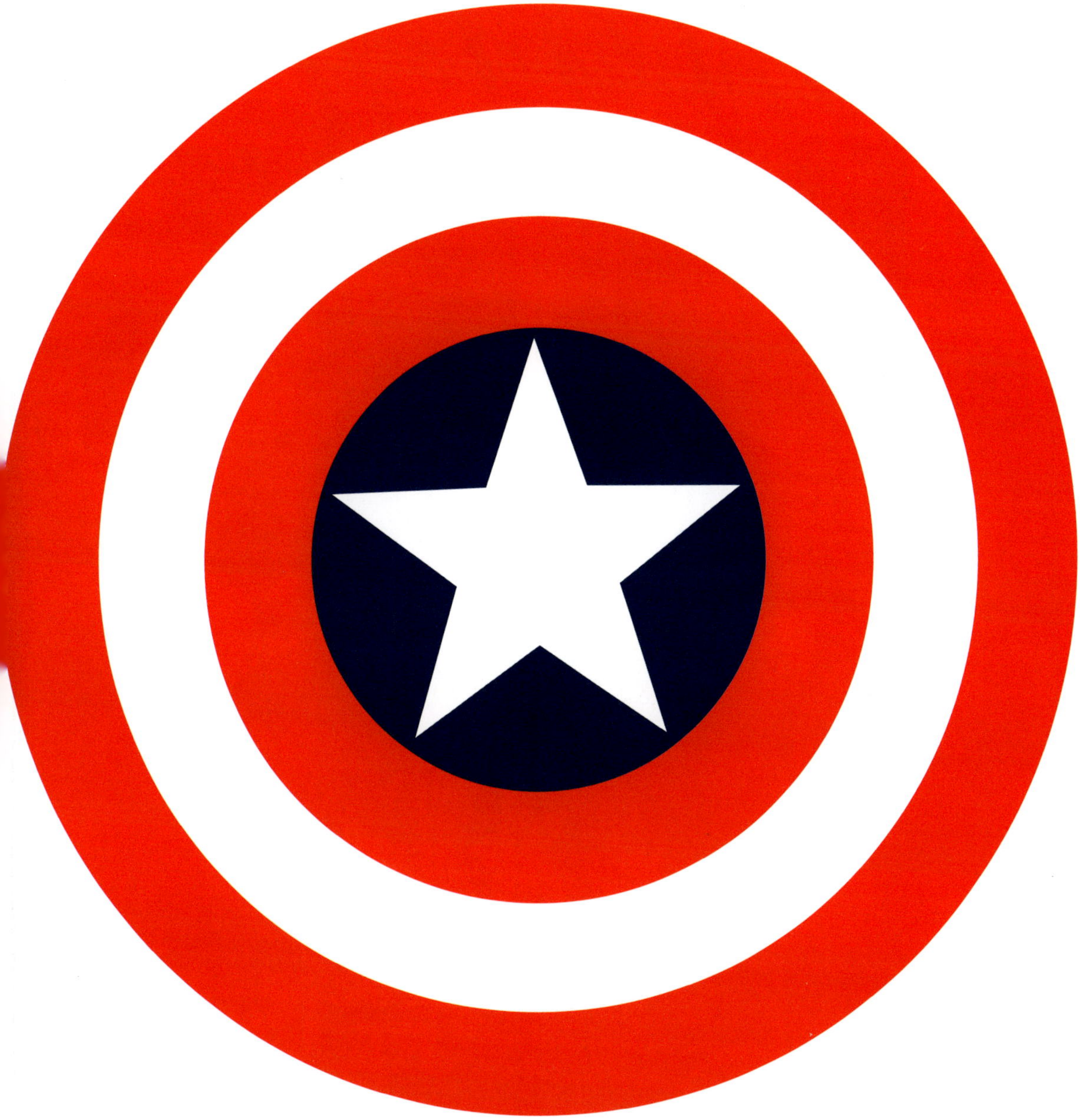

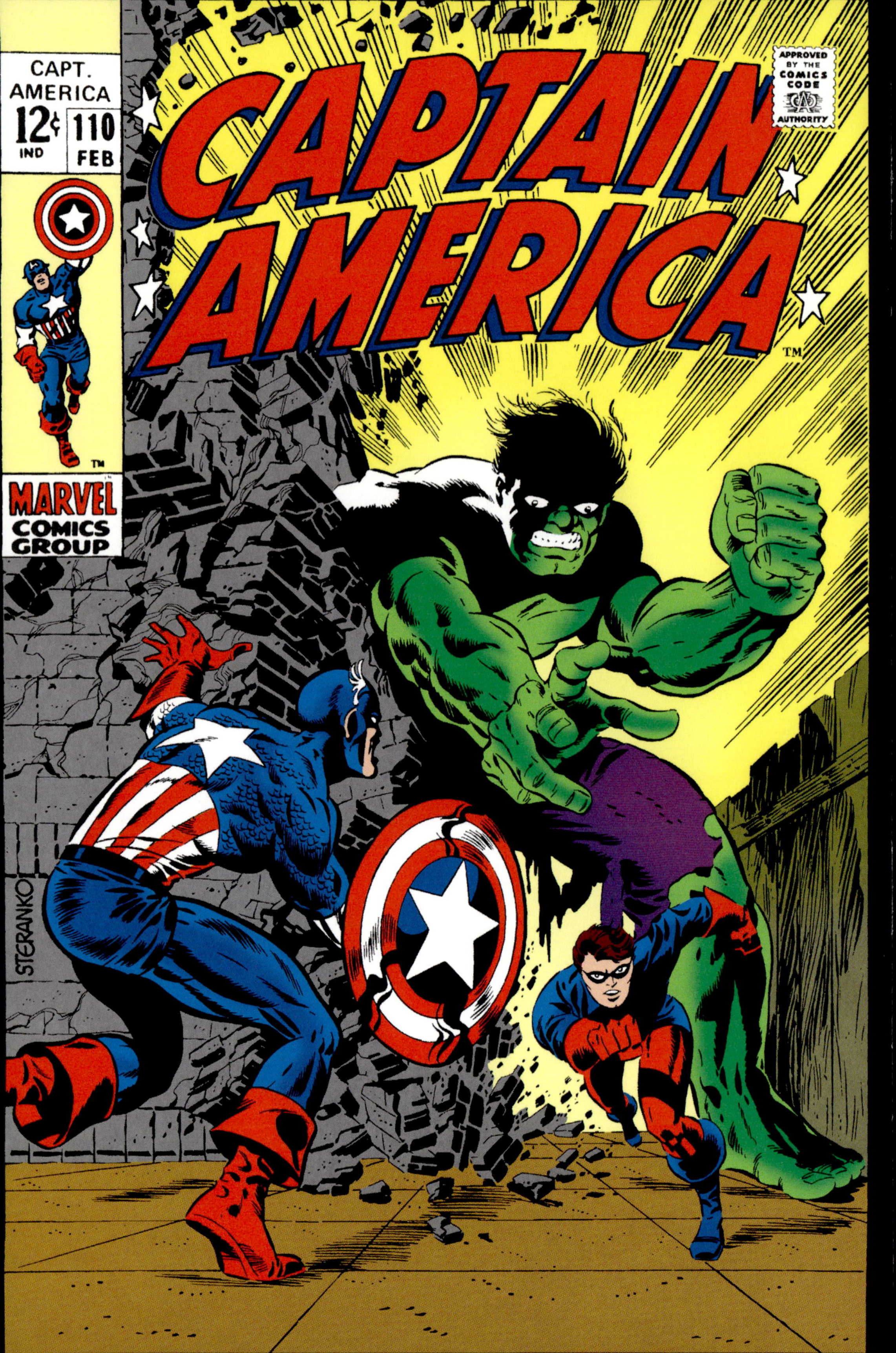
CAPT. AMERICA
12¢
IND
110
FEB
APPROVED BY THE COMICS CODE AUTHORITY
CAPTAIN AMERICA
TM
MARVEL COMICS GROUP
STERANKO

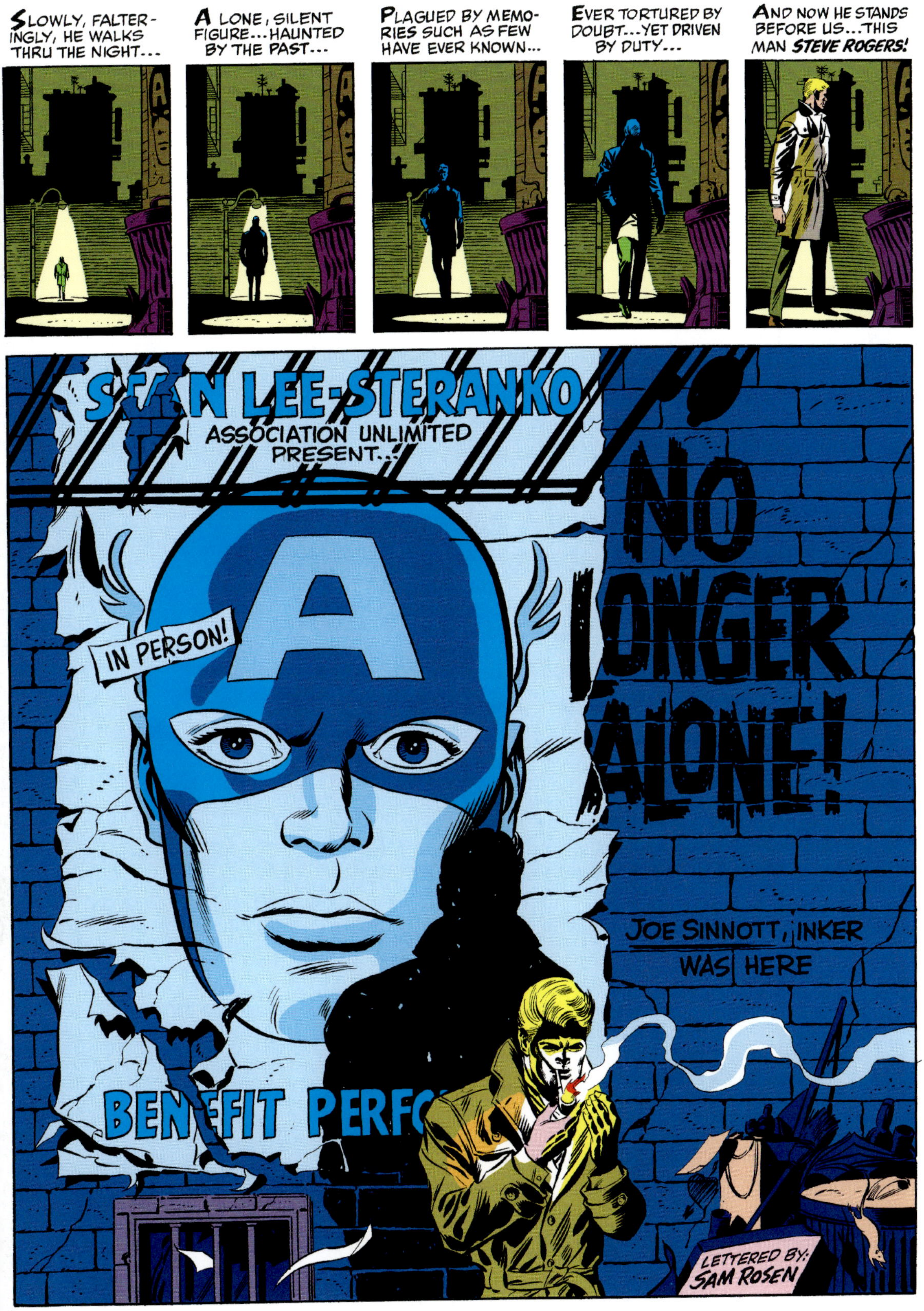
SLOWLY, FALTER-INGLY, HE WALKS THRU THE NIGHT...
A LONE, SILENT FIGURE...HAUNTED BY THE PAST...
PLAGUED BY MEMO-RIES SUCH AS FEW HAVE EVER KNOWN...
EVER TORTURED BY DOUBT...YET DRIVEN BY DUTY...
AND NOW HE STANDS BEFORE US...THIS MAN STEVE ROGERS!
N LEE-STERANKO
ASSOCIATION UNLIMITED
PRESENT...
IN PERSON!
NO LONGER ALONE!
JOE SINNOTT, INKER WAS HERE
BEN FIT PERF
LETTERED BY: SAM ROSEN

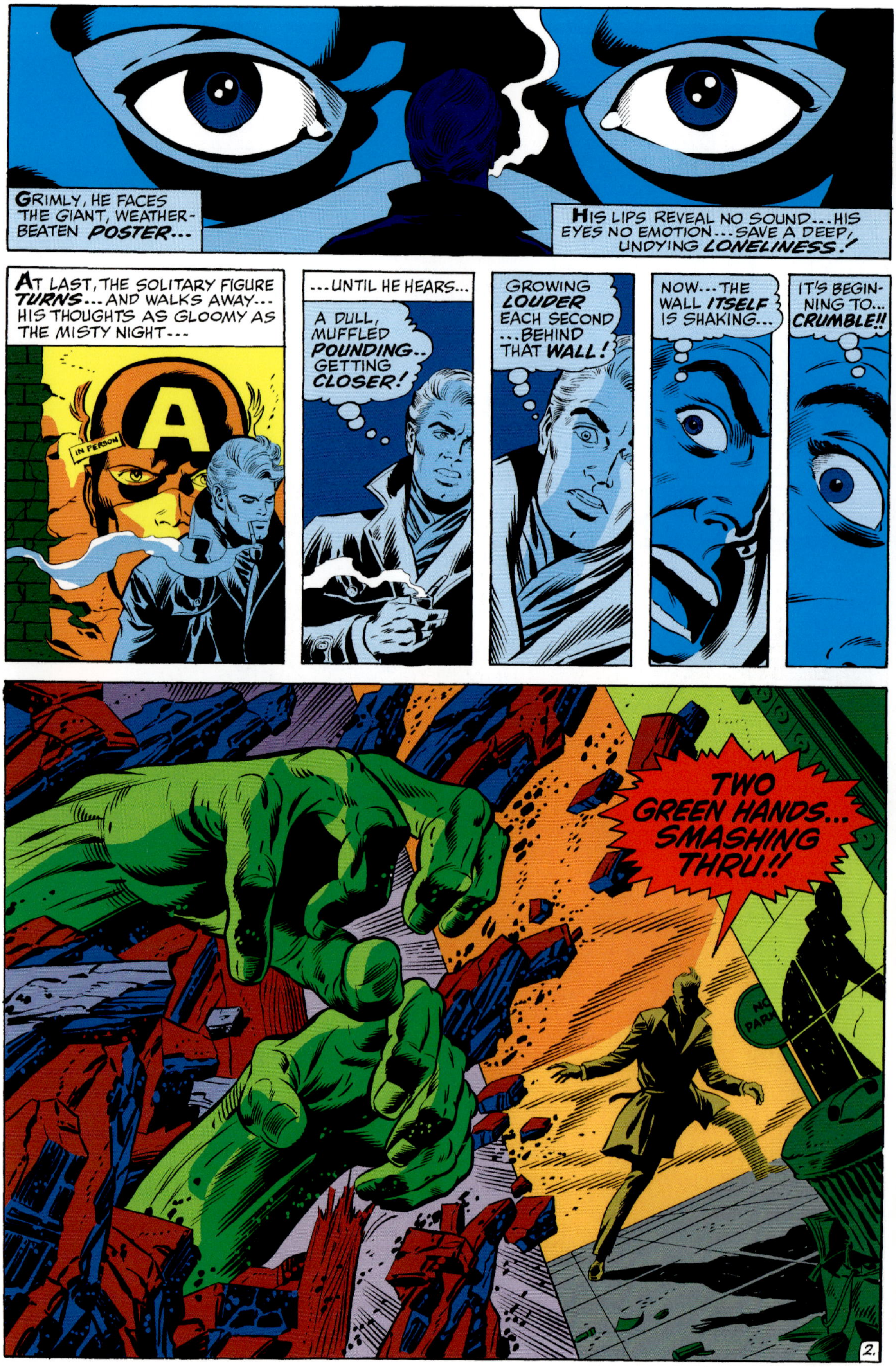
GRIMLY, HE FACES THE GIANT, WEATHER-BEATEN POSTER...
HIS LIPS REVEAL NO SOUND...HIS EYES NO EMOTION...SAVE A DEEP, UNDYING LONELINESS!
AT LAST, THE SOLITARY FIGURE TURNS...AND WALKS AWAY...HIS THOUGHTS AS GLOOMY AS THE MISTY NIGHT...
IN PERSON
...UNTIL HE HEARS...
A DULL, MUFFLED POUNDING.. GETTING CLOSER!
GROWING LOUDER EACH SECOND ...BEHIND THAT WALL!
NOW...THE WALL ITSELF IS SHAKING...
IT'S BEGINNING TO... CRUMBLE!!
TWO GREEN HANDS... SMASHING THRU!!
2.

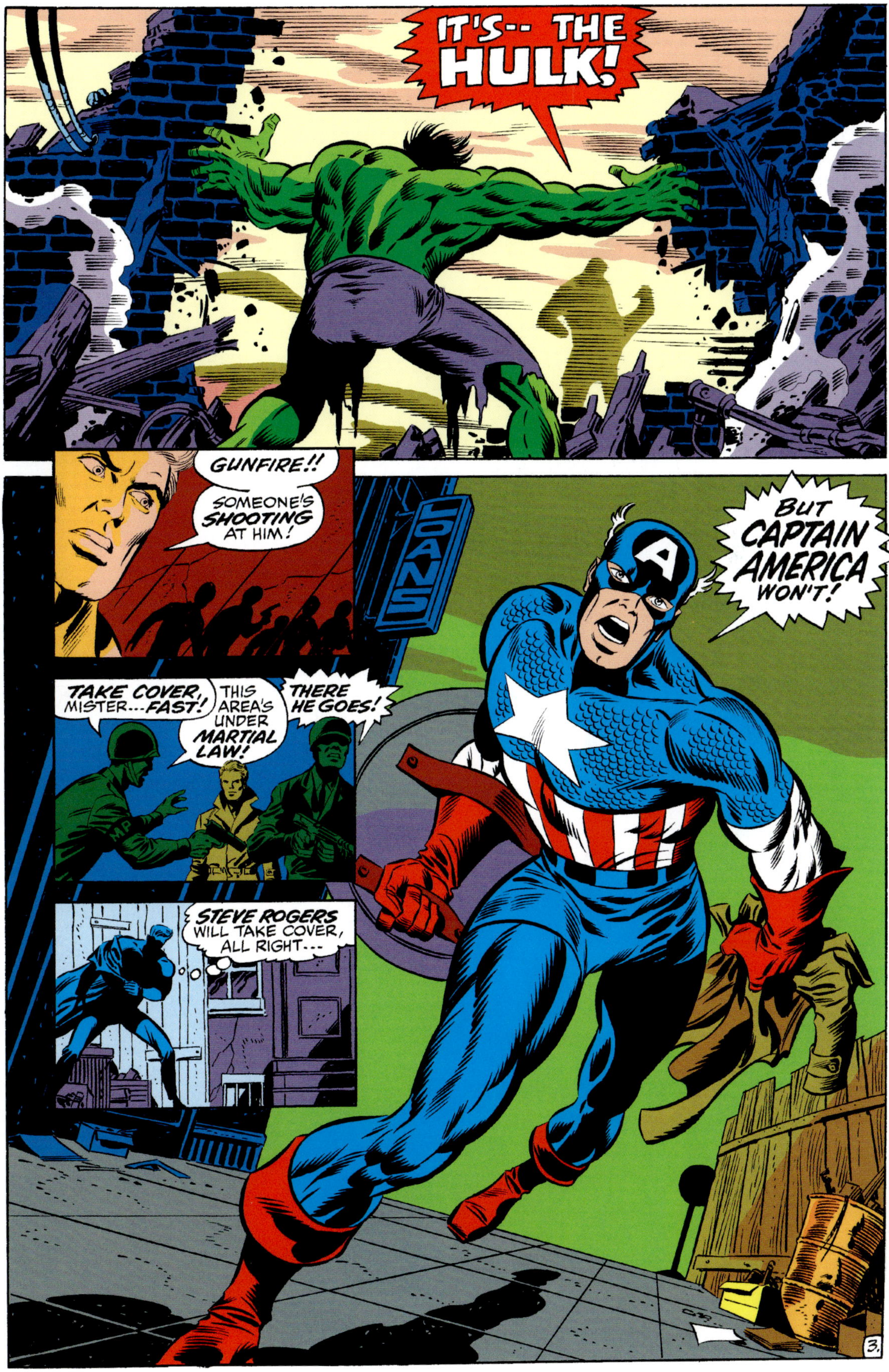

IT'S-- THE HULK!
GUNFIRE!!
SOMEONE'S SHOOTING AT HIM!
TAKE COVER, MISTER... FAST!
THIS AREA'S UNDER MARTIAL LAW!
THERE HE GOES!
STEVE ROGERS WILL TAKE COVER, ALL RIGHT---
BUT CAPTAIN AMERICA WON'T!
LOANS
3.

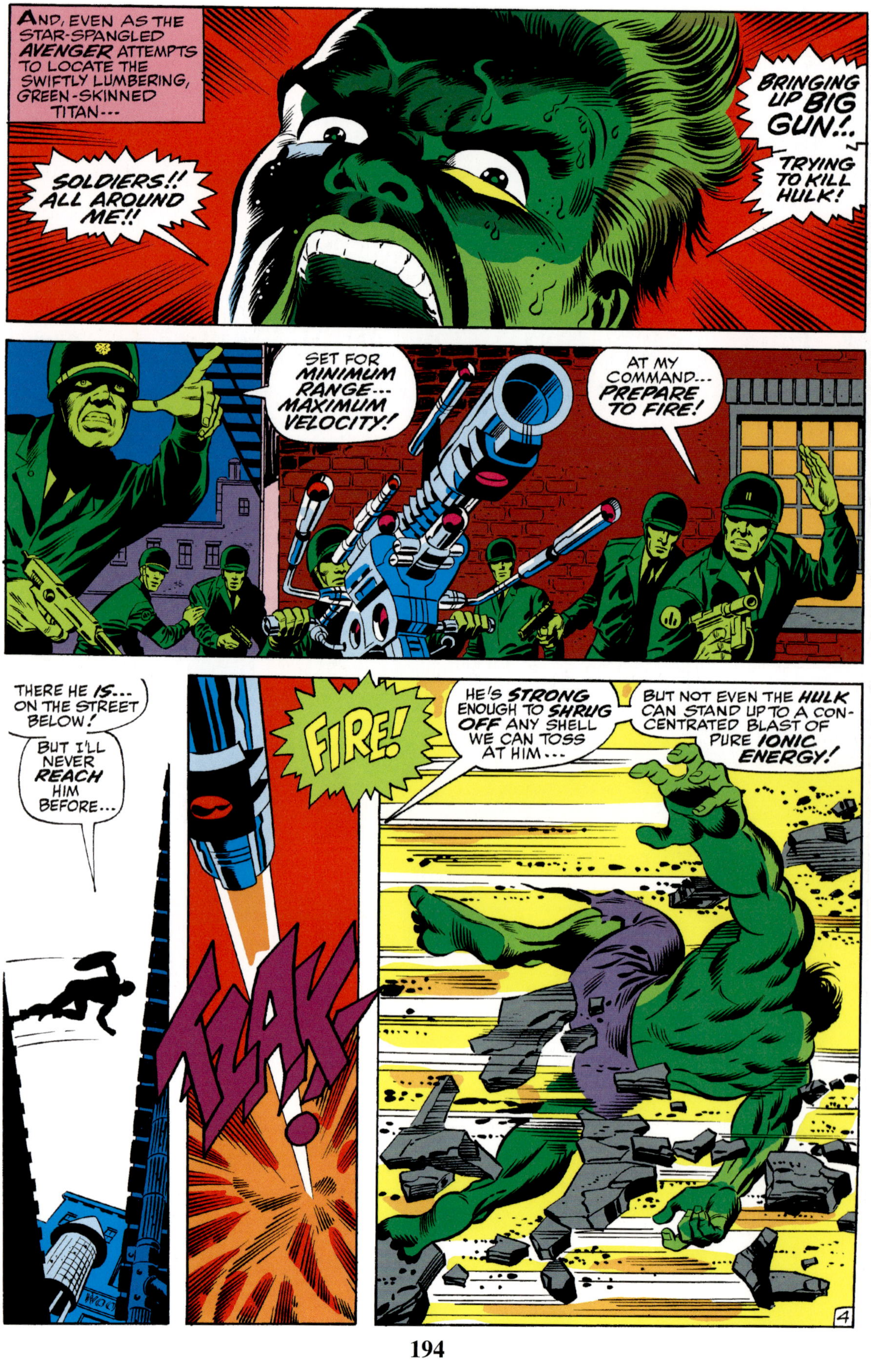
AND, EVEN AS THE STAR-SPANGLED AVENGER ATTEMPTS TO LOCATE THE SWIFTLY LUMBERING, GREEN-SKINNED TITAN---
SOLDIERS!! ALL AROUND ME!!
BRINGING UP BIG GUN!..
TRYING TO KILL HULK!
SET FOR MINIMUM RANGE--- MAXIMUM VELOCITY!
AT MY COMMAND--- PREPARE TO FIRE!
THERE HE IS... ON THE STREET BELOW!
BUT I'LL NEVER REACH HIM BEFORE...
FIRE!
HE'S STRONG ENOUGH TO SHRUG OFF ANY SHELL WE CAN TOSS AT HIM...
BUT NOT EVEN THE HULK CAN STAND UP TO A CONCENTRATED BLAST OF PURE IONIC ENERGY!
FZAK!
4

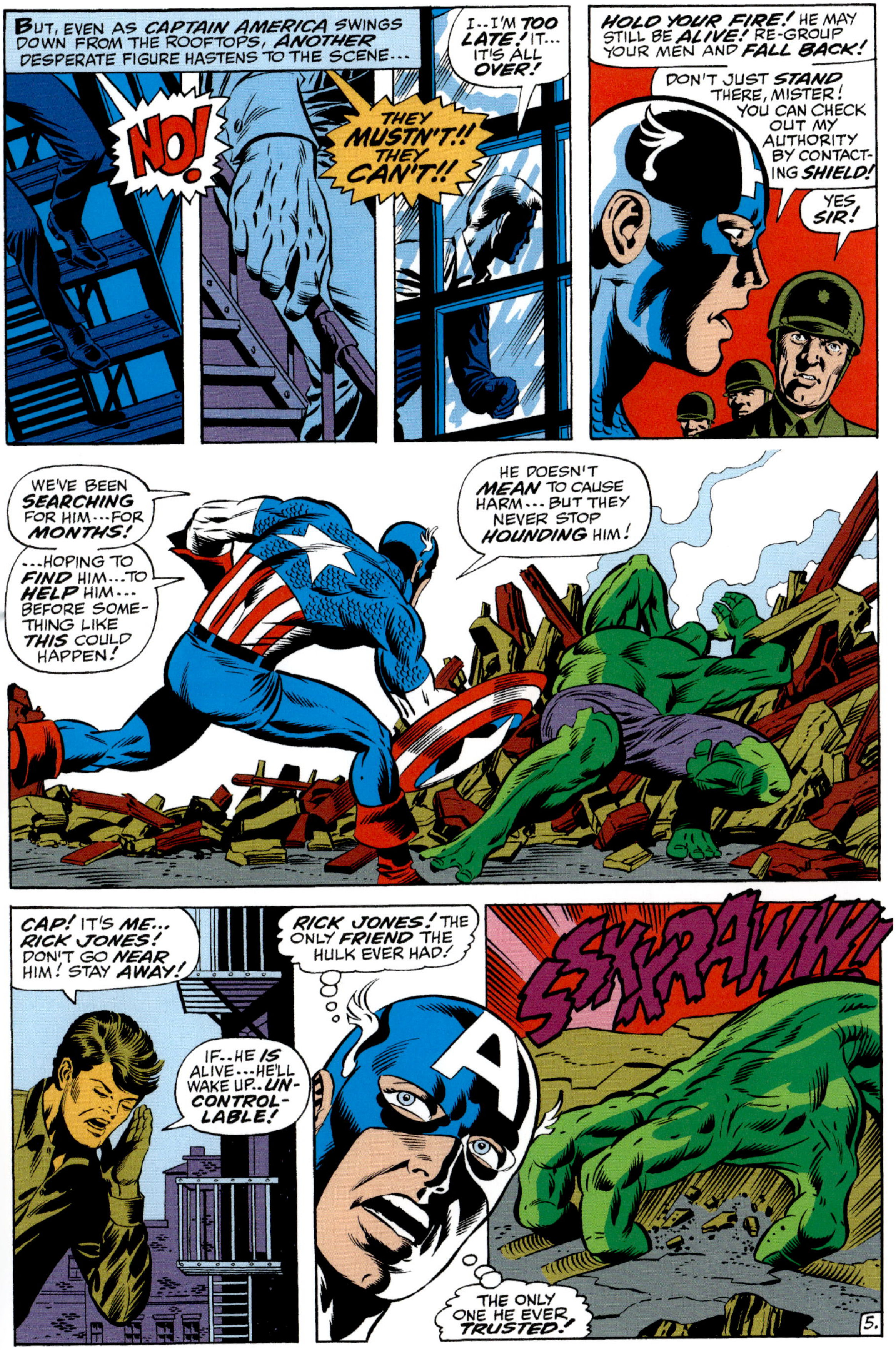

BUT, EVEN AS CAPTAIN AMERICA SWINGS DOWN FROM THE ROOFTOPS, ANOTHER DESPERATE FIGURE HASTENS TO THE SCENE...
NO!
THEY MUSTN'T!! THEY CAN'T!!
I..I'M TOO LATE! IT... IT'S ALL OVER!
HOLD YOUR FIRE! HE MAY STILL BE ALIVE! RE-GROUP YOUR MEN AND FALL BACK!
DON'T JUST STAND THERE, MISTER! YOU CAN CHECK OUT MY AUTHORITY BY CONTACTING SHIELD!
YES SIR!
WE'VE BEEN SEARCHING FOR HIM---FOR MONTHS!
...HOPING TO FIND HIM...TO HELP HIM... BEFORE SOMETHING LIKE THIS COULD HAPPEN!
HE DOESN'T MEAN TO CAUSE HARM... BUT THEY NEVER STOP HOUNDING HIM!
CAP! IT'S ME... RICK JONES! DON'T GO NEAR HIM! STAY AWAY!
RICK JONES! THE ONLY FRIEND THE HULK EVER HAD!
IF..HE IS ALIVE...HE'LL WAKE UP..UNCONTROLLABLE!
SSKRAWW!
THE ONLY ONE HE EVER TRUSTED!
5.

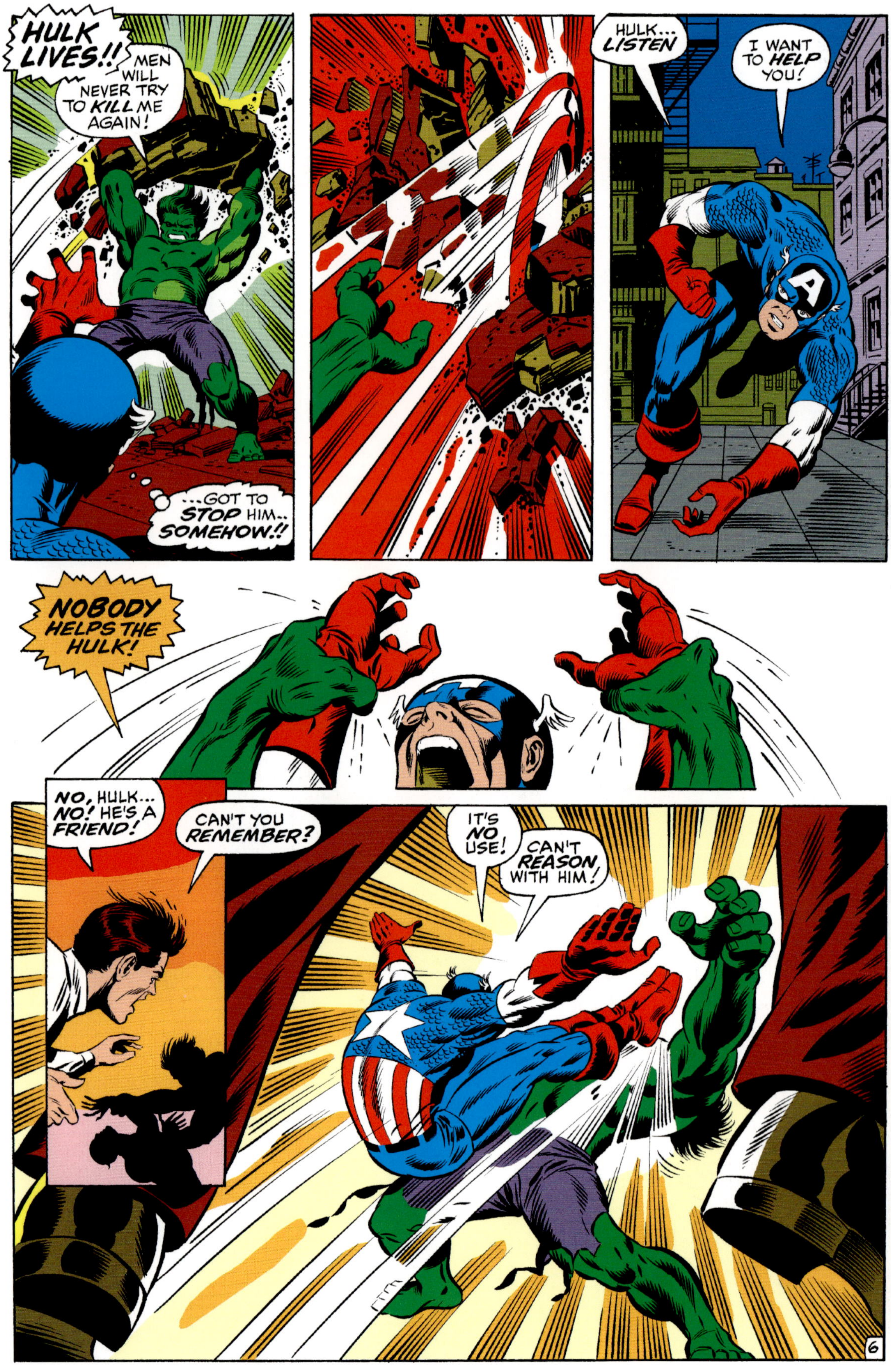
HULK LIVES!!
MEN WILL NEVER TRY TO KILL ME AGAIN!
...GOT TO STOP HIM.. SOMEHOW!!
HULK... LISTEN
I WANT TO HELP YOU!
NOBODY HELPS THE HULK!
NO, HULK... NO! HE'S A FRIEND!
CAN'T YOU REMEMBER?
IT'S NO USE!
CAN'T REASON WITH HIM!
6

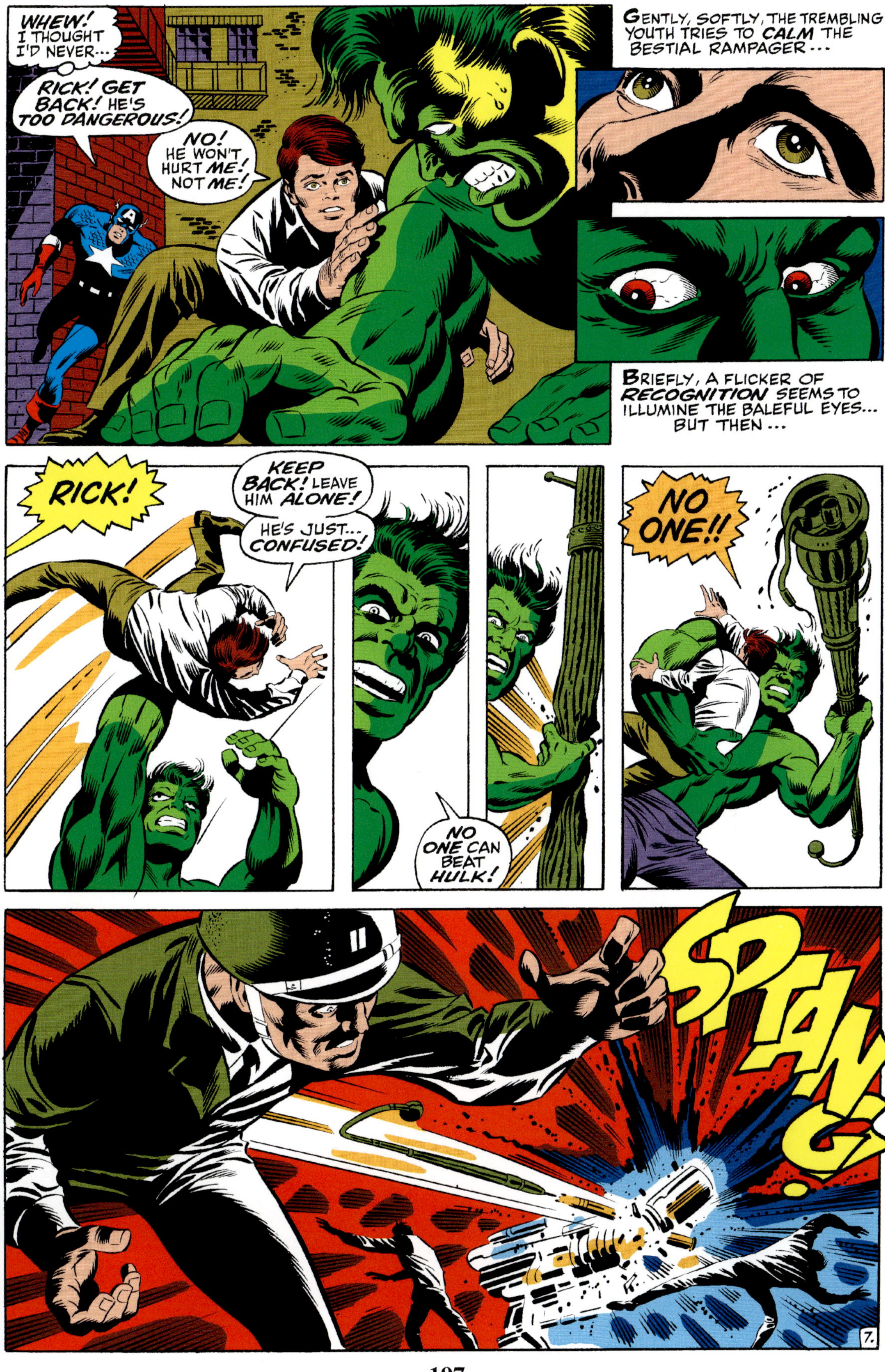
WHEW! I THOUGHT I'D NEVER...
RICK! GET BACK! HE'S TOO DANGEROUS!
NO! HE WON'T HURT ME! NOT ME!
GENTLY, SOFTLY, THE TREMBLING YOUTH TRIES TO CALM THE BESTIAL RAMPAGER...
BRIEFLY, A FLICKER OF RECOGNITION SEEMS TO ILLUMINE THE BALEFUL EYES... BUT THEN...
RICK!
KEEP BACK! LEAVE HIM ALONE!
HE'S JUST... CONFUSED!
NO ONE CAN BEAT HULK!
NO ONE!!
SPTANG!
7.

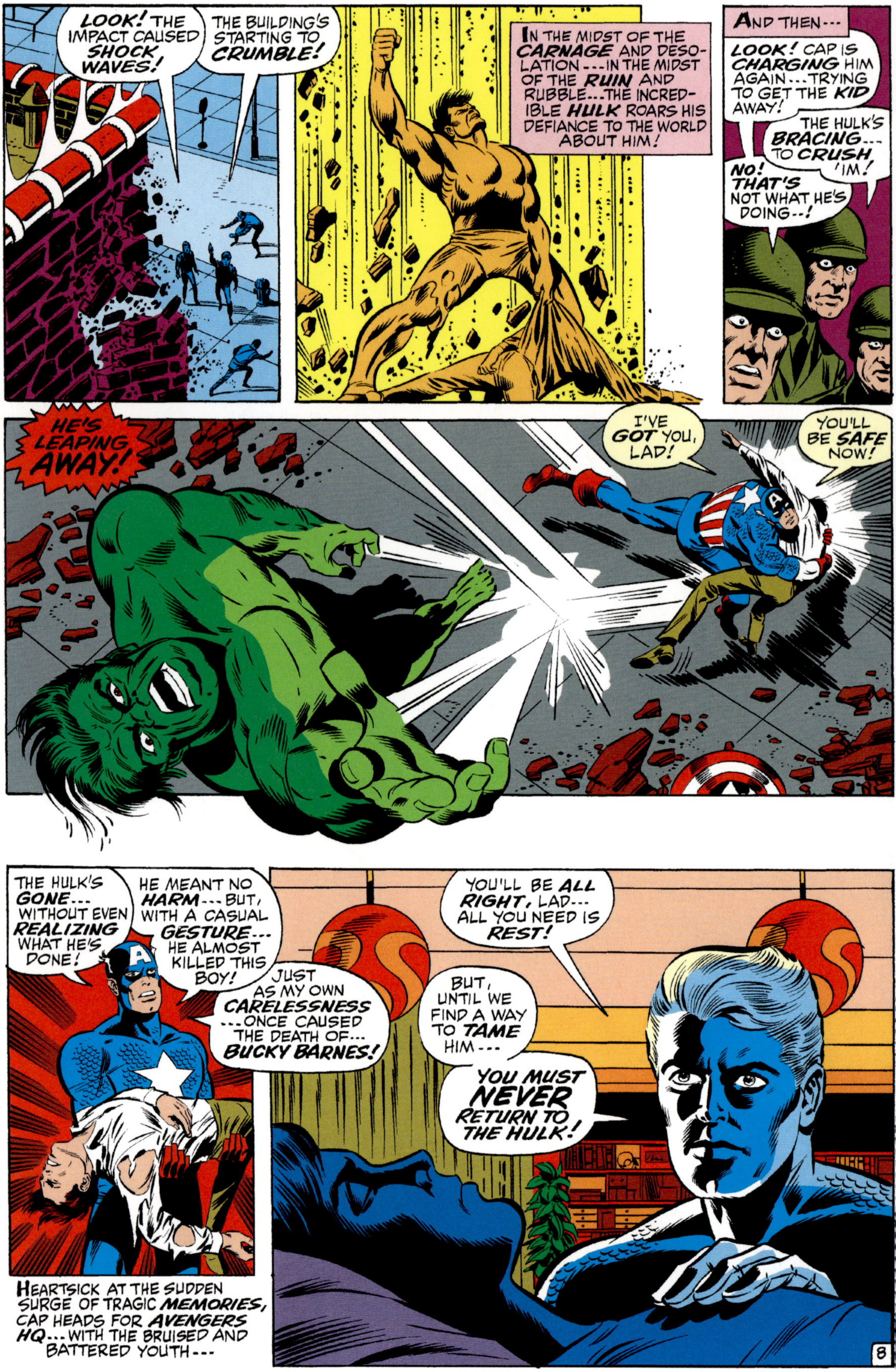
LOOK! THE IMPACT CAUSED SHOCK WAVES!
THE BUILDING'S STARTING TO CRUMBLE!
IN THE MIDST OF THE CARNAGE AND DESOLATION---IN THE MIDST OF THE RUIN AND RUBBLE---THE INCREDIBLE HULK ROARS HIS DEFIANCE TO THE WORLD ABOUT HIM!
AND THEN---
LOOK! CAP IS CHARGING HIM AGAIN---TRYING TO GET THE KID AWAY!
THE HULK'S BRACING---TO CRUSH 'IM!
NO! THAT'S NOT WHAT HE'S DOING--!
HE'S LEAPING AWAY!
I'VE GOT YOU, LAD!
YOU'LL BE SAFE NOW!
THE HULK'S GONE---WITHOUT EVEN REALIZING WHAT HE'S DONE!
HE MEANT NO HARM---BUT, WITH A CASUAL GESTURE---HE ALMOST KILLED THIS BOY!
JUST AS MY OWN CARELESSNESS---ONCE CAUSED THE DEATH OF---BUCKY BARNES!
HEARTSICK AT THE SUDDEN SURGE OF TRAGIC MEMORIES, CAP HEADS FOR AVENGERS HQ---WITH THE BRUISED AND BATTERED YOUTH---
YOU'LL BE ALL RIGHT, LAD---ALL YOU NEED IS REST!
BUT, UNTIL WE FIND A WAY TO TAME HIM---
YOU MUST NEVER RETURN TO THE HULK!
8

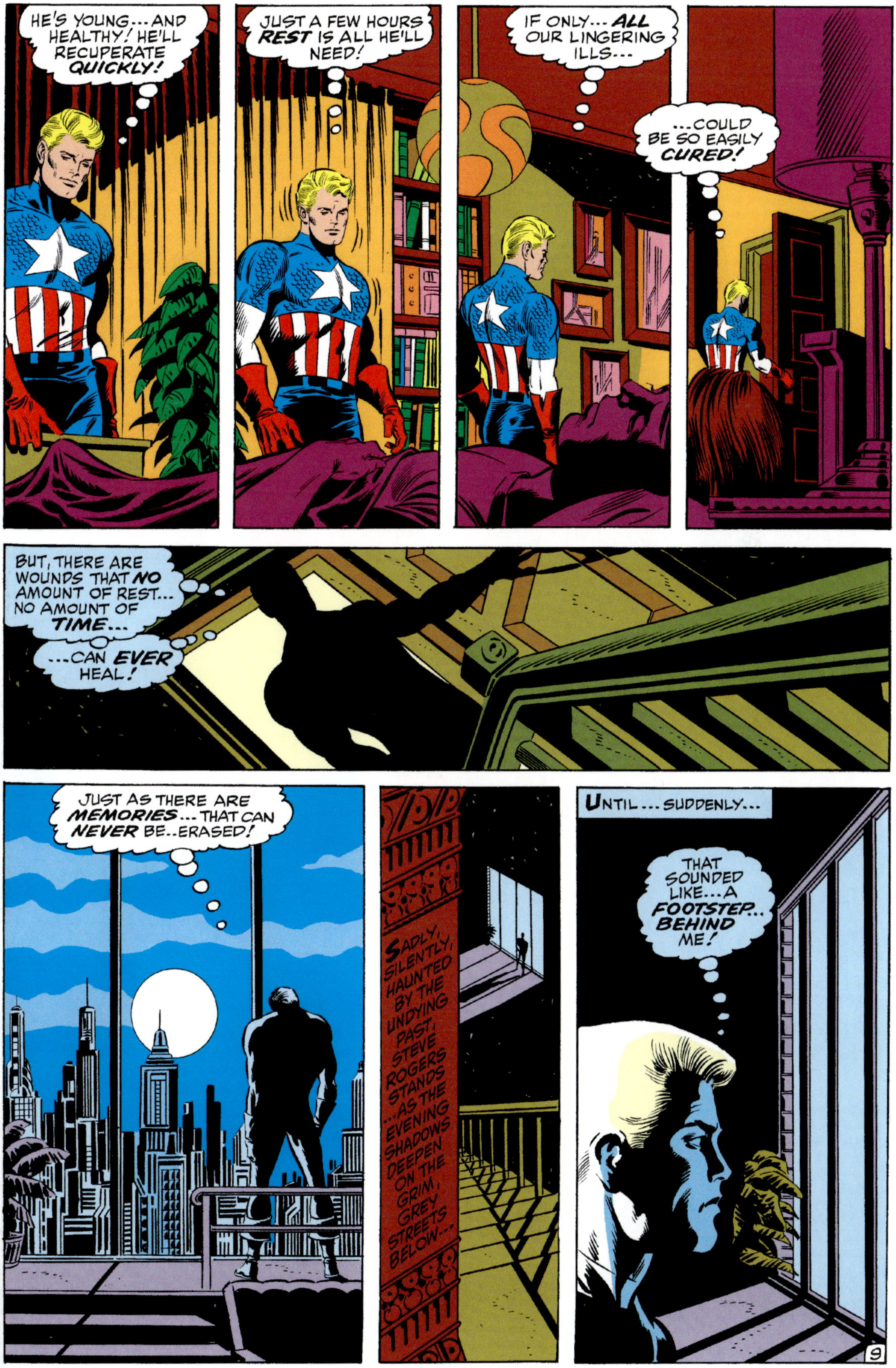

HE'S YOUNG... AND HEALTHY! HE'LL RECUPERATE QUICKLY!
JUST A FEW HOURS REST IS ALL HE'LL NEED!
IF ONLY... ALL OUR LINGERING ILLS...
...COULD BE SO EASILY CURED!
BUT, THERE ARE WOUNDS THAT NO AMOUNT OF REST... NO AMOUNT OF TIME...
...CAN EVER HEAL!
JUST AS THERE ARE MEMORIES... THAT CAN NEVER BE..ERASED!
SADLY, SILENTLY, HAUNTED BY THE UNDYING PAST, STEVE ROGERS STANDS ...AS THE EVENING SHADOWS DEEPEN ON THE GRIM, GREY STREETS BELOW...
UNTIL... SUDDENLY...
THAT SOUNDED LIKE... A FOOTSTEP... BEHIND ME!
9

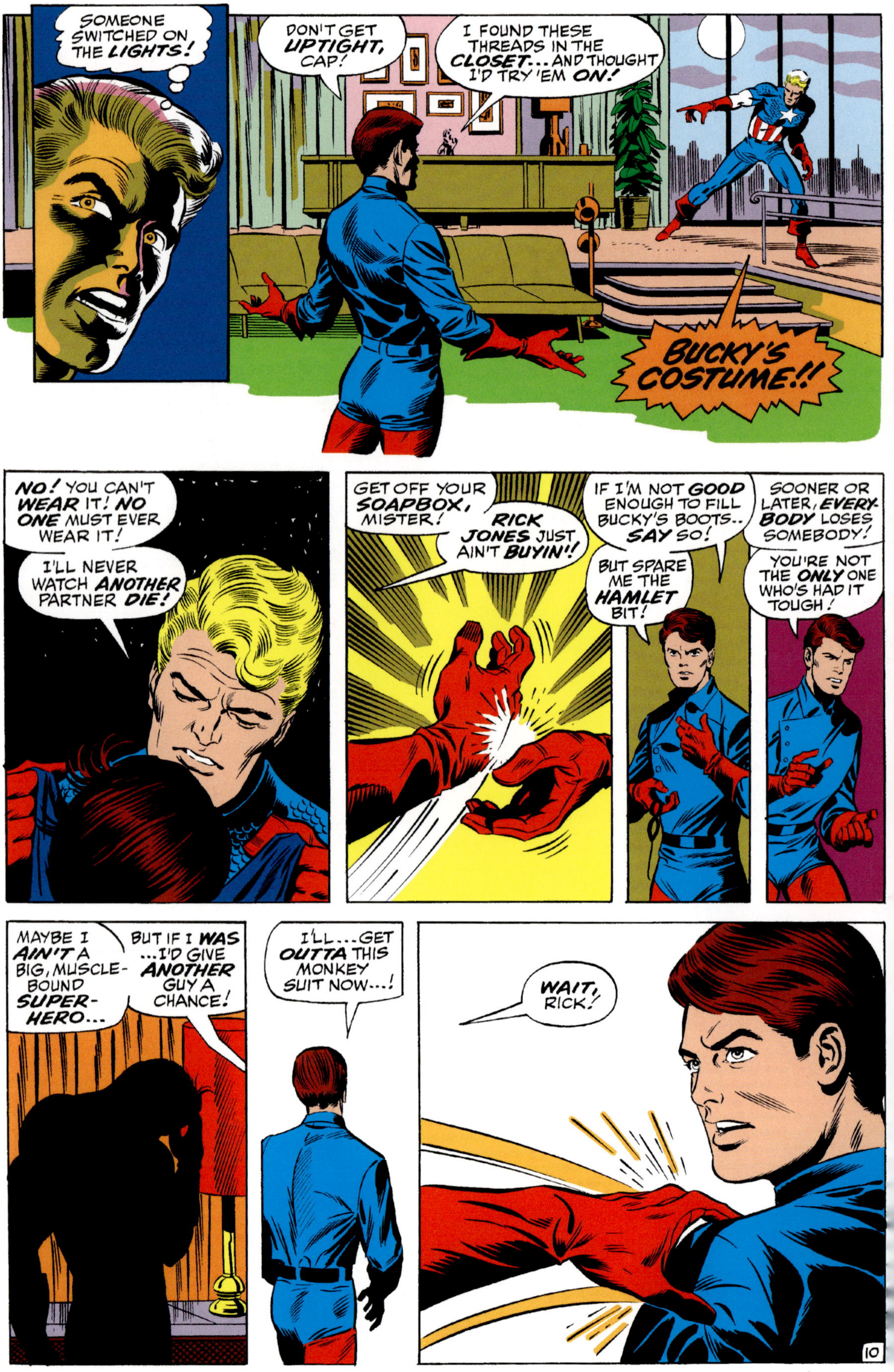
SOMEONE SWITCHED ON THE LIGHTS!
DON'T GET UPTIGHT, CAP!
I FOUND THESE THREADS IN THE CLOSET... AND THOUGHT I'D TRY 'EM ON!
BUCKY'S COSTUME!!
NO! YOU CAN'T WEAR IT! NO ONE MUST EVER WEAR IT!
I'LL NEVER WATCH ANOTHER PARTNER DIE!
GET OFF YOUR SOAPBOX, MISTER!
RICK JONES JUST AIN'T BUYIN'!
IF I'M NOT GOOD ENOUGH TO FILL BUCKY'S BOOTS.. SAY SO!
BUT SPARE ME THE HAMLET BIT!
SOONER OR LATER, EVERYBODY LOSES SOMEBODY!
YOU'RE NOT THE ONLY ONE WHO'S HAD IT TOUGH!
MAYBE I AIN'T A BIG, MUSCLE-BOUND SUPER-HERO...
BUT IF I WAS ...I'D GIVE ANOTHER GUY A CHANCE!
I'LL... GET OUTTA THIS MONKEY SUIT NOW...!
WAIT, RICK!
10

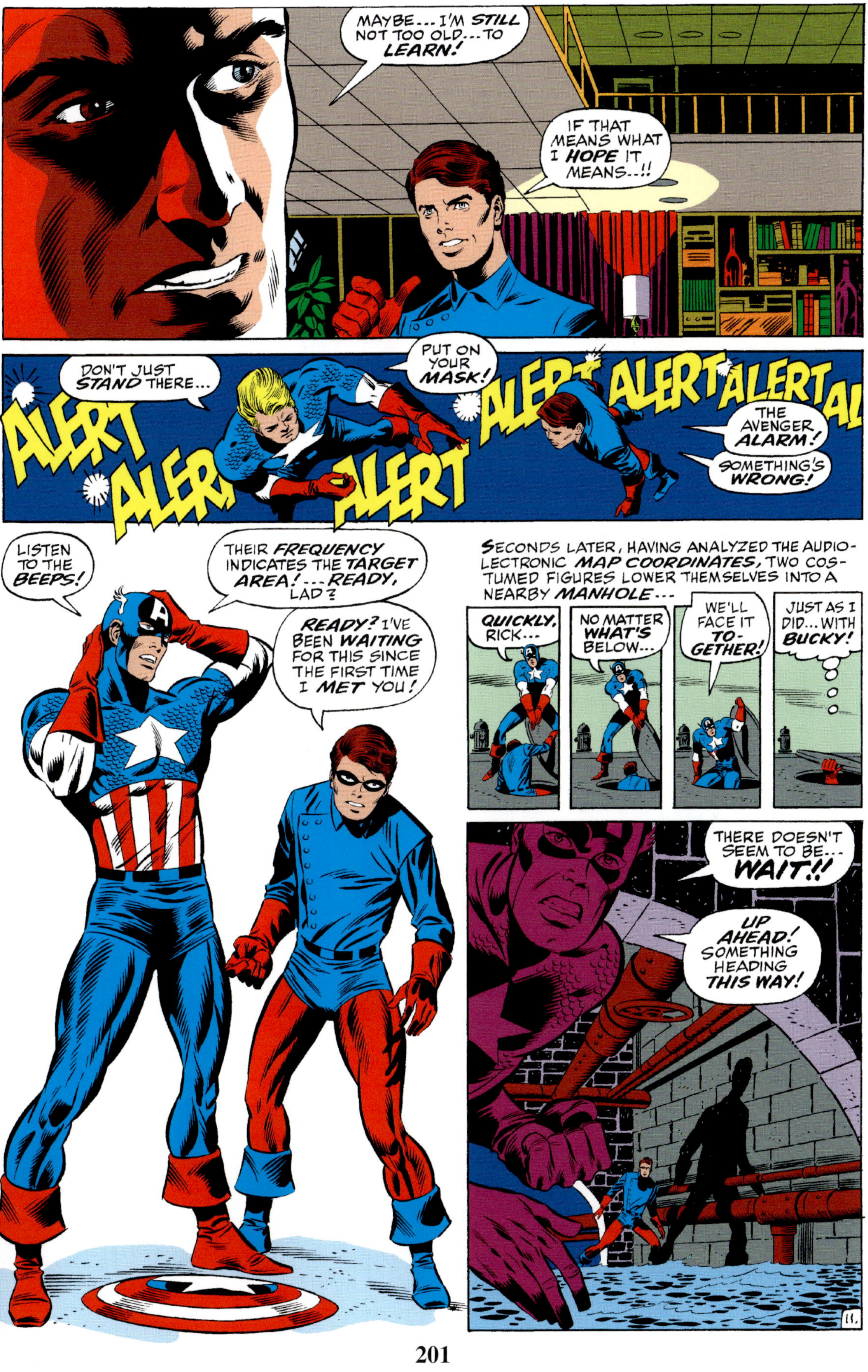
MAYBE... I'M STILL NOT TOO OLD... TO LEARN!
IF THAT MEANS WHAT I HOPE IT MEANS--!!
DON'T JUST STAND THERE...
PUT ON YOUR MASK!
ALERT ALERT ALERT ALERT ALERT ALERT ALERT AL
THE AVENGER ALARM!
SOMETHING'S WRONG!
LISTEN TO THE BEEPS!
THEIR FREQUENCY INDICATES THE TARGET AREA! ... READY, LAD?
READY? I'VE BEEN WAITING FOR THIS SINCE THE FIRST TIME I MET YOU!
SECONDS LATER, HAVING ANALYZED THE AUDIO-LECTRONIC MAP COORDINATES, TWO COSTUMED FIGURES LOWER THEMSELVES INTO A NEARBY MANHOLE...
QUICKLY, RICK...
NO MATTER WHAT'S BELOW...
WE'LL FACE IT TO-GETHER!
JUST AS I DID... WITH BUCKY!
THERE DOESN'T SEEM TO BE... WAIT!!
UP AHEAD! SOMETHING HEADING THIS WAY!
11.

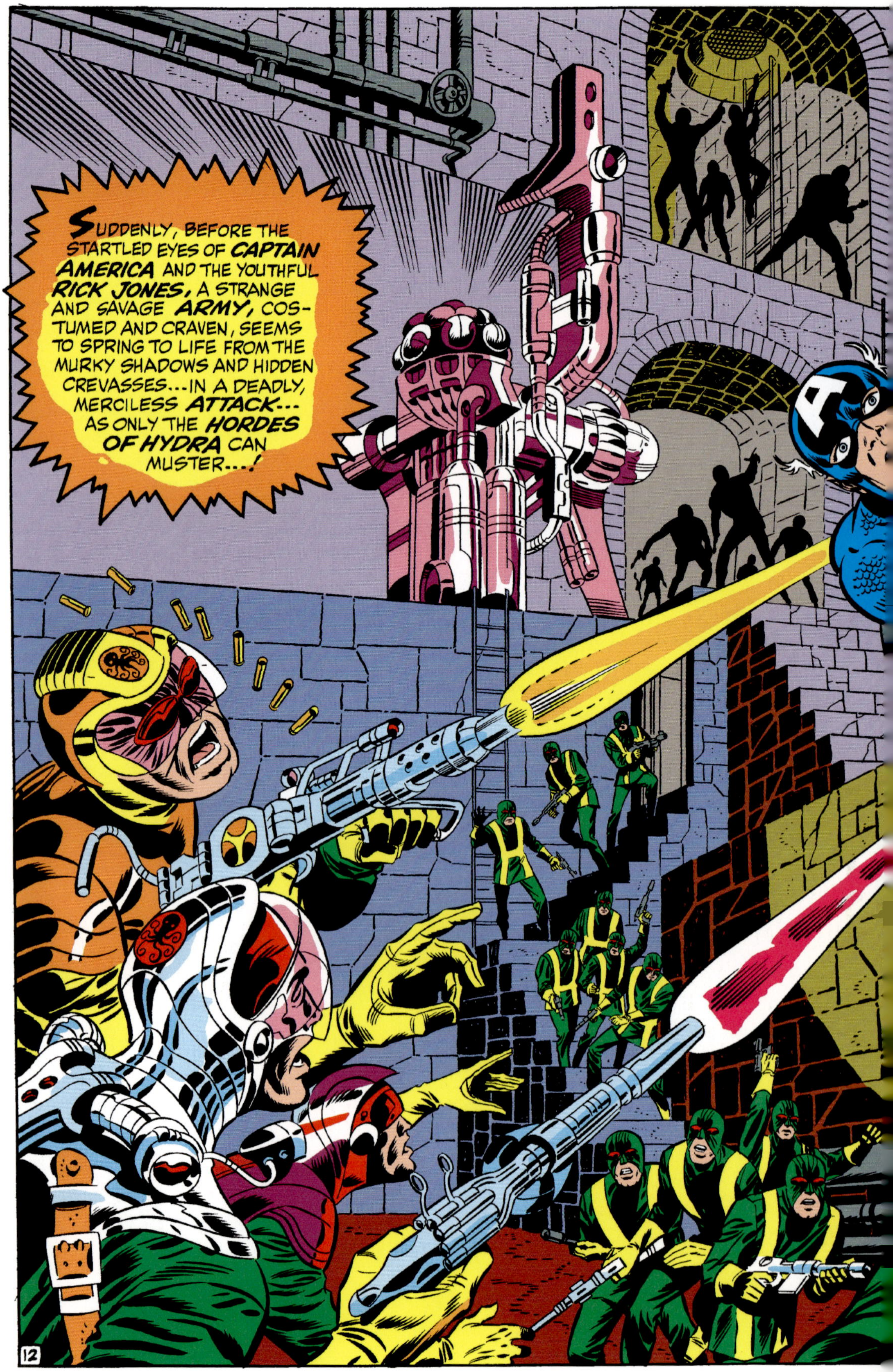
SUDDENLY, BEFORE THE STARTLED EYES OF CAPTAIN AMERICA AND THE YOUTHFUL RICK JONES, A STRANGE AND SAVAGE ARMY, COSTUMED AND CRAVEN, SEEMS TO SPRING TO LIFE FROM THE MURKY SHADOWS AND HIDDEN CREVASSES...IN A DEADLY, MERCILESS ATTACK...AS ONLY THE HORDES OF HYDRA CAN MUSTER...!
12

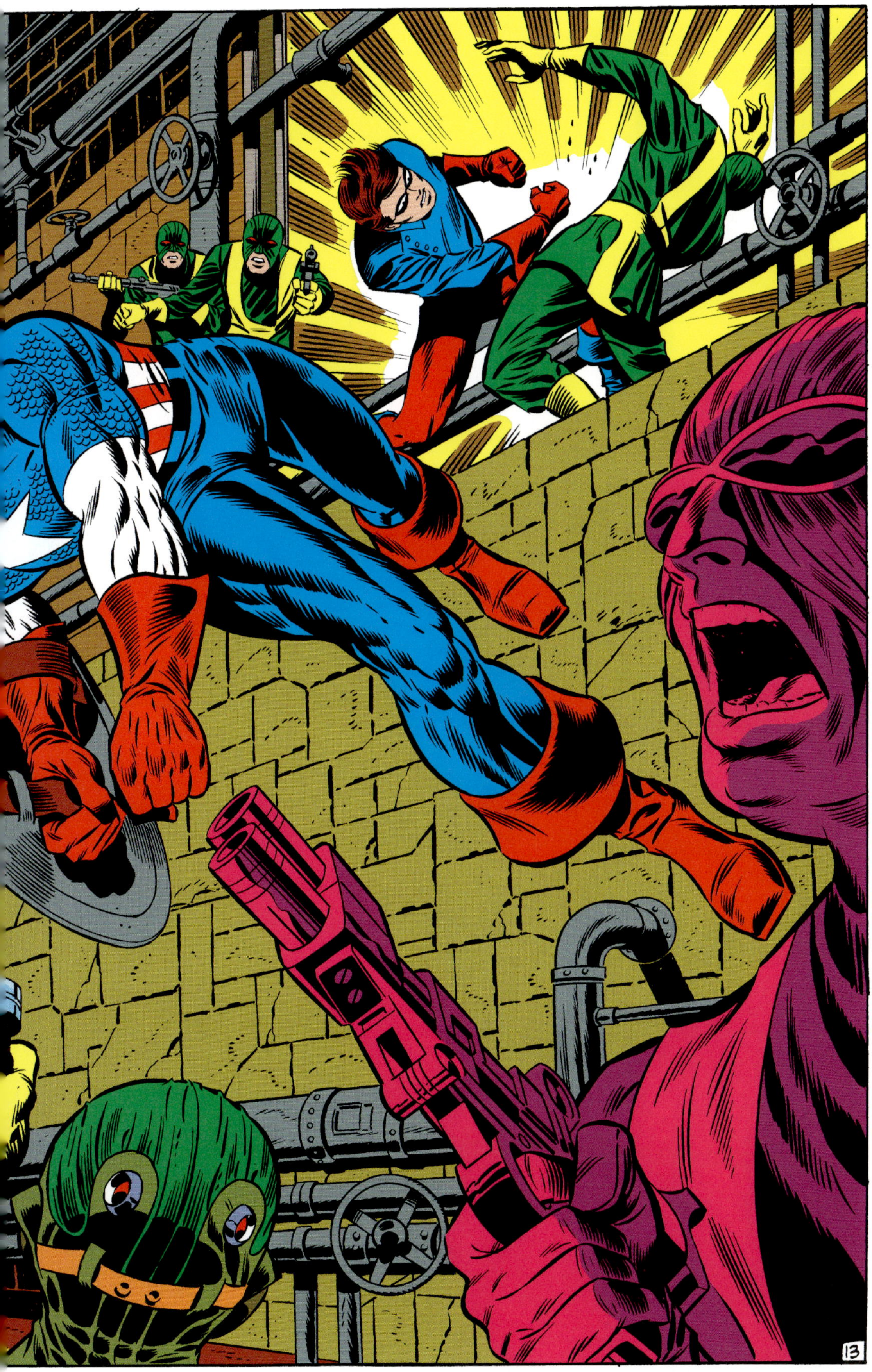
13

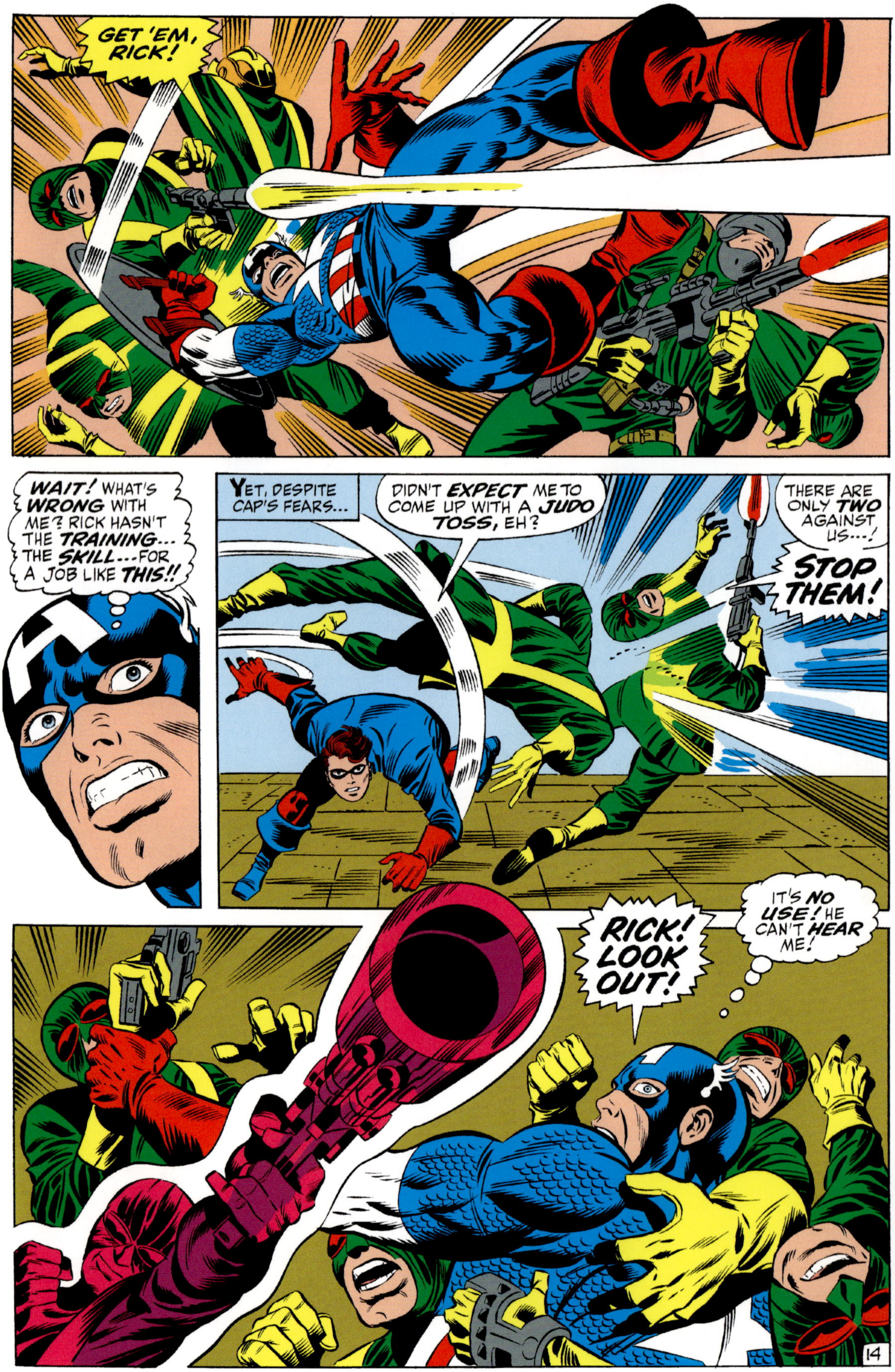
GET 'EM, RICK!
WAIT! WHAT'S WRONG WITH ME? RICK HASN'T THE TRAINING... THE SKILL...FOR A JOB LIKE THIS!!
YET, DESPITE CAP'S FEARS...
DIDN'T EXPECT ME TO COME UP WITH A JUDO TOSS, EH?
THERE ARE ONLY TWO AGAINST US...!
STOP THEM!
RICK! LOOK OUT!
IT'S NO USE! HE CAN'T HEAR ME!
14

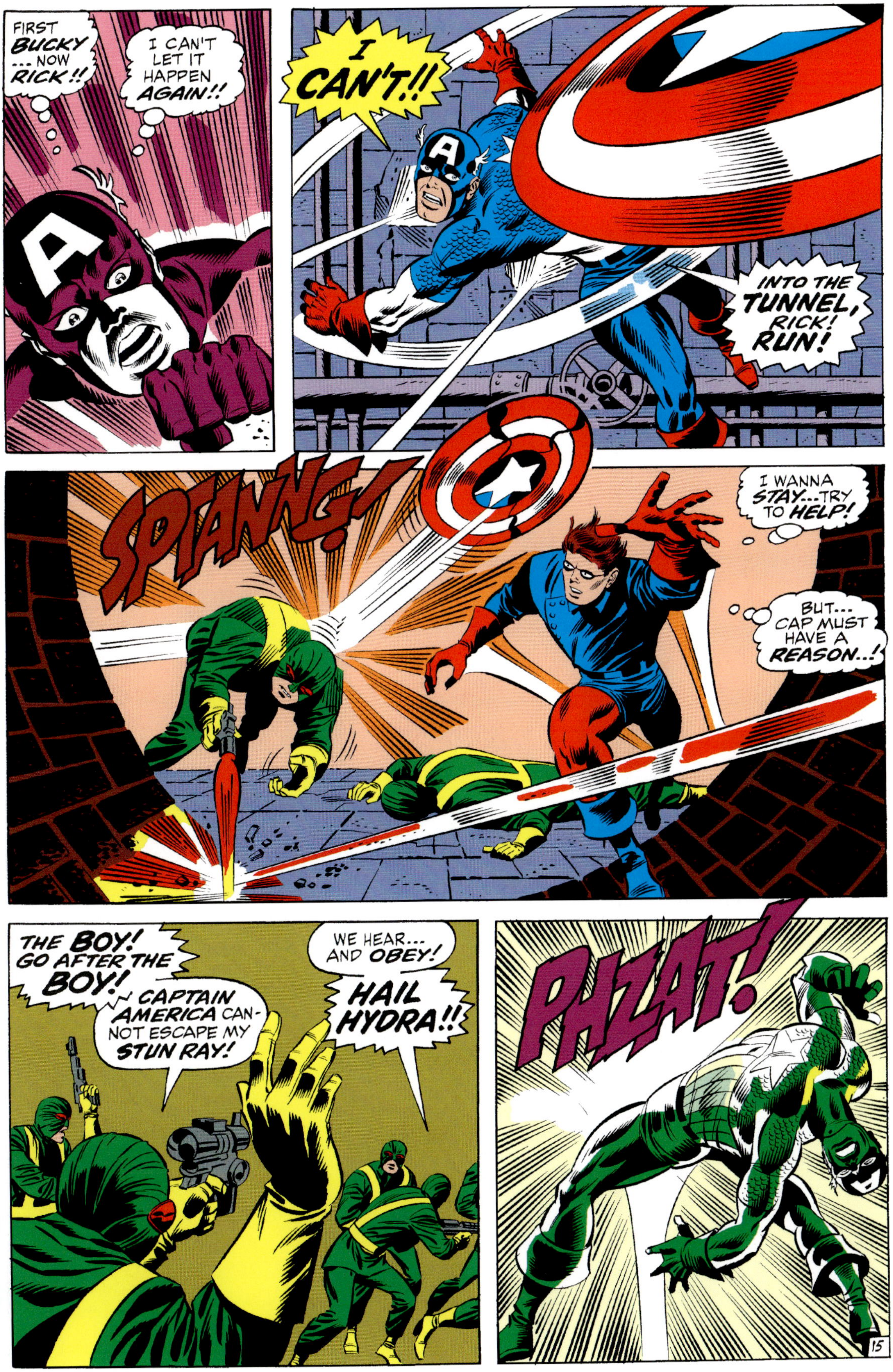
FIRST BUCKY ...NOW RICK!!
I CAN'T LET IT HAPPEN AGAIN!!
I CAN'T!!
INTO THE TUNNEL, RICK! RUN!
SPTANNG!
I WANNA STAY...TRY TO HELP!
BUT... CAP MUST HAVE A REASON..!
THE BOY! GO AFTER THE BOY!
CAPTAIN AMERICA CAN-NOT ESCAPE MY STUN RAY!
WE HEAR... AND OBEY!
HAIL HYDRA!!
PHZAT!
15

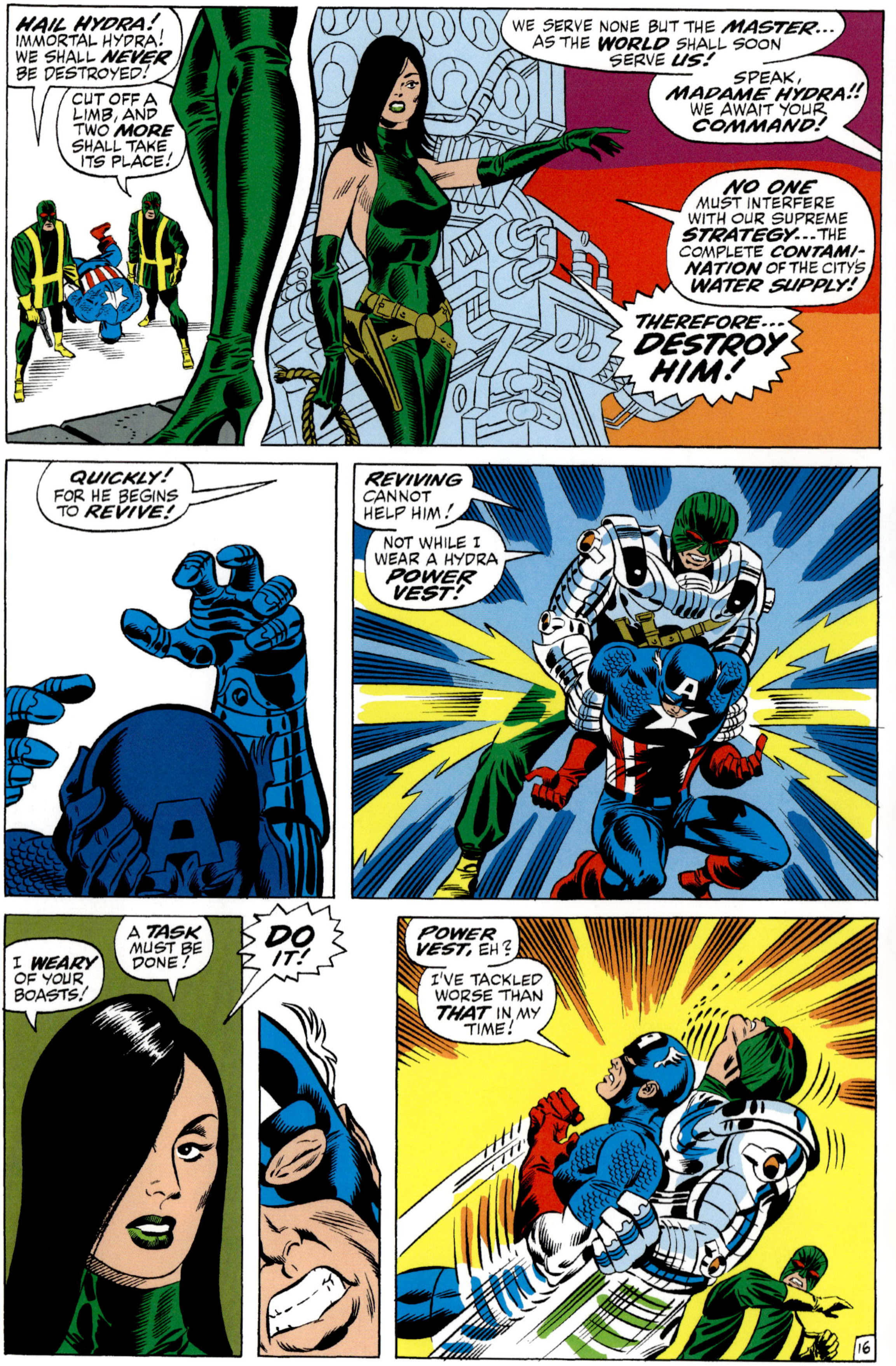

HAIL HYDRA! IMMORTAL HYDRA! WE SHALL NEVER BE DESTROYED!
CUT OFF A LIMB, AND TWO MORE SHALL TAKE ITS PLACE!
WE SERVE NONE BUT THE MASTER... AS THE WORLD SHALL SOON SERVE US!
SPEAK, MADAME HYDRA!! WE AWAIT YOUR COMMAND!
NO ONE MUST INTERFERE WITH OUR SUPREME STRATEGY... THE COMPLETE CONTAMINATION OF THE CITY'S WATER SUPPLY!
THEREFORE... DESTROY HIM!
QUICKLY! FOR HE BEGINS TO REVIVE!
REVIVING CANNOT HELP HIM!
NOT WHILE I WEAR A HYDRA POWER VEST!
I WEARY OF YOUR BOASTS!
A TASK MUST BE DONE!
DO IT!
POWER VEST, EH?
I'VE TACKLED WORSE THAN THAT IN MY TIME!
16

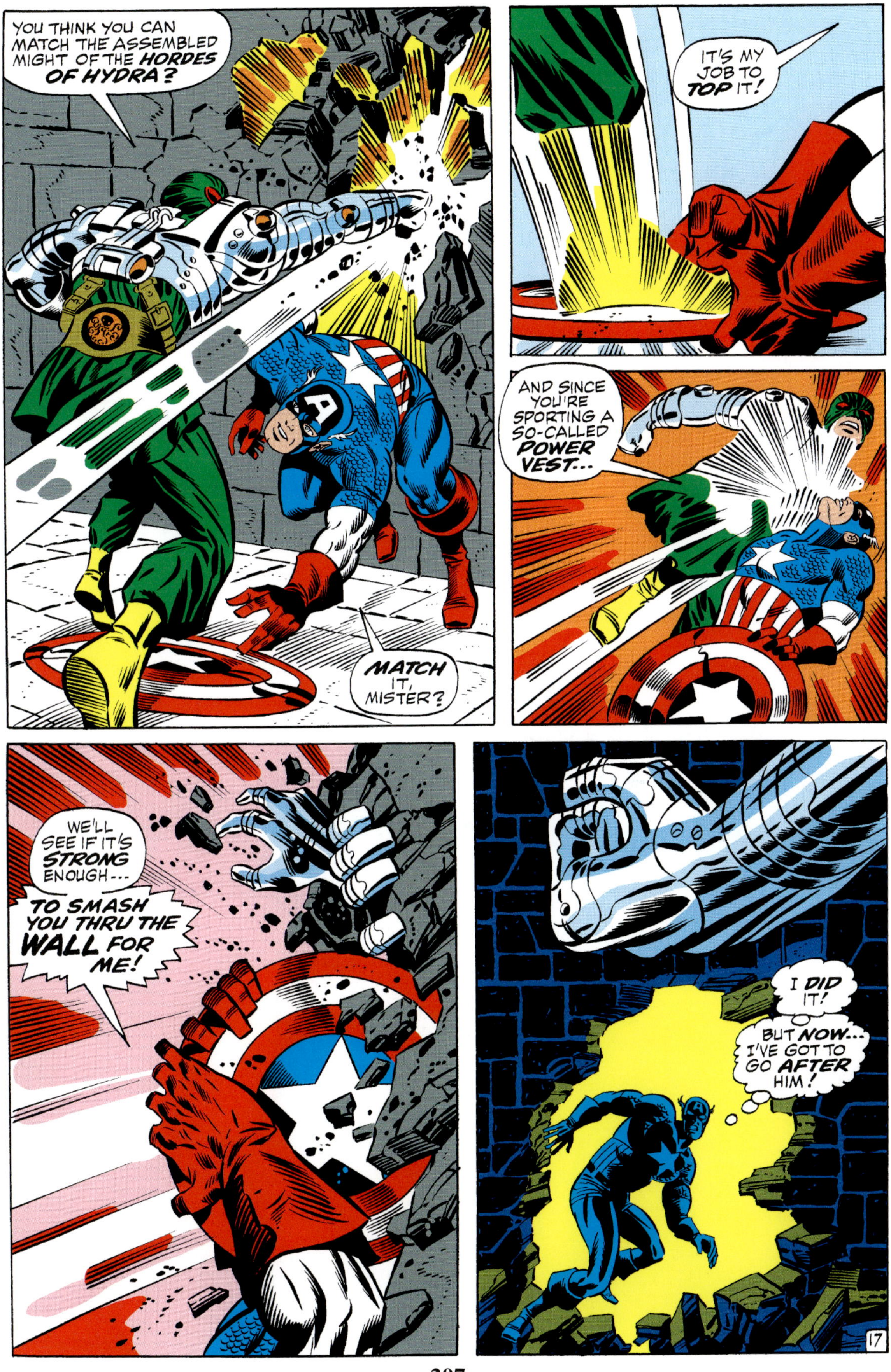
YOU THINK YOU CAN MATCH THE ASSEMBLED MIGHT OF THE HORDES OF HYDRA?
MATCH IT, MISTER?
IT'S MY JOB TO TOP IT!
AND SINCE YOU'RE SPORTING A SO-CALLED POWER VEST...
WE'LL SEE IF IT'S STRONG ENOUGH---
TO SMASH YOU THRU THE WALL FOR ME!
I DID IT!
BUT NOW... I'VE GOT TO GO AFTER HIM!
17

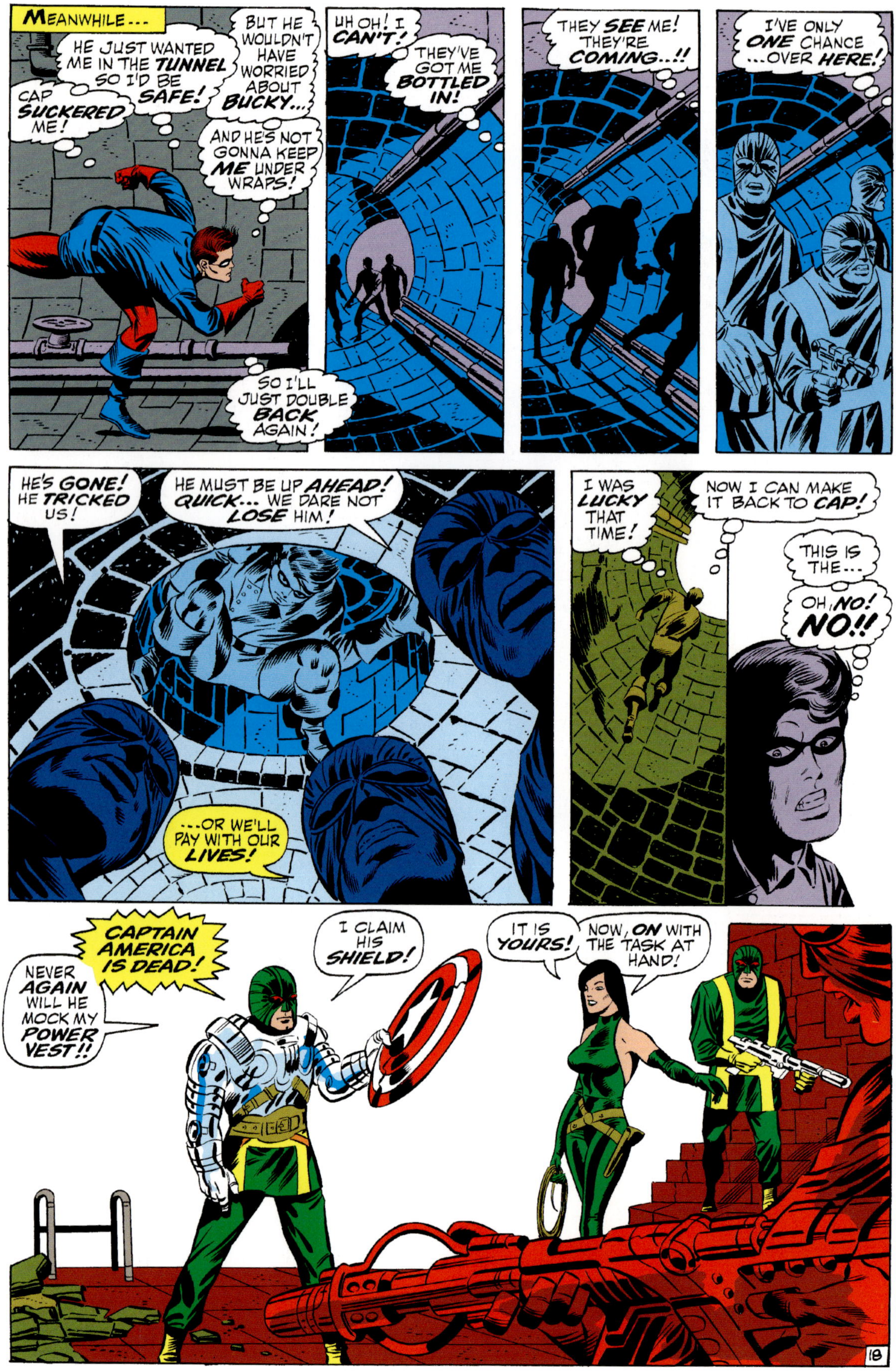
MEANWHILE...
CAP SUCKERED ME!
HE JUST WANTED ME IN THE TUNNEL SO I'D BE SAFE!
BUT HE WOULDN'T HAVE WORRIED ABOUT BUCKY...
AND HE'S NOT GONNA KEEP ME UNDER WRAPS!
SO I'LL JUST DOUBLE BACK AGAIN!
UH OH! I CAN'T!
THEY'VE GOT ME BOTTLED IN!
THEY SEE ME! THEY'RE COMING...!!
I'VE ONLY ONE CHANCE ...OVER HERE!
HE'S GONE! HE TRICKED US!
HE MUST BE UP AHEAD! QUICK... WE DARE NOT LOSE HIM!
...OR WE'LL PAY WITH OUR LIVES!
I WAS LUCKY THAT TIME!
NOW I CAN MAKE IT BACK TO CAP!
THIS IS THE...
OH, NO! NO!!
CAPTAIN AMERICA IS DEAD!
NEVER AGAIN WILL HE MOCK MY POWER VEST!!
I CLAIM HIS SHIELD!
IT IS YOURS!
NOW, ON WITH THE TASK AT HAND!
18

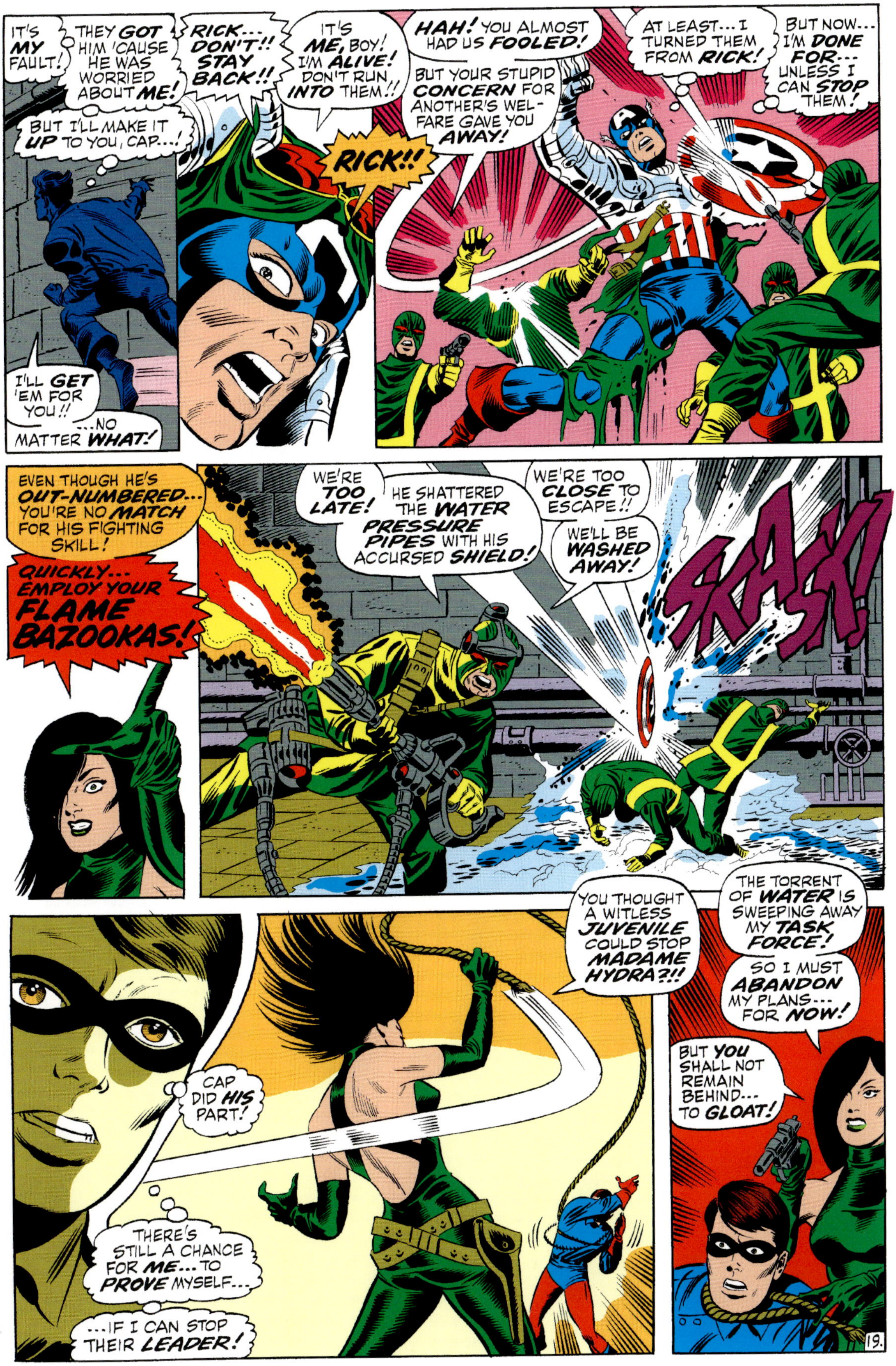
IT'S MY FAULT!
THEY GOT HIM 'CAUSE HE WAS WORRIED ABOUT ME!
BUT I'LL MAKE IT UP TO YOU, CAP...!
I'LL GET 'EM FOR YOU!!
...NO MATTER WHAT!
RICK... DON'T!! STAY BACK!!
IT'S ME, BOY! I'M ALIVE! DON'T RUN INTO THEM!!
RICK!!
HAH! YOU ALMOST HAD US FOOLED!
BUT YOUR STUPID CONCERN FOR ANOTHER'S WEL-FARE GAVE YOU AWAY!
AT LEAST... I TURNED THEM FROM RICK!
BUT NOW... I'M DONE FOR... UNLESS I CAN STOP THEM!
EVEN THOUGH HE'S OUT-NUMBERED... YOU'RE NO MATCH FOR HIS FIGHTING SKILL!
QUICKLY... EMPLOY YOUR FLAME BAZOOKAS!
WE'RE TOO LATE!
HE SHATTERED THE WATER PRESSURE PIPES WITH HIS ACCURSED SHIELD!
WE'RE TOO CLOSE TO ESCAPE!!
WE'LL BE WASHED AWAY!
SKASH!
CAP DID HIS PART!
THERE'S STILL A CHANCE FOR ME... TO PROVE MYSELF...
...IF I CAN STOP THEIR LEADER!
YOU THOUGHT A WITLESS JUVENILE COULD STOP MADAME HYDRA?!!
THE TORRENT OF WATER IS SWEEPING AWAY MY TASK FORCE!
SO I MUST ABANDON MY PLANS... FOR NOW!
BUT YOU SHALL NOT REMAIN BEHIND... TO GLOAT!
19.

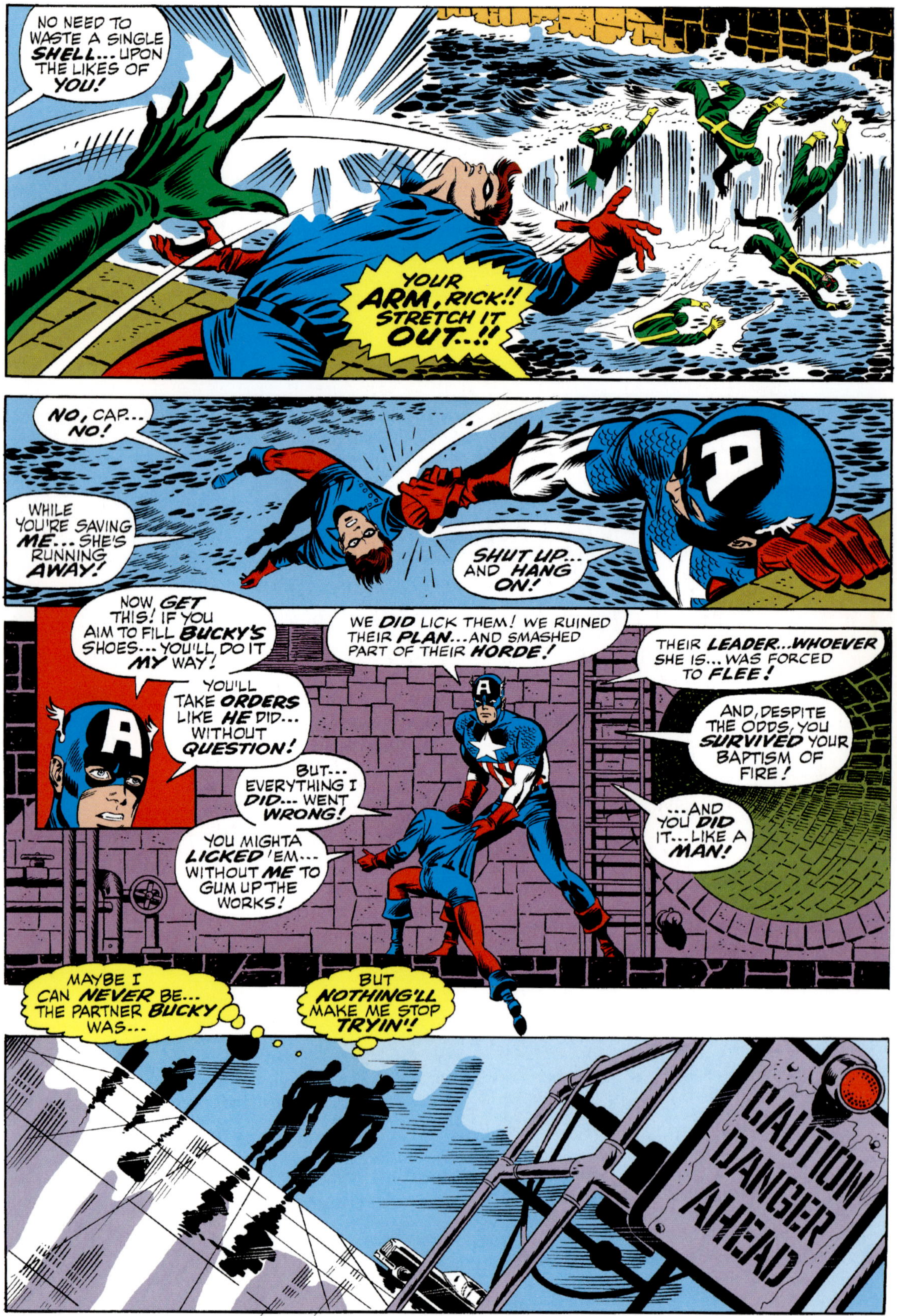
NO NEED TO WASTE A SINGLE SHELL... UPON THE LIKES OF YOU!
YOUR ARM, RICK!! STRETCH IT OUT..!!
NO, CAP... NO!
WHILE YOU'RE SAVING ME... SHE'S RUNNING AWAY!
SHUT UP... AND HANG ON!
NOW GET THIS! IF YOU AIM TO FILL BUCKY'S SHOES... YOU'LL DO IT MY WAY!
YOU'LL TAKE ORDERS LIKE HE DID... WITHOUT QUESTION!
WE DID LICK THEM! WE RUINED THEIR PLAN... AND SMASHED PART OF THEIR HORDE!
THEIR LEADER...WHOEVER SHE IS... WAS FORCED TO FLEE!
AND, DESPITE THE ODDS, YOU SURVIVED YOUR BAPTISM OF FIRE!
BUT... EVERYTHING I DID... WENT WRONG!
YOU MIGHTA LICKED 'EM... WITHOUT ME TO GUM UP THE WORKS!
...AND YOU DID IT... LIKE A MAN!
MAYBE I CAN NEVER BE... THE PARTNER BUCKY WAS...
BUT NOTHING'LL MAKE ME STOP TRYIN'!
CAUTION DANGER AHEAD

WRAPPED IN A SILENCE, MORE MEANINGFUL THAN WORDS, TWO WEARY FIGURES SLOWLY MELT INTO THE RAINSWEPT SHADOWS OF THE GATHERING DAWN... AND WHO ARE WE TO SAY WHETHER A LEGEND HAS DIED... OR IS JUST A'BORNING?

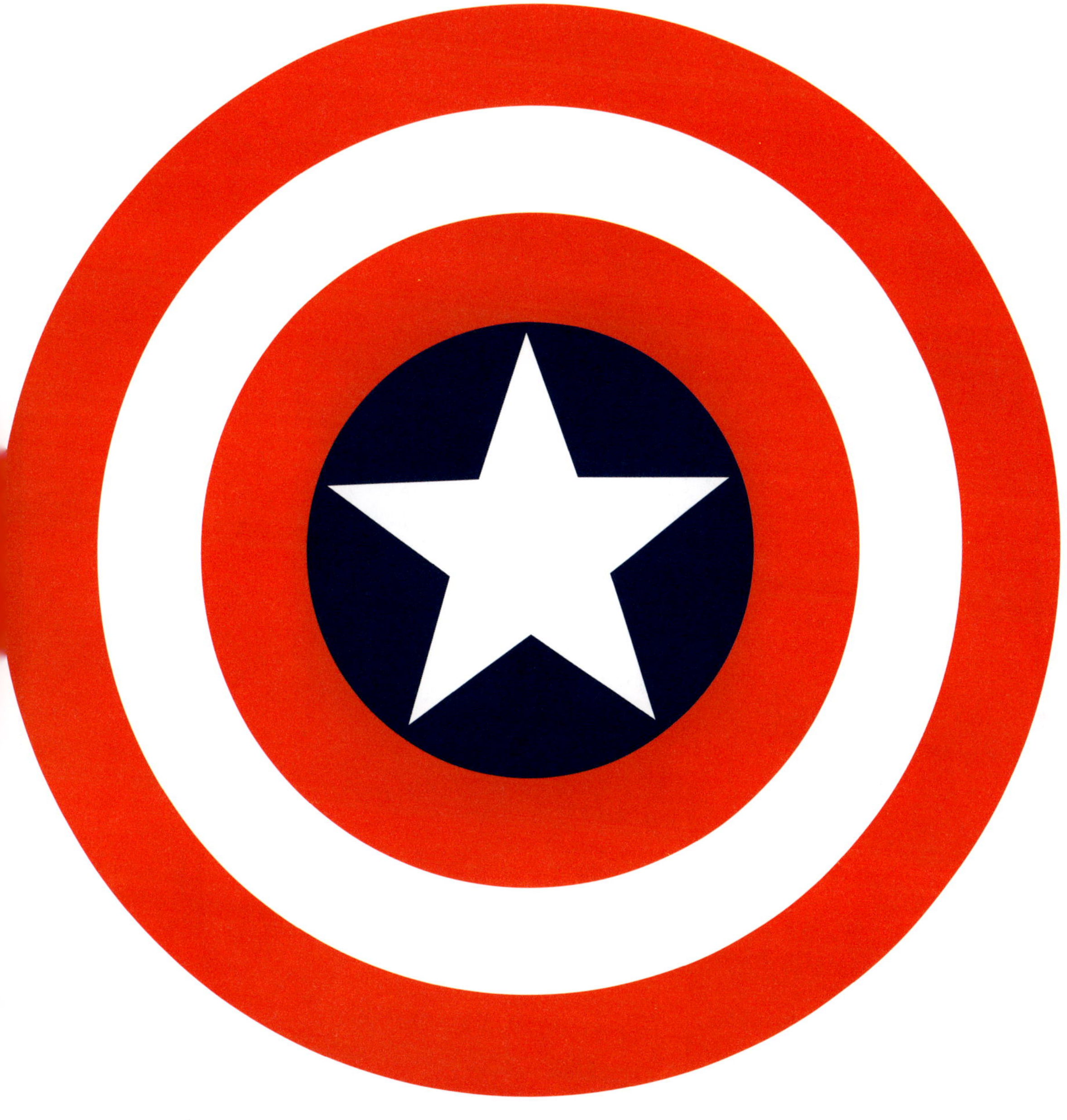

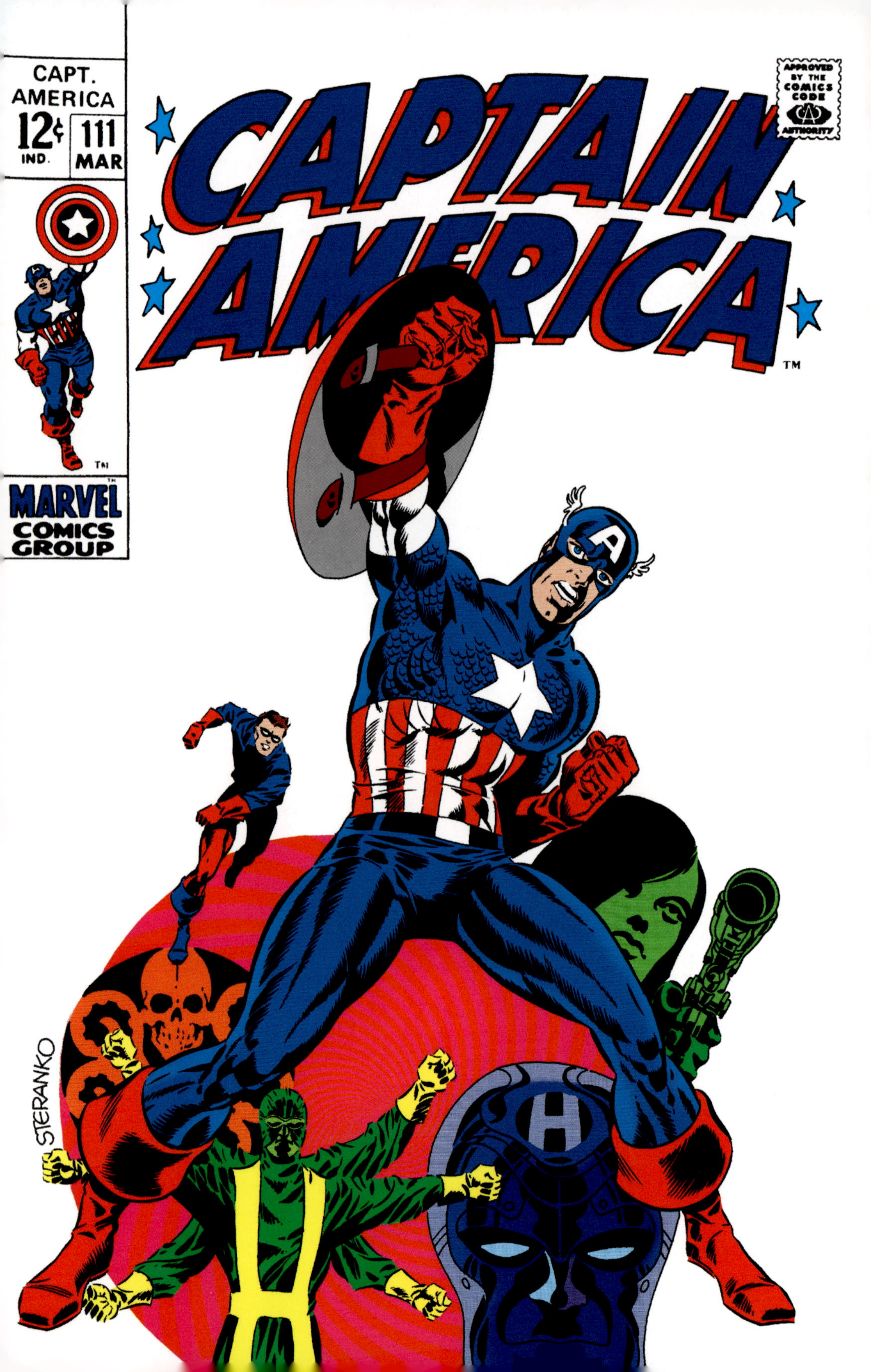
CAPT. AMERICA
12¢ IND.
111 MAR
CAPTAIN AMERICA
MARVEL COMICS GROUP
APPROVED BY THE COMICS CODE AUTHORITY
STERANKO

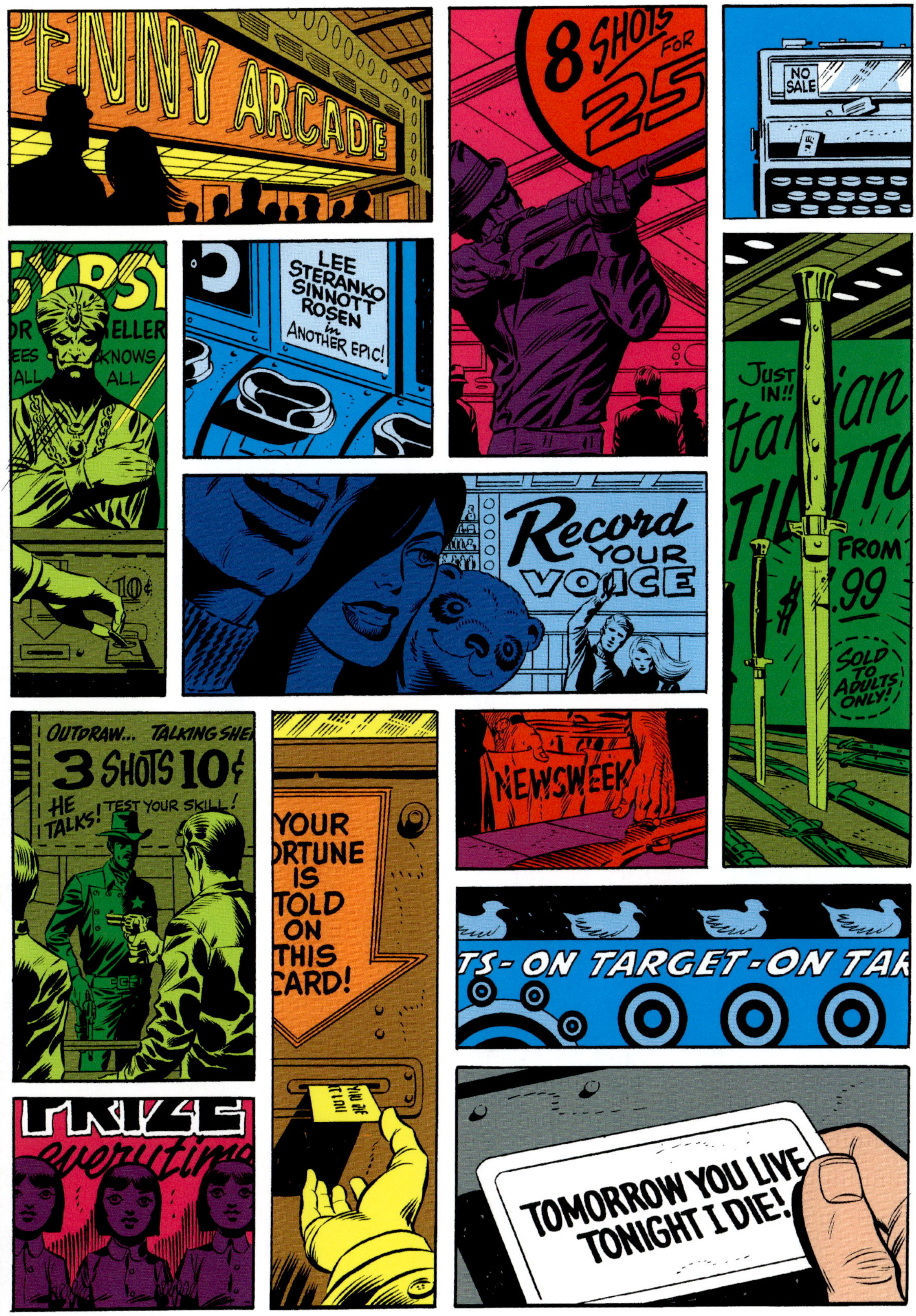
PENNY ARCADE
8 SHOTS FOR 25
NO SALE
GYPSY
FORTUNE TELLER
SEES ALL
KNOWS ALL
LEE
STERANKO
SINNOTT
ROSEN
in
ANOTHER EPIC!
10¢
Record YOUR VOICE
JUST IN!!
FROM
.99
SOLD TO ADULTS ONLY!
OUTDRAW... TALKING SHE
3 SHOTS 10¢
HE TALKS!
TEST YOUR SKILL!
YOUR
ORTUNE
IS
TOLD
ON
THIS
CARD!
NEWSWEEK
TS-ON TARGET-ON TAR
PRIZE
everytim
TOMORROW YOU LIVE
TONIGHT I DIE!

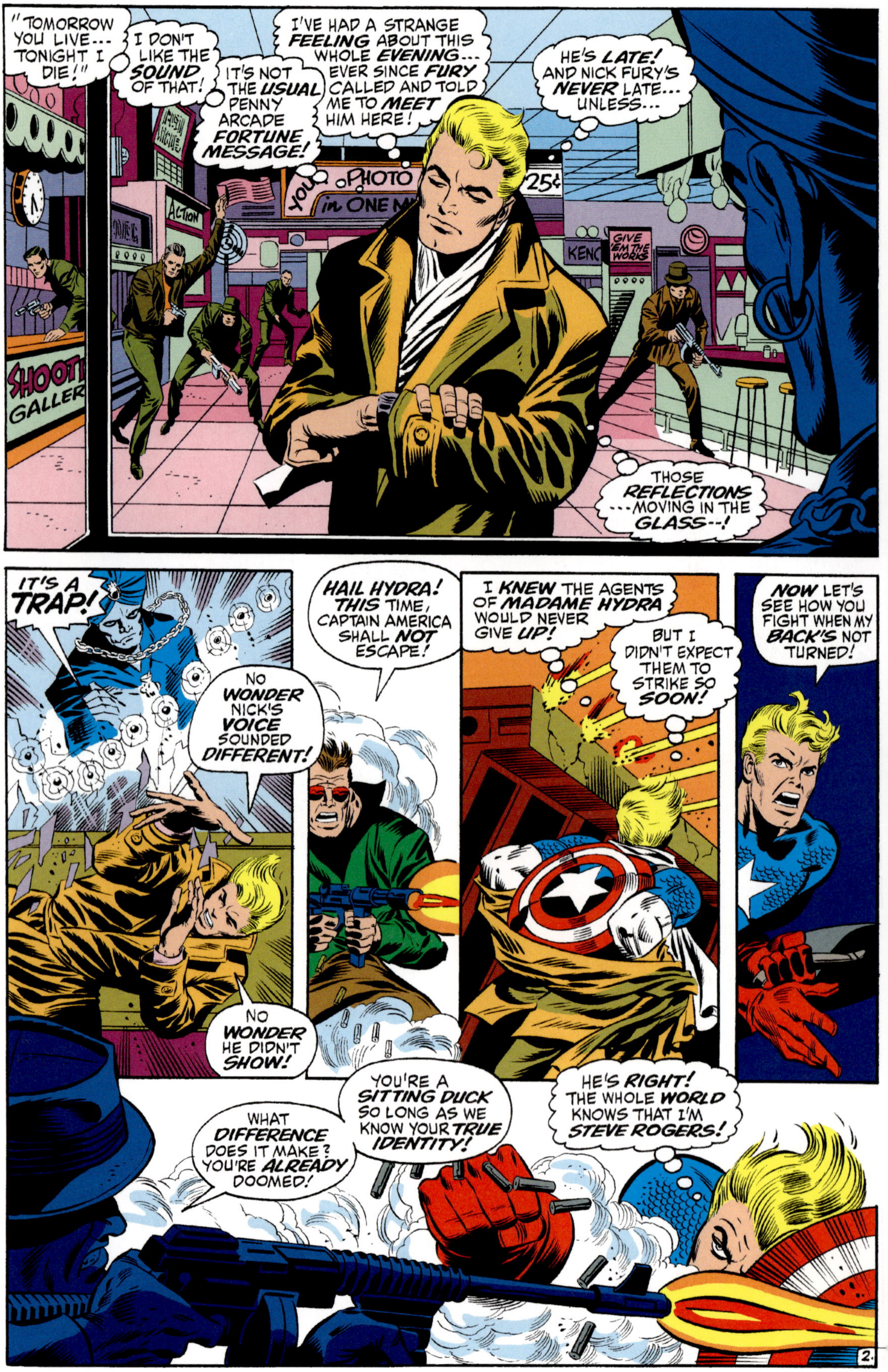
"TOMORROW YOU LIVE... TONIGHT I DIE!"
I DON'T LIKE THE SOUND OF THAT!
IT'S NOT THE USUAL PENNY ARCADE FORTUNE MESSAGE!
I'VE HAD A STRANGE FEELING ABOUT THIS WHOLE EVENING... EVER SINCE FURY CALLED AND TOLD ME TO MEET HIM HERE!
HE'S LATE! AND NICK FURY'S NEVER LATE... UNLESS...
THOSE REFLECTIONS ---MOVING IN THE GLASS--!
IT'S A TRAP!
NO WONDER NICK'S VOICE SOUNDED DIFFERENT!
NO WONDER HE DIDN'T SHOW!
HAIL HYDRA! THIS TIME, CAPTAIN AMERICA SHALL NOT ESCAPE!
I KNEW THE AGENTS OF MADAME HYDRA WOULD NEVER GIVE UP!
BUT I DIDN'T EXPECT THEM TO STRIKE SO SOON!
NOW LET'S SEE HOW YOU FIGHT WHEN MY BACK'S NOT TURNED!
WHAT DIFFERENCE DOES IT MAKE? YOU'RE ALREADY DOOMED!
YOU'RE A SITTING DUCK SO LONG AS WE KNOW YOUR TRUE IDENTITY!
HE'S RIGHT! THE WHOLE WORLD KNOWS THAT I'M STEVE ROGERS!
2.

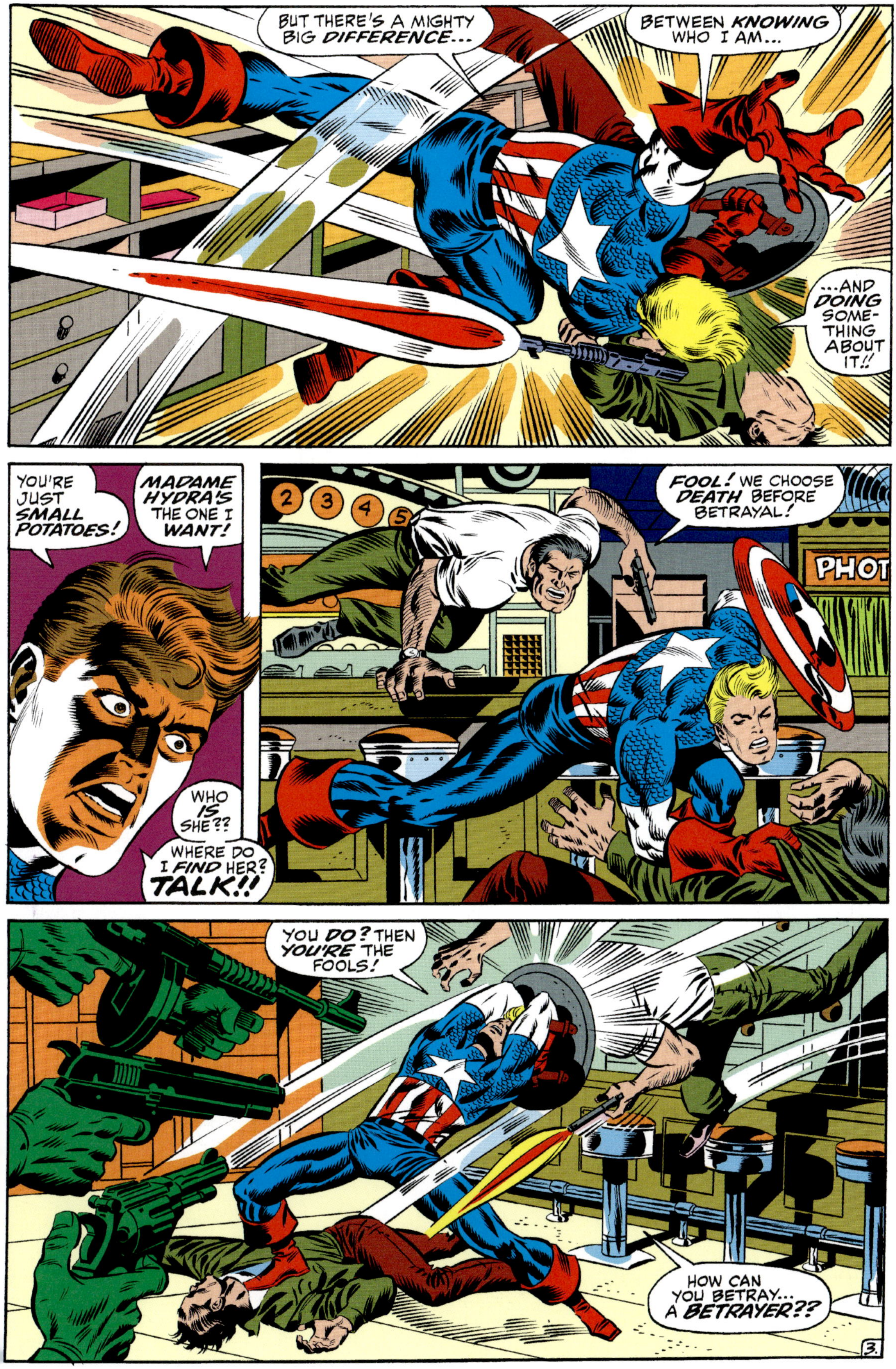
BUT THERE'S A MIGHTY BIG DIFFERENCE...
BETWEEN KNOWING WHO I AM...
...AND DOING SOMETHING ABOUT IT!!
YOU'RE JUST SMALL POTATOES!
MADAME HYDRA'S THE ONE I WANT!
WHO IS SHE??
WHERE DO I FIND HER? TALK!!
2 3 4 5
FOOL! WE CHOOSE DEATH BEFORE BETRAYAL!
PHOT
YOU DO? THEN YOU'RE THE FOOLS!
HOW CAN YOU BETRAY... A BETRAYER??
3.

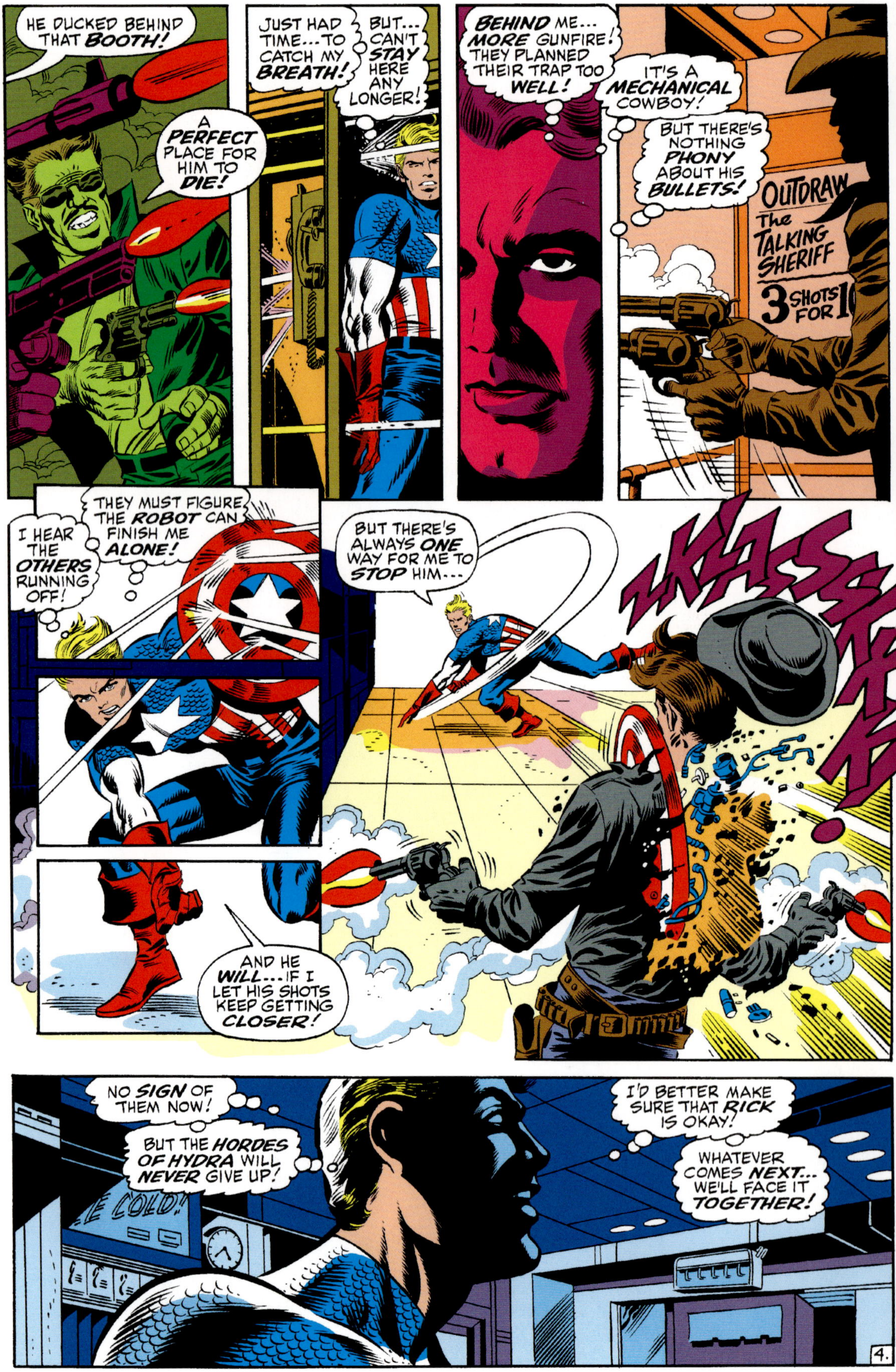
HE DUCKED BEHIND THAT BOOTH!
A PERFECT PLACE FOR HIM TO DIE!
JUST HAD TIME... TO CATCH MY BREATH!
BUT... CAN'T STAY HERE ANY LONGER!
BEHIND ME... MORE GUNFIRE! THEY PLANNED THEIR TRAP TOO WELL!
IT'S A MECHANICAL COWBOY!
BUT THERE'S NOTHING PHONY ABOUT HIS BULLETS!
OUTDRAW The TALKING SHERIFF 3 SHOTS FOR 1
I HEAR THE OTHERS RUNNING OFF!
THEY MUST FIGURE THE ROBOT CAN FINISH ME ALONE!
AND HE WILL... IF I LET HIS SHOTS KEEP GETTING CLOSER!
BUT THERE'S ALWAYS ONE WAY FOR ME TO STOP HIM---
NO SIGN OF THEM NOW!
BUT THE HORDES OF HYDRA WILL NEVER GIVE UP!
I'D BETTER MAKE SURE THAT RICK IS OKAY!
WHATEVER COMES NEXT... WE'LL FACE IT TOGETHER!
4.

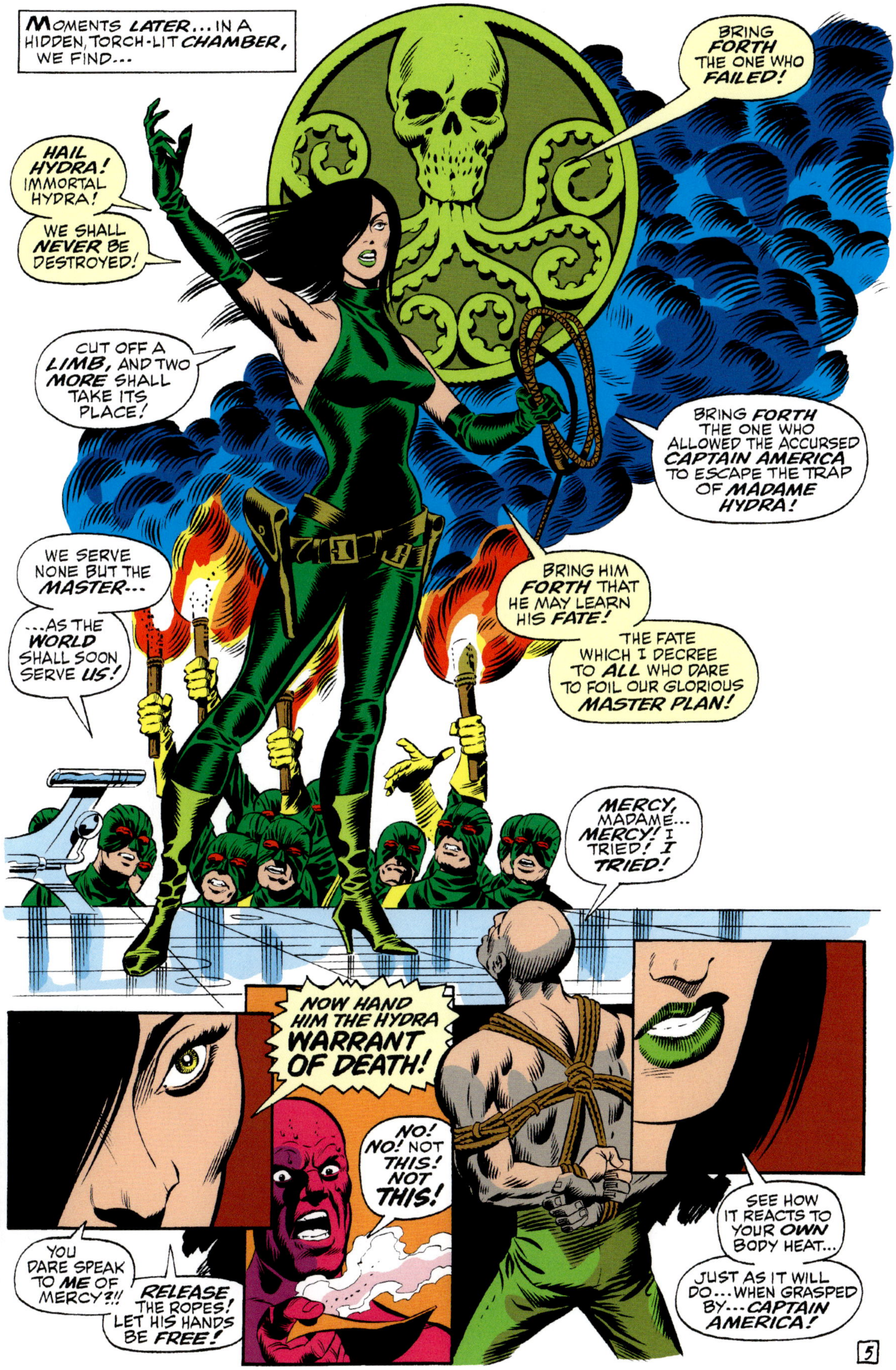

MOMENTS LATER... IN A HIDDEN, TORCH-LIT CHAMBER, WE FIND...
BRING FORTH THE ONE WHO FAILED!
HAIL HYDRA! IMMORTAL HYDRA!
WE SHALL NEVER BE DESTROYED!
CUT OFF A LIMB, AND TWO MORE SHALL TAKE ITS PLACE!
BRING FORTH THE ONE WHO ALLOWED THE ACCURSED CAPTAIN AMERICA TO ESCAPE THE TRAP OF MADAME HYDRA!
WE SERVE NONE BUT THE MASTER--
...AS THE WORLD SHALL SOON SERVE US!
BRING HIM FORTH THAT HE MAY LEARN HIS FATE!
THE FATE WHICH I DECREE TO ALL WHO DARE TO FOIL OUR GLORIOUS MASTER PLAN!
MERCY, MADAME... MERCY! I TRIED! I TRIED!
NOW HAND HIM THE HYDRA WARRANT OF DEATH!
YOU DARE SPEAK TO ME OF MERCY?!!
RELEASE THE ROPES! LET HIS HANDS BE FREE!
NO! NO! NOT THIS! NOT THIS!
SEE HOW IT REACTS TO YOUR OWN BODY HEAT...
JUST AS IT WILL DO... WHEN GRASPED BY... CAPTAIN AMERICA!
5

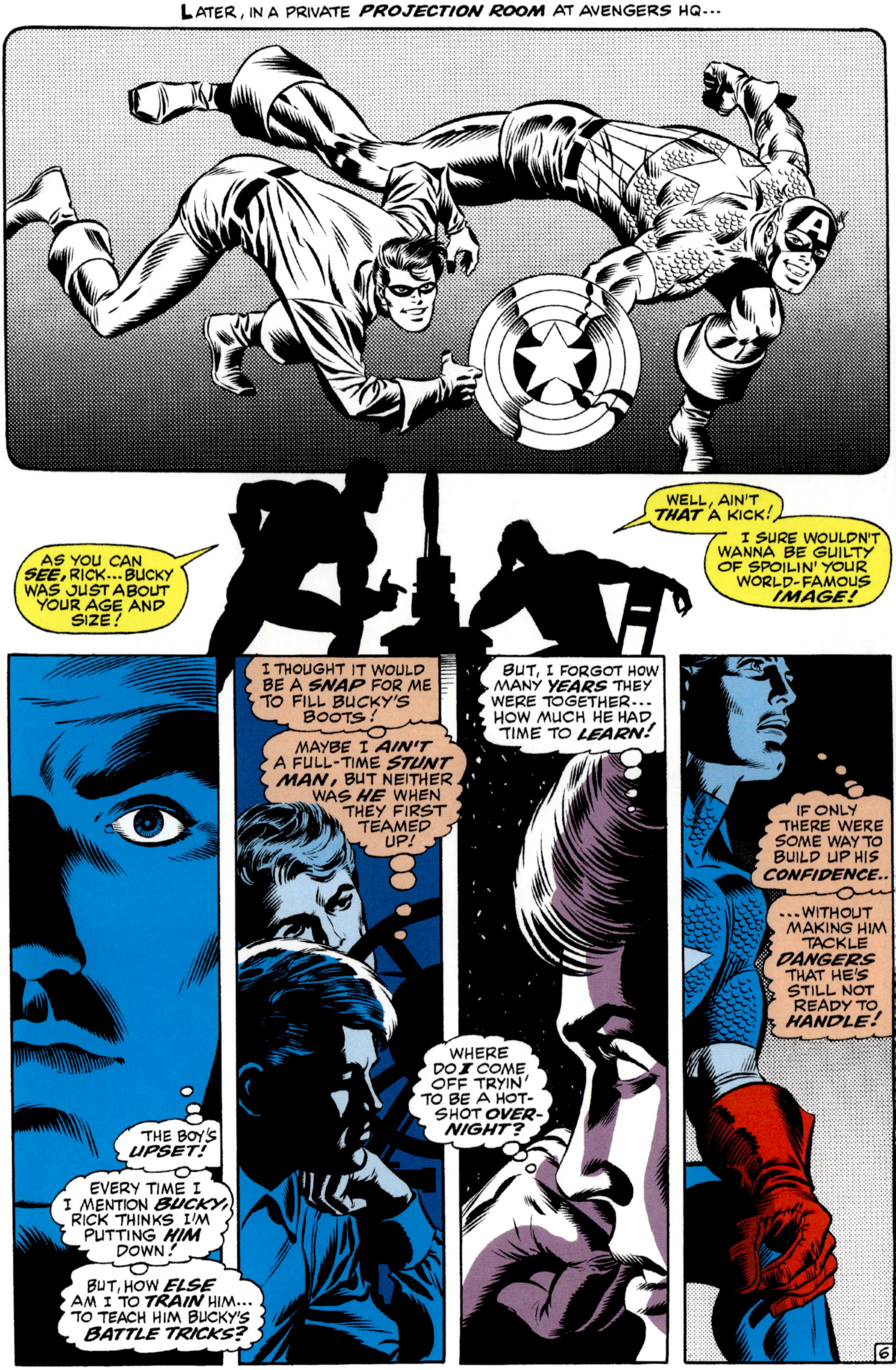
LATER, IN A PRIVATE PROJECTION ROOM AT AVENGERS HQ...
AS YOU CAN SEE, RICK... BUCKY WAS JUST ABOUT YOUR AGE AND SIZE!
WELL, AIN'T THAT A KICK!
I SURE WOULDN'T WANNA BE GUILTY OF SPOILIN' YOUR WORLD-FAMOUS IMAGE!
THE BOY'S UPSET!
EVERY TIME I I MENTION BUCKY, RICK THINKS I'M PUTTING HIM DOWN!
BUT, HOW ELSE AM I TO TRAIN HIM... TO TEACH HIM BUCKY'S BATTLE TRICKS?
I THOUGHT IT WOULD BE A SNAP FOR ME TO FILL BUCKY'S BOOTS!
MAYBE I AIN'T A FULL-TIME STUNT MAN, BUT NEITHER WAS HE WHEN THEY FIRST TEAMED UP!
BUT, I FORGOT HOW MANY YEARS THEY WERE TOGETHER... HOW MUCH HE HAD TIME TO LEARN!
WHERE DO I COME OFF TRYIN' TO BE A HOT-SHOT OVER-NIGHT?
IF ONLY THERE WERE SOME WAY TO BUILD UP HIS CONFIDENCE..
...WITHOUT MAKING HIM TACKLE DANGERS THAT HE'S STILL NOT READY TO HANDLE!
6

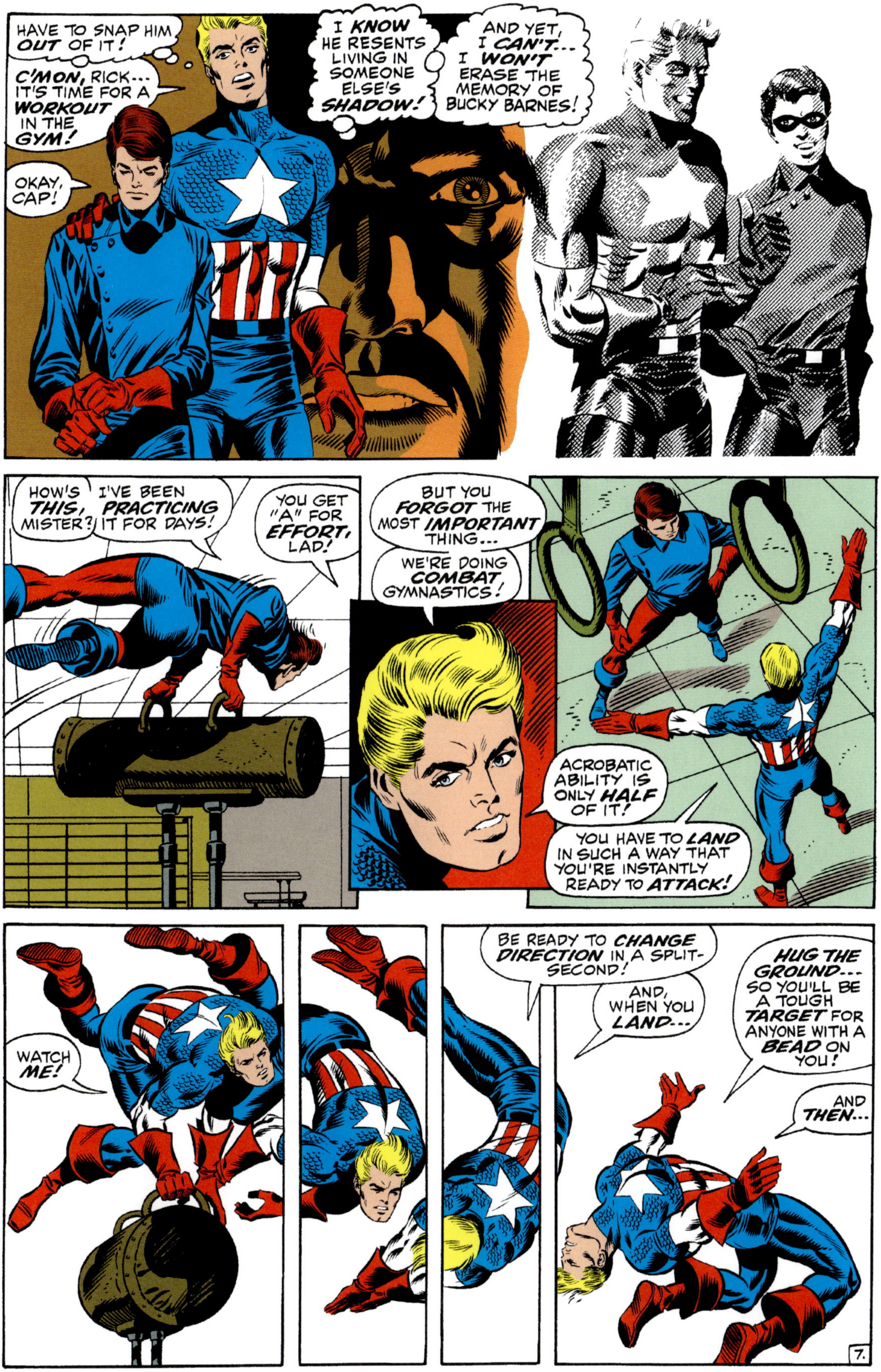
HAVE TO SNAP HIM OUT OF IT!
C'MON, RICK... IT'S TIME FOR A WORKOUT IN THE GYM!
OKAY, CAP!
I KNOW HE RESENTS LIVING IN SOMEONE ELSE'S SHADOW!
AND YET, I CAN'T... I WON'T ERASE THE MEMORY OF BUCKY BARNES!
HOW'S THIS, MISTER?
I'VE BEEN PRACTICING IT FOR DAYS!
YOU GET "A" FOR EFFORT, LAD!
BUT YOU FORGOT THE MOST IMPORTANT THING...
WE'RE DOING COMBAT GYMNASTICS!
ACROBATIC ABILITY IS ONLY HALF OF IT!
YOU HAVE TO LAND IN SUCH A WAY THAT YOU'RE INSTANTLY READY TO ATTACK!
WATCH ME!
BE READY TO CHANGE DIRECTION IN A SPLIT-SECOND!
AND, WHEN YOU LAND...
HUG THE GROUND... SO YOU'LL BE A TOUGH TARGET FOR ANYONE WITH A BEAD ON YOU!
AND THEN...
7.

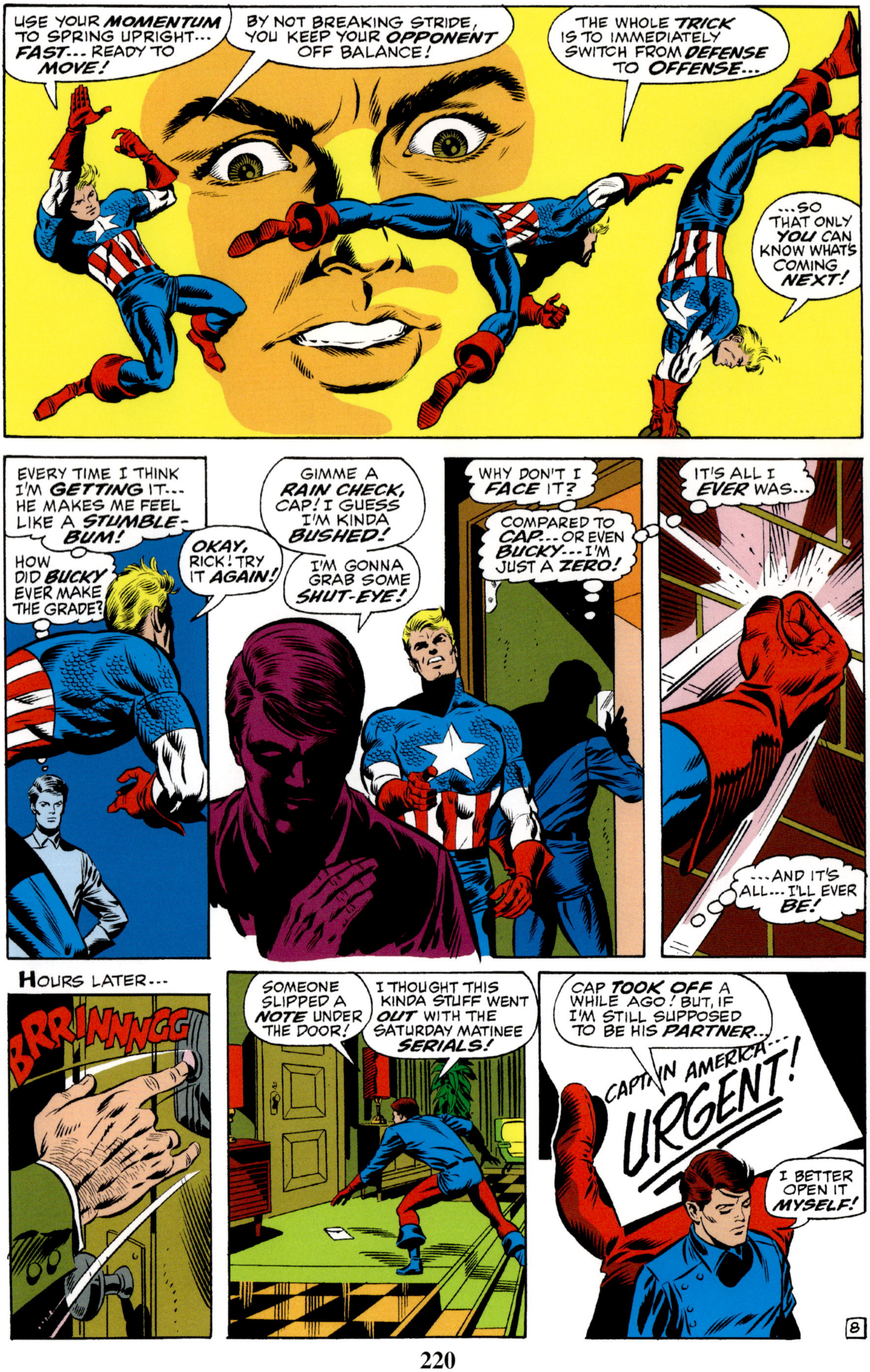
USE YOUR MOMENTUM TO SPRING UPRIGHT... FAST... READY TO MOVE!
BY NOT BREAKING STRIDE, YOU KEEP YOUR OPPONENT OFF BALANCE!
THE WHOLE TRICK IS TO IMMEDIATELY SWITCH FROM DEFENSE TO OFFENSE...
...SO THAT ONLY YOU CAN KNOW WHAT'S COMING NEXT!
EVERY TIME I THINK I'M GETTING IT--- HE MAKES ME FEEL LIKE A STUMBLE-BUM!
HOW DID BUCKY EVER MAKE THE GRADE?
OKAY, RICK! TRY IT AGAIN!
GIMME A RAIN CHECK, CAP! I GUESS I'M KINDA BUSHED!
I'M GONNA GRAB SOME SHUT-EYE!
WHY DON'T I FACE IT?
COMPARED TO CAP--- OR EVEN BUCKY--- I'M JUST A ZERO!
IT'S ALL I EVER WAS...
...AND IT'S ALL... I'LL EVER BE!
HOURS LATER...
BRRINNNGG
SOMEONE SLIPPED A NOTE UNDER THE DOOR!
I THOUGHT THIS KINDA STUFF WENT OUT WITH THE SATURDAY MATINEE SERIALS!
CAP TOOK OFF A WHILE AGO! BUT, IF I'M STILL SUPPOSED TO BE HIS PARTNER...
CAPTAIN AMERICA... URGENT!
I BETTER OPEN IT MYSELF!
8

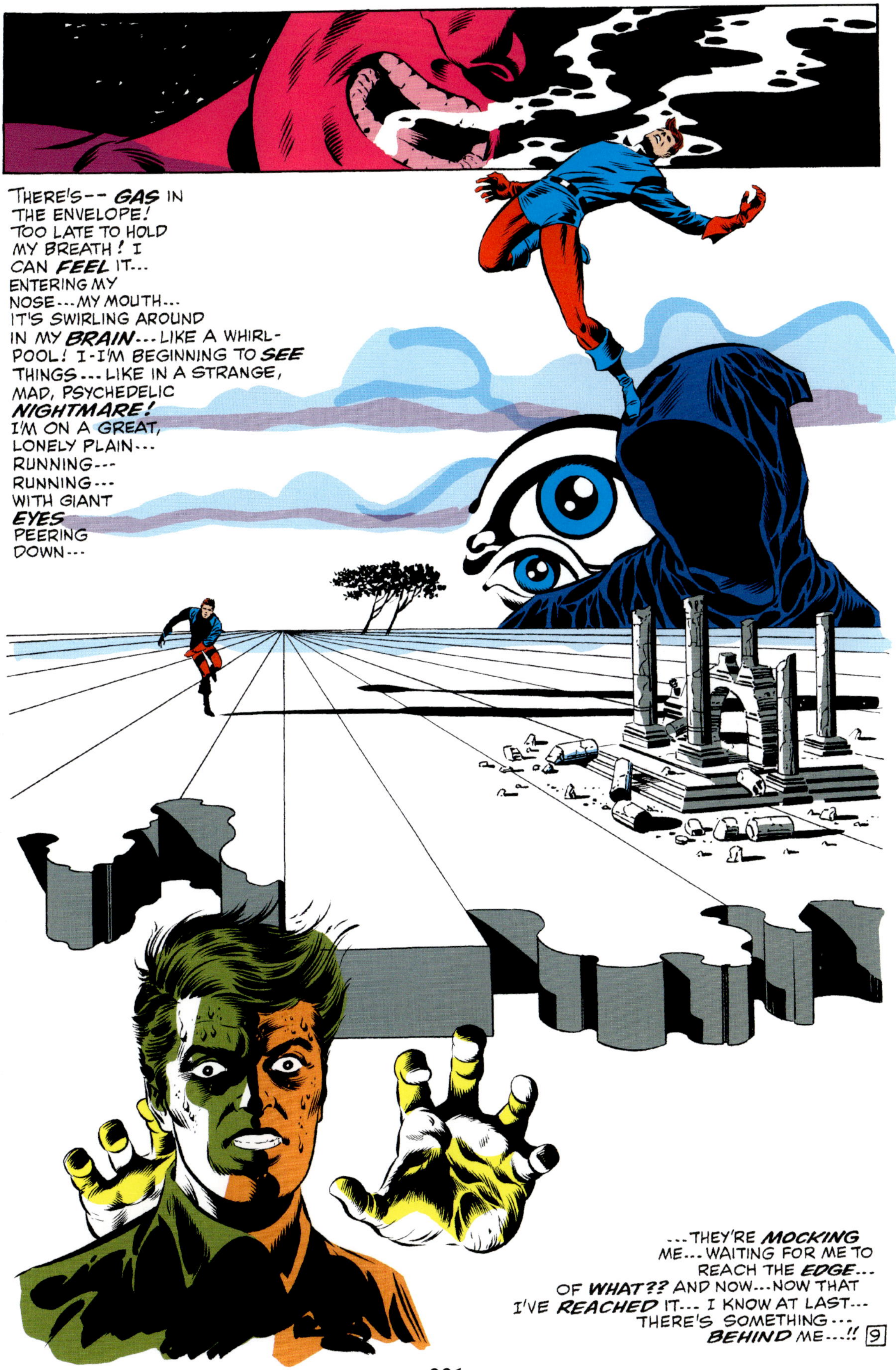

THERE'S-- GAS IN THE ENVELOPE! TOO LATE TO HOLD MY BREATH! I CAN FEEL IT... ENTERING MY NOSE... MY MOUTH... IT'S SWIRLING AROUND IN MY BRAIN... LIKE A WHIRLPOOL! I-I'M BEGINNING TO SEE THINGS... LIKE IN A STRANGE, MAD, PSYCHEDELIC NIGHTMARE! I'M ON A GREAT, LONELY PLAIN... RUNNING--- RUNNING--- WITH GIANT EYES PEERING DOWN---
...THEY'RE MOCKING ME... WAITING FOR ME TO REACH THE EDGE... OF WHAT?? AND NOW... NOW THAT I'VE REACHED IT... I KNOW AT LAST... THERE'S SOMETHING... BEHIND ME...!!
9

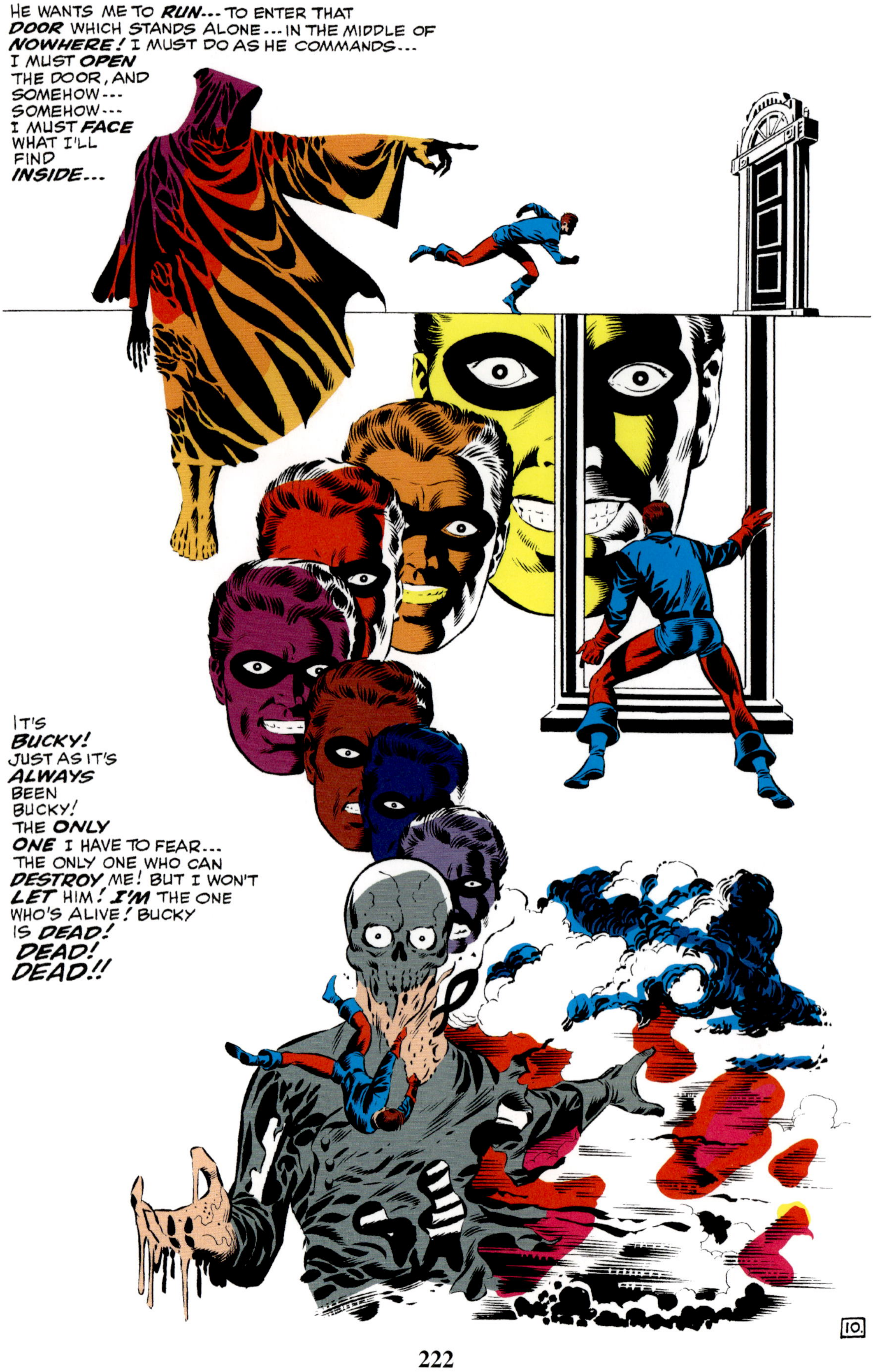
HE WANTS ME TO RUN--- TO ENTER THAT DOOR WHICH STANDS ALONE --- IN THE MIDDLE OF NOWHERE! I MUST DO AS HE COMMANDS--- I MUST OPEN THE DOOR, AND SOMEHOW--- SOMEHOW--- I MUST FACE WHAT I'LL FIND INSIDE...
IT'S BUCKY! JUST AS IT'S ALWAYS BEEN BUCKY! THE ONLY ONE I HAVE TO FEAR... THE ONLY ONE WHO CAN DESTROY ME! BUT I WON'T LET HIM! I'M THE ONE WHO'S ALIVE! BUCKY IS DEAD! DEAD! DEAD!!
10.

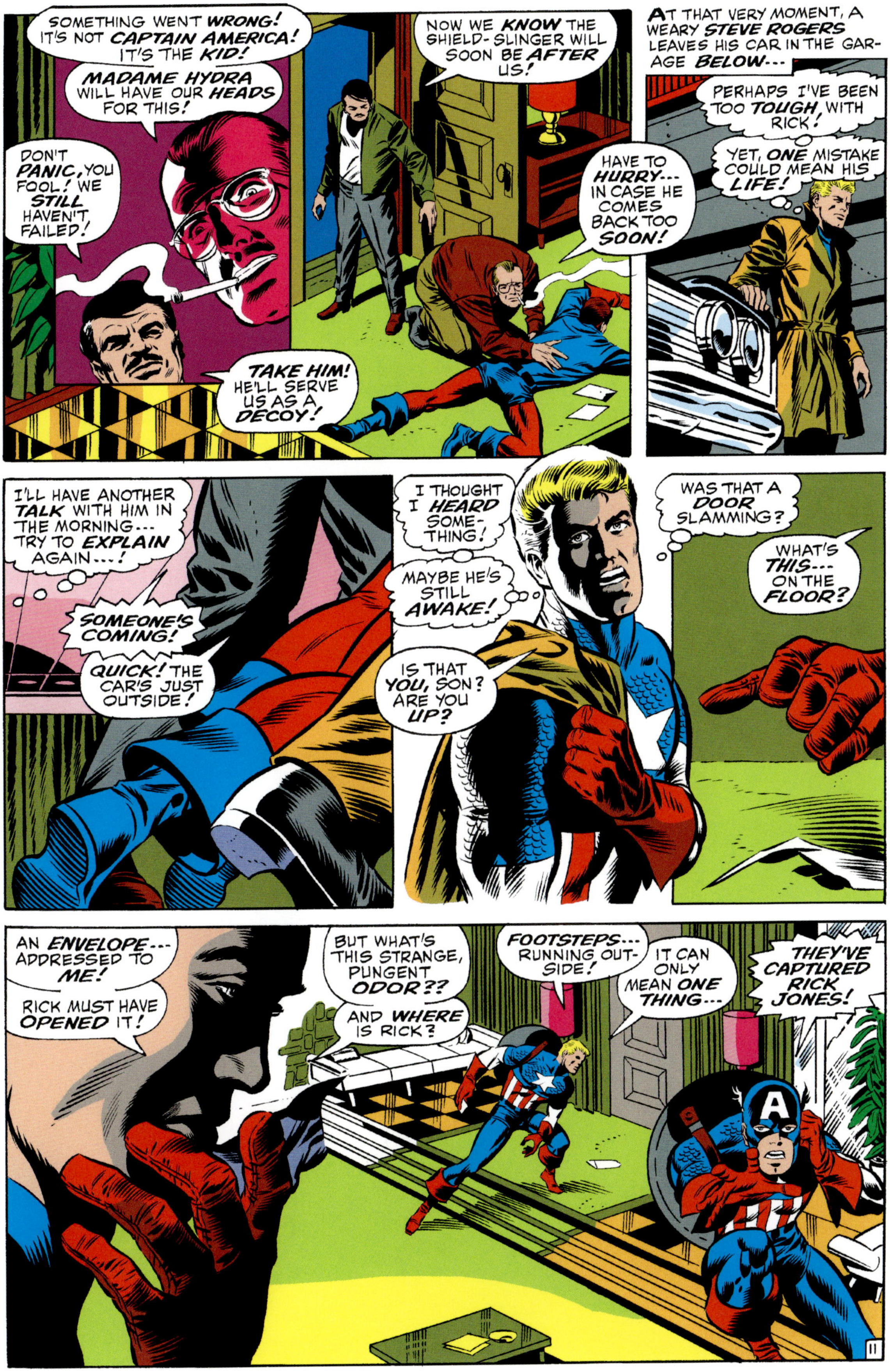
SOMETHING WENT WRONG! IT'S NOT CAPTAIN AMERICA! IT'S THE KID!
MADAME HYDRA WILL HAVE OUR HEADS FOR THIS!
DON'T PANIC, YOU FOOL! WE STILL HAVEN'T FAILED!
TAKE HIM! HE'LL SERVE US AS A DECOY!
NOW WE KNOW THE SHIELD-SLINGER WILL SOON BE AFTER US!
HAVE TO HURRY... IN CASE HE COMES BACK TOO SOON!
AT THAT VERY MOMENT, A WEARY STEVE ROGERS LEAVES HIS CAR IN THE GARAGE BELOW---
PERHAPS I'VE BEEN TOO TOUGH, WITH RICK!
YET, ONE MISTAKE COULD MEAN HIS LIFE!
I'LL HAVE ANOTHER TALK WITH HIM IN THE MORNING--- TRY TO EXPLAIN AGAIN---!
SOMEONE'S COMING!
QUICK! THE CAR'S JUST OUTSIDE!
I THOUGHT I HEARD SOMETHING!
MAYBE HE'S STILL AWAKE!
IS THAT YOU, SON? ARE YOU UP?
WAS THAT A DOOR SLAMMING?
WHAT'S THIS--- ON THE FLOOR?
AN ENVELOPE--- ADDRESSED TO ME!
RICK MUST HAVE OPENED IT!
BUT WHAT'S THIS STRANGE, PUNGENT ODOR??
AND WHERE IS RICK?
FOOTSTEPS--- RUNNING OUTSIDE!
IT CAN ONLY MEAN ONE THING---
THEY'VE CAPTURED RICK JONES!
11

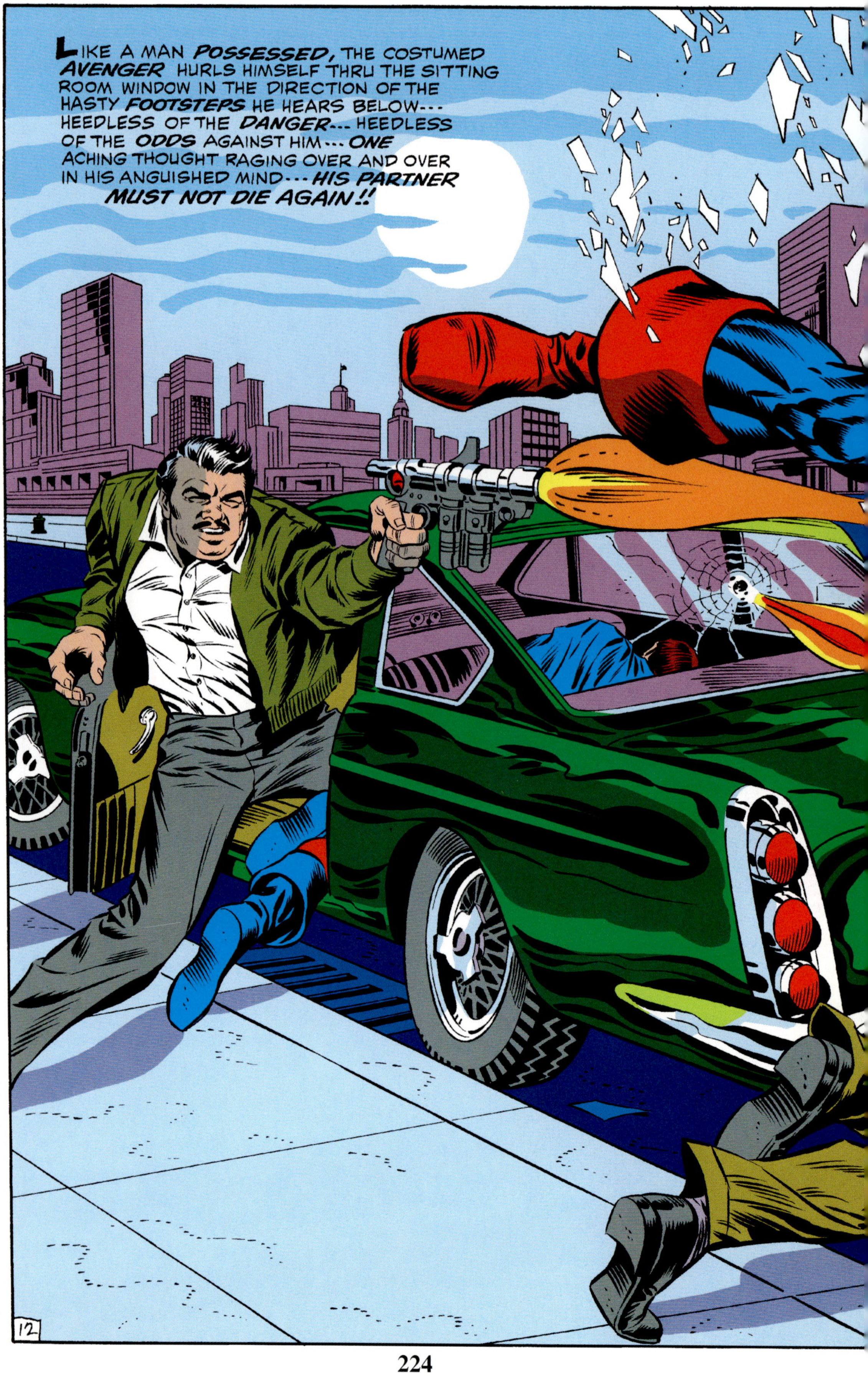
LIKE A MAN POSSESSED, THE COSTUMED AVENGER HURLS HIMSELF THRU THE SITTING ROOM WINDOW IN THE DIRECTION OF THE HASTY FOOTSTEPS HE HEARS BELOW--- HEEDLESS OF THE DANGER--- HEEDLESS OF THE ODDS AGAINST HIM--- ONE ACHING THOUGHT RAGING OVER AND OVER IN HIS ANGUISHED MIND--- HIS PARTNER MUST NOT DIE AGAIN!!
12

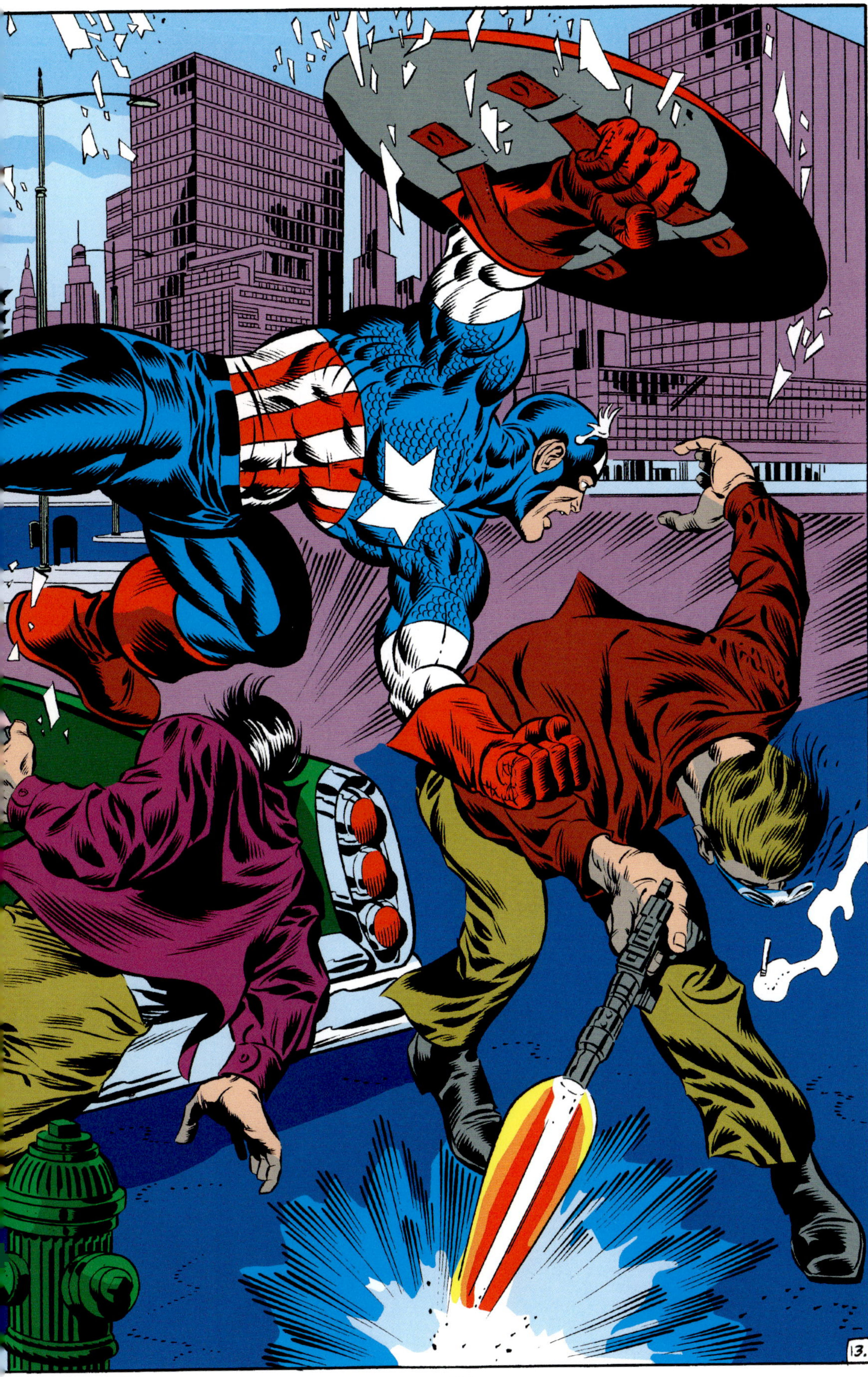
13.

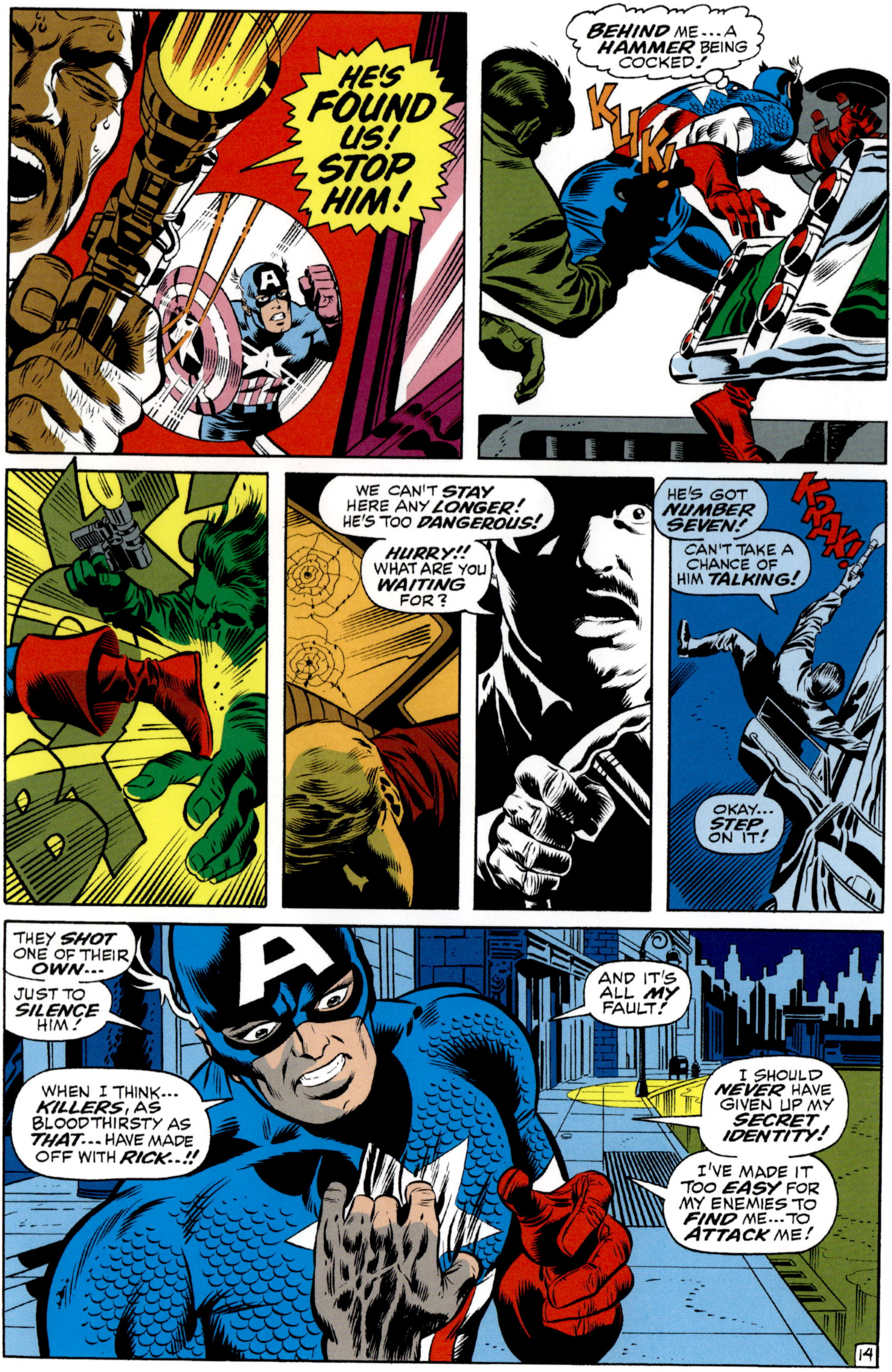
HE'S FOUND US! STOP HIM!
BEHIND ME... A HAMMER BEING COCKED!
KLIK
WE CAN'T STAY HERE ANY LONGER! HE'S TOO DANGEROUS!
HURRY!! WHAT ARE YOU WAITING FOR?
HE'S GOT NUMBER SEVEN!
CAN'T TAKE A CHANCE OF HIM TALKING!
KRAK!
OKAY... STEP ON IT!
THEY SHOT ONE OF THEIR OWN...
JUST TO SILENCE HIM!
WHEN I THINK... KILLERS, AS BLOODTHIRSTY AS THAT... HAVE MADE OFF WITH RICK..!!
AND IT'S ALL MY FAULT!
I SHOULD NEVER HAVE GIVEN UP MY SECRET IDENTITY!
I'VE MADE IT TOO EASY FOR MY ENEMIES TO FIND ME... TO ATTACK ME!
14

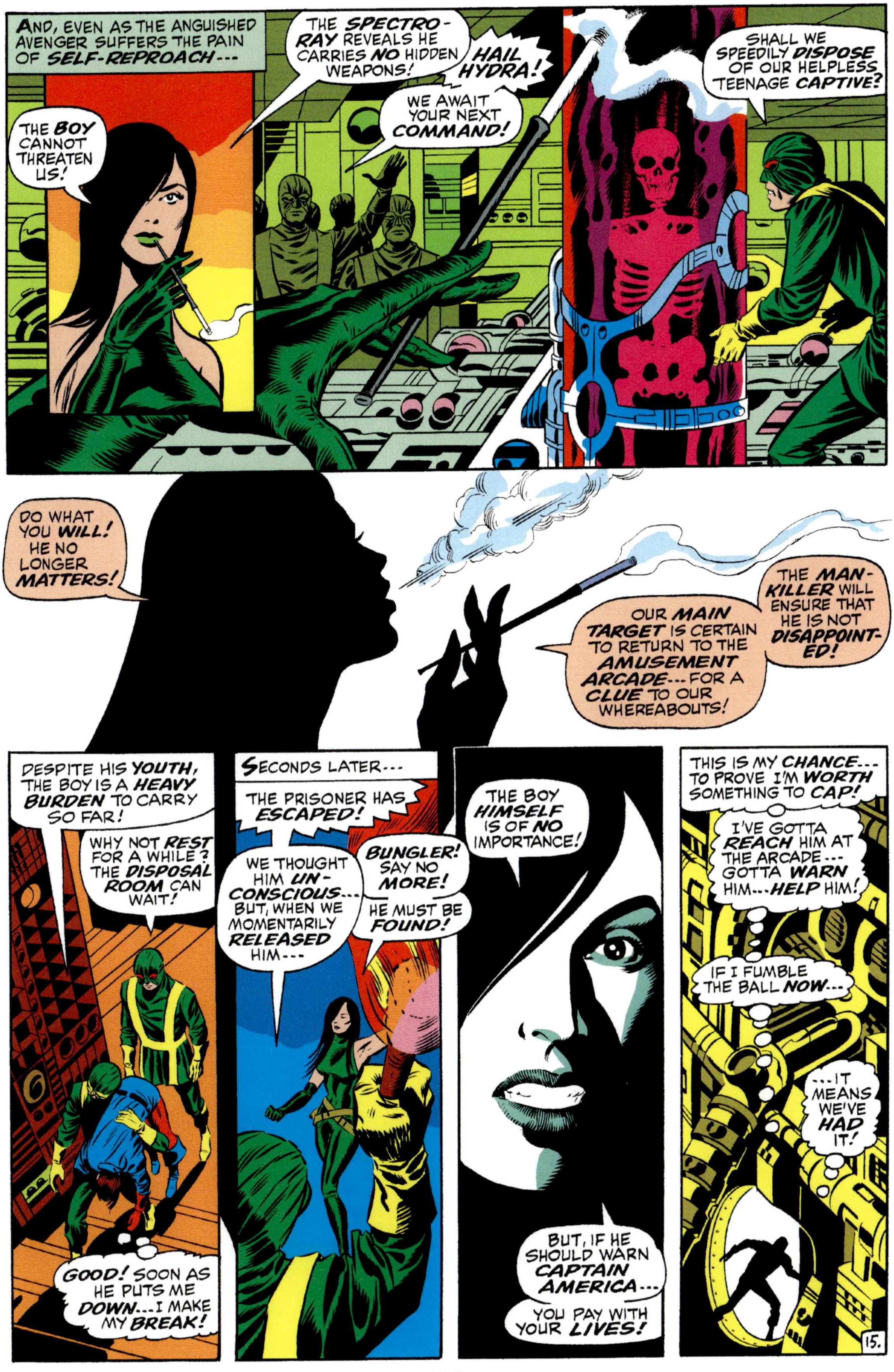

AND, EVEN AS THE ANGUISHED AVENGER SUFFERS THE PAIN OF SELF-REPROACH---
THE BOY CANNOT THREATEN US!
THE SPECTRO-RAY REVEALS HE CARRIES NO HIDDEN WEAPONS!
HAIL HYDRA!
WE AWAIT YOUR NEXT COMMAND!
SHALL WE SPEEDILY DISPOSE OF OUR HELPLESS TEENAGE CAPTIVE?
DO WHAT YOU WILL! HE NO LONGER MATTERS!
OUR MAIN TARGET IS CERTAIN TO RETURN TO THE AMUSEMENT ARCADE--- FOR A CLUE TO OUR WHEREABOUTS!
THE MAN-KILLER WILL ENSURE THAT HE IS NOT DISAPPOINTED!
DESPITE HIS YOUTH, THE BOY IS A HEAVY BURDEN TO CARRY SO FAR!
WHY NOT REST FOR A WHILE? THE DISPOSAL ROOM CAN WAIT!
GOOD! SOON AS HE PUTS ME DOWN--- I MAKE MY BREAK!
SECONDS LATER---
THE PRISONER HAS ESCAPED!
WE THOUGHT HIM UN-CONSCIOUS--- BUT, WHEN WE MOMENTARILY RELEASED HIM---
BUNGLER! SAY NO MORE!
HE MUST BE FOUND!
THE BOY HIMSELF IS OF NO IMPORTANCE!
BUT, IF HE SHOULD WARN CAPTAIN AMERICA---
YOU PAY WITH YOUR LIVES!
THIS IS MY CHANCE--- TO PROVE I'M WORTH SOMETHING TO CAP!
I'VE GOTTA REACH HIM AT THE ARCADE--- GOTTA WARN HIM--- HELP HIM!
IF I FUMBLE THE BALL NOW---
---IT MEANS WE'VE HAD IT!
15.

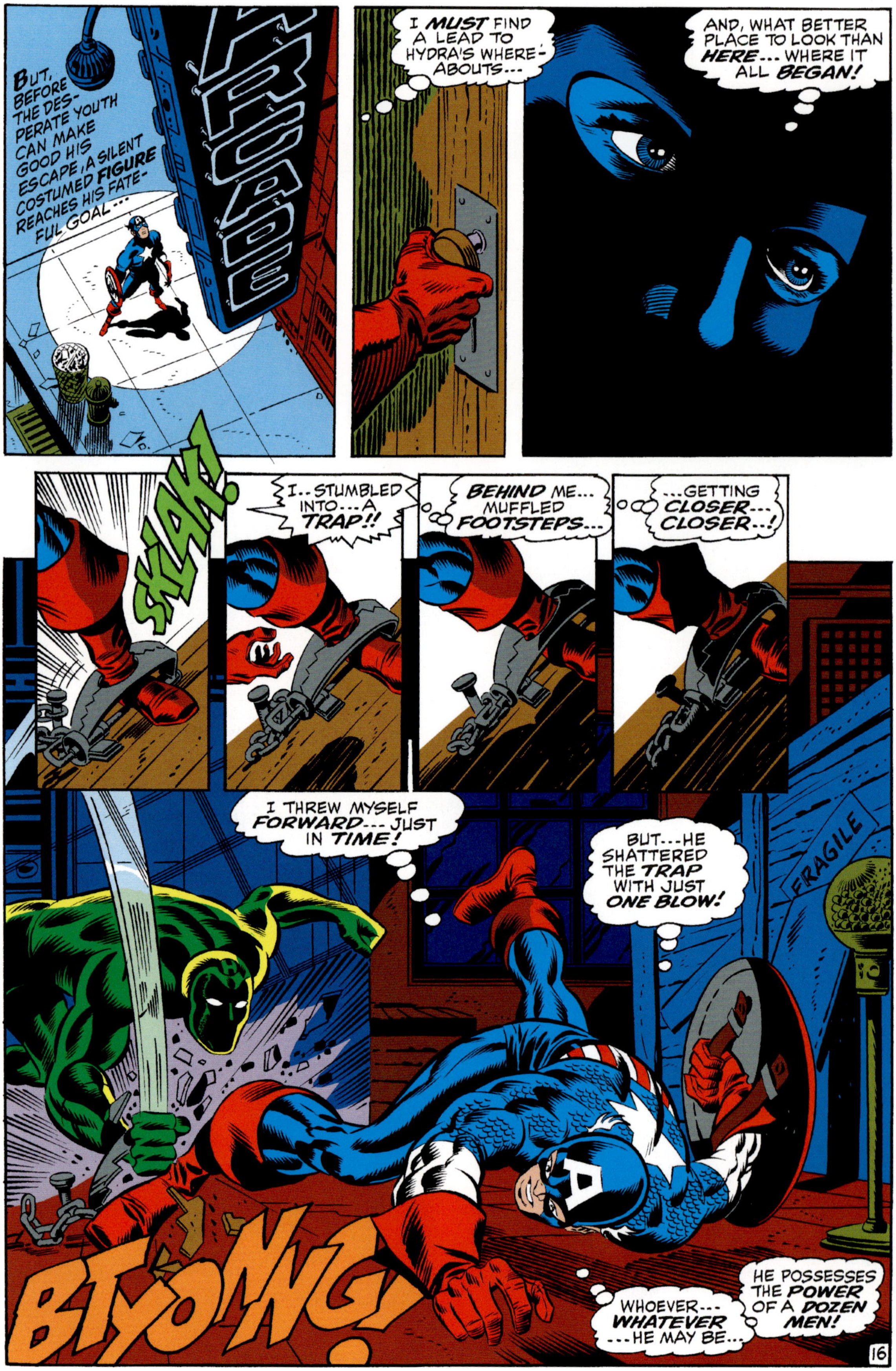
BUT, BEFORE THE DESPERATE YOUTH CAN MAKE GOOD HIS ESCAPE, A SILENT COSTUMED FIGURE REACHES HIS FATEFUL GOAL...
ARCADE
I MUST FIND A LEAD TO HYDRA'S WHEREABOUTS...
AND, WHAT BETTER PLACE TO LOOK THAN HERE... WHERE IT ALL BEGAN!
SKLAK!
I.. STUMBLED INTO... A TRAP!!
BEHIND ME... MUFFLED FOOTSTEPS...
...GETTING CLOSER... CLOSER..!
I THREW MYSELF FORWARD--- JUST IN TIME!
BUT---HE SHATTERED THE TRAP WITH JUST ONE BLOW!
FRAGILE
BTYONNG!
WHOEVER--- WHATEVER ---HE MAY BE...
HE POSSESSES THE POWER OF A DOZEN MEN!
16

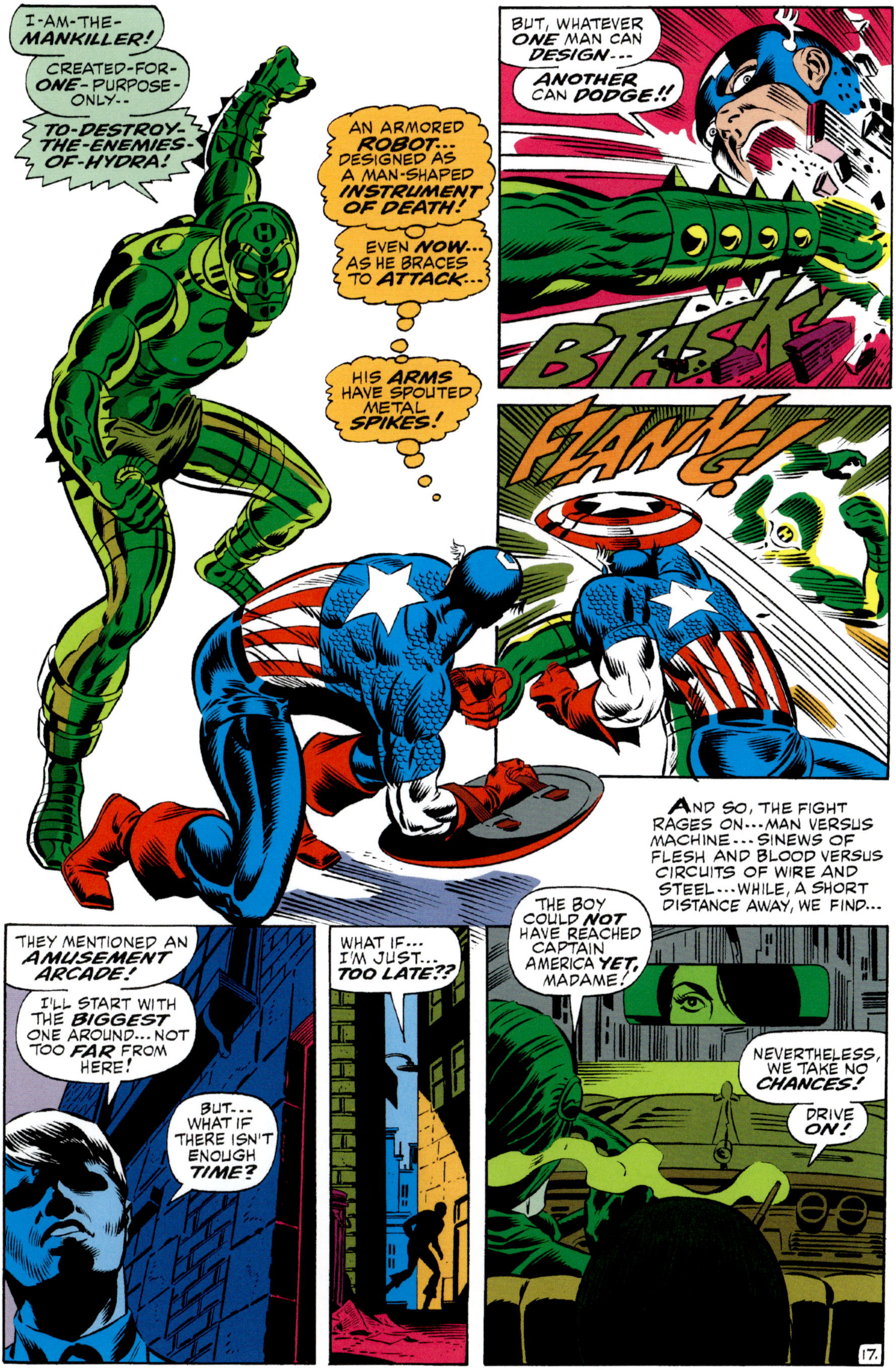

I-AM-THE-MANKILLER!
CREATED-FOR-ONE-PURPOSE-ONLY--
TO-DESTROY-THE-ENEMIES-OF-HYDRA!
AN ARMORED ROBOT... DESIGNED AS A MAN-SHAPED INSTRUMENT OF DEATH!
EVEN NOW... AS HE BRACES TO ATTACK...
HIS ARMS HAVE SPOUTED METAL SPIKES!
BUT, WHATEVER ONE MAN CAN DESIGN---
ANOTHER CAN DODGE!!
BTASK!
FLANNG!
AND SO, THE FIGHT RAGES ON---MAN VERSUS MACHINE---SINEWS OF FLESH AND BLOOD VERSUS CIRCUITS OF WIRE AND STEEL---WHILE, A SHORT DISTANCE AWAY, WE FIND...
THEY MENTIONED AN AMUSEMENT ARCADE!
I'LL START WITH THE BIGGEST ONE AROUND... NOT TOO FAR FROM HERE!
BUT--- WHAT IF THERE ISN'T ENOUGH TIME?
WHAT IF... I'M JUST... TOO LATE??
THE BOY COULD NOT HAVE REACHED CAPTAIN AMERICA YET, MADAME!
NEVERTHELESS, WE TAKE NO CHANCES!
DRIVE ON!
17.

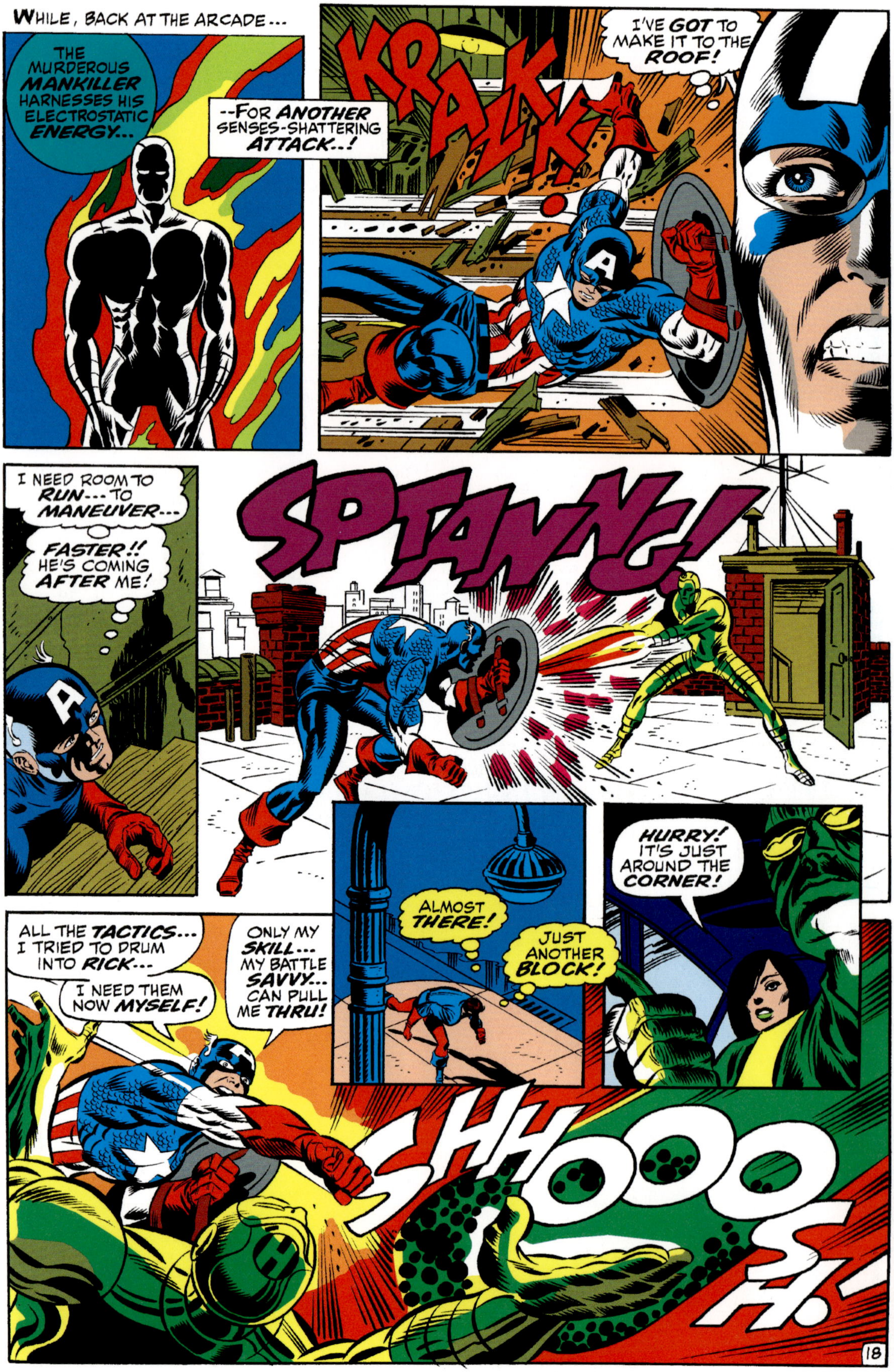

WHILE, BACK AT THE ARCADE...
THE MURDEROUS MANKILLER HARNESSES HIS ELECTROSTATIC ENERGY...
--FOR ANOTHER SENSES-SHATTERING ATTACK..!
KRAKK!
I'VE GOT TO MAKE IT TO THE ROOF!
I NEED ROOM TO RUN--- TO MANEUVER---
FASTER!! HE'S COMING AFTER ME!
SPTANNG!
ALL THE TACTICS... I TRIED TO DRUM INTO RICK---
I NEED THEM NOW MYSELF!
ONLY MY SKILL... MY BATTLE SAVVY... CAN PULL ME THRU!
ALMOST THERE!
JUST ANOTHER BLOCK!
HURRY! IT'S JUST AROUND THE CORNER!
SHHOOOSH!
18

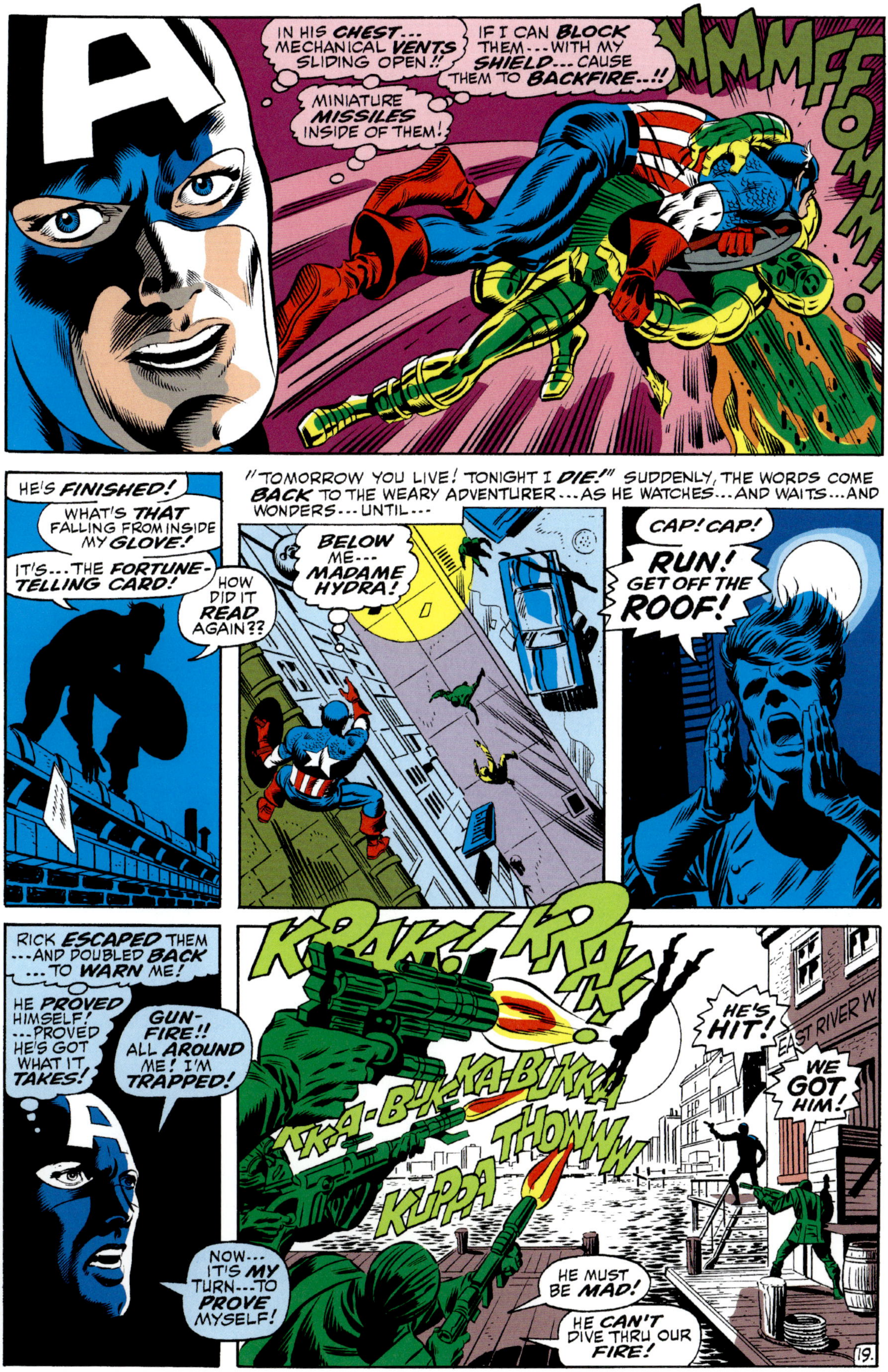
IN HIS CHEST... MECHANICAL VENTS SLIDING OPEN!!
MINIATURE MISSILES INSIDE OF THEM!
IF I CAN BLOCK THEM---WITH MY SHIELD... CAUSE THEM TO BACKFIRE...!!
MMMFFOMMM!
HE'S FINISHED!
WHAT'S THAT FALLING FROM INSIDE MY GLOVE!
IT'S...THE FORTUNE-TELLING CARD!
HOW DID IT READ AGAIN??
"TOMORROW YOU LIVE! TONIGHT I DIE!" SUDDENLY, THE WORDS COME BACK TO THE WEARY ADVENTURER... AS HE WATCHES...AND WAITS...AND WONDERS...UNTIL...
BELOW ME--- MADAME HYDRA!
CAP! CAP!
RUN! GET OFF THE ROOF!
RICK ESCAPED THEM ...AND DOUBLED BACK ...TO WARN ME!
HE PROVED HIMSELF! ...PROVED HE'S GOT WHAT IT TAKES!
GUN-FIRE!! ALL AROUND ME! I'M TRAPPED!
NOW... IT'S MY TURN...TO PROVE MYSELF!
KRAK! KRAK!
KA-BUKKA-BUKKA
KUPPA THOWWW
HE'S HIT!
EAST RIVER W
WE GOT HIM!
HE MUST BE MAD!
HE CAN'T DIVE THRU OUR FIRE!
19.

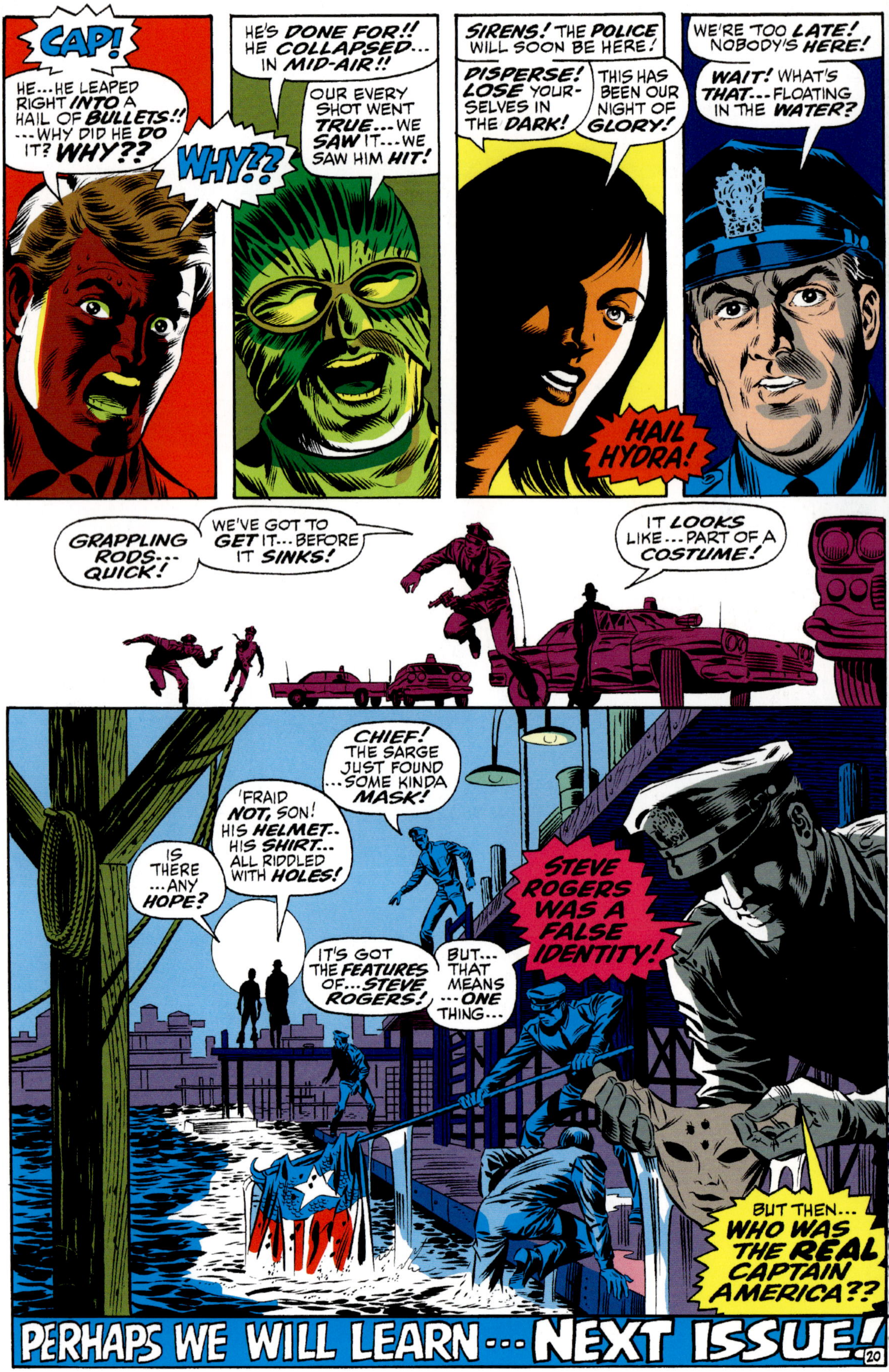
CAP!
HE...HE LEAPED RIGHT INTO A HAIL OF BULLETS!! ...WHY DID HE DO IT? WHY??
WHY??
HE'S DONE FOR!! HE COLLAPSED... IN MID-AIR!!
OUR EVERY SHOT WENT TRUE... WE SAW IT...WE SAW HIM HIT!
SIRENS! THE POLICE WILL SOON BE HERE!
DISPERSE! LOSE YOURSELVES IN THE DARK!
THIS HAS BEEN OUR NIGHT OF GLORY!
HAIL HYDRA!
WE'RE TOO LATE! NOBODY'S HERE!
WAIT! WHAT'S THAT...FLOATING IN THE WATER?
GRAPPLING RODS... QUICK!
WE'VE GOT TO GET IT... BEFORE IT SINKS!
IT LOOKS LIKE...PART OF A COSTUME!
CHIEF! THE SARGE JUST FOUND ...SOME KINDA MASK!
'FRAID NOT, SON! HIS HELMET.. HIS SHIRT... ALL RIDDLED WITH HOLES!
IS THERE ...ANY HOPE?
IT'S GOT THE FEATURES OF...STEVE ROGERS!
BUT... THAT MEANS ...ONE THING...
STEVE ROGERS WAS A FALSE IDENTITY!
BUT THEN... WHO WAS THE REAL CAPTAIN AMERICA??
PERHAPS WE WILL LEARN...NEXT ISSUE!
20

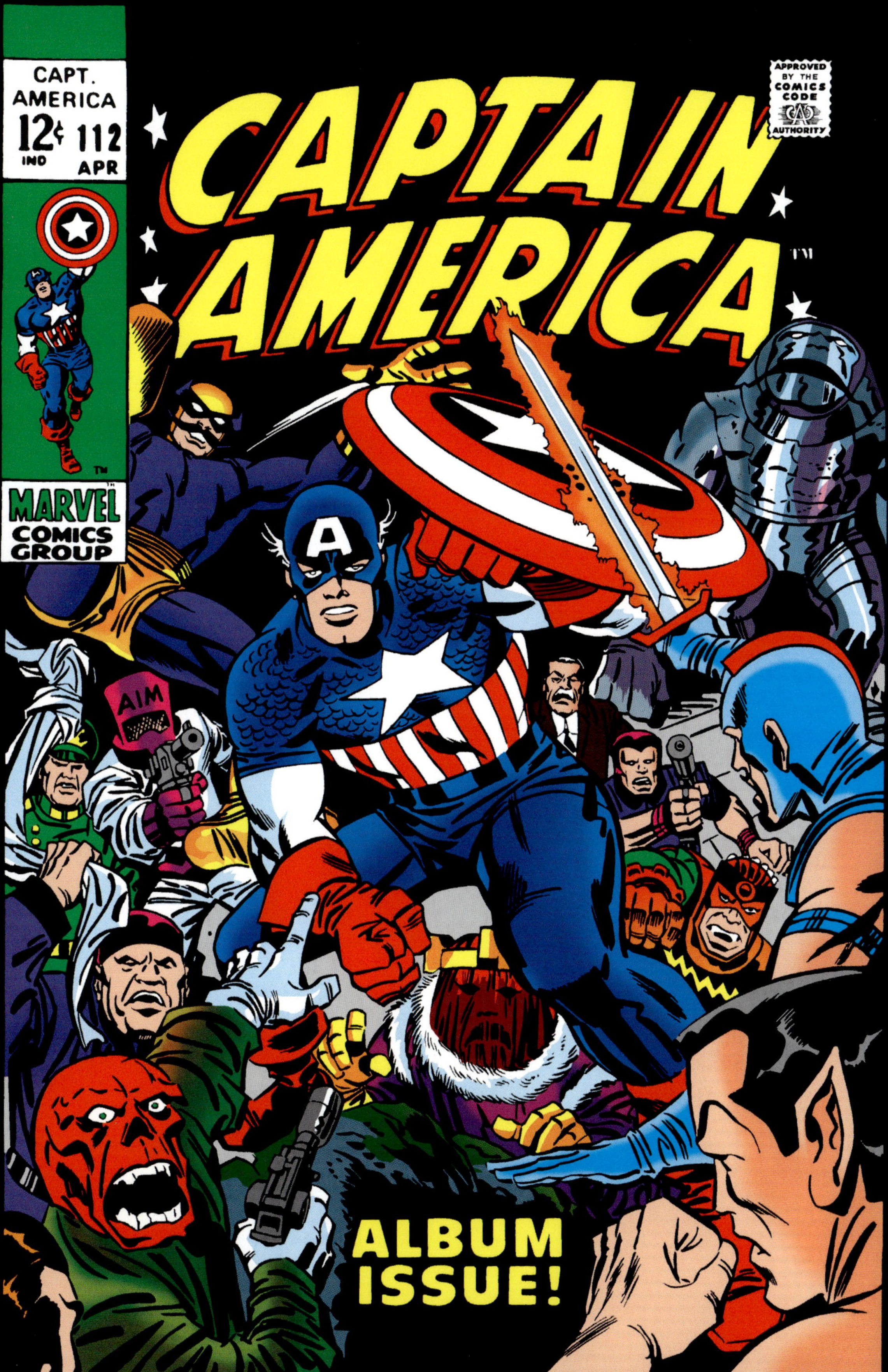

CAPT. AMERICA
12¢ 112
IND APR
MARVEL COMICS GROUP
APPROVED BY THE COMICS CODE AUTHORITY
CAPTAIN AMERICA
AIM
ALBUM ISSUE!

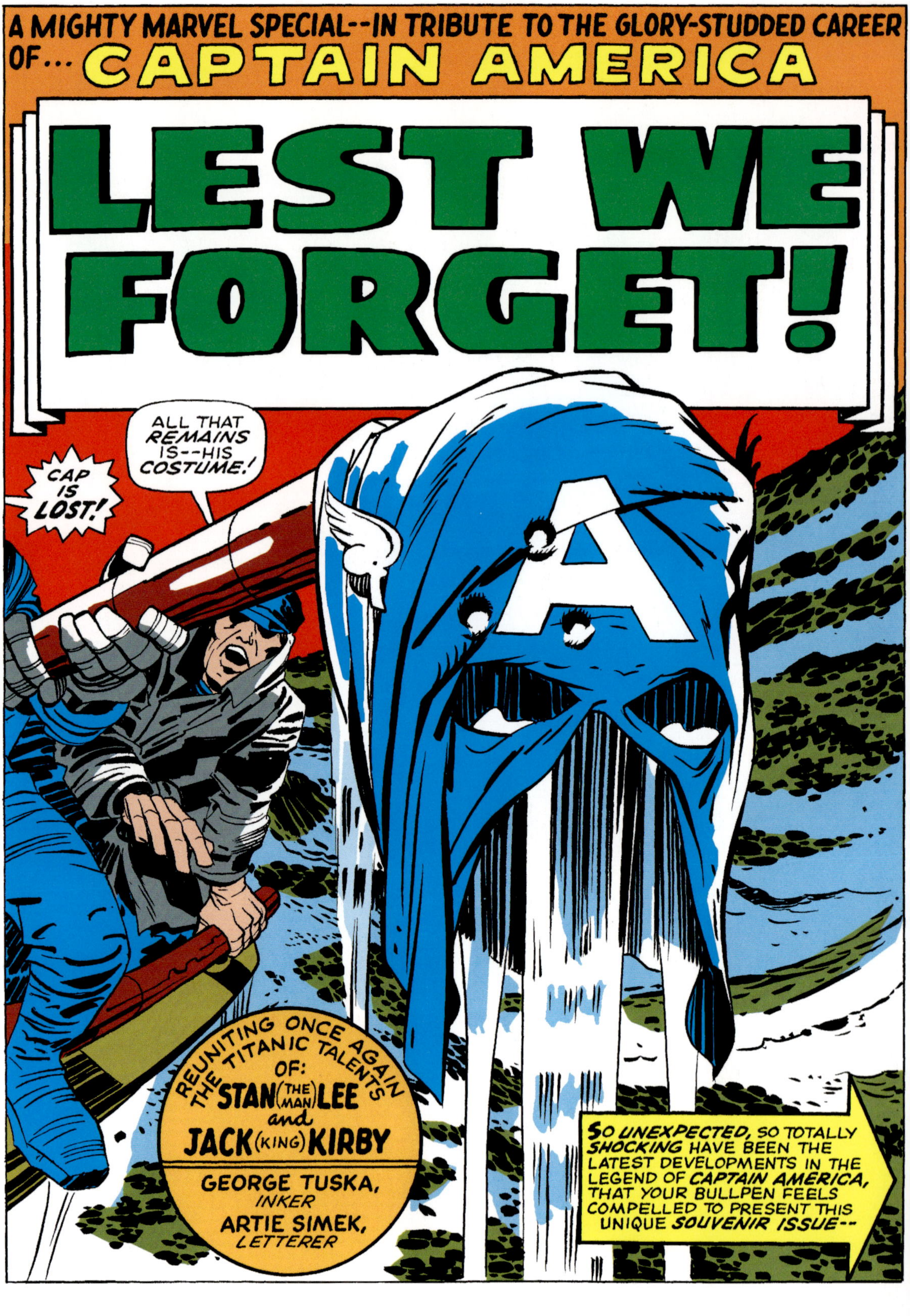
A MIGHTY MARVEL SPECIAL--IN TRIBUTE TO THE GLORY-STUDDED CAREER OF... CAPTAIN AMERICA
LEST WE FORGET!
CAP IS LOST!
ALL THAT REMAINS IS--HIS COSTUME!
REUNITING ONCE AGAIN THE TITANIC TALENTS OF: STAN (THE MAN) LEE and JACK (KING) KIRBY
GEORGE TUSKA, INKER
ARTIE SIMEK, LETTERER
SO UNEXPECTED, SO TOTALLY SHOCKING HAVE BEEN THE LATEST DEVELOPMENTS IN THE LEGEND OF CAPTAIN AMERICA, THAT YOUR BULLPEN FEELS COMPELLED TO PRESENT THIS UNIQUE SOUVENIR ISSUE--

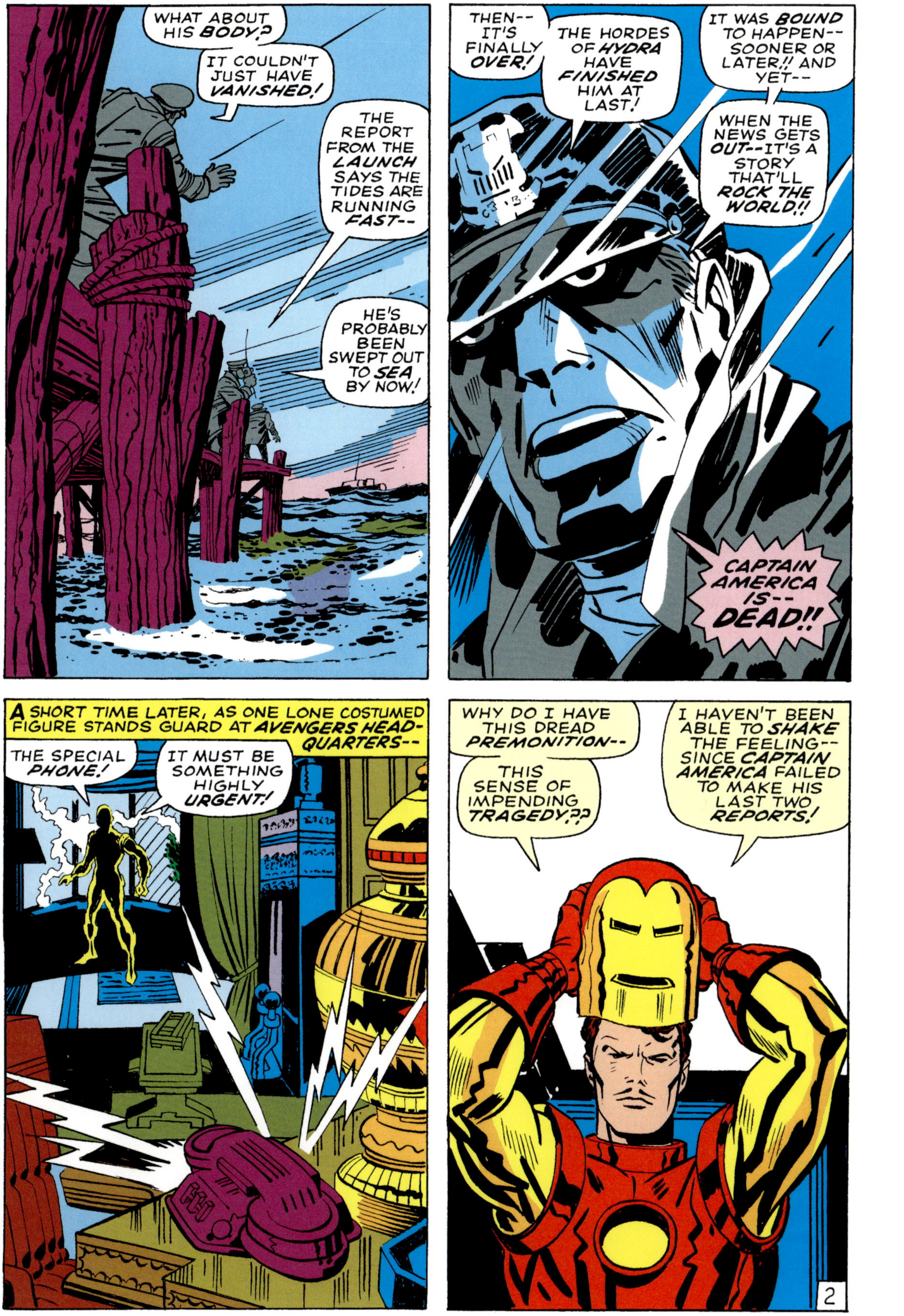
WHAT ABOUT HIS BODY?
IT COULDN'T JUST HAVE VANISHED!
THE REPORT FROM THE LAUNCH SAYS THE TIDES ARE RUNNING FAST--
HE'S PROBABLY BEEN SWEPT OUT TO SEA BY NOW!
THEN-- IT'S FINALLY OVER!
THE HORDES OF HYDRA HAVE FINISHED HIM AT LAST!
IT WAS BOUND TO HAPPEN-- SOONER OR LATER!! AND YET--
WHEN THE NEWS GETS OUT--IT'S A STORY THAT'LL ROCK THE WORLD!!
CAPTAIN AMERICA IS--DEAD!!
A SHORT TIME LATER, AS ONE LONE COSTUMED FIGURE STANDS GUARD AT AVENGERS HEAD-QUARTERS--
THE SPECIAL PHONE!
IT MUST BE SOMETHING HIGHLY URGENT!
WHY DO I HAVE THIS DREAD PREMONITION--
THIS SENSE OF IMPENDING TRAGEDY???
I HAVEN'T BEEN ABLE TO SHAKE THE FEELING-- SINCE CAPTAIN AMERICA FAILED TO MAKE HIS LAST TWO REPORTS!
2

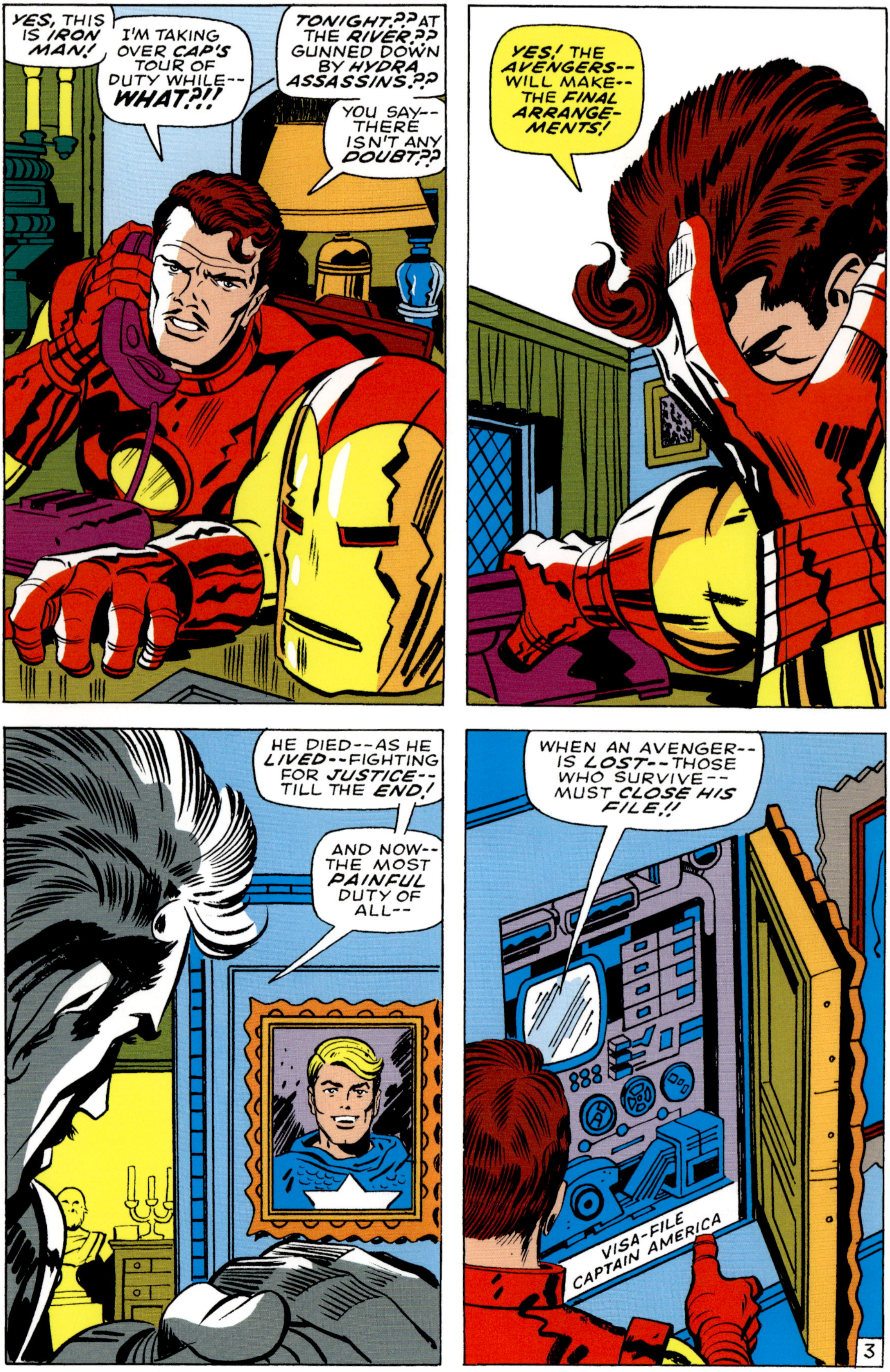
YES, THIS IS IRON MAN!
I'M TAKING OVER CAP'S TOUR OF DUTY WHILE-- WHAT?!!
TONIGHT?? AT THE RIVER?? GUNNED DOWN BY HYDRA ASSASSINS??
YOU SAY-- THERE ISN'T ANY DOUBT??
YES! THE AVENGERS-- WILL MAKE-- THE FINAL ARRANGE-MENTS!
HE DIED--AS HE LIVED--FIGHTING FOR JUSTICE-- TILL THE END!
AND NOW-- THE MOST PAINFUL DUTY OF ALL--
WHEN AN AVENGER-- IS LOST--THOSE WHO SURVIVE-- MUST CLOSE HIS FILE!!
VISA-FILE CAPTAIN AMERICA
3

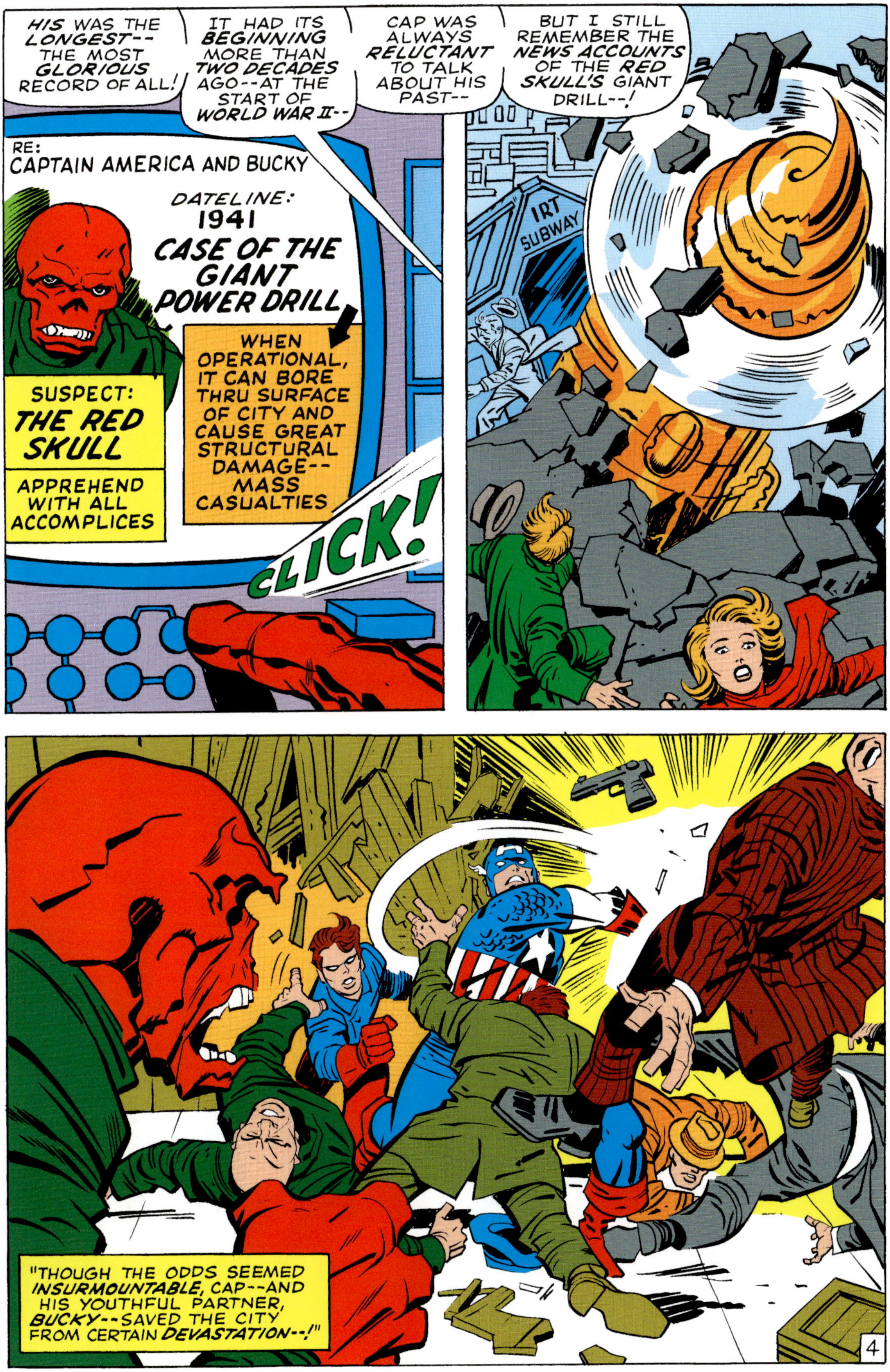
HIS WAS THE LONGEST-- THE MOST GLORIOUS RECORD OF ALL!
IT HAD ITS BEGINNING MORE THAN TWO DECADES AGO--AT THE START OF WORLD WAR II--
CAP WAS ALWAYS RELUCTANT TO TALK ABOUT HIS PAST--
BUT I STILL REMEMBER THE NEWS ACCOUNTS OF THE RED SKULL'S GIANT DRILL--!
RE: CAPTAIN AMERICA AND BUCKY
DATELINE: 1941
CASE OF THE GIANT POWER DRILL
SUSPECT: THE RED SKULL
APPREHEND WITH ALL ACCOMPLICES
WHEN OPERATIONAL, IT CAN BORE THRU SURFACE OF CITY AND CAUSE GREAT STRUCTURAL DAMAGE--MASS CASUALTIES
CLICK!
IRT SUBWAY
"THOUGH THE ODDS SEEMED INSURMOUNTABLE, CAP--AND HIS YOUTHFUL PARTNER, BUCKY--SAVED THE CITY FROM CERTAIN DEVASTATION--!"
4

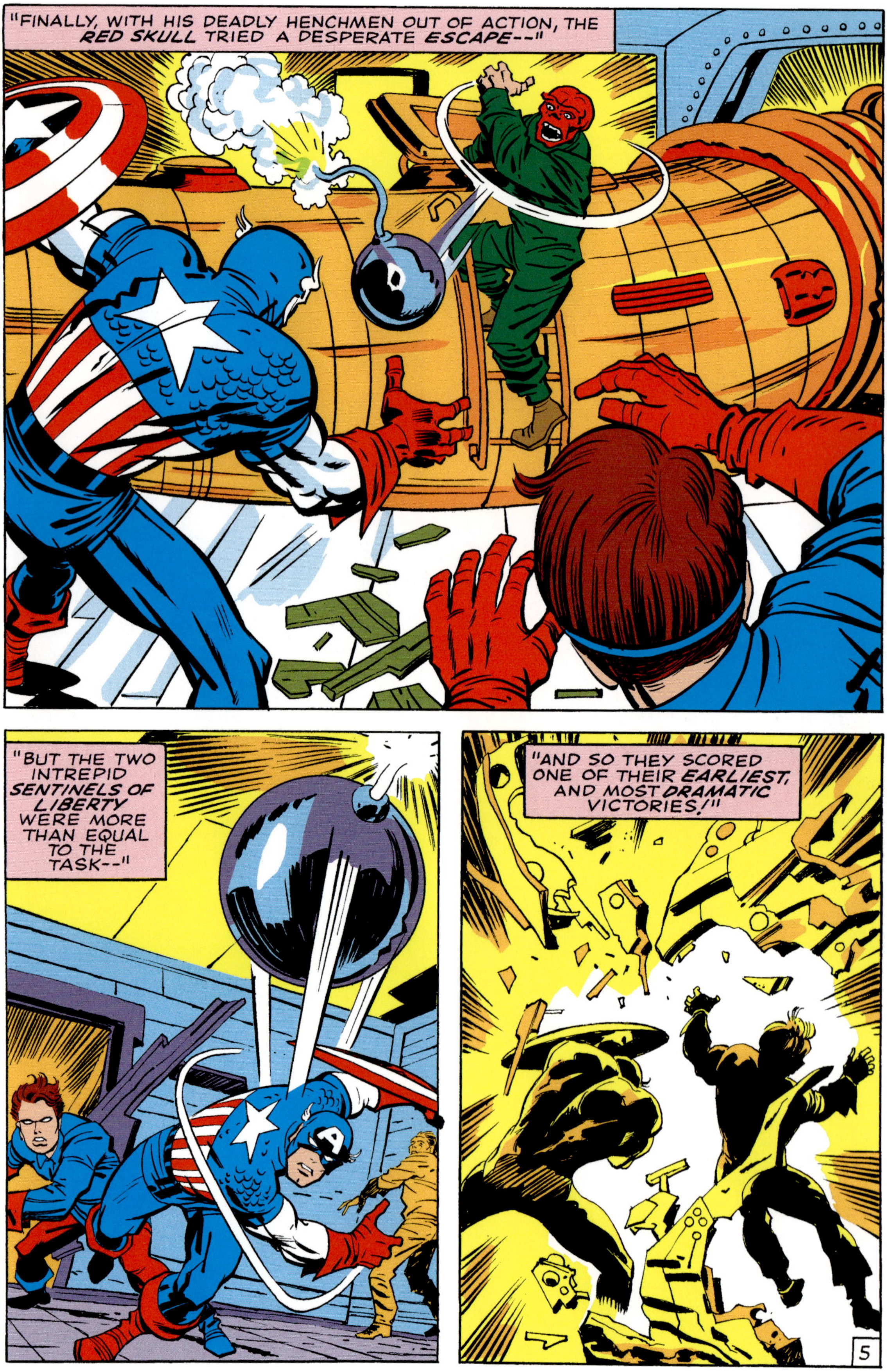
"FINALLY, WITH HIS DEADLY HENCHMEN OUT OF ACTION, THE RED SKULL TRIED A DESPERATE ESCAPE--"
"BUT THE TWO INTREPID SENTINELS OF LIBERTY WERE MORE THAN EQUAL TO THE TASK--"
"AND SO THEY SCORED ONE OF THEIR EARLIEST, AND MOST DRAMATIC VICTORIES!"
5

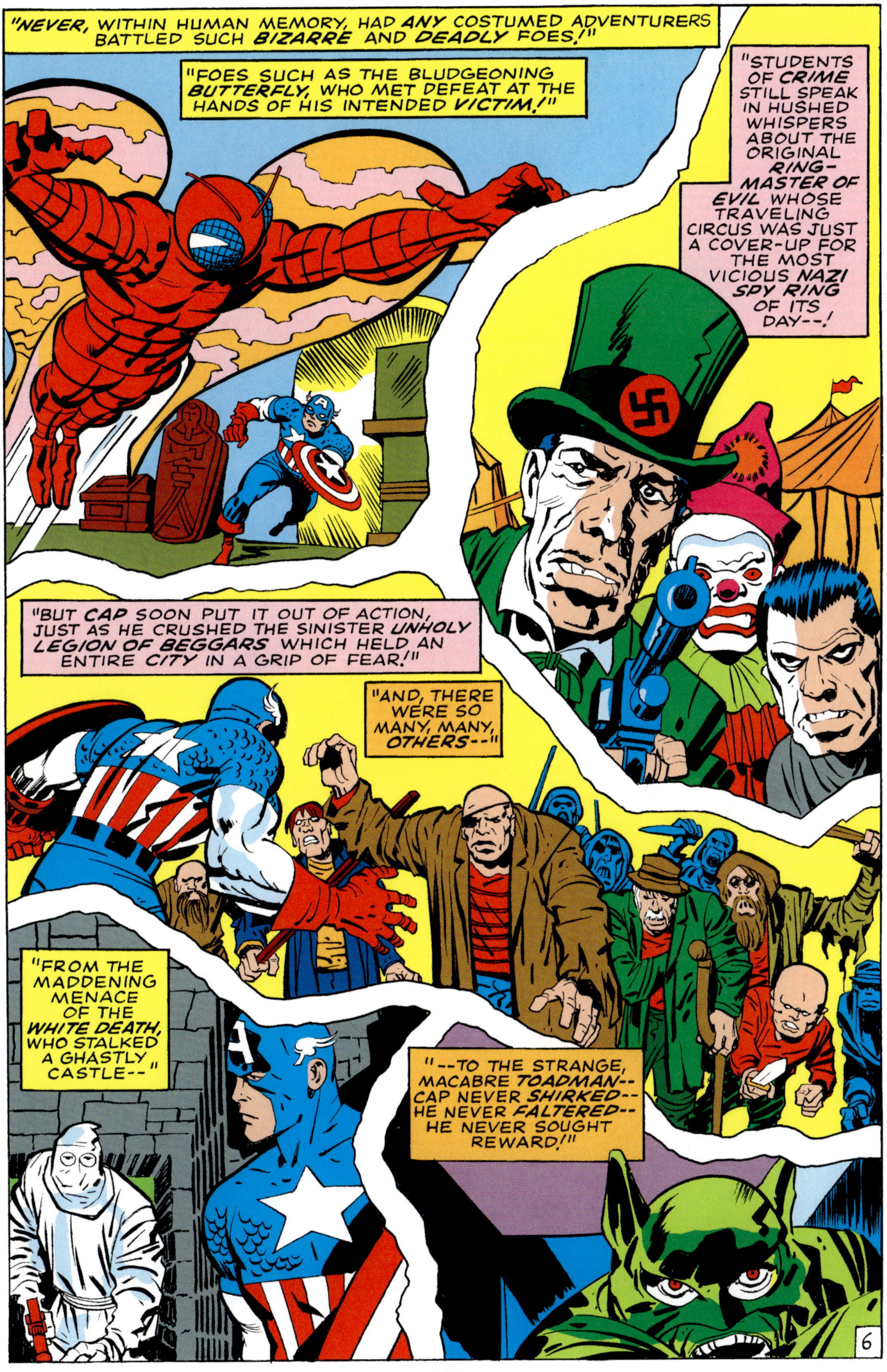
"NEVER, WITHIN HUMAN MEMORY, HAD ANY COSTUMED ADVENTURERS BATTLED SUCH BIZARRE AND DEADLY FOES!"
"FOES SUCH AS THE BLUDGEONING BUTTERFLY, WHO MET DEFEAT AT THE HANDS OF HIS INTENDED VICTIM!"
"STUDENTS OF CRIME STILL SPEAK IN HUSHED WHISPERS ABOUT THE ORIGINAL RING-MASTER OF EVIL WHOSE TRAVELING CIRCUS WAS JUST A COVER-UP FOR THE MOST VICIOUS NAZI SPY RING OF ITS DAY--!
"BUT CAP SOON PUT IT OUT OF ACTION, JUST AS HE CRUSHED THE SINISTER UNHOLY LEGION OF BEGGARS WHICH HELD AN ENTIRE CITY IN A GRIP OF FEAR!"
"AND, THERE WERE SO MANY, MANY, OTHERS--"
"FROM THE MADDENING MENACE OF THE WHITE DEATH, WHO STALKED A GHASTLY CASTLE--"
"--TO THE STRANGE, MACABRE TOADMAN--CAP NEVER SHIRKED--HE NEVER FALTERED--HE NEVER SOUGHT REWARD!"
6

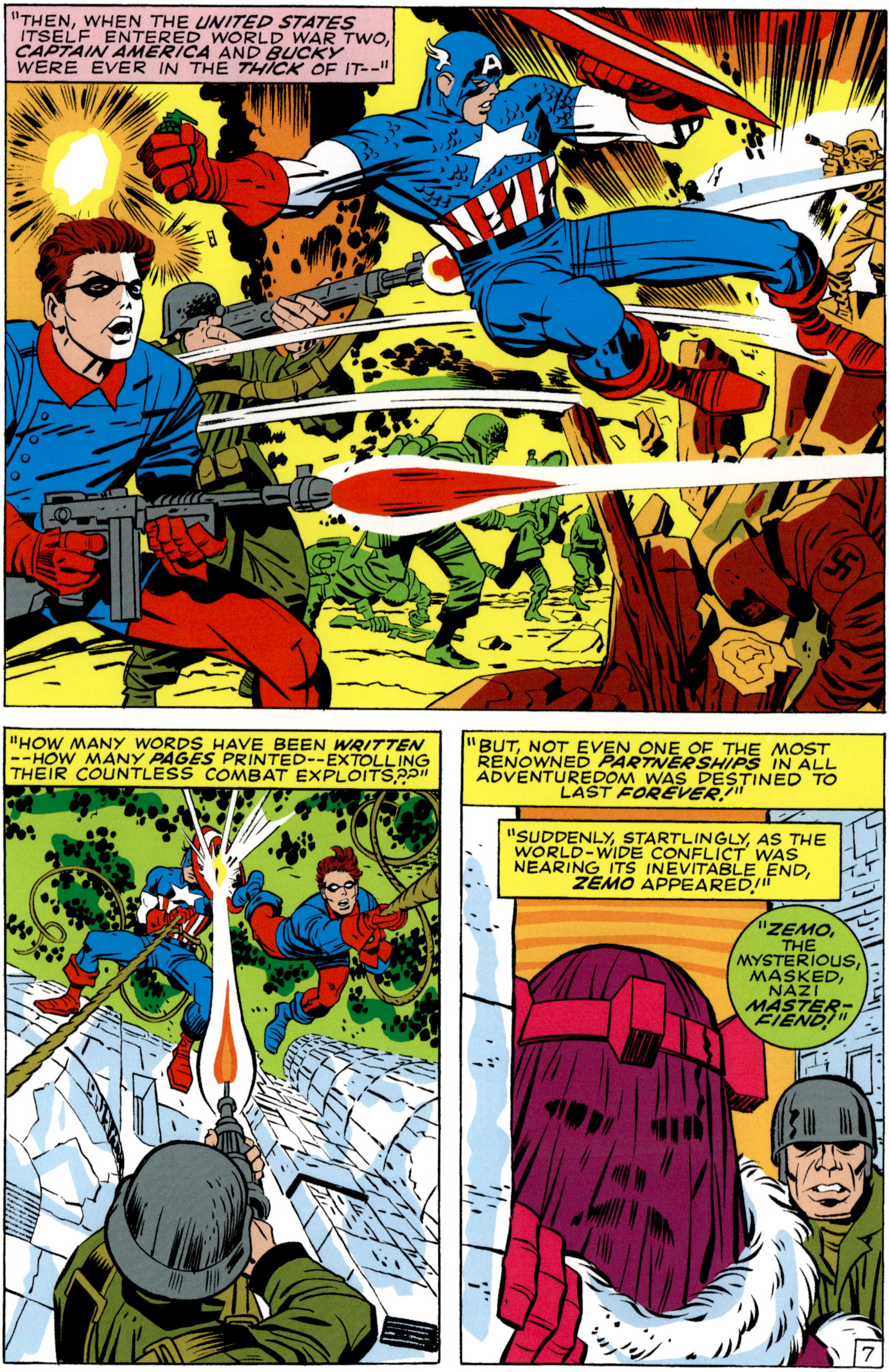
"THEN, WHEN THE UNITED STATES ITSELF ENTERED WORLD WAR TWO, CAPTAIN AMERICA AND BUCKY WERE EVER IN THE THICK OF IT--"
"HOW MANY WORDS HAVE BEEN WRITTEN --HOW MANY PAGES PRINTED--EXTOLLING THEIR COUNTLESS COMBAT EXPLOITS??"
"BUT, NOT EVEN ONE OF THE MOST RENOWNED PARTNERSHIPS IN ALL ADVENTUREDOM WAS DESTINED TO LAST FOREVER!"
"SUDDENLY, STARTLINGLY, AS THE WORLD-WIDE CONFLICT WAS NEARING ITS INEVITABLE END, ZEMO APPEARED!"
"ZEMO, THE MYSTERIOUS, MASKED, NAZI MASTER-FIEND!"
7

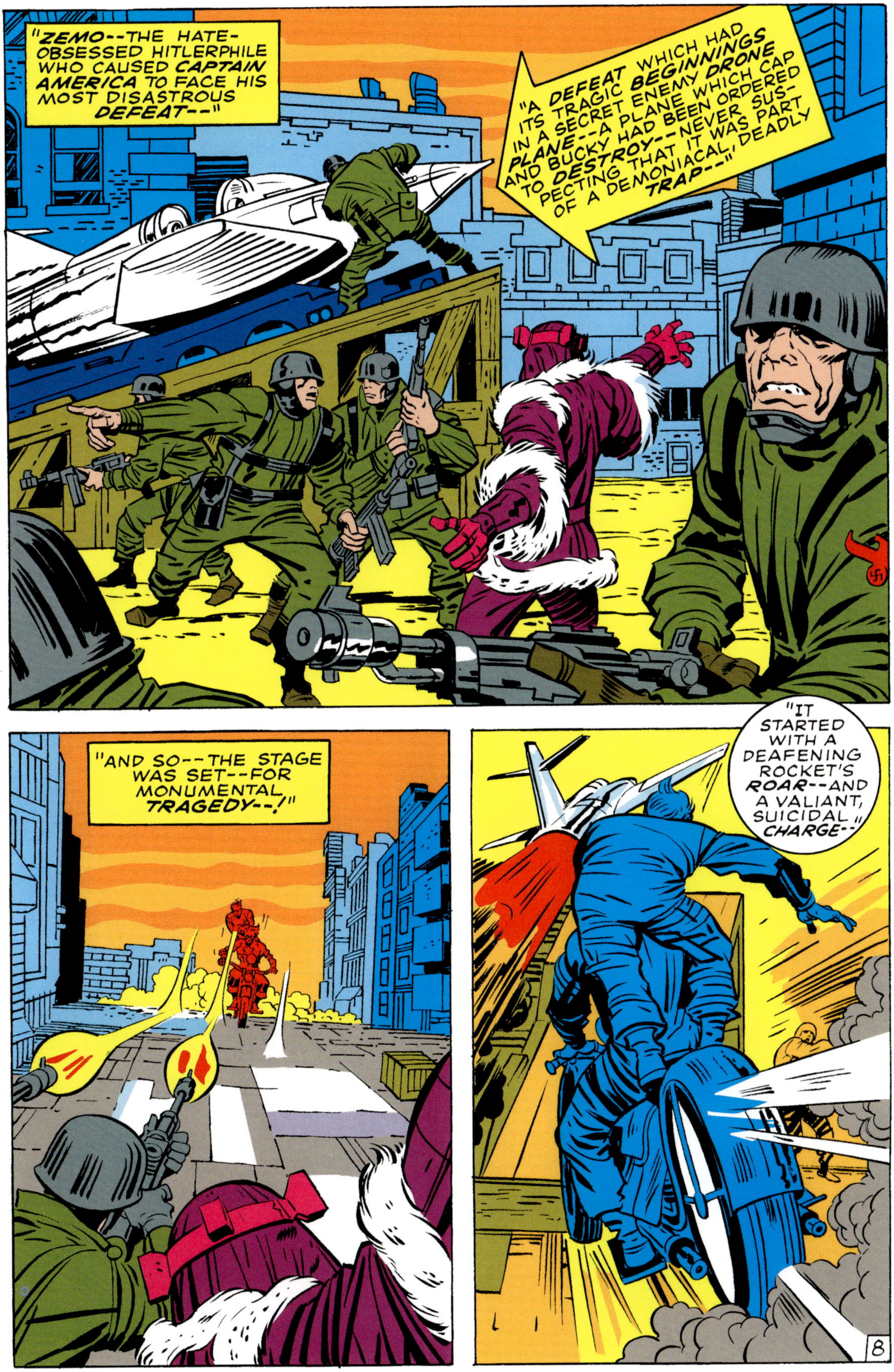

"ZEMO--THE HATE-OBSESSED HITLERPHILE WHO CAUSED CAPTAIN AMERICA TO FACE HIS MOST DISASTROUS DEFEAT--"
"A DEFEAT WHICH HAD ITS TRAGIC BEGINNINGS IN A SECRET ENEMY DRONE PLANE--A PLANE WHICH CAP AND BUCKY HAD BEEN ORDERED TO DESTROY--NEVER SUSPECTING THAT IT WAS PART OF A DEMONIACAL, DEADLY TRAP--"
"AND SO--THE STAGE WAS SET--FOR MONUMENTAL TRAGEDY--!"
"IT STARTED WITH A DEAFENING ROCKET'S ROAR--AND A VALIANT, SUICIDAL CHARGE--"
8

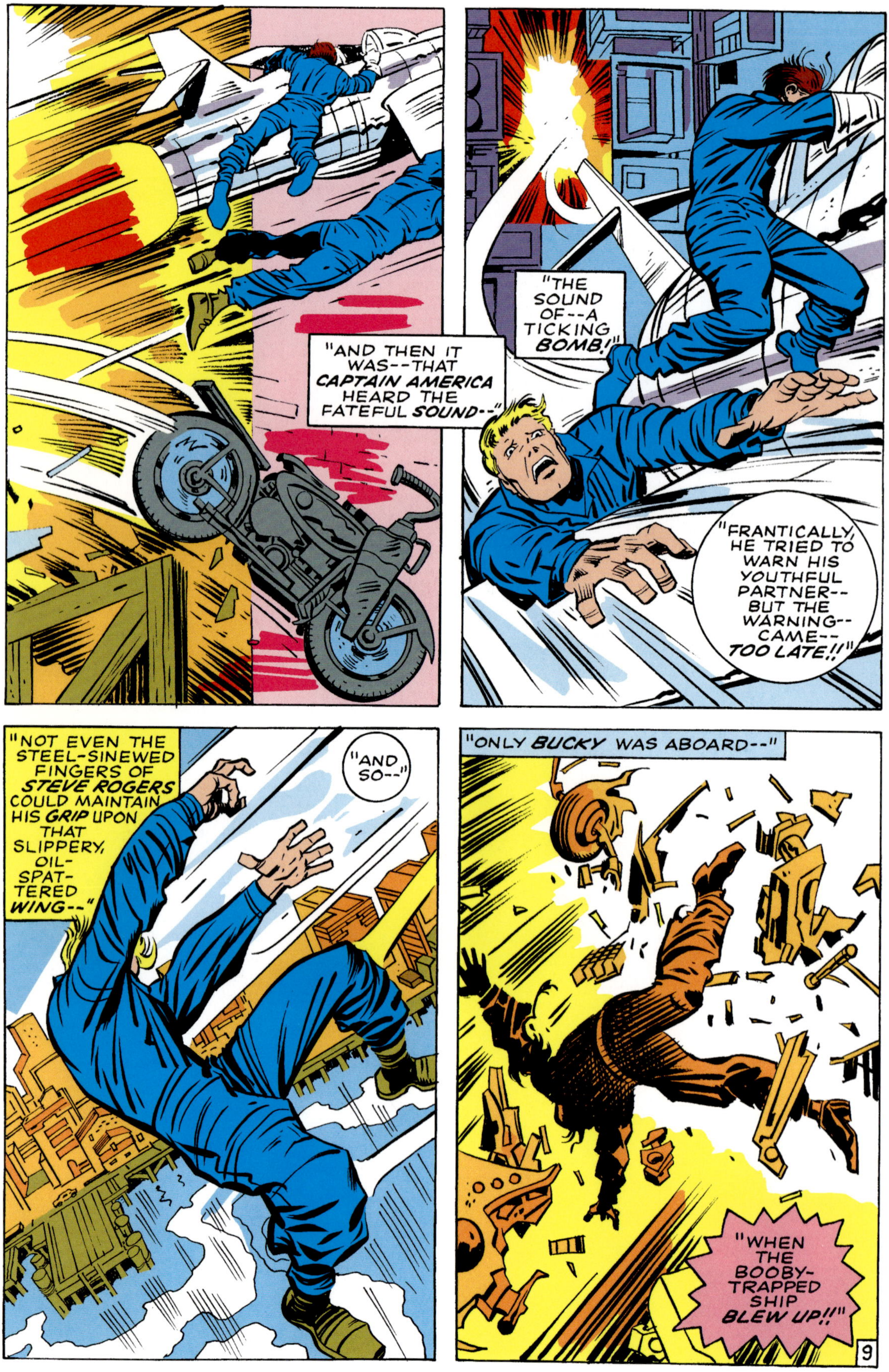
"AND THEN IT WAS--THAT CAPTAIN AMERICA HEARD THE FATEFUL SOUND--"
"THE SOUND OF--A TICKING BOMB!"
"FRANTICALLY, HE TRIED TO WARN HIS YOUTHFUL PARTNER--BUT THE WARNING--CAME--TOO LATE!!"
"NOT EVEN THE STEEL-SINEWED FINGERS OF STEVE ROGERS COULD MAINTAIN HIS GRIP UPON THAT SLIPPERY, OIL-SPATTERED WING--"
"AND SO--"
"ONLY BUCKY WAS ABOARD--"
"WHEN THE BOOBY-TRAPPED SHIP BLEW UP!!"
9

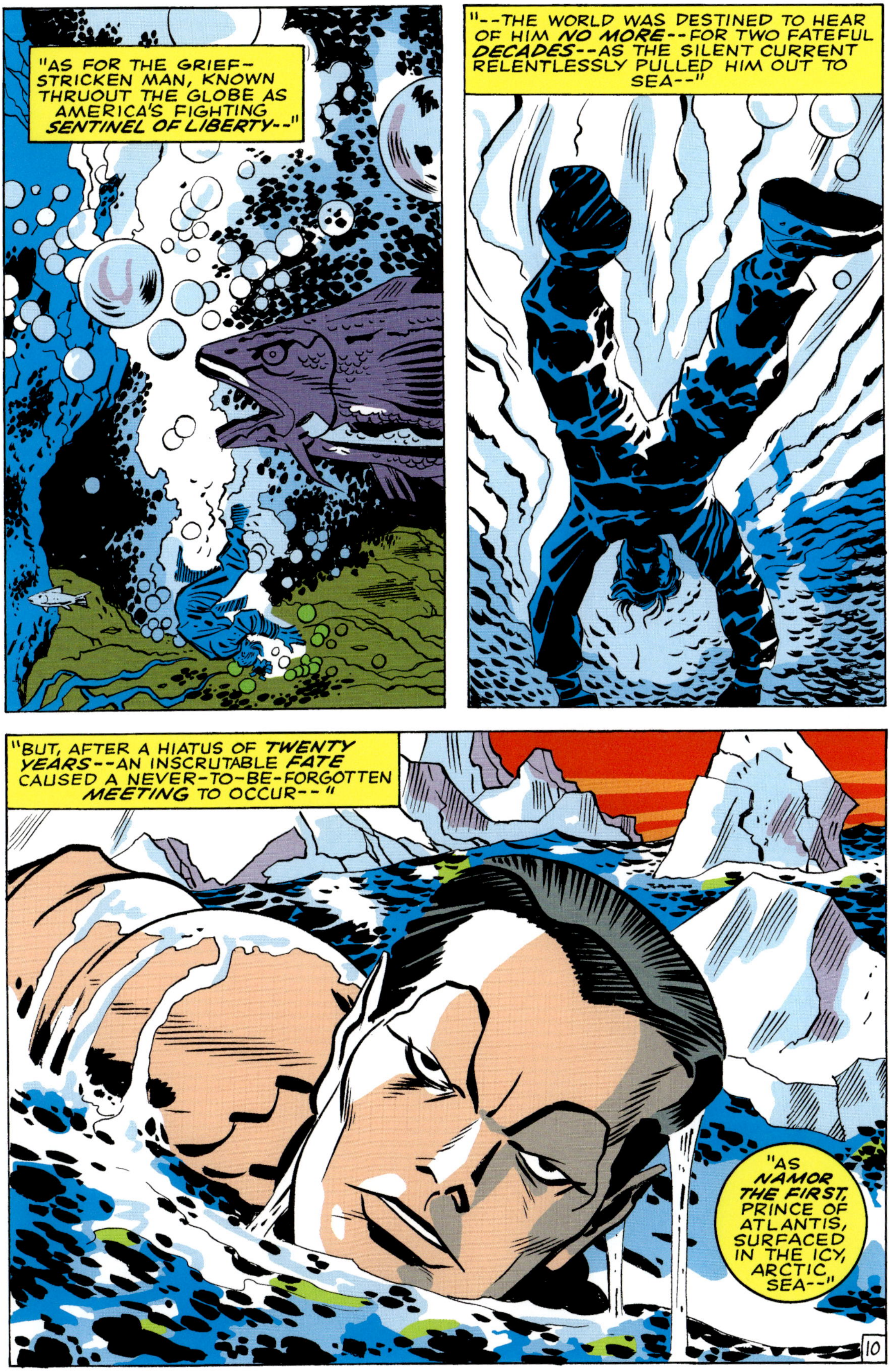
"AS FOR THE GRIEF-STRICKEN MAN, KNOWN THRUOUT THE GLOBE AS AMERICA'S FIGHTING SENTINEL OF LIBERTY--"
"--THE WORLD WAS DESTINED TO HEAR OF HIM NO MORE--FOR TWO FATEFUL DECADES--AS THE SILENT CURRENT RELENTLESSLY PULLED HIM OUT TO SEA--"
"BUT, AFTER A HIATUS OF TWENTY YEARS--AN INSCRUTABLE FATE CAUSED A NEVER-TO-BE-FORGOTTEN MEETING TO OCCUR--"
"AS NAMOR THE FIRST, PRINCE OF ATLANTIS, SURFACED IN THE ICY, ARCTIC SEA--"
10

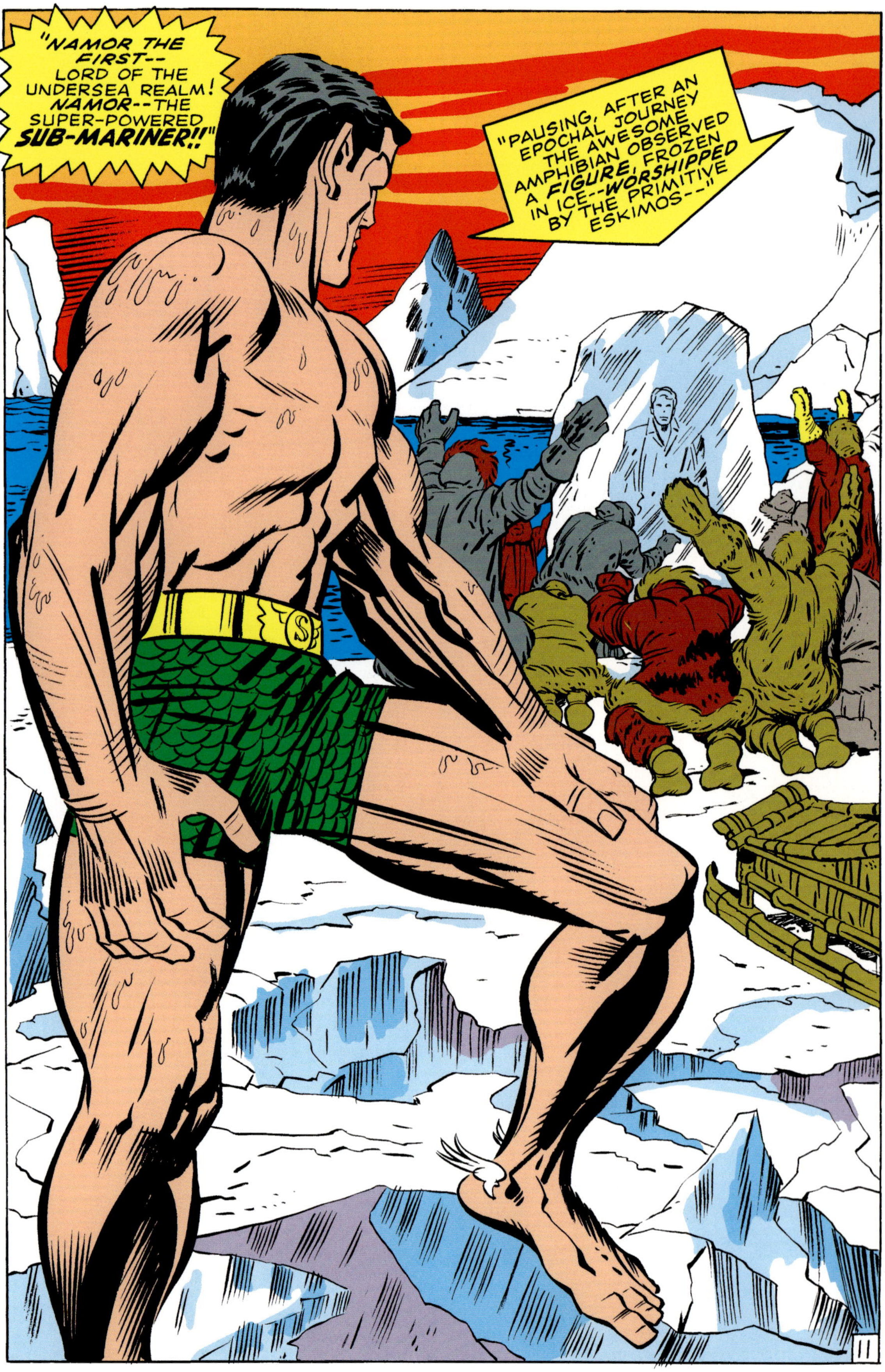
"NAMOR THE FIRST-- LORD OF THE UNDERSEA REALM! NAMOR--THE SUPER-POWERED SUB-MARINER!!"
"PAUSING, AFTER AN EPOCHAL JOURNEY THE AWESOME AMPHIBIAN OBSERVED A FIGURE, FROZEN IN ICE--WORSHIPPED BY THE PRIMITIVE ESKIMOS--"
11

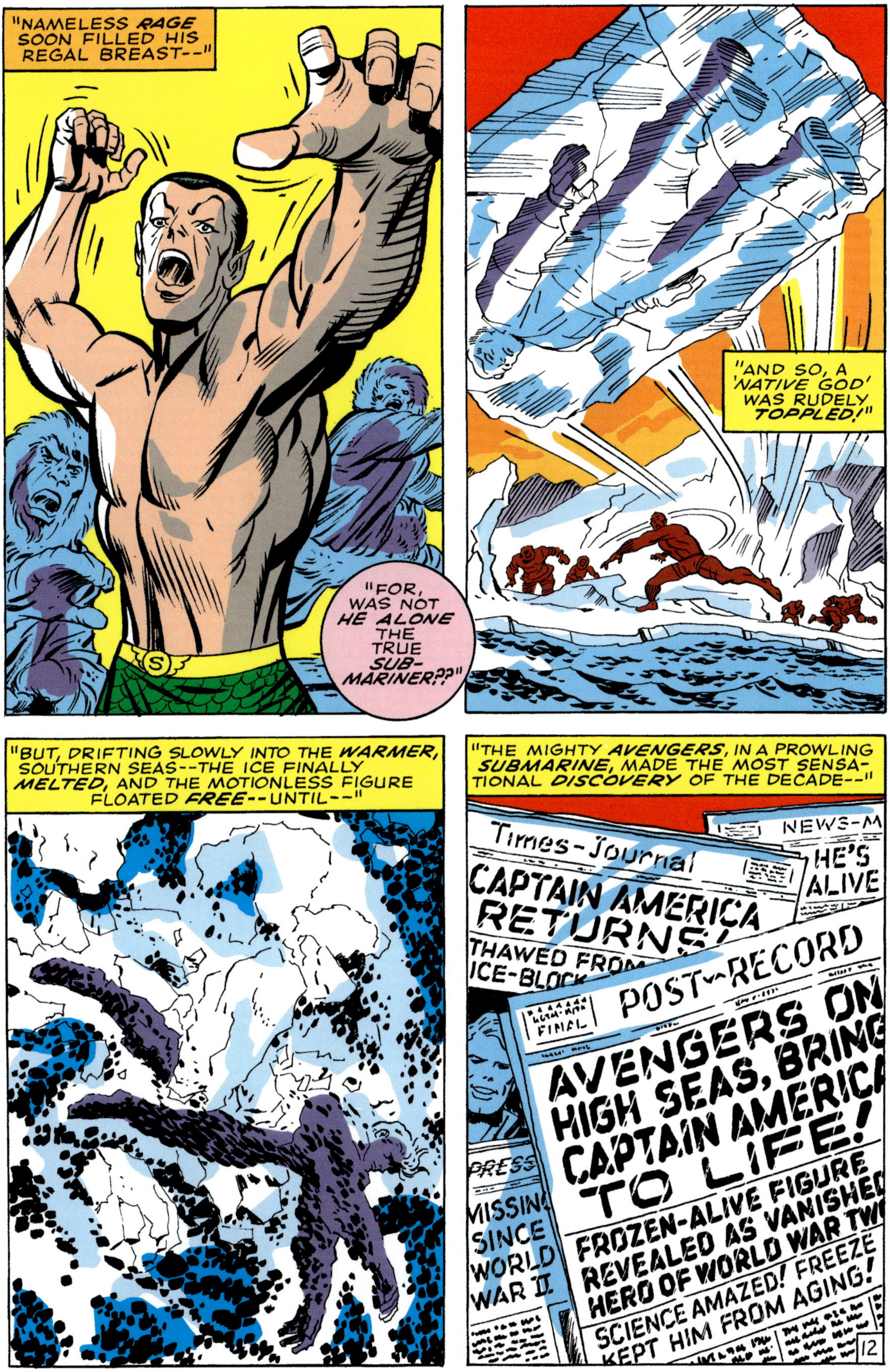
"NAMELESS *RAGE* SOON FILLED HIS REGAL BREAST--"
"FOR, WAS NOT *HE ALONE* THE TRUE *SUB-MARINER??*"
"AND SO, A *'NATIVE GOD'* WAS RUDELY *TOPPLED!*"
"BUT, DRIFTING SLOWLY INTO THE *WARMER*, SOUTHERN SEAS--THE ICE FINALLY *MELTED*, AND THE MOTIONLESS FIGURE FLOATED *FREE*--UNTIL--"
"THE MIGHTY *AVENGERS*, IN A PROWLING *SUBMARINE*, MADE THE MOST SENSATIONAL *DISCOVERY* OF THE DECADE--"
Times-Journal
CAPTAIN AMERICA RETURNS!
THAWED FROM ICE-BLOCK
NEWS-M
HE'S ALIVE
POST-RECORD
FINAL
AVENGERS ON HIGH SEAS, BRING CAPTAIN AMERICA TO LIFE!
FROZEN-ALIVE FIGURE REVEALED AS VANISHED HERO OF WORLD WAR TWO
SCIENCE AMAZED! FREEZE KEPT HIM FROM AGING!
PRESS
MISSING SINCE WORLD WAR II
12

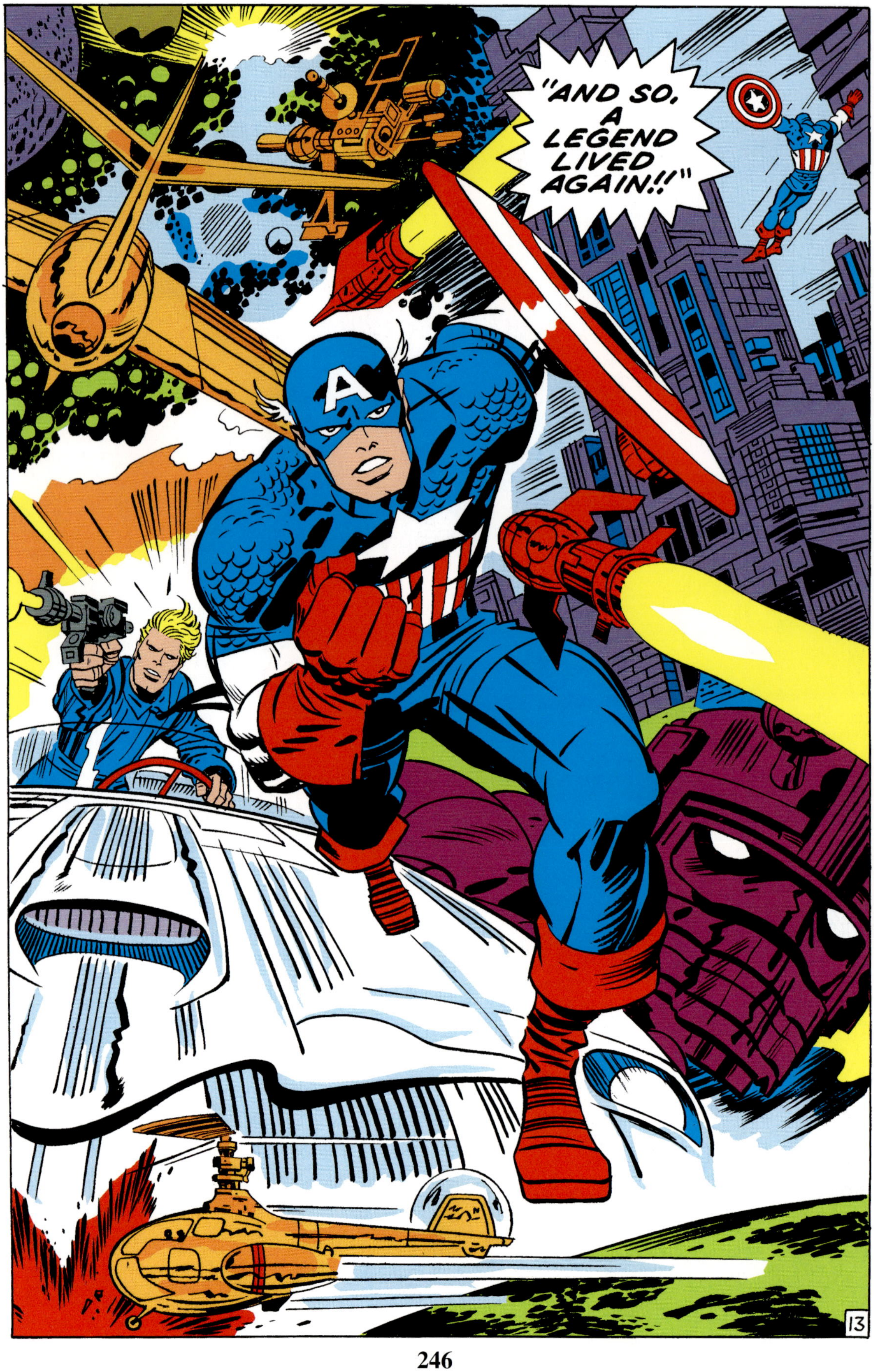
"AND SO, A LEGEND LIVED AGAIN!!"
13

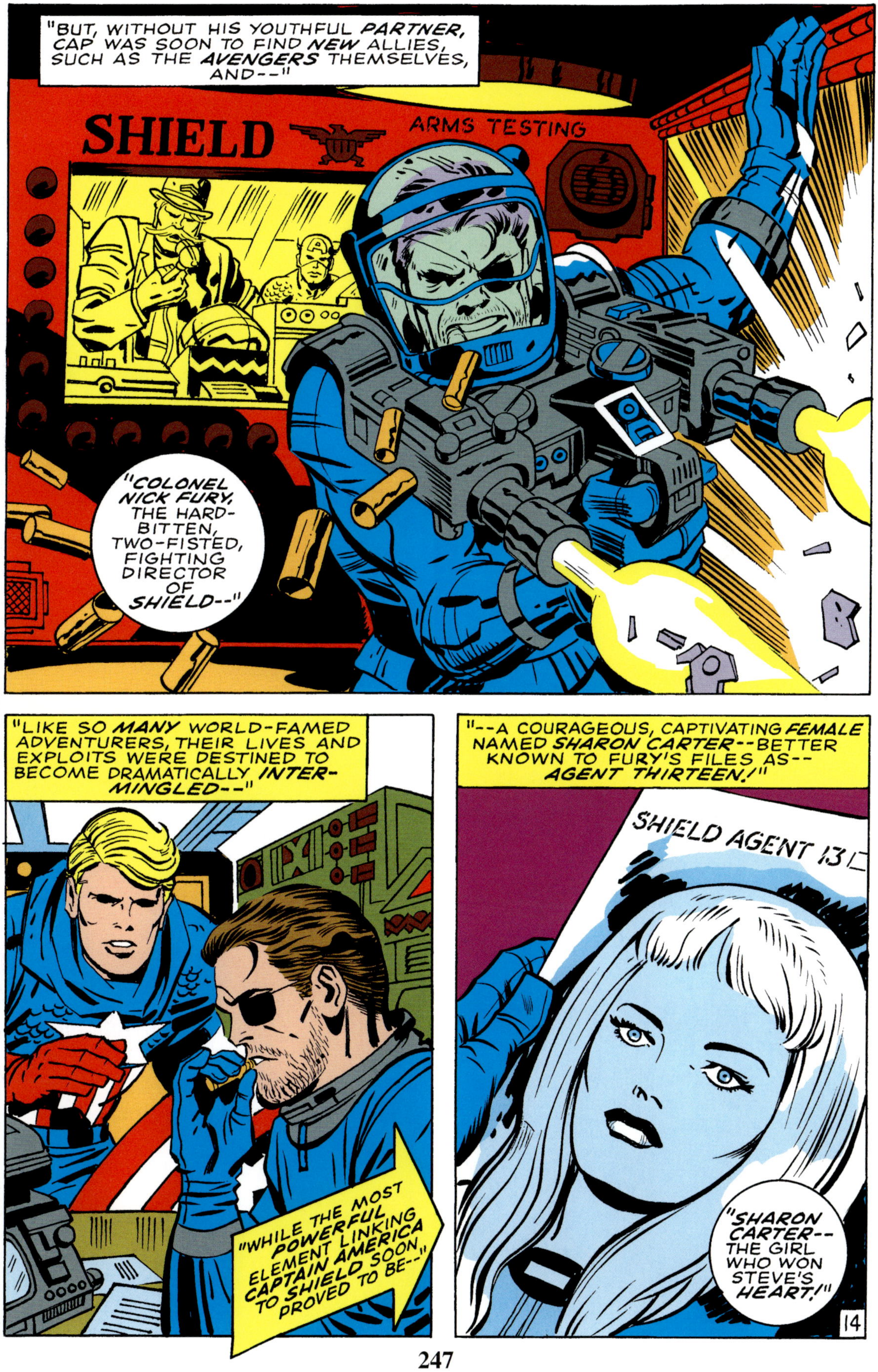
"BUT, WITHOUT HIS YOUTHFUL PARTNER, CAP WAS SOON TO FIND NEW ALLIES, SUCH AS THE AVENGERS THEMSELVES, AND--"
SHIELD
ARMS TESTING
"COLONEL NICK FURY, THE HARD-BITTEN, TWO-FISTED, FIGHTING DIRECTOR OF SHIELD--"
"LIKE SO MANY WORLD-FAMED ADVENTURERS, THEIR LIVES AND EXPLOITS WERE DESTINED TO BECOME DRAMATICALLY INTER-MINGLED--"
"WHILE THE MOST POWERFUL ELEMENT LINKING CAPTAIN AMERICA TO SHIELD SOON PROVED TO BE--"
"--A COURAGEOUS, CAPTIVATING FEMALE NAMED SHARON CARTER--BETTER KNOWN TO FURY'S FILES AS-- AGENT THIRTEEN!"
SHIELD AGENT 13
"SHARON CARTER-- THE GIRL WHO WON STEVE'S HEART!"
14

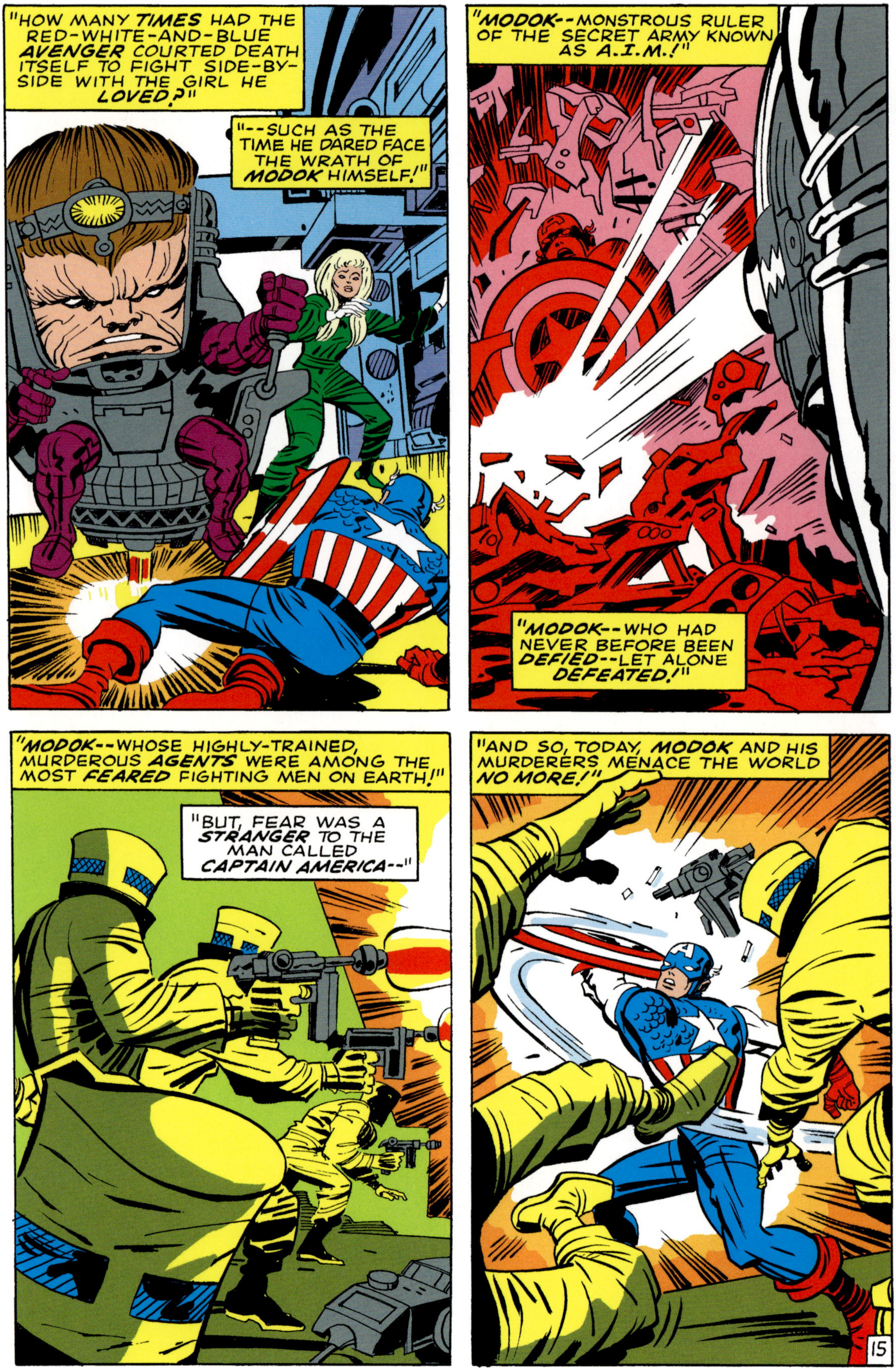
"HOW MANY TIMES HAD THE RED-WHITE-AND-BLUE AVENGER COURTED DEATH ITSELF TO FIGHT SIDE-BY-SIDE WITH THE GIRL HE LOVED?"
"--SUCH AS THE TIME HE DARED FACE THE WRATH OF MODOK HIMSELF!"
"MODOK--MONSTROUS RULER OF THE SECRET ARMY KNOWN AS A.I.M.!"
"MODOK--WHO HAD NEVER BEFORE BEEN DEFIED--LET ALONE DEFEATED!"
"MODOK--WHOSE HIGHLY-TRAINED, MURDEROUS AGENTS WERE AMONG THE MOST FEARED FIGHTING MEN ON EARTH!"
"BUT, FEAR WAS A STRANGER TO THE MAN CALLED CAPTAIN AMERICA--"
"AND SO, TODAY, MODOK AND HIS MURDERERS MENACE THE WORLD NO MORE!"
15

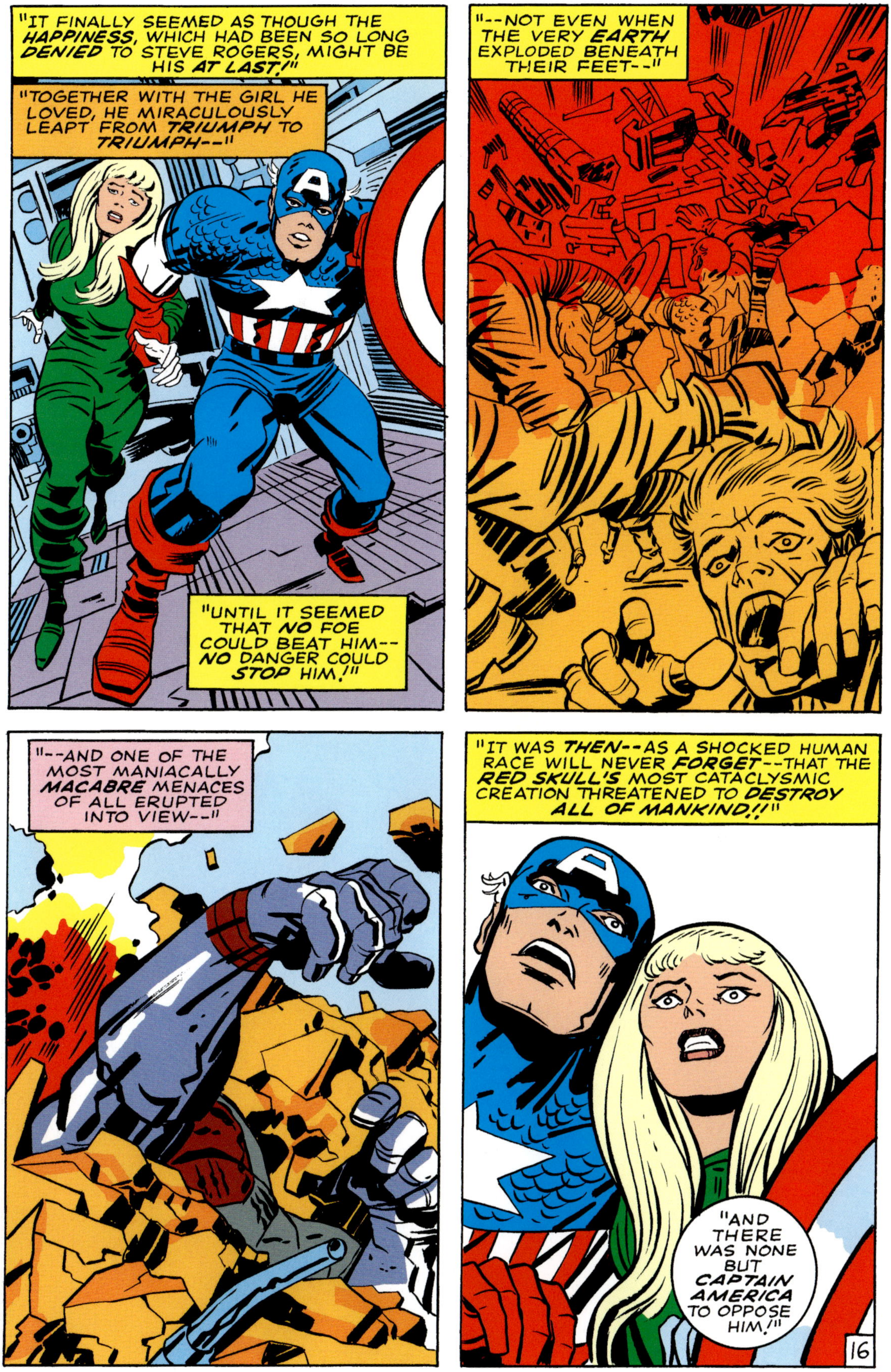
"IT FINALLY SEEMED AS THOUGH THE HAPPINESS, WHICH HAD BEEN SO LONG DENIED TO STEVE ROGERS, MIGHT BE HIS AT LAST!"
"TOGETHER WITH THE GIRL HE LOVED, HE MIRACULOUSLY LEAPT FROM TRIUMPH TO TRIUMPH--"
"UNTIL IT SEEMED THAT NO FOE COULD BEAT HIM-- NO DANGER COULD STOP HIM!"
"--NOT EVEN WHEN THE VERY EARTH EXPLODED BENEATH THEIR FEET--"
"--AND ONE OF THE MOST MANIACALLY MACABRE MENACES OF ALL ERUPTED INTO VIEW--"
"IT WAS THEN--AS A SHOCKED HUMAN RACE WILL NEVER FORGET--THAT THE RED SKULL'S MOST CATACLYSMIC CREATION THREATENED TO DESTROY ALL OF MANKIND!!"
"AND THERE WAS NONE BUT CAPTAIN AMERICA TO OPPOSE HIM!"
16

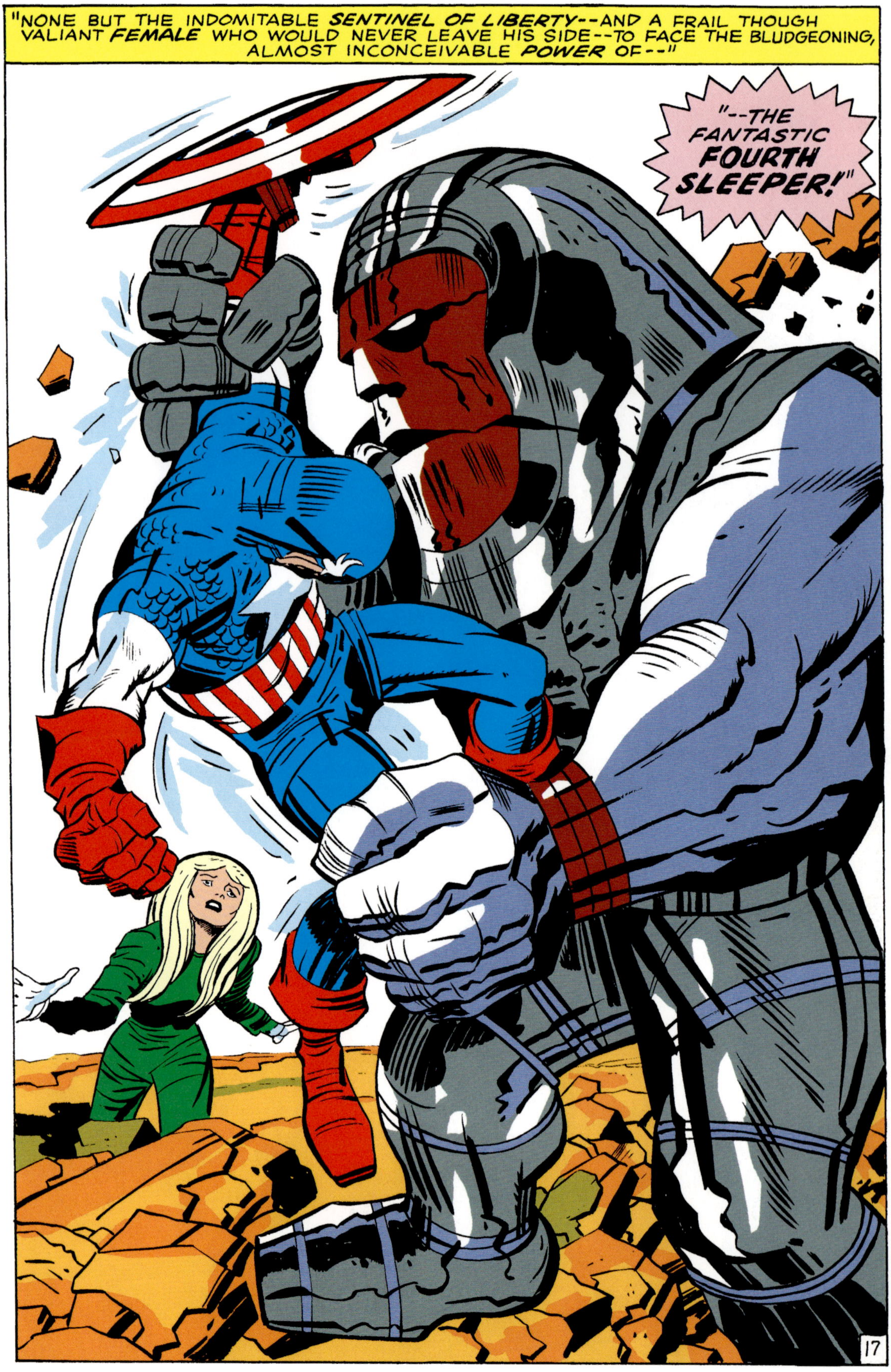
"NONE BUT THE INDOMITABLE SENTINEL OF LIBERTY--AND A FRAIL THOUGH VALIANT FEMALE WHO WOULD NEVER LEAVE HIS SIDE--TO FACE THE BLUDGEONING, ALMOST INCONCEIVABLE POWER OF--"
"--THE FANTASTIC FOURTH SLEEPER!"
17

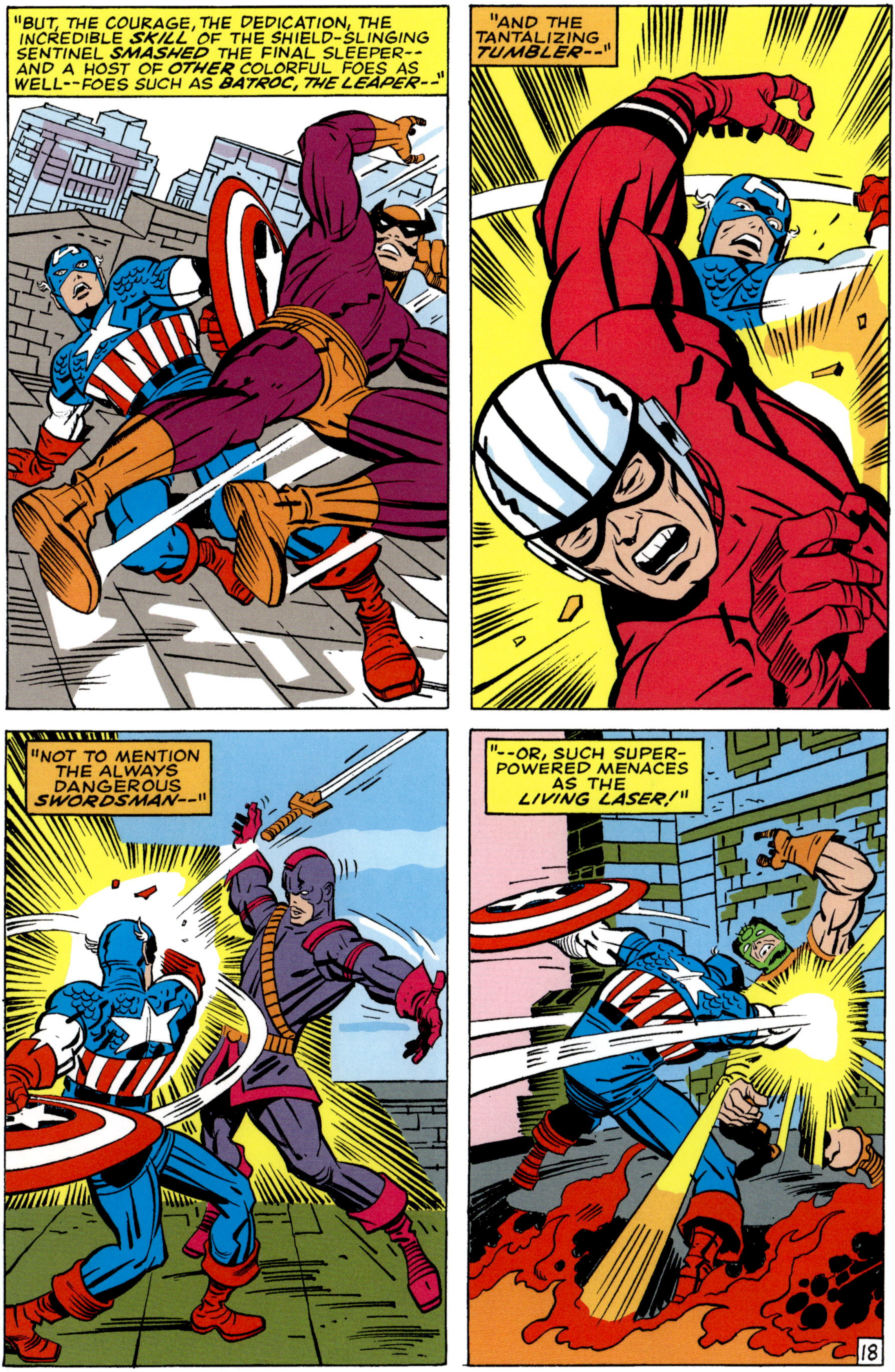

"BUT, THE COURAGE, THE DEDICATION, THE INCREDIBLE SKILL OF THE SHIELD-SLINGING SENTINEL SMASHED THE FINAL SLEEPER-- AND A HOST OF OTHER COLORFUL FOES AS WELL--FOES SUCH AS BATROC, THE LEAPER--"
"AND THE TANTALIZING TUMBLER--"
"NOT TO MENTION THE ALWAYS DANGEROUS SWORDSMAN--"
"--OR, SUCH SUPER-POWERED MENACES AS THE LIVING LASER!"
18

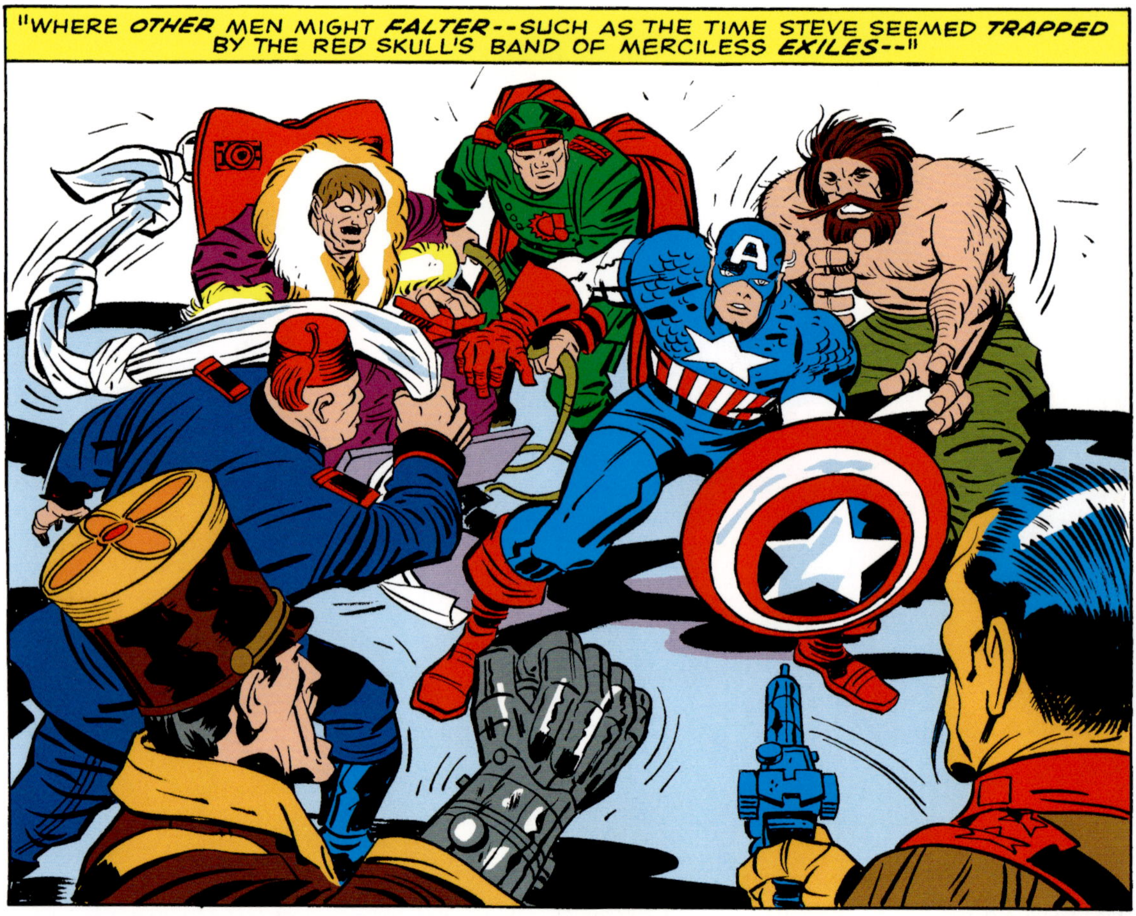
"WHERE OTHER MEN MIGHT FALTER--SUCH AS THE TIME STEVE SEEMED TRAPPED BY THE RED SKULL'S BAND OF MERCILESS EXILES--"

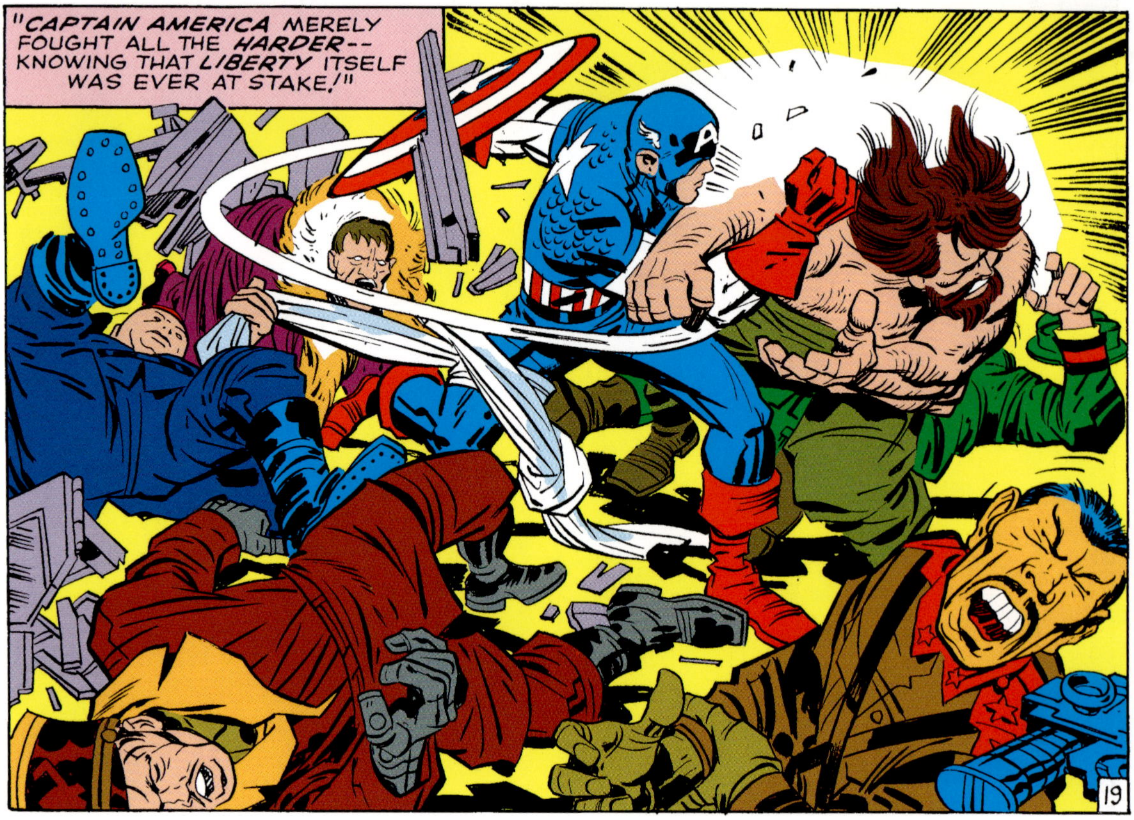
"CAPTAIN AMERICA MERELY FOUGHT ALL THE HARDER--KNOWING THAT LIBERTY ITSELF WAS EVER AT STAKE!"
19

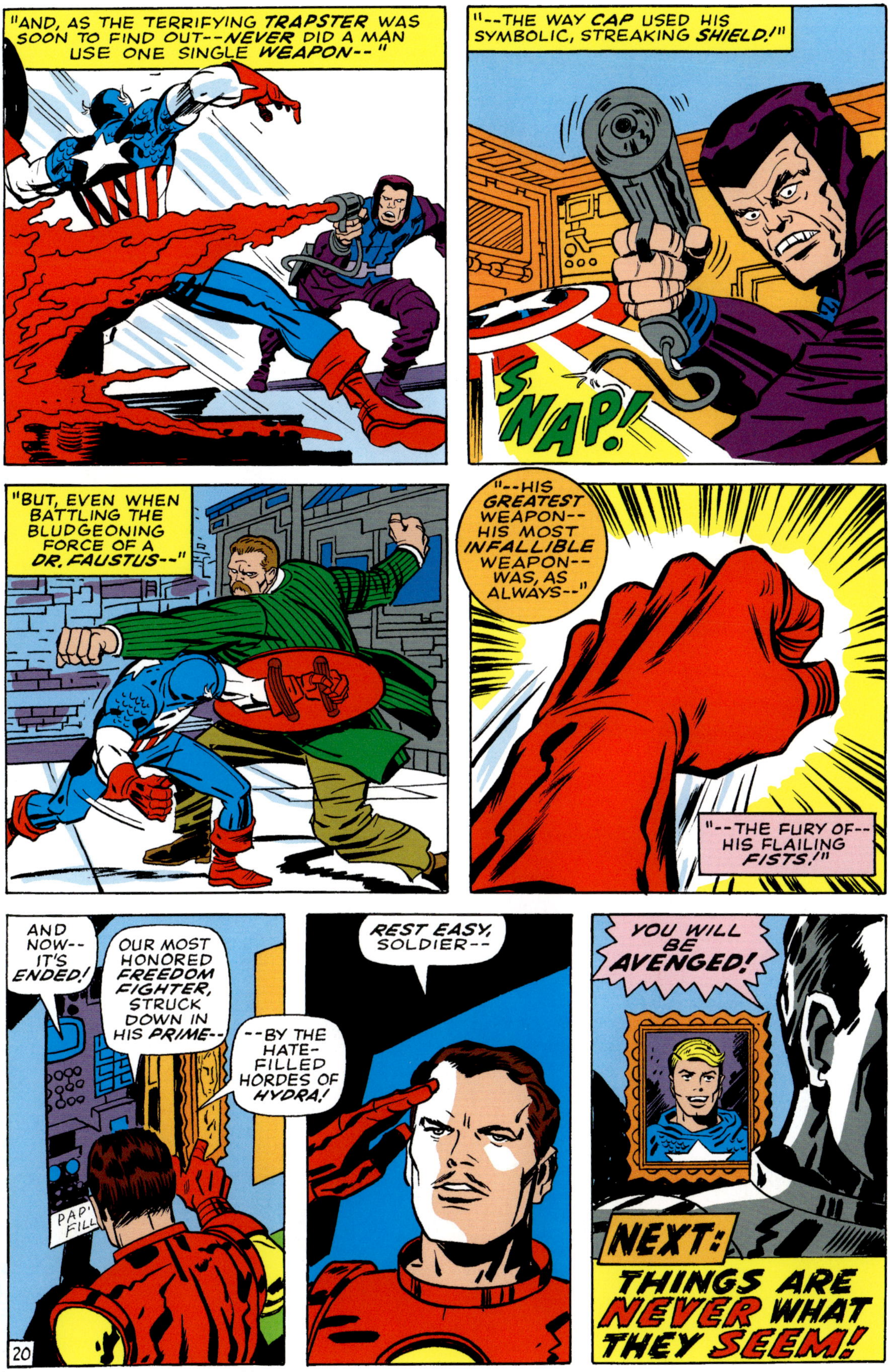
"AND, AS THE TERRIFYING TRAPSTER WAS SOON TO FIND OUT--NEVER DID A MAN USE ONE SINGLE WEAPON--"
"--THE WAY CAP USED HIS SYMBOLIC, STREAKING SHIELD!"
SNAP!
"BUT, EVEN WHEN BATTLING THE BLUDGEONING FORCE OF A DR. FAUSTUS--"
"--HIS GREATEST WEAPON--HIS MOST INFALLIBLE WEAPON--WAS, AS ALWAYS--"
"--THE FURY OF--HIS FLAILING FISTS!"
AND NOW--IT'S ENDED!
OUR MOST HONORED FREEDOM FIGHTER, STRUCK DOWN IN HIS PRIME--
--BY THE HATE-FILLED HORDES OF HYDRA!
20
REST EASY, SOLDIER--
YOU WILL BE AVENGED!
NEXT:
THINGS ARE NEVER WHAT THEY SEEM!

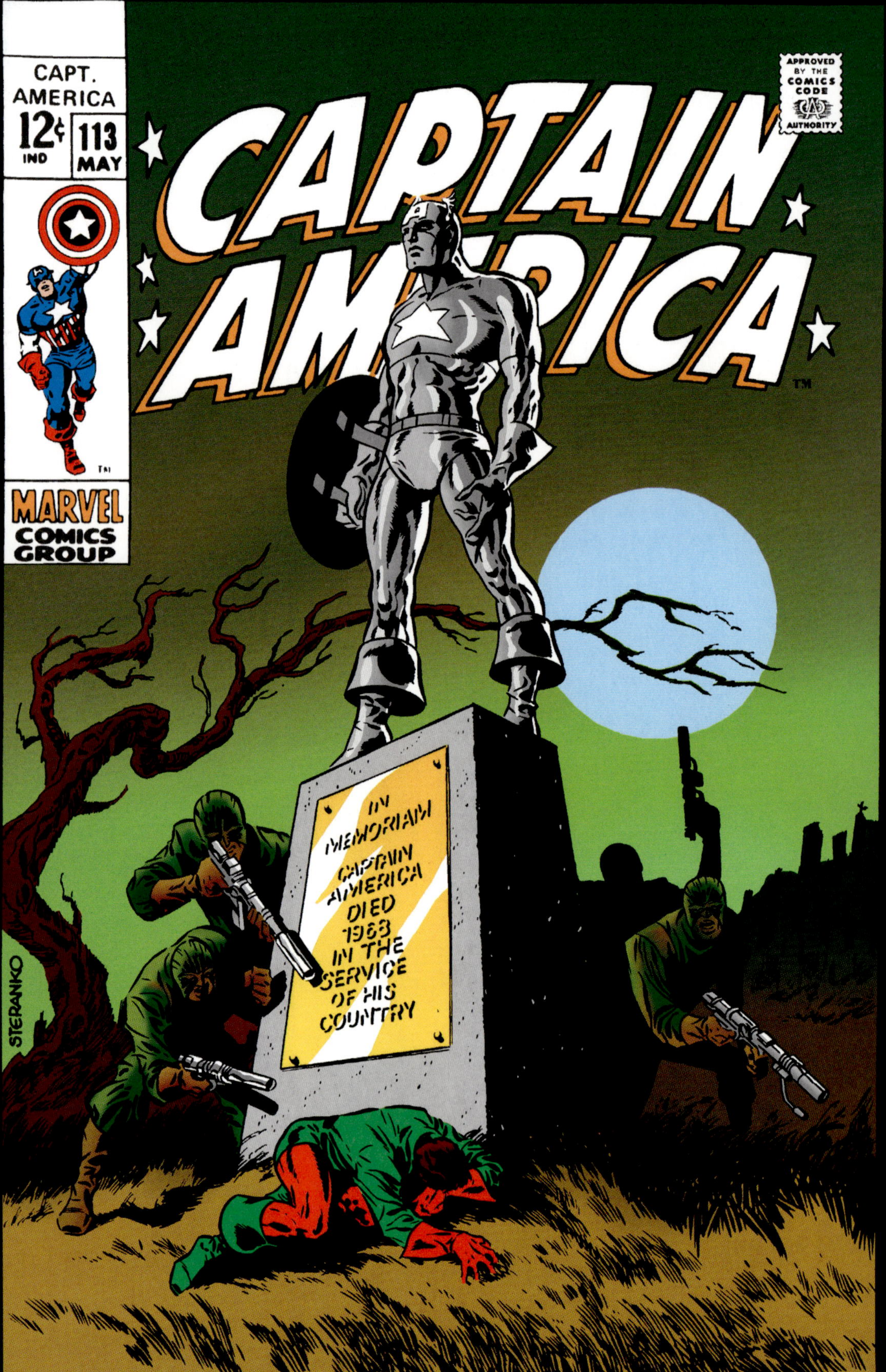
CAPT. AMERICA
12¢ IND
113 MAY
MARVEL COMICS GROUP
APPROVED BY THE COMICS CODE AUTHORITY
CAPTAIN AMERICA
IN MEMORIAM
CAPTAIN AMERICA DIED 1968 IN THE SERVICE OF HIS COUNTRY
STERANKO

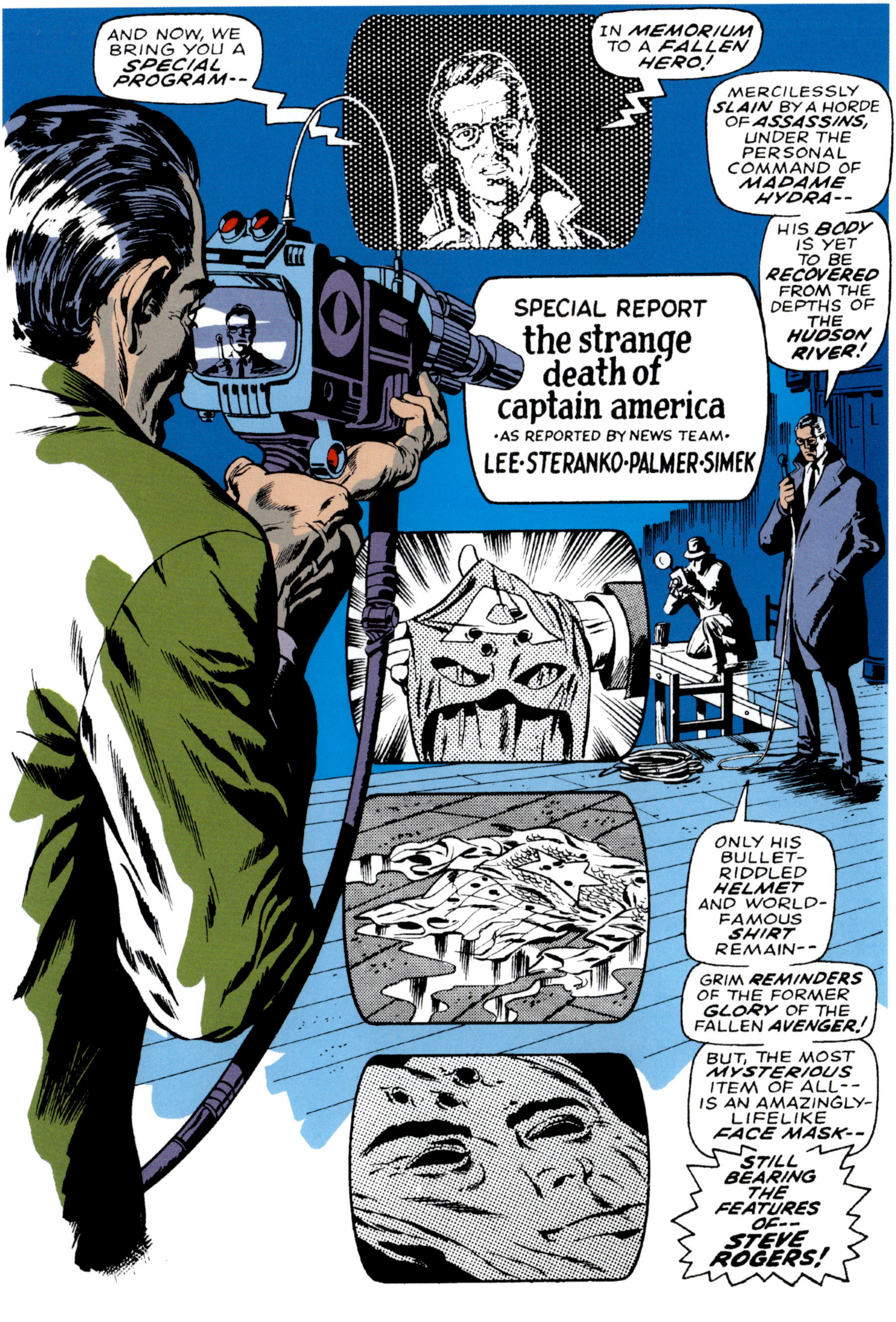
AND NOW, WE BRING YOU A SPECIAL PROGRAM--
IN MEMORIUM TO A FALLEN HERO!
MERCILESSLY SLAIN BY A HORDE OF ASSASSINS, UNDER THE PERSONAL COMMAND OF MADAME HYDRA--
HIS BODY IS YET TO BE RECOVERED FROM THE DEPTHS OF THE HUDSON RIVER!
SPECIAL REPORT
the strange death of captain america
•AS REPORTED BY NEWS TEAM•
LEE•STERANKO•PALMER•SIMEK
ONLY HIS BULLET-RIDDLED HELMET AND WORLD-FAMOUS SHIRT REMAIN--
GRIM REMINDERS OF THE FORMER GLORY OF THE FALLEN AVENGER!
BUT, THE MOST MYSTERIOUS ITEM OF ALL-- IS AN AMAZINGLY-LIFELIKE FACE MASK--
STILL BEARING THE FEATURES OF-- STEVE ROGERS!

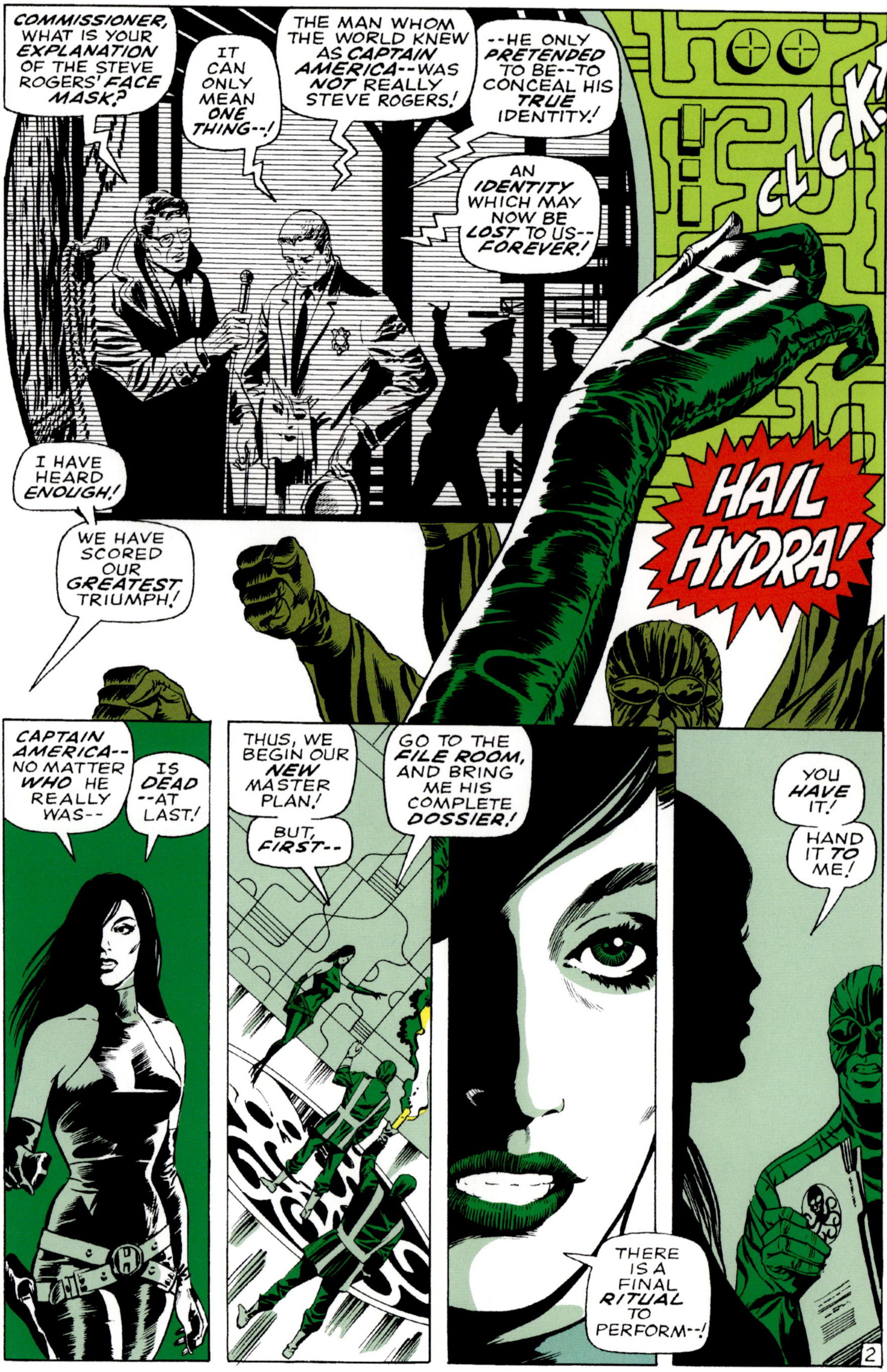

COMMISSIONER, WHAT IS YOUR EXPLANATION OF THE STEVE ROGERS' FACE MASK?
IT CAN ONLY MEAN ONE THING--!
THE MAN WHOM THE WORLD KNEW AS CAPTAIN AMERICA--WAS NOT REALLY STEVE ROGERS!
--HE ONLY PRETENDED TO BE--TO CONCEAL HIS TRUE IDENTITY!
AN IDENTITY WHICH MAY NOW BE LOST TO US--FOREVER!
CLICK!
I HAVE HEARD ENOUGH!
WE HAVE SCORED OUR GREATEST TRIUMPH!
HAIL HYDRA!
CAPTAIN AMERICA--NO MATTER WHO HE REALLY WAS--
IS DEAD--AT LAST!
THUS, WE BEGIN OUR NEW MASTER PLAN!
BUT, FIRST--
GO TO THE FILE ROOM, AND BRING ME HIS COMPLETE DOSSIER!
THERE IS A FINAL RITUAL TO PERFORM--!
YOU HAVE IT!
HAND IT TO ME!
2

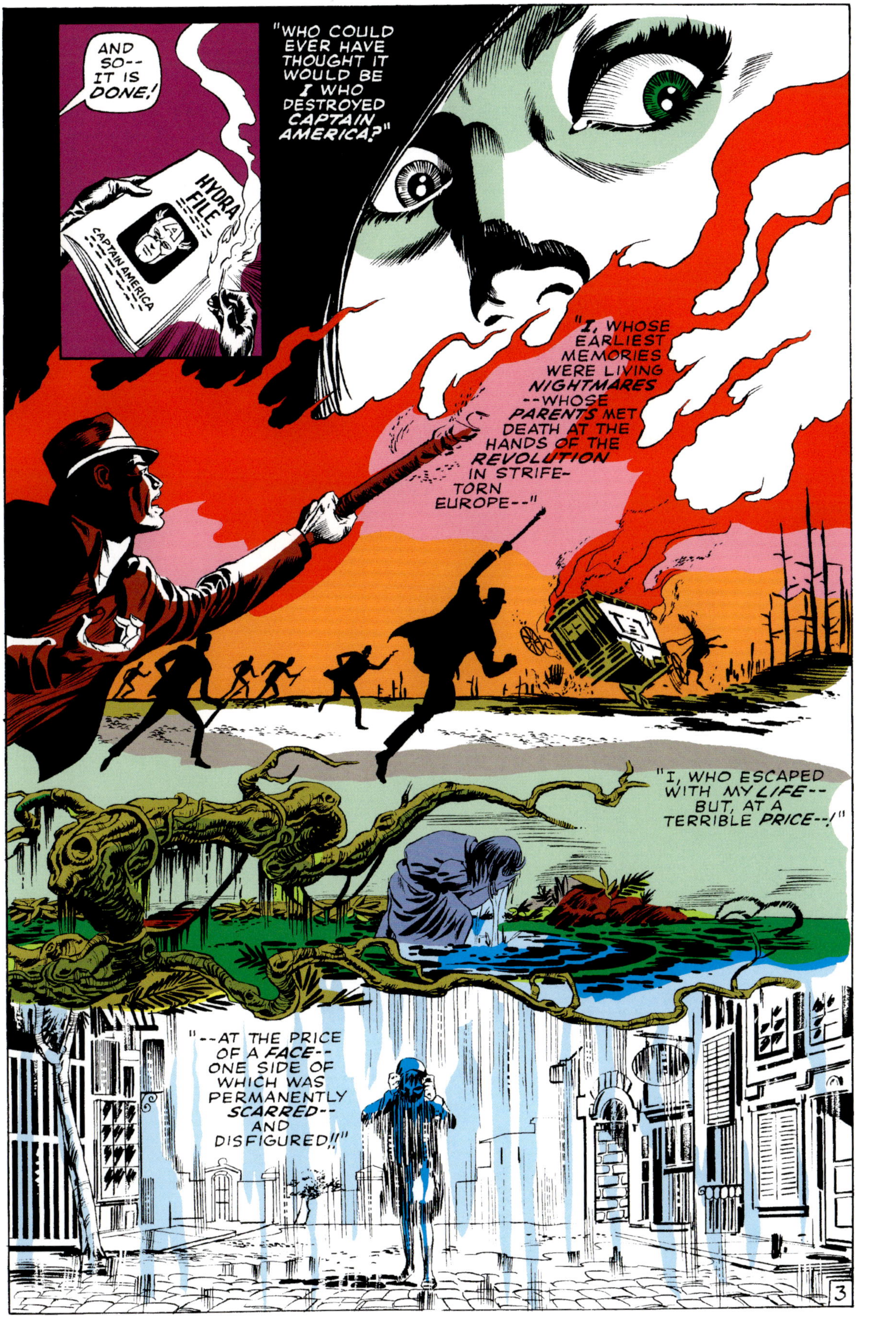
AND SO-- IT IS DONE!
"WHO COULD EVER HAVE THOUGHT IT WOULD BE I WHO DESTROYED CAPTAIN AMERICA?"
HYDRA FILE
CAPTAIN AMERICA
"I, WHOSE EARLIEST MEMORIES WERE LIVING NIGHTMARES --WHOSE PARENTS MET DEATH AT THE HANDS OF THE REVOLUTION IN STRIFE-TORN EUROPE--"
"I, WHO ESCAPED WITH MY LIFE-- BUT, AT A TERRIBLE PRICE--!"
"--AT THE PRICE OF A FACE-- ONE SIDE OF WHICH WAS PERMANENTLY SCARRED-- AND DISFIGURED!!"
3

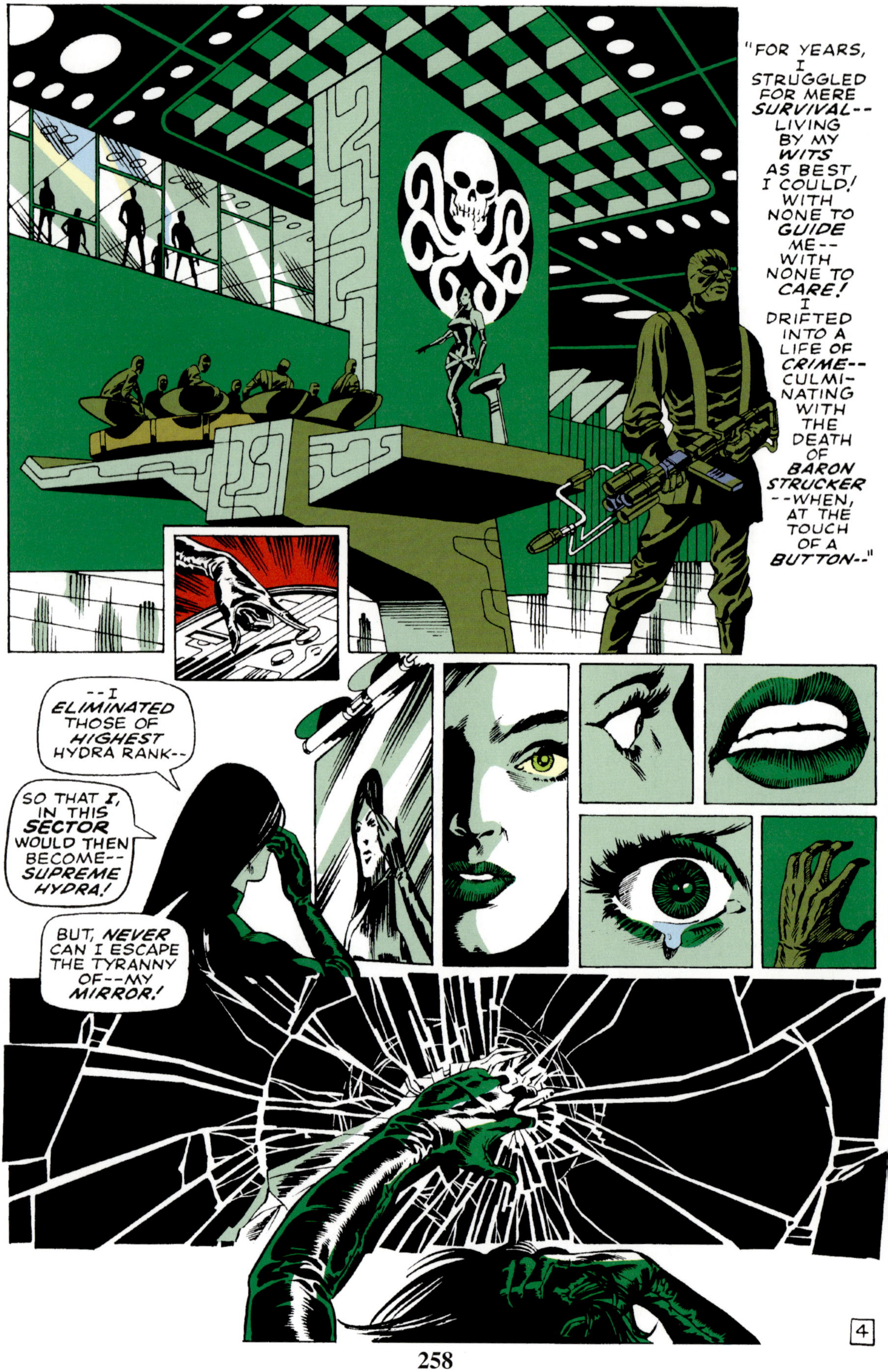
"FOR YEARS, I STRUGGLED FOR MERE SURVIVAL--LIVING BY MY WITS AS BEST I COULD! WITH NONE TO GUIDE ME--WITH NONE TO CARE! I DRIFTED INTO A LIFE OF CRIME--CULMINATING WITH THE DEATH OF BARON STRUCKER--WHEN, AT THE TOUCH OF A BUTTON--"
--I ELIMINATED THOSE OF HIGHEST HYDRA RANK--
SO THAT I, IN THIS SECTOR WOULD THEN BECOME--SUPREME HYDRA!
BUT, NEVER CAN I ESCAPE THE TYRANNY OF--MY MIRROR!
4

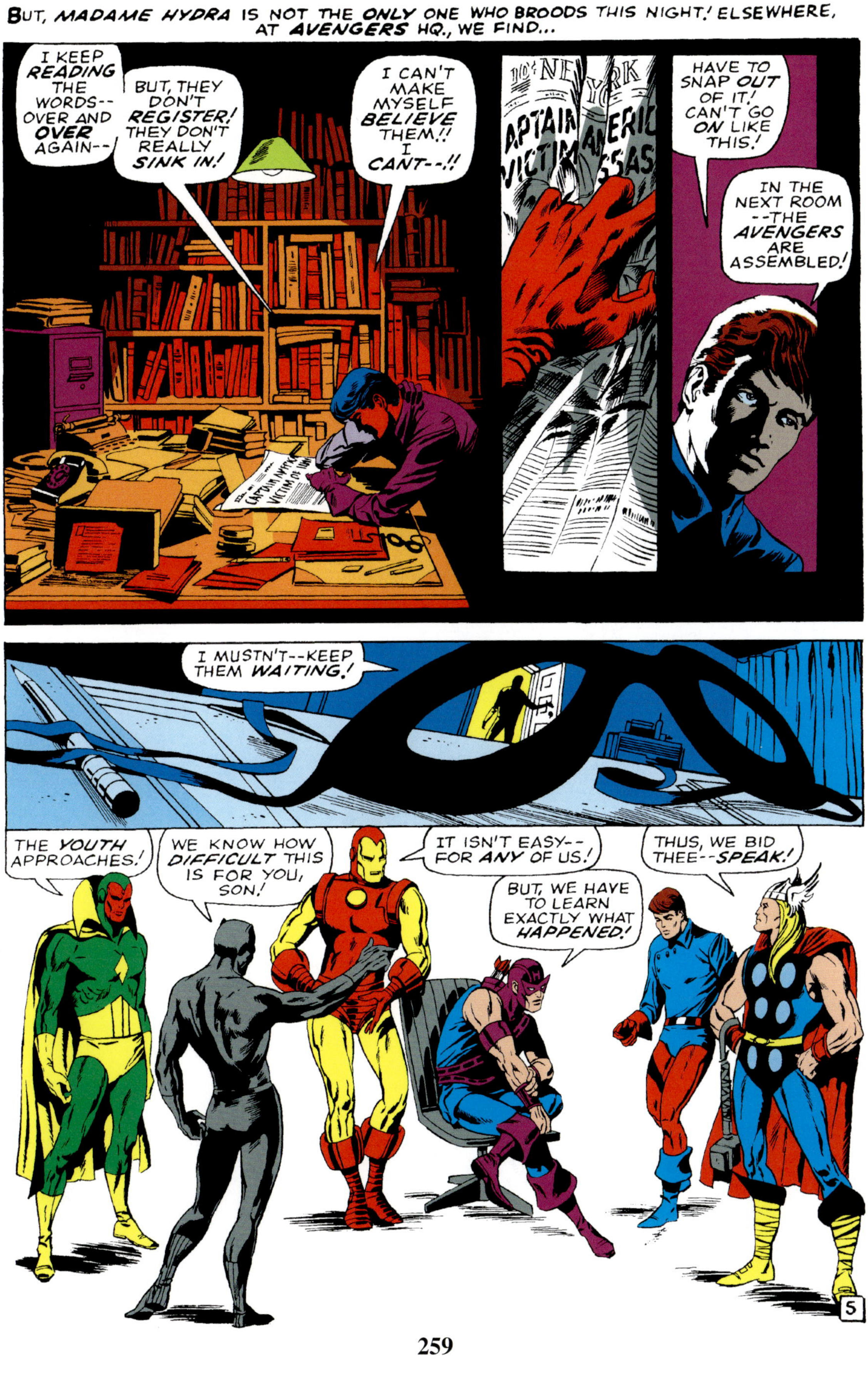

BUT, MADAME HYDRA IS NOT THE ONLY ONE WHO BROODS THIS NIGHT! ELSEWHERE, AT AVENGERS HQ., WE FIND...
I KEEP READING THE WORDS-- OVER AND OVER AGAIN--
BUT, THEY DON'T REGISTER! THEY DON'T REALLY SINK IN!
I CAN'T MAKE MYSELF BELIEVE THEM!! I CANT--!!
HAVE TO SNAP OUT OF IT! CAN'T GO ON LIKE THIS!
IN THE NEXT ROOM --THE AVENGERS ARE ASSEMBLED!
I MUSTN'T--KEEP THEM WAITING!
THE YOUTH APPROACHES!
WE KNOW HOW DIFFICULT THIS IS FOR YOU, SON!
IT ISN'T EASY-- FOR ANY OF US!
BUT, WE HAVE TO LEARN EXACTLY WHAT HAPPENED!
THUS, WE BID THEE--SPEAK!
5

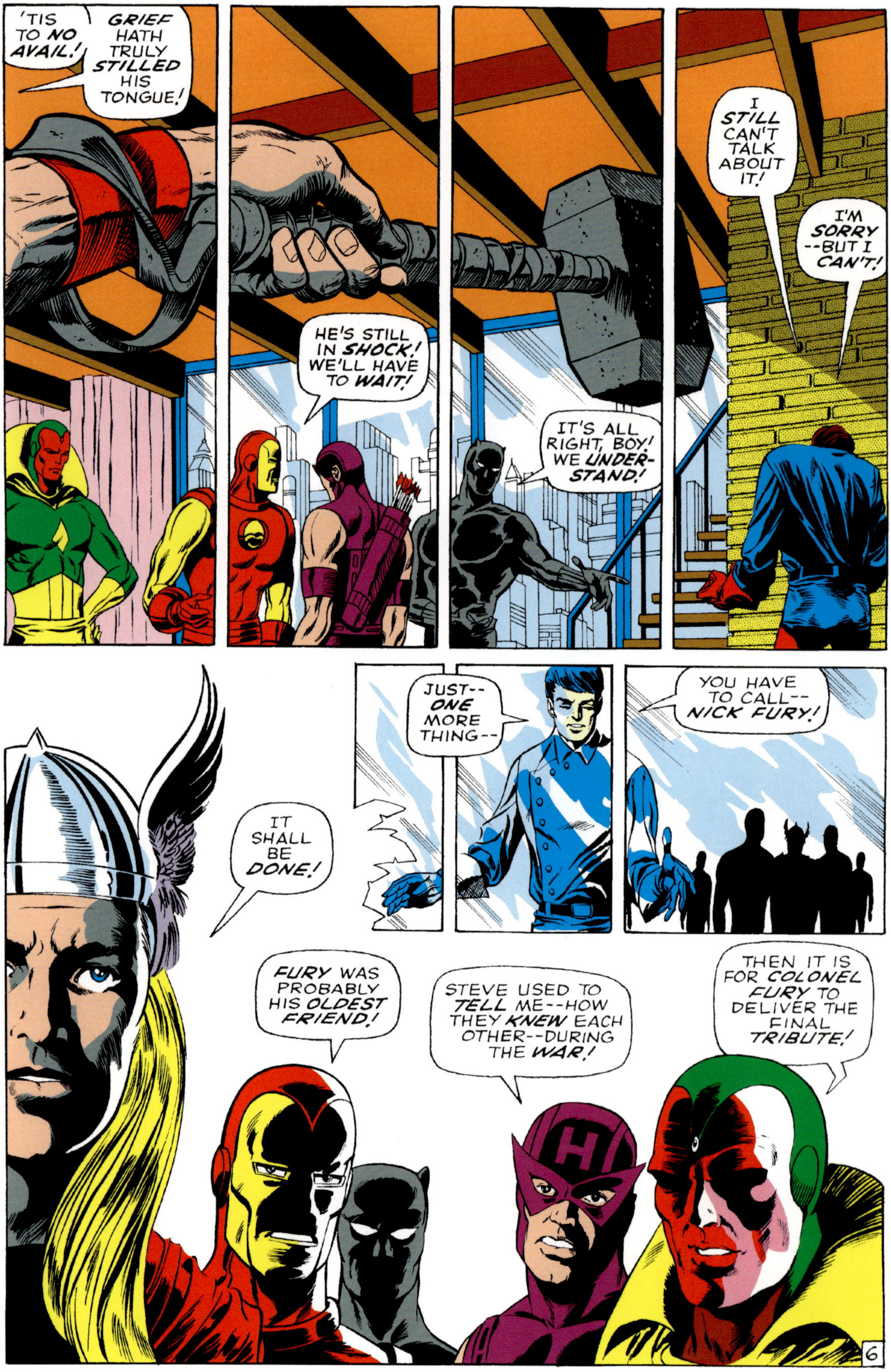
'TIS TO NO AVAIL!
GRIEF HATH TRULY STILLED HIS TONGUE!
HE'S STILL IN SHOCK! WE'LL HAVE TO WAIT!
IT'S ALL RIGHT, BOY! WE UNDERSTAND!
I STILL CAN'T TALK ABOUT IT!
I'M SORRY--BUT I CAN'T!
JUST--ONE MORE THING--
YOU HAVE TO CALL--NICK FURY!
IT SHALL BE DONE!
FURY WAS PROBABLY HIS OLDEST FRIEND!
STEVE USED TO TELL ME--HOW THEY KNEW EACH OTHER--DURING THE WAR!
THEN IT IS FOR COLONEL FURY TO DELIVER THE FINAL TRIBUTE!
6

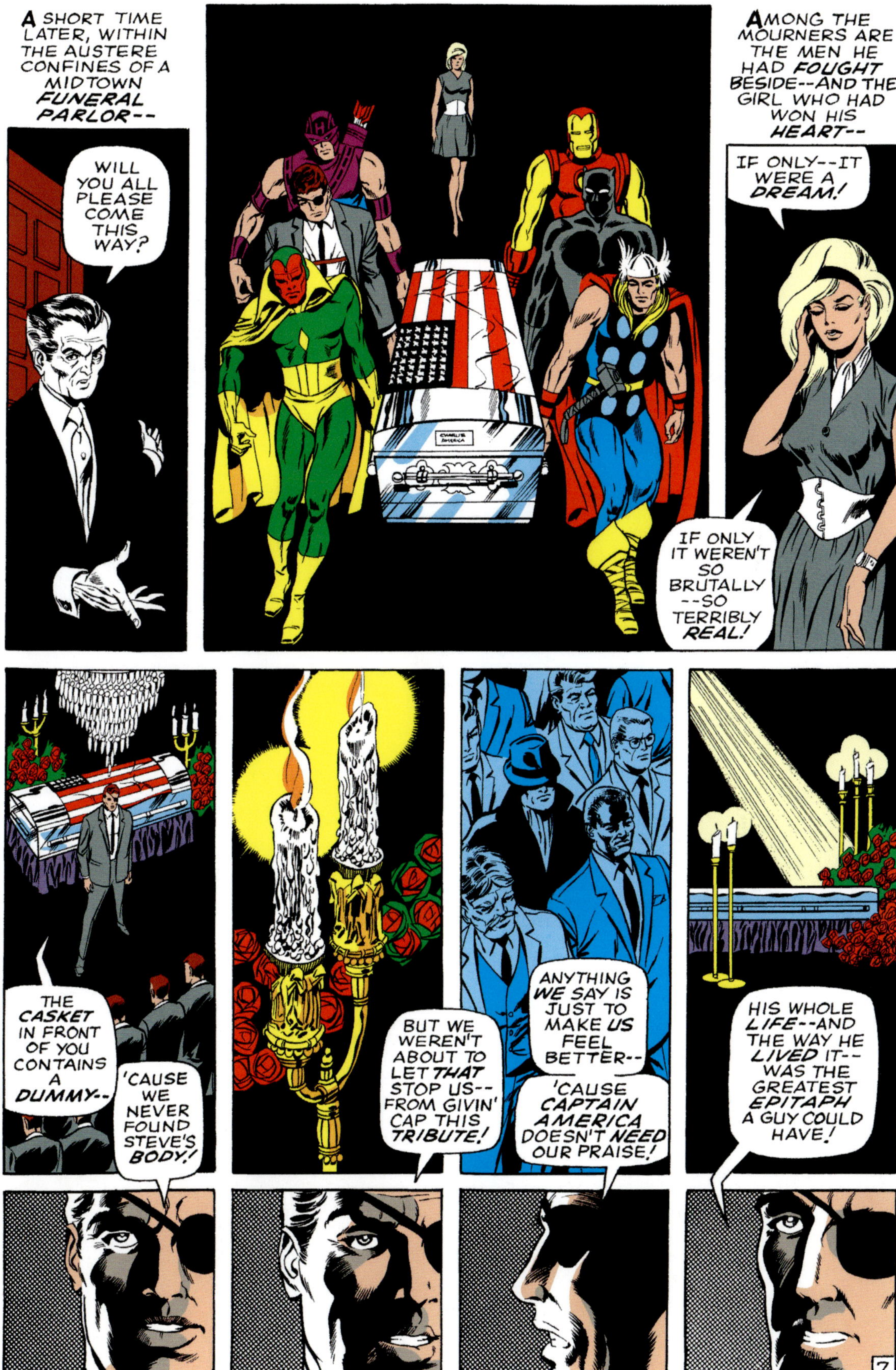
A SHORT TIME LATER, WITHIN THE AUSTERE CONFINES OF A MIDTOWN FUNERAL PARLOR--
WILL YOU ALL PLEASE COME THIS WAY?
AMONG THE MOURNERS ARE THE MEN HE HAD FOUGHT BESIDE--AND THE GIRL WHO HAD WON HIS HEART--
IF ONLY--IT WERE A DREAM!
IF ONLY IT WEREN'T SO BRUTALLY --SO TERRIBLY REAL!
THE CASKET IN FRONT OF YOU CONTAINS A DUMMY--
'CAUSE WE NEVER FOUND STEVE'S BODY!
BUT WE WEREN'T ABOUT TO LET THAT STOP US--FROM GIVIN' CAP THIS TRIBUTE!
ANYTHING WE SAY IS JUST TO MAKE US FEEL BETTER--
'CAUSE CAPTAIN AMERICA DOESN'T NEED OUR PRAISE!
HIS WHOLE LIFE--AND THE WAY HE LIVED IT--WAS THE GREATEST EPITAPH A GUY COULD HAVE!
7

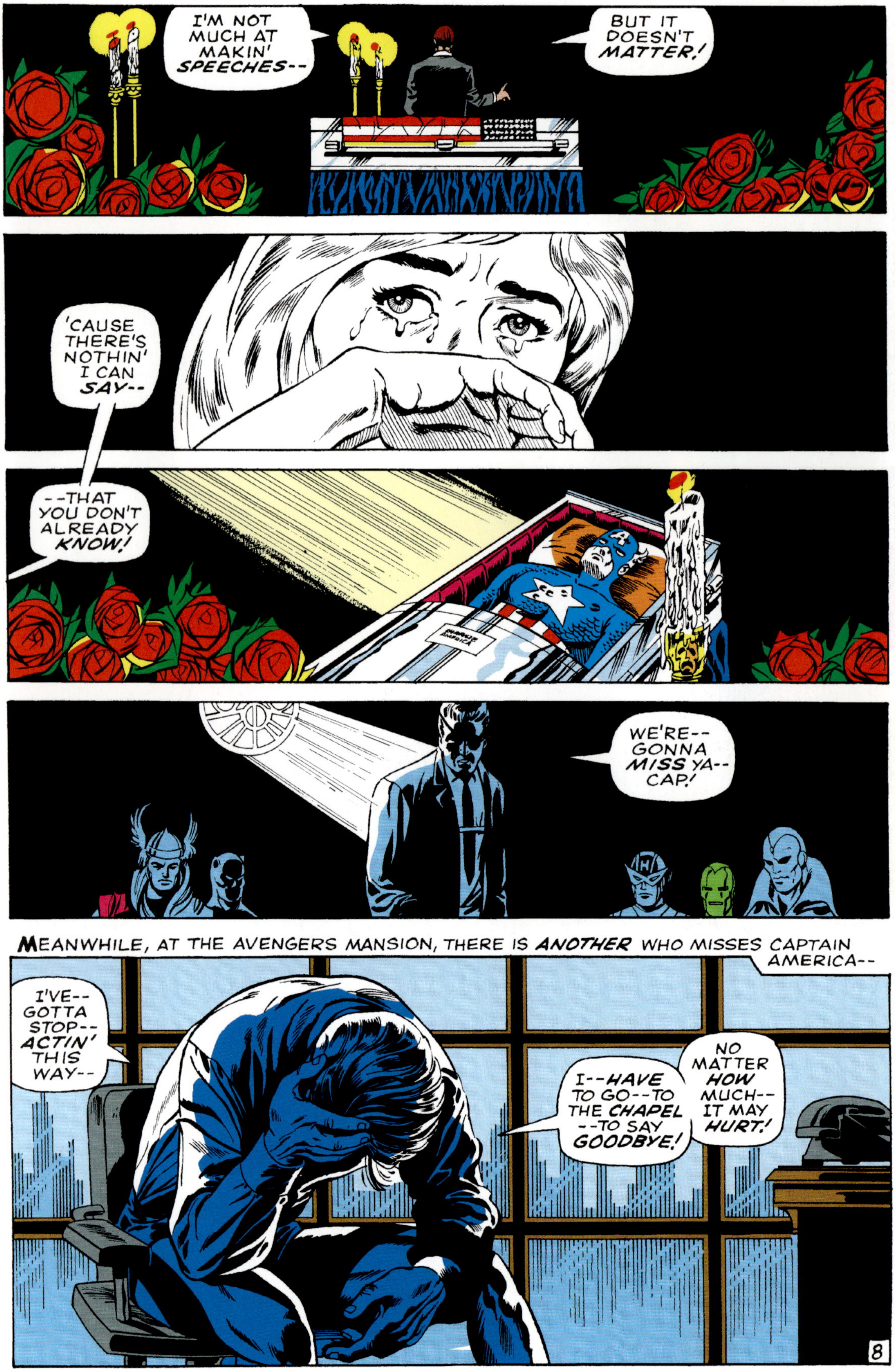
I'M NOT MUCH AT MAKIN' SPEECHES--
BUT IT DOESN'T MATTER!
'CAUSE THERE'S NOTHIN' I CAN SAY--
--THAT YOU DON'T ALREADY KNOW!
WE'RE--GONNA MISS YA--CAP!
MEANWHILE, AT THE AVENGERS MANSION, THERE IS ANOTHER WHO MISSES CAPTAIN AMERICA--
I'VE--GOTTA STOP--ACTIN' THIS WAY--
I--HAVE TO GO--TO THE CHAPEL--TO SAY GOODBYE!
NO MATTER HOW MUCH--IT MAY HURT!
8

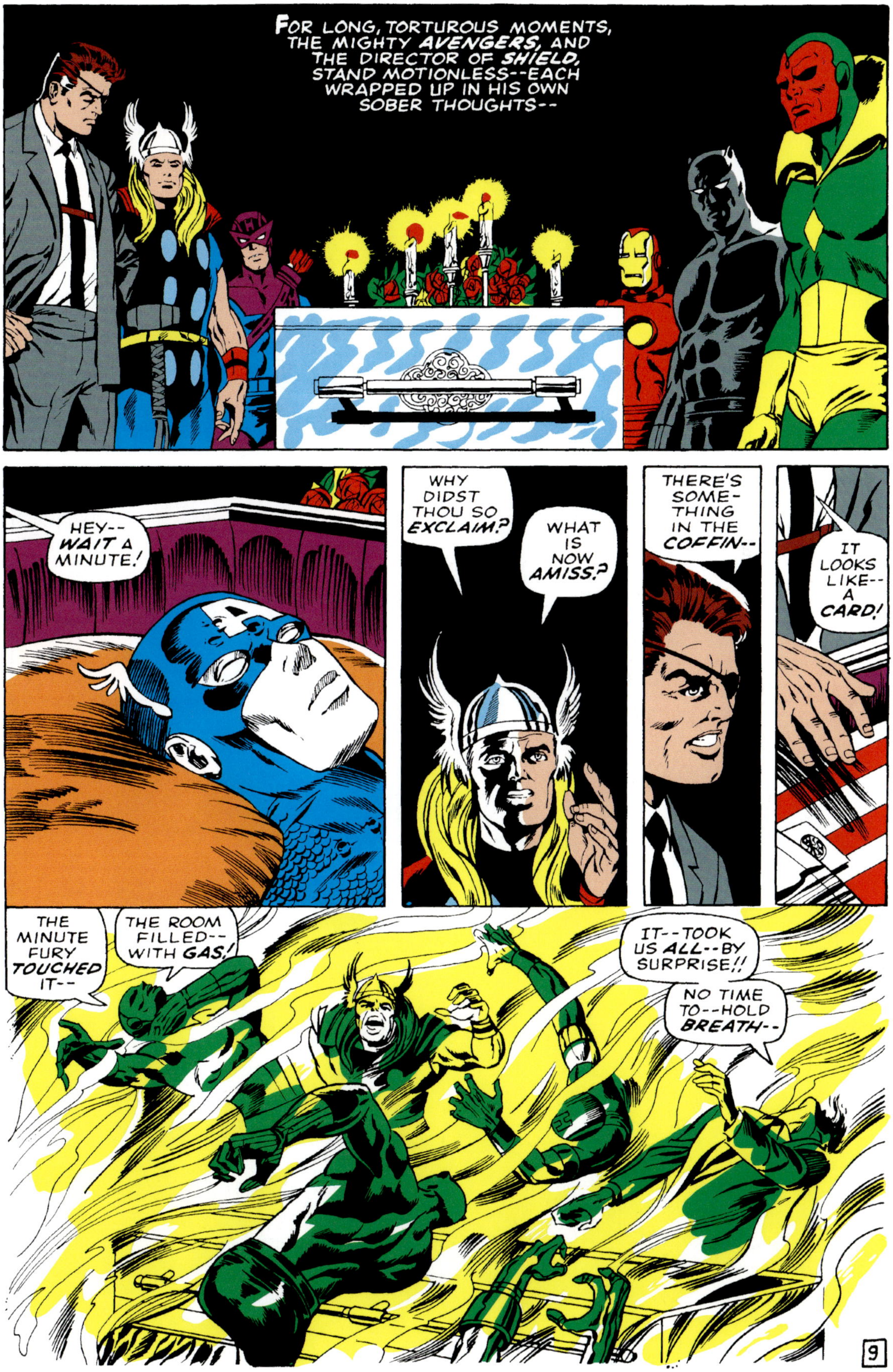
FOR LONG, TORTUROUS MOMENTS, THE MIGHTY AVENGERS, AND THE DIRECTOR OF SHIELD, STAND MOTIONLESS--EACH WRAPPED UP IN HIS OWN SOBER THOUGHTS--
HEY-- WAIT A MINUTE!
WHY DIDST THOU SO EXCLAIM?
WHAT IS NOW AMISS?
THERE'S SOME-THING IN THE COFFIN--
IT LOOKS LIKE-- A CARD!
THE MINUTE FURY TOUCHED IT--
THE ROOM FILLED-- WITH GAS!
IT--TOOK US ALL--BY SURPRISE!!
NO TIME TO--HOLD BREATH--
9

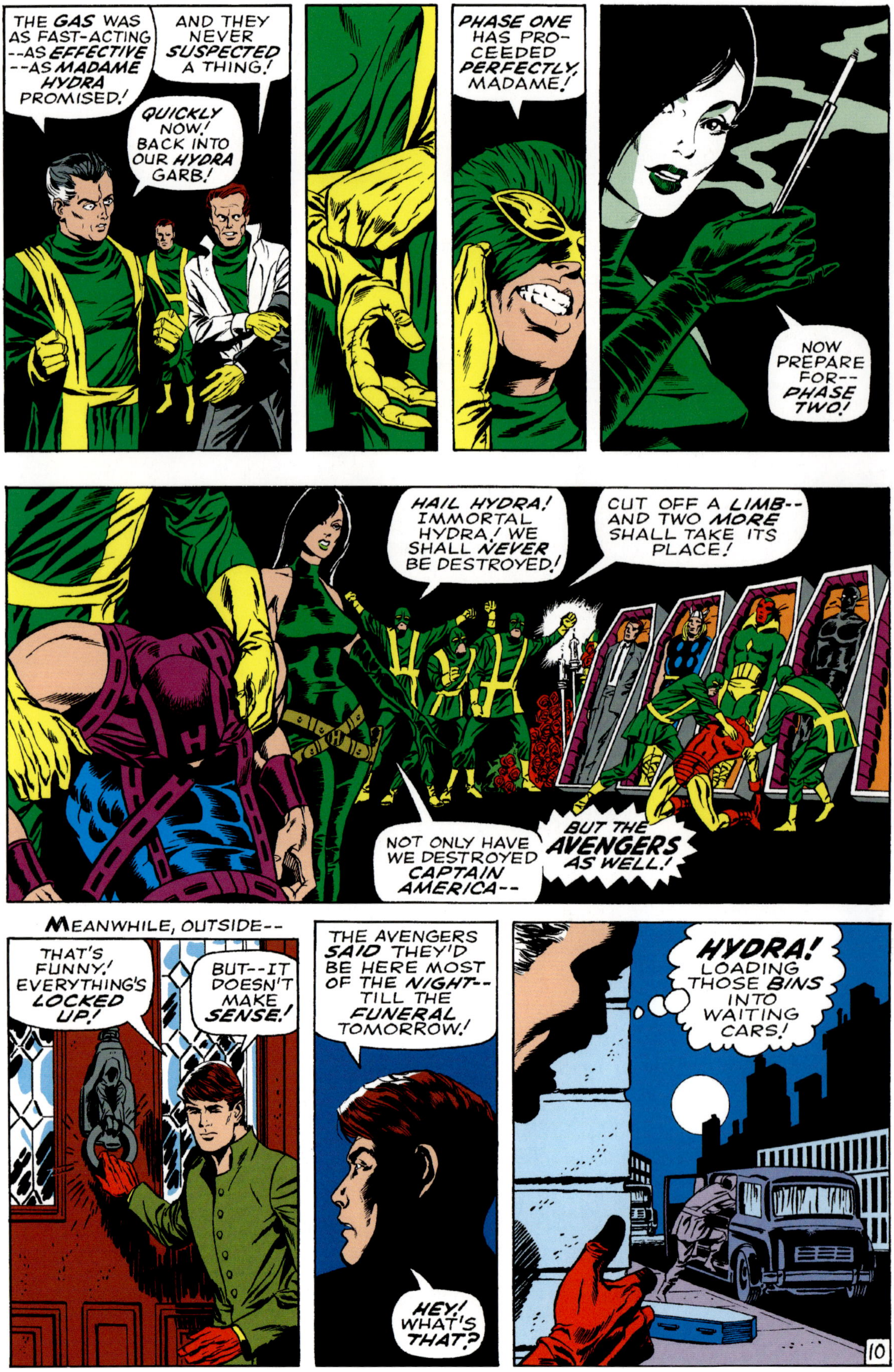

THE GAS WAS AS FAST-ACTING --AS EFFECTIVE --AS MADAME HYDRA PROMISED!
AND THEY NEVER SUSPECTED A THING!
QUICKLY NOW! BACK INTO OUR HYDRA GARB!
PHASE ONE HAS PRO-CEEDED PERFECTLY, MADAME!
NOW PREPARE FOR-- PHASE TWO!
HAIL HYDRA! IMMORTAL HYDRA! WE SHALL NEVER BE DESTROYED!
CUT OFF A LIMB-- AND TWO MORE SHALL TAKE ITS PLACE!
NOT ONLY HAVE WE DESTROYED CAPTAIN AMERICA--
BUT THE AVENGERS AS WELL!
MEANWHILE, OUTSIDE--
THAT'S FUNNY! EVERYTHING'S LOCKED UP!
BUT--IT DOESN'T MAKE SENSE!
THE AVENGERS SAID THEY'D BE HERE MOST OF THE NIGHT-- TILL THE FUNERAL TOMORROW!
HEY! WHAT'S THAT?
HYDRA! LOADING THOSE BINS INTO WAITING CARS!
10

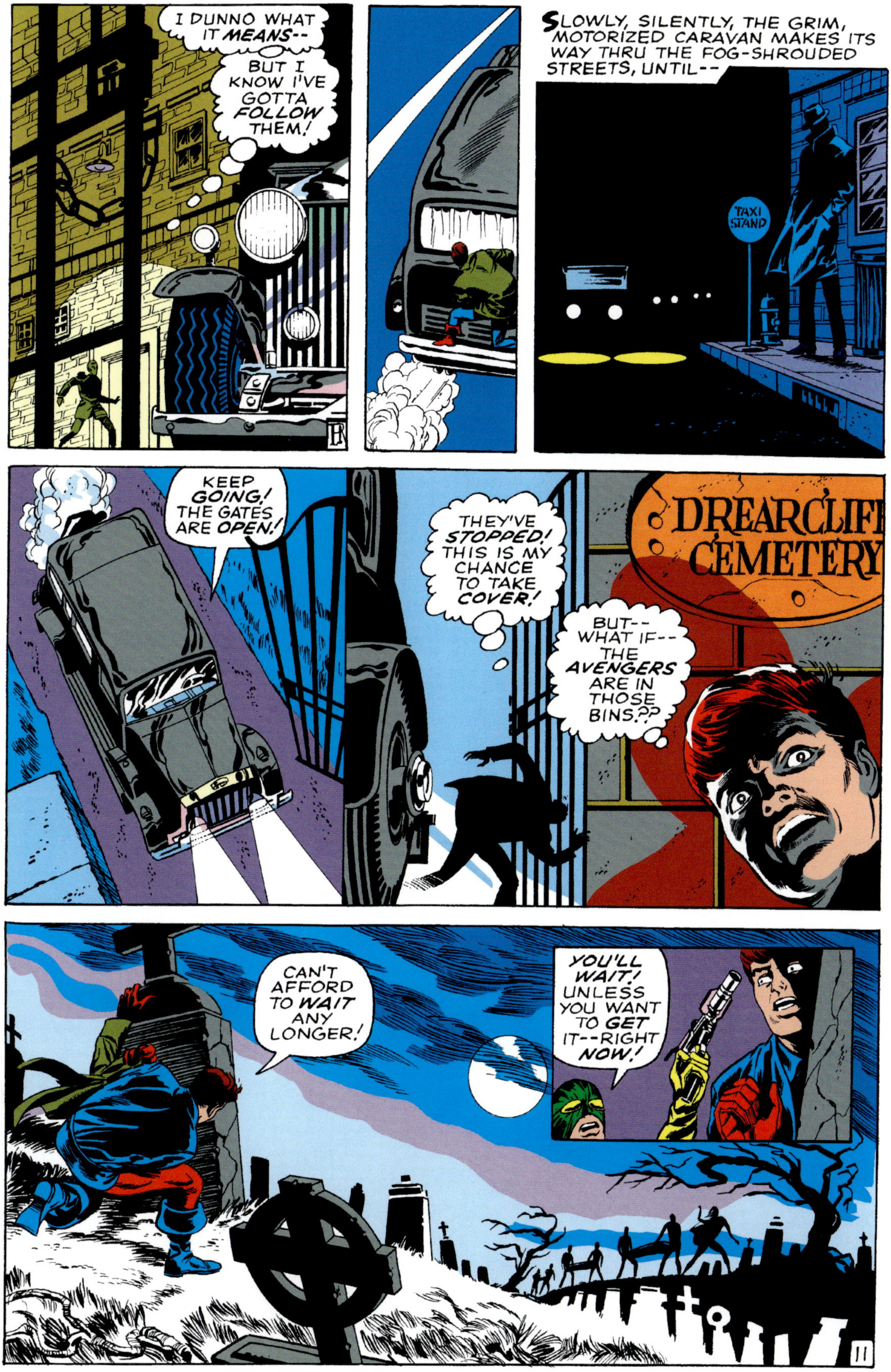
I DUNNO WHAT IT MEANS--
BUT I KNOW I'VE GOTTA FOLLOW THEM!
SLOWLY, SILENTLY, THE GRIM, MOTORIZED CARAVAN MAKES ITS WAY THRU THE FOG-SHROUDED STREETS, UNTIL--
TAXI STAND
KEEP GOING! THE GATES ARE OPEN!
THEY'VE STOPPED! THIS IS MY CHANCE TO TAKE COVER!
DREARCLIFF CEMETERY
BUT--WHAT IF--THE AVENGERS ARE IN THOSE BINS??
CAN'T AFFORD TO WAIT ANY LONGER!
YOU'LL WAIT! UNLESS YOU WANT TO GET IT--RIGHT NOW!
11

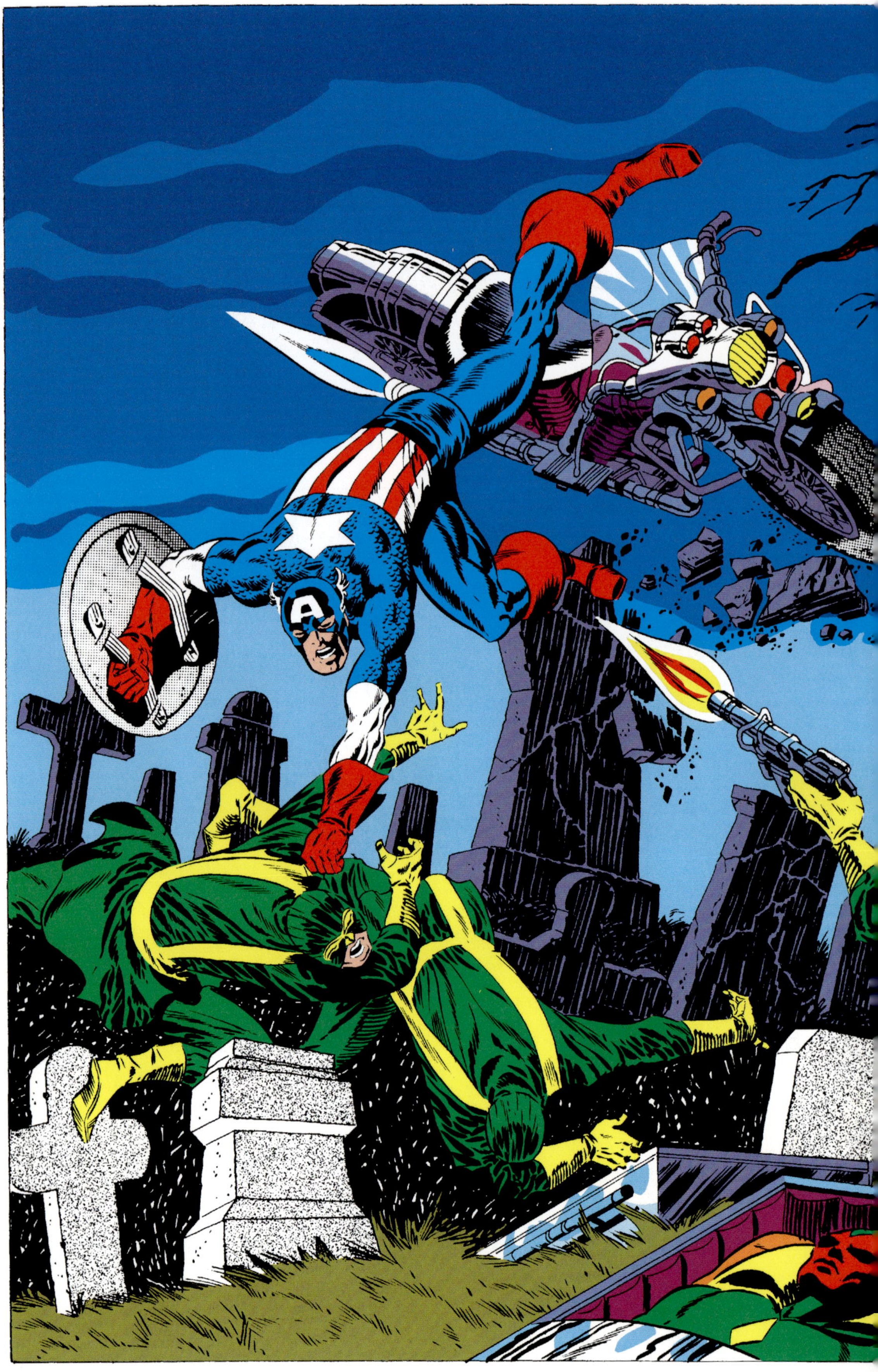

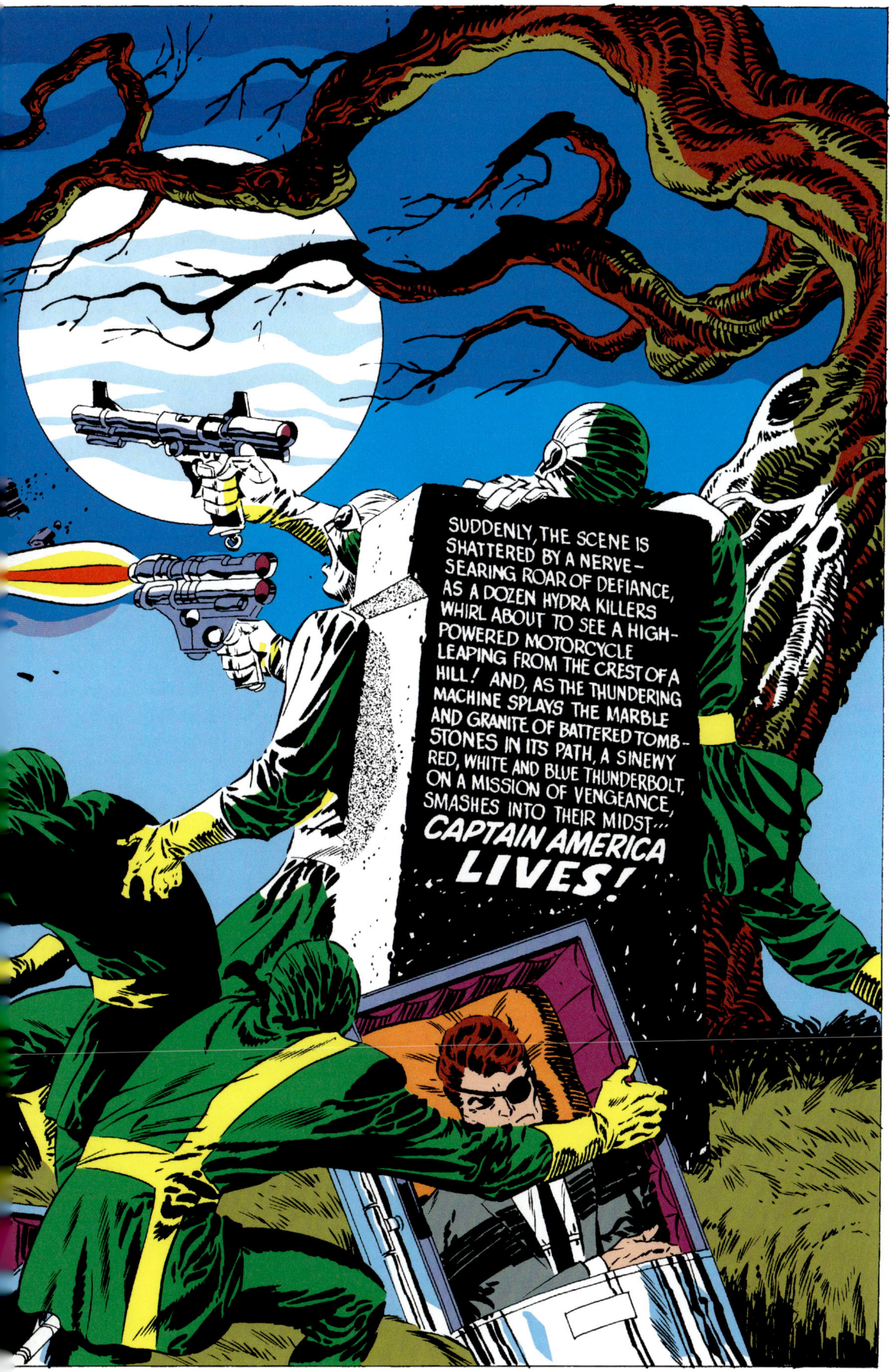
SUDDENLY, THE SCENE IS SHATTERED BY A NERVE-SEARING ROAR OF DEFIANCE, AS A DOZEN HYDRA KILLERS WHIRL ABOUT TO SEE A HIGH-POWERED MOTORCYCLE LEAPING FROM THE CREST OF A HILL! AND, AS THE THUNDERING MACHINE SPLAYS THE MARBLE AND GRANITE OF BATTERED TOMB-STONES IN ITS PATH, A SINEWY RED, WHITE AND BLUE THUNDERBOLT, ON A MISSION OF VENGEANCE, SMASHES INTO THEIR MIDST...
CAPTAIN AMERICA LIVES!

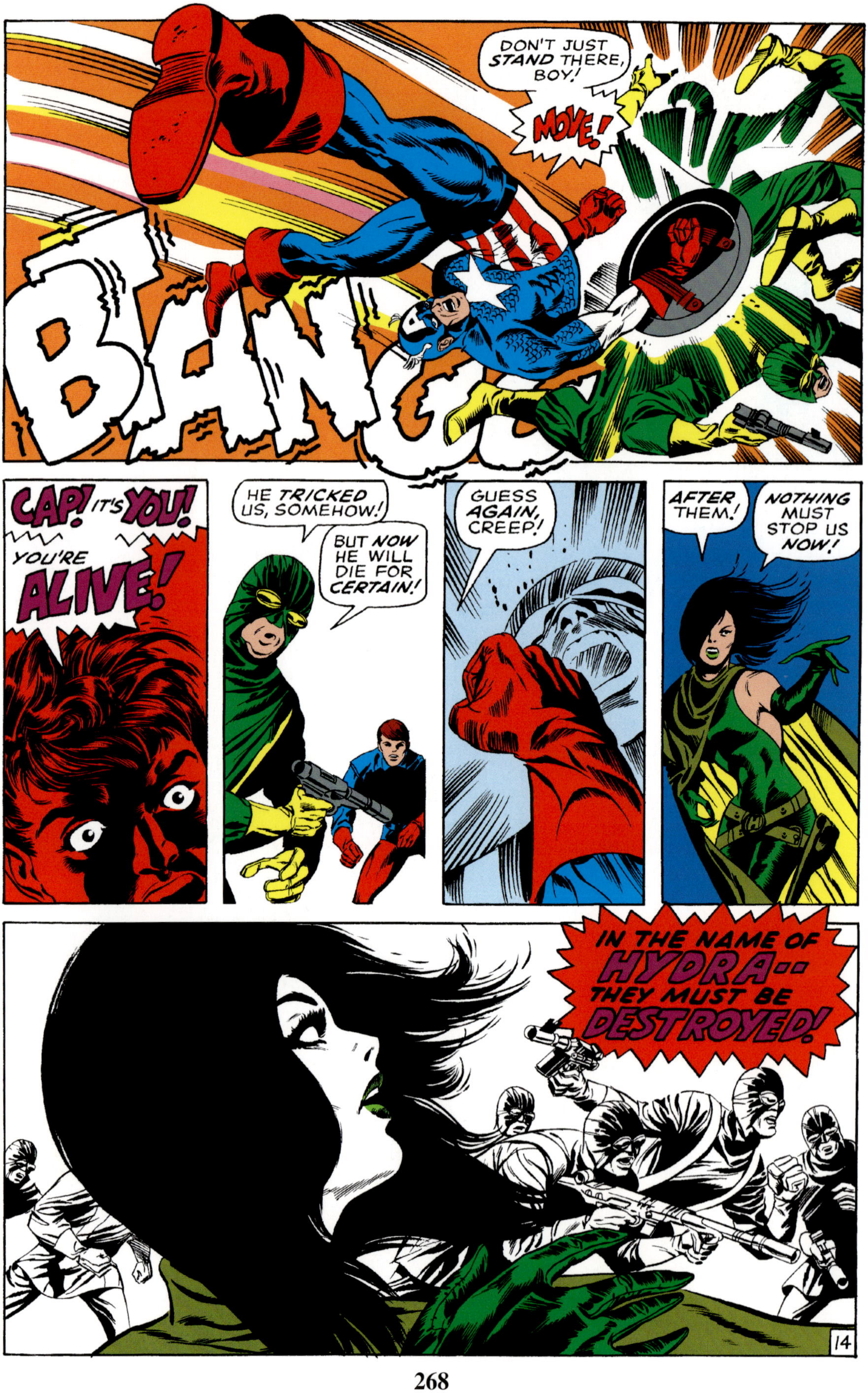
DON'T JUST STAND THERE, BOY!
MOVE!
BANG
CAP! IT'S YOU! YOU'RE ALIVE!
HE TRICKED US, SOMEHOW!
BUT NOW HE WILL DIE FOR CERTAIN!
GUESS AGAIN, CREEP!
AFTER THEM!
NOTHING MUST STOP US NOW!
IN THE NAME OF HYDRA-- THEY MUST BE DESTROYED!
14

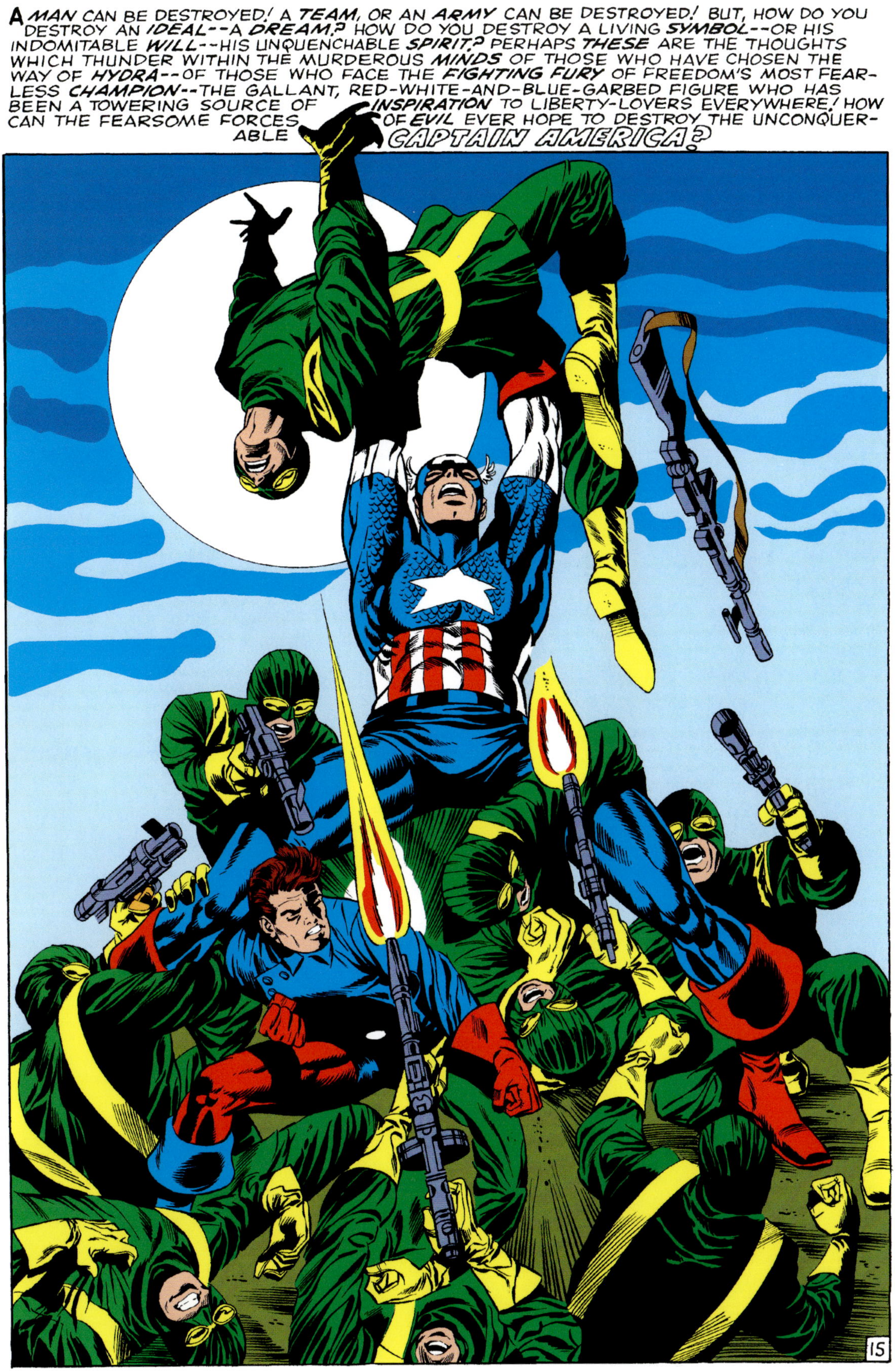
A MAN CAN BE DESTROYED! A TEAM, OR AN ARMY CAN BE DESTROYED! BUT, HOW DO YOU DESTROY AN IDEAL--A DREAM? HOW DO YOU DESTROY A LIVING SYMBOL--OR HIS INDOMITABLE WILL--HIS UNQUENCHABLE SPIRIT? PERHAPS THESE ARE THE THOUGHTS WHICH THUNDER WITHIN THE MURDEROUS MINDS OF THOSE WHO HAVE CHOSEN THE WAY OF HYDRA--OF THOSE WHO FACE THE FIGHTING FURY OF FREEDOM'S MOST FEARLESS CHAMPION--THE GALLANT, RED-WHITE-AND-BLUE-GARBED FIGURE WHO HAS BEEN A TOWERING SOURCE OF INSPIRATION TO LIBERTY-LOVERS EVERYWHERE! HOW CAN THE FEARSOME FORCES OF EVIL EVER HOPE TO DESTROY THE UNCONQUERABLE CAPTAIN AMERICA?
15

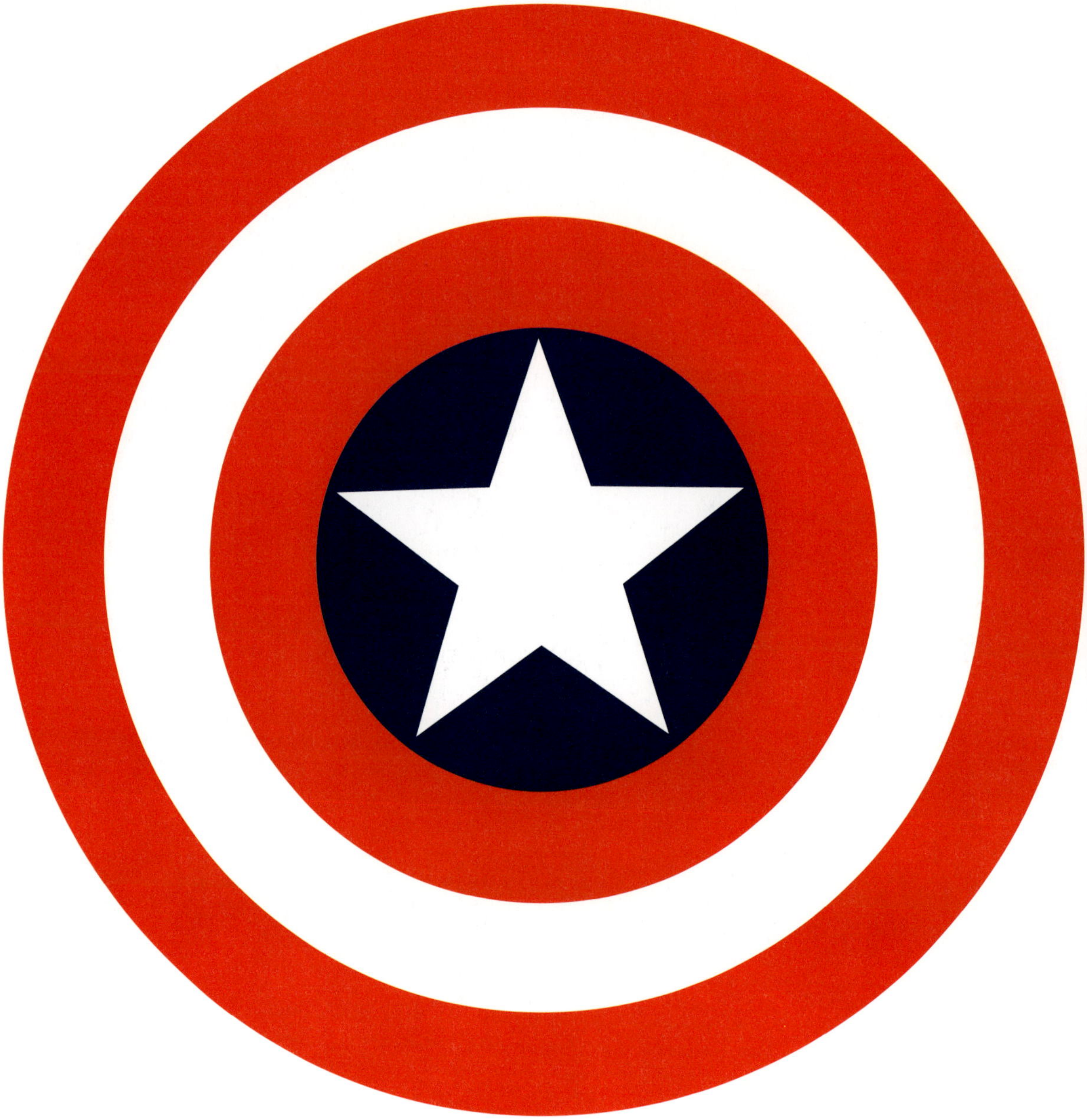

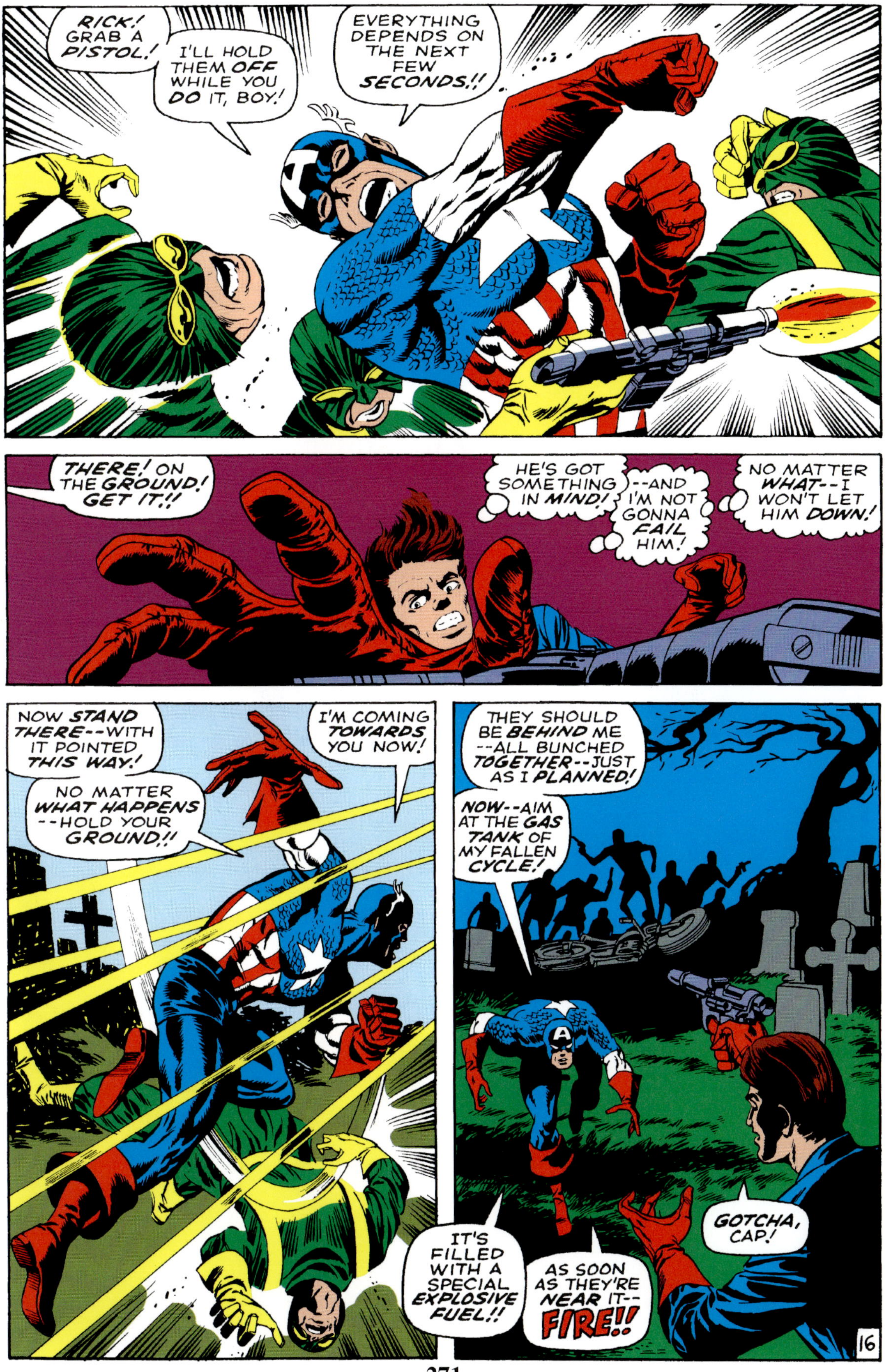
RICK! GRAB A PISTOL!
I'LL HOLD THEM OFF WHILE YOU DO IT, BOY!
EVERYTHING DEPENDS ON THE NEXT FEW SECONDS!!
THERE! ON THE GROUND! GET IT!!
HE'S GOT SOMETHING IN MIND!
--AND I'M NOT GONNA FAIL HIM!
NO MATTER WHAT--I WON'T LET HIM DOWN!
NOW STAND THERE--WITH IT POINTED THIS WAY!
NO MATTER WHAT HAPPENS --HOLD YOUR GROUND!!
I'M COMING TOWARDS YOU NOW!
THEY SHOULD BE BEHIND ME --ALL BUNCHED TOGETHER--JUST AS I PLANNED!
NOW--AIM AT THE GAS TANK OF MY FALLEN CYCLE!
IT'S FILLED WITH A SPECIAL EXPLOSIVE FUEL!!
AS SOON AS THEY'RE NEAR IT-- FIRE!!
GOTCHA, CAP!
16

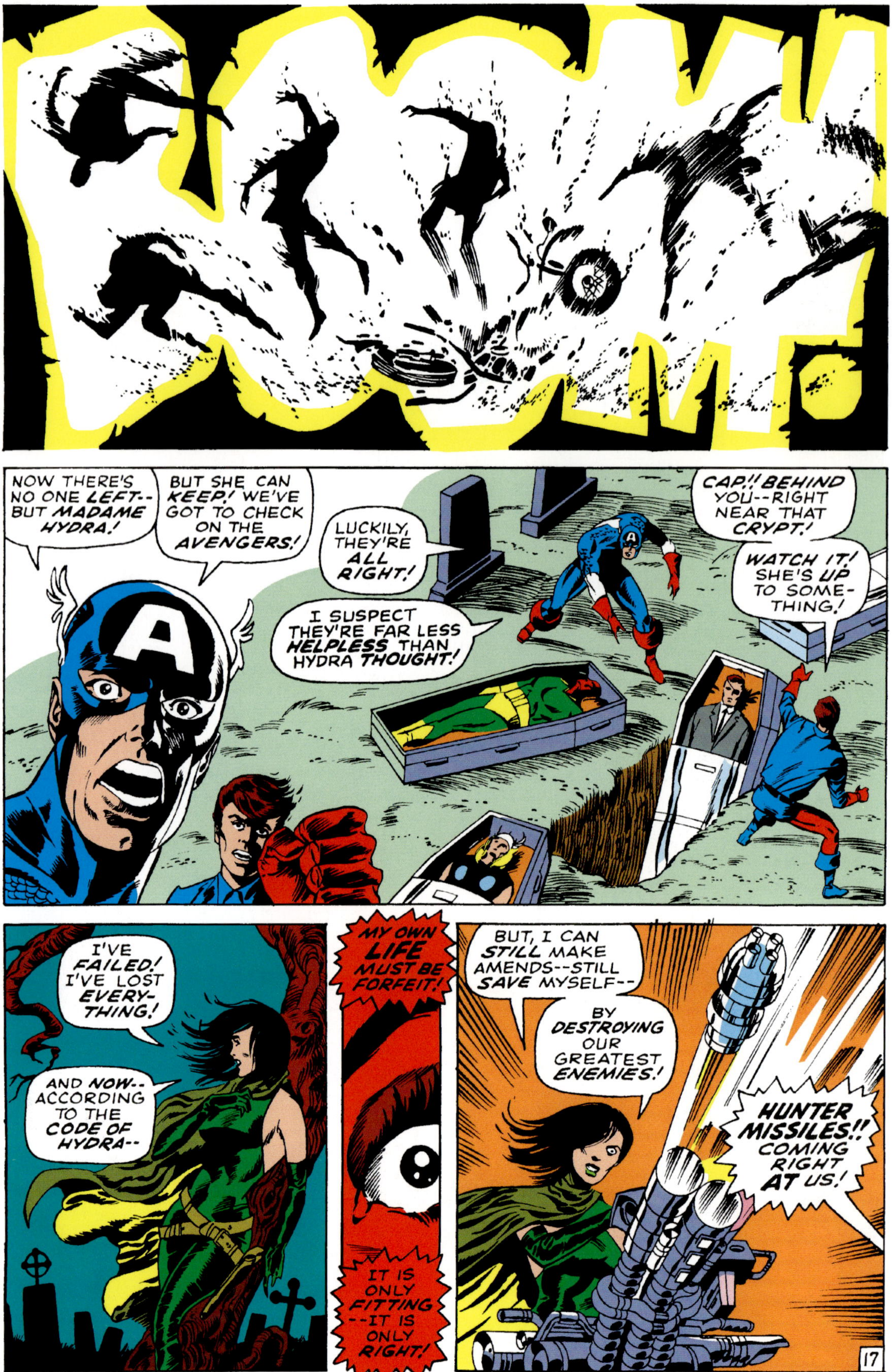
BOOM!
NOW THERE'S NO ONE LEFT-- BUT MADAME HYDRA!
BUT SHE CAN KEEP! WE'VE GOT TO CHECK ON THE AVENGERS!
LUCKILY, THEY'RE ALL RIGHT!
I SUSPECT THEY'RE FAR LESS HELPLESS THAN HYDRA THOUGHT!
CAP!! BEHIND YOU--RIGHT NEAR THAT CRYPT!
WATCH IT! SHE'S UP TO SOME-THING!
I'VE FAILED! I'VE LOST EVERY-THING!
AND NOW-- ACCORDING TO THE CODE OF HYDRA--
MY OWN LIFE MUST BE FORFEIT!
IT IS ONLY FITTING --IT IS ONLY RIGHT!
BUT, I CAN STILL MAKE AMENDS--STILL SAVE MYSELF--
BY DESTROYING OUR GREATEST ENEMIES!
HUNTER MISSILES!! COMING RIGHT AT US!
17

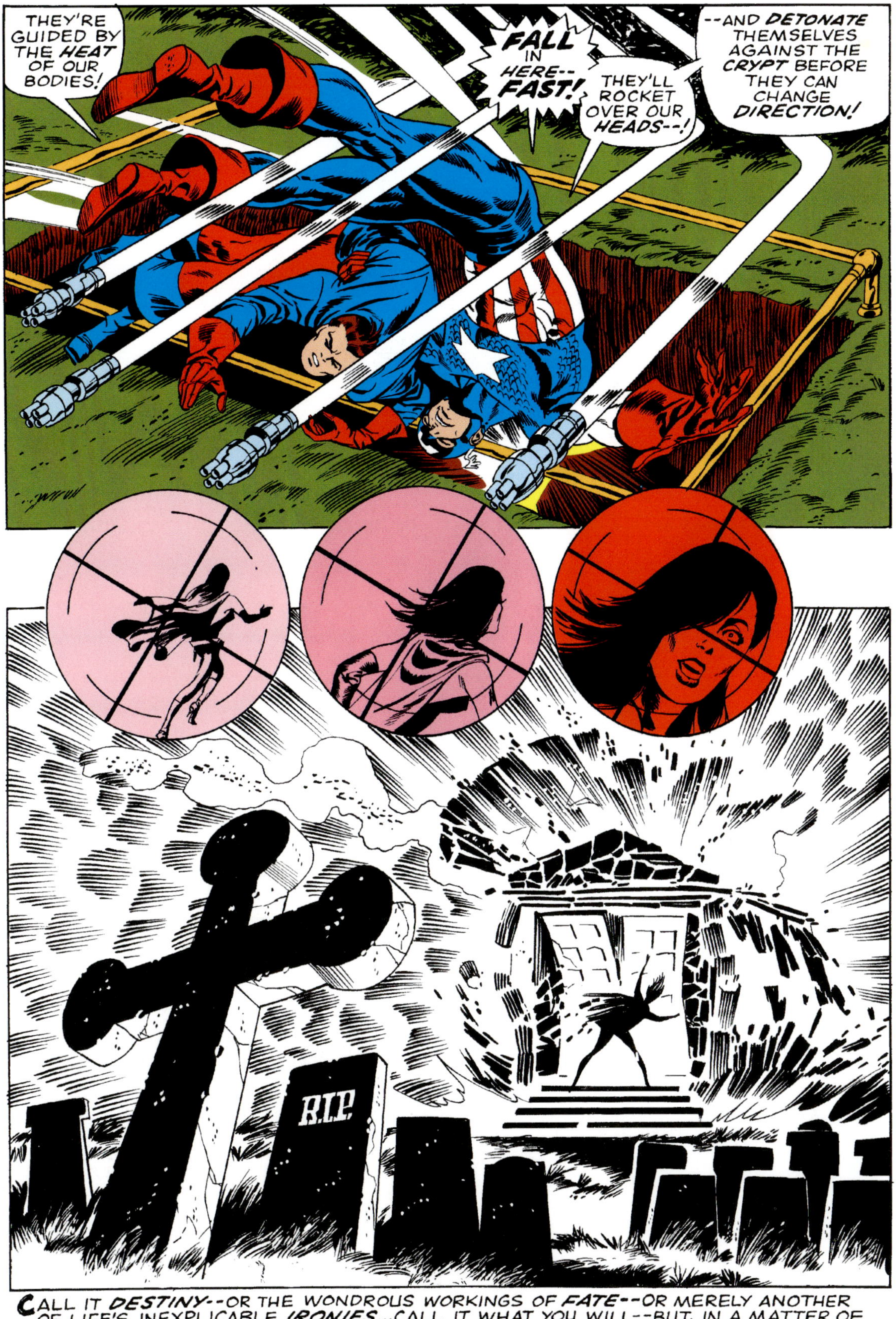
THEY'RE GUIDED BY THE HEAT OF OUR BODIES!
FALL IN HERE-- FAST!
THEY'LL ROCKET OVER OUR HEADS--!
--AND DETONATE THEMSELVES AGAINST THE CRYPT BEFORE THEY CAN CHANGE DIRECTION!
R.I.P.
CALL IT DESTINY--OR THE WONDROUS WORKINGS OF FATE--OR MERELY ANOTHER OF LIFE'S INEXPLICABLE IRONIES...CALL IT WHAT YOU WILL--BUT, IN A MATTER OF SPLIT-SECONDS, SHE WHO HAD BEEN MADAME HYDRA REAPS THE GRIM HARVEST SHE HAD SO MERCILESSLY SOWN--!
18

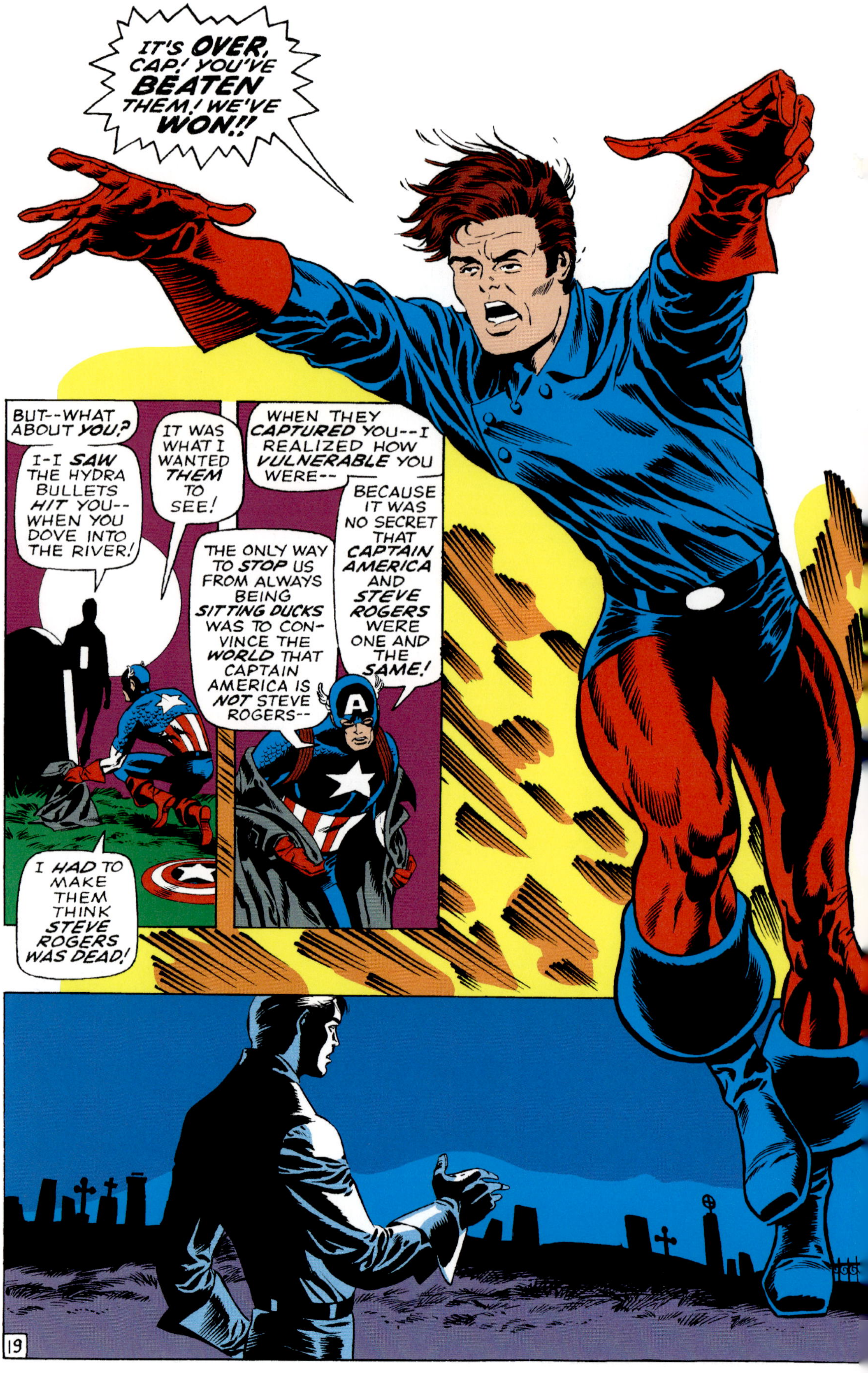
IT'S OVER, CAP! YOU'VE BEATEN THEM! WE'VE WON!!
BUT--WHAT ABOUT YOU?
I-I SAW THE HYDRA BULLETS HIT YOU-- WHEN YOU DOVE INTO THE RIVER!
IT WAS WHAT I WANTED THEM TO SEE!
I HAD TO MAKE THEM THINK STEVE ROGERS WAS DEAD!
WHEN THEY CAPTURED YOU--I REALIZED HOW VULNERABLE YOU WERE--
BECAUSE IT WAS NO SECRET THAT CAPTAIN AMERICA AND STEVE ROGERS WERE ONE AND THE SAME!
THE ONLY WAY TO STOP US FROM ALWAYS BEING SITTING DUCKS WAS TO CONVINCE THE WORLD THAT CAPTAIN AMERICA IS NOT STEVE ROGERS--
19

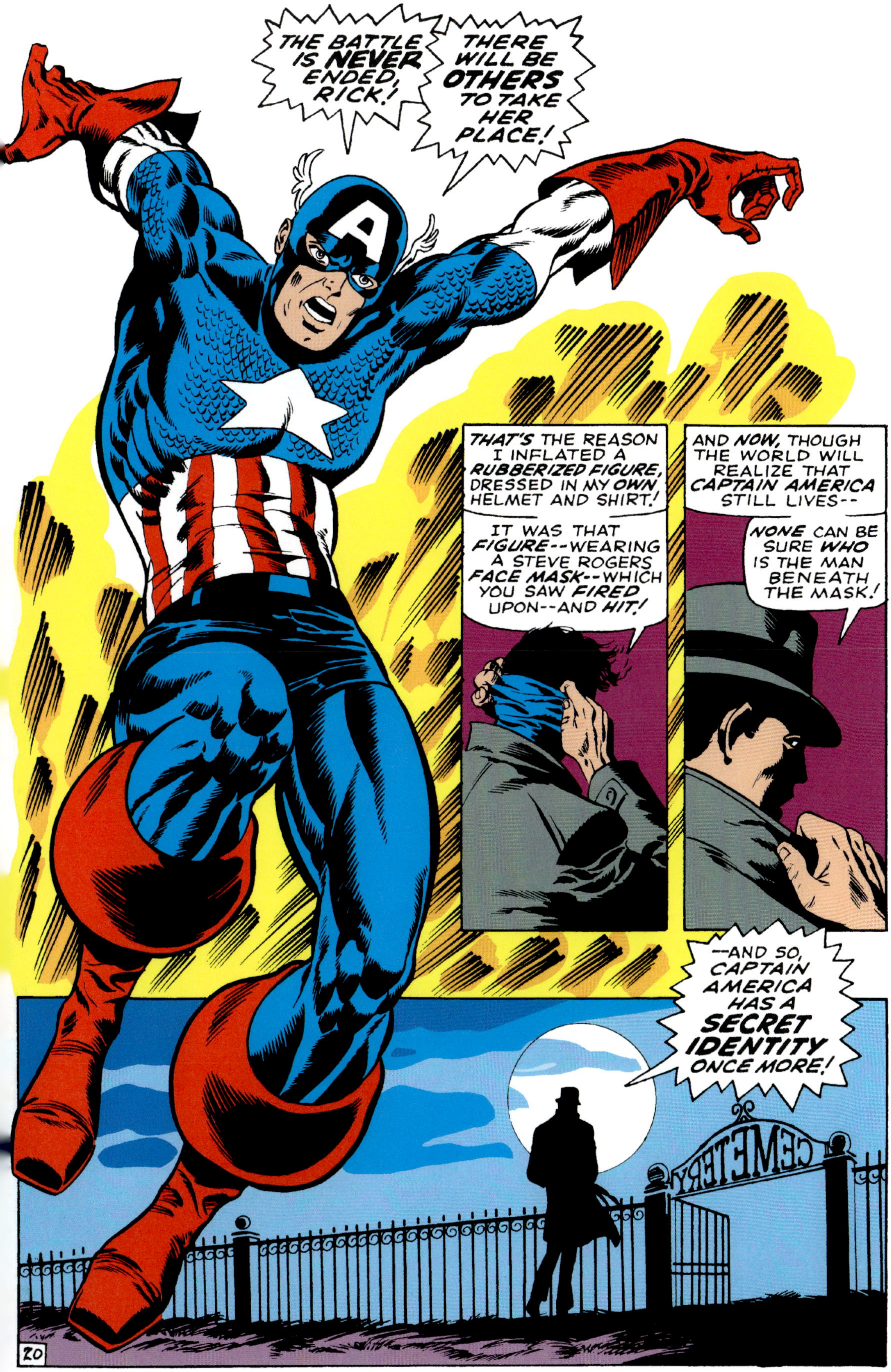
THE BATTLE IS NEVER ENDED, RICK!
THERE WILL BE OTHERS TO TAKE HER PLACE!
THAT'S THE REASON I INFLATED A RUBBERIZED FIGURE, DRESSED IN MY OWN HELMET AND SHIRT!
IT WAS THAT FIGURE--WEARING A STEVE ROGERS FACE MASK--WHICH YOU SAW FIRED UPON--AND HIT!
AND NOW, THOUGH THE WORLD WILL REALIZE THAT CAPTAIN AMERICA STILL LIVES--
NONE CAN BE SURE WHO IS THE MAN BENEATH THE MASK!
--AND SO, CAPTAIN AMERICA HAS A SECRET IDENTITY ONCE MORE!
CEMETERY
20

SPECIAL BONUS:

Captain America #105 original cover pencils by Jack Kirby

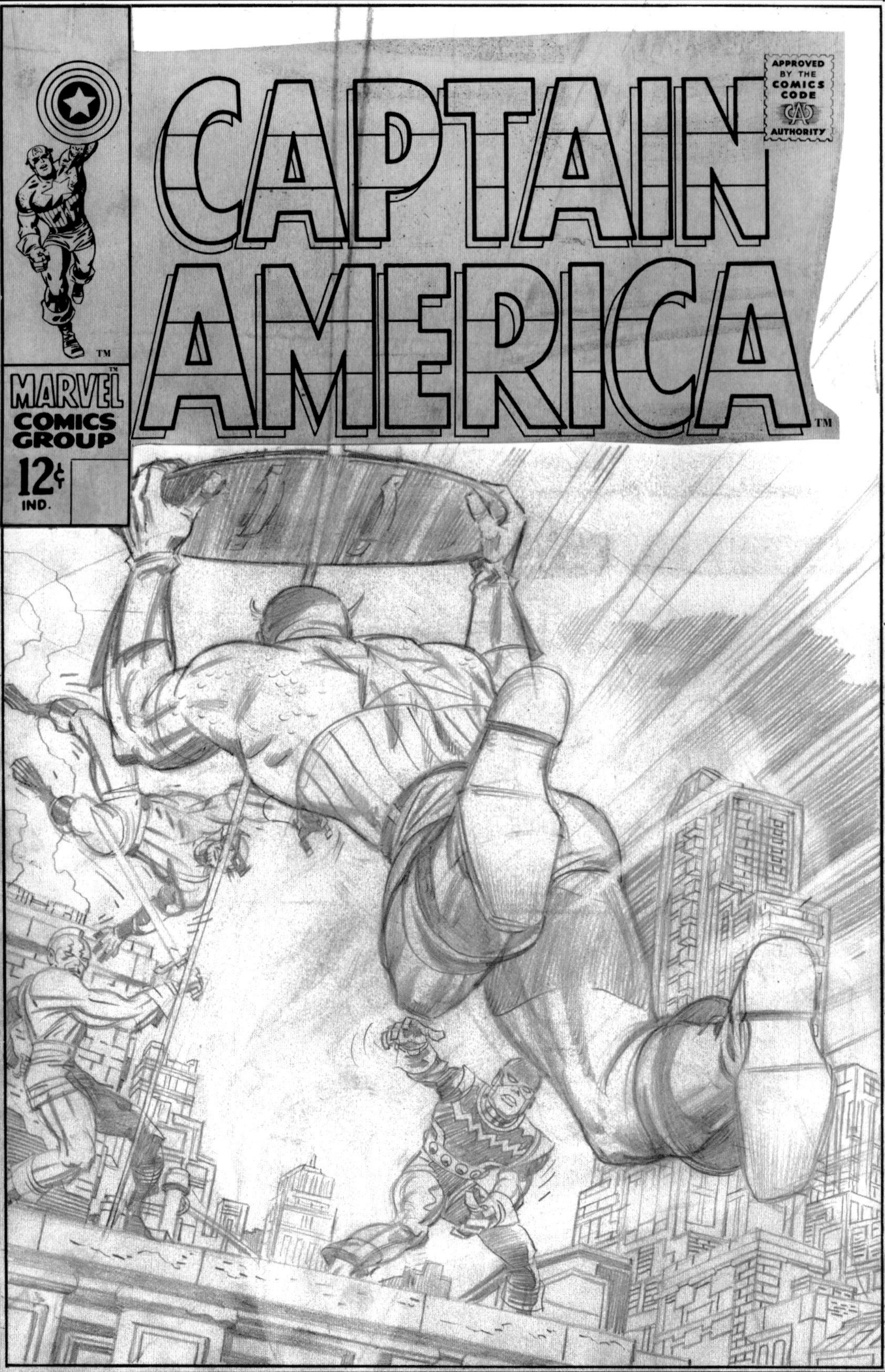
CAPTAIN AMERICA
TM
APPROVED BY THE COMICS CODE AUTHORITY
MARVEL COMICS GROUP
12¢ IND.

Captain America #112, page 1 original art by Jack Kirby & George Tuska

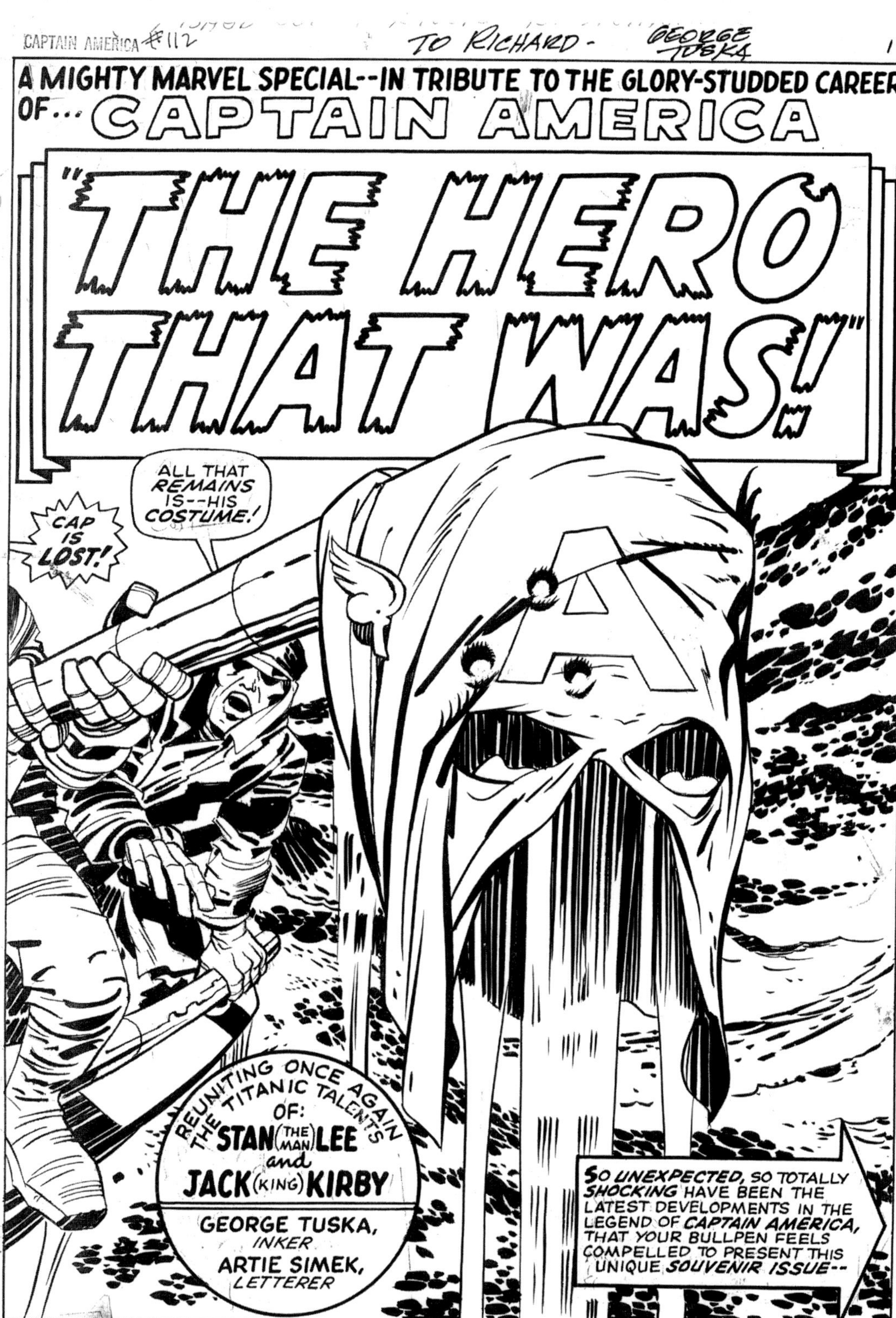

CAPTAIN AMERICA #112
TO RICHARD - GEORGE TUSKA
1
A MIGHTY MARVEL SPECIAL--IN TRIBUTE TO THE GLORY-STUDDED CAREER OF... CAPTAIN AMERICA
"THE HERO THAT WAS!"
ALL THAT REMAINS IS--HIS COSTUME!
CAP IS LOST!
REUNITING ONCE AGAIN THE TITANIC TALENTS OF: STAN (THE MAN) LEE and JACK (KING) KIRBY
GEORGE TUSKA, INKER
ARTIE SIMEK, LETTERER
SO UNEXPECTED, SO TOTALLY SHOCKING HAVE BEEN THE LATEST DEVELOPMENTS IN THE LEGEND OF CAPTAIN AMERICA, THAT YOUR BULLPEN FEELS COMPELLED TO PRESENT THIS UNIQUE SOUVENIR ISSUE--

CAPTAIN AMERICA is published by MAGAZINE MANAGEMENT CO. OFFICE OF PUBLICATION 625 MADISON AVENUE, NEW YORK, N. Y. 10022. SECOND CLASS POSTAGE PAID AT NEW YORK, N. Y. AND AT ADDITIONAL MAILING OFFICES. Published monthly. Copyright ©1969 by Magazine Management Co., Marvel Comics Group, all rights reserved, 625 Madison Avenue, New York, N. Y. 10022. Vol. 1, No. 112, April, 1969 issue. Price 12¢ per copy. No similarity between any of the names, characters, persons and/or institutions in this magazine with those of any living or dead person or institution is intended, and any such similarity which may exist is purely coincidental. Printed in the U.S.A. by World Color Press, Inc., Sparta, Illinois 62286. **Subscription rate $1.75 and $2.25 Canada for 12 issues including postage. Foreign subscriptions $3.25.**

BIOGRAPHIES

STAN LEE

Stanley Lieber was born in New York City in 1922, the oldest son of Jewish immigrants from Romania. Upon an early graduation from high school, Stan was thrust out into the post-Depression wartime economy. Through family connections, he was able to land a job with Martin Goodman's comic-book publishing start-up Timely Comics as an assistant editor. His youthful aspiration was to one day write the "Great American Novel," so when his first professional writing job came in the form of a humble two-page text story in *Captain America Comics* #3, he adopted a pseudonym: Stan Lee. This way, he could reserve his real name for that novel-to-be.

But the world of comics managed to keep Stan Lee constantly employed. His proficiency on the job got him the position of managing editor at an extremely young age. He graduated from simple text pieces to full-length stories in *All-Winners*, *USA Comics*, and other Timely anthologies. His tenure in the '50s saw him expand the company (now called Atlas Comics) output to include more genre experimentation, with westerns, war, horror and crime comics.

All this activity was a prelude to the Marvel Age of Comics, ushered in under the auspices of Stan Lee and a small stable of artists topped off by the formidable talents of Jack Kirby and Steve Ditko. Responding to Martin Goodman's challenge to do something to find a way to revitalize dwindling sales, Stan figured he would co-opt the successful super-hero revival at competitor DC Comics and add his own magic to the mix: Instead of being perfect invulnerable champions, Stan's Marvel Age heroes would be normal, fallible, imperfect people, forced to cope with their newfound superhuman traits just like the average person might.

Stan's innovation sent shockwaves through the comics industry, and within a few years, Marvelmania was taking hold: unlike other fads of the time, it wasn't letting go. Under his direction, creations like Fantastic Four, Spider-Man, Iron Man, Thor, Doctor Strange and Incredible Hulk flourished in the shared universe they inhabited. Stan developed the idea that these larger-than-life heroes would meet each other in crossovers from title to title, thus exploding the story possibilities for the kids who became eager fans.

In addition to bringing a new twist to the life of the super hero, Stan also brought the reader inside Marvel's "Batty Bullpen," creating a sense of camaraderie and special membership. His friendly and enthusiastic banter in letters pages, house ads, and Bullpen Bulletins brought Marvel Comics to a level of familiarity with their fans that had kids and college students proudly professing themselves to be "True Believers."

At one time, Stan wrote virtually every comic that appeared from Marvel during the 1960s. But when he was promoted to Publisher in 1971, his writing had to take a back seat, and by the mid-'70s, he semi-retired from scripting duties. Over the years, Stan has returned to write scripts for the odd single issue or series, focusing on Marvel's ventures into television and movie development. To this day, he remains Marvel Comics' single greatest ambassador to the world.

JACK KIRBY

Jacob Kurtzberg was born in 1917 into a gritty upbringing on the streets of New York's Lower East Side. It would be many years before he would adopt the more familiar name of Jack Kirby, but his experiences on the street would help inform the work that later made him a legend. Unlike many of his rough-and-tumble peers, his imagination inspired him to look beyond the commonality of everyday life. He was inclined at an early age to pursue drawing, and he was also a guy who wanted to "get things done." This hard work ethic and ambition took him places most men of humble stations like him would never dream of going,

After some early strip work helped get his name out to prospective employers, a fateful meeting with artist Joe Simon connected the two at the hip, and vaulted both of them into comics prominence. Together, they developed *Captain America* for Timely Comics, and Jack immediately helped redefine what comics could be with his innovative page designs and proportion-exploding panels.

Soon, Simon & Kirby were working with National Publications, turning out hit kid-gang comics like *Newsboy Legion* and *Boy Commandos*, as well as super-hero fare like *Sandman* and *Manhunter*. Like many of his peers, he served honorably in WWII, with combat duties that took him through the European theater.

In the '50s, Jack returned to comics, helping establish the romance genre with its first title, *Young Romance Comics*. More genre work followed for Timely/Atlas, with a prolific output that covered western, war, and monster genres. When it came time to launch the Marvel Age of Comics, Jack brought his dynamic layouts, unparalleled bombast and unbridled creativity to the fore in books like *Fantastic Four*, *Avengers*, *X-Men*, *Incredible Hulk* and *Thor*, leaving his unmistakable stamp on the characters he created.

The King's way of doing things was so popular that it set the tone for many of Stan Lee's editorial decisions throughout the '60s; before they were entrusted with taking over completely, new artists were often assimilated onto books by drawing over Jack's layouts. Jack left Marvel for DC in 1970, this time handling the scripting chores as well as the art duties. Jack's "Fourth World" books, along with *Kamandi*, *OMAC* and *The Demon*, were just a few of the highlights of his tenure at DC before returning to Marvel in the '70s to lend his unbridled imagination to a new cast of creations: *The Eternals*, *Devil*

Dinosaur, and *Machine Man*. In addition, he returned to the pages of *Captain America*, the character he had first made famous 35 years previously.

Jack continued creating comics throughout the '90s until passing away in 1994, a creative giant for whom the word "legend" may be too small a title.

JIM STERANKO

When Jim Steranko burst onto the comic scene, he worked furiously for a few short years and then was gone. What sets Steranko apart from other creators who may have had equally short tenures is the considerable significance of his creative output in that brief period. He came to comics with a mission to change them, to move comic art from what he perceived to be a moribund stagnation to something more evolved and exciting.

Though known for later, more iconic work for Marvel, Jim Steranko actually saw his first comic art published in *Spyman*, a comic in the short-lived Harvey Thriller imprint. Drafted to help create the visual look for editor Joe Simon, it wasn't long before he made his move to Marvel in the fall of 1966. There, his art caught the eye of young staffer Roy Thomas, who liked Jim's portfolio well enough to recommend him for a job at the House of Ideas. Stan Lee agreed, and before the day was over, Jim had the job drawing "Nick Fury, Agent of S.H.I.E.L.D." in the pages of *Strange Tales*. Initially drawing over Kirby's layouts, it wasn't long before Jim had transformed the book into something that reflected his own unique vision, so much so that he eventually took on both script and art chores combined. He covered a lot of bases in his bid to include a heavy dose of pop-art sensationalism into his work: psychedelia and op art was the rule, and it wasn't unexpected to see such things as an homage to artists like Salvador Dali, most notably on the cover to *Nick Fury* #7. Another thing that really blew the doors open were his splash pages, borrowing heavily from the luxuriously stylized pages of Will Eisner's *The Spirit*, merging title design and art into a single graphic whole.

As his two-year run on *Nick Fury* concluded, Jim drew a two-part feature in *X-Men* #50-51, designing the team's classic title logo in the process. Drawing *Captain America* was a lifelong ambition of Jim's and after *X-Men*, he drew three seminal issues of the red, white and blue Avenger's comic. Both these titles were given a quick jolt from Steranko's visceral new approach to graphic design, and serve as milestone issues for longtime fans.

He did quick turns drawing short stories in Marvel's horror title *Tower of Shadows* and romance title *Our Love Story*, as well as a small handful of covers for *Incredible Hulk*, *Fantastic Four*, *Shanna the She-Devil* and a handful of western titles, and then he was gone from Marvel Comics.

Seeking new creative horizons, Jim took up employment drawing the covers to dozens of science fiction, fantasy, and pulp paperback novels. He also wrote the seminal *Steranko History of Comics* in the early '70s, a well-considered look back at comics history from one of its contemporary elites. By the late '70s, Steranko had begun working in conceptual design for films including *Raiders of the Lost Ark* and *Bram Stoker's Dracula*. Though Steranko art appearances are a rare event in comics today, he is still active on the convention circuit.

Biographical material researched and written by John Rhett Thomas.

THE
MARVEL MASTERWORKS
LIBRARY

The Amazing Spider-Man Vols. 1-7 By Stan Lee, Steve Ditko & John Romita
    Sensational stories of everybody's favorite wall-crawler—your friendly neighborhood Spider-Man.

Ant-Man/Giant-Man Vol. 1 By Stan Lee, Jack Kirby, Don Heck & Larry Lieber
    Thrilling science and microscopic adventures abound in the action-packed world of Hank Pym, Ant-Man and Janet Van Dyne, the Wasp!

Atlas Era Tales to Astonish Vol. 1 By Jack Kirby, Steve Ditko, Don Heck, Joe Sinnott & Stan Lee
    Amazing tales of monsters and the farthest reaches of the imagination by comics' greatest talents.

The Avengers Vols. 1-5 By Stan Lee, Roy Thomas, Jack Kirby, Don Heck & John Buscema
    Marvel's greatest stars assemble to form Earth's Mightiest Heroes.

Captain America Vols. 1-3 By Stan Lee, Jack Kirby, Gil Kane & Jim Steranko
    America's Sentinel of Liberty in action-packed stories of amazing adventure and suspense.

Captain Marvel Vol. 1 By Stan Lee, Roy Thomas, Arnold Drake, Gene Colan & Don Heck
    Born of the Kree, Marvel's Space-Born Super-Hero, Captain Mar-Vell protects planet Earth!

Doctor Strange Vols. 1-2 By Stan Lee, Steve Ditko, Bill Everett, Marie Severin & Dan Adkins
    The original otherworldly tales of Dr. Stephen Strange, Master of the Mystic Arts!

Daredevil Vols. 1-3 By Stan Lee, Wallace Wood, John Romita & Gene Colan
    Blind lawyer Matt Murdock is Daredevil, the Man Without Fear.

The Fantastic Four Vols. 1-10 By Stan Lee & Jack Kirby
    Presenting the First Family of Super Heroes' unparalled adventures beyond your wildest imagination.

Golden Age All-Winners Vol. 1 By Joe Simon, Jack Kirby, Carl Burgos, Bill Everett & Stan Lee
    The greatest heroes of the Golden Age band together to fight the Nazi hordes and the forces of evil!

Golden Age Captain America Vol. 1 By Joe Simon & Jack Kirby
    A top-secret serum turns Steve Rogers, 98-pound weakling, into America's greatest wartime weapon in battles with his kid sidekick, Bucky.

Golden Age Marvel Comics Vols. 1-2 By Carl Burgos & Bill Everett
    Experience the birth of Marvel Comics from the very beginning! Featuring the Sub-Mariner, Ka-Zar, the Human Torch and more!

Golden Age Human Torch Vol. 1 By Carl Burgos & Bill Everett
    Fiery adventures of the amazing creation, the Human Torch and Toro, the Flaming Kid.

Golden Age Sub-Mariner Vol. 1 By Bill Everett & Paul Gustavson
    From his undersea kingdom of Atlantis, the mighty Sub-Mariner protects the Seven Seas from tyranny.

The Incredible Hulk Vols. 1-3 By Stan Lee, Jack Kirby, Steve Ditko, Bill Everett, John Buscema, Gil Kane & Marie Severin
    When Dr. Robert Bruce Banner loses control, he becomes the unstoppable Hulk!

The Invincible Iron Man Vols. 1-2 By Stan Lee & Don Heck
    Gravely injured, Tony Stark built a suit of amazing armor to become the Invincible Iron Man!

Rawhide Kid Vol. 1 By Stan Lee & Jack Kirby
    Johnny Bart brings justice to the American frontier with the fastest six-shooters this side of the Mississippi. He is the Rawhide Kid!

Sgt. Fury Vol. 1 By Stan Lee, Jack Kirby & Dick Ayers
    WWII tales of America's toughest army team, the Howling Commandos!

The Silver Surfer Vols. 1-2 By Stan Lee & John Buscema
    The Sentinel of the Spaceways in his galaxy-spanning saga throughout the stars.

The Sub-Mariner Vol. 1 By Stan Lee, Gene Colan & Bill Everett
    Namor, Prince of Atlantis, in his original adventures under the Seven Seas.

The Mighty Thor Vols. 1-4 By Stan Lee & Jack Kirby
    The Asgardian Thunder God in mythic tales of epic battle and mystical adenture.

The X-Men Vols. 1-6 By Stan Lee, Roy Thomas, Arnold Drake, Jack Kirby & Werner Roth
    Gifted with strange and amazing powers, Professor Charles Xaiver's teen team, the X-Men, lead the way in the quest to bring together man and mutant.

The Uncanny X-Men Vols. 1-5 By Chris Claremont, Dave Cockrum & John Byrne
    Children of the Atom, they fight to defend a world that fears and hates them. They are the All-New, All-Different X-Men.